Text, Speech and Language Technology

Volume 49

Series Editor

Nancy Ide, Poughkeepsie, NY, USA

Due to the recent availability of large bodies of text and speech in electronic form, data-based research of all kinds has increased dramatically in areas such as computational linguistics and language engineering (especially corpus-based linguistics), speech, humanities computing, psycho-linguistics, and information retrieval. This series is intended to explore the methodologies and technologies that are emerging as a result of this work. In addition, while each of these disciplines has developed methodologies appropriate to its particular problem area, there is emerging a clearly defined set of technologies and methodologies common to all areas of research involving large quantities of electronic data. The series will be particularly concerned with methodologies and technologies with either actual or potential applicability to other areas. The topics covered by the series include but are not limited to:

- encoding and representation of text and speech;
- lexical statistics and quantitative word studies;
- computational lexicography;
- morphological analysis and part-of-speech tagging;
- grammars and parsing technologies;
- automated content and thematic analysis;
- text databases and retrieval;
- document analysis, automatic indexing and abstracting;
- stylometry and computerized authorship discrimination;
- text generation;
- message understanding;
- text-to-speech and dictation systems;
- speech synthesis and speech recognition;
- phonological and prosodic analysis

The series will contain three general types of books:

methodologies - which survey major methodological approaches in a given domain. Many of the methodologies emerging for text-based work have never been considered collectively or comprehensively, and there is a serious need for books which provide an overview of the important approaches to certain problem areas. **advanced research topics** - which treat in depth specific areas of interest or projects at the state of the art. This type of book will describe leading edge research on specific topics, whose methodologies may only have begun to develop. **tutorials** - which provide a general introduction to a particular topic.

Because text based research has developed so rapidly in recent years, there is a large number of researchers who are unfamiliar with basic concepts and approaches. In addition, applicable methodologies which may be well-developed within one discipline are often completely unknown to researchers in another discipline. Supplementary materials, such as, software, demonstrations, program libraries, etc. in appropriate forms (diskettes, web sites, etc.) will be included where appropriate.

For inquiries and submission of proposals please contact the Series Editor, Nancy Ide- ide@vassar.edu

Chu-Ren Huang • Shu-Kai Hsieh • Peng Jin
Editors

Chinese Language Resources

Data Collection, Linguistic Analysis, Annotation and Language Processing

Springer

Editors
Chu-Ren Huang
Department of Chinese and Bilingual Studies
The Hong Kong Polytechnic University
Kowloon, Hong Kong

Shu-Kai Hsieh
Graduate Institute of Linguistics
National Taiwan University
Taipei, Taiwan

Peng Jin
School of Electronic Information and Artificial Intelligence
Leshan Normal University
Leshan City, Sichuan, China

ISSN 1386-291X
Text, Speech and Language Technology
ISBN 978-3-031-38912-2 ISBN 978-3-031-38913-9 (eBook)
https://doi.org/10.1007/978-3-031-38913-9

This Springer imprint is published by the registered company Springer Nature Switzerland AG
The registered company address is: Gewerbestrasse 11, 6330 Cham, Switzerland

Paper in this product is recyclable.

谨以此书 敬献给 我们敬爱的

俞士汶 教授

1938-2021

This volume is dedicated to our beloved

Professor Shiwen Yu

1938-2021

路漫漫其修远兮

吾将上下而求索

屈原《离骚》

The road winding with no end in sight,
I will seek truth high and low, despite the setting sun.

"The Lament" by Qu Yuan (c. 342 BC – 278 BC)

Biography of Prof. Shiwen Yu

Yu, Shiwen was a professor in the Department of Computer Science and Technology, School of Electronics Engineering and Computer Science, Peking University. As a leading scholar and trailblazer in Chinese information processing, he laid a solid foundation for the research of Chinese information processing technology. At the Institute of Computational Linguistics of Peking University, Professor Yu set the research focus on the construction of language knowledge bases for Chinese NLP, based on his keen vision of the vital role of language knowledge resources in natural language processing and his own experience gained from developing application systems.

A Dictionary of Modern Chinese Grammar Information, a large-scale electronic lexicon for language information processing, represents the accumulated research work of more than a decade and contains more than 73,000 entries organized according to both grammatical function and meaning. In 1998, this achievement won the Tier Two Award in the Science and Technology Progress Awards of the Ministry of Education in China. In 2011, a Tier Two Award in the Chinese National Science and Technology Progress Awards was given for developing a *Comprehensive Language Knowledge Base* on the basis of *A Dictionary of Modern Chinese Grammar Information*. In the same year, Professor Yu was awarded the Lifetime Achievement Award of the Chinese Information Processing Society of China.

俞士汶教授小传

俞士汶先生是北京大学信息学院计算机科学技术系教授，是中文信息处理领域的主要开创者与引领者之一，为中文信息处理技术研究奠定了坚实的基础。俞先生领悟到语言知识资源对自然语言处理系统的重要意义，又吸取开发应用系统的实践经验，果断地将北京大学计算语言学研究所研究重点确定为语言知识库的建设。集十余年之努力研制成功的《现代汉语语法信息词典》，是一部面向语言信息处理的大型电子词典，按照语法功能和意义相结合的准则收录了7.3万余词语。1998年，　这项成果获教育部科技进步二等奖。2011年，　在《现代汉语语法信息词典》基础上进一步发展形成的《综合型语言知识库》荣获国家科技进步二等奖。同年，俞先生获得中国中文信息学会首届终身成就奖。

A Chronological Biography of Professor Shiwen Yu

December 8, 1938	Born, in Xuancheng 宣城, Anhui Province, China
1958–1964	Studied at the Department of Physics, and the Department of Mathematics and Mechanics at Peking University Graduated with a major in Computational Mathematics
1964–1979	Teaching assistant in the Department of Mathematics and Mechanics, and the Institute of Computer Science, Peking University
1979–1985	Lecturer at the Institute of Computer Technology, Peking University
1982–1983	Visiting scholar in the Department of Electronic Engineering, Osaka University
1985–1990	Associate professor at the Institute of Computer Technology, Peking University
1990–2004	Professor in the School of Computer Science and the School of Electronics Engineering and Computer Science, Peking University
1990–2004	Deputy director of the Institute of Computational Linguistics, Peking University
2005–2010	Professor at the Institute of Computational Linguistics, Peking University (Retained after retirement)
November 4, 2021	Passed away

生平简历

1938年12月8日 出生于安徽省宣城县。

1958年—1964年 在北京大学物理系、数学力学系学习，毕业于计算数学专业。

1964年—1979年 任北京大学数学力学系和计算机研究所助教。

1979年—1985年 任北京大学计算机研究所讲师。

1982年—1983年 日本大阪大学电子工学科访问学者。

1985年—1990年 任北京大学计算机研究所副教授。

1990年—2004年　任北京大学计算机科学技术系和信息科学技术学院教授。

1990年—2004年 任北京大学计算语言学研究所负责人、副所长。

2005年—2010年 任北京大学计算语言学研究所返聘教授。

2021年11月4日 逝世

Acknowledgments

To 俞士汶 Shiwen Yu and 陳克健 Keh-Jiann Chen

To all ICLers and CKIPers

And to all like-minded scholars who dedicate their time to building language resources

The preparation and editing of *Chinese Language Resources: Data Collection, Linguistic Analysis, Annotation, and Language Processing* is sponsored by the Hong Kong Polytechnic University and Peking University Research Centre on Chinese Linguistics (RP2U2).

Contents

Editors and Contributors

About the Editors

Chu-Ren Huang is a Chair Professor in the Department of Chinese and Bilingual Studies at the Hong Kong Polytechnic University. Focusing on Chinese, computational, and corpus linguistics, he is fascinated by what language can tell us about human cognition and our collective reactions to natural and social environments. He approaches these questions with a deep and comprehensive study of the Chinese language. His recent books on Chinese include *A Reference Grammar of Chinese* (Cambridge), the Routledge Handbook on Chinese Applied Linguistics, and *the Cambridge Handbook of Chinese Linguistics*. His recent papers appeared in *Behavior Research Methods; Computational Linguistics; Cognitive Linguistics; Corpus Linguistics and Linguistic Theories; Humanities and Social Sciences Communications, Knowledge-Based Systems; Language, Cognition, and Neuroscience; Language Resources and Evaluation; Lingua; Natural Language Engineering; PLoS One; etc.*

Shu-Kai Hsieh is Associate Professor of Linguistics at the National Taiwan University, Taiwan. He received his PhD in Computational Linguistics from the University of Tübingen, Germany. He is the supervisor of NTU Lab of Ontologies, Language Processing, and e-Humanities and the founder of Taiwan Olympiad in Linguistics (TOL) and serves as the team leader and head coach of the Taiwanese national teams for International Olympiad in Linguistics.

Peng Jin is a full professor at Leshan Normal University. He co-founded the Sichuan Provincial Key Laboratory of Philosophy and Social Science for Language Intelligence in Special Education in 2022. He also founded the Key Laboratory of Internet Natural Language Processing of Sichuan Provincial Education Department in 2014. He has published tens of top journals and conference papers on natural language processing and has been granted two NSFC projects. He received his PhD degree from Peking University in July 2009, working on word sense disambiguation for his thesis. As a visiting scholar and student, he worked and studied at the University of Sussex, UK, in 2007 and 2014, respectively.

Contributors

Kathleen Ahrens Department of English and Communication, The Hong Kong Polytechnic University, Hong Kong, China

Wenlei Bai School of Computer Science and Technology, Nanjing Normal University, Nanjing, China
Information Security and Confidential Technology Engineering Research Center of Jiangsu Province, Nanjing, China

Xiaojing Bai Language Centre, Tsinghua University, Beijing, China

Baobao Chang Key Laboratory of Computational Linguistics, Peking University, Ministry of Education, Beijing, China
School of Electronic Engineering and Computer Science, Peking University, Beijing, China

Kai-Chun Chang Department of Information Management, Yuan Ze University, Taoyuan, Taiwan

Paul Yu-Chun Chang LMU Munich, Munich, Germany

Ru-Yng Chang AI Clerk International Co. LTD., New Taipei City, Taiwan
Computational Intelligence Technology Center, Industrial Technology Research Institute, Hsinchu, Taiwan

Wanxiang Che Computer Science and Technology College, Harbin Institute of Technology, Harbin, China

Chao-Jan Chen Department of Foreign Languages and Literature, National Chi Nan University, Puli, Taiwan

Chengyao Chen JP Morgan Asset Management, Kansas City, MO, USA

Helen Kai-Yun Chen National Central University, Taoyuan City, Taiwan

Keh-Jiann Chen Institute of Information Science, Taipei, Taiwan

Yu-Hsuan Chen Computational Intelligence Technology Center, Industrial Technology Research Institute, Hsinchu, Taiwan

Christopher Cieri Linguistic Data Consortium, University of Pennsylvania, Philadelphia, PA, USA

Yu Ding Computer Science and Technology College, Harbin Institute of Technology, Harbin, China

Zhao-Ming Gao Department of Foreign Languages and Literatures, National Taiwan University, Taipei, Taiwan

Min Gu School of Computer Science and Technology, Nanjing Normal University, Nanjing, China
Information Security and Confidential Technology Engineering Research Center of Jiangsu Province, Nanjing, China

Yanhui Gu School of Computer Science and Technology, Nanjing Normal University, Nanjing, China
Information Security and Confidential Technology Engineering Research Center of Jiangsu Province, Nanjing, China

Jia-Fei Hong Department of Chinese as a Second Language, National Taiwan Normal University, Taipei, Taiwan

Shu-Kai Hsieh Graduate Institute of Linguistics, National Taiwan University, Taipei, Taiwan

Hui-Ju Hsiung Department of English, National University of Tainan, Tainan, Taiwan

Hai Hu School of Foreign Languages, Shanghai Jiao Tong University, Shanghai, China

Chu-Ren Huang Department of Chinese and Bilingual Studies, The Hong Kong Polytechnic University, Hong Kong, China

Peng Jin Sichuan Provincial Key Laboratory of Philosophy and Social Science for Language Intelligence in Special Education, Leshan Normal University, Leshan, China

Shiyin Kang Department of Systems Engineering and Engineering Management, The Chinese University of Hong Kong, Hong Kong, China

Wei Lai AI Data, Amazon Website Services, Seattle, WA, USA

Sophia Yat Mei Lee Department of Chinese and Bilingual Studies, The Hong Kong Polytechnic University, Hong Kong, China

Anran Li Department of Chinese and Bilingual Studies, The Hong Kong Polytechnic University, Hong Kong, China

Qiang Li College of Liberal Arts, Shanghai University, Shanghai, China

Shida Li School of Software and Microelectronics, Peking University, Beijing, China

Shoushan Li Natural Language Processing Lab, Soochow University, Taipei, Taiwan

Wenjie Li Department of Computing, The Hong Kong Polytechnic University, Hong Kong, China

Mark Liberman Linguistic Data Consortium, University of Pennsylvania, Philadelphia, PA, USA

Bo-Lin Lin Computational Intelligence Technology Center, Industrial Technology Research Institute, Hsinchu, Taiwan
Department of Information Management, Yuan Ze University, Taoyuan, Taiwan

Chien-Jer Charles Lin Department of East Asian Languages and Cultures, Indiana University Bloomington, Bloomington, IN, USA

Yen-Hsi Lin Delta Electronics, Inc., Taipei, Taiwan

Meichun Liu Department of Linguistics and Translation, City University of Hong Kong, Hong Kong, China

Nien-Chi Liu Computational Intelligence Technology Center, Industrial Technology Research Institute, Hsinchu, Taiwan
Department of Information Management, Yuan Ze University, Taoyuan, Taiwan

Qun Liu Huawei Noah's Ark Lab, Hong Kong, China

Ting Liu Computer Science and Technology College, Harbin Institute of Technology, Harbin, China

Xunying Liu Department of Systems Engineering and Engineering Management, The Chinese University of Hong Kong, Hong Kong, China

Wei-Yun Ma Institute of Information Science, Taipei, Taiwan

Diana McCarthy Department of Theoretical and Applied Linguistics, University of Cambridge, Cambridge, UK

Fuyong Meng School of Foreign Languages, Huazhong University of Science and Technology, Wuhan, China

Helen Meng Department of Systems Engineering and Engineering Management, The Chinese University of Hong Kong, Hong Kong, China

Weiguang Qu School of Artificial Intelligence, Nanjing Normal University, Nanjing, China

Yanqiu Shao College of Information Sciences, Beijing Language and Culture University, Beijing, China

Yueh-Yin Shih Institute of Information Science, Taipei, Taiwan

Zhifang Sui Key Laboratory of Computational Linguistics, Peking University, Ministry of Education, Beijing, China
School of Electronics Engineering and Computer Science, Peking University, Beijing, China

Lifa Sun Department of Systems Engineering and Engineering Management, The Chinese University of Hong Kong, Hong Kong, China

Weiwei Sun Department of Computer Science, University of Cambridge, Cambridge, UK

Xuri Tang School of Foreign Languages, Huazhong University of Science and Technology, Wuhan, China

Chiu-Yu Tseng Institute of Linguistics, Academia Sinica, Taipei, Taiwan

Ruben G. Tsui Graduate Program in Translation and Interpretation, College of Liberal Arts, National Taiwan University, Taipei, Taiwan

Houfeng Wang Key Laboratory of Computational Linguistics, Peking University, Ministry of Education, Beijing, China

Kexiang Wang Key Laboratory of Computational Linguistics, Peking University, Ministry of Education, Beijing, China
School of Electronic Engineering and Computer Science, Peking University, Beijing, China

Lei Wang Key Laboratory of Computational Linguistics, Peking University, Ministry of Education, Beijing, China
School of Foreign Languages, Peking University, Beijing, China

Longyue Wang Tencent AI Lab, Shenzhen, China

Lulu Wang Department of Linguistics, Communication University of China, Beijing, China

Meng Wang School of Humanities, Jiangnan University, Wuxi, China

Zhitao Wang Wechat Pay, Tencent Inc., Shenzhen, China

Andy Way ADAPT Centre, Dublin City University, Dublin, Ireland

Tingxin Wei International College for Chinese Studies, Nanjing Normal University, Nanjing, China

Guoxiang Wu School of Foreign Languages, Huaqiao University, Quanzhou, China

Yunfang Wu Institute of Computational Linguistics, Peking University, Beijing, China
Key Laboratory of Computational Linguistics, Peking University, Ministry of Education, Beijing, China

Liang-Chih Yu Department of Information Management, Yuan Ze University, Taoyuan, Taiwan

Shiwen Yu Key Laboratory of Computational Linguistics, Peking University, Ministry of Education, Beijing, China
Institute of Computational Linguistics, Peking University, Beijing, China

Jiahong Yuan Interdisciplinary Studies of Linguistic Sciences Research Center, School of Humanities and Social Sciences, University of Science and Technology of China, Hefei, China

Yulin Yuan Department of Chinese Language and Literature, Faculty of Arts and Humanities, University of Macau, Zhuhai, China
Department of Chinese Language and Literature, Peking University, Beijing, China

Hongying Zan School of Computer and Artificial Intelligence, Zhengzhou University, Zhengzhou, China

Weidong Zhan Department of Chinese Language and Literature, Peking University, Beijing, China

Kunli Zhang School of Computer and Artificial Intelligence, Zhengzhou University, Zhengzhou, China

Xiaojun Zhang Xi'an Jiaotong-Liverpool University, Suzhou, China

Ren Zhou Department of Chinese Language and Literature, Peking University, Beijing, China

Wenjie Zhou Key Laboratory of Computational Linguistics, Peking University, Ministry of Education, Beijing, China

Xuefeng Zhu Institute of Computational Linguistics, Peking University, Beijing, China
Key Laboratory of Computational Linguistics, Peking University, Beijing, China

Part I
Overview

Chapter 1
Chinese Language Resources Through One-Third of a Century

Chu-Ren Huang

Abstract This chapter provides a comprehensive overview of the co-development of Chinese language resources and Chinese language processing in the past three decades. The overview highlights the contribution of the Institute of Computational Linguistics at Peking University and the CKIP group at Academia Sinica, as they are the two groups that constructed most to building a robust infrastructure for Chinese language processing. Adopting the metaphor of "language resources is water," the chapter focuses on the power of accessibility, interoperability, and shareability, as well as the synergetic nature of language resources, language processing, and linguistic knowledge.

Keywords Language resources · Chinese language processing · Accessibility · Interoperability · Shareability

1.1 Headwater 濫觴

The recent rapid developments in computational linguistics and Chinese language processing is built upon more than 33 years of painstaking research on Chinese language resources. It is difficult for us to conceptualize that just 50 years ago, there was still doubt about whether the Chinese language could be effectively encoded and represented by a computer (Wang 1973; Zong et al. 宗成慶等 2009; Lu 2019). Similarly, just 35 years ago, Chinese documents were typically manually typeset, and electronic files of texts were the rare exception, rather than the norm. Fortunately, the constraints on accessible data allowed researchers to direct their efforts toward deeply understanding the linguistic characteristics of Chinese, as well as analyzing how the systematic knowledge of these characteristics can be best represented and annotated computationally.

C.-R. Huang (✉)
Department of Chinese and Bilingual Studies, The Hong Kong Polytechnic University, Hong Kong, China
e-mail: churen.huang@polyu.edu.hk

C.-R. Huang et al. (eds.), *Chinese Language Resources*, Text, Speech and Language Technology 49, https://doi.org/10.1007/978-3-031-38913-9_1

Two major research groups, the Institute of Computational Linguistics (ICL) at Peking University in Beijing and the Chinese Knowledge Information Processing (CKIP) group at Academia Sinica in Taipei, among others, located on either side of the Taiwan Strait, took a similar approach and marked the inception of computational linguistics and natural language processing scholarship in the Chinese language by launching long-term projects to construct sharable language resources at nearly the same time in 1986. Unsurprisingly, the language resources constructed by ICL and CKIP are now the essential infrastructure supporting Chinese language processing research.

The first paper that introduced research on Chinese language resources to the international academic community was most likely Huang and Chen's (1992) COLING paper, although both teams began publishing papers and technical reports regionally soon after the formation of their teams. In fact, the beginning of sustained efforts in Chinese language resource construction also heralded the new field of Chinese language processing and computational linguistics. The flagship computational linguistics journal in Chinese, *Journal of Chinese Information Processing* 中文信息學報, was founded in 1986 (Zong et al. 宗成慶等 2009). Chen and Huang (1989) were likely the first special issue on Chinese computational linguistics published in an internationally recognized journal. The development of the field can be tracked by several subsequently published edited volumes on Chinese language processing (Huang et al. 1996; Huang and Lenders 2004; Wong et al. 2009; etc.), and of course, by the growing number of papers on Chinese NLP in prestigious conferences and journals in the world.

1.2 Vision: Of Peaks and Giants 高瞻遠矚

Newton famously and aptly used the metaphor of standing on the shoulders of giants to describe scientific achievements. The shoulders of giants provided the height to extend our otherwise limited vision. In Chinese, vision is also linked to great height for great scholars, but the metaphor is instead of a tall mountain. The great height for one to look up to, and to hope to, at best, replicates 高山仰止景行行止. Fortunately, neither of the two visionary scholars who inspired and set up the infrastructure for research on Chinese language resources at Peking University and at Academia Sinica wanted to be immobile great mountains. Professor Zhu Dexi 朱德熙 of Peking University foresaw the potential impact of data-driven computational tools for Chinese language sciences and gracefully provided support with his stature and knowledge in Chinese linguistics while still entrusting the ICL team with full confidence. Professor Hsieh Ching-Chun謝清俊, a pioneer in Chinese language processing, continued to participate and support the computational environment, but also allowed the fledging computational linguists at CKIP to develop their new interdisciplinary expertise without the baggage of an existing paradigm. These two professors are the giants who not only carried their teams but also guided them, with their acumen and vision, to the source of the spring water so that they could carry out research.

1.3 From the Great Mountains Long Streams Flow 高山流水

The vision that the shareability and versatility of Chinese language resources would be the cornerstone of Chinese language technology was a catalyst for the digital revolution in the Chinese-speaking world. Before 1986, research on Chinese language technology focused almost exclusively on character encoding (see, e.g., Wang 1973; Lu 2019); however, the research topics broadened to those that are linguistically significant, such as word segmentation, parts-of-speech (PoS) tagging, and parsing. This research, in turn, enabled research on automatic processing of Chinese language content both online and offline. Such developments often went hand in hand with the systematic acquisition, organization, and documentation that was needed to build up a comprehensive linguistic knowledge of Chinese. The resources and linguistic knowledge milestones include the segmentation standards that amount to the first set of operable definitions of words in Chinese, e.g., Huang et al. (1996) and Liu et al. 劉源等 (1994). Additionally, using a large-scale corpus, both teams published works, both in the form of sharable databases and as monographs, following a rigorous methodology to analyze wordhood and PoS of millions of words of Chinese, so as to provide a comprehensive grammatical knowledge of Chinese. Yu et al. 俞士汶等 (1998) is the summary work of the PKU team and Huang et al. (2017) is the summary work in English of the Academia Sinica team, based on the many papers and technical report documentation that were published in Chinese in the 1990s. Huang and Xue (2019) also provided a comprehensive view of the state-of-the-art language resources and a general trajectory of development. In this handbook, the influence and cumulative impact of the language resource research of the two teams can be clearly witnessed.

The need to synergize linguistic and computational expertise, as well as the required attention to linguistic details starting at the lexical level to ensure robustness and coherence throughout these million-word corpora, necessitated the investment of a significant amount of talent. It is estimated that each team maintained a research group the size of at least 10–20 people for over 20 years, most of whom worked on language resources or linguistic analysis issues daily. These trained researchers were not only keenly attuned to linguistic facts but also well-versed in computational and quantitative methodologies. ICLers and CKIPers, as well as honorary members who visited, now form the core of the scholarly community espousing empirical approaches to computational and Chinese linguistics in greater China; much of their research can be found in this volume.

1.4 The Versatility of Language Resources 上善若水

Like water, the versatility of language resources does not come from what it is, nor because it has a highly specified designed function. The functional versatility of water and language resources is derived from their extremely adaptable shapes and the power from their accumulative volume. Just as water is shaped by its channel, conduit, or container, language resources are shaped by their design criteria, and especially by the annotation schemes. Water can cleanse, quench thirst, generate power, cut metal, fight fire, and carry ships, among other functions. The way that water is used depends on how the water body is shaped and directed to create kinetic energy. The many uses of language resources also depend on how they are shaped and directed by annotation and by all kinds of stochastic tools.

This metaphor of versatility provides an overarching design for papers included in this volume. We start with two overview papers from ICL and CKIP, respectively, introducing the vision, the roadmap, and the design criteria for their respective language resource infrastructures. Of special interest is the remarkable parallelisms in their approaches, in spite of inevitable variations and sociocultural differences due to over 30 years of separation, which severed most forms of academic exchange of information. Success for both teams bears witness to the soundness of the approaches they adopted to build language resources from scratch and to their vision and mission to build language resources that would support language technology and linguistic research in Chinese.

1.5 Giving Shape to Water 長溝流月

The second part, with the title of **Language Resources: Annotation and Processing**, contains 13 papers. These papers focus on the process that converts unstructured documentation of language uses to structured data that contains extractable linguistic knowledge. In this process, the special considerations are how to highlight and leverage linguistic characteristics of Chinese and the shareability and reusability of the resources. In other words, they focus on how collective instances of actual daily language uses can be harvested and harnessed with design criteria and enriched with annotation in order to be shareable and interoperable (Bird and Simons 2003; Stede and Huang 2012) for various corpus linguistics and NLP applications. In general, annotation can either be conceptually classified as linguistic annotation designed to be applicable for all genres/tasks or telic (purpose-driven) annotation for specific applications (such as emotion detection or opinion mining). Although the types of annotations that are reported do not cover the full range of possibilities reported in Ide and Pustejovsky's (2017) comprehensive handbook, it rivals the richness of annotation types of any other human language, including English.

Word segmentation, or tokenization, is the crucial first step for Chinese language resources and computing. Huang's Chap. 4 addresses this issue and proposes an approach that is significantly different than the dominant resource-dependent statistical learning approaches. His paper identifies that segmentation becomes a bottleneck for robust, real-time NLP applications in Chinese when short novel texts that lack suitable training data are encountered. This is also the only context where segmentation can directly contribute to new information. Yet, this is the exact context where the state-of-the-art segmentation algorithms fail because of their reliance on sizable, labeled data for training. The complexity of segmentation is minimized as a unary boundary decision model, which, when coupled with active learning, requires minimal training data.

The next five papers deal with lexical knowledgebases, both as the primary resources of lexical information for NLP and the structured and accessible repository of linguistic knowledge acquired through processing large-scale language resources. Bai's Chap. 5 provides an overview of the grammatical information in the PKU ICL lexical knowledgebase. Under this structure, and as part of the general lexical knowledgebase described in Chap. 2, Zhang et al.'s Chap. 7 introduces a knowledgebase for function word and Wang et al.'s Chap. 8 focuses on idioms. These two chapters tackle two of the most challenging linguistic constructions for lexical knowledge description. Function words are called *xuci* "empty words" 虛詞 in Chinese because of the abstractness of their meaning. Zhang et al.'s Chap. 7 clearly shows that a data-driven approach to capture the meaning of function words according to their context of usage and grammatical function is an effective one. Wang et al.'s Chap. 8, on the other hand, deals with the issue of the highly conventionalized and contextual knowledge-dependent lexical information of idioms and benefits from the perspective of treating idioms as lexical constructions. Shih et al.'s Chap. 9 describes a linguistic ontology-driven approach to the lexical knowledgebase. One of the strengths of this approach is the ability to describe the composition of the meaning of compounds, which are not compositional by definition yet are dependent and derivable from the meanings of their component words. The adaptation of an ontological database (E-HowNet in this case) also allows lexical meaning to be decomposed. Lastly, Hsieh's Chap. 6 introduces the linked data approach to enriching lexical databases and to creating connectivity for additional versatility in usages.

The next group is of three papers, Chaps. 10–12. These papers all deal with how to ascribe word senses to words in a corpus. Interestingly, they take different approaches. Liu's Chap. 12 relies heavily on linguistic knowledge already analyzed and stored in *VerbNet*. Jin et al.'s Chap. 11 introduces a supervised way of automatic tagging based on the abovementioned lexical databases from PKU. Finally, Bai et al.'s Chap. 10 adopts the powerful word-embedding algorithm to tackle the issue of senses of unknown words. This chapter represents an NLP approach to meaning prediction and can be read in contrast to the paper (Chap. 19) by Hong, which adopts an interdisciplinary approach.

The last group of the four papers in this part consists of four chapters introducing different types of specialized Chinese language resources. The construction of a semantic dependency bank in Chap. 13 by Shao et al. is a good example of the recent semantic turn in NLP and computational linguistics. Notably missing from our current volume are papers dealing with syntactic annotation, such as treebanks (Chen et al. 2003; Huang and Chen 2017). Earlier work on language resources, probably with parsing in mind, tended to attempt to add deeper structural information. More recent studies focus instead on the various types of information content that is carried by the words and texts. As such, we can see that Chap. 13 deals with the representation of semantic relationship among different components in a sentence. Li et al.'s Chap. 14 focuses instead on the context of conversation and dialogue acts. Similarly, Zhang et al.'s Chap. 15 approaches conversation and discourse from the perspective of translation. Lee et al.'s emotion corpus in Chap. 16 highlights one of the most productive direction in NLP and computational linguistic research that should have important implications for theoretical studies: the relation between language and emotion, as well as emotion and causes. A separate compendium of Chinese language resources, Li et al.'s Chap. 32, can be found in part five, at the end of the book.

1.6 Deriving Sharable and Versatile Knowledge 水善利萬物而不爭

The third part, entitled **Language Resources and Linguistic Analysis**, includes eight papers. While the chapters in the last part focus more on issues directly related to resource construction, they also briefly discuss the fundamental linguistic issues. The papers in this section take the perspective of linguistic theories, but with a focus on how principled arguments in linguistics can affect the study of language resources and language processing. Their shared theme is the new perspectives that afford linguists the versatility of shareable annotated language resources.

Yuan et al.'s Chap. 17 deals with the most basic issues in language processing: how to identify a speech sound segment without prior linguistic knowledge. The forced alignment algorithm has been developed and proven to be a very powerful tool for automatic speech recognition. Yuan's team applied this tool to gain important insights into phonetic studies. Chapters 18 (by Yuan et al.) and 20 (by Hsiung) can be described as more typical corpus linguistic studies. Yuan et al. underline the importance of annotating deep linguistic knowledge on the corpora, while Hsiung leverages an annotated corpus to resolve the long-standing issue of preposition versus localizer in Mandarin. The next group of three papers shows that frequency information, as the most straightforward quantitative measure from a corpus, can be leveraged to shed light on different linguistic issues. Chen in Chap. 21 uses quantitative data to establish a correlation between polysemy and the productivity of compounds. Ahrens and Chang in Chap. 22 apply the frequency of lexical patterns to study political discourse, especially how politicians engage their perceived audiences. In Chap. 23, frequency data plays a pivotal role in Lin and Hu's psycholinguistic study of the processing of relative clauses in Chinese. This is a good example of how structurally annotated corpora, such as treebanks, can be used in research on language processing. Hong et al.'s Chap. 19 can be related back to work on sense annotation in the last section. This paper takes a multidisciplinary approach to predict word senses, to construct a theory of how word senses are conceptualized, and to verify with behavioral studies. Lastly, Chap. 24 by Chen and Tseng leverages prosodic information to study how speakers align with each other in a conversation, linking the most basic acoustic information to the complex discourse interaction.

1.7 The Power of Language Data as Water 沛然莫之能禦

The fourth part of seven papers is given the title of **Language Processing: Models and Applications**. These papers demonstrate that based on the shared language resources and the reusable annotation and information, tools and systems can be built to tackle a wide range of language technology tasks. In Chap. 25, Sun et al. give us a very comprehensive overview of work on speech recognition and TTS (text-to-speech) synthesis. The next two chapters deal with noun phrases, as their identification (Chap. 26, Gao et al.) and interpretation (Chap. 27, Wang and Wang) underline some of the crucial tasks in language technology, such as name entity identification, paraphrasing, and question answering. Sun's Chap. 28 revisits one of the most fundamental technical issues in language resource construction: quality assurance for annotation. Chapter 29 (Wang et al.) looks even deeper at language resources and examines the issue of ontology matching and the issue of integrating different knowledge systems. The final two papers focus even more on the real world. Chang et al. (Chap. 30) explore an automatic question and answering system, trying to simulate humanlike behavior based on language resources. Wang et al.'s Chap. 31 leads us to the ubiquitous social media, underlining the importance of social media as language resources, as well as how language technology can help us to extract collective human behavior patterns from social media.

1.8 Conclusion and Dedication 水深無聲 有容乃大

At the beginning of the two research groups at Academia Sinica and Peking University, more than a third-century ago, the biggest challenges included character encoding (Lu 2019) and the cost of digitizing sizable language resources because of the lack of digitized content. Both teams took years to collect and annotate the first one million words of the corpus. It was nearly impossible at that time to imagine our current surge of Big Data, with web-as-corpus and gigabyte size (1000 million words, e.g., Huang 2009) corpus as the norm. Yet, without the small spring at the headwater, the whole content-based digital economy would exist in Chinese-speaking communities today.

In the past 30 plus years, more than 200 linguists and computer scientists have worked on Chinese language resources at either CKIP/CWN at Academia Sinica or at ICL, Peking University. Many of them continue to develop their academic careers in computational or theoretical linguistics, and we have gladly included some of their excellent academic contributions in this volume. The key people behind this sustained growth of the language resources are the two long-time group leaders who have preferred to speak softly and to overcome challenges with the persistence and power of dripping water 滴水穿石. We dedicate this volume to them as they are the giants whose shoulders we currently stand on, looking at the bright future of language big data-driven research.

References

Bird, Steven, and Gary Simons. 2003. Seven dimensions of portability for language documentation and description. *Language* 79(3):557–582.

Chen, Keh-Jiann, and Chu-Ren Huang. 1989. R.O.C. computational linguistics Workshops I. *Journal of Chinese Linguistics* 17(1):172–179.

Chen, Keh-Jiann, Chi-Ching Luo, Ming-Chung Chang, Feng-Yi Chen, Chao-Jan Chen, Chu-Ren Huang, and Zhao-Ming Gao. 2003. Sinica treebank. In *Treebanks*, ed. Anne Abeillé, 231–248. Dordrecht: Springer.

Huang, Chu-Ren. 2009. Tagged Chinese Gigaword version 2.0, ldc2009t14. *Linguistic Data Consortium.*

Huang, Chu-Ren, and Keh-Jiann Chen. 1992. A Chinese corpus for linguistic research. In *Proceedings of COLING 1992 Volume 4: The 15th International Conference on Computational Linguistics*, 1214–1217.

Huang, Chu-Ren, and Keh-Jiann Chen. 2017. Sinica treebank. In *Handbook of linguistic annotation*, ed, N. Ide and J. Pustejovsky, 641–657. Dordrecht: Springer.

Huang, Chu-Ren, and Winfried Lenders. (eds.). 2004. *Computational linguistics and Beyond.* Frontiers in Linguistics Monograph No, 1. Institute of Linguistics, Academia Sinica. Beijing: The Commercial Press.

Huang, Chu-Ren, and Nianwen Xue. 2019. Digital language resources and NLP tools. In *The Routledge handbook of Chinese applied linguistics*, ed. Chu-Ren Huang, Zhuo Jing-Schmidt, and Barbara Meisterernst, 483–497. London: Routledge.

Huang, Chu-Ren, Keh-Jiann Chen, and Benjamin K. Tsou. (eds) 1996. *Readings in Chinese Natural Language Processing*. Journal of Chinese Linguistics Monograph No. 9.

Huang, Chu-Ren, Shu-Kai Hsieh, and Keh-Jiann Chen. 2017. *Mandarin Chinese words and parts of speech: A corpus-based study*. London: Routledge.

Ide, Nancy, and James Pustejovsky. (eds.) 2017. *Handbook of linguistic annotation* (Vol. 1). Berlin: Springer.

Liu, Yuan, Qiang Tan, and Xukun Shen 劉源, 譚強, 沈旭昆. 1994. *Contemporary Chinese word segmentation standard used for information processing, and automatic word segmentation methods*信息處理用現代漢語分詞規範及自動分詞方法. Beijing: Tsing Hua University Press.

Lu, Qin. 2019. Computers and Chinese writing systems. In *The Routledge handbook of Chinese applied linguistics*, ed. Chu-Ren Huang, Zhuo Jing-Schmidt, and Barbara Meisterernst, 461–482. London: Routledge.

Stede, Manfred, and Chu-Ren Huang. 2012. Inter-operability and reusability: the science of annotation. *Language Resources and Evaluation* 46(1):91–94.

Wang, William S.Y. 1973. The Chinese language. *Scientific American* 228(2):50–63.

Wong, Kam-Fai, Wenjie Li, Ruifeng Xu, and Zheng-sheng Zhang. 2009. Introduction to Chinese natural language processing. *Synthesis Lectures on Human Language Technologies*. Morgan and Claypool.

Yu, Shiwen, Xuefeng Zhu, Hui Wang, and Yunyun Zhang 俞士汶, 朱學鋒, 王惠, 張蕓蕓. 1998. The grammatical knowledge-base of contemporary Chinese—a complete specification 現代漢語語法信息詞典詳解. Beijing: Tsing Hua University Press.

Zong, Chengqing, Youqi Cao, and Shiwen Yu 宗成慶, 曹右琦, 俞士汶. 2009. Sixty years of Chinese information processing中文信息處理 60 年. Applied Linguistics語言文字應用 2009 (4):53–61.

Chapter 2
Chinese Comprehensive Language Knowledge Base

Lei Wang, Zhifang Sui, Xuefeng Zhu, and Shiwen Yu

Abstract Natural language processing (NLP) aims to enable computers to understand human language and, moreover, to interact with humans to obtain information and knowledge more efficiently and more effectively. To this end, relevant resources—knowledge bases—can provide assistance and significant support to applications such as machine translation, information extraction, text processing, human-computer dialogue, and even language education. This paper will introduce the rationale for and the process of constructing the Comprehensive Language Knowledge Base (CLKB) by the Institute of Computational Linguistics at Peking University (ICL/PKU), as well as illustrate its importance as the infrastructure for Chinese information processing (CIP) in various domains.

Keywords Comprehensive Language Knowledge Base · Chinese information processing · Natural language processing · Grammatical knowledge base of contemporary Chinese

L. Wang (✉)
Key Laboratory of Computational Linguistics, Peking University, Beijing, China

School of Foreign Languages, Peking University, Beijing, China
e-mail: wangleics@pku.edu.cn

Z. Sui
Key Laboratory of Computational Linguistics, Peking University, Beijing, China

School of Electronics Engineering and Computer Science, Peking University, Beijing, China
e-mail: szf@pku.edu.cn

X. Zhu · S. Yu
Key Laboratory of Computational Linguistics, Peking University, Beijing, China

Institute of Computational Linguistics, Peking University, Beijing, China

C.-R. Huang et al. (eds.), *Chinese Language Resources*, Text, Speech and Language Technology 49, https://doi.org/10.1007/978-3-031-38913-9_2

2.1 Why Was the Chinese Language Knowledge Base Constructed?

Language knowledge resources serve as the infrastructure of research on computational linguistics, and natural language processing (NLP) systems are usually added to language knowledge bases. Researchers whose native language is Chinese have focused on Chinese language processing, the advantages of which can meet social needs. In addition, Chinese information processing (CIP) can contribute significantly to the overall development of computational linguistics and the expected breakthrough of NLP technologies. Chinese linguist Lü 吕叔湘 (1984) once remarked: "The grammatical analysis is relatively easy when a language has inflection; however, the job will become hard to do when the inflection is absent." In spite of Lü's comments on researchers' works on grammatical analysis, it is enlightening for those who are working on automatic computer analysis. Pertaining to automatic analysis, the Chinese language has the following characteristics: (1) in Chinese texts, there is no clear-cut definition between language units, and the borderlines between morphemes and words, compounds and phrases, phrases and sentences, and sentences and paragraphs remain fuzzy; moreover, the rules for constructing compounds and phrases, and phrases and sentences, are almost the same (Zhu 朱德熙 1999); (2) Chinese words lack morphological variations, and there is no direct corresponding relationship between word classes and their syntactic functions (Lü 吕叔湘 1984; Zhu 朱德熙 1999); (3) the Chinese 虚词 *xuci* "function word" (similar to English prepositions and Japanese postpositionals) is the same as 实词 *shici* "content word" in word form, and their erratic pragmatics and frequent omission increase analysis difficulties when they are regarded as leads for automatic analysis; (4) a Chinese subject-predicate structure can serve as the predicate of another subject-predicate structure, and a nested Chinese syntactic structure does not need additional elements such as conjunctions; and (5) the tense, voice, and mood of Chinese are not formal indicators.

In all natural languages, there is no simple direct corresponding relationship between form and meaning. The above characteristics of the Chinese language increase the complexity of this relationship. To conduct research on Chinese information processing, much more work needs to be done, and the construction of Chinese language knowledge bases has become a must as well as a great challenge for Chinese researchers who also regard it as their obligation. Based on such knowledge, as well as to employ strength in both science and humanity studies at Peking University, the Institute of Computational Linguistics at Peking University (ICL/PKU) has been dedicated to building various Chinese language knowledge bases since its foundation in 1986. The 30-plus-year effort has resulted in the completion of the Comprehensive Language Knowledge Base (CLKB) (Yu et al. 俞士汶等 2011: 12–20), a National Science and Technology Progress Award winner (second prize) in China in 2011.

The CLKB consists of six language knowledge bases, along with their specifications, including the software toolkits for building these bases and several application systems to test them. The bases complement each other as an organic entity whose serialized structure consists of various language units, such as words, phrases, sentences, and discourse, and covers different aspects of lexicography, syntax, semantics, and so on. The CLKB can also expand from Chinese to other languages and from general domains to professional domains.

2.2 Cornerstone of the CLKB: Grammatical Knowledge Base of Contemporary Chinese

If CLKB is comparable to a building, then its cornerstone is the grammatical knowledge base (GKB) of contemporary Chinese (Yu et al. 俞士汶等 2003: 19–136), an electronic lexicon for NLP research. Developed over 30 years beginning in 1986, it includes the following:

1. Over 80,000 word entries (one 词形 *cixing* "word form" may correspond to many word entries according to its pronunciation, meaning, and grammatical functions)
2. An NLP-oriented word class system established in accordance with the principle of superior distribution of grammatical functions
3. Classification of all words in the lexicon
4. Various grammatical features of each word based on its classification

The GKB adopted a relational database to depict the features of words by contingency tables, and it has a total of 34 files. Its general file describes all the common features of all the words and their attributes, including 词语 *ciyu* "word," 拼音 *pinyin* "phonetic symbol," 词类 *cilei* "word class," 同形 *tongxing* "homograph," 虚实 *xushi* "function or content," 体谓 *tiwei* "substantive or predicative," and 单合 *danhe* "simple or compound." Among them, *ciyu*, *pinyin*, and *cilei* can be understood literally, whereas *xushi*, *tiwei*, and *danhe* indicate whether a word is a function or content word, substantive or predicative, and simple or compound. The feature *tongxing* will be explained in the following.

Except for punctuation marks, the value of the field "word" in every file is marked with Chinese characters. However, because a character can have different pronunciations, word classes, or meanings, the field "word" cannot distinguish different entries using the same characters. 地道 *di4dao4*[1] is a noun (n),[2] while 地道 *di4dao5* is an adjective (a), so respective letters are inputted into the "word class" field in the GKB. For example, 当年 has two pronunciations— *dang1nian2* and *dang4nian2*— and both are 时间词 *shijianci* "temporal nouns (t)." The values of the word classes are both "t," but their differences cannot be distinguished. Thus, "A" and "B" are both inputted into the field "*tongxing*." In another example, there are two 仪表 in the

[1]Hereafter 1, 2, 3, 4, and 5 indicate the five tones—level, rising, falling-rising, falling, and soft—in Mandarin Chinese.

[2]The lowercase letters in parentheses represent the codes for the word classes.

Table 2.1 Samples from the GKB's general file

词语	词类	同形	拼音	虚实	体谓	单合	...
背	a		*bei4*	实	谓	单	
背	n		*bei4*	实	体	单	
背	v	A	*bei1*	实	谓	单	
背	v	B1	*bei4*	实	谓	单	
背	v	B2	*bei4*	实	谓	单	
当年	t	A	*dang1nian2*	实	体		
当年	t	B	*dang4nian2*	实	体		
地道	n		*di4dao4*	实	体		
地道	a		*di4dao5*	实	谓		
进行	v		*jin4xing2*	实	谓		
虽然	c		*sui1eran2*	虚			
枇杷	n	1	*pi2pa5*	实	体		
枇杷	n	2	*pi2pa5*	实	体		
希望	v		*xi1wang4*	实	谓		
仪表	n	A	*yi2biao3*	实	体		
仪表	n	B	*yi2biao3*	实	体		

GKB and both are nouns that are pronounced the same—*yi2biao3*. Nevertheless, they are two different words: one refers to instruments, whereas the other refers to a person's appearance or disposition. Thus, "A" and "B" are both inputted into the field "*tongxing*." Moreover, there are also two entries for 枇杷 *pi2pa5* in the GKB and their *tongxing* are 1 and 2, representing different senses of the same word (i.e., "plant" and "fruit"). Therefore, "word" + "word class" + "*tongxing*" is the key of the database file, and every record has a unique ID. Another more complex example is 背, which is a verb when pronounced as "*bei1*," meaning "to carry"; an adjective when pronounced as "*bei4*," meaning "unlucky"; a noun when pronounced as "*bei4*," referring to one's back; or a verb when pronounced as "*bei4*," referring to an action. To distinguish between their different pronunciations, it can be inputted into the field "*tongxing*" using the letters "A" or "B." Further, "*bei4*" as a verb can be distinguished as two senses: (1) to move in an opposite direction, to avoid, to go against, or to hide and (2) to recite. Therefore, the values 1 and 2 are added after "B." Some samples from the general file are listed in Table 2.1 (with incomplete fields).

The word classes and their tags in the GKB are shown in Table 2.2. It should be clarified that the additional classes are not defined by the principle of superior distribution of grammatical functions. However, the setup of their attribute fields in various data files and possible subclasses describe their grammatical functions.

After the establishment of word classes, every word had to be classified into a proper class, which proved to be a complicated and intricate task. 50,000 words were classified in 1998 and 70,000 in 2003, resulting in an unprecedented project of language engineering in the history of Chinese grammar research. Currently, 80,000 words have been classified. During the process of classification, it was crucial not only to distinguish the *tongxing* of words but also to confirm the superior distribution

Table 2.2 The word classes and their tags in the GKB

	中文	拼音	英文	代码
基	名词	*Mingci*	Noun	n
本	时间词	*Shijianci*	Temporal noun	t
词	处所词	*Chusuoci*	Place noun	s
类	方位词	*Fangweici*	Locative word	f
	数词	*Shuci*	Numeral	m
	量词	*Liangci*	Classifier	q
	区别词	*Qubieci*	Non-predicative adjective	b
	代词	*Daici*	Pronoun	r
	动词	*Dongci*	Verb	v
	形容词	*Xingrongci*	Adjective	a
	状态词	*Zhuangtaici*	State adjective	z
	副词	*Fuci*	Adverb	d
	介词	*Jieci*	Preposition	p
	连词	*Lianci*	Conjunction	c
	助词	*Zhuci*	Particle	u
	语气词	*Yuqici*	Mood particle	y
	拟声词	*Nishengci*	Onomatopoeia	o
	叹词	*Tanci*	Interjection	e
附	前接成分	*Qianjiechengfen*	Prefix	h
加	后接成分	*Houjiechengfen*	Suffix	k
类	语素	*Yusu*	Morpheme	g
别	非语素字	*Feiyusuzi*	Non-morpheme character	x
	成语	*Chengyu*	Idiom	i
	习用语	*Xiyongyu*	Social idiom	l
	简称略语	*Jianchenglueyu*	Abbreviation	j
	标点符号	*Biaodianfuhao*	Punctuation	w

of the words' grammatical functions in a real corpus. For some words that were semantically similar but grammatically different, the GKB regarded them as a double class. For example, 自动 *zidong* is an adverb in 门自动关上了*men zidong guan shang le* "the door closed automatically," as well as a *qubieci* in 自动阀门 *zidong famen* "automatic value."

In addition to the general file, the GKB created an individual file for each word class to describe their unique attributes and to reduce redundancy. However, there are only 25 files for the 26 word classes because non-morpheme characters were included in the morpheme file, and a file for punctuation marks was also produced. Moreover, to describe more attributes of verbs and pronouns, six subclasses were generated under the verb class: 体宾动词文件 *tibin dongci wenjian* "substantive object verb file," 谓宾动词文件 *weibin dongci wenjian* "predicative object verb file," 双宾动词文件 *shuangbin dongci wenjian* "double object verb file," 动结式文件 *dongjieshi wenjian* "verb and resultative construction file," 动趋式文件 *dongqushi wenjian* "verb and directional verb construction file," and 离合词文件

Table 2.3 Samples from the GKB's verb file

词语	同形	释义	体宾	谓宾	准谓宾	双宾	兼语	形式	很	...
背	A	用脊背驮；负担，承担。	体				兼			
背	B1	朝反方向；躲避；违反；瞒。	体							
背	B2	背诵	体							
进行		从事	体		准			形		
希望				谓					很	

liheci wenjian "segregatory verb file." 人称代词文件 *rencheng daici wenjian* "personal pronoun file" and 指示/疑问代词文件 *zhishi/yiwen daici wenjian* "demonstrative/interrogative pronoun file" were included in the pronoun class. Thus, altogether there are 34 files in the GKB.

Word classification is the foundation of the GKB. Nevertheless, it is only the foundation, as Chinese linguist Zhu 朱德熙 (1999) once said: "Words in the same class have similarities. But that is not to say they are grammatically identical ... Because words in the same class have individual characteristics, there shall be sub-classes. For instance, there are transitive and intransitive verbs in the verb class." Without mechanically understanding Zhu's exposition, creating more sub-classes would have made the whole scheme more difficult to work with and possibly inapplicable. The GKB's primary scheme is to place emphasis on describing the different grammatical attributes of each word based on its word class. The maturation of database management technology in the mid-1980s provided technical support for the computerization of the GKB. Obviously, the GKB not only grasped the essence of Zhu's 朱德熙 (1999) theory but also made innovations in technology. The methods of classification and attribute description are equivalent. If the different attributes of n ($n > =1$ and has the value 1 or 0) are given, a maximum of 2^n individual subsets can be obtained. Or, if a set of objects can be classified into N different subsets, then at least $[\log_2(N-1)+1]$ (square brackets are used to obtain an integer) different attributes will be required. The idea of combining classifications and attribute descriptions in designing the lexicon's framework was influenced by grammar theories from the mid-1980s, such as the lexical-functional grammar (LFG) theory (Kaplan and Bresnan 1982), which is represented by a set of complex features, and the unification theory. The GKB is indeed a complex feature set that is capable of describing the syntactical and semantic attributes of the Chinese language. Table 2.3 gives examples of some verbs and their attributes in the verb file:

体宾 *tibin* "substantive object," 谓宾 *weibin* "predicative object," 准谓宾 *zhunweibin* "quasi-predicative object," and 双宾语 *shuangbinyu* "double object" indicate whether a verb can take a substantive object, predicative object, quasi-predicative object, or double object and its value is 可否 *kefou* "can/cannot," whereas 兼语 *jianyu* "pivotal" and 形式 *xingshi* "formal" indicate whether the verb is a pivotal verb or a formal verb and its value is 是非 *shifei* "yes/no." 很 *hen* "very" indicates whether a verb can be modified by adverbs such as 很 and its value is also "*kefou*." However, the tags in the GKB are not simply "可/1" or "否/0" and "是/y" or "否/n" but vivid Chinese characters that are helpful in recognizing the meanings of the attributes. For instance, the value 很 in the "很" field in Table 2.3 amounts to "可/1" and "" amounts to "否/0." Since the GKB can be loaded onto machines where it will be stored and read, it was necessary to digitalize and normalize it. Nevertheless, its research, development, and redevelopment in applying NLP required human participation, such as linguists and NLP experts. For example, if the database is filled with "1/0" or "y/n," the data risks becoming monotonous, which could lead to a loss of efficiency and applicability.

Complemented with the above strategies, the choice of granularity also shows the true mission of the GKB. Rule-based methods such as context-free grammar (CFG) were adopted in most NLP technologies in the 1980s to describe the relationships between word classes. This resulted in a coarse granularity of knowledge, which was considered a bottleneck in improving the performance of NLP systems. Refining knowledge granularity has greatly improved the performance of rule-based systems and has met the needs in developing Chinese information processing technology, which has alleviated the shortage of Chinese language resources. The GKB essentially describes the relationship between a word and other word classes, while the relationships between words are naturally the language knowledge of fine granularity, but knowledge as such can only be obtained from a real corpus. However, there were no corpora available when digitalized texts still needed to be created manually. Today, defining the value of a field in the GKB as one information unit, the total information units in the 34 files are now 3.6 million.

2.3 Profile of the CLKB

After the completion of the GKB, which has made considerable contributions to Chinese information processing, an overall plan for constructing language knowledge bases was proposed in 1995 (Zhu and Yu 朱学锋, 俞士汶 1996). The CLKB was constructed step by step and reached the achievement of winning a National Science and Technology Progress Award by China's Ministry of Education in 2007. Thereafter, the CLKB has been continuously developing nonstop.

Two language knowledge bases form the body of the CLKB, including the phrase structure knowledge base (PSKB) of contemporary Chinese and the basic POS-tagged corpus (BPTC) of contemporary Chinese.

2.3.1 *PSKB*

Phrases (or phrasal expressions) are the basis of the Chinese grammar system. The Chinese phrase-based grammar system proposed by Zhu (1999) suggested that "[i]f we can describe clearly the structure and function of all phrases, Chinese syntactic structure will be clear since sentences are merely independent phrases." The 600 rules in the PSKB were written with extended CFG and describe the composition of various phrases. These rules can be highly abstract, such as "a verb can take nouns to form a 述宾 *shubin* 'predicate-object' phrase" and "a verb with certain attributes can take the types of nouns with matching attributes to form certain phrases (e.g., *shubin*, 定中 *dingzhong* 'modifier-head', or 主谓 *zhuwei* 'subject-predicate')," with the attributes of the verb and the nouns all from the GKB. The rules can also indicate that the phrase inherited attributes from its head, lost attributes, and derived new attributes. Two simple examples are given below:

lbvnnp::= *v*(双宾 = "双") + *n* + *n*/*例:送她礼物*/
jyvnvp::= *v*(兼语 = "兼") + *n* + *v*/*例:背老人上楼*/

2.3.2 BPTC

A corpus stores texts that are composed of sentences, which are formed by phrases (plus mood particles and punctuation marks), and then by words. The class, meaning, and pragmatics of every language unit in a text are all definite and enriched with concrete language knowledge. However, the knowledge may be implicit, and the purpose of corpus processing is to explicate implicit knowledge. Sentences are usually processed in the CLKB, for example:

S1: 坐久了, 腰疼、背疼。
S2: 他今天手气背, 打牌总输。
S3: 明明小时候就会背很多唐诗。
S4: 孩子常背着家长干冒险的事。
S5: 过去农村妇女背着孩子干活是常事。

S_i (i = 1, 2, 3, 4, and 5) is the ID of sentences. Formally, a sentence in written Chinese is a sequence of characters. To tag a sequence of characters is to change it to a sequence of words with POS tags, which are the codes for the word classes in the GKB. Therefore, the sentences above would be tagged as follows:

S1-1: 坐/v 久/a 了/y , /y 腰/n 疼/v 、 /w 背/n 疼/v 。 /w
S2-1: 他/r 今天/t 手气/n 背/a , /w 打牌/v 总/d 输/v 。 /w
S3-1: 明明/zr 小/a 时候/n 就/d 会/v 背/v 很多/m 唐诗/n 。 /w
S4-1: 孩子/n 常/d 背/v 着/u 家长/n 干/v 冒险/v 的/u 事/n 。 /w
S5-1: 过去/t 农村/n 妇女/n 背/v 着/u 孩子/n 干活/v 是/v 常事/n 。 /w

Thus, it is quite clear that 今天, 手气, 很多, and 冒险 are words, while 天手, 气背, 多唐, and 是常 are not. 今天, 手气, 很多, and 冒险 are a temporal noun (t),

Table 2.4 背in the CSD's verb file

词语	同形	义项	释义	语义类	配价数	主体	客体	与事	英译	. . .
背	A	1	用脊背驮	身体活动	2	人	具体事务		Carry	
背	A	2	负担, 承担	社会活动	2	人	抽象事物		Shoulder	
背	B1	1	背部对着, 朝反方向	位移	2	人	具体事务		Turn away	
背	B1	2	躲避；瞒	动态行为	2	人	人		Hide	
背	B1	3	违背；违反	社会活动	2	人	抽象事物		Violate	
背	B2		背诵	身体活动	2	人	创作物|信息|法规		Learn by rote	

noun (n), numeral (m), and verb (v), respectively. Machines learn explicit knowledge easily in that they know words and their frequencies and collocations once statistics are conducted for the BPTC. Knowledge such as word relations is finer in granularity than that in the GKB and PSKB. Based on knowledge as such, software can be developed to segment and POS-tag words automatically. Once software for automatic processing is available, a POS-tagged corpus on a larger scale can be created. Of course, human correction is required if automatic processing cannot reach the expected precision. At present, the thoroughly processed BPTC has 52 million Chinese characters with manual correction and the expectation that deeper processing from different aspects will be completed in the future. The CLKB also includes the *tongxing* attribute in the BPTC, for example:

S3-2: 明明/zr 小/a 时候/n 就/d 会/v 背/v!B2 很多/m 唐诗/n 。/w
S4-2: 孩子/n 常/d 背/v!B1 着/u 家长/n 干/v 冒险/v 的/u 事/n 。/w
S5-2: 过去/t 农村/n 妇女/n 背/v!A 着/u 孩子/n 干活/v 是/v 常事/n 。/w

An exclamation mark is added after the verb tag "v" to separate the following "A," "B1," and "B2" in the GKB (see Table 2.2). The *tongxing*-tagged corpus in the CLKB has 28 million characters.

The CLKB is still in progress and many new knowledge bases have been developed, such as the Chinese Semantic Dictionary (CSD), the Compound Structure Database, the Abbreviation Database, and the Chinese Idiom Knowledge Base. Table 2.4 provides the semantic information for the verb 背 in the CSD:

The CSD directly inherits information, such as word, word class, *pinyin*, and *tongxing*, and follows the GKB's principle of design and data format. *Tongxing* in the GKB is only a coarse granulation of word sense, while in the CSD, the word sense is decomposed further and the field "义项 *yixiang* 'word sense'" has been added. For instance, the *yixiang* of *tongxing* "A" are "1" and "2," respectively, while the field "释义 *shiyi* 'explanation'" has also been modified. In the CSD, the ID of each record is "word" + "word class" + "*tongxing*" + "word sense." To describe the semantic information of every word, fields such as "语义类 *yuyilei* 'semantic class'," "配价数 *peijiashu* 'valence'," "主体 *zhuti* 'agent'," "客体 *keti* 'patient'," and "与事 *yushi* 'dative'" have been added, and the field "English translation" has also been added to meet the demands of the Chinese-English machine translation system.

With the CSD, it is easy to see that the sense of "背/v!B1" in S4-2 above is "2" (i.e., "to avoid or hide"), whereas the sense of "背/v!A" in S5-2 above is "1" (i.e., "to carry on one's back"). Further tagging the word sense (i.e., the number after the hyphen is the "word sense" in Table 2.3.) in the corpus, which has seven million characters, produced the following:

S4-3: 孩子/n 常/d 背/v!B1-2 着/u 家长/n 干/v 冒险/v 的/u 事/n 。/w
S5-3: 过去/t 农村/n 妇女/n 背/v!A-1 着/u 孩子/n 干活/v 是/v 常事/n 。/w

2.4 What Was Learned from the Development of the CLKB?

The following is what was learned from the development of the CLKB over the past 30 years.

2.4.1 Fundamental Research and Application Research

Fundamental research is driven by application research. From 1986 to 1990, the ICL/PKU developed two NLP applications: one was Chinese input software based on words that considered sentences as transformation units (Yu 俞士汶 1988), and the other was automatic evaluation software for the output quality of machine translation systems (Yu 1993). Both were equipped with lexicons and rule bases that were separate from the program. Past research found that language knowledge bases were crucial in NLP systems, which led to large-scale research on Chinese information processing. Responding to the extensive demand for universal language knowledge bases, the CLKB came into being based on the GKB. The knowledge base projects in the CLKB were launched after the call for application systems, but a knowledge base did not necessarily apply to only one application system because fundamental research showed that it was not limited to the view that it applied to only the current needs of an application. The process of constructing language knowledge bases began with dictionaries and then extended to tagged corpora, focusing on morphology, syntax, and then semantics, starting with Chinese and then expanding to other languages and from general fields to professional fields. The stages and rhythm presented above coordinated the development of supporting technologies for the construction of language knowledge bases.

2.4.2 Theoretical Research and Engineering Practices

In the 1980s, grammar theories such as a set of complex features (e.g., lexical functional grammar) and unification were introduced, and at that time, the Chinese phrase-based grammar system began to grow. Guidance from those theories enabled the GKB and other knowledge bases to be widely applied. During that time, research practices were helpful in understanding and applying the theories. Although the design of the GKB was inspired by those theories, simply by looking at its data structure and knowledge representation, it is clear that the GKB did not simply copy their conclusions and expositions mechanically.

2.4.3 Development Goals and Process Monitoring

Although the GKB's top-level design was completed in 1995, the actual construction was not launched until the data analysis was complete. Large-scale corpus processing was only possible with good automatic segmentation, tagging tools, and technical human resources, all elements that went into the construction of the GKB. During the process, plans needed to be adjusted from time to time. With the GKB and its large-scale multi-level tagged corpus available, it became possible to propose and explore integrating heterogeneous knowledge bases and building probabilistic knowledge bases (Yu et al. 俞士汶等 2006: 227–283; Yu and Zhu 俞士汶, 朱学锋 2015). To fulfill these plans, there is still much work to do. Nevertheless, our research has confirmed the applicability and quality of our present work.

2.4.4 Balance of Scale and Quality

Without a scale large enough, a language knowledge base is an inapplicable toy. Quality is the lifeline of a language knowledge base. Although assisted development software is crucial to ensure quality, it is humans (or experts) who guarantee the quality of a language knowledge base. In the process of developing the CLKB, we trained talents and made scientific achievements at the same time. However, quality assurance can only be improved in development. If we had rigidly adhered to every detail from the beginning, our work would have stalled. Fortunately, in its 30-plus years of life, the CLKB has been put into application, and its quality has continued to improve, while its defects have been eliminated.

2.5 Conclusion

The main battlefield of language computation research has been transferred to the deep computing of language big data, especially semantic computation. Deep semantic computation requires support from semantic knowledge resources. Although "the available semantic resources have expanded to certain scale and depth, there are still problems and room for reaching the goal of Internet-oriented deep computation" (Sun et al. 孙茂松等 2014: 1–8). There are still expansive virgin lands to be found in constructing semantic knowledge resources. Nevertheless, although the CLKB involves some semantic knowledge, it only focuses on lexical and syntactic aspects. From the perspective of the Internet, the CLKB is only a drop in the ocean in language big data. Therefore, constructing new Chinese semantic knowledge bases is our current aim.

The ICL/PKU started a new language engineering project recently, the goal of which is to build a Chinese language knowledge consortium that is oriented to Chinese deep computation in the Internet environment and that will be able to cover all language units, such as morphemes, words, phrases, sentences, and discourse. We aim to build a static semantic dictionary, with no less than 100,000 words and about one million semantic knowledge items, including the framework for the semantic role of predicates and conducting multi-level tagging for a dynamic corpus with 10 million characters, for instance, labeling semantic roles for predicate arguments. To ensure the quality, scale, and successful development of the new semantic knowledge base, we intend to conduct research on technologies that integrate heterogeneous language resources and semantic knowledge acquisition based on weakly annotated resource interactions to build a semantic knowledge base platform based on collective intelligence.

Acknowledgments Our work was supported by the Key Project of Chinese National Programs for Fundamental Research and Development (No. 2014CB340504) and the National Natural Science Foundation of China (Grant No. 61772278). The authors also want to extend our thanks to all who have offered sincere support and contributions through grants, expertise, and hard work on the CLKB.

References

Editing Team of *Dexi Zhu's collection* 《朱德熙文集》编辑小组. 1999. *Dexi Zhu's collection* (Vol. 1) *《朱德熙文集》第1卷*. Beijing: The Commercial Press.

Kaplan, Ronald M., and Joan Bresnan. 1982. Lexical-functional grammar: A formal system for grammatical representation. In *The mental representation of grammatical relations*, ed. Joan Bresnan. Cambridge, MA: MIT Press.

Lü, Shuxiang 吕叔湘. 1984. *800 words in modern Chinese 现代汉语八百词*. Beijing: The Commercial Press.

Sun, Maosong, Ting Liu, Donghong Ji, Zhifang Sui, Jun Zhao, Bo Zhang, Silamu Wushouer, Shiwen Yu, Jun Zhu, Jianmin Li, Yang Liu, Houfeng Wang, Ibrah Turgun, Qun Liu, and

Zhiyuan Liu 孙茂松, 刘挺, 姬东鸿, 穗志方, 赵军, 张钹, 吾守尔·斯拉木, 俞士汶, 朱军, 李建民, 刘洋, 王厚峰, 吐尔根·依布拉音, 刘群, 刘知远. 2014. Frontiers of language computing 语言计算的重要国际前沿. *Journal of Chinese Information Processing 中文信息学报* 28(1): 1–8.

Yu, Shiwen 俞士汶. 1988. Application of grammar analysis technology in Chinese input 中文输入中语法分析技术的应用, *Journal of Chinese Information Processing 中文信息学报* 2(3): 20–26.

Yu, Shiwen. 1993. Automatic evaluation of output quality for machine translation systems. In *Machine translation* (Vol. 8), 117–126. Netherlands: Kluwer Academic Publishers.

Yu, Shiwen and Xuefeng Zhu 俞士汶, 朱学锋. 2015. Quantitative lexicon study and knowledge base construction for commonly used words 词汇计量研究与常用词知识库建设. *Journal of Chinese Information Processing 中文信息学报* 29(3):16–20.

Yu, Shiwen, Xuefeng Zhu, Hui Wang 俞士汶, 朱学锋, 王惠. 2003. *Specification of grammatical knowledge base of modern Chinese* (2nd ed.) *现代汉语语法信息词典详解(第二版)*. Beijing: Tsinghua University Press.

Yu, Shiwen, Huiming Duan, and Xuefeng Zhu 俞士汶, 段慧明, 朱学锋. 2006. Research and achievements on describing word probabilistic attributes 词的概率语法属性描述研究及其成果. In *Chinese information processing—Vocabulary research of modern Chinese 中文信息处理——现代汉语词汇研究*, ed. Jialu Xu and Yonghe Fu 许嘉璐, 傅永和, 227–283. Guangzhou: Guangdong Education Press.

Yu, Shiwen, Zhifang Sui and Xuefeng Zhu 俞士汶, 穗志方, 朱学锋. 2011. Comprehensive language knowledge base and its prospect 综合型语言知识库及其前景. *Journal of Chinese Information Processing 中文信息学报* 25(6):12–20.

Zhu, Xuefeng and Shiwen Yu 朱学锋, 俞士汶. 1996. Natural language processing and language knowledge base 自然语言处理与语言知识库. In *Research on Chinese characters at computer age 计算机时代的汉语汉字研究*, ed. Zhensheng Luo and Yulin Yuan 罗振声, 袁毓林, 107–118. Beijing: Tsinghua University Press.

Chapter 3
Introduction to CKIP's Language Resources and Their Applications

Zhao-Ming Gao, Chu-Ren Huang, and Keh-Jiann Chen

Abstract In this chapter, we will introduce the language resources developed by the Chinese Knowledge Information Processing (CKIP) Group at Academia Sinica in Taiwan over the past 30 years. These include monolingual and bilingual lexical knowledge bases (CKIP lexical knowledge base, Hantology, Chinese WordNet, Sinica BOW, and E-HowNet), Chinese grammar (Information-based Case Grammar), annotated corpora (Sinica Chinese Corpus, Sinica Ancient Chinese Corpus, Sinica Chinese Treebank, and Chinese Sketch Engine), and online Chinese word segmentation and parsing systems. After a brief overview, we will show how some of these resources can be employed to generate natural language processing (NLP) applications using machine learning algorithms.

Keywords Hantology · Chinese wordnet · E-HowNet · Sinica Chinese Treebank · Sinica Chinese Copus

3.1 Background

Research on Chinese information processing dates back to the pioneering work by Dougherty and Martin (1964) (cf. Huang 2004; T'sou 2004). Early research focused primarily on two areas, namely, the treatment of Chinese characters and the construction of Chinese dialect databases (cf. Wang 1973). It was not until the mid-1980s that the technical difficulties related to the input of traditional Chinese

Z.-M. Gao (✉)
Department of Foreign Languages and Literatures, National Taiwan University, Taipei, Taiwan
e-mail: zmgao@ntu.edu.tw

C.-R. Huang
Department of Chinese and Bilingual Studies, The Hong Kong Polytechnic University, Hong Kong, China
e-mail: churen.huang@polyu.edu.hk

K.-J. Chen
Institute of Information Science, Taipei, Taiwan
e-mail: kchen@iis.sinica.edu.tw

C.-R. Huang et al. (eds.), *Chinese Language Resources*, Text, Speech and Language Technology 49, https://doi.org/10.1007/978-3-031-38913-9_3

characters into computers were completely resolved. This was attributed to the invention of the Cangjie input method (倉頡輸入法) by Bong-Foo Chu 朱邦復 in 1976 and the release of the Big5 code in 1984 by the Institute for Information Industry (資策會), both of which have had far-reaching impacts in areas where traditional Chinese characters are used, including Taiwan, Hong Kong, and Macau.

Subsequent to the release of the Big5 code marked the beginning of a new epoch in Chinese language processing in Taiwan. Large-scale construction of language resources started after an ambitious project on the digitalization of archaic Chinese historical archives was launched by Ching-Chun Hsieh 謝清俊 at the Institute of Information Science, Academia Sinica, in 1984. Influenced by Hsieh's work, the Chinese Knowledge Information Processing (CKIP) Group 詞庫小組 was founded at Academia Sinica in 1986 under the joint leadership of Keh-Jiann Chen 陳克健 and Chu-Ren Huang 黃居仁. Over the past three decades, CKIP has established itself as one of the most important catalysts for research on Chinese computational linguistics as well as an internationally active research center on Chinese natural language processing (NLP). CKIP has made significant contributions to the construction of language resources as well as research on Chinese computational linguistics. In addition, CKIP has trained hundreds of research assistants and dozens of postdoctoral researchers.

This chapter will introduce the language resources developed by the CKIP Group at Academia Sinica and suggest how these resources can be used in conjunction with other NLP toolkits to create applications for Chinese information processing. For discussions on Chinese information processing in different periods, Zong et al. 宗成慶等 (2009), T'sou (2004), and Huang and Chen (1996) are recommended. Readers are also referred to Huang 黃居仁 (2009a, 2009b, 2016), Huang et al. (2010a, 2010b), and Huang and Shi (2016) for more detailed discussions on CKIP's Chinese language resources.

3.2 Language Resources

3.2.1 Chinese Writing System Resources

Database of Component Parts of Chinese Characters

Chinese characters are essential to Chinese information processing. In the early research on Chinese characters, Chinese character encoding only involved the creation of tables that contained the mapping of Chinese character symbols to an arbitrary code. This simple method was effective in handling most Chinese characters. However, it fell short when handling different variants of the same characters in Chinese dialects, Japanese, and archaic Korean, in which Chinese characters are used. In projects that digitalized archaic Chinese texts at Academia Sinica, Ching-Chun Hsieh 謝清俊 realized that the problem could be solved by dividing the characters into smaller parts and analyzing the configurations of these parts. The Document Processing Lab Hsieh led at Academia Sinica collaborated with the team led by Ning Wang 王寧 at Beijing Normal University. After scrutinizing the configurations of the component parts of Chinese characters, a Chinese database was created.

In the framework developed by Hsieh's and Wang's team, any Chinese character can be analyzed as a combination of a unique sequence of its component parts, which is exactly the same sequence of writing Chinese characters taught at schools. Component parts in each character can form a larger unit, which in turn form even larger unit. The component parts are merged from left to right and from top to bottom. For instance, the Chinese character 件 is made up of a combination of the two component parts 亻 and 牛 in sequence, whereas 部 consists of a combination of the three component parts 立, 口, and 阝 in sequential order, in which 立 and 口 are merged to form a unit before merging with 阝. No two Chinese characters are identical in the sequential order of their component parts. In other words, sequential order and component parts can uniquely determine any Chinese character. If two characters have the same component parts but in different sequential order, they refer to different characters, as 力 and 口 make up 加, while 口 and 力 constitute 叻. Likewise, 口 and 木 make up 呆, whereas 木 and 口 constitute 杏. The sequential order of the component parts determines the configuration and is therefore equivalent to the unique coding scheme of Chinese characters.

The integration of Chinese character coding with sequential order associated with the configuration of component parts has solved several fundamental problems in the information processing of Chinese characters, such as the uniqueness of coding, the coding of character variants, and the insufficiency of Chinese character sets. The technique, which has been an important pedagogical concept for teaching and learning Chinese characters for centuries, has been adopted by the ISO technical subcommittee of coded character sets. The database arising from this concept, namely, the Database of Component Parts of Chinese Characters at Academia Sinica 《中研院漢字部件檢字系統》, was made available to the public by Ching-Chun Hsieh 謝清俊 and Der-ming Juang 莊德明 (cf. Juang and Hsieh 莊德明, 謝清俊 2005). The same technique has also been employed in the user interfaces of learning tools in digital library and computer-assisted language learning projects, such as SouWenJieZi 《「搜」文解字》 and Adventures in Wen-Lan 《文國尋寶記》 at Academia Sinica (Huang et al. 2000a, 2000b; Huang et al. 黃居仁等 2004).

Hantology

Another feature of the Chinese writing system is that it is ideographic and contains semantic information, which presented a big challenge in converting the inherent semantic information in Chinese characters into a representation that could be used in information processing, particularly in the context of the Semantic Web. What was needed was a new language resource rich in semantic information based on Chinese characters. Hantology 《漢字知識本體》 was constructed by Ya-Ming Chou 周亞民 and Chu-Ren Huang 黃居仁 (Chou and Huang 2010; Chou and Huang 周亞民, 黃居仁 2013) to address this need. Based on the 540 Chinese radicals in 說文解字 *Shuowenjiezi*, Hantology categorizes Chinese ideographs based on the ontologies of the IEEE Suggested Upper Merged Ontology (SUMO) (cf. Niles and Pease 2001).

Different from traditional databases of Chinese characters, Hantology takes advantage of the knowledge representations in Chinese characters by making use of formal language in the Semantic Web. The framework of this language resource leverages the knowledge inherent in Chinese characters across different NLP applications, allowing its semantic information to be manipulated and computed. Hantology treats the entire Chinese writing system as an ontology, with the fundamental concepts associated with Chinese radicals serving as the top ontologies (cf. Huang et al. 2013a, 2013b). Within this framework, the relationship between radicals and characters and the intercharacter relationship can be interpreted as hyponyms and hypernyms, respectively. These concepts and relationships have been described by SUMO. The Hantology database (Chou & Huang, n.d.) was constructed based on Protégé, an open-source ontology editor and knowledge management system using OWL-DL, the formal language of the Semantic Web. The database's content includes the evolution of characters at the structural level, the description of ideograms and phonograms, the configurations of the component parts, the original meaning and the derived meaning of the characters, the relationship between variant characters, and the evolution of the pronunciation of the characters. This database also makes cross-lingual comparisons between the conceptual structures of Chinese and those of Japanese, Korean, and English possible. The theoretical assumptions of Hantology were further tested using the Generative Lexicon Theory proposed by Pustejovsky (1991). The exploration of radicals in Chinese characters and their relationship to event structures have been discussed in Huang et al. (2013a, 2013b) and Huang and Hsieh (2015).

3.2.2 Lexical Databases and Grammar

CKIP Lexical Knowledge Base

The CKIP lexical knowledge base contains 80,000 lexical entries with rich linguistic information, including pronunciation, frequency in the corpus, parts of speech, argument structure, selectional restrictions, co-occurring adjuncts, semantic features for nominals, and the syntactic environments in which a word occurs. The rationale behind the part-of-speech (POS) tags and their distinctions are described in detail in CKIP (1993) and Huang et al. (2017). Verbs are divided into stative and dynamic following Chao (1968). The syntactic and semantic information is designed to be used in Information-based Case Grammar (ICG) and for Chinese linguistic information processing. For instance, the verb 開始 "start" is specified as both a stative transitive verb with the syntactic category VI2 and the argument structure [theme, goal] mapping to its subject and object and a stative intransitive verb with the syntactic category Vh11 and the argument structure [theme] corresponding to its subject. Nouns are given semantic features, for example, 房子 "house" is a common noun with the syntactic category Nab and the semantic feature [+building]. In addition, the lexical database also specifies the classifiers that can co-occur with the word, for instance, 房子 "house" is often modified by the following classifiers {棟, 間, 幢, and 座}.

Information-Based Case Grammar

CKIP adopted ICG (cf. Chen and Huang 1990), under the framework of which the syntax and semantics of a word are represented using feature structures. As ICG is head-driven and unification-based, all the features must be in accordance with the restrictions imposed on the features when words are combined to form phrases and phrases are further combined to form sentences. Syntax and semantics are derived by the unification of features.

3.2.3 Corpora

Sinica Chinese Corpus

Corpus linguistic research in Taiwan dates back to two pioneering projects, namely, the Sinica Modern Chinese Corpus and the Sinica Ancient Chinese Corpus, which started in 1990 and 1993, respectively. These two projects were supported by the Chiang Ching-kuo Foundation for International Scholarly Exchange 蔣經國國際學術交流基金會 and later by funding from Academia Sinica and the National Science Council in Taiwan. The principal investigator of these two projects was Chu-Ren Huang 黃居仁, and Keh-Jiann Chen 陳克健 was the co-principal investigator in charge of computational aspects. The other two co-principal investigators of the Sinica Ancient Chinese Corpus Project were Pei-chun Wei 魏培泉 and Paul Thompson.

Sinica Corpus 1.0 was released in 1997, with over five million tokens. It was the first Chinese corpus that could be accessed via the Internet and was among the earliest corpora publicly available on the Internet. It was expanded to 10 million words in 2007. The main sources of the Sinica Corpus are newspaper and magazine articles, complemented by speeches and dialogues. The Sinica Corpus is balanced in terms of topics and genres, with 19,247 articles, 11,245,330 tokens, and 239,598 types.

The Sinica Corpus (CKIP, n.d.-a) is characterized by the following features (cf. Chen et al. 1996): (1) it conforms to the CKIP Chinese word segmentation criteria; (2) the articles included are complete texts; (3) users can select a subcorpus based on a given genre, register, topic, and media; and (4) the corpus has been processed with a part-of-speech tagger and manually corrected by a group of well-trained linguistic assistants. Since no tagged Chinese corpus was available at that

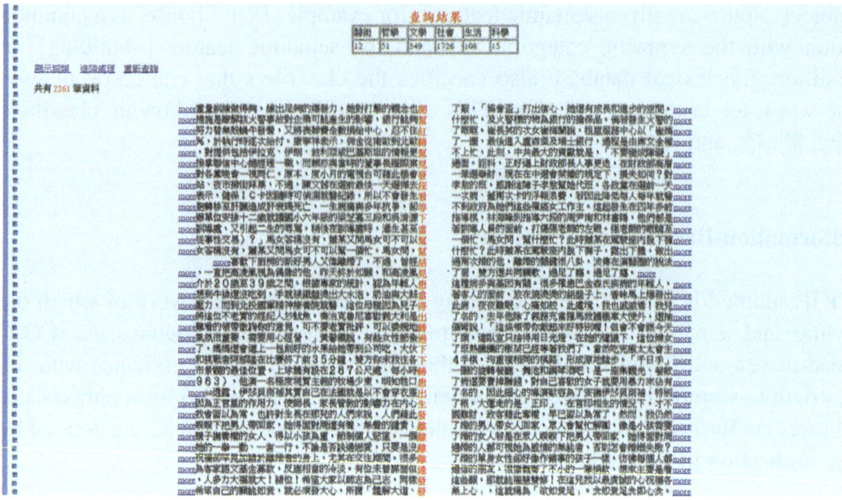

Fig. 3.1 The output of a search based on the +spv feature in the Sinica Chinese Corpus

time, the part-of-speech tagger was developed using a hybrid approach that integrated relaxation labeling and rule-based methods (cf. Chen et al. 1994).

The web interface of the corpus allows four types of searches based on keywords, morphological reduplications (i.e., AAB, ABB, AABB, ABAB, AA), part-of-speech (POS) tags, and features that are syntactic or morphological, including nominals, proper nouns, and displaced elements of separable verb-object (VO) or verb-resultative compounds. Users can choose to display the POS information. The system also supports multistage queries. Users can refine the initial keyword-based search results using one or more of the filtering methods based on binary (inclusion/exclusion) conditions: (1) immediate adjacent word before or after the keyword, (2) co-occurrences of word(s) within a window, (3) mutual information, and (4) parts of speech of keywords or collocating words. These functions make the Sinica Chinese Corpus a convenient tool for linguistic research on Chinese syntax, morphology, and semantics. Figure 3.1 shows the output of a search based on the +spv feature, which refers to the verbal element of a displaced verb-object compound. With this function, it is very convenient to retrieve instances of Chinese VO compounds in the Sinica Chinese Corpus that have been displaced.

Sinica Ancient Chinese Corpus

The Academia Sinica Ancient Chinese Corpus was the first of its kind with part-of-speech information (Wei et al. 魏培泉等 1997). The project was initiated by Chu-Ren Huang 黃居仁 and has been taken over by Pei-chun Wei 魏培泉. It contains archaic Chinese 上古漢語 (from the Pre-Qin 先秦 period to the Western Han Dynasty 西漢), medieval period Chinese 中古漢語 (from the Eastern Han

Dynasty 東漢 to the Wei Jin Northern and Southern Dynasty 魏晉南北朝), and early modern Chinese 近代漢語 dating from the Tang Dynasty 唐朝. Corpora in the archaic and early modern Chinese periods have been annotated with part-of-speech information using a tagset similar to the one adopted by the Sinica Modern Chinese Corpus. The public can access the corpora via the Internet.

Sinica Treebank

The Sinica Treebank project was initiated in 1997. The Sinica Treebank is now in its third edition, with 61,087 syntactic trees separated by punctuation marks and a total of 361,834 tokens. It is the first treebank in the world annotated with semantic roles. The Sinica Chinese Treebank was developed under the framework of ICG and adopted the head-driven principle, which labels the head of a syntactic unit as well as other syntactic and semantic information (cf. Chen et al. 1999; Chen et al. 2003; Huang and Chen 2017). As shown in Fig. 3.2, the head of a noun phrase is annotated with its semantic role. Each node is labeled with both syntactic and semantic information. Each tree represents a text segment delimited by punctuation marks. In other words, a tree can be a phrase or a sentence. These features make it distinct from the Penn Chinese Treebank (cf. Xue et al. 2005), in which only periods, exclamation marks, and question marks are used to delimit a text segment.

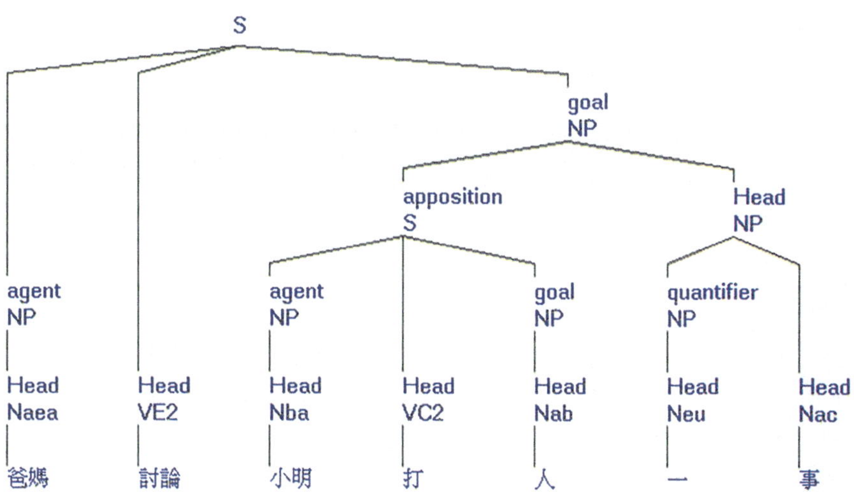

Fig. 3.2 Example of the Sinica Chinese Treebank represented by tree structures (http://godel.iis.sinica.edu.tw/CKIP/treebank/apposition.htm)

Language Resources Derived from the Sinica Corpus

The Word Frequency List of the Sinica Corpus was derived from the Sinica Corpus. It is the only one of its kind with part-of-speech information. It provides Chinese word frequency and cumulative frequency (cf. CKIP 中研院詞庫小組 1997).

The List of the Most Common Word-initial and Word-final Chinese Characters (CKIP, n.d.-c) contains 1135 word-initial characters and 1427 word-final characters from nouns, as well as 735 word-initial characters and 282 word-final characters from verbs (cf. Chiu et al. 邱智铭等 2004). For nouns, the English translations, part-of-speech information, the category in the Chinese synonym dictionary *Cilin* (*同義詞詞林*), *and examples are given. For verbs, the English translations, morphological rules, and examples are provided.*

3.2.4 WordNet and Ontologies

Bilingual Ontological WordNet

Bilingual Ontological WordNet (BOW) represents the ontological information in WordNet using SUMO and contains the linking between word senses and word forms in both English and Chinese (cf. Huang et al. 2010a, 2010b). In other words, given a Chinese word as an input, Sinica BOW can provide the sense corresponding to English WordNet and SUMO. Figure 3.3 shows the partial output of the search of the verb 蓋 *gai* "cover; build" in the Sinica BOW, displaying their equivalents in SUMO:

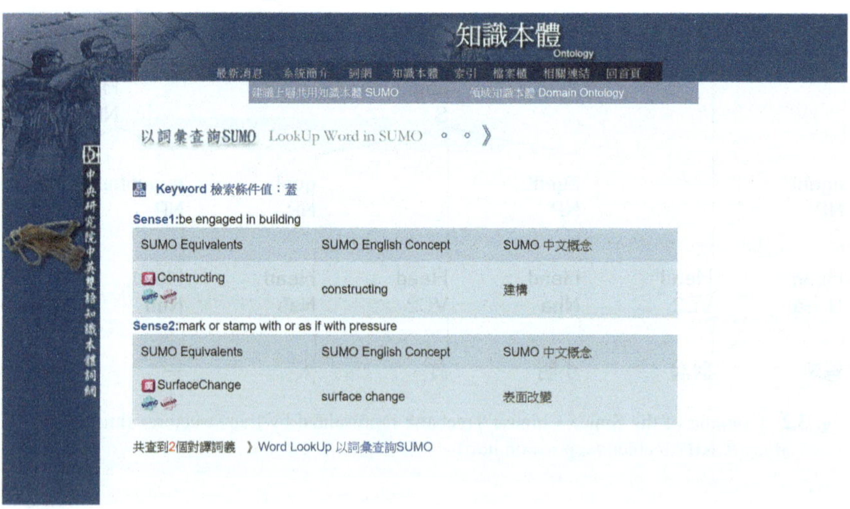

Fig. 3.3 Two verb senses of 蓋 *gai* in the Sinica BOW and their equivalents in SUMO

Chinese WordNet

Chinese WordNet (CWN), modeled after WordNet for the English language, was developed by Chu-Ren Huang 黃居仁 and Shu-Kai Hsieh 謝舒凱. CWN is a Chinese lexical semantic database with enumerations of word senses, definitions, and examples, along with parts of speech and synonyms (also known as synsets) for each sense (Huang et al. 黃居仁等 2010a, 2010b). The example in (3.1) below shows partial information for one of the verb meanings of 蓋 *gai* in Chinese WordNet. Notice that the part-of-speech information provided in Chinese WordNet is based on the same tagset used in the Sinica Chinese Corpus, in which VC is a transitive verb. To reduce the manual work required in constructing CWN, an effort was made to bootstrap information for CWN from English WordNet and other bilingual lexicons. For instance, Lee et al. (2009) used bootstrapping methods to automatically annotate word senses in Chinese WordNet using the semantic labels of WordNet Domains.

(3.1)
蓋
及物動詞 (VC) 將材料依照設計規格, 建造後供人類活動的房屋或土木工程。
同義詞: 建造 建^{1} 建築 造^{1} 作^{1} 構^{1}
例句
這間浴室是專門為我而蓋的。
香港政府在此蓋了兩間飯堂供膳。
她在肯亞蓋了一個專門收容動物寶寶的孤兒院。

Extended-HowNet

The Extended-HowNet (E-HowNet) ontology (CKIP, n.d.-d) (cf. Chen and Huang 2009) was adapted from HowNet (cf. Dong and Dong 2006) and provides lexical semantic representations for Chinese words that are used in Taiwan. The content in E-HowNet has been modified. There are four semantic types, namely, objects, acts, attributes, and values. Following HowNet, E-HowNet adopted a special form of knowledge representation language that encoded lexical knowledge, related common sense, and event structures in a way that computers can manipulate. The semantic primitives in HowNet and E-HowNet are called sememes. Meanings of a word are represented by structured information with sememes and attribute-value pairs. For instance, 老師 *laoshi* "teacher" is represented in HowNet as {human|人: HostOf = {Occupation |職位},domain = {education |教育},{teach |教: agent = {~}}}; that is, 老師 *laoshi* "teacher" is defined as a person with an occupation in the educational domain and as the agent in the teaching event. The ontology of the word is represented by the first sememe. For instance, the sememe {human| 人} denotes that 老師 *laoshi* "teacher" is a person. Note that each Chinese

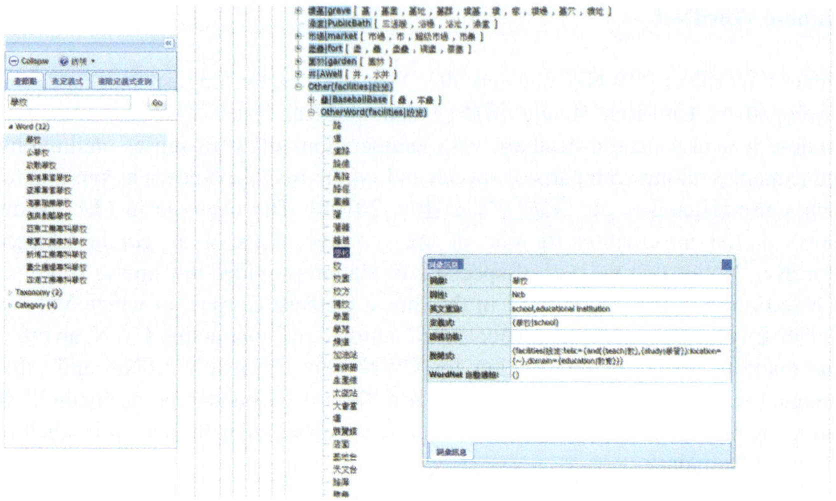

Fig. 3.4 E-HowNet representation of 學校 *xuexiao* "school" and its semantic hierarchies

word in HowNet contains Chinese-English bilingual information. In E-HowNet, however, 老師 *laoshi* "teacher" is represented slightly differently as {專業人士|professional:domain = {education |教育},predication = {teach |教:agent = {~}}}. Figure 3.4 is the E-HowNet representation of 學校 *xuexiao* "school." Like English WordNet, HowNet and E-HowNet have semantic hierarchies. The major differences between WordNet and HowNet are that WordNet uses English for its definitions, whereas HowNet employs a knowledge representation language for its definitions. WordNet is based on semantic networks and contains less common-sense knowledge. In contrast, HowNet contains more common-sense knowledge and encodes the events, semantic roles, and domains typically associated with a word.

3.2.5 Integrated Resources

Chinese Sketch Engine

Chinese Sketch Engine (Chinese WordNet Group, n.d.) was developed by Adam Kilgarriff, Chu-Ren Huang 黃居仁, and Wei-Yun Ma 馬偉雲 (cf. Kilgarriff et al. 2005). The system, drawing on the Chinese Giga-word Corpus (cf. Huang 2009a, 2009b), which includes 1.4 billion words from Taiwan, China, and Singapore, is one of the largest Chinese corpora available. Huang et al. (2005) used Chinese Sketch Engine to extract Chinese collocations, while Hong and Huang 洪嘉馡, 黃居仁 (2008) semiautomatically derived the different usages between the Mandarin Chinese words used in Taiwan and China in terms of collocations using the Word Sketch function in Chinese Sketch Engine.

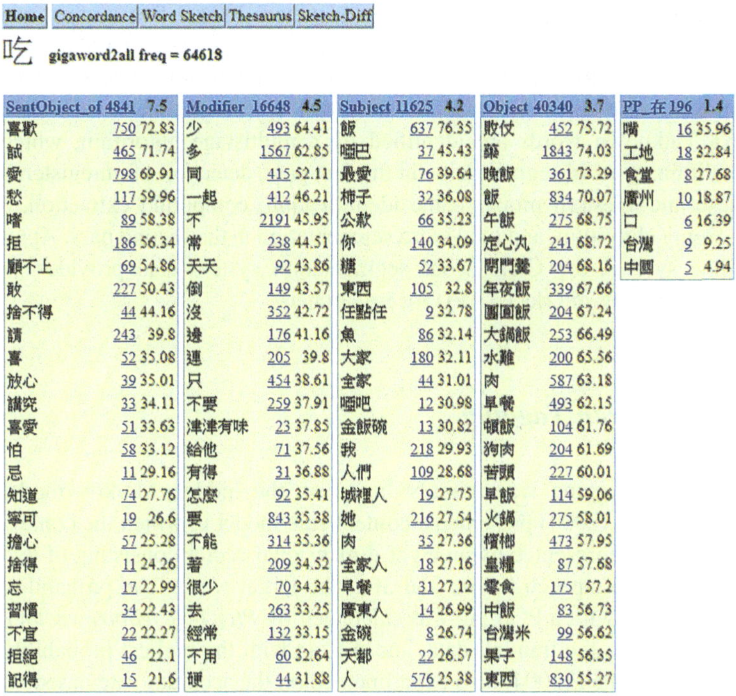

Home | Concordance | Word Sketch | Thesaurus | Sketch-Diff

吃 gigaword2all freq = 64618

SentObject_of 4841		7.5	Modifier 16648		4.5	Subject 11625		4.2	Object 40340		3.7	PP_在 196		1.4
喜歡	750	72.83	少	493	64.41	飯	637	76.35	敗仗	452	75.72	嘴	16	35.96
試	465	71.74	多	1567	62.85	啞巴	37	45.43	藥	1843	74.03	工地	18	32.84
愛	798	69.91	同	415	52.11	最愛	76	39.64	晚飯	361	73.29	食堂	8	27.68
愁	117	59.96	一起	412	46.21	柿子	32	36.08	飯	834	70.07	廣州	10	18.87
嗜	89	58.38	不	2191	45.95	公款	66	35.23	午飯	275	68.75	口	6	16.39
拒	186	56.34	常	238	44.51	你	140	34.09	定心丸	241	68.72	台灣	9	9.25
顧不上	69	54.86	天天	92	43.86	糖	52	33.67	閉門羹	204	68.16	中國	5	4.94
敢	227	50.43	倒	149	43.57	東西	105	32.8	年夜飯	339	67.66			
捨不得	44	44.16	沒	352	42.72	任點任	9	32.78	團圓飯	204	67.24			
請	243	39.8	邊	176	41.16	魚	86	32.14	大鍋飯	253	66.49			
喜	52	35.08	連	205	39.8	大家	180	32.11	水雞	200	65.56			
放心	39	35.01	只	454	38.61	全家	44	31.01	肉	587	63.18			
講究	33	34.11	不要	259	37.91	啞吧	12	30.98	早餐	493	62.15			
喜愛	51	33.63	津津有味	23	37.85	金飯碗	13	30.82	頓飯	104	61.76			
怕	58	33.12	給他	71	37.56	我	218	29.93	狗肉	204	61.69			
忌	11	29.16	有得	31	36.88	人們	109	28.68	苦頭	227	60.01			
知道	74	27.76	怎麼	92	35.41	城裡人	19	27.75	早飯	114	59.06			
寧可	19	26.6	要	843	35.38	她	216	27.54	火鍋	275	58.01			
擔心	57	25.28	不能	314	35.36	肉	35	27.36	檳榔	473	57.95			
捨得	11	24.26	著	209	34.52	全家人	18	27.16	皇糧	87	57.68			
忘	17	22.99	很少	70	34.34	早餐	31	27.12	零食	175	57.2			
習慣	34	22.43	去	263	33.25	廣東人	14	26.99	中飯	83	56.73			
不宜	22	22.27	經常	132	33.15	金碗	8	26.74	台灣米	99	56.62			
拒絕	46	22.1	不用	60	32.64	天都	22	26.57	果子	148	56.35			
記得	15	21.6	硬	44	31.88	人	576	25.38	東西	830	55.27			

Fig. 3.5 Output of the query for 吃 *chi* "eat" using the Word Sketch function in Chinese Sketch Engine

Ma and Huang (2006) discussed how to tag a heterogeneous giga-word corpus in a uniform way. Apart from its large corpus size, it was characterized by the powerful Word Sketch function, which highlighted collocations based on grammatical dependency relations such as subject-verb, verb-object, and modifier-noun automatically derived from the corpus (cf. Fig. 3.5 for the output of the query for 吃 "eat" using the Word Sketch function). The Word Sketch function also extracted synonymous words based on the distribution of the words in the context. In addition, it displayed the differences of two words based on the words that co-occurred in their grammatical dependency relations.

3.3 Core Tools in Chinese Language Processing

3.3.1 Word Segmentation and POS Tagging

The CKIP word segmentation system is based on a statistical algorithm, morphological rules, and a lexical database consisting of roughly 100,000 words, along with information such as their parts of speech, frequencies, frequencies of each part of speech, and frequencies of bigrams (cf. Ma and Chen 2004). The system can automatically identify words that are not included in the lexicon. Unlike most Chinese word segmentation systems, it not only relies on language models and corpus statistics but also takes into account the statistical information derived from the input text. Unknown words are identified by a multistage algorithm, which consists of preliminary word segmentation in the first pass, detection of unregistered words, Chinese and Western proper name identification, compound extraction, a bottom-up merging algorithm, and final word segmentation in the second pass. Apart from the online system, the CKIP word segmentation system also provides an application programming interface (API) for researchers.

3.3.2 Part-of-Speech Tagging

CKIP part-of-speech tagging was initially based on the hidden Markov model (HMM). Tsai and Chen (2004) presented a context-rule model in which the context feature of a word was represented by an eight-dimensional vector consisting of two words and their parts of speech before and after the target word. The probability associated with a word with a POS tag was calculated by $P(c_0 \mid w_0, \textit{feature vector})$, which was derived from the training data, and the tag with the highest probability was chosen. Tsai and Chen (2004) also experimented on the accuracy rate based on the proposed context-rule model, the Markov bigram model, and the word-dependent Markov bigram model. The findings showed that the proposed context-rule model outperformed both the word-dependent Markov bigram model and the Markov bigram model.

3.3.3 Parsing

If a large manually corrected treebank is available, the probability of each context-free grammar (CFG) rule can be computed, and the probability of a tree structure is the multiplication of all the CFG rules (also known as the phrase structure rules in linguistics) in a derivation (cf. Jurafsky and Martin 2008; Manning and Schütze 1999). The most likely structure of a sentence is the one with the highest probability. This is the essence of probabilistic context-free grammar (PCFG), in which the maximum likelihood is used to calculate probability. The Viterbi PCFG parser is a bottom-up parser that uses dynamic programming to find the single most likely parse (cf. Bird et al. 2009). The Viterbi PCFG parser analyzes the structure of a sentence by iteratively creating a "most likely constituents table," which keeps track of the most likely syntactic structures and their spans and nodes, as shown in Table 3.1:

Two types of information have been proven useful to the improvement of PCFG parsers, namely, lexicalized information and word-to-word dependency information (cf. Jurafsky and Martin 2008; Manning and Schütze 1999). PCFG parsers do not

Table 3.1 Construction of a most likely constituents table using the Viterbi PCFG parser

Most likely constituents table			
Span	Node	Syntactic structure tree	Probability
[0:1]	NP	(NP 我)	0.3
[2:3]	NP	(NP 樓梯)	0.3
[5:6]	NP	(NP 教授)	0.3
[1:4]	PP	(PP 在 (NP 樓梯) 上)	0.05
[4:6]	VP	(VP 看到 (NP 教授))	0.03
[0:4]	NP	(NP (NP 我) (PP 在 (NP 樓梯) 上))	0.01
[0:6]	S	(S (NP (NP 我) (PP 在 (NP 樓梯) 上)) (VP 看到 (NP 教授)))	0.0001

S sentence, *NP* noun phrase, *PP* prepositional phrase, *VP* verb phrase

consider the properties of individual words. Lexicalized PCFG, however, makes use of the lexical head of a CFG rule and its probability and reflects individual lexical properties of words such as transitivity and complementation of verbs. This is why the performance of a lexicalized PCFG parser outperforms that of a non-lexicalized PCFG parser. However, the size of the Sinica Chinese Treebank (CKIP, n.d.-e) was not large enough to train a lexicalized PCFG parser. To tackle this problem, Hsieh et al. (2007) proposed using a self-learning method to derive the association strengths of dependency word pairs from the Chinese Giga-word Corpus. Hsieh et al. (2012) further proposed a context-dependent probability re-estimation model (CDM), which integrated the contextual features, including words, parts of speech, and word sense features, derived from probabilities from PCFG with contextual probabilities. Hsieh et al. (2012) also showed that the performance of this parser outperformed the Berkeley statistical parser when both parsers used the same training data from the Sinica Chinese Treebank.

3.3.4 Automatic Semantic Role Assignment

You and Chen (2004) presented dependency decision-making and example-based approaches to semantic role labeling by drawing on the Sinica Chinese Treebank, which has 74 semantic roles. The intuitive idea of the example-based approach is that semantic relations in the same event will be roughly the same. Thus, semantic relations can be revealed by looking for similar dependency relations such as head-argument. The probability of each semantic role in a constituent structure is calculated by $P(r \mid constituent)$. Figure 3.6 shows the output of the CKIP parser (CKIP, n.d.-b) with semantic role labeling:

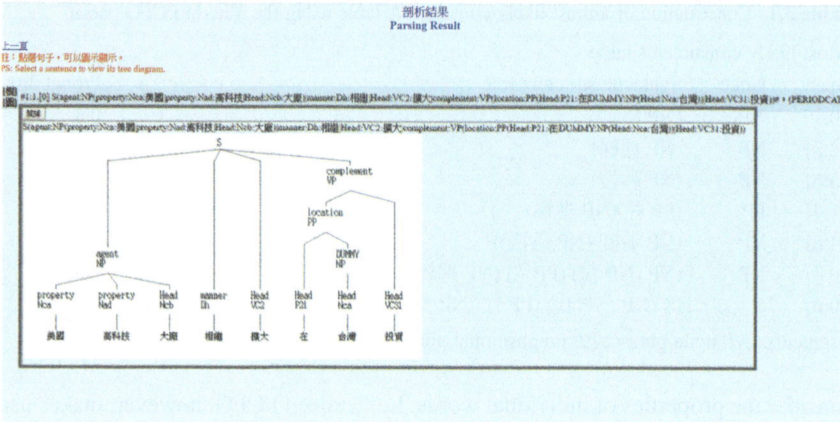

Fig. 3.6 Output of the CKIP parser with semantic role labeling

3.4 Applications of CKIP's Resources

As discussed above, CKIP has many language resources that can be used in NLP applications. For instance, in Hsieh et al. (2005), a grammar binarization method was proposed to increase the coverage of probabilistic context-free grammar. Based on CKIP's annotated corpora, Huang et al. (2015) semiautomatically extracted grammar rules.

When creating NLP applications, researchers can use the API in the CKIP word segmentation and part-of-speech tagging program. Alternatively, they can employ the corpora from CKIP to train their own word segmentation and POS tagging systems. In this section, we will demonstrate how CKIP's resources can be used to create NLP applications such as Chinese word segmentation, part-of-speech tagging, dependency parsing, extraction of lexical semantic patterns, and word sense induction.

3.4.1 Word Segmentation and Part-of-Speech Tagging Using YamCha and CRF++

We will start with Chinese word segmentation programs. With the Sinica Chinese Corpus, it is relatively easy to implement word segmentation and POS tagging programs using YamCha or CRF++, both of which were developed by Taku Kudo (cf. Kudo 2001, 2005). Both of these NLP toolkits were based on support vector machine (SVM) and conditional random field (CRF), respectively, and were designed for word segmentation, part-of-speech tagging, and NP chunking (cf. Kudo and Matsumoto 2000). The input format that YamCha and CRF++ take is the same. By converting the Sinica Corpus into the format adopted by the shared tasks of the CoNLL 2000, a classifier for Chinese word segmentation programs can be easily trained. For instance, the B, E, and I tags can be used for word segmentation, in which B and E represent word-initial and word-final position, respectively, and I indicates that it is inside a word that is not in the word-initial or word-final position, as shown in (3.2) below. The recent release of the Python package NAER Chinese word segmentation and part-of-speech tagging programs was developed using CRF++ and the Sinica Corpus, which significantly outperformed Jieba's open-source software for Chinese word segmentation.

(3.2)	
人	B
工	I
智	I
慧	E
超	B
越	E
專	B
家	E

YamCha and CRF++ can both be used for part-of-speech tagging. There are only a few differences between training a word segmentation program and a part-of-speech tagger. A part-of-speech tagger is trained using part-of-speech tags. In addition, in POS tagging, the unit is a word instead of a character, as illustrated in (3.3) below. There are in fact three versions of the CKIP tagsets, ranging from fine-grained to coarse-grained. If the corpus size is not very large, coarse-grained POS tags are preferred.

(3.3)		
保證	VE	(active verb with a sentential object)
一定	D	(adverb)
會	D	
請	VF	(active verb with a verbal object)
大家	Nh	(pronoun)

3.4.2 Viterbi PCFG Parser, Syntactic Complexity, and Chinese Readability

Several tools can be used to train a Chinese parser. The NLTK toolkit (cf. Bird et al. 2009), for example, provides functions for deriving the Viterbi PCFG parser. However, as the format of the Sinica Chinese Treebank is different from that of most existing parsers, it needs to be preprocessed first. The format of the Sinica Chinese Treebank in (3.4) below can be converted into a format that can train the

1	1	S->NP V_11 NP	(S(NP(N))(V_11)(NP(DM(TT)(M))(N)))	(S(NP(Nh(我)))(V_11(是))(NP(DM(Neu(一))(Nf(名)))(Na(秘書))))	我是一名秘書
2	1	S->NP V	(S(NP(N))(V))	(S(NP(Nh(你)))(VH(好)))	你好。
3	1	S->NP V_11 NP	(S(NP((N)(ADV))(N))(V_11)(NP(N)))	(S(NP(N•的(Nh(我))(DE(的)))(Na(名字)))(V_11(是))(NP(Nb(愛麗絲))))	我的名字是愛麗絲，
4	1	S->NP V_11 NP	(S(NP(N))(V_11)(NP(DM(TT)(M))(N)))	(S(NP(Nh(我)))(V_11(是))(NP(DM(Neu(一))(Nf(名)))(Na(秘書))))	我是一名秘書。
5	1	S->NP V_11 NP	(S(NP(TT)(NP(M)))(V_11)(NP(N)(N)))	(S(NP(Nep(那))(NP(Nf(位))))(V_11(是))(NP(Nb(王))(Na(小姐))))	那位是王小姐，
6	1	S->NP V_11 NP	(S(NP(N))(V_11)(NP((N)(ADV))(N)))	(S(NP(Nh(她)))(V_11(是))(NP(N•的(Nh(我))(DE(的)))(Na(老闆))))	她是我的老闆。
7	1	S->NP V_11 NP	(S(NP(TT)(NP(M)))(V_11)(NP((N)(ADV))(N)))	(S(NP(Nep(這))(NP(Nf(位))))(V_11(是))(NP(N•的(Nh(我))(DE(的)))(Na(哥哥))))	這位是我的哥哥，大衛。
7	1	S->NP	(S(NP(N)))	(S(NP(Nb(大衛))))	這位是我的哥哥，大衛。
8	1	S->NP V_11 NP	(S(NP(N))(V_11)(NP(DM(TT)(M))(N)))	(S(NP(Nh(他)))(V_11(是))(NP(DM(Neu(一))(Nf(名)))(Na(記者))))	他是一名記者。
9	1	S->NP ADV V_11 NP	(S(NP(N))(ADV)(V_11)(NP((N)(ADV))(N)))	(S(NP(Nb(馬克)))(D(也))(V_11(是))(NP(N•的(Nh(我))(DE(的)))(Na(哥哥))))	馬克也是我的哥哥。
10	1	S->NP V_11 NP	(S(NP(N))(V_11)(NP(N)))	(S(NP(Nh(他)))(V_11(是))(NP(Na(軍人))))	他是軍人。

Fig. 3.7 Context-free grammar rules in an article

Viterbi PCFG parser using the NLTK toolkit, while (3.5) below shows the output of the Viterbi PCFG parser trained with the Sinica Chinese Treebank. The performance of the parser can be evaluated using the PARSEVAL metric or the Leaf-Ancestor (LA) metric proposed by Sampson (2000).

(3.4)

S(theme:VP(Head:VC33:噴灑| theme:NP(Head:Nab:農藥))| evaluation:Dbb:只有| Head:VC2: 威脅到| goal:NP(property:Nab:生物| Head:Nad:多樣性))

(3.5)

(S (NP (NP (NP (VP (PP (P 由) (NP (N 哈爾濱))) (Vt 開往) (NP (N 上海)) (T 的)) (N 高速)) (N 電車)) (DM (DET 28) (M 日))) (Vi 正式) (VP (Vi 開通) (Vi 發車)))

One application of this Chinese parser is the study of syntactic complexity. By counting the frequency of each sentence structure in a graded reader in Chinese, the relationship between syntactic complexity and readability can be explored. The assumption is that the more frequently a word or structure occurs in a lower-grade textbook, the easier it is. By counting the frequency of each word and each context-free grammar rule in each article of each level, the difficulty level of a text can be modeled. Figure 3.7 shows the sentence structures in an article in the form of context-free grammar:

3.4.3 *Chinese Dependency Parser*

Yamada and Matsumoto (2003) proposed using SVM to train an English dependency parser. Following the algorithm by Yamada and Matsumoto (2003), we developed a Chinese dependency parser to parse and extract dependency relations from the Sinica Chinese Treebank using the three tags R, L, and O to represent the three relations between any two words, where R and L denoted the position of the head of the phrase (R for right, L for left) and O indicated that no dependency relation existed between the two words. Using the syntactic information in the Sinica Treebank, the SVM algorithm can be used to train a classifier to predict Chinese dependency relations. We further deduced the grammatical dependency relations by drawing on the part-of-speech tags and the extra information about the head of the phrase. The output of the program is shown in (3.6) below. Note that the symbols => and <= represent the direction in which the head of the two words lies, and S, O, ADV, and V denote subject, object, adverb, and verb, respectively.

(3.6)

Word	Directionality	Word	Dependency relation
他	=>	吃	S V
怎麼	=>	吃	ADV V
一直	=>	吃	ADV V
吃	<=	螺絲	V O

3.4.4 *Chinese Dependency Relations Database and Lexicology*

With the Chinese dependency parser, we developed a database of Chinese dependency relations similar to that in Chinese Sketch Engine. We also compiled a web corpus by automatically downloading texts from the web. The corpus contained more than 0.1 billion Chinese words from newspapers, magazines, and social media in Taiwan. All the Chinese texts were preprocessed by the CKIP Chinese word segmentation and part-of-speech tagging system and by our own dependency parser. We created a Chinese dependency relations database in which the words that formed dependency relations and grammatical relations, as well as their examples, were stored. The Chinese dependency relations database was a convenient tool for exploring the phraseology of Chinese. For instance, by inputting the verb 沈 *chen* "sink" and choosing the subject-verb relation, we were able to retrieve the examples shown in (3.7) below. These examples show that 心 *xin* "heart," 眼皮 *yanpi* "eyelid," and 暮色 *mushe* "dusk" often served as the subjects of the verb 沈 *chen* "sink" apart from the common collocate 船 *chuan* "boat."

(3.7)	(a) 船(Na) 會(D) 沈(VH)
	boat will sink
	The boat will sink.
	(b) 心(Na) 沈(VH) 下來(Ng)
	heart sank down
	(Someone's) heart sank.
	(c) 眼皮(Na) 直(D) 往(P) 下(Ncd) 沈(VH)
	eyelids continuously toward down sink
	(Someone's) eyelids felt heavy.
	(d) 暮色(Na) 漸(D) 沈(VA)
	dusk gradually sink
	Dusk fell.

Similarly, we extracted the subject of the predicate 冷 *leng* "cold," such as 天氣 *tianqi* "weather," a date like 明天 *mingtian* "tomorrow," a place like 北極 *beiji* "North Pole," and something like 水 *shui* "water." Combinations of these words with 冷 "cold" were predictable and may exist across languages. However, as shown in (3.8) below, when the predicate 冷 *leng* "cold" co-occurred with subjects such as 聲音 *shengyin* "sound," 心 "heart," 眼神 *yanshen* "eyes," 表情 *biaoqing* "expression," 笑話 *xiaohua* "joke," 口氣 *kouqi* "tone," 內需 *neixu* "domestic needs," and 文字 *wenzi* "language," these word combinations seemed to be arbitrary, idiosyncratic, and language-specific collocations, metaphorical expressions, and novel usages. Thus, 冷 *leng* "cold" in these contexts is negative and means "indifferent," "disillusioned," "uninteresting," or "downturn."

(3.8)	(a) 眼神(NA) 冷(VH)
	eyes cold
	(Someone's) eyes are cold.
	(b) 表情(NA) 冷(VH)
	expression indifferent
	(Someone's) got an indifferent expression.
	(c) 內需(NA) 很(D) 冷(VH)
	domestic needs very cold
	The domestic market is in recession.
	(d) 文字(Na) 也許(D) 稍(D) 冷(VH) 些(Dfb)
	words perhaps slightly cold a bit
	The tone of the article is a bit cold.
	(e) 笑話(Na) 冷(VH) 呀(T) !
	joke cold particle
	The joke is not funny!

As discussed above, the dependency relations database is a powerful tool for lexicology and lexicography that can be used for research on collocations, metaphors, lexical syntax, and lexical semantics. For instance, our database showed that 獨家 *dujia* "exclusive" could only modify a noun and was never used as a predicate.

3.4.5 Selectional Preferences

While the dependency relations database can facilitate research on Chinese collocations and phraseology, it is still not very convenient for exploring lexical semantics based simply on syntactic dependency relations. If nouns in the dependency relations were further classified in terms of semantic features, it would be much easier to identify semantic patterns and novel usages. With the semantic information in HowNet, it is possible to automatically derive lexical semantic patterns. To save space, we will only show the English ontologies of the Chinese nouns that formed dependency relations with the verb 蓋 *gai* "cover; build" in our corpus using curly brackets { }. As we were unable to determine the sense in each instance when a word had more than one meaning, all the possible senses were taken into account and calculated. Semantic patterns like selectional restrictions were expected to emerge after this procedure. The examples in (3.9) below reveal some of the semantic classes of the objects of the verb 蓋 *gai*, which can mean "to construct," "to cover," and "to make a mark; to stamp." The numbers in parentheses indicate the frequency of the nouns that co-occurred with the verb 蓋 *gai*.

(3.9) (a) {facilities}
捷運 "metro" (16), 公園 "park" (6), 機場 "airport" (6), 廟 "temple" (6), 水庫 "reservoir" (5), 球場 "(tennis/basketball) court; (baseball) field" (4)
(b) {InstitutePlace}
廟 "temple" (6), 醫院 "hospital" (6), 賭場 "casino" (4), 電廠 "power plant" (4), 旅館 "hotel" (3), 劇場 "theater" (2)
(c) {tool}
棉被 "quilt" (34), 布袋 "cloth bag" (22), 被子 "quilt" (11), 火鍋 "hot pot" (8), 毯子 "blanket" (3), 棺 "coffin" (2), 帳篷 "tent" (1)
(d) {house}
房子 "house" (133), 大樓 "tall building" (53), 農舍 "farmhouse" (15), 高樓 "tall building" (9), 豪宅 "mansion" (6), 宿舍 "dormitory" (6), 別墅 "villa" (3)
(e) {image}
手印 "handprint" (10), 指印 "fingerprint" (3), 指紋 "fingerprint" (2)
(f) {LandVehicle}
纜車 "gondola" (3), 地鐵 "metro" (1), 水車 "waterwheel" (1)
(g) {clothing}
外套 "coat" (18), 衣服 "clothing" (1), 夾克 "jacket" (1), 大衣 "overcoat" (1)
(h) {room}
廁所 "toilet" (3), 屋 "house" (2), 教室 "classroom" (2), 新房 "new house" (2)

(continued)

(i) {stationery}
印章 "seal" (7), 章 "seal" (3), 私章 "seal" (2), 圖章 "seal" (1)

The relationship between a verb and the selectional preferences of its object can be modeled in probabilistic terms. Resnik (1997) dubbed this "selectional associations." To derive the selectional association of a semantic class and a verb, Resnik (1997) computed relative entropy $S_R(p)$ in (3.10) below first, in which $Pr(c)$ is the probability of a semantic class, c is a dependency relation, and $Pr(c|p)$ is the probability of a semantic class in a dependency relation with a given verb p.

(3.10) $S_R(p) = \sum_{c} Pr(c|p) \log \frac{Pr(c|p)}{Pr(c)}$

Then, selectional association $A_R(p, c)$ was computed using the formula in (3.11) below. The stronger the selectional association, the stronger the selectional preference.

(3.11) $A_R(p, c) = \frac{1}{S_R(p)} Pr(c|p) \log \frac{Pr(c|p)}{Pr(c)}$

In fact, with the information of selectional association, the meaning of a polysemous verb can be revealed by choosing the maximal selectional association, as provided, using the formula in (3.12) below (Resnik 1997).

(3.12) $C_i = \{c \mid c \textit{ is an ancestor of } s_i\}$

$a_i = \max A_R(p, c)$, c *belongs to* C_i

3.4.6 Unsupervised and Minimally Supervised Approaches to Word Sense Disambiguation

Large-scale sense-tagged corpora are valuable resources for natural language understanding. However, to date, no such Chinese resource is available to researchers. A well-known unsupervised method of semantic class labeling was proposed by Yarowsky (1992), who used a corpus and the semantic classes in *Roget's International Thesaurus* for an experiment in which the semantic class of each word in the corpus was annotated. If a word had more than one semantic class, each possible semantic class was tagged. Yarowsky (1992) collected the context of a given semantic class by recording 100 words on each side of it. If a semantic class occurred k times, each of the contexts contributed to $1/k$ of the meaning. The weight of the word was computed as shown in (3.13) below, where w is a word and $RCat$ is the semantic class of a word, and $Pr(w|RCat)$ is the conditional probability of a word given a semantic class.

(3.13) $log\ (Pr(w|RCat)/Pr(w))$

According to Yarowsky (1992), the semantic class of a polysemous word can be derived by choosing the semantic class that maximizes when summing up the weight of 100 words on both sides of it, as shown in (3.14) below. Yarowsky (1992) reported an accuracy of 92%.

(3.14) $$\underset{RCat}{ARGMAX} \sum_{w \text{ in context}} log \frac{Pr(w|Rcat) * Pr(RCat)}{Pr(w)}$$

Yarowsky (1995) employed a self-learning approach to word sense disambiguation that resulted in a performance greatly superior to methods that used only labeled data. In a given discourse, how is the meaning of the word *plant*, which could refer to *botanical life* or a *factory building*, determined? Yarowsky (1995) proposed two assumptions: (I) a word has only one sense in a given discourse; and (II) words exhibit only one sense in a given collocation. From the unlabeled data, Yarowsky (1995) first extracted a small amount of data (about 2% of the entire training set) and labeled the answers. For example, if *plant* referred to *botanical life* in a sentence, then it was classified as Class A, and if it meant *factory*, then it was labeled Class B. Based on assumption (I), collocations in similar sentences were identified. For example, for Class A data in the selected sentences, the word *life* occurred next to *plant*, and for Class B data, the word *manufacturing* happened to be a collocate. Sentences with these same features were then located in the unlabeled data and included in the training set. At the same time, a number of decision functions were also used to find new collocation pairs in the newly labeled sentences. With assumption (II), if multiple sentences in the same text were grouped into the same category, then the remaining sentences in that same text were also assigned to the same category. This assumption not only was applied to expand the training set but also to correct sentences that were incorrectly classified in the previous step. These steps were repeated to expand the training data and to use new data to train the model until the number of unlabeled data no longer changed too much. Compared with supervised learning using only labeled data, the experimental results indicated that with models trained using this approach, performance was improved and at the same time manual annotation efforts were also reduced.

3.4.7 Vector Semantics and Deep Neural Net

The power of deep neural net has been manifested by its tremendous success in various domains, including computer go programs, automated driving systems, and facial recognition programs. In NLP, word embedding (also known as word vectors) is one of the most widely used deep learning algorithms in addition to convolutional neural network (CNN), recurrent neural network (RNN), long short-term memory (LSTM), and the sequence-to-sequence model (seq2seq) (cf. Goldberg 2017). In

Table 3.2 Words most similar to the word 籃球 "basketball" in word2vec

Chinese	English	Similarity
足球	Soccer	0.7878
排球	Volleyball	0.7669
棒球	Baseball	0.7601
桌球	Table tennis	0.7584
橄欖球	Football	0.7454
高爾夫球	Golf	0.7435
羽球	Badminton	0.7383
撞球	Snooker	0.7296
拳擊	Boxing	0.7295
網球	Tennis	0.7244

traditional vector space models, a word in a corpus with *n* distinct words can be represented by *n* dimensional vectors, with each distinct word corresponding to one dimension. The similarity of two words can be computed by the cosine function of the two vectors. As such a representation has difficulty finding semantically similar words, singular value decomposition (SVD) has been proposed to overcome this problem, which reduces the dimensions of the vectors. This method, however, is computationally costly when the number of documents is large.

Mikolov et al. (2013) presented a computationally efficient learning method called word2vec, which is capable of representing words using dense vectors. Word2vec is a two-layer neural net whose input is a text corpus and whose output is a set of vectors. Under the word2vec model, words (or phrases) in the vocabulary are mapped to real numbers. Compared with traditional vector space models, vectors in word2vec are continuous and have much fewer dimensions (typically with no more than a few thousand). The similarity of two words is measured using the cosine function. Word2vec has been proven as a very efficient way to cluster semantically similar words when the corpus size is large and it has been widely used in many NLP tasks. Table 3.2 shows some of the words that are near the vector of 籃球 "basketball" using word2vec and a Chinese newspaper corpus with over 1.5 billion words. As can be seen in Table 3.2, the results seem to suggest that word2vec can cluster semantically related words quite well, as the words in the cluster all belong to sports:

In fact, word2vec clusters not only words with related meanings such as synonyms, antonyms, and semantic fields but also collocates. For instance, Table 3.3 shows that the words that are most similar to the word 存 "save" in word2vec are synonyms like 掙 "save," 存進 "save...in," 存下 "save," 存下來 "save," 存到 "save...to," 攢 "save," and 存滿 "save more than..."; antonyms like 領出來 "withdraw...from" and 掏 "take...out"; and collocates like 養老金 "pension." As shown in the examples in Table 3.3, word2vec mainly clusters words with paradigmatic relations, but sometimes it also clusters words with syntagmatic relations, typically words that occur before or after the word under study:

While word2vec can generate semantic resources based on a large corpus only, the relation among the words is not entirely clear. If word2vec can cluster words with similar meanings very well, we would expect that it would be able to cluster the

Table 3.3 Words most similar to 存 "save" in word2vec

Chinese	English	Similarity
掙	Save	0.548
存下	Save	0.538
存進	Save. . .in	0.536
存下來	Save	0.528
存到	Save. . .to	0.527
攢	Save	0.524
存滿	Save more than. . .	0.509
養老金	Pension	0.508
領出來	Withdraw. . .from	0.504
掏	Take. . .out	0.503

Table 3.4 Two clusters of the verb 打卡 *daka*

Sense #1 of 打卡 *daka* "check-in"	Sense #2 of 打卡 *daka* "punch card"
Facebook_打卡#1 0.928036	準時_打卡#1 0.788486
合照_打卡#1 0.925906	早到晚_退#2 0.754307
FB_打卡#1 0.921325	中視_女王#2 0.753268
打卡_拍照#1 0.911354	自願_加班#1 0.752856
拍照_打卡#2 0.906916	周休_三日#1 0.727778
打卡_按#1 0.902463	照常_上班#2 0.727206
打卡_即可#1 0.896281	打卡_下班#1 0.726511
拍照_打卡#1 0.888326	衛勤#2 0.724331
粉絲團_按#1 0.885469	大小夜班#1 0.720800
	朝九晚六#1 0.709096

objects of a polysemous word like the examples created by HowNet in (3.9). However, our experiments showed that the results using word2vec were worse than those created by a thesaurus or HowNet, suggesting that word2vec cannot replace a manually created lexical semantic database or a thesaurus, at least in some applications.

Word2vec has several limitations. For instance, it cannot draw distinctions between different meanings of polysemous words because a word is represented in one vector only. Furthermore, word2vec relies on large corpora and cannot integrate existing semantic resources. Several researches have been proposed to address these problems. Reisinger and Mooney (2010) and Huang et al. (2012) further decomposed word embedding into multiple sense-specific vectors. Bartunov et al. (2015) proposed the adaptive Skip-gram model capable of inducing different senses of a word in different contexts. Based on word2vec, Pelevina et al. (2016) further clustered the ego-network of related words and derived the different meanings of a word. Iacobacci et al. (2015) proposed a method that integrated existing semantic resources and derived sense embeddings. These are all promising approaches.

Table 3.4 shows one interesting example from the results of our experiment using the SenseGram toolkit of Pelevina et al. (2016), in which the conventional meaning and the new meaning of 打卡 *daka* were successfully distinguished. 打卡 *daka*, which literally means "to punch cards," is often used to record the times employees arrive at and leave their workplace. The new sense of 打卡 *daka* is the act of informing your friends on social media where you are, typically by posting pictures, especially happy moments. The cluster on the left (Sense#1) in Table 3.4 is associated with the new meaning, whereas the cluster on the right (Sense#2) is related to the old meaning. As can be seen, Sense#1 contains words related to social media, such as Facebook, 拍照 "taking pictures," and 粉絲團 "fans," whereas Sense#2 contains words related to work and time, such as 準時 "punctual," 早到晚退 "arrive early and leave late," 加班 "work extra time," 上班 "on duty," 下班 "off duty," and 夜班 "night shift."

SenseGram (cf. Pelevina et al. 2016) is able to discriminate which sense is used in a given context. The examples in (3.15) and (3.16) below show that SenseGram can output the probabilities associated with the senses, as SenseGram assigned higher probability to the correct sense in the two examples. Like word2vec and SenseGram, the algorithms derived or inspired by word2vec seem promising in solving some NLP problems. However, a comprehensive evaluation of these algorithms requires further investigation.

(3.15) (a) 這個 景點 每天 都 吸引 不少 人 來 打卡
this scenic spot everyday all attract not few people come check in
This scenic spot attracts many people to check in.
(b) ('打卡#1', [-0.003623650289649795, -0.009384661201232311])
(3.16) (a) 這 家 公司 上 下班 都 要打卡
this classifier company on off duty all require punch cards
The company requires employees to punch cards when they arrive or leave.
(b) ('打卡#2', [-0.025133929472191133, 0.37259653407996307])

3.5 Conclusion: Interdisciplinary Impact and Future Research

In this chapter, we introduced the NLP resources from Academia Sinica and some of their applications. We showed that corpora released from CKIP can be used to train models in word segmentation, part-of-speech tagging, and dependency-based parsing, along with other NLP toolkits. We also demonstrated the integration of a dependency parser with HowNet in constructing a Chinese dependency relations database enriched with semantic information. Such a database has been shown to be useful in the study of collocations, lexical semantic patterns, selectional preferences, and word sense disambiguation. As illustrated in the preceding section, deep learning has become quite successful at word sense induction and other applications. While some recent researches seem to suggest that deep learning algorithms are capable of performing NLP tasks by learning from scratch, traditional NLP resources will continue to play an important role, as illustrated by Niu et al. (2017), which shed light on how deep learning and knowledge resources such as HowNet may be combined to generate new knowledge.

In addition to serving as the foundational resources and catalyst of research in Chinese computational and corpus linguistics, CKIP language resources have also been widely used in interdisciplinary language studies on Chinese. Redington et al. (1995), for instance, were the first to build a machine learning model for Mandarin POS based on the Sinica Corpus. Other research on psychological language processing based on the Sinica Corpus include Hsu et al.'s (2009) neurolinguistic work on reading Chinese, Myers' (2000) work on classifier selection, and Huang et al. (2002) on the nature of categorical ambiguity in Chinese. The Sinica Corpus is frequently used in the study of Chinese linguistics and has generated many interesting new topics, for instance, the Module-Attribute Representation of Verbal Semantics (MARVS) theory for Chinese verbal semantics (Huang et al. 2000a, 2000b), repairs in Chinese conversation (Tseng 2006), and work on a general reference grammar (Huang and Shi 2016). The Sinica Treebank has had the largest impact on the field of dependency parsing (Buchholz and Marsi 2006) and in quantitative linguistics (Hou et al. 2017), and it has been widely consulted for role and discourse labeling. Sinica BOW and Chinese WordNet have supported new research on Global WordNet and the extraction of semantic relations, as well as studies on metaphors and other nonliteral meanings (Ahrens et al. 2003). As the world turns more and more toward data sciences and sharable digital resources, we can expect foundational language resources such as those built on CKIP to continue to play a central role in language, information, and computation.

References

Ahrens, Kathleen, Siaw Fong Chung, and Chu-Ren Huang. 2003. Conceptual metaphors: Ontology-based representation and corpora driven mapping principles. In *Proceedings of the ACL 2003 Workshop on Lexicon and Figurative Language—Volume 14*, Association for Computational Linguistics, 36–42. Sapporo, Japan.

Bartunov, Sergey, Dmitry Kondrashkin, Anton Osokin, and Dmitry Vetrov. 2015. Breaking sticks and ambiguities with adaptive Skip-gram. arXiv preprint arXiv:1502.07257.

Bird, Steven, Ewan Klein, and Edward Loper. 2009. *Natural language processing with Python: Analyzing text with the natural language toolkit* (1st ed.). Sebastopol, CA: O'Reilly Media, Inc.

Buchholz, Sabine, and Erwin Marsi. 2006. CoNLL-X shared task on multilingual dependency parsing. In *Proceedings of the Tenth Conference on Computational Natural Language Learning*, Association for Computational Linguistics, 149–164. New York City, New York.

Chao, Yuen Ren. 1968. *A grammar of spoken Chinese*. Berkeley: University of California Press.

Chen, Keh-Jiann, and Chu-Ren Huang. 1990. Information-based Case Grammar. In *Proceedings of the 13th International Conference on Computational Linguistics (COLING '90)*, (2): 54–59. Helsinki, Finland.

Chen, Keh-Jiann, and Shu-Ling Huang. 2009. A step toward compositional semantics: E-HowNet a lexical semantic representation system. In *Proceedings of the 23rd Pacific Asia Conference on Language, Information and Computation*, 1–8. Hong Kong.

Chen, Keh-Jiann, Shing-Huan Liu, Li-ping Chang, and Yeh-Hao Chin. 1994. A practical tagger for Chinese corpora. In *Proceedings of ROCLING VII*, 111–126. Hsinchu, Taiwan.

Chen, Keh-Jiann, Chu-Ren Huang, Li-ping Chang, and Hui-Li Hsu. 1996. Sinica corpus: Design methodology for balanced corpora. In *Proceeding of the 11th Pacific Asia Conference on Language, Information and Computation*, ed. Byung-Soo Park and Jong Bok Kim, 167–176. Seoul, Korea.

Chen, Feng-Yi, Pi-Fang Tsai, Keh-Jiann Chen, and Chu-Ren Huang 陳鳳儀, 蔡碧芳, 陳克健, 黃居仁. 1999. The construction of Sinica Chinese Treebank. 中文句結構樹資料庫的構建. *Computational Linguistics and Chinese Language Processing* 中文計算語言學期刊 4(2): 87–104.

Chen, Keh-Jiann, Chi-Ching Luo, Ming-Chung Chang, Feng-Yi Chen, Chao-Jan Chen, Chu-Ren Huang, and Zhao-Ming Gao. 2003. Sinica treebank: Design criteria, representational issues and implementation. In *Treebanks: Building and using parsed corpora*, ed. Anne Abeillé: 231–248. Dordrecht and Boston: Kluwer Academic Publishers.

Chinese WordNet Group, Institute of Linguistics, Academia Sinica. 中央研究院語言學研究所中文詞彙網路小組. n.d.. *Chinese Word Sketch* 中文詞彙特性速描系統. Available at http://wordsketch.ling.sinica.edu.tw/. Accessed 18 August 2018.

Chiu, Chih-Ming, Chi-Ching Luo, and Keh-Jiann Chen 邱智銘, 駱季青, 陳克健. 2004. A Study of the Prefixes and Suffixes of Compound Verbs in Modern Chinese 現代漢語複合動詞之詞首詞尾研究. In *Proceedings of ROCLING XVI: Conference on Computational Linguistics and Speech Processing* 第十六屆自然語言與語音處理論文集: 1-9. Taipei.

Chou, Ya-Min, and Chu-Ren Huang. 2010. Hantology: Conceptual system discovery based on orthographic convention. In *Ontology and the lexicon: A natural language processing perspective*, ed. Chu-ren Huang, Nicoletta Calzolari, Aldo Gangemi, Alessandro Lenci, Alessandro Oltramari, and Laurent Prévot, 122–143. Cambridge: Cambridge University Press.

Chou, Ya-min, and Chu-Ren Huang. 周亞民, 黃居仁 2013. The formal representation for Chinese characters 漢字知識的形式表達. *Contemporary Linguistics* 當代語言學 2:142–161.

Chou, Ya-min, and Chu-Ren Huang. 周亞民, 黃居仁. n.d.. *Hantology* 漢字知識本體. Available at http://hantology.sinica.edu.tw. Accessed 15 October 2018.

CKIP (Chinese Knowledge and Information Processing) Group, Academia Sinica 中央研究院詞庫小組. 1997. *Word List with Accumulated Word Frequency in Sinica Corpus 3.0: CKIP Technical Report, Academia Sinica* 中央研究院平衡語料庫詞集及詞頻統計. 中研院資訊所詞庫小組技術報告.

CKIP (Chinese Knowledge and Information Processing) Group, Academia Sinica. 中央研究院詞庫小組. n.d.-a. *Academia Sinica Balanced Corpus of Modern Chinese (Sinica Corpus) 4.0* 中央研究院現代漢語平衡語料庫 *4.0* 版. Available at http://lingcorpus.iis.sinica.edu.tw/modern/. Accessed 18 August 2018.

CKIP (Chinese Knowledge and Information Processing) Group, Academia Sinica 中央研究院詞庫小組. n.d.-b. *CKIP Chinese Parser* 中文剖析器線上測試. Available at http://parser.iis.sinica.edu.tw. Accessed 18 August 2018.

CKIP (Chinese Knowledge and Information Processing) Group, Academia Sinica 中央研究院詞庫小組. n.d.-c. *Common Chinese Prefix and Suffix Characters Database* 常用詞首、詞尾字資料庫查詢. Available at http://140.109.19.103/affix/. Accessed 18 August 2018.

CKIP (Chinese Knowledge and Information Processing) Group, Academia Sinica 中央研究院詞庫小組. n.d.-d. *E-HowNet 2.0* 廣義知網知識本體架構 *2.0*. Available at http://ehownet.iis.sinica.edu.tw. Accessed 18 August 2018.

CKIP (Chinese Knowledge and Information Processing) Group, Academia Sinica 中央研究院詞庫小組. n.d.-e. *On-line Interface for Searching the Sinica Treebank* 中文句結構樹檢索系統. Available at http://turing.iis.sinica.edu.tw/treesearch/. Accessed 18 August 2018.

Dong, Zendong, and Qiang Dong. 2006. *HowNet and the computation of meaning*. Singapore: World Scientific Publishing Co.

Dougherty, Ching-Yi, and Samuel E. Martin. 1964. *Chinese syntactic rules for machine translation. The project for machine translation and general automated linguistic systems*. Berkeley: University of California.

Goldberg, Yoav. 2017. *Neural network methods for natural language processing*. Morgan & Claypool Publishers, Inc.

Hong, Jia-Fei, and Chu-Ren Huang 洪嘉馡, 黃居仁. 2008. A Corpus-Based Approach to the Discovery of Cross-Strait Lexical Contrasts 語料庫為本的兩岸對應詞彙發掘. *Language and Linguistics* 語言暨語言學 9(2): 221–238.

Hou, Renkui, Chu-Ren Huang, and Hongchao Liu. 2017. A study on Chinese register characteristics based on regression analysis and text clustering. *Corpus Linguistics and Linguistic Theory*. Ahead of print. Available at https://doi.org/10.1515/cllt-2016-0062. Accessed 15 October 2018.

Hsieh, Yu-Ming, Duen-Chi Yang, and Keh-Jiann Chen. 2005. Linguistically motivated grammar extraction, generalization, and adaptation. In In *Proceedings of the Second International Joint Conference on Natural Language Processing (IJCNLP 2005)*, ed. Robert Dale, Kam-Fai Wong, Jian Su, and Oi Yee Kwong, 177–187. Jeju Island, Korea.

Hsieh, Yu-Ming, Duen-Chi Yang, and Keh-Jiann Chen. 2007. Improve parsing performance by self-learning. *International Journal of Computational Linguistics and Chinese Language Processing* 12(2):195–216.

Hsieh, Yu-Ming, Ming-Hong Bai, Jason S. Chang, and Keh-Jiann Chen. 2012. Improving PCFG Chinese parsing with context-dependent probability re-estimation. *Proceedings of the Second CIPS-SIGHAN Joint Conference on Chinese Language Processing*, 216–221. Tianjin, China.

Hsu, Chun-Hsien, Jie-Li Tsai, Chia-Ying Lee, and Ovid J.-L. Tzeng. 2009. Orthographic combinability and phonological consistency effects in reading Chinese phonograms: An event-related potential study. *Brain and Language* 108(1):56–66.

Huang, Chu-Ren. 2004. Introduction to Chinese language processing at the dawn of the 21st century. In *Computational linguistics and beyond*, ed. Chu-Ren Huang and Winfried Lenders, 187–188. Taipei: Institute of Linguistics, Academia Sinica.

Huang, Chu-Ren. 2009a. Tagged Chinese Gigaword. Version 2.0. Philadelphia: Linguistic Data Consortium, University of Pennsylvania. Available at http://www.ldc.upenn.edu/Catalog/catalogEntry.jsp?catalogId=LDC2009T14. Accessed 15 October 2018.

Huang, Chu-Ren 黃居仁. 2009b. Language resources integration and contrastive analysis: a case study of cross-strait lexical contrasts. 語言資源整合與對比研究—以兩岸詞匯對比研究為例. In *Chinese Language Resources Series (1).中國語言資源論叢(一)*, ed. Pu Zhang and Tienkun Wang 張普, 王鐵琨 (主編), 52–66. Beijing: The Commercial Press.

Huang, Chu-Ren 黃居仁. 2016. Corpus and language resource construction in Taiwan. 臺灣語料庫與語言資源建設. In *Report of the of the Chinese Langauges and Life*. 中國語言生活狀況報告, ed. Division of Langauge and Information Management, Ministry of Education. 教育部語言資訊管理司(組編), 259–267. Beijing: The Commercial Press.

Huang, Chu-Ren, and Keh-Jiann Chen. 1996. Issues and topics in Chinese natural language processing. In *Readings in Chinese natural language processing. Journal of Chinese Linguistics Monograph Series (9)*, ed. Chu-Ren Huang, Keh-Jiann Chen, and Benjamin K. T'sou, 1–22. Berkeley, CA: Journal of Chinese Linguistics.

Huang, Chu-Ren, and Keh-Jiann Chen. 2017. Sinica treebank. In *Handbook of Linguistic Annotation*, ed. Nancy Ide and James Pustejovsky, 641–657. Dordrecht: Springer.

Huang, Chu-Ren, and Shu-Kai Hsieh. 2015. Chinese lexical semantics: From radicals to event structure. In *The Oxford handbook of Chinese linguistics*, ed. William S.-Y. Wang and Chao-Fen Sun, 290–305. New York: Oxford University Press.

Huang, Chu-Ren, and Dingxu Shi (eds.). 2016. *A reference grammar of Chinese*. Cambridge: Cambridge University Press.

Huang, Chu-Ren, Kathleen Ahrens, Li-Li Chang, Keh-Jiann Chen, Mei-Chun Liu, and Mei-Chih Tsai. 2000a. The module-attribute representation of verbal semantics: From semantic to argument structure. *International Journal of Computational Linguistics & Chinese Language Processing, February 2000: Special Issue on Chinese Verbal Semantics* 5(1): 19–46.

Huang, Chu-Ren, Feng-Chu Luo, Puo-Sheng Chung, Hui-Chun Shiao, Mei-Ling Li, Chiu-Jung Lu, and Mei-Ling Tsao 黃居仁, 羅鳳珠, 鍾柏生, 蕭慧君, 李美齡, 盧秋蓉, 曹美琳. 2000b.

Adventures in Wen-Land and SouWenJieZi: Two digital museums for Chinese language learning. 「文國尋寶記」與「搜文解字」—為華語文教學設計的兩個數位博物館網站。 *The Sixth International Conference on Chinese Language Teaching and Learning*. 第六屆世界華語文教學研討會. Dec 27–30, 2000. Taipei.

Huang, Chu-Ren, Chao-Jan Chen, and Claude C. C. Shen. 2002. The nature of categorical ambiguity and its implications for language processing: A corpus-based study of Mandarin Chinese. In *Sentence processing in East Asian languages*, ed. Mineharu Nakayama, 53–83. Stanford, CA: CSLI Publications.

Huang, Chu-Ren, Ju-Ying Chang, and Chiu-Jung Lu 黃居仁, 張如瑩, 盧秋蓉. 2004. Linguistic knowledge network and digital learning: Using Adventures in Wen-Land as an example 語言知識網路與數位學習:以「文國尋寶記」為例. In *Language, literature, and information* 語言, 文學與資訊, ed. Feng-Chu Luo, 羅鳳珠, 487–53. Hsinchu: National Tsing Hua University Press.

Huang, Chu-Ren, Adam Kilgarriff, Yiching Wu, Chih-Min Chiu, Simon Smith, Pavel Rychly, Ming-Hong Bai, and Keh-Jiann Chen. 2005. Chinese Sketch Engine and the extraction of collocations. In *Proceedings of the Fourth SigHAN Workshop*, 48–55. Jeju Island, Korea.

Huang, Chu-Ren, Ru-Yng Chang, and Hsiang-bin Lee. 2010a. Sinica BOW (Bilingual Ontological WordNet): Integration of bilingual WordNet and SUMO. In *Ontology and the lexicon: A natural language processing perspective*, ed. Chu-Ren Huang, Nicoletta Calzolari, Aldo Gangemi, Alessandro Lenci, Alessandro Oltramari, and Laurent Prévot, 201–211. Cambridge: Cambridge University Press.

Huang, Chu-Ren, Shu-Kai Hsieh, Jia-Fei Hong, Yi-Li Su, Yong-Xiang Chen, and Sheng-Wei Huang 黃居仁, 謝舒凱, 洪嘉馡, 陳韻竹, 蘇依莉, 陳永祥, 黃勝偉. 2010b. Chinese WordNet: Design and implementation of a cross-lingual knowledge processing infrastructure. 中文詞滙網絡:跨語言知識處理基礎架構的設計理念與實踐. *Journal of Chinese Information Science*. 中文資訊學報. 24(2):14–23.

Huang, Eric, Richard Socher, Christopher Manning, and Andrew Ng. 2012. Improving word representations via global context and multiple word prototypes. In *Proceedings of the 50th Annual Meeting of the Association for Computational Linguistics*, 1:873–882. Jeju Island, South Korea.

Huang, Chu-Ren, Jia-Fei Hong, Sheng-Yi Chen, and Ya-Min Chou 黃居仁, 洪嘉馡, 陳聖怡, 周亞民. 2013a. Knowledge system in Chinese characters: Ideographs as the fundamental concept-driven event structure. 漢字所表達的知識系統:意符為基本概念導向的事件結構. *Contemporary Linguistics* 當代語言學 9.2(6):221–238.

Huang, Chu-Ren, Ya-Jun Yang, and Sheng-Yi Chen. 2013b. Radicals as ontologies: Concept derivation and knowledge representation of four-hoofed mammals as semantic symbols. In *Breaking down the barriers: Interdisciplinary studies in Chinese linguistics and beyond*, ed. Guangshun Cao, Hilary Chappell, Redouane Djamouri, and Thekla Wiebusch, 1117–1133. Taipei: Institute of Linguistics, Academia Sinica.

Huang, Chu-Ren, Jia-Fei Hong, Wei-Yun Ma, and Petr Šimon. 2015. From corpus to grammar: Automatic extraction of grammatical relations from annotated corpus. *Journal of Chinese Linguistics Monograph Series* 25:192–221.

Huang, Chu-Ren, Shu-Kai Hsieh, and Keh-Jiann Chen. 2017. *Mandarin Chinese words and parts of speech: A corpus-based study*. London: Routledge.

Iacobacci, Ignacio, Mohammad Taher Pilehvar, and Roberto Navigli. 2015. SensEmbed: Learning sense embeddings for word and relational similarity. In *Proceedings of the 50th Annual Meeting of the Association for Computational Linguistics*. Jeju Island, South Korea.

Juang, Der-Ming, and Ching-Chun Hsieh. 莊德明, 謝清俊. 2005. Database of the Configurations of Radicals in the Chinese Characters: Implementation and Applications 漢字構形資料庫的建置與應用. In *Proceedings of the International Symposium on Chinese Characters and Globalization* 漢字與全球化國際學術研討會論文集.119–133.

Jurafsky, Daniel, and James Martin. 2008. *Speech and language processing* (2nd ed.). Upper Saddle River, NJ: Prentice Hall.

Kilgarriff, Adam, Chu-Ren Huang, Pavel Rychly, Simon Smith, and David Tugwell. 2005. Chinese word sketches. In *ASIALEX 2005: Words in Asian Cultural Context*. Singapore.
Kudo, Taku. 2001. YamCha: Yet another multipurpose chunk annotator. Available at http://chasen.org/~taku/software/yamcha/. Accessed 15 October 2018.
Kudo, Taku. 2005. CRF++: Yet another CRF toolkit. Available at http://taku910.github.io/crfpp/. Accessed 15 October 2018.
Kudo, Taku, and Yuji Matsumoto. 2000. Use of support vector learning for chunk identification. In *Proceedings of CoNLL-2000*. Lisbon, Portugal.
Lee, Lung-Hao, Yu-Ting Yu, and Chu-Ren Huang. 2009. Chinese WordNet domains: Bootstrapping Chinese WordNet with semantic domain labels. In *Proceedings of the 23rd Pacific Asia Conference on Language, Information and Computation (PACLIC)*, 288–296. Hong Kong.
Ma, Wei-Yun, and Keh-Jiann Chen. 2004. Design of CKIP Chinese word segmentation system. *International Journal of Asian Language Processing* 14(3):235–249.
Ma, Wei-Yun, and Chu-Ren Huang. 2006. Uniform and effective tagging of a heterogeneous giga-word corpus. In *Proceedings of Language Resources and Evaluation Conference*. Genoa, Italy.
Manning, Christopher, and Hinrich Schütze. 1999. *Foundations of statistical natural language processing*. Cambridge, MA: The MIT Press.
Mikolov, Tomas, Kai Chen, Greg Corrado, and Jeffrey Dean. 2013. Efficient estimation of word representations in vector space. arXiv:1301.3781.
Myers, James. 2000. Rules vs. analogy in Mandarin classifier selection. *Language and Linguistics* 1(2):187–209.
Niles, Ian, and Adam Pease. 2001. Towards a standard upper ontology. In *Proceedings of the International Conference on Formal Ontology in Information Systems*, 2–9. Ogunquit, Maine.
Niu, Yilin, Ruobing Xie, Zhiyuan Liu, and Maosong Sun. 2017. Improved Word Representation Learning with Sememes. In Proceedings of the 55th Annual Meeting of the Association for Computational Linguistics, Vol 1, 2049–2058, Vancouver, Canada. Association for Computational Linguistics.
Pelevina, Maria, Nikolay Arefyev, Chris Biemann, and Alexander Panchenko. 2016. Making sense of word embeddings. In *Proceedings of the 1st Workshop on Representation Learning for NLP*, 174–183. Berlin, Germany.
Pustejovsky, James. 1991. The generative lexicon. *Computational Linguistics* 17(4):409–441.
Redington, Martin, Nick Chater, Chu-Ren Huang, Li-Ping Chang, Steve Finch, and Keh-Jiann Chen. 1995. The universality of simple distributional methods: Identifying syntactic categories in Mandarin Chinese. In *Proceedings of the International Conference on Cognitive Science and Natural Language Processing*. Dublin, Ireland.
Reisinger, Joseph, and Raymond Mooney. 2010. Multi-prototype vector-space models of word meaning. In *Proceedings of Human Language Technologies: The 2010 Annual Conference of the North American Chapter of the Association for Computational Linguistics*, 109–117. Los Angeles, California.
Resnik, Philip. 1997. Selectional preference and sense disambiguation. In *Proceedings of the ACL SIGLEX Workshop on Tagging Text with Lexical Semantics: Why, What, and How?*, in conjunction with ANLP-97. Washington, DC.
Sampson, Geoffrey. 2000. A proposal for improving the measurement of parse accuracy. *International Journal of Corpus Linguistics* 5:53–68.
T'sou, Benjamin K. 2004. Chinese language processing at the dawn of the 21st century. In *Computational linguistics and beyond*, ed. Chu-Ren Huang and Winfried Lenders, 189–205, Taipei: Institute of Linguistics, Academia Sinica.
Tsai, Yu-Fang, and Keh-Jiann Chen. 2004. Reliable and cost-effective pos-tagging. *Computational Linguistics and Chinese Language Processing* 9(1):83–96.
Tseng, Shu-Chuan. 2006. Repairs in Mandarin conversation. *Journal of Chinese Linguistics* 34(1): 80.
Wang, William S.-Y. 1973. The Chinese language. *Scientific American* 228:50–60.

Wei, Pei-chuan, Paul Thompson, Cheng-Hui Liu, Chu-Ren Huang, and Chaofen Sun 魏培泉, 譚樸森, P. M. Thompson, 劉承慧, 黃居仁, 孫朝奮. 1997. Constructing a historical corpus for synchronic and diachronic linguistic study. 建構一個以共時與歷時語言研究為導向的歷史語料庫. *Computational Linguistics & Chinese Language Processing* 中文計算語言學期刊 2(2):131–145.

Xue, Nianwen, Fei Xia, Fu-Dong Chiou, and Martha Palmer. 2005. The Penn Chinese Tree Bank: Phrase structure annotation of a large corpus. *Natural Language Engineering* 11(2):207–238.

Yamada, Hiroyasu, and Matsumoto, Yuji. 2003. Statistical dependency analysis with support vector machines. In *Proceedings of the 8th International Workshop on Parsing Technologies (IWPT)*, 195–206. Nancy, France.

Yarowsky, David. 1992. Word sense disambiguation using statistical models of Roget's categories trained on large corpora. In *Proceedings of COLING-92*, 454–460. Nantes, France.

Yarowsky, David. 1995. Unsupervised word sense disambiguation rivaling supervised methods. In *Proceedings of the 33rd Annual Meeting of the Association for Computational Linguistics*, 189–196. Cambridge, Massachusetts.

You, Jia-Ming, and Keh-Jiann Chen. 2004. Automatic semantic role assignment for a tree structure. In *Proceedings of the Third SIGHAN Workshop on Chinese Language Processing*. Barcelona, Spain.

Zong, Chengqing, Youqi Cao, and Shiwen Yu 宗成慶, 曹右琦, 俞士汶. 2009. Sixty Years of Chinese Information Processing 中文資訊處理 60 年. *Applied Linguistics* 語言文字應用 4: 54–62.

Part II
Language Resources: Annotation and Processing

Chapter 4
Practical and Robust Chinese Word Segmentation and PoS Tagging

Chu-Ren Huang

Abstract The ability to automatically segment and PoS tag any Chinese text at any time with high accuracy and recall is a prerequisite for the online processing of Chinese texts. While this goal is within reach, it has yet to be attained even after more than 30 years of Chinese language processing research. Most recent achievements in Chinese adopt either stochastic or deep learning models that rely heavily on the availability of training data. As such, these state-of-the-art algorithms are not designed for texts without enough training data, such as texts on novel topics, in new genres, or from linked heterogeneous sources. In this paper, we propose practical and robust Chinese word segmentation and PoS tagging methodologies to address these challenges. The goals are to achieve real-time adaptation of unfamiliar texts, as well as to gain high quality with consistency among heterogeneous texts. For segmentation, we propose a semi-supervised approach, which performs online learning with either labeled or unlabeled data. This approach adopts the word boundary decision (WBD) model and is capable of using only the bigram information of the target article to train for better performance in almost real-time and on heterogeneous texts. For PoS tagging, we introduce the idea of tagset mapping and active learning. The result is the first realistic Chinese segmentation system that is able to support a wide range of HLT applications, which will have important implications in Chinese language processing.

Keywords Part-of-speech tagging · Word segmentation · Word boundary decision · Active learning approach · Robustness

C.-R. Huang (✉)
Department of Chinese and Bilingual Studies, The Hong Kong Polytechnic University, Hong Kong, China
e-mail: churen.huang@polyu.edu.hk

C.-R. Huang et al. (eds.), *Chinese Language Resources*, Text, Speech and Language Technology 49, https://doi.org/10.1007/978-3-031-38913-9_4

4.1 Introduction

Tokenization and part-of-speech (PoS) tagging are two prerequisites for sharable language resources for both language technology and linguistic research. They are exceptionally important for Chinese for the following two reasons, respectively. For tokenization, the challenges come from the lack of conventionalized word breaks to follow as default (Huang and Xue 2015). Tokenization in Chinese is commonly referred to as Chinese word segmentation (CWS, e.g., Chen and Liu 1992; Chiang et al. 1992; Huang and Zhao 2007). It is well-known that state-of-the-art Chinese word segmentation systems routinely achieve high f-scores, around 98–99 in shared tasks. However, the shared task setting typically involves large amounts of tagged training data, which is significantly larger than the testing set, in matching variety, domain, and genre; this necessitates computing resources and long training time. Furthermore, shared tasks typically last at least 1–2 months from task announcement to deadline. These conditions are drastically different from real-world needs for word segmentation or PoS tagging tasks. The most in-demand and challenging real-world applications typically involve real-time segmentation of a target article with neither prior domain knowledge nor a large-scale corpus of similar texts for training. Similarly, PoS tagging in Chinese is challenging due to its lack of inflectional morphology and fluidity of categorical changes without overt morphological marking (e.g., Chao 1968; Huang et al. 2017). Past research and bakeoff competition of Chinese PoS tagging similarly require a sizable previously PoS-tagged training dataset that has been manually tagged or checked. One of the largest PoS-tagged Chinese corpus, the 14-billion-word-tagged Chinese Gigaword II (Huang 2009), for instance, relied on the high-quality tagging of the 10-million-word Sinica Corpus 2.0 (Chen et al. 1996) as training data (Ma and Huang 2006).

Ma and Huang's (2006) tagging of the Chinese Gigaword Corpus points to another challenging context: heterogeneous language big data. Language technology applications nowadays routinely require the processing of gargantuan-sized texts containing billions of words. In this scenario, there is no real-time processing requirement, but instead a set of different challenges, including a reliable uniform tagset for data from different sources and with possibly different grammatical features, a reliable and scalable quality assurance method, and suitable training data.

Given the goal of robust and practical segmentation and PoS tagging of Mandarin Chinese, the two most challenging scenarios that state-of-the-art methodologies cannot handle satisfactorily are (1) novel domain or variety without sufficient tagged data for training and (2) gargantuan size big data that are so big that comprehensive word-level quality assurance tasks are not practical. These two challenging scenarios can be summarized as three closely related issues.

1. Resource dependency: training and adaptation must be carried out effectively and quickly without large-scale labeled data.
2. Domain dependency: systems need to be able to maintain robustness when applied to a new and unknown domain without (significant) performance degradation.

3. Robust and effective quality assurance: quality assurance measures that an existing gold standard (of labeling) from the same dataset or manual checking is not required.

Robustness is the ability to handle unexpected challenges in real-life applications. However, there is currently no robustness measurement for Chinese word segmentation tools as all bakeoffs rely on pre-prepared gold standards and do not have any test for domain adaptation. This may be the reason why, even though winning teams in SIGHAN International Word Segmentation Bakeoffs score high f-scores, they are rarely developed into viable real-time applications. This is an area where research in Chinese word segmentation needs urgent improvement, and an updated measurement of performance to reflect robustness and domain adaptability should help.

Another area that has received little attention so far is the efficiency of segmentation. The state-of-the-art segmentation algorithms typically require large-scale training and computing resources. Leading systems now routinely use training data in the range of billions or tens of billions of words with machine learning algorithms. Although computing capacity may develop, resource dependency is still a crucial weakness. In real life, any domain that can provide tens of billions of words of verified segmented data does not have an urgent need for word segmentation. The field either produces pre-segmented data regularly or already has a large-scale and reliable lexicon compiled; hence, it can easily have content keywords tokenized using various lexicon-driven approaches. The areas and domains where segmentation tools can really make impacts are typically low in resources, not unlike a low-resource language.

A truly robust and practical Chinese word segmentation system should have the capacity of fast online adaptation to a text from an unknown domain or variety, requiring no more than a small set of labeled or unlabeled data. This is not unlike the requirements of the LORELEI project (Christianson et al. 2018). Such capacity relies crucially on the success of addressing the three issues previously raised. In this paper, we propose a two-pronged approach: On one hand, we propose to reduce the complexity of the word segmentation by modeling it as a word boundary decision (WBD, Huang et al. 2007; Huang and Xue 2012) task. On the hand other hand, we propose to reduce the reliance on large homogeneous labeled data from the same source by actively learning (Li and Huang 李壽山, 黃居仁 2010) ways to model these two tasks as well as possible ways to implement the new models effectively.

In what follows, we will first overview the WBD model for word segmentation and discuss how this model not only reduces the complexity of the word segmentation task but also lays the foundation for active learning without labeled data. We next explicate how active learning would allow for fast and robust adaption with a small set of unfamiliar data. This is followed by how a similar approach can be applied to PoS tagging, especially in the context of grammatical differences belonging to different varieties of language or the application of different tagsets. A conclusion section will summarize the proposed approach, as well as potential future directions.

4.2 Word Boundary Detection Model Robust Word Segmentation

Huang and Xue (2012) provided a succinct summary of the evolution of models of Chinese word segmentation. They showed that models improve through reduction of dependence on lexical information, as well as of the complexity of classification.

4.2.1 From Word Identification to Boundary Decision

Chinese word segmentation is intuitively modeled as word identification by early research. The task of word segmentation is envisioned in two steps: looking up and identifying known and unknown words in a text and then segmenting the text before and after each word. This approach (e.g., Chen and Liu 1992, Chiang et al. 1992) faces the immediate challenges of unknown words (or out-of-vocabulary words, OOV), as well as segmentation ambiguity (where a single string can be segmented in different ways to yield different words). In addition, by the inclusion of word identification as part of the task, the simple segmentation task is compounded by the fact that the linguistic definition of words in Chinese cannot be comprehensively operationalized, and words are often not interoperable between the two systems (Huang and Zhao 2007; Huang and Xue 2015; Huang et al. 2017). So far, regardless of whether heuristic or statistic approaches are adopted, the performance of the word identification approach has not been ideal.

An important breakthrough in Chinese word segmentation recast it as a character classification task, word identification task. By taking an unsegmented text as a string of characters just like previous models, Xue (2003) and Xue and Shen (2003) conceptualized word segmentation as identification of characters that are at word boundaries. That is, the string of characters can be classified as those at the beginning of a word, in the middle of a word, and at the end of a word. Word segmentation is achieved without reliance on a dictionary; hence, there is no need for special treatment of OOVs. This model fundamentally changed the nature and performance baseline of Chinese word segmentation. Note that word identification-driven approaches, including those relying on n-gram or other stochastic models, is a classification task with n classes where n is the number of potential words in the language. Unfortunately, words in Chinese or any other language in the world form an open set. Characters, on the other hand, form a close set that contains roughly 10,000 members. This model reduces the scale of classification. In addition, they adopted an annotation scheme similar to name entity recognition that tags characters according to their position in a word. Thus, the task of classification can be further simplified as the classification of characters (order of 10,000) into three classes according to their position in the word: begin, middle, and end. A robust, supervised method can be developed by training the segmentation program as a classifier of characters based on a large collection of labeled data (Xue and Shen 2003). Several subsequent studies proposed different variations of the annotation schemes following the same conceptual model. The model achieved significantly improved results over the word identification models and has been the most popular model in the past 20 years.

Semi-supervised methods have the advantage of being able to learn from unlabeled data, hence adding robustness in dealing with novel genre, variety, and topical areas. Such approaches have the potential to offer a comparable performance to the supervised method. Ando and Lee (2003) proposed a semi-supervised approach (called mostly unsupervised) for the segmentation of Japanese kanji sequences. They used very few labeled data for parameter tuning rather than direct supervision segmentation. Their approach works fine on large-scale unlabeled data; however, this approach is not applicable to very small-scale unlabeled data because such data have poor coverage of the n-grams needed for learning.

4.2.2 Word Boundary Decision (WBD)

Huang et al. (2007) streamlined the conceptual model of word segmentation further. They distilled the essence of word segmentation as a unary decision on whether to mark a word boundary between each two characters, called word boundary decision (WBD). The proposal is based on the observation that the character classification model is a secondary derivation based on the question of whether there is a wordbreak before or after a certain character or not. In other words, it answers the question of what does a word begin with and what does a word end with, but not what a word is. Logically, the essence of word segmentation is simply a unary decision of whether a word boundary exists or not. The challenge is how to build a linguistic data-driven model of this concept.

Huang et al. (2007) conceptualized Chinese text as a sequence of characters and intervals by explicitly modelling the space that separates characters:

$$c_1 I_1 c_2 I_2, \ldots, c_{n-1} I_{n-1} c_n$$

where c_i stands for a character and I_i are the natural intervals occurring between two neighboring characters. Note that such a model is, in fact, well corroborated in languages that conventionalized spaces to mark words in orthography, such as English. In reading and writing, an implicit assumption is that a space is inserted to mark the boundary of a word and recognized as such. Contrary to some previous accounts, it is not true that Chinese orthography does not employ blank space to mark boundaries between words. Since each character as a basic writing unit is also the sociological word (Chao 1968) in Chinese, a space follows each character and hence marks both sociological and linguistic words (Huang and Xue 2015). As such, each blank could also be a mark for a word boundary, and there are no other possible positions for word boundaries. Based on this fact, WBD models word boundary according to the on ($I_i = 1$) or off ($I_i = 0$) status of the interval. The classification problem in WBD is to classify the intervals into word boundaries or non-boundaries. Based on the fact that the average word length in Chinese is between 1.3 and 1.4 characters (e.g., Huang et al. 2002), we can estimate that roughly 70–80% of the I's defined in WBD are word boundaries.

Implementation of WBD typically consists of two main steps: The first is the generation of a set of character n-gram probabilities as training data. The probabilities are defined in terms of contextual probability for an I to be a word boundary, as shown below. The second step is the classifier training and testing using probability vectors built based on the training data. In the first step, different kinds of character n-gram probabilities are estimated from training data. Five different unigram and bigram probabilities are usually used in WBD. They may include unigram probabilities of P_{CB}, P_{BC} and bigram probabilities of P_{CCB}, P_{CBC}, P_{BCC}. The definition of P_{CCB} is given as

$$P_{CCB}(I_i = 1 | c_{i-1}, c_i) = \frac{C(c_{i-1}, c_i, I_i = 1)}{C(c_{i-1}, c_i)}$$

where $C(c_i, I_i = 1)$ is the number of appearances of a character immediately before a word boundary. $C(c_i)$ is the total number of the same character c_i in the training data. Intuitively, this is the probability of a word boundary occurring immediately after a character. Similarly, the definition of P_{CCB} is given in terms of a bigram to capture the probability of a word boundary occurring immediately after the bigram. c_{i-1}, c_i. P_{BC} is the probability of a word boundary occurring immediately before a certain character. P_{BCC} is the probability of a word boundary occurring immediately before a bigram. Lastly, P_{CBC} is the probability of a word boundary occurring in between a bigram. The set of probabilities defines the full range of immediate edge conditions around a word boundary. If necessary, it can be expanded to include longer contexts in the same manner.

After the probability extraction based on the training data, all unigrams and bigrams will get their boundary probability information. The probabilities are then applied to generate the vectors in the second step. Once the frequency and probability information of all character n-grams are obtained, it can be easily preserved in a database (n-gram database).

In the second step, each boundary I_i is represented as a vector:

$$< P_{CCB}(I_i), P_{CB}(I_i), P_{CBC}(I_i), P_{BC}(I_i), P_{BCC}(I_i) >$$

The WBD model is not a language-specific model. In fact, it applies to all language that uses space to separate writing units. In language, such as English, where a space is the conventionalized orthographic mark for word boundary, there are also notable exceptions such as multiword expressions (MWE), such as *the White House*, or *to keep an eye on*. As such MWEs are relatively rare in English, the ensuing space and word boundary mismatches do not typically pose serious challenges in NLP implementations. English language processing typically accepts the default of spaces equal to word boundaries and deal with the issue of MWEs separately. Given the possible mismatches between orthographic convention and linguistic wordhood, the rationale of the WBD model for tokenization should also be applicable in other languages, such as English.

Similarly, the character classification model can also be applied to other languages as a model for tokenization with some adjustment. For languages that do not use characters, the basic unit of such a model could be either a letter, a syllable, or a morpheme.

4.3 From Online Learning to Active Learning

The ultimate test for robustness of a segmentation algorithm is to segment a text without knowing its source and with limited training data, labeled or unlabeled. It is possible that information available during online learning could be restricted to the target text itself. In machine learning, online learning is a model of induction that learns one instance at a time (Blum 1998). One big benefit of this model is its ability to quickly learn from new labeled data without retraining from previously labeled data. We adopt a similar concept of online learning on the premise that online learning helps to address the three unresolved issues facing robust and practical Chinese word segmentation. In order to make the segmentation system versatile and effective, it needs to be able to handle newly introduced and unfamiliar domains, varieties, genres, and neologisms, which are not covered by the labeled training data. Robust online training needs to be carried out with new data alone and cannot presuppose the availability of original training data.

4.3.1 Online Semi-supervised Learning with Labeled Data

Huang et al. (2008) show that 1000 vectors are enough to optimize a good WBD classifier. Based on this result, we assume that we can retain as the sharable baseline training data an n-gram dataset obtained from a large-scale comparable corpus containing different varieties and genres, such as the tagged Chinese Gigaword Corpus 2.1 (Huang 2009). Semi-supervised learning can be applied to novel data accompanied by a small set of labeled data. The crucial step is to update the probability information in the n-gram database with the following formula. Note that the n-gram database here contains both probability and frequency information:

$$P'_{\mathrm{CCB}}(I_i = 1 | c_{i-1}, c_i) = \frac{C(c_{i-1}, c_i, I_i = 1) + C_{new}(c_{i-1}, c_i, I_i = 1)}{C(c_{i-1}, c_i) + C_{new}(c_{i-1}, c_i)}$$

In this formula, $C(c_{i-1}, c_i, l_i = 1)$ and $C(c_{i-1}, c_i)$ are frequency information reserved in the baseline n-gram database; it would be zero if this n-gram was not included. $C_{new}(c_{i-1}, c_i, l_i = 1)$ and $C_{new}(c_{i-1}, c_i)$ are the frequency information collected from the new labeled data.

4.3.2 Online Semi-supervised Learning with Unlabeled Data

For a novel target dataset without labeled data, Li et al. (2012) designed an approach based on the observation that domain-specific words often appear more often in a domain-specific text (e.g., a person names in a news article). We assume that the bigrams that appear more than once are likely to be parts of the new words. We try to preserve those bigrams unsegmented to guarantee that the new words remain unsegmented as well.

Specifically, we first acquire all bigrams from the target text (seen as our unlabeled data). The bigrams that appear more than M times are considered to be nonsegmented parts, while the other bigrams are considered to be segmented. As a result, the short text becomes virtual labeled data.

For example, we set $M = 1$ and have an unlabeled character string:

$$c_1c_2c_3c_4c_5c_6c_1c_2c_3c_7c_2c_3c_8$$

Among all the bigrams, only c_1c_2, c_2c_3 appear more than once. Thus, they are both considered segmented units, and we obtain labeling information from unlabeled data.

Given the virtual labeled data, we can get the target n-gram database of those unsegmented bigrams, e.g., c_1c_2 and c_2c_3 in the above example. Then the target n-gram database is used to update the former n-gram data with our online learning approach (proposed in Sect. 4.3.1). Note that we do not need to collect unigram information because we assume the unigram information in the former n-gram database (obtained through training a big-scale labeled data) is stable and need not be updated.

4.3.3 Performances of WBD

Adopting SIGHAN Bakeoff 2 data, Li et al. (2012) designed their study to showcase the robustness of WBD. For comparison, we also implement a best performance character-based approach with conditional random field (CRF) following Ng and Low (2004). The first study involves two different simplified Chinese datasets from Peking University (PKU) and Microsoft Research Centre Asia (MSR). A pair of close-tests on two bakeoff datasets are performed as baselines, while two cross-dataset training and testing are also performed to mimic novel testing data

Table 4.1 Comparison of two segmentation approaches

	CRF	WBD
PKU→PKU	0.931	0.914
MSR→MSR	0.962	0.949
PKU → MSR	0.856	0.850
MSR → PKU	0.850	0.851

conditions. We use *F*-score as the performance measurement. *F*-score is defined as $F = 2PR/(P + R)$ where *P* is precision and *R* is recall. The results are shown in Table 4.1.

From this table, we can see that WBD performs slightly worse than CRF when the training and testing data come from the same source (PKU → PKU and MSR → MSR), although the training process of WBD is much faster than CRF. Take PKU, for instance, WBD takes less than 2 min of training, while CRF takes more than 1 h. Furthermore, we cross datasets to simulate a real-world application scenario where the existing large-scaled labeled training data is not necessarily matched with the novel text to be segmented. The results are also shown in Table 4.1, where "PKU → MSR" means the classifier is trained with training data from PKU but used to test the gold testing data from MSR. As expected, the performances dropped compared to homogeneous testing/training. It is important to observe that under this mimicked real-world scenario, there is no significant gap of performance between character-based CRF and WBD, with WBD being more efficient with time and resources required.

4.3.4 Results of Online Learning with Unlabeled Data

In addition to the mimic robustness test, we apply our online semi-supervised approach to tackle a more realistic and challenging real-world scenario of segmenting with only small-scale unlabeled data. Our system uses Sinica Corpus (Chen et al. 1996) to generate n-gram frequency and probability information as default pre-compiled knowledge.

In order to refer to existing evaluation tools for comparison, we adopt testing data from CityU data in SIGHAN Bakeoff 3. Note that ASBC data is collected in Taiwan and CityU data is collected in Hong Kong; they are both in traditional Chinese characters. To perform the evaluation, we randomly selected ten articles in CityU data, each about 20–40 sentences long. Each article was processed independently as unlabeled data, without other training. We set the frequency threshold *M* to 1, which means we consider a bigram as a non-segmented part if it appears more than once. The *F*-score results are shown in Table 4.2. Note that the *F*-score score is 0.892 when testing the complete set of data without any semi-supervised process.

Table 4.2 shows that online learning with unlabeled data improves the performance in eight of ten articles and maintains the same performance for the other two. It is also important to underline that the achieved scores are comparable to most

Table 4.2 *F*-score results of using testing data as unlabeled data with our approach

	Without online learning	With online learning
A1	0.906	**0.940**
A2	0.931	**0.947**
A3	0.831	**0.838**
A4	**0.890**	**0.890**
A5	0.920	**0.943**
A6	0.925	**0.936**
A7	0.915	**0.927**
A8	0.935	**0.941**
A9	**0.929**	0.928
A10	0.892	**0.913**

state-of-the-art systems, which use the large-scale training data from the same source. This study confirms the feasibility of the WBD approach in a real-world context of segmenting a short, novel text without matching training data.

4.3.5 Active Learning Approach for CWS: Meeting the Three Challenges

As mentioned above, current CWS systems lack practicality due to two thresholds: reliance on existing homogeneous large-scale labeled data and the need for significant training time. We have shown that adopting WBD with supervised learning based on a small unlabeled dataset can produce results comparable to the traditional approach. To further improve the results to achieve realistic real-time segmentation, we implement active learning where *informative* samples are selected for manually annotating and used for training the segmentation model. This approach reduces the annotation cost as redundant samples are filtered without annotation. In addition, the computational cost of the training and testing phases is also reduced because fewer samples are used for training.

To investigate the effectiveness of active learning for CWS quickly, we employ the WBD segmentation approach as discussed in Sect. 4.3.2. Figure 4.1 shows the framework of WBD-based active learning for CWS.

In this study, we adopt one popular selections strategy known as uncertainty sampling, where a learner queries the instance which is most uncertain (Lewis and Gale 1994). The uncertainty sampling will identify the most challenging data to be labeled a human oracle for training. As WBD is a binary classification problem, uncertainty can simply be measured by querying the boundary whose posterior probability is nearest to 0.5. Therefore, we can define the uncertainty confidence value as follows:

Input:

Labeled set L, unlabeled pool U, selection strategy $\phi(x)$

Procedure:

Repeat

(1). Learn a segmenter using current L with WBD

(2). Use current segmenter to label all the unlabeled boundaries

(3). Use the selection strategy $\phi(x)$ to select a batch of most informative boundaries for oracle labeling

(4). Put the new labeled boundaries together with their context (automatically labeled) into L

Until the predefined stopping criterion is met

Fig. 4.1 WBD-based active learning for CWS

Table 4.3 The segmentation performance of the WBD approach when selecting a part of training data using either random selection or active learning in PKU dataset

Proportion of the selected data	5%	10%	25%	100%
Random selection	0.906	0.913	0.92	0.945
Active learning	0.925	0.936	0.945	0.945

Table 4.4 The segmentation performance of WBD approach when selecting a part of training data using either random selection or active learning with CityU dataset

Proportion of the selected data	5%	10%	25%	100%
Random selection	0.890	0.901	0.912	0.946
Active learning	0.920	0.930	0.945	0.946

$$\phi^{Un}(b_k) = \max_{y \in \{0,1\}} P(y|I_k) - 0.5$$

In this equation, $P(y|I_k)$ denotes the posterior probability that boundary I_k is labeled as y. The lower the confidence value is, the more informative the segmentation decision would be. After computing the confidences, all the boundaries in the unlabeled pool U are ranked according to their uncertainty values. In this way, a batch of most uncertain boundaries can be picked as the most informative ones to be labeled by a human oracle, and for ensuing learning.

We use three datasets in the SIGHAN Bakeoff 2, including PKU, MSR, and CityU, for evaluating the uncertainty sampling-based active learning approach for CES. To perform active learning, 10% of the labeled training data in each corpus are used as the initial training data L, and the remaining are used as the unlabeled data U. In all experiments, we use standard F1 score as our main performance measurement. Tables 4.3, 4.4, and 4.5 report the segmentation performance of the WBD approach when selecting a part of training data using either random selection or active learning in each dataset. From these tables, we can see that when using the same size of training data, active learning apparently outperforms random selection strategy.

Table 4.5 The segmentation performance of the WBD approach when selecting a part of training data using either random selection or active learning with MSR dataset

Proportion of the selected data	5%	10%	25%	100%
Random selection	0.918	0.923	0.928	0.961
Active learning	0.937	0.948	0.957	0.961

When using only 25% of the training data with active learning, the performances in all datasets approach those that use all the training data. For example, in PKU, when 25% of training data is selected for annotating by our active learning approach, the segmentation performance on the testing data is 0.945 in terms of F1 score, which is the same as the one when all training data is used. These findings demonstrate that active learning is an effective way to reduce the annotation cost. Meanwhile, since the training data is reduced when an active learning approach is applied, the computational cost can also be greatly decreased.

4.4 Robustness of PoS Tagging and Quality Assurance: A Two-Tagset Model

PoS tagging is considered to be a must for sharable corpora as well as for language technology applications (Atkins et al. 1992; Huang and Yao 2015). Tokenization or word segmentation is the prerequisite of PoS tagging. As an input to PoS tagging, however, the model of segmentation has no direct impact on PoS tagging performances. That is, all different models or algorithms of segmentation produce the same type of information about words in a text that is required for PoS tagging. The adaptation of different annotation schemes for PoS tagging, i.e., different tagsets, however, would have crucial implications for syntactic and semantic processing. For instance, a sortal classifier is tagged as Nf in Sinica Corpus (Chen et al. 1996) but as q in the PKU-ICL tagset (Yu et al. 2002.), and as Cl or CL in linguistic grammars. These names are more than just different labels as they also suggest slightly different definitions of each category and therefore have implications for subsequent processing.

Compared to the process of word segmentation, however, the conceptual model of PoS tagging involves the straightforward classification of words according to their grammatical functions. Given a well-defined and linguistically motivated PoS tagset, automatic tagging typically achieves good results, especially with machine learning approaches trained on labeled data. This can be attributed to several contributing factors, including the relatively small and enumerable number of PoS, the fact that an even smaller number of possible PoS are compatible with each word, and each context. However, when dealing with language changes and variations, such as the processing of similar languages (Zampieri et al. 2019; Xu et al. 2020), the system of PoS tagging poses a dilemma. On the one hand, differences in the definition of parts of speech should be one of the fundamental issues to consider for language variations and changes. On the other hand, in a corpus-driven approach, direct comparison would be extremely difficult (if not outright impossible) if different annotation systems are used. On the most mundane level, two datasets may have different annotation systems in terms of PoS simply because they were prepared by different research teams (or at different times). As such, the three issues for robust and practical PoS tagging, resources dependency, domain dependency, and quality assurance, can be narrowed down to the context of dealing with two or more different tagsets.

Quality assurance of automatically tagged corpora has become a central issue as very large corpora, such as those constructed from the web-as-corpus approach (Kilgarriff and Grefenstette 2003), have become the norm. Manual checking of tagging and other textual markups is obviously not practical for such corpora. It has been a standard practice for previous research on quality assurance to assume one unique gold standard, which in turn presupposed a single PoS tagset. We propose an innovative approach with two competing tagsets. When two similar but different linguistic analysis systems are available, a substantial number of discrepancies can be expected. The comparison between two versions of the same corpus allows for the discovery of both regular mapping and non-regular mapping. Non-regular mapping can be further analyzed to identify both potential errors and systematic correspondences. This two-tagset model is a viable alternative and even necessary when a language contains significant varieties, such as in Mandarin Chinese. In Mandarin Chinese, it is generally believed that PRC corpora are best processed with PRC tagset and Taiwan corpora with Taiwan tagset. Although such judgments are subjective and hard to verify empirically, it is extremely unlikely to find Mainland data with a Taiwan tagset and vice versa. The bottom line is that the most direct way to test the robustness of a PoS tagging system is to apply it to a new and unfamiliar set of data, such as texts from a different language variety.

Huang et al. (2008) proposed a set of heuristics for improving annotation quality in a gargantuan corpus. They examined the Xinhua News portion of the tagged Chinese Gigaword Corpus (Huang 2009) as it tagged independently with both the Peking University ICL tagset and the Academia Sinica CKIP tagset. They empirically attested mapping between the two tagsets. The corpus-based mapping, annotated with the probability of mapping relations, will serve as basic data for two very different purposes. First, it will serve as the basis for the possible contrast in grammatical systems between PRC and Taiwan. Second, it will serve as the basic model for quality assurance.

The CKIP tagset was adopted for Sinica Corpus and a hybrid HMM (hidden Markov model) and morpheme analysis-based method was adopted for tagging (Tseng and Chen 2002). Figure 4.1 shows an example with the CKIP-PoS tagset, which was inspired by Chao (1968) and detailed in both CKIP 詞庫小組 (1993) and Huang et al. (2017).

```
<DOC id="XIN_CMN_20010101.0004" type="story">
<HEADLINE>
印度(Nca) 平靜(VH11) 迎接(VC2) 新(VH11) 千(Neu) 年(Nfg)
</HEADLINE>
<DATELINE>
新華社(Nca) 新德里(Nca) 1月(Nd) 1日(Nd) 電(Naa)
</DATELINE>
<TEXT>
<P>
((PARENTHESISCATEGORY)    記 者 (Nab)    熊昌義
(Nb) )(PARENTHESISCATEGORY)    10億(Neu)    印度
人(Nab)    以(P11)  平靜(VH11)  的(DE)  心情(Nad)  迎(VC2)
來(VA11    了(Di)    新(VH11)    千(Neu)    年(Nfg)  。
(PERIODCATEGORY) ........
</P>
<P>
1日(Nd) 凌晨(Ndabe)  , (COMMACATEGORY)
新德里(Nca) 雖(Cbba) 下(VC) 起(Di) 了(Di) 小(VH13)
雨 (Naa)  , (COMMACATEGORY)
</P>
........
</TEXT>
</DOC>
```


The Institute of Computational Linguistics, Peking University PoS tagset was proposed and defined by Yu et al. (2002). The most popular PoS tagger for simplified Chinese is the ICTCLAS (Institute of Computing Technology, Chinese Lexical Analysis System) tagger (Zhang et al. 2003a, b). The tagger adopts a hierarchical hidden Markov model (HHMM).

4.4.1 Corpus-Based POS Tag Mapping

The POS-tagged documents of China's Xinhua News Agency from 2001 to 2004 were used for tags mapping. First, both versions of the tagged corpus were aligned in order to compare their segmentation results. This comparison shows that the two systems have about 85% agreement in terms of segmentation. Next, for all words where both systems agree in segmentation, we obtain mappings from the CKIP-AS tagset to the ICL-PKU tagset and ICL-PKU tagset to CKIP-AS tagset. There are 48 tags in the CKIP system and 40 tags in the ICL system. The main difference between these two tagsets is that the CKIP POS tags is hierarchy designed.

Tables 4.6 and 4.7 show all the possible mappings as well as their probabilities in two different directions. Table 4.6 shows that 87.5% (42 of 48) of CKIP PoS tags are mapped to a single dominant ICL PoS; we use the heuristic rule of having the top mapping be higher than 40%, as well as at least twice as frequent as the second highest mapping. The six PoS that do not map to a clearly dominant ICL PoS are Dfb, I, Nc, Ncd, Neqb, and T. All the other tags, to varying degrees, are mapped to

Table 4.6 CKIP to ICL tag mapping table

CKIP tag	PKU mapping tag
A (non-predicative adjective)	b (53.6%)
Caa (conjunctive conjunction)	c (84.8%)
Cab (conjunction, e.g., 等等)	u (87.5%)
Cba (conjunction, e.g., 的話)	u (92.4%)
Cbb (correlative conjunction)	c (82.9%)
D (adverb)	d (67.5%)
Da (quantitative adverb)	d (88.5%)
DE (的,之,得,地)	u (91.5%)
Dfa (pre-verbal adverb of degree)	d (91.4%)
Dfb (post-verbal adverb of degree)	t (34.6%); q (24.9%)
Di (aspectual adverb)	u (93.3%)
Dk (sentential adverb)	v (49.1%); n (15.8%)
FW (foreign word)	m (82.5%)
I (interjection)	e (34.7%); j (27.4%)
Na (common noun)	n (82.6%)
Nb (proper noun)	nr (47.6%); ns (10%)
Nc (place noun)	ns (47.2%); n (36.4%)
Ncd (localizer)	f (45.4%); m (37.9%)
Nd (time noun)	t (88.3%)
Nep (demonstrative determinatives)	r (98.5%)
Neqa (quantitative determinatives)	m (55.1%)
Neqb (post-quantitative determinatives)	m (48%); a (32.7%)
Nes (specific determinatives)	r (55.7%)
Neu (numeral determinatives)	m (99.6%)
Nf (measure)	q (90%)
Ng (postposition)	f (76.7%)
Nh (pronoun)	r (89.5%)
Nv (verbal nominalization)	vn (65.2%)
P (preposition)	p (87.3%)
SHI (是)	v (95.2%)
T (particle)	y (47.7%); u (43%)
VA (active intransitive verb)	v (52.7%)
VAC (active causative verb)	v (83.8%)
VB (active pseudo-transitive verb)	v (59.3%)
VC (active transitive verb)	v (70.8%)
VCL (active verb with a locative object)	v (82.7%)
VD (ditransitive verb)	v (73.2%)
VE (active verb with a sentential object)	v (85.1%)
VF (active verb with a verbal object)	v (82.9%)
VG (classificatory verb)	v (70.8%)
VH (stative intransitive verb)	a (43.1%); v (16.3%)
VHC (stative causative verb)	v (63.2%)

(continued)

Table 4.6 (continued)

CKIP tag	PKU mapping tag
VI (stative pseudo-transitive verb)	v (70.7%)
VJ (stative transitive verb)	v (81.8%)
VK (stative verb with a sentential object)	v (88.4%)
VL (stative verb with a verbal object)	v (79.1%)
V_2 (有)	v (95%)
*CATEGORY (punctuation)	w (96.1%)

one dominant corresponding PoS tag with other less dominant mappings. Note that Dfb, I, and T are minor categories without concrete semantic meaning, while Nc and Ncd are highly dependent on semantic interpretation. 65% (26 of 40) of ICL POS tags in Table 4.7 have a single dominant mapped category. There are 14 that do not map to one dominant corresponding PoS. The high degree of correspondences, in both directions, confirms that the two linguistic systems are still very similar and that comparative studies based on these two different tagsets are valid.

All exceptional mappings are investigated after the regular and default tag-to-tag mapping between CKIP and ICL systems are established based on the above data and manual analysis. Some of these mappings will be explained as non-homomorphism between the systems, yet others will be identified as potential tagging errors. We will investigate the possible error patterns when the segmented words were inconsistent. Once these error patterns are successfully found, models for automatic correction and the estimation of confidence for automatic tags will be devised. An iteration algorithm that will improve the quality of both versions of the tagged corpus will be proposed and tested.

4.5 Linguistic Ramification

The fact that word boundaries are not conventionalized in Chinese orthography presents computational Chinese word segmentation as a possible way to computationally model how words are identified linguistically. It is interesting to note that the two most promising approaches are the ones that involve the least amount of lexical knowledge. For the character tagging approach, no explicit knowledge of words or word lists are referred to. It refers to the knowledge of words indirectly by marking the position of each character in a word. The word boundary decision (WBD) approach requires no knowledge of word lists at all. The fact that these two approaches achieve the most promising results so far supports the modular view of language processing. That is, word identification as the most preliminary task of language processing and as the prerequisite of lexicon construction should not refer to knowledge of the lexicon.

Both the character tagging approach and the WBD approach can also be viewed as implicitly modeling morphological information. Although Chinese does not have

Table 4.7 ICL to CKIP tag mapping table

ICL PKU tag	CKIP mapping tag
a (adjective)	VH (75.5%)
ad (adjective)	VH (72.6%)
an (noun adjective)	VH (65.7%)
ag (adjectival morpheme)	Caa (45.6%); VH (21%)
b (distinguishing word)	DE (33.5%); A (29.2%)
c (conjunction)	Caa (50.5%)
d (adverb)	D (74.5%)
dg (adverbial morpheme)	P (34.6%); D (12.6%); VJ (8%)
e (interjection)	DE (43.9%); T (15.7%)
f (location)	Ng (58.3%)
g (morpheme)	FW (52.1%)
h (pre-adjective of degree)	A (21.8%); Nes (20%); Nc (14.9%)
i (phrase)	VH (64%)
j (abbreviation)	Nc (36.3%); Na (31.6%)
k (post-adjective of degree)	Na (80.1%)
l (idiom)	Na (35.9%); VH (28.4%)
m (measure)	Neu (72.2%)
n (noun)	Na (78.7%)
ng (noun morpheme)	Na (34.9%); Ng (31.5%)
nr (proper noun)	Nb (80.3%)
ns (place noun)	Nc (92.2%)
nt (affiliation)	Nc (74.4%)
nx (non-Chinese character)	*CATEGORY (98.9%)
nz (other special noun)	Nb (44.2%); Na (26.5%)
o (onomatopoeia)	D (36.4%); VC (17%)
p (preposition)	P (86%)
q (classifier)	Nf (90.2%)
r (pronoun)	Nh (42.2%); nep (27.8%)
s (locational noun)	Nc (80.3%)
t (time noun)	Nd (96.9%)
tg (time morpheme)	Nd (54%)
u (auxiliary)	DE (76.8%)
v (verb)	VC (32.7%); VE (11.4%); VJ (8.2%)
vd (adverbial verb)	VH (17.5%); VC (14%); VL (12.9%); D (10.8%)
vg (verbal morpheme)	VC (22%); Na (19.3%); D (10.4%)
vn (noun verb)	VC (34.7%); Na (28.2%)
w (punctuation marks)	*CATEGORY (95.3%)
x (non-morpheme)	FW (68.2%)
y (modal particle)	T (61.3%)
z (stative modifier)	VH (68.4%)

very productive derivational morphology, it does have many productive prefixes and suffixes, such as the suffix 度 du4 "-ity" and 阿 a1 "prefix for informal names." In addition, compounding is very productive in Chinese, and the most productive compound roots do tend to occur in either word-initial or word-final positions. In other words, word boundaries correlate highly with these edge items.

In terms of the WBD approach, what is most surprising about the experiment's result so far is that it only requires 1000 randomly chosen vectors to achieve optimal results of word segmentation. It is important to note that even though we have reduced the task of segmentation to the decision of whether existing inter-character breaks are also word boundaries, there are still nearly 6000 characters in context to define the intervals. There are two possible explanations for this fact. The first is that the space of word boundaries is well clustered, hence not a difficult problem to solve. On the other hand, recall that each vector contains the immediate context of four characters for each interval and is recorded with five features. Also, recall that the WBD approach models segmentation as a unary decision on whether to segment or not at the intervals. A unary decision means that the classifier only needs to be trained to make word segmentation at less than 70% of the intervals and no action is needed for the remaining more than 30% of the intervals, based on the estimated average word length of roughly 1.4 characters. Based on these two crucial facts, 1000 vectors do seem to be sufficient to provide the information for training the classifier. In fact, these two possible explanations are not mutually exclusive and may be related to the reference to morphological edges in the last paragraph. Future studies may shed better light on how words are distributed and clustered in the space of character strings.

4.6 Conclusion: The Convergence of Linguistic and Stochastic Modeling

We discuss the issues involving modeling and performance evaluation of Chinese word segmentation in this paper. Our survey shows that a modular processing model can be supported and that word identification and segmentation may not be as complicated a problem as it may have seemed originally since words may have strong clustering features that make them easy to be detected in a text. Recent developments in modeling of Chinese word segmentation tend to take a more modular approach minimizing the role of prior lexical knowledge. They also tend to model the task as a simple classification problem, such as character-labeling approaches, four-character position tags, or the WBD approach classification of whether an interval is a word boundary or not. The newest models are also shown to be easily adapted with model combination and active learning. These new trends offer great promise for the development of a truly robust and realistic solution for Chinese word segmentation for human language technology applications in the near future.

References

Ando, Rie Kubota, and Lillian Lee. 2003. Mostly-unsupervised statistical segmentation of Japanese kanji sequences. *Natural Language Engineering* 9(2):127–149.

Atkins, Sue, Jeremy Clear, and Nicholas Ostler. 1992. Corpus design criteria. *Literary and Linguistic Computing* 7(1):1–16.

Blum, Avrim. 1998. On-line algorithms in machine learning. *Lecture Notes in Computer Science* 1442:306–325.

Chao, Yuen Ren. 1968. *A grammar of spoken Chinese*. Berkeley: University of California Press.

Chen, Keh-Jiann, and Shing-Huan Liu. 1992. Word identification for Mandarin Chinese sentences. In *Proceedings of the 15th International Conference on Computational Linguistics*, 101–107. Nantes.

Chen, Keh-Jiann, Chu-Ren Huang, Li-ping Chang, and Hui-Li Hsu. 1996. Sinica Corpus: Design methodology for balanced corpora. In *Proceeding of the 11th Pacific Asia Conference on language, information and computation*, ed. Byung-Soo Park and Jong-Bok Kim, 67–176. Seoul: Kyung Hee University.

Chiang, Tung-Hui, Jing-Shin Chang, Ming-Yu Lin, and Keh-Yih Su. 1992. Statistical models for word segmentation and unknown word resolution. In *Proceedings of ROCLING V*, 123–146. Taipei, Taiwan.

Chinese Knowledge and Information Processing Group (CKIP) 詞庫小組. 1993. *The analysis of Chinese parts of speech* 中文詞類分析. CKIP Technical Report 93–105. Taipei: Academia Sinica.

Christianson, Caitlin, Jason Duncan, and Boyan Onyshkevych. 2018. Overview of the DARPA LORELEI Program. *Machine Translation* 32(1):3–9

Huang, Chu-Ren. 2009. *Tagged Chinese Gigaword version 2.0*. Philadelphia: Lexical Data Consortium, University of Pennsylvania.

Huang, Chu-Ren, and Nianwen Xue. 2012. Words without boundaries: Computational approaches to Chinese word segmentation. *Language and Linguistics Compass* 6(8): 494–505.

Huang, Chu-Ren, and Nian-Wen Xue. 2015. Modeling word concepts without convention: linguistic and computational issues in Chinese word identification. In *The Oxford Handbook of Chinese Linguistics*, ed. William S.-Y. Wang and Chao-Fen Sun, 348–361. New York: Oxford University Press.

Huang, Chu-Ren, and Yao Yao. 2015. Corpus Linguistics. In *International encyclopedia of the social and behavioral sciences* (2nd edition), ed, James D. Wright, 4:949–953. Oxford: Elsevier.

Huang, Changning, and Hai Zhao. 2007. Chinese word segmentation: A decade review. *Journal of Chinese Information Processing* 21(3):8–20.

Huang, Chu-Ren, Chao-Jan Chen, and Claude C. C. Shen. 2002. The nature of categorical ambiguity and its implications for language processing: A corpus-based study of Mandarin Chinese. In *Sentence processing in east Asian languages*, ed. Mineharu Nakayama, 53–83. Stanford, California: CSLI Publications.

Huang, Chu-Ren, Petr Šimon, Shu-Kai Hsieh, and Laurent Prévot. 2007. Rethinking Chinese word segmentation: Tokenization, character classification, or wordbreak identification. In *Proceedings of the 45th Annual Meeting of the ACL on Interactive Poster and Demonstration Sessions*, 69–72. Stroudsburg, PA: Association for Computational Linguistics.

Huang, Chu-Ren, Lung-Hao Lee, Jia-Fei Hong, Weiguang Qu, and Shiwen Yu. 2008. Quality assurance of automatic annotation of very large corpora: A study based on heterogeneous tagging system. In *The Proceedings of the 6th International Conference on Language Resources and Evaluation (LREC 2008)*, 2725–2729. Marrakech, Morocco.

Huang, Chu-Ren, Shu-Kai Hsieh, and Keh-Jiann Chen. 2017. *Mandarin Chinese words and parts of speech: A corpus-based study*. London: Routledge.

Kilgarriff, Adam, and Gregory Grefenstette. 2003. Introduction to the special issue on the web as corpus. *Computational Linguistics* 29(3):333–347.

Lewis, David D., and William A. Gale. 1994. A sequential algorithm for training text classifiers. In *Proceedings of the Seventeenth Annual International ACM-SIGIR Conference on Research and Development in Information Retrieval (SIGIR '94)*, 3–12. Springer, London.

Li, Shou-Shan, and Chu-Ren Huang, 李壽山 黃居仁. 2010. Chinese word segmentation based on word boundary decision 基於詞邊界分類的中文分詞方法. *Journal of Chinese Information Processing* 中文信息學報 *24*(1):3–7.

Li, Shoushan, Guodong Zhou and Chu-Ren Huang. 2012. Active learning for Chinese word segmentation. In *Proceedings of the 24th International Conference on Computational Linguistics (COLING 24)*, 683–692. Mumbai, India.

Ma, Wei-Yun, and Chu-Ren Huang. 2006. Uniform and effective tagging of a heterogeneous Gigaword corpus. In *Proceedings of the 5th International Conference on Language Resources and Evaluation (LREC 2006)*, 2182–2185. Genoa, Italy.

Ng, Hwee Tou, and Jin Kiat Low. 2004. Chinese part-of-speech tagging: One-at-a-time or all-at-once? Word-based or character-based? In *Proceedings of the 2004 Conference on Empirical Methods in Natural Language Processing (EMNLP)*, 277–284. Available at https://aclanthology.org/W04-3236.pdf.

Tseng, Huihsin, and Keh-Jiann Chen. 2002. Design of Chinese morphological analyzer. In Proceedings of COLING-02: The 1st SIGHAN Workshop on Chinese Language Processing. Available at https://aclanthology.org/W02-1811.pdf.

Xu, Hongzhi, Menghan Jiang, Jingxia Lin, and Chu-Ren Huang. 2020. Light verb variations and varieties of Mandarin Chinese: Comparable corpus driven approaches to grammatical variations. *Corpus Linguistics and Linguistic Theory*.

Xue, Nianwen. 2003. Chinese word segmentation as character tagging. *Computational Lingusitcs and Chinese Language Processing* 8(1):29–48.

Xue, Nianwen, and Libin Shen. 2003. Chinese word segmentation as LMR tagging. In *Proceedings of Second SIGHAN Workshop on Chinese Language Processing*, 176–179. Sapporo, Japan. Available at https://doi.org/10.3115/1119250.1119278.

Yu, Shi-wen, Hui-ming Duan, Xue-feng Zhu, and Bin Sun. 2002. The basic processing of contemporary Chinese corpus at Peking University- Specification. Journal of Chinese Information Processing, 16(5):49–64.

Zampieri, Marcos, Shervin Malmasi, Yves Scherrer, Tanja Samardžic, Francis Tyers, Miikka Silfverberg, Natalia Klyueva, Tung-Le Pan, Chu-Ren Huang, Radu Tudor Ionescu, Andrei Butnaru, and Tommi Jauhiainen. 2019. A report on the third VarDial evaluation campaign. *In Proceedings of the Sixth Workshop on NLP for Similar Languages, Varieties and Dialects (VarDial 2019)*, 1–16. Minneapolis, USA.

Zhang, Hua-Ping, Qun Liu, Xue-Qi Cheng, Hao Zhang, and Hong-Kui Yu. 2003a. Chinese lexical analysis using hierarchical hidden Markov model. In *Proceedings of the 2nd SIGHAN Workshop on Chinese Language Processing*, 63–70. Sapporo, Japan.

Zhang, Hua-Ping, Hong-Kui Yu, De-Yi Xiong, and Qun Liu. 2003b. HHMM-based Chinese lexical analyzer ICTCLAS. In *Proceedings of the 2nd SIGHAN Workshop on Chinese Language Processing*, 184–187. Sapporo, Japan.

Chapter 5
Describing the Grammatical Knowledge of Chinese Words for Natural Language Processing

Xiaojing Bai

Abstract The grammar of a language tells people how smaller linguistic units combine to form larger ones. This chapter will introduce a grammatical knowledge base of Chinese words, which was developed for natural language processing, assisting the automatic analysis and generation of Chinese sentences. The overall design of the knowledge base, the classification of words, and the formal description of their grammatical functions will be outlined, and some semantic issues will be discussed. From a computational perspective, the knowledge base offers new insights into the long-running introspection and exploration of grammar issues in Chinese.

Keywords Grammatical knowledge base · Formal description · Word class · Grammatical properties · Computational linguistics · Natural language processing

5.1 Introduction

The grammar of a language tells people how smaller linguistic units, which have sound and meaning, combine to form larger ones. These linguistic units mainly include morphemes, words, phrases, and sentences. The grammar of the Chinese language has been studied for more than 2000 years (Gong 龚千炎 2000), the purpose of which, in general, is to discover the rules of linguistic facts that can help and are helping people express ideas in Chinese appropriately, clearly, and precisely. Computational approaches were adopted in the mid-twentieth century to process the Chinese language (Zong et al. 宗成庆等 2009) to aid human-human and human-machine communication, and new goals have been set for research on the grammar of Chinese (Yu 俞士汶 2000). Language models have been built for computers to analyze and generate natural languages, taking either rationalist or empirical positions (Church 2011; Feng 冯志伟 2008; Zong 宗成庆 2008). With the

X. Bai (✉)
Language Centre, Tsinghua University, Beijing, China
e-mail: bxj@tsinghua.edu.cn

C.-R. Huang et al. (eds.), *Chinese Language Resources*, Text, Speech and Language Technology 49, https://doi.org/10.1007/978-3-031-38913-9_5

rationalist positions, particularly, the grammatical knowledge of Chinese has been described in machine-readable dictionaries (lexicons) and rule banks and marked up in corpus data.

For quite a long time in the history of natural language processing (NLP), rule systems have been widely used to capture grammatical knowledge. A rule system, with its high level of abstraction, can describe the syntagmatic relation between words from different word classes. The richness and complexity of language, however, make it impossible for a rule system to cover all the syntagmatic relations between individual words as their properties tend to vary significantly. The statistical approach, which has been used to investigate the co-occurrence between words in large corpora, is a promising alternative. There are constraints on this alternative approach, namely, the amount of computing power and the availability of large corpora with rich annotation, though dramatic progress has been made in these two aspects over the past 20 years (Hirschberg and Manning 2015).

This chapter will introduce an intermediate approach between rule systems and the statistical approach, which was adopted to describe the grammatical knowledge of Chinese words in the Grammatical Knowledge Base (GKB) of Contemporary Chinese developed by the Institute of Computational Linguistics (ICL) at Peking University. The knowledge base is independent of any specific NLP system, irrelevant even to any computational theory or algorithm. This general-purpose knowledge base stores the basic facts about the grammatical functions of commonly used Chinese words. A specific application system can access the data in the GKB, which is, in most cases, a subset of the abundant grammatical knowledge stored. It is also possible and necessary to add new entries and properties to adapt the GKB to a particular system. The knowledge base has supported a wide range of NLP tasks and applications since the 1980s. From a computational perspective, the GKB offers new insights into the long-running exploration of grammar issues in Chinese (Yu et al. 俞士汶等 2011).

This chapter will present a brief introduction to the formal description of the grammatical knowledge of Chinese words in the GKB, including the overall design of the knowledge base, the classification of words, and the description of their grammatical functions. Semantic considerations for the GKB will be discussed, considering the significance of semantics to grammar in a broad sense. The conclusion will highlight the features of the GKB and its implications for both theoretical linguistic studies and natural language processing.

5.2 Overall Design of the Knowledge Base

The GKB is a large-scale electronic dictionary that was developed for natural language processing. As a language knowledge base in NLP systems, the GKB facilitates the automatic analysis and generation of language. It features the classification of words and the description of their grammatical properties in a fine-grained way. There are approximately 80,000 entries of words with distinctive functions and meanings. The grammatical properties of each word are recorded as attribute-value pairs, describing how the word combines with other words. The knowledge base contains more than 3,600,000 attribute values in total.

5.2.1 Databases

The GKB is organized as 34 relational databases, which makes it easy to manage the data, eliminate redundancy, and convert the stored grammatical knowledge of Chinese words to other formal mechanisms, such as complex feature structures. As shown in Fig. 5.1, a general database keeps a record of all the selected words and their shared properties. There are 26 databases that store different classes of words and their properties, respectively. Within each database, one row represents a single entry, and its properties are described by the values in the corresponding columns that represent grammatical attributes. Sample entries in the GKB are shown in Table 5.1.

Table 5.1 lists sample entries taken from the database of verbs, where, for example, the value of the attribute 外内 "taking a true object" suggests the transitivity of a verb. Verbs and pronouns are further divided, and the typical properties of each subclass are described in a separate database. Therefore, for a verb taking nominal objects, such as 拜访 *baifang* "to visit," there is actually an entry in each of the three databases (i.e., the general database, the database of verbs, and the database of verbs taking nominal objects). The three entries can be linked if required to provide more information about the verb.

Theoretically, classification and property description are equivalent methods of distinguishing words. Suppose n attributes are designated for a set of words (where $n \geq 1$ and the attribute value is 1 or 0); there will be at most 2^n distinct subsets of the

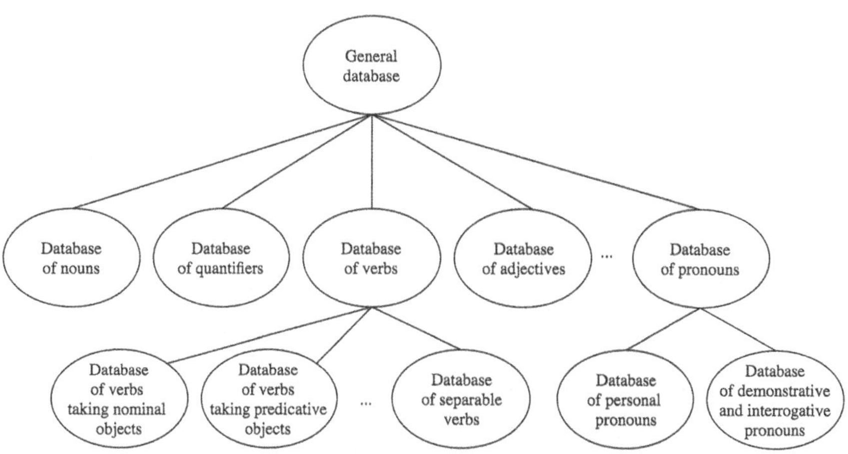

Fig. 5.1 The overall design of the GKB (Source: Yu et al. 俞士汶等 2011)

Table 5.1 Sample entries in the GKB

词语	同形	义项	助动	外内	体谓准	双宾	着了过	重叠	VVO	离合	单作谓语	单作补语	兼类
交给					体	双	了过						
理发				内			了过		VVO	离	可		
会	A	见面			体		着了过	VV					n
会	B1	理解			体谓		了				可	可	n
会	B2	可能	助		谓						可		n
会	C	付账			体		了过				可		n
加强					体准		了						
进行					体准		着了过						
能够			助		谓						可		
保管	1	保存			体		着了过	ABAB			可		
保管	2	担保			谓								
帮		帮助			体	双	着了过	VV			可		q
冒险				内			过		VVO	离			a
上去				内			了过			离	可	可	

Attribute (column) names in Table 5.1 are translated as follows. 词语, word entry; 同形, homograph; 义项, sense; 助动, auxiliary; 外内, taking a true object; 体谓准, taking a nominal/predicative/quasi-object; 双宾, taking two objects; 着了过, taking zhe/le/guo; 重叠, reduplicated form; VVO, variation of a separable verb; 离合, separable; 单作谓语, as an independent predicate; 单作补语, as an independent complement; 兼类, multi-class word
Source: Yu et al. 俞士汶等 (2003)

words. On the contrary, to divide these words into N distinct subsets (where $N \geq 2$), there needs to be at least $[\log_2(N - 1) + 1]$ attributes (the square brackets denote rounding the number to the nearest integer) (Yu et al. 俞士汶等 2011).

Word classification and property description have their own strengths and weaknesses. The former helps to sort a multitude of words quickly, but it is difficult to define an infallible classification scheme, which is particularly true in the case of Chinese. The latter is time-consuming but allows more fine-grained linguistic expertise. In the GKB, both methods were adopted to complement each other.

5.2.2 Selection of Words

The GKB includes words listed in important reference books of Chinese grammar compiled for humans, but more typically, high-frequency words were carefully selected from corpus data. All GKB entries satisfy the definitions of words by the National Standard of Contemporary Chinese Word Segmentation for Information Processing (GB 13715). Closed classes, such as locative particles, pronouns, prepositions, conjunctions, auxiliaries, modal particles, and interjections, are all included. With open classes, such as nouns, verbs, adjectives, numerals, time words, location words, stative words, classifying words, onomatopoeic words, and fixed expressions like Chinese idioms, idiomatic expressions, and abbreviations, representativeness and frequency of the candidates were considered. However, words typically used during a limited period of time were not selected despite their possible high frequency, such as 士大夫 *shidafu* "scholar-official" and 臭老九 *choulaojiu* "a derogatory label for intellectuals." Likewise, words from classical Chinese, dialects, and special technical fields were excluded.

Detailed considerations have been given to reduplicated forms, ensuring as much coverage as possible while avoiding conceivable redundancy, for instance, whether the basic form (e.g., 亮晶 *liangjing*) and its reduplicated form (e.g., 亮晶晶 *liangjingjing* "glittering") are words, whether the basic form (e.g., 往 *wang* 'toward') and its reduplicated form (e.g., 往往 *wangwang* "often") mean the same thing, and whether the basic form (e.g., 大方 *dafang* "generous") and its reduplicated form (e.g., 大大方方 *dadafangfang* "generous") belong to the same word class.

To increase its coverage of Chinese words, the GKB includes as many word components as possible, which are limited in number but highly productive in word formation. Prefixes and suffixes are included as word components, such as 老 *lao* "used before surnames to indicate seniority," 超 *chao* "super-," 准 *zhun* "quasi-," 们 *men* "used after a personal pronoun or a noun to show plural number," 者 *zhe* "used after a noun phrase to indicate a person doing the stated work or following the stated doctrine," 化 *hua* "-ify," etc. There is also a table in the GKB for morphemes that are not considered words when standing alone, such as 脐 *qi* in 肚脐 *duqi* "navel," 贝 *bei* in 贝壳 *beike* "shell," 冬 *dong* in 冬天 *dongtian* "winter," etc.

5.3 Classification of Words

In Chinese language processing, grammatical units mainly include characters, words, phrases, and sentences. No consensus has been reached so far on the classification of Chinese words. From the perspective of language engineering, a viable classification scheme has been applied to the GKB, which is mainly based on Zhu's grammatical theory (Zhu 朱德熙 1982, 1983), and word classes have thereby been defined. Accordingly, all GKB entries have been classified, and a corpus of more than 10 million Chinese characters has been segmented and POS-tagged to assess the viability of the classification system.

5.3.1 Basic Word Classes

There are 18 basic classes of Chinese words in the GKB, as listed in Table 5.2. Among them, nouns, time words, location words, locative particles, numerals, and quantifiers are called nominals; verbs, adjectives, and stative words are predicates; and pronouns are divided between nominals and predicates. Moreover, nominals, predicates, classifying words, and adverbs are referred to as content words, while prepositions, conjunctions, auxiliaries, and sentence-final particles are called function words. Distinct from these, there are also onomatopoeic words and interjections. In addition, there are eight types of non-lexical items: prefixes, suffixes, morphemes, non-morpheme characters, Chinese idioms, idiomatic expressions, abbreviations, and punctuation marks (Yu et al. 俞士汶等 2003).

5.3.2 Purpose of Word Classification

Word classes help to describe how words combine to form larger syntactic structures (i.e., phrases and sentences). There are two kinds of relations involved: the syntagmatic relation, where words combine to form a certain syntactic structure, and the paradigmatic relation, where words can replace each other in a certain syntactic position. As illustrated in the following examples, words from the same class, such as 爸爸 *baba* "father" and 学校 *xuexiao* "school," bear a paradigmatic relation, meaning that they can take the same syntactic position w1, acting as the subject, in a syntactic structure, as shown in (5.1) and (5.2) below:

w1__w2__w3__w4__w5__w6__w7__w8
(5.1) 爸爸__昨天__买__了__两__本__新__书
baba__zuotian__mai__le__liang__ben__xin__shu
father__yesterday__bought__u__two__q__new__books
My father bought two new books yesterday
(5.2) 学校__去年__增添__了__三__台__先进__设备
xuexiao__qunian__zengtian__le__san__tai__xianjin__shebei
school__last-year__got __u__three__pieces__advanced__equipment
The school got three more pieces of advanced equipment last year

Table 5.2 The classification system of Chinese words and their part-of-speech (POS) tags in the GKB

Word classes	POS tags	Examples
Nouns	n	书 *shu* "book," 教授 *jiaoshou* "professor," 心胸 *xinxiong* "breath of mind," 北京 *beijing* "Beijing"
Time words	t	明天 *mingtian* "tomorrow," 元旦 *yuandan* "New Year's Day," 唐朝 *tangchao* "Tang Dynasty," 现在 *xianzai* "now," 春天 *chuntian* "spring"
Location words	s	空中 *kongzhong* "space above the ground," 低处 *dichu* "lower place," 郊外 *jiaowai* "suburbs"
Locative particles	f	上 *shang* "above," 前 *qian* "before," 东 *dong* "east," 外头 *waitou* "outside," 中间 *zhongjian* "middle"
Numerals	m	一 *yi* "one," 第一 *diyi* "first," 千 *qian* "thousand," 零 *ling* "zero," 许多 *xuduo* "many," 百万 *baiwan* "million"
Quantifiers	q	个 *ge* "used before a noun that does not have a fixed measure word of its own," 群 *qun* "group," 克 *ke* "gram," 杯 *bei* "cup," 片 *pian* "slice," 种 *zhong* "kind," 些 *xie* "some"
Classifying words	b	男 *nan* "male," 公共 *gonggong* "public," 微型 *weixing* "miniature," 初级 *chuji* "elementary"
Pronouns	r	你 *ni* "you," 这 *zhe* "this," 哪儿 *nar* "where," 谁 *shui* "who/whom"
Verbs	v	走 *zou* "to go," 同意 *tongyi* "to agree," 能够 *nenggou* "to be able to," 出去 *chuqu* "to go out," 是*shi* "to be," 繁荣 *fanrong* "to flourish"
Adjectives	a	好 *hao* "good," 红 *hong* "red," 温柔 *wenrou* "gentle," 突然 *turan* "sudden," 繁荣 *fanrong* "prosperous"
Stative words	z	雪白 *xuebai* "snow-white," 泪汪汪 *leiwangwang* "tearful," 满满当当 *manmandangdang* "full," 灰不溜秋 *huibuliuqiu* "grayish"
Adverbs	d	不 *bu* "not," 很 *hen* "very," 都 *dou* "all," 刚刚 *ganggang* "just," 忽然 *huran* "suddenly"
Prepositions	p	把 *ba* "used to advance the object of a verb to the position before it," 被 *bei* "by," 对于 *duiyu* "for," 以 *yi* "with," 按照 *anzhao* "according to"
Conjunctions	c	和 *he* "and," 或 *huo* "or," 虽然 *suiran* "although," 但是 *danshi* "but," 不但 *budan* "not only," 而且 *erqie* "but also"
Auxiliaries	u	着 *zhe* "used to indicate the continuation of an action or a state," 的 *de* "used to indicate a relationship of modification," 所 *suo* "used with 为 *wei* or 被 *bei* to indicate passive voice," 似的 *shide* "like"
Sentence-final particles	y	吗 *ma* "used at the end of a question," 呢 *ne* "used at the end of a special, alternative, or rhetorical question," 呗 *bei* "used to indicate reluctant agreement or concession"
Onomatopoeic words	o	呜 *wu* "hoot," 啪 *pa* "bang," 叮咚 *dingdong* "tinkle," 哗啦 *huala* "splash"
Interjections	e	唉 *ai* "oops," 喔 *o* "oh," 哎哟 *aiyo* "oh dear," 嗯 *ng* "eh," 啊 *a* "wow"

Source: Yu et al. 俞士汶等 (2003)

Not considered an urgent task in human-oriented linguistic studies, the classification of words and the tagging of word classes are indispensable in computational linguistics and natural language processing.

In rule-based parsing with a context-free grammar (CFG), for instance, each leaf node, or terminal, of a parse tree produced by the CFG rules represents a word class in the context-free language. A grammatical sentence is simply a legitimate tree that is derivable from the production rules, and syntactic parsing starts with rewriting words by their corresponding word classes. The classification of words is in fact the description of their fundamental grammatical properties, which are the most important clues for natural language analysis and generation.

In statistical parsing with N-grams, for instance, data sparseness can be endemic when the probabilities of word sequences are computed. Alternatively, when the probabilities of word class sequences are computed, the classification of words is required as well. With real-world applications like document retrieval and information extraction, where deep syntactic analysis may not be required, word segmentation and POS-tagging will also contribute to higher accuracy, and word class definitions in this sense are also essential.

5.3.3 Word Class Definitions by Grammatical Functions

Theoretically speaking, a word can be classified according to its grammatical functions, which are generally taken as the role and the distribution of the word in the syntactic structure: (1) what role it plays as a syntactic constituent and (2) which words or word classes it collocates with. In the GKB, the specification of grammatical functions constitutes a solid ground for the proper classification of words. Here are some of the functions specified for adjectives:

(a) Acting as the predicate in a subject-predicate construction but taking no true object. In (5.3), 安静 *anjing* "quiet" acts as the predicate and takes no object. The word sometimes takes an object, as in (5.4), but the numeral-quantifier phrase 两天 *liang tian* "two days" is not a true object.

(5.3)	教室_安静
	jiaoshi_anjing
	classroom_quiet
	The classroom is quiet
(5.4)	他_安静_了_两_天
	ta_anjing_le_liang_tian
	he_quiet_u_two_days
	He remained quiet for two days

(b) Taking a modifying degree adverb like 很 *hen* "very," 挺 *ting* "pretty," or 特别 *tebie* "particularly" as in 很 长 *hen chang* "very long," 挺 安静 *ting anjing* "pretty quiet," and 特别 雄伟 *tebie xiongwei* "particularly magnificent."
(c) Acting as the complement in a predicate-complement construction, such as 干净 *ganjing* "clean" in 洗 干净 *xi ganjing* "to wash clean" and 结实 *jieshi* "tight" in 捆 得 结实 *kun de jieshi* "to be fastened tight."

Word classes can thus be distinguished broadly. For instance, nouns cannot perform functions (b) and (c), and they do not perform function (a) in most cases. Similarly, some functions of nouns cannot be performed by adjectives. However, as word classes in Chinese are often multifunctional, functions can be shared by different classes and the distinction between classes is then obscured. In the GKB, therefore, the probability distribution of grammatical functions has been carefully considered and examined.

On the one hand, although a certain word class may be able to play different syntactic roles, the probability of performing these roles is different as can be observed in a large corpus of real texts. Nouns in Chinese, for example, may function either as the subject, the object, the attributive, or even the predicate if in a nominal-predicate sentence. In real texts, however, a noun is mostly used as the subject, the object, or the head in a nominal phrase, but seldom as the predicate. Similarly, verbs and adjectives can be used as the subject, the object, or the predicate, but in real texts, they are mostly used as the predicate.

On the other hand, probability also varies when a specific syntactic role is played by different word classes respectively. In a subject-predicate construction, the position of the subject is mainly taken by a noun and that of the predicate by a verb; in a predicate-object construction, the predicate is often a verb and the object a noun; and in a predicate-complement construction, the predicate is often a verb and the complement an adjective or a stative word.

When a word class is defined in the GKB, its grammatical functions with predominant distributions are identified first, and the selectional preference for the word class to play certain syntactic roles is often specified as well. In the case of adjectives, its predominant functions do not include "acting as the modifier of a noun," because (1) an adjective alone does not modify nouns very often, as it usually needs to be combined with 的 *de* to play such a role, and (2) it is quite common that the modifier of a noun is a noun or even a verb. With such a simplified model of complicated grammatical phenomena, words in the GKB are classified based on which grammatical functions of each word can be inferred.

Words in the same class may share some similarity in meaning, but it does not follow that words expressing the same meaning can perform the same grammatical function. For instance, 战争 *zhanzheng* "war" and 打仗 *dazhang* "to go to war" are related semantically but their grammatical functions diverge significantly. Likewise, 红 *hong* "red" and 红色 *hongse* "red" denote the same color; whereas the former can serve as the predicate in a sentence and the latter as the subject or object, the grammatical function of these words cannot be reversed. The meaning of a word, though not the main criterion for its classification, is important in the GKB, more details of which will be discussed in Sect. 5.5.

5.3.4 Multi-class Words, Homographs, and Homonyms

According to word class definitions, a word can be put into a specific class. However, part-of-speech ambiguity may arise when one word has different grammatical functions typical of more than one word class and is thus taken as belonging to two or more classes. The words 共同 *gongtong* and 定期 *dingqi* are adverbs in (5.5a) and (5.6a), respectively, but are classifying words in (5.5b) and (5.6b), respectively. These words are treated as multi-class words in the GKB, and they have their own entries in the databases of adverbs and classifying words, respectively.

(5.5a)	共同_完成_一_些_任务
	gongtong_wancheng_yi_xie_renwu
	together_accomplish_one_q_task
	to accomplish some tasks together
(5.5b)	我们_的_共同_愿望
	women_de_gongtong_yuanwang
	we_u_common_aspriations
	our common aspirations
(5.6a)	定期_检查_机器
	dingqi_jiancha_jiqi
	regularly_check_machine
	to check the machine regularly
(5.6b)	一_笔_定期_存款
	yi_bi_dingqi_cunkuan
	one_q_fixed_deposit
	a fixed deposit

Homographs are words that share the same form but have different pronunciations. They may belong to the same word class, such as 和 *huo* "to mix" in 和稀泥 *huo xini* "blur the line between right and wrong" and 和 *he* "to tie" in 和一盘棋 *he yi pan qi* "to tie in a game of chess," both of which are verbs. However, there is another homograph 和 *he* "and," which is a conjunction.

When two or more words share both the same form and the same pronunciation, they are called homonyms. They may belong to the same word class, such as 抄 *chao* "to copy" in 抄稿子 *chao gaozi* "to copy a draft" and 抄 *chao* "to take" in 抄近道 *chao jindao* "to take a shortcut," respectively. But in many cases, they belong to different word classes, which gives rise to part-of-speech ambiguity in natural language processing. For instance, 花 *hua* is a verb in 花时间 *hua shijian* "to spend time," but it is a noun in 石榴花 *shiliu hua* "pomegranate flower."

Both homographs and homonyms are distinguishable in meaning, as can be seen in the examples above. In contrast, the semantic distinction between the adverb 共同 *gongtong* and the classifying word 共同 *gongtong*, as well as that between the adverb 定期 *dingqi* and the classifying word 定期 *dingqi*, is hardly discernible. Despite these differences, the GKB treats homographs and homonyms as multi-class words in a broad sense. Each homograph or homonym is stored as a separate entry and is classified mainly according to its grammatical functions. In the GKB, there is a column for the attribute 兼类 "multi-class word" in the databases of each word class, the value of which indicates the other word classes that an entry may belong to, be it a multi-class word in a strict sense or in a broad sense.

5.4 Description of Grammatical Properties

Word class definitions constitute the criteria by which words can be properly classified. As has been discussed previously, the complexity and ambiguity of linguistic phenomena make it extremely hard to carry through some of the "strict" criteria prescribed by linguists, such as "adverbs are function words that only serve as the adverbial modifier" (Zhu 朱德熙 1982), which would definitely exclude 很 *hen* "very" and 极 *ji* "extremely" because the two words, though commonly recognized as adverbs, can also be used as a complement, as in 舒服 得 很 *shufu de hen* "very comfortable" and 痛快 极 了 *tongkuai ji le* "extremely happy."

Consequently, the predominant functions of adverbs have been considered, resulting in a more practical definition that "adverbs are function words mainly used as the adverbial modifier," which allows *hen* and *ji* to be included. The less strict criteria, however, gives rise to a new problem—words that are grouped in a particular class can display inconsistent grammatical properties. As a partial but practical solution to this dilemma, a more delicate approach has been adopted for the GKB to describe the grammatical attributes of each word, with its word class being only one of them, and to provide more detailed information about Chinese words for NLP tasks and application systems.

5.4.1 Selection of Grammatical Attributes

The grammatical attributes described in the GKB were selected with respect to the special requirements of NLP tasks, as this knowledge base was originally designed to assist computers in analyzing and generating Chinese sentences. More specifically, grammatical attributes help resolve ambiguities that either are intrinsic to natural languages or arise when natural languages are analyzed by computers; on the other hand, they help computers generate fluent Chinese sentences. When analyzing Chinese sentences, computers may rely on different grammatical theories and algorithms, but they also follow four basic steps: (1) segment the sequence of

Chinese characters into words; (2) add a POS tag to each word; (3) combine words to form phrases and then sentences; and (4) identify the syntactic or semantic role of each word or phrase in a phrase or sentence. Following these steps, the GKB manages to provide as much information as possible.

Morphological Attributes

The Chinese language, though much less inflectional than English or Russian, has some classes of words that can form new words through reduplication and affixation. In the database of nouns, for instance, there is a column for the attribute 重叠 "reduplicated form." For single-character nouns like 人 *ren* "person" and 家 *jia* "family," the value of this attribute is NN, indicating that their reduplicated forms are 人人 *renren* "everyone" and 家家 *jiajia* "every family." For double-character nouns like 方面 *fangmian* "aspect" and 风雨 *fengyu* "hardships," the value is AABB, indicating that their reduplicated forms are 方方面面 *fangfangmianmian* "every aspect" and 风风雨雨 *fengfengyuyu* "all kinds of hardships," respectively.

Both prefixes and suffixes are used to form words. In the database of prefixes, there is a column for the attribute 后接词性 "POS of the word that the prefix is added to" and another column for the attribute 结构词性 "POS of the word to be formed." Similarly, the attributes 前接词性 "POS of the word that the suffix is added to" and 结构词性 "POS of the word to be formed" are specified in the database of suffixes. In addition, the general database has a column for the attribute 单合 "simple/compound" to distinguish between simple and compound words. These attributes are selected to assist in the detection of unknown words.

Syntactic Attributes

Syntactic attributes, which constitute the bulk of the grammatical attributes in the GKB, describe whether and how a word can be combined with other words or word classes to form syntactic structures and what syntactic role the word can play therein. In the database of adjectives, for instance, there is a column for the attribute 很 "very." The value of this attribute is 否 "no" if an adjective cannot be modified by the degree adverb 很 *hen* "very"; otherwise, the corresponding field is left blank. In the database of verbs, the same attribute is described, indicating whether a verb can be modified by *hen*. Interestingly, the values of this attribute help to further distinguish between verbs describing mental activities, which are assumed to be able to take *hen* as the modifier. It is appropriate to say 很 爱 *hen ai* "to love . . . very much," 很 喜欢 *hen xihuan* "to like . . . very much," and 很 想念 *hen xiangnian* "to miss . . . very much," but the modifier does not go well with 盘算 *pansuan* "to figure," which is also a verb for mental activities.

In many cases, the syntactic attributes may suggest the syntactic role that a word plays in certain syntactic structures. For example, if an adjective takes the degree modifier *hen*, this implies that an adverbial-head structure can be formed, with the adjective as the head. In the database of nouns, the attribute 前名 "preceded by a noun" helps to describe whether an attributive-head structure can be formed by a noun as the head and its preceding noun as the modifier.

In each database, there are also attributes that explicitly describe whether a word can play certain syntactic roles. For instance, the attribute 宾语 "object" in the database of nouns specifies not only whether a noun alone can be an object but also whether the noun needs to take an attributive modifier to play such a role. The value of this attribute for the noun 方面 *fangmian* "aspect" is 定 "attributive modifier," as the word itself cannot be the object of a predicate-object construction. Instead, it takes the attributive modifier 各个 *gege* "each" as in 兼顾 各个 方面 *jiangu gege fangmian* "to give consideration to each aspect."

Semantic Attributes

In a broad sense, grammatical studies involve syntax, semantics, and pragmatics. The attributes described in the GKB are mainly morphological and syntactic, but some semantic attributes are included as well. Each entry in the GKB has a field for its sense and another field for its sample usages as a reference for human users. Other attributes are described to facilitate computer processing.

The database of time words includes the semantic attribute 时态 "tense," the values of which can be 过 "past" when a word refers to past time, such as 从前 *congqian* "before" and 昨天 *zuotian* "yesterday," and 未 "future" when a word refers to future time, such as 将来 *jianglai* "future" and 明天 *mingtian* "tomorrow."

More semantic attributes can be found in the databases of verbs. With verbs taking nominal objects, for instance, there are different columns for 受事 "patient," 结果 "result," 与事 "beneficiary," 工具 "instrument," 方式 "manner," 处所 "location," 时间 "time," 目的 "purpose," 原因 "reason," 致使 "cause," 施事 "agent," etc., specifying the possible semantic roles that the nominal object of a verb can play.

Collocation

Two words may co-occur very often in a sentence but do not combine to form a syntactic construction. For example, the preposition 在 *zai* "at" collocates significantly with the locative particles 上 *shang* "on top of, above," 下 *xia* "under, below," 中 *zhong* "in, in the center of," and 里 *li* "in, inside" to form different patterns, which allows the insertion of other words to form phrases like 在 理论 上 *zai lilun shang* "in theory," 在 他 的 帮助 下 *zai ta de bangzhu xia* "with his help," 在 群众 中 *zai qunzhong zhong* "among the masses," and 在 女儿 的 房间 里 *zai nüer de fangjian li* "in the daughter's room." Knowledge about collocations like these will help the analysis and generation of Chinese sentences. Therefore, the database of prepositions includes the attributes 后照应词 "collocate" and 后照应类 "POS of collocate." Similar attributes can be found in the databases of locative particles, adverbs, conjunctions, and auxiliaries.

5.4.2 Data Redundancy

As grammatical attributes are specified for each database in the GKB, the problem of data redundancy has been carefully considered. For instance, nouns like 中国 *zhongguo* "China," 学校 *xuexiao* "school," 图书馆 *tushuguan* "library," and 财政部 *caizhengbu* "Ministry of Finance" can also be used as location words, which means that they can be the object of 在 *zai* "at," 到 *dao* "to," and 往 *wang* "to." To minimize redundancy, the attribute 处所 "location" has been added to the database of nouns, the value of which suggests that a noun can also be a location word. Otherwise, there are two separate entries in two databases for such words, a large number of which can be found in Chinese.

There is, however, a trade-off between data redundancy and computational cost. For example, the general database has a column to record the number of homographs for an entry, which seems redundant as the number can be computed automatically whenever queried. However, the number is stored in this column to reduce query execution time. In the task of ambiguity resolution, the number in this column tells the computer immediately whether or not to end the search for all the possible homographs of a word. Similar considerations have also been given to other attributes in different databases.

5.4.3 Value Types

A relational database organizes data into a table of rows and columns. In the GKB, one row in a database constitutes a word entry. For each entry, there are different columns for the values of different attributes, respectively. The values can be one of two data types—numeric data and character string data. Numeric values are found only in the general database for attributes like 字数 "number of characters," 同字词 "number of homographs," 音节数 "number of syllables," 同音调 "number of homophones," 使用频度 "frequency," etc. Attribute values in the GKB are mostly character strings, of which there are four kinds.

Some attributes can have one of two possible values, which is the most common case. For example, in the database of verbs, there is a column for the attribute 很 "very," the value of which can be 很 "very" or null depending on whether a verb can take degree adverbs like 很 *hen* "very," 极 *ji* "extremely," 极其 *jiqi* "extremely," 非常 *feichang* "very," and 太 *tai* "so" as its modifier. There are columns named 系词 "copula," 助动词 "auxiliary verb," 趋向动词 "directional verb," 形式动词 "dummy verb," and so on for verbs, the values of which can be 是 *shi* "yes" or 否 *fou* "no" depending on whether a verb belongs to those subclasses. Values of this kind are similar to but more evident than the logical type and are thus adopted to ease the input and validation of grammatical knowledge by human annotators.

Some attributes can have one of many possible values. For example, in the database of pronouns, there is a column for the attribute 子类 "subclass," the value of which can be 人 "personal pronoun," 指 "demonstrative pronoun," or 疑 "interrogative pronoun." In the database of personal pronouns, the value of the attribute 人称 "person" can be 一 "first person", 二 "second person," 三 "third person," or null. Values of this kind vary considerably in length.

Theoretically, nonatomic values should be eliminated in relational databases. In the GKB, as in the common practice of database management, not all values are atomic. In the database of nouns, for example, there are columns for attributes like 度量 "measure quantifier," 容器量词 "container quantifier," 形量词 "shape quantifier," 不定量词 "indefinite quantifier," etc. The values of these attributes for the noun 白糖 *baitang* "sugar" can be either atomic or nonatomic, listing its possible collocates respectively: 克 *ke* "gram," 千克 *qianke* "kilogram," 公斤 *gongjin* "kilogram," and 吨 *dun* "ton" as measure quantifiers; 瓶 *ping* "bottle," 袋 *dai* "sack," and 包 *bao* "bag" as container quantifiers; 撮 *cuo* "pinch" as a shape quantifier; and 些 *xie* "some" and 点 *dian* "a little" as indefinite quantifiers.

Two attributes are added to each database in the GKB, the values of which are character strings specifying the sense of each entry and its sample usages. Originally set to assist human annotators, these values can also be used in natural language processing, such as word sense disambiguation.

5.5 Semantic Considerations in the GKB

With a repertoire of grammatical knowledge, semantic concerns are indispensable. Setting its focus on morphology and syntax, the GKB includes careful considerations for the semantic information of Chinese words as well.

5.5.1 Word Entries Distinguished by Their Meanings

As mentioned in Sect. 5.3.4, multi-class words, homographs, and homonyms are treated the same way in the GKB, which helps to solve problems caused by shared word forms in machine translation, spelling correction, speech recognition, speech synthesis, and many other NLP tasks. In the case of homographs and homonyms, particularly, word meanings are the main consideration for setting entries. In other words, a word form is represented as different entries if it can be used to refer to different things, ideas, activities, etc., such as 和 *huo/he*, 抄 *chao*, and 花 *hua*.

5.5.2 Semantic Properties Described for Word Entries

As mentioned in Sect. 5.4.1, some properties described in the GKB are straightforwardly semantic, such as the attribute 格标 "case marker" in the database of prepositions and the database of verbs taking nominal objects. For the preposition 被 *bei*, a case marker for the semantic role of agent, the attribute value is 施 "agent"; for 把 *ba*, a case marker for the semantic role of patient, the attribute value is 受 "patient"; and for 用 *yong*, a case marker for the semantic role of tool, the attribute value is 工 "tool."

5.5.3 Grammatical Properties Distinguished Based on Semantic Clues

Some grammatical properties are distinguished with regard to not only the syntactic behaviors but also the semantic clues of a word or the words in its context. For instance, there is a column 兼语 "pivotal" for all verb entries in the GKB, the value of which suggests that a verb can take the position of v1 in the pivotal construction "v1 + n + v2." To decide this, however, semantic knowledge is required. For the word sequence to be a pivotal construction, n should be a noun denoting the agent of the action specified by v2, where the role "agent" is a semantic category. The semantic clue thus helps to confirm that the verb 选 *xuan* "to elect" in (5.7) below can take the position of v1, as 他 *ta* "he/him" is the agent of 当 *dang* "to act as." In contrast, the verb 帮 *bang* "to help" in (5.8) below cannot take the position of v1, as 他 *ta* "he/him" is not the agent of 洗 *xi* "to wash," and the sequence therefore forms a serial verb construction:

(5.7)	选_他_当_班长
	xuan_ta_dang_banzhang
	elect_him_as_monitor
	to elect him as the monitor
(5.8)	帮_他_洗_衣服
	bang_ta_xi_yifu
	help_him_wash_cloth
	to help him wash the cloth

5.6 Conclusion

It is evident that language resources play an increasingly important role in the progress of computational linguistics and natural language processing, but the development of language resources is also evidently tedious, difficult, and time-consuming. The GKB started as an electronic dictionary in the 1980s, and it has taken three decades for the dictionary to develop into the knowledge base it is today, during which linguists and computer scientists have gone hand in hand to unravel the grammatical properties of Chinese words and describe them as computational attributes that can be used by NLP systems. The knowledge base relies heavily on the expert knowledge of linguists to set the guidelines and to carry them out in the selection of words, the definitions of word classes and grammatical attributes, the classification of words, and the descriptions of attribute values.

The knowledge base differs tremendously from traditional printed dictionaries in form, content, and size, which is greatly motivated by the computational perspective of computer scientists, or more precisely, computational linguists. These formalisms allow the GKB to assist in natural language processing as a repository of grammatical knowledge, the data structure of which enables easy conversion between different knowledge representations. The classification system and all word entries have been validated and optimized with corpus data of different sizes, which involved automatic processing tasks—word segmentation, POS-tagging, phrase boundary detection, phrase type tagging, etc. As a working component of an NLP system, the GKB is a huge repository with high accuracy, appropriate granularity, and optimal resource cost. All of these features may add a computational perspective to the introspective studies of Chinese, from which the complicated grammatical knowledge of Chinese words is observed, distinguished, and described.

References

Church, Kenneth. 2011. A pendulum swung too far. *Linguistic Issues in Language Technology* 6(5):1–27.

Feng, Zhiwei 冯志伟. 2008. Preface II 序二. In *Statistical natural language processing 统计自然语言处理*, Chengqing Zong 宗成庆, 5–18. Beijing: Tsinghua University Press.

Gong, Qianyan 龚千炎. 2000. A review of studies on the grammar of Chinese 汉语语法研究的回顾. In *An introduction to studies on grammar 汉语研究入门*, ed. Qingzhu Ma 马庆株, 69–87. Beijing: The Commercial Press.

Hirschberg, Julia, and Christopher D. Manning. 2015. Advances in natural language processing. *Science* 349(6245):261–266.

Yu, Shiwen 俞士汶. 2000. Natural language understanding and studies on grammar 自然语言理解与语法研究的回顾. In *An introduction to studies on grammar 汉语研究入门*, ed. Qingzhu Ma 马庆株, 240–251. Beijing: The Commercial Press.

Yu, Shiwen, Xuefeng Zhu, Hui Wang, Huarui Zhang, Yunyun Zhang, Dexi Zhu, Jianming Lu, and Rui Guo 俞士汶, 朱学锋, 王慧, 张化瑞, 张芸芸, 朱德熙, 陆俭明, 郭锐. 2003. *The grammatical knowledge-base of contemporary Chinese—A complete specification* (2nd ed.) *现代汉语语法信息词典详解(第二版)*. Beijing: Tsinghua University Press.

Yu, Shiwe, Zhifang Sui, and Xuefeng Zhu 俞士汶, 穗志方, 朱学锋. 2011. The comprehensive language knowledge base and its prospect 综合型语言知识库及其前景. *Journal of Chinese Information Processing* 中文信息学报 25(6):12–20.

Zhu, Dexi 朱德熙. 1982. *Lecture notes on grammar 语法讲义*. Beijing: The Commercial Press.

Zhu, Dexi 朱德熙. 1983. *Questions and answers on grammar 语法问答*. Beijing: The Commercial Press.

Zong, Chengqing 宗成庆. 2008. *Statistical natural language processing 统计自然语言处理*. Beijing: Tsinghua University Press.

Zong, Chengqing, Youqi Cao, and Shiwen Yu 宗成庆, 曹右琦, 俞士汶. 2009. Sixty years of Chinese information processing 中文信息处理 60 年. *Applied Linguistics 语言文字应用* 4: 53–61.

Chapter 6
DeepLEX

Shu-Kai Hsieh

Abstract This chapter will introduce a dynamically integrated lexical resource called DeepLEX. With its modularized architecture, DeepLEX aims to be a fine-grained yet scaled multilingual lexical resource that empowers linguists to pursue a wide array of previously unanswerable research questions. Our approach expands on previous efforts and calls for an open collaboration in which lexical knowledge is semantically founded, symbolically operationalized, and empirically gleaned.

Keywords DeepLEX · Fluid annotation · Lexical resource · Multilingual · Chinese wordnet

6.1 Introduction

Among most of the lexical resources, *wordhood*, or the clear-cut existence of word boundary, has been assumed. However, recent cognitive-functional approach to language has revealed the significant role of gradience and variation and put the usage at the very foundations of linguistic units and structure (Bybee 2010), and the form-meaning pair is argued to become entrenched and filtered through repeated use. The emergent view of language has challenged the way we view lexical storage and processing, which motivated the current study toward a dynamic representation of the gradient nature of the form-meaning pair.

The DeepLEX project features the following key aspects:

1. It takes a functional linguistic position in determining units and patterns (in Chinese), as well as the ontological grounding on the relationship between linguistic objects and situations (i.e., bits of reality). Following the observation of Wray (2005), a huge amount of our everyday language is formulaic and seems to be stored in (semi-fixed) chunks, as well as appears to be prefabricated (i.e., retrieved whole from memory at the time of use).

S.-K. Hsieh (✉)
Graduate Institute of Linguistics, National Taiwan University, Taipei, Taiwan
e-mail: shukaihsieh@ntu.edu.tw

C.-R. Huang et al. (eds.), *Chinese Language Resources*, Text, Speech and Language Technology 49, https://doi.org/10.1007/978-3-031-38913-9_6

2. Lexical data at different levels are flexibly modularized, such as the syntax-semantics module, emotion module, discourse and pragmatic module, diachronic module, etc. The architecture does not serve as a theoretical assumption but, rather, as a way to draw together various perspectives so that researchers from different fields can initiate new cooperation based upon the architecture. In addition to multidimensional data, it also provides various quantitative measures (via application programming interfaces) for exploring the data in a reproducible manner.
3. The rich information of DeepLEX can facilitate (semi-)automatic multilevel corpus annotation and deep text analytics (i.e., ease of vectorization). From a technical aspect, the goals of DeepLEX are to be an open-source, scaled, dynamic, reproducible lexical resource for everyone. With its modularized architecture and multilingual mapping, it should empower linguists to pursue a wide array of previously unanswerable research questions. In a similar vein, Lynott and Connell (2013) reported that concreteness/imageability norms do not account for what people normally intend with concrete and abstract words; as observed from the data, concreteness effects are predicted more by perceptual strength than by concreteness/imageability norms.

At the moment, there are 30,000 units (ranging from characters to lexical chunks), with over 120 variables in total. The scope and size of DeepLEX are still evolving, and with concerted and long-term efforts, we believe that this resource will be valuable for the deep processing of natural language processing (NLP) and intelligent applications.

6.2 Current Approaches and Issues

Lexicon, originated from the Greek *λεξικόν* ("of or for words"), has been used as a collective expression in linguistic terminology in the sense of "vocabulary" or a language's inventory of lexemes (Singleton 2016). This is based on *λέξις* ("lexis," "words"), which is deemed central to linguistic theorizing; however, defining what a word is, is debatable. Depending on the level of linguistic classification, a word can be seen from different points of view, and finding common characteristics of words among languages in the world can be difficult. For instance, a word in Finnish with word-stress and vowel-harmony is rather different from a word in languages where neither word-stress nor vowel-harmony operates (Singleton 2016).

The lexico-centricity hypothesis has greatly influenced the study of (computational) linguistics as well as language resource construction. The design of a lexicon or lexical resources often involves the determination of the lexical items to be selected. It has been recognized that there are many ways of viewing words—either by way of the distinction of types/tokens, lexemes/word-forms, or phonological/grammatical/semantic/orthographic units—particularly when cross-language studies are presented. However, the concept of word (i.e., its "wordhood") has been

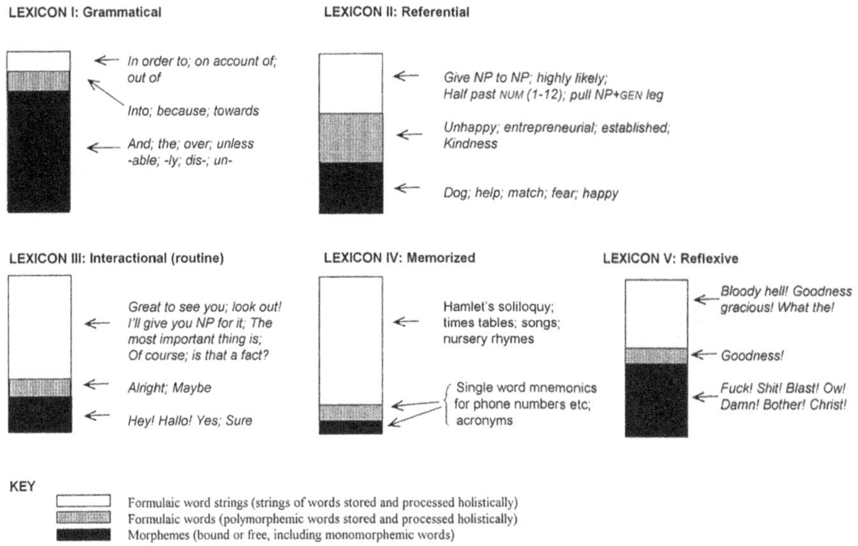

Fig. 6.1 The Heteromorphic Distributed Lexicon model (Wray 2005): distribution of the notional balance of three types of lexical units (in formulaic sequence)

circumvented by way of the dominant orthographic approach, where a word seems to be inevitably defined as a sequence of letters bounded on either side by a blank space (Singleton 2016). This definition, though it seems quite odd to define words via the written medium, works up to a point for languages using Roman and Cyrillic writing systems, but not for those languages whose writing systems do not have explicit markers for word boundaries (e.g., Chinese, Lao, Khmer, etc.) or those that have never been written down (e.g., Formosan languages).

We consider the current stance in constructing lexical resources the closed model, as it employs form/token-oriented information, which is less capable of accounting for dynamic conceptualization as encoded in language. In contrast, the open lexicon model uses a functional approach that aims to rebuild the form-meaning relationship from language usages. Wray's (2005) heteromorphic distributed lexicon (HDL) model (see Fig. 6.1) is regarded as the pioneering open lexicon model to handle this kind of form-meaning relationship. Wray (2005) proposed the HDL model, where no irregularity needs to be assumed. As a result, no linguistic units are holistic units in the sense that they are not subjected to further segmentation, that is, "a polymorphemic word or a word string can qualify simply by virtue of its not needing to be segmented in normal use, rather than its being unable to undergo segmentation."

The second main issue is contextual sparseness. Recall that the lexicon is the Anglicized version of a Greek word meaning "dictionary." Thus, over the past few decades, lexical resources have provided general characteristics of the word by making reference to quite a wide variety of lexical properties, including orthographic, morpho-syntactic, lexical semantic, social variational information, and even more experimental data. However, a point worth making in this connection is that context plays a trigger role in the symbiosis process of form and meaning. Not many formulaic sequences exist in an equal manner, so most of the lexicon models fail to capture the diverse context of the units adopted. A very simple example in Chinese is 還在那邊 V/A ("still there verb/adjective"). This sequence would quickly be triggered with negative polarity in the affective context and would resist further word segmentation from being semantically saturated.

6.2.1 Chinese Lexical Resources

The past several years have witnessed dramatic progress in NLP and text analytics. This section will briefly introduce two main types of lexical resources in Chinese, the first of which is Chinese Wordnet. Princeton's English WordNet (PWN) (Fellbaum 1998) has become a de facto lexical resource standard in English computational linguistics. Modeled on PWN, Chinese Wordnet (Huang et al. 黃居仁等 2010)[1] is a lexical database comprising different parts of speech. Synonyms following linguistic criteria are grouped into synsets, each expressing a distinct concept. Synsets are interconnected with lexical semantic relations, such as hyperonymy, meronymy, and entailment, making it a comprehensive lexical semantic network. Chinese Wordnet is now part of the Open Multilingual Wordnet.[2]

The second type of lexical resource in Chinese is the Chinese psychological lexicon. Driven by advances in machine learning models and lexical resource construction, the extraction of individual or collective psychological makeup has become possible. In particular, through psychological text analysis, the detection and analysis of personalities, individual differences, social processes, and even mental health can be conducted in a computerized way (Boyd 2017). How language reveals the affective state and other psychological phenomena has been a long-standing attempt in psychology and related NLP fields, and well-established approaches have been developed, such as Linguistic Inquiry and Word Count (LIWC) (Tausczik and Pennebaker 2010), Sundararajan-Schubert Word Count (SSWC) (Sundararajan and Schubert 2002, 2005), and machine reading comprehension (MRC).

Among the psychology-oriented lexical databases, LIWC, the latest version of which is LIWC2015 (Pennebaker et al. 2015) and has been translated into Chinese (Huang et al. 黃金蘭等 2012), is one of the first mainstream examples. At its core, the LIWC lexicon contains word-to-category mappings for around 80 categories of words, including both common content words and function words. In a similar vein, SSWC provides a taxonomy of 15 types of verbal expressions of self and emotions but is more flexible in allowing patterns to follow a regular-expression syntax whose

[1] http://lope.linguistics.ntu.edu.tw/cwn2/

[2] http://compling.hss.ntu.edu.sg/omw/

primitives can be words, stems, parts of speech, and even negation.[3] By assessing whether and where a verbal expression is distributed in texts, both resources can be utilized as a word count approach that gives percentages of the production of any categories out of the total number of words in a particular text, which "indicates the extent to which one specific category has out-competed others for the cognitive resources allotted to the production of a text of certain length" (Sundararajan and Schubert 2005).

From experimental fields, Sze et al. (2014) developed a database of the numerical information of lexical variables, as well as lexical decision reaction times and accuracy rates, for more than 25,000 traditional Chinese two-character compound words. Recently, Sun et al. (2018)[4] presented a new large-scale Chinese Lexical Database (CLD) that provides over 150 descriptive and lexical-distributional variables for more than 30,000 words in simplified Chinese.

6.3 DeepLEX

Langacker's (1987) usage-based model constitutes the foundation of DeepLEX, that is, all language units hover between various levels and can be recognized as arising from usage events in context. As a consequence, 14 modules (dimensions) in the current version were constructed either from scratch or from third-party open-source resources, which include orthographical, morpho-syntactic, lexical-semantic, ontological, psychological, stylistic, social, affect, computational modules, etc. In addition, a novel annotation architecture was proposed to handle context issues.

6.3.1 Modules

DeepLEX aims to be a large-scale lexical resource in Chinese. Currently, the affect module alone comprises a seed list of 22,852 lexical units (LUs), with a portion of LUs (1288) related to language-as-emotion in 16 dimensions. While it is not exhaustive, it does contain a large selection of emotionally related lexical units in Mandarin Chinese used in Taiwan. In addition to the common measures used in corpus linguistics, interaction between lexical semantics and emotions is taken into account. The measures include frequency variation (frequency distribution across different corpora, e.g., Academia Sinica Balanced Corpus, LDC Chinese Gigaword Corpus, NTU Plurk Corpus, PTT Corpus, TMMC Corpus, etc.); pos variation; sense density (extracted from Chinese Wordnet); semantic relation variation (extracted from Chinese Wordnet ver.2); polarity coercive force (emotion type coercion

[3] The Chinese SSWC has been completed and the release is in progress.

[4] http://www.chineselexicaldatabase.com

Table 6.1 DeepLEX affect table

	sense. num	rel.num emo. type polarity			freq. plurk	emo. trigger	freq. div	collocates	collostructure	…
擔心	3	5	c	–1	0.0025	0.48	0.66	NA	NA	…
高興	4	6	a	1	0.036	0.53	0.59	NA	NA	…
沒你的事	NA	NA	d	–1	0.0006	0.55	0.23	NA	NA	…
考試	3	2	NA	–1	0.0042	0.68	0.46	NA	NA	…
愛面子	2	NA	NA	-1	0.0009	0.43	0.21	NA	NA	…
…	…	…	…	…	…	…	…	…	…	…

Extracted Patterns	Instances	Polarity
[N 直逼 N] 'N can nearly compete with N'	設計感 直逼 Whotel 'its design can compete with WHotel'	+
[N 有梗] 'N is interesting'	空間 有梗 'the space is interesting'	+
[N 破表] 'it's quite over of the degree of the N'	浪漫指數 破表 'it's quite over of the degree of the romance'	+
[讓你有種 N 的感覺] 'to make you have the feeling of N'	讓你有種 家 的感覺 'to make you have to feeling to be home'	+
[N 級 N] 'N level's N'	貴婦 級 享受 'rich people's level of enjoyment'	+
[絕對是N 的 N] 'it's definite N to me'	絕對是 飯店 的 基本設備 'it's definitely the basic equipment in a hotel'	-
[N 對我來說已是 N] 'N is already N to me'	甜度 對我來說已是 極限 'the sweetness is already the limit to me'	+
[非常有 N 味] ' it's so full of N's feeling'	非常有 家鄉 味 'it's so full of home's feeling'	+
[N 與 N 都在] 'N and N still remain'	Q度 與 脆度 都在 'the springy and crunchy texture remains'	+
[N 十足] 'a lot of N; high degree of N'	咬勁 十足 'high degree of texture'	+
[光是 V N 就知它的 N] 'can feel it's N just by V'	光是 看 顏色 就知它的 粉嫩程度 'can feel it's freshness just by looking at its color'	+
[ADJ 翻了] 'so ADJ'	美 翻了 'so beautiful'	+
[N ADJ 到爆] 'N is extremely ADJ'	天氣 好 到爆 'the weather is extremely perfect'	+

Fig. 6.2 Affect patterns

measure); etc. (see Table 6.1).[5] Figure 6.2 (extracted from Lee and Hsieh 2016) shows some affective expressions that go beyond word level.

---

[5]The seed items and reference measures were retrieved from our previous experiments published on different occasions. In the future, much effort will be put into determining the proper weights and measures for this huge sparse matrix.

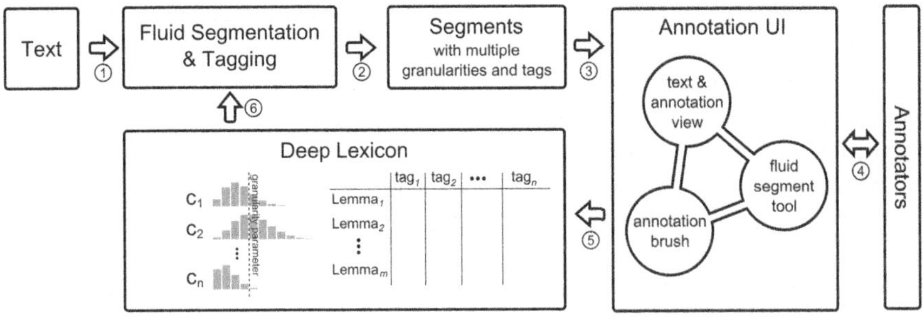

Fig. 6.3 Overview of fluid annotation scheme and its six critical steps: (1) input text; (2) preprocess text; (3) prepare segments with multiple granularities and automatic tagging; (4) revise segmentations and tags; (5) input annotations into deep lexicon; and (6) improve segmentation and tagging with new lexical information

6.3.2 Fluid Annotation

To capture the contexts in a fine-grained and dynamic way, we proposed an annotation scheme called fluid annotation coupled with DeepLEX. Specifically, the scheme was comprised of three main components: DeepLEX, fluid segmentation and tagging, and annotation user interface (UI) (see Fig. 6.3). DeepLEX provided all the candidate words and tag data associated with the given words used in segmentation and tagging. Distinctively, DeepLEX features lemma of different granularity that facilitates fluid segmentation. Six crucial steps were identified in the scheme: (1) unprocessed text was fed into the fluid segmentation and tagging preprocessor, where (2) text was segmented into different granularities and automatically labeled with possible tags; (3) an annotation UI with these segments and tags was provided, with which (4) annotators could further refine (by regrouping or dividing) the segmentation with the fluid segmentation tool, or annotate the segmentation (with the annotation "brush"), and view the annotation in a natural text context; (5) the annotations created by users were then fed into the deep lexicon, where the granularity parameters of the lexical bundles and the lexicon tag set table were updated; and (6) the updated lexicon provided the latest information for fluid segmentation and tagging in the next session. As a result, a cycle was established where not only the flexibility of the linguistic patterns was assured, but annotators' efforts were accumulated in the process.

Chinese words have a strong tendency to be monosyllabic and disyllabic. However, in segmentation or other practical annotation scenarios, a word is just one level of information among other linguistic components, such as multiword expressions, compounds, idioms, and lexical bundles. Previous segmenters relied on a "gold standard" to achieve a high performance in a word segmentation task, virtually eliminating other possibilities of looking into groups larger than words. To alleviate the "hard-cut" issue brought by standard segmentation, DeepLEX and fluid segmentation used in this scheme feature words of different granularity.

"Word granularity" refers to a sequence of lexical patterns of different length. These patterns occur regularly in different contexts and carry out a relatively stable communication function. In this sense, "words with different granularities" encompass other linguistic constructs, such as multiword expressions, compounds, idioms, and lexical bundles. For ease of interpretation, granularity was defined as a number ranging from 0 to 1, where we assigned granularities of 0 as more fine-grained (i.e., shorter patterns in the unit of character count) and 1 as a pattern more coarse-grained (i.e., more characters).

To operate granularity formally, we further defined the granularity of any given word by first calculating the word-length distribution of all the words starting with the same leading character. Second, the value of granularity resulted from the cumulative probabilities of the word-length distribution:

$$\text{Granularity}(w) = p(l; \text{leadChar}(w)) = \sum_{l=1}^{L(w)}$$

where w is the word of interest, leadChar(w) is w's leading character, $L(w)$ denotes the word length of word w, and $p(l;\text{leadChar}(w))$ is the probability density function of word length l, given the word's leading character.

The current pilot lexicon includes 135,424 lemmas, which were collected from various sources. Besides conventional texts, the lexicon also contains neologisms extracted from Taiwan's largest Internet forum, emotion expressions, and academic lexical bundles commonly found in Chinese academic writings. The resulting word list contained considerably long bundles, as revealed in Fig. 6.4. The distribution distinctively called for a novel segmentation procedure that could accommodate the dynamic patterns frequently observed in Chinese discourse. An example of word segmentations under different granularities is shown in Fig. 6.5.

It is noteworthy that, although the base lexicon already had abundant lexical entries, the lexicon here was designed to be incremental with annotators' collaboration. When annotators grouped/divided a sequence of words using the annotation UI (see Fig. 6.6), the granularity of the corresponding lemma was automatically adjusted accordingly, and the segmentation results also reflected the changes made. Furthermore, we posed few limitations on what could be considered a "word" in the lexicon. Annotators could add their new lemma appropriately in their studies, as long as the pattern was a valid character sequence representable by Unicode. Flexibility is particularly vital when dealing with unconventional and unstructured text, which is dominant in social media, micro-blogging, and forums.

In addition to the "word" information itself, DeepLEX also stores linguistic information from other linguistic resources and user feedback from the annotation UI. For instance, sentiment polarity, mood, and frequency are predefined in DeepLEX. As annotators created new annotations, this information was fed back into DeepLEX and new tag sets were created. This new tag information along with the predefined tag data in turn provided a more probable tag through fluid tagging. That is to say, DeepLEX expanded new lemma and tag information as the annotation

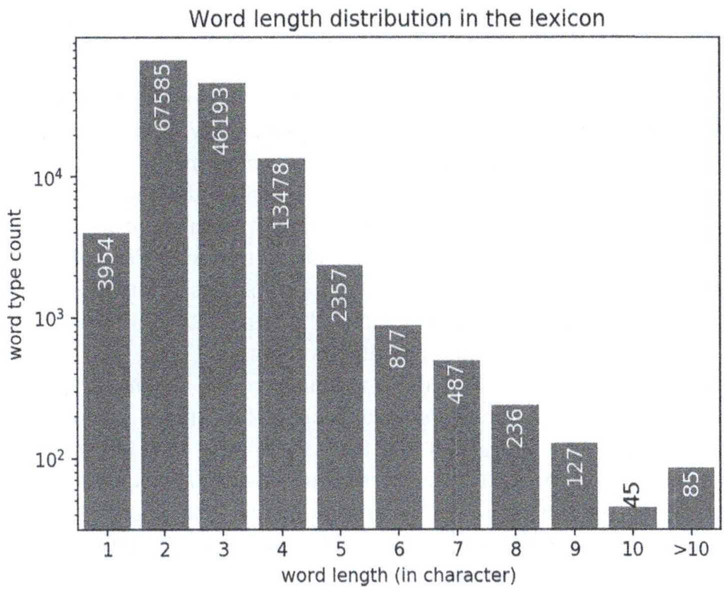

Fig. 6.4 Word length distribution in the lexicon

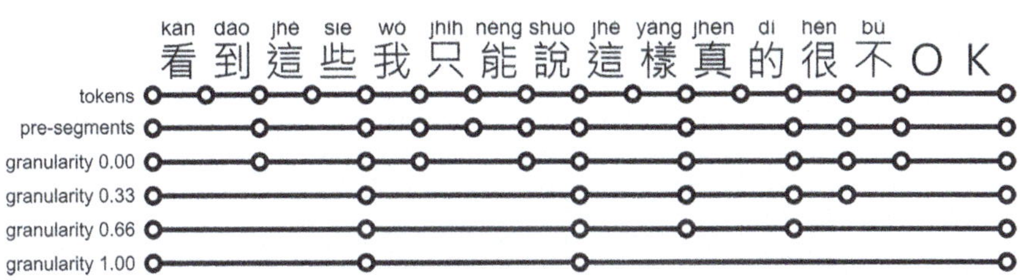

Fig. 6.5 Word segmentations under different granularities

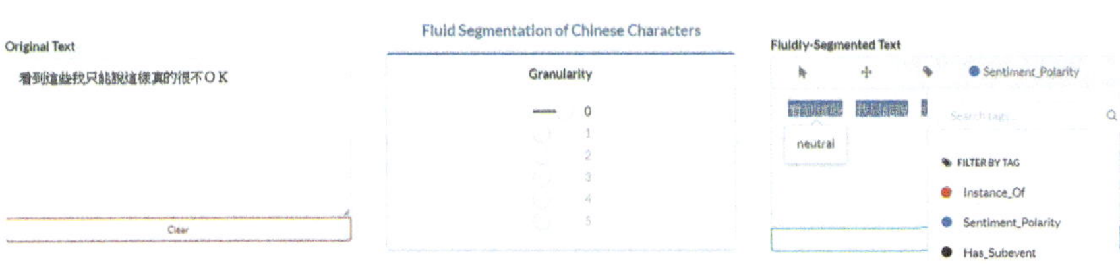

Fig. 6.6 Annotation UI

process progressed. Different annotators could work on a text and share their annotations with others, so the annotation effort accumulated in a systematic fashion.

6.4 Conclusion

In this chapter, we introduced our ongoing work on a novel Chinese lexicon architecture that features a large quantity and deep quality. The goal of this project was multifaceted. First, the aim was to construct a multidimensional lexicon. Instead of being restricted to words and phrases, the targets of the collection crossed the syntax boundary and involved longer expressions, such as lexical chunks. The project also made a breakthrough in restrictions on the usual elements in language use and included symbolic units such as emoticons. Based on these broader elements, the design of the construction contained multivariate information at different linguistic levels that merged with previous resources.

This resource has highlighted the importance of the nature of lexicons. The findings of this research have provided insights for further exploration of the phenomenon for pattern-extraction and the development of a larger lexicon with balanced genres. Moreover, further experimental investigations are needed to estimate the weight of the units. With the multilingual mappings in progress, this lexicon in Chinese will be a fruitful lexical resource for future fields involving different tasks in natural language processing.[6]

References

Boyd, Ryan L. 2017. Psychological text analysis in the digital humanities. In *Data analytics in digital humanities*, ed. Shalin Hai-Jew, 161–189. Springer Science.

Bybee, Joan. 2010. *Language, usage and cognition*. Cambridge University Press.

Fellbaum, Christiane. 1998. *WordNet*. Wiley Online Library.

Huang, Chu-Ren, Shu-Kai Hsieh, Jia-Fei Hong, Yun-Zhu Chen, I-Li Su, Yong-Xiang Chen, and Sheng-Wei Huang 黄居仁, 谢舒凯, 洪嘉馡, 陈韵竹, 苏依莉, 陈永祥, 黄胜伟. 2010. Chinese Wordnet: Design, implementation, and application of an infrastructure for cross-lingual knowledge processing 中文词汇网络:跨语言知识处理基础架构的设计理念与实践. *Journal of Chinese Information Processing* 中文信息学报 24(2):14–23.

Huang, Chin-Lan, Cindy K. Chung, Natalie Hui, Yi-Cheng Lin, Yi-Tai Seih, Ben C. P. Lam, Wei-Chuan Chen, Michael H. Bond, and James W. Pennebaker 黃金蘭, Cindy K. Chung, Natalie Hui, 林以正, 謝亦泰, Ben C. P. Lam, 程威銓, Michael H. Bond, and James W. Pennebaker. 2012. The development of the Chinese linguistic inquiry and word count dictionary 中文版「語文探索與字詞計算」詞典之建立. *Chinese Journal of Psychology 中華心理學刊* 54(2):185–201.

Langacker, Ronald W. 1987. *Foundations of cognitive grammar: Theoretical prerequisites* (Vol 1). Stanford, CA: Stanford University Press.

Lee, Chia-Chen and Shu-Kai Hsieh. 2016. Evaluative pattern extraction for automated text extraction. In: *Proceedings of the 9th International Natural Language Generation Conference*. Edinburgh, Scotland.

[6]The system will be available at lope.linguistics.ntu.edu.tw/deeplex

Lynott, Dermot, and Louise Connell. 2013. Modality exclusivity norms for 400 nouns: The relationship between perceptual experience and surface word form. *Behavior Research Methods* 45(2):516–526.

Pennebaker, James W., Ryan L. Boyd, Kayla Jordan, and Kate Blackburn. 2015. *The development and psychometric properties of LIWC 2015*. Austin, TX: University of Texas at Austin.

Singleton, David. 2016. *Language and the lexicon: An introduction*. Routledge.

Sun, Ching Chu, Peter Hendrix, Jianqiang Ma, and Rolf Harald Baayen. (2018). Chinese Lexical Database (CLD): A large-scale lexical database for simplified Mandarin Chinese. *Behavior Research Methods*, https://doi.org/10.3758/s13428-018-1038-3.

Sundararajan, Louise, and Schubert, Lenhart K. 2002. The externalizing scale: A pattern-matching word count program. Unpublished manuscript, Computer Science Department, University of Rochester, NY.

Sundararajan, Louise, and Schubert, Lenhart K. 2005. Verbal expressions of self and emotions: A taxonomy with implications for alexithymia and. *Conscious Emotions: Agency, Conscious Choice, and Selective Perception* 1:243.

Sze, Wei Ping, Susan J. Rickard Liow, and Melvin J. Yap. 2014. The Chinese lexicon project: A repository of lexical decision behavioral responses for 2,500 Chinese characters. *Behavior Research Methods* 46(1):263–273.

Tausczik, Yla R., and James W. Pennebaker. 2010. The psychological meaning of words: LIWC and computerized text analysis methods. *Journal of Language and Social Psychology* 29(1): 24–54.

Wray, Alison. 2005. *Formulaic language and the lexicon*. Cambridge University Press.

Chapter 7
The Chinese Generalized Function Word Usage Knowledge Base and Its Applications

Kunli Zhang, Hongying Zan, Xuefeng Zhu, and Shiwen Yu

Abstract The study of modern Chinese function word usage is of great significance in Chinese syntax analysis and semantic understanding. In this chapter, we will first describe the triune Chinese generalized function word usage knowledge base, which includes a usage dictionary, a usage rule base, a usage corpus, and defined function words such as adverbs, prepositions, conjunctions, auxiliaries, modal particles, and location words. With this constructed knowledge base, we were able to examine the automatic recognition of Chinese function word usages using the rule-based method, the statistics-based method, and the combined rule-based/statistics-based method, respectively. In this chapter, we will also discuss the applications of the Chinese function word usage knowledge base (CFKB) in syntactic analysis, grammar error analysis, information extraction, and Chinese deep semantic understanding.

Keywords Function word usage knowledge base · Function word usage dictionary · Function word usage rule base · Function word usage corpus · Applications

7.1 Introduction

In Chinese, function words, the meanings of which are intangible, play an important role in describing the relationship between content words, as Chinese lacks morphological changes in the strict sense (Lü 吕叔湘 1979). In comparison with other languages, such as English, Chinese function words undertake a more onerous grammatical task and play a key role in understanding the semantic analysis and grammatical analysis of texts. As such, research on function words is important in

K. Zhang (✉) · H. Zan
School of Computer and Artificial Intelligence, Zhengzhou University, Zhengzhou, China
e-mail: ieklzhang@zzu.edu.cn; iehyzan@zzu.edu.cn

X. Zhu · S. Yu
Key Laboratory of Computational Linguistics, Peking University, Ministry of Education, Beijing, China

Institute of Computational Linguistics, Peking University, Beijing, China

C.-R. Huang et al. (eds.), *Chinese Language Resources*, Text, Speech and Language Technology 49, https://doi.org/10.1007/978-3-031-38913-9_7

the study of contemporary Chinese. In studying Chinese function words, researchers should focus on understanding both the meaning of each function word and the usage of each function word (Lu and Ma 陆俭明, 马真 1999). Meanwhile, language processing systems need knowledge bases for support (Dong and Dong 董振东, 董强 n.d.). In particular, lexical knowledge bases play an important role in natural language processing (NLP).

In the field of linguistics, many researchers have focused on the meaning and the usage of Chinese function words. Some research papers and monographs have focused on detailed descriptions of function words. There are also some function word dictionaries, such as *The Contemporary Chinese 800 words* (Lü 吕叔湘 1999), *The Contemporary Common Chinese Function Word Dictionary* (Wu 武克忠 1998), *The Contemporary Chinese Function Word Dictionary* (Hou 侯学超 1999), and *The Contemporary Chinese Function Word Dictionary* (Zhang 张斌 2001), in which the function words are differentiated, analyzed, and discussed in detail combined with examples. The abovementioned studies were all human-oriented. Current contemporary Chinese lexical knowledge bases mainly include HowNet, Chinese FrameNet (CFN), *TongYiCi CiLin*, and the grammatical knowledge base (GKB) of contemporary Chinese (Yu et al. 俞士汶等 2003a). However, these lexical knowledge bases are weak in terms of the information on Chinese function words included (Yu et al. 俞士汶等 2003b).

Based on the weaknesses in the current lexical knowledge bases, it is urgent that NLP construct a perfect Chinese function word lexical knowledge base following the achievements of linguists. Yu et al. 俞士汶等 (2003b) proposed the "trinity" design concept of the Chinese function word usage knowledge base (CFKB). Liu 刘云 (2004) discussed the basic framework of the CFKB, while Peng 彭爽 (2006) studied the grammatical functions of Chinese prepositions and created a preliminary dictionary of Chinese prepositions. On this basis, Zan et al. 昝红英等 (2007), Zan and Zhu 昝红英, 朱学锋 (2009), Zan et al. (2011a), Zhang et al. (2013), and Zhang et al. 张坤丽等 (2015) constructed and improved the CFKB.

Aimed at the needs of research on NLP and its applications, the Chinese generalized function words in this chapter include adverbs, prepositions, conjunctions, auxiliaries, modal particles, and location words to avoid getting bogged down in the boundary between content words and function words. Starting with function word usage, the CFKB includes a usage dictionary, a usage rule base, and a usage corpus. In this chapter, we will describe the CFKB in detail and introduce the automatic identification of function word usages supported by the CFKB rule base and corpus. Moreover, the applications of the CFKB in syntactic analysis, grammar error analysis, information extraction, and Chinese deep semantic understanding will also be discussed.

The rest of this chapter is organized as follows. Section 7.2 will present the construction process of the CFKB and its recent results. In Sect. 7.3, the results of the automatic identification of function word usages using the CFKB will be presented, while Sect. 7.4 will examine the overall applications of the CFKB. Finally, the conclusion and directions for future works will be presented in Sect. 7.5.

7.2 Chinese Function Word Usage Knowledge Base

7.2.1 Framework and Construction Process of the CFKB

The CFKB includes three parts—a function word usage dictionary, a function word usage rule base, and a function word usage tagged corpus—which are associated with the automatic identification of function word usages and form an organic whole. The complete framework of the CFKB is shown in Fig. 7.1.

In the process of construction, the dictionary was built first. Then, based on the usage descriptions in the dictionary, the rule base was built, which was used as a rule-based method to automatically annotate the usages in the corpus. The corpus texts were initially proofread by two researchers, and a third person discussed the inconsistencies between the two researchers and determined the final usage tag. The usage dictionary and usage rule base were modified and gradually improved according to the proofreading feedback. In the current CFKB, the dictionary contains 2401 function words and 4337 usages, the rule base contains 4696 rules, and the corpus includes 7 months of texts from the *People's Daily*, which were used to tag function word usage.

7.2.2 Function Word Usage Dictionary

In the function word usage dictionary, the attributes of the function words are divided into four categories: identity attribute, usage description, syntactic function description, and category. The identity attributes are the same for the six part-of-speech (POS) words, and each usage has a unique ID in the usage dictionary, which links the usage dictionary, the rule base, and the corpus. In general, the coding frame of the IDs is "p_z[_tn][_m][x][y]," which represents the words POS, Pinyin (Chinese pronunciation notation), homophone, sequent number, word sense sequent number, usage sequent number, and sub-usage sequent number, respectively.

In the coding frame, "[]" represents "optional." For instance, one usage ID of the auxiliary 的 *de* "DE" is "u_de5_t2_1bc," where "u" represents the auxiliary's POS, "de5" is the pronunciation notation, "t2" represents the second homophone word, and "1bc" represents the third sub-usage of the second usage in the first sense. A further detail about IDs is presented in Zan et al. 昝红英等 (2007). In the dictionary, the usage descriptions, syntactic function descriptions, and categories vary for each POS. For instance, with regard to category attributes, conjunction usages focus on relationship, adverb usages focus on classification, and preposition usages focus on object type. Further details on the dictionary's framework can be found in Zan et al. 昝红英等 (2007), Zan and Zhu 昝红英, 朱学锋 (2009) and Zan et al. (2011a). As a whole, in the design of the framework, all word classes in the CFKB have both uniform attributes and different ones because of their distinctive properties, which enables the CFKB to serve a more important function in NLP.

The word and usage descriptions included in the dictionary are mainly referred to in Lü 吕叔湘 (1999), Zhang 张斌 (2001), Yu et al. 俞士汶等 (2003a), the *Contemporary Chinese Dictionary*, and the segmentation and POS corpus from the *People's Daily*. In the usage dictionary, combined with the practical usage of Chinese functions, every usage of a function word was decomposed and regarded as a record. Based on the demands of language processing, the usage descriptions of every word were decomposed, differentiated, and then fulfilled in the dictionary after the operational features were extracted. An example from the function word usage dictionary is shown in Fig. 7.2.

We adopted the words in the function word usage dictionary following the principle of respecting classical authority and adjusting the usages according to actual semantics. For instance, in (7.1) below, if the words 又 *you* "and" and 既 *ji* "both" occur together, the POS of 又 *you* "and" is labeled "/c" (conjunction).

(7.1) 这样/rz 既/c 方便/v 广大/b 市民/n 参加/v 活动/vn , /wd 又/c 能/vu 更/d 好/a 地
/ui 维持/v 秩序/n , /wd 确保/v 安全/an 。 /wj (20000101-10-014-006/m)
zheyang_ji_fangbian_guangda_shimin_canjia_huodong_you_neng_geng_hao_de
_weichi_zhixu_quebao_anquan
So_both_offer_convenience_masses_citizen_take-part-in_activity_and_can_more
_good DE_keep_order_ensure_safety
So this can both offer convenience for the masses to take part in activities and better
keep order to ensure safety

According to the labeled POS in the corpus, the word 又 *you* "and" should be adopted as a conjunction, but through analysis, the semantic meaning of 又 *you* "and" in (7.1) is "several actions, states, conditions accumulated together," which

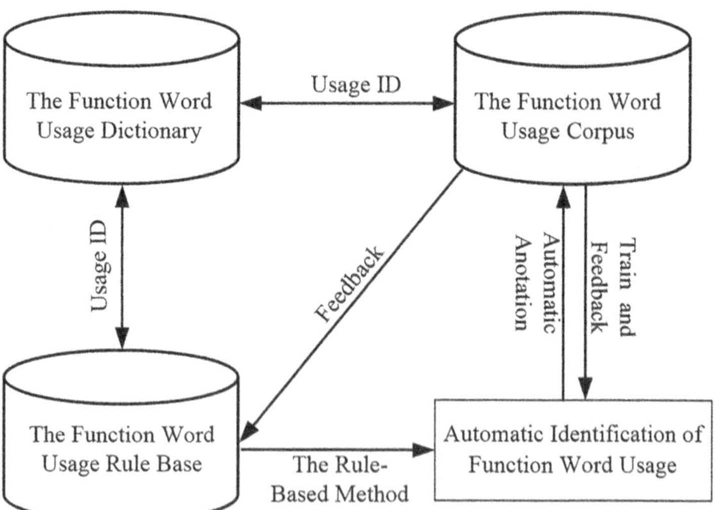

Fig. 7.1 The framework of the CFKB

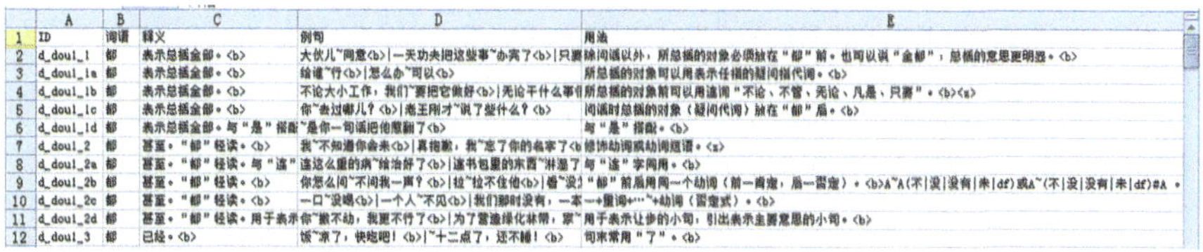

Fig. 7.2 Example from the function word usage dictionary

belongs to the adverb category, so this word was not adopted as a conjunction in the usage dictionary.

Additionally, each usage adopted in the usage dictionary was examined carefully. For instance, when the adverb 也 *ye* "also" represented an association relationship, besides progressive, alternative, adversative, suppositional, concessions, conditional, and causal relationships, the transition relationship was also found in the corpus. Therefore, a new usage of the word 也 *ye* "also" was added to the usage dictionary.

In the function word usage dictionary, the usages of common words (i.e., high-frequency occurrences in the corpus) are complicated in general, so the senses and usages of common words have been divided into smaller particle sizes than those of uncommon words. For instance, the auxiliary word 的 *de* "DE" had a high frequency in the corpus, as it occurred 54,928 times in the *People's Daily* in January 1998, and its usages were very complicated and were thus divided into 39 senses in the dictionary.

The construction of the usage dictionary is a process of continuous improvement. In the 2007 version (Zan et al. 昝红英等 2007), the usage dictionary contained 1153 adverbs and 1946 usages. The word and usage distribution in the 2009 version (Zan and Zhu 昝红英, 朱学锋 2009) and the 2013 version are shown in Table 7.1.

In Table 7.1, N_u represents the number of usages, and N_w represents the number of words. It can be seen that except for auxiliary, the number and usages of each function word has changed significantly.

7.2.3 *Function Word Usage Rule Base*

Based on the usage descriptions in the Chinese function word usage dictionary, we distilled feasible criteria, including the features of the first word in a sentence (F), words to the left of the function word in a sentence (M), words close to the left of the function word in a sentence (L), words close to the right of the function word in a sentence (R), words to the right of the function word in a sentence (N), and end word or punctuation in a sentence (E), and determined the rule descriptions in Backus Normal Form (BNF). Using the principle of detailed descriptions, a general form of the usage rules is shown below:

@<ID>→[F][M][L][R][N][E]^F→<word1>|<word2>|. . .|a|v|n|. . .

^M→<word1>|<word2>|. . .|a|v|n|. . .^L→<word1>|<word2>|. . .|a|v|n|. . .

^R→<word1>|<word2>|. . .|a|v|n|. . .^N→<word1>|<word2>|. . .|a|v|n|. . .

^E→<word1>|<word2>|. . .|a|v|n|. . .

In the usage rules, "@" represents the rule start symbol, "^" represents the connector between feature definitions that indicate the conjunction relationship of the features, "ID" is the usage ID, "<word 1>" and "|a|v|n|" represent the words and POS that appear in the feature position, respectively, the symbol "~" represents the observed function word itself, and the other meta symbols, such as "→", "|", "*", "()", and "[]", are general notations in BNF. In addition to these six features, the framework and semantic field are employed in the rules, which have three description forms:

(i) The meta symbols "A" or "B" will be adopted by the rule if the framework is formed by the same words or the same POS, for example:

$不 *bu* "not"

@<d_bu4_2a>→A~A ^A→a//"A" represents the same word before and after 不 *bu* "not," such as 干净不干净 *ganjing bu ganjing* 'clean or not clean'

@<d_bu4_2e>→~B~B ^B→f //"B" represents the same POS for 不 *bu* "not," such as 不上不下 *bushangbuxia* "be in a dilemma"

(ii) The meta symbols "T" and "S" will be adopted by the rule, with "%" as a marker, if the two words are before and after the observed function word, for example:

$不 *bu* 'not'

@<d_bu4_2a>→%S%~%T%//Such as in the phrase 吃饭不吃 *chifanbuchi* "eat or not eat," where the word 吃 *chi* "eat" (T) is the subset of the word 吃饭 *chifan* "eat" (S)

(iii) Each semantic field is saved in a file named for the usage rule, with a pair of single quotes as the marker, for example:

$十分 *shifen* "very"

@<d_shi2fen1_1b>→R^R→'xinli_v.txt'//Semantic field of psychological verbs is saved in the file named "xinli_v.txt"

According to the descriptions and specifications above, the original rule base was built manually. The rules in the rule base and their usage in the dictionary do not have a one-to-one relationship. If one usage is complex, multiple rules can be used to describe it. Based on the proofread corpus, which was automatically tagged using this original rule base, there were two ways to modify the usage rules, the first of which was manual modification. For the content of the rules, we analyzed sentences that had been tagged with error usage using the rule-based method, distilled the feasible features, and then modified the usage rule. For the order of the rules, rules

Table 7.1 Distribution of Chinese function word usages in the CFKB

N_u												Words in total	Usages in total	Words in total	Usages in total
N_w															
POS	1	2	3	4	5	6	7	8	9	10	Above 10	2013	2013	2009	2009
Adverb	1214	179	84	38	21	12	4	3	2	1	8	1566	2356	1566	2356
Preposition	66	30	23	7	4	5	7	0	1	1	2	141	331	141	331
Conjunction	156	50	55	24	16	7	4	0	1	2	0	315	696	315	696
Auxiliary	30	4	3	1	0	1	2	0	0	0	1	45	144	45	144
Modality	30	7	7	4	2	0	1	4	0	0	2	58	169	58	169
Locality	164	34	11	24	19	6	6	4	6	1	1	276	641	276	641

that showed a high-frequency occurrence or rules that resulted in a good effect in automatic identification were put in a prior position in the rules queue to ensure that each function word was annotated by the best usage rule for automatic identification based on the rules.

The second way to modify the usage rules was automatic modification. For the function word usages that could not be automatically recognized using the rule-based method and were tagged "<FAIL>" in the corpus, an error-driven learning approach was adopted to generate new usage rules (Wu and Zan 吴云鹏, 昝红英 2010). This approach consisted of three steps: first, conversion templates were set up to generate candidate rules; second, the candidate rules were scored using the objective function; and third, the highest-scored rule was chosen as the updated rule.

Through multiple modifications and adjustments, the Chinese function word usage rule base currently includes 2456 adverb rules, 385 preposition rules, 747 conjunction rules, 165 auxiliary rules, 182 modality rules, and 761 locality rules.

7.2.4 Function Word Usage Corpus

The Chinese function word usage corpus was formed using the segmented and POS-tagged texts from the *People's Daily*. First, the function words in the corpus were automatically annotated using the rule-based method. Second, the machine-tagged corpus was proofread by two researchers from the linguistics and computer science fields, respectively. A third person joined them to discuss the inconsistent usages between the two researchers and that person determined the final usage tag. The tagging criterion for each function word was established in the discussions, which guaranteed tagging consistency for each of the function words.

Except for the auxiliary word 的 *de* "DE" in the *People's Daily* from February to March 2000, all of the function words, including adverbs, prepositions, conjunctions, auxiliaries, modal particles, and location words, in 7 months of texts from the *People's Daily* corpus were tagged and proofread, which resulted in about 1.42 million words in the standard contemporary Chinese function word usage corpus. Usage annotation annotated the corresponding labels of the usage IDs next to the function words in the Chinese function word usage corpus, an example of which is shown in (7.2) below:

(7.2) 20000401-01-001-006/m 中国/ns 和/c<c_he2_1> 印度/ns 都/d<d_dou1_1> 是/vl 世
界/n 文明/a 古国/n , /wd 两/m 国/n 之间/f<f_zhi1jian1_1c> 的/ud<u_de5_t2_1a>
友好/a 交往/vn 源远流长/iv 。/wj
Zhongguo_he yindu dou shi shijie wenming guguo liang guo zhijian de
youhao jiaowang_yuanyuangliuchang
China_and_India_both_SHI_world_civilization_ancient_state_two_country_between
DE_friendly_exchange_a-long-history
Both China and India are ancient civilization countries of the world, and the friendly

(continued)

exchanges between them have a long history

During the process of manual proofreading, the original word segmentation and POS tags in the corpus were also analyzed and modified. Meanwhile, some word segmentation or POS tagging errors were automatically found by analyzing the words that were marked with "<FAIL>" using the rule-based method (Han et al. 韩英杰等 2011b).

7.3 Automatic Identification of Function Word Usages

The automatic identification of function word usages is an important part of the construction and application of the CFKB. Automatic identification was achieved in three ways: the rule-based method, the statistics-based method, and the combined rule-based/statistics-based method.

7.3.1 Rule-Based Method

The rule-based method places corpus and usage rules into memory and then uses six types of matching and a special framework matcher to match and parse usage rules and determine the annotating results. Yuan et al. 袁应成等 (2010) introduced the design requirements for all kinds of verifiers and the realization of automatic annotation of function word usage based on rules. Zan et al. (2011b), Zhou et al. 周溢辉等 (2010), and Han et al. 韩英杰等 (2011a) described the detailed process of automatic usage identification based on rules for conjunction, modality, and auxiliary function words, respectively.

This automatic identification method found commonalities and disparities among different word classes. For instance, modalities and auxiliaries match and parse usage rules only within a sentence (with the ".", ",", "!", and "?" punctuation marks as the standard), while conjunction usage identification considers sentences or paragraphs matching units depending on the connecting characteristics of the conjunctions because they can connect causes, sentences, and paragraphs. Currently, the accuracy rates of automatically recognizing function words in the 7 months of texts in the *People's Daily*, using the rule-based method, are 84.36% for adverbs, 71.71% for prepositions, 83.68% for conjunctions, 40.71% for auxiliaries, 78.85% for modalities, and 88.14% for localities, respectively. The low accuracy rate of auxiliaries was due to the word 的 *de* "DE"; its complex usage and high frequency led to the low recognition rate of 的 *de* "DE" and reduced the overall accuracy rate of auxiliaries.

The accuracy rates of the rule-based method depended on rule descriptions. Although some strategies such as modifying the rules and adjusting the order of the rules were used in building the rule base, "phrasal verbs" and "cause" in the usage descriptions were difficult to formalize, which limited the automatic recognition accuracy rates of the rule-based method.

7.3.2 Statistics-Based Method

In view of the limitations of the rule-based method, using the standard function word usage corpus mentioned in Sect. 7.2.4 as the training data, statistical models, such as the support vector machine (SVM), maximum entropy (ME), and conditional random fields (CRF), were used to automatically identify the usages of common function words that did not attain high accuracy rates using the rule-based method.

When function word usages were automatically identified using the statistics-based method, each function word needed to train a classifier because there were great differences among the usages of the function words. Zan and Zhu 昝红英, 朱学锋 (2009), Zan et al. (2010), Zan et al. (2011b), Zhang et al. 张坤丽等 (2012a), and Zhang et al. (2012b) examined the automatic identification of the adverb 就 *jiu* "as soon as," the adverb 才 *cai* "just," common conjunctions, common adverbs, and prepositions, respectively. These studies used different models and features to identify function word usages, respectively, and the best macro-accuracy rate of usage identification based on the statistical models was about 27% more than that of the rule-based method.

7.3.3 Combined Rule-Based/Statistics-Based Method

Although the overall accuracy of the statistics-based method was high, some of the usage results of the rule-based method were better than those of the statistics-based method. Based on this finding, we combined the rule-based method and the statistics-based method to automatically identify function word usages.

Zhang and Zan 张静杰, 昝红英 (2013) performed statistical analysis on the usage distribution of the adverb 都 *dou* "all" in the *People's Daily* corpus in March, April, and May 2000 and analyzed the accuracy and recall rates of the rule-based method and the statistics-based method, which found that the accuracy rates of the rule-based method were higher than those of the statistics-based method when the frequency of one function word was low in the corpus. Zhang and Zan 张静杰, 昝红英 (2013) adopted usage distribution in the corpus and the usage accuracy rates of the two methods as parameters and examined the automatic identification of the adverb 都 *dou* "all." The accuracy rate reached 98.54%, which was 16.54% and 8.92% higher than that of the rule-based method and the statistics-based method, respectively. Zhou et al. (2013) examined the automatic identification of conjunctions using the hybrid rules and statistics method, and the accuracy rates of usage identification improved across methods, which showed that there is high complementation between the rule-based method and the statistics-based method.

7.4 Applications Based on the CFKB

The achievements of the CFKB can be used directly in NLP. The applications of the CFKB in syntactic analysis, grammar error analysis, information extraction, and Chinese deep semantic understanding are now in full swing.

7.4.1 Syntactic Analysis

In the process of constructing the bilingual phrase structure treebank, it was found that the errors in automatic Chinese syntactic analysis mainly focused on three aspects: the conjunction phrase structure, prepositional phrases, and noun phrases, including 的 *de* "DE," which is related to function words (Zhang et al. 2014). In terms of the influence of preposition usages in the syntactic analysis, Zhang et al. 张坤丽等 (2011) examined prepositional phrase boundary identification based on the preposition usage identification results. In terms of the influence of conjunction usages in the syntactic analysis, in Zan et al. 昝红英等 (2012), the conjunction usage identification results were integrated into the conjunction phrase structure analysis, and the accuracy rate based on the rules reached 48.67%. Then, a statistics-based method was adopted in conjunction with the phrase structure analysis, and conjunction usage as a feature was integrated into the CRF model. Compared with not adding usage features, the highest accuracy rate improved by 4%.

Zan et al. 昝红英等 (2013a) employed usage identification to modify the dependency syntactic analysis results from the Language Technology Platform (LTP) at Harbin Institute of Technology, which improved the accuracy rates in the dependency syntactic analysis. For instance, (7.3) below includes the conjunction 还是 *haishi* "or." Its standard dependency syntactic analysis result is shown in Fig. 7.3, and its automatic tagging result using the LTP is shown in Fig. 7.4.

(7.3) 认为李自成占领北京后，中国面临的是统一还是分裂问题
renwei_lizicheng_zhanling_beijing_hou_zhongguo_minalin_de_shi_tongyi_haishi _fenlie_wenti
think_LiZicheng_occupy_Peking_after_China_face_DE_is_unification_or_division _problem
They thought after Li Zicheng occupied Peking, the problem China faced was its unification or division

In comparing Fig. 7.4 with Fig. 7.3, it was found that there were some errors in the coordinate phrases in Fig. 7.4, so the usage of the conjunction word 还是 *haishi* "or" was automatically tagged, and then the boundaries of the corresponding coordinate phrase were automatically tagged based on the usage. The coordinate phrase in Fig. 7.4 is "<CP_bl> 统一/n还是 /c <c_hai2shi4_1a> 分裂/n</CP_bl>," among which "<c_hai2shi4_1a>" is the usage tag, "<CP_bl>" is the left border, and "</CP_bl>" is the right border. The LPT result was modified according to the tagged result. The modified result is shown in Fig. 7.5. As can be seen in Figs. 7.3, 7.4, and 7.5, the coordinate relation COO was correctly identified by introducing the conjunction usage and coordinated structure, and the additional relation LAD was also affected, which improved the accuracy rates in the dependency syntactic analysis.

Zhang 张静杰 (2013) integrated the preposition usage identification results into the post-process of the dependency syntactic analysis using the LTP, and Pang 庞熠雅 (2013) integrated the conjunction usage identification results into the post-process of the phrase structure syntactic analysis using the Stanford Parser, both of which improved the accuracy rates in the syntactic analysis. Feng et al. 冯晓波等 (2016) used the rule-based approach, the CRF model, and the convolutional neural network model to identify the phrase boundaries by integrating the function word usage rules and then examined the syntactic analysis based on phrase boundaries. The results showed that integrating function word usage rules improved the accuracy rates in the syntactic analysis.

7.4.2 Grammar Error Analysis

Foreign students learning Chinese always make grammar errors because of the negative transfer of their mother tongue. Among all grammar errors, misuses of function words account for about half of the errors. Han et al. (2013) analyzed the HSK Dynamic Composition Corpus and extracted conjunction error sentences in the conjunction usage category of the corpus. Then, they summarized the correct and incorrect usages of conjunctions based on the descriptions in the CFKB and proposed a rule-based method to detect conjunction grammar errors such as addition, overrepresentation, and omission. The results based on the HSK Dynamic

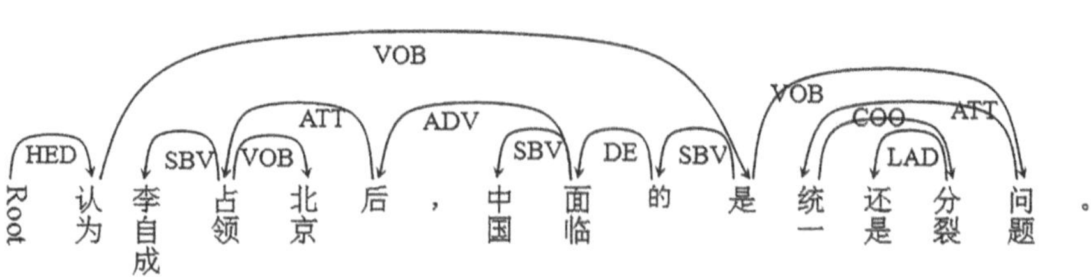

Fig. 7.3 Standard dependency syntactic analysis result

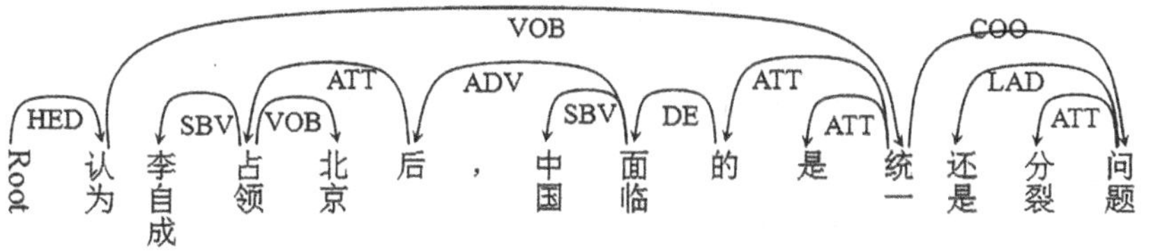

Fig. 7.4 LTP dependency syntactic analysis result

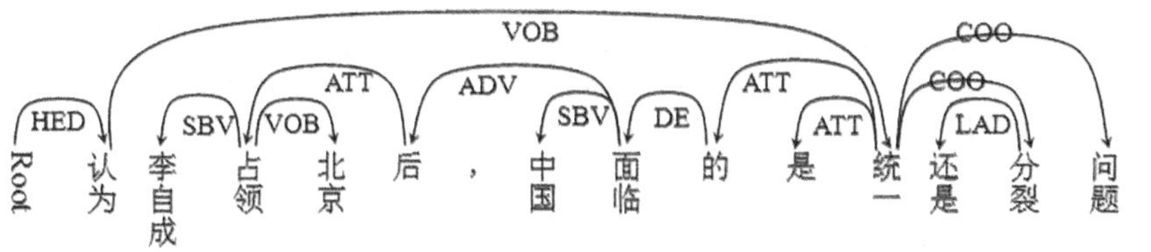

Fig. 7.5 Modified dependency syntactic analysis result

Composition Corpus proved that the rule-based method to detect errors was simple, practicable, and effective in the automatic recognition of conjunction grammar errors.

Taking the conjunction 和 *he* "and" as an example, in addition to using the appropriate usage rules in the CFKB to recognize possible grammatical errors, Han et al. (2013) summarized and extracted inappropriate usage rules of typical conjunction grammar errors according to the rule form shown in Sect. 7.2.3. The problematic usage rules of 和 *he* "and" are shown below:

$和 *he* 'and'.

(i) @<c_he2_e>→F^F→~
(ii) @<c_he2_e>→E^E→~
(iii) @<c_he2_e>→LR^L→v^R→{d}v
(iv) @<c_he2_e>→L|R^L→p|d|a|c|, |、|。|?|!^R→, |。|、|?|!
(v) @<c_he2_e>→M^M→*!(》)
(vi) @<c_he2_e>→MLR^M→(n|r)*v*(n|r)^L→(n|r)^R→(n|r)*v*n

An error sentence from the HSK Dynamic Composition Corpus is shown in (7.4) below. "{CD}" indicates an addition followed by additional words. In general, 和 *he* "and" can be used to connect nouns and pronouns, and it indicates a coordinative relation. The problematic usage of 和 *he* "and" in sentence (7.4) was detected using rule (iii) @<c_he2_e>→LR^L→v^R→{d}v.

(7.4) *你们两位自己小心{CD 和 *he* 'and'}照顾吧。
nimen_liang_wei_ziji_xiaoxin_zhaogu_ba_
you_two_CL_yourselves_carefully_take-care-of_BA

Based on the automatic recognition of conjunction usage errors, He 贺娟 (2014) constructed an aided teaching system. This system gathered the functions of understanding conjunction semantics, identifying the differences and similarities of conjunction usages, detecting grammar errors, and automatically modifying errors into one organic whole, which could be of great help in teaching Chinese as a second language.

7.4.3 Information Extraction

Event extraction is mainly the research of information extraction, which extracts the semantic roles of the predefined target event. The objects introduced by prepositions are often the related time and location elements in event extraction. The objects introduced by some prepositions may be different elements. For instance, the preposition 在 *zai* "in" introduces the location element "郑州大学 *zhengzhoudaxue* 'Zhengzhou University'" in (7.5) and the time element "五月份 *wuyufen* 'May'" in (7.6), respectively. In the CFKB, the usage of the preposition 在 *zai* "in" is "1a" in sentence (7.5) and "2a" in sentence (7.6). Placing the usage information into the information extraction template, the time element and the location element can be extracted correctly.

(7.5) CLSW将在郑州大学举行。
CLSW_jiang zai zhengzhoudaxue juxing
CLSW_will_in Zhengzhou University hold
CLSW will be held in Zhengzhou University.
(7.6) CLSW将在五月份举行。
CLSW_jiang_zai_wuyufen juxing
CLSW_will_in_May hold
CLSW will be held in May.

Zan et al. 昝红英等 (2013b) integrated the results of the preposition usage identification into the CFKB to extract the elements of the meeting event and the time and location elements associated with five commonly used prepositions. Compared with the existed method, the accuracy rate of the results improved approximately 9%, which showed that the integration of preposition usage had a certain effect on event extraction.

7.4.4 Chinese Deep Semantic Understanding

In the abstract semantics structure of the sentence "{[<|(preposition component) (tense and aspect component)|modal component>mood component] tone component}," the basic logic meaning conveyed by the preposition component should not only focus on the understanding of the logic complement, as the negative, the degree, the tense and aspect, the modal, the mood, and the tone components are also important levels for the deep semantic understanding of a sentence. It is interesting to note that most formal features, which are called operators of the logic complement, are function words. Zhang et al. (2016) examined modal operators in a Chinese modality tagging framework and found that most of the modal operators were adverbs whose attributes could be extracted directly from the adverb usage category in the CFKB. The constructed modal operator dictionary contained 298 operators and 186 were from the CFKB, accounting for 62.4% of the total. Using the CFKB's results of automatic recognition for further automatic modality annotation, the words from the CFKB in the modal operator dictionary represented the granularity partitioning of usage, and those from other sources were described according to semantic granularity.

Furthermore, the operators of the negative and the degree components in logical complement semantics are almost all words that belong to the negative subclass and the degree subclass in the adverb usage category, while the operators of the mood component and the tone component are almost all auxiliaries and modal particles, which are included in the CFKB. Thus, complement semantic operators can be obtained directly from the usage dictionary in the CFKB, and automatic recognition and understanding can also use the CFKB's results of automatic recognition.

7.5 Conclusion

The research on contemporary Chinese function word usage plays an important role in semantic and syntactic analysis. In this chapter, we introduced the construction process and current situation of the CFKB, which includes the Chinese function word usage dictionary, the Chinese function word usage rule base, and the Chinese function word usage corpus. In addition, the automatic identification of function word usages was examined according to the rule base and the corpus. The applications of the CFKB were also discussed, such as syntactic analysis, grammar error analysis, information extraction, and Chinese deep semantic understanding, as well as the automatic identification of function word usages. Next, we will continue to improve the quality of the CFKB, ensuring that the three parts of the CFKB are in concordance. We will also use the applications more extensively based on the CFKB.

Acknowledgments We gratefully acknowledge the support of the National Basic Research Program of China (2014CB340504), the National Natural Science Foundation of China (No.61402419, No.60970083), the National Social Science Foundation (No.14BYY096), the Basic Research Project of the Science and Technology Department of Henan Province (No. 142300410231, No.142300410308), and the Key Technology Project of the Education Department of Henan Province (No.12B520055, No. 13B520381, No.15A520098).

References

Dong, Zhendong, and Qiang Dong 董振东, 董强. n.d. *Wordnet* 知网. Available at http://www.keenage.com/. Accessed 17th April 2014.

Feng, Xiaobo, Lingling Mu, Hongying Zan, and Kunli Zhang 冯晓波, 穆玲玲, 昝红英, 张坤丽. 2016. Studies on boundary identification of phrases with function words and its application in syntactic parsing 汉语虚词相关的短语边界在句法分析中的应用研究. Paper presented at the *China Workshop on Machine Translation*, 38–46. Urumchi, China. Available at http://www.cips-cl.org/static/anthology/CCL-2013/CCL-13-054.pdf. Accessed 1 April 2019.

Han, Yingjie, Kunli Zhang, Hongying Zan, and Yumei Chai 韩英杰, 张坤丽, 昝红英, 柴玉梅. 2011a. Automatic annotation of auxiliary words usage in rule-based Chinese language 基于规则的现代汉语常用助词用法自动识别. *Computer Applications* 计算机应用 31(4):1318–1321.

Han, Yingjie, Kunli Zhang, Hongying Zan, and Yumei Chai 韩英杰, 张坤丽, 昝红英, 柴玉梅. 2011b. Automatic discovery on auxiliary word usage-based POS and segmentation errors for Chinese language 基于助词用法的汉语词性、分词错误自动发现. *Application Research of Computers* 计算机应用研究 28(4):1318–1321.

Han, Yingjie, Aiying Lin, Yonggang Wu, and Hongying Zan. 2013. Usage-Based Automatic Recognition of Grammar Errors of Conjunctions in Teaching Chinese as a Second Language. *Lecture Notes in Computer Science* 8229:519–528.

He, Juan 贺娟. 2014. *HSK composition corpus-oriented automatic recognition of wrong conjunction usages and application* 面向 *HSK* 作文库的连词偏误用法自动识别及其应用研究. Master's thesis. Zhengzhou University, Zhengzhou.

Hou, Xuechao 侯学超. 1999. *The contemporary Chinese function word dictionary* 现代汉语虚词词典. Beijing: Press of Peking University.

Liu, Yun 刘云. 2004. *The building of knowledge database of contemporary Chinese functional words* 汉语虚词知识库的建设. Postdoctoral report. Beijing: Peking University.

Lü, Shuxiang 吕叔湘. 1979. *The problem on grammatical analysis of the contemporary Chinese* 汉语语法分析问题, 23–25. Beijing: Commercial Press.

Lü, Shuxiang 吕叔湘. 1999. *Contemporary Chinese 800 words* 现代汉语八百词. Beijing: The Commercial Press.

Lu, Jianmin, and Zhen Ma 陆俭明, 马真. 1999. *Some comments on the Modern Chinese function word* 现代汉语虚词散论, 49–51. Beijing: Language and Culture Press.

Pang, Yiya 庞熠雅. 2013. *Studies on the usage of preposition and conjunction in phrase structure syntactic parsing* 介词、连词用法在短语结构句法分析中的应用研究. Master's thesis. Zhengzhou University, Zhengzhou.

Peng, Shuang 彭爽. 2006. *The building of knowledge base of contemporary Chinese prepositions and related research* 现代汉语介词知识库的建设与相关研究. Postdoctoral report. Beijing: Peking University.

Wu, Kezhong 武克忠. 1998. *The contemporary common Chinese function word dictionary* 现代汉语常用虚词词典. Hangzhou: Zhejiang Education Publishing House.

Wu, Yunpeng, and Hongying Zan 吴云鹏, 昝红英. 2010. Automatic updates of position words usage rules in Modern Chinese based on error-driver 基于错误驱动的现代汉语方位词用法规则的自动更新. Paper presented at *The 5th Youth Computational Linguistics Workshop*, 43–49. Wuhan, China. Available at http://cips-cl.org/static/anthology/2010-76/YWCL-10-007.pdf. Accessed 1 April 2019.

Yu, Shiwen, Xuefeng Zhu, and Hui Wang 俞士汶, 朱学峰, 王惠. 2003a. *The grammatical knowledge base of contemporary Chinese* 现代汉语语法信息词典详解. Beijing: Tsinghua University Press.

Yu, Shiwen, Xuefeng Zhu, and Yun Liu 俞士汶, 朱学锋, 刘云. 2003b. Knowledge-base of generalized functional words of contemporary Chinese 现代汉语广义虚词知识库的建设. *Journal of Chinese Language and Computing* 汉语语言与计算学报 13(1):89–98.

Yuan, Yingcheng, Hongying Zan, Kunli Zhang, and Yihui Zhou 袁应成, 昝红英, 张坤丽, 周溢辉. 2010. The automatic annotation algorithm design and system implementation rule- base function word usage 基于规则的虚词用法自动标注算法设计与系统实现. Paper presented at *The 11th Chinese Lexical Semantics Workshop*, 163–169. Taipei, Taiwan.

Zan, Hongying, and Xuefeng Zhu 昝红英, 朱学锋. 2009. NLP oriented studies on Chinese functional words and the construction of their generalized knowledge base 面向自然语言处理的汉语虚词研究与广义虚词知识库构建. *Contemporary Linguistics* 当代语言学 2:124–135.

Zan, Hongying, Kunli Zhang, Yumei Chai, and Shiwen Yu 昝红英, 张坤丽, 柴玉梅, 俞士汶. 2007. Studies on the functional word knowledge base of Modern Chinese 现代汉语虚词知识库的研究. *Journal of Chinese Information Processing* 中文信息学报 21(5):107–111.

Zan, Hongying, Junhui Zhang, Xue-Feng Zhu, and Shi-Wen Yu. 2010. The studies on the usages and their automatic identification of Chinese adverb JIU. *Recent Advances of Chinese Lexical Semantics* 37–43.

Zan, Hongying, Kunli Zhang, Xuefeng Zhu, and Shiwen Yu. 2011a. Research on the Chinese function word usage knowledge base. *International Journal on Asian Language Processing* 21(4):185–198.

Zan, Hongying, Lijuan Zhou, and Kunli Zhang. 2011b. Studies on the automatic recognition of Modern Chinese conjunction usages. *Lecture Notes in Computer Science* 6838:472–479.

Zan, Hongying, Lijuan Zhou, and Kunli Zhang 昝红英, 周丽娟, 张坤丽. 2012. Modern Chinese conjunction phrase recognition based on usage 基于用法的现代汉语连词结构短语识别研究. *Journal of Chinese Information Processing* 中文信息学报 6:72–78.

Zan, Hongying, Jingjie Zhang, and Xinpo Lou 昝红英, 张静杰, 娄鑫坡. 2013a. Studies on the application of Chinese functional words usages in dependency parsing 汉语虚词用法在依存句法分析中的应用研究. *Journal of Chinese Information Processing* 中文信息学报 27(5):35–42.

Zan, Hongying, Tengfei Zhang, and Aiying Lin 昝红英, 张腾飞, 林爱英. 2013b. Research on event information extraction based on preposition's usages 基于介词用法的事件信息抽取研究. *Computer Engineering and Design* 计算机工程与设计 34(7):2152–2157.

Zhang, Bin 张斌. 2001. *The contemporary Chinese function word dictionary* 现代汉语虚词词典. Beijing: The Commercial Press.

Zhang, Jingjie 张静杰. 2013. *Studies on automatic recognition of functional words usages and application on dependency parsing* 虚词用法自动识别及其在依存句法分析中的应用. Master's thesis. Zhengzhou University, Zhengzhou.

Zhang, Jingjie, and Hongying Zan 张静杰, 昝红英. 2013. Automatic recognition research on Chinese adverb DOU's usages 副词"都"用法自动识别研究. *Journal of Peking University (Natural Science)* 北京大学学报(自然科学版) 49(1):165–169.

Zhang, Kunli, Yingjie Han, Hongying Zan, and Yumei Chai 张坤丽, 韩英杰, 昝红英, 柴玉梅. 2011. Prepositional phrase boundary identification based on statistical models 基于统计的介词短语边界识别研究. *Journal of Henan University* 河南大学学报 41(6):636–640.

Zhang, Kunli, Dan Zhao, Hongying Zan, and Yumei Chai 张坤丽, 赵丹, 昝红英, 柴玉梅. 2012a. Studies on automatic recognition of Modern Chinese common adverbs' usages 常用现代汉语副词用法自动识别研究. *Journal of Chinese Information Processing* 中文信息学报 26(6):65–71.

Zhang, Kunli, Hongying Zan, Yingjie Han, and Tengfei Zhang. 2012b. Studies on automatic recognition of contemporary Chinese common preposition usage. *Chinese Lexical Semantics* 2012:219–229.

Zhang, Kunli, Hongying Zan, Yumei Chai, Yingjie Han, and Dan Zhao. 2013. Construction and application of the Chinese function word usage knowledge base. *International Journal of Knowledge and Language Processing* 4(4):32–42.

Zhang, Kunli, HongYing Zan, Yingjie Han, and Lingling Mu. 2014. Preliminary study on the construction of bilingual phrase structure treebank. *Lecture Notes in Computer Science* 8922: 403–413.

Zhang, Kunli, Hongying Zan, Yumei Chai, and Dan Zhao 张坤丽, 昝红英, 柴玉梅, 赵丹. 2015. A survey on the Chinese function word usage knowledge base 现代汉语虚词用法知识库建设综述. *Journal of Chinese Information Processing* 中文信息学报 29(3):1–8.

Zhang, Kunli, Lingling Mu, Hongying Zan, and Yingjie Han. 2016. Study on Chinese modality tagging framework. *Chinese Lexical Semantics* 2016:291–305.

Zhou, Yihui, Lingling Mu, and Hongying Zan 周溢辉, 穆玲玲, 昝红英. 2010. Research on automatic recognition of Chinese modality usage 汉语语气词用法的自动识别研究. *Computer Engineering* 计算机工程 36(23):155–157.

Zhou, Lijuan, Hongying Zan, and Kunli Zhang. 2013. Studies on a hybrid way of rules and statistics for Chinese conjunction usages recognition. *Lecture Notes in Computer Science* 8229:416–424.

Chapter 8
A Generic Study of Linguistic Information Based on the Chinese Idiom Knowledge Base and Its Expansion

Lei Wang, Weiguang Qu, Houfeng Wang, and Shiwen Yu

Abstract The Chinese language is rich in set phrases and idiomatic expressions of various types. By definition, a set phrase is an inclusive concept that consists of not only lexical units, such as idioms and proper nouns, but also non-lexical units, such as proverbs, maxims, adages, and poems, as long as they are "fixed" in form. These constructions are regarded as multiword expressions (MWEs) in linguistics. This chapter will describe the linguistic information obtained from a generic investigation of the Chinese Idiom Knowledge Base (CIKB), along with its expansion to other similar language resources. In Chinese information processing, idiomatic expressions play an important role in word segmentation, which is a prerequisite for other natural language processing (NLP) tasks. The current challenge is constructing knowledge bases for Chinese idiomatic expressions with relatively complete entries and annotations. In our study, we focused on how the constituents in a fossilized composition like an idiom affect semantic and grammatical properties. As an important Chinese language resource, our knowledge base of Chinese idiomatic expressions is expected to play a major role in practices such as linguistic research,

L. Wang (✉)
Key Laboratory of Computational Linguistics, Peking University, Ministry of Education, Beijing, China

School of Foreign Languages, Peking University, Beijing, China
e-mail: wangleics@pku.edu.cn

W. Qu
School of Artificial Intelligence, Nanjing Normal University, Nanjing, China
e-mail: wgqu@njnu.edu.cn

H. Wang
Key Laboratory of Computational Linguistics, Peking University, Ministry of Education, Beijing, China
e-mail: wanghf@pku.edu.cn

S. Yu
Key Laboratory of Computational Linguistics, Peking University, Ministry of Education, Beijing, China

Institute of Computational Linguistics, Peking University, Beijing, China

C.-R. Huang et al. (eds.), *Chinese Language Resources*, Text, Speech and Language Technology 49, https://doi.org/10.1007/978-3-031-38913-9_8

teaching Chinese as a foreign language, and as a tool for preserving non-material Chinese cultural and historical heritage.

Keywords Linguistic information · Chinese idiom knowledge base · Expansion

8.1 Introduction

For Chinese idioms, the most important issue has always been definition, which remains controversial. One of the aims of our work was to attempt to bring the dispute to an end by referring to commonly acknowledged standards and considering the actual situation of Chinese idiomatic expressions. As a language evolves and develops, some combinations of words with good prevalence and high frequency of usage will become "set" or "habitual," as in the Chinese 熟语 *shuyu* "idiomatic expressions" and 习语 *xiyu* "habitual expressions,"[1] which appeared before the concept of "multiword expressions" (MWEs) was introduced into Chinese linguistics. *Lexic Sea* (Xia and Chen 2009) defines *shuyu* as a fixed expression in a language that is not decomposable and must be understood as a whole and that should include idioms, idiomatic expressions, proverbs, adages, 歇后语 *xiehouyu*,[2] etc. In other words, the composition of these types of expressions is not readily changed.

Indeed, *shuyu*, *xiyu*, and 成语 *chengyu* are all MWEs from a linguistic perspective because they all meet Baldwin et al.'s (2003) definition: (1) decomposable into multiple simplex words and (2) lexically, syntactically, semantically, pragmatically, and/or statistically idiosyncratic. Thus, by definition, it is essential for MWEs as such to be "fixed" no matter whether in Chinese or in English. Nevertheless, there are still many disputes on how to define the term "idiom" accurately, be it from a semantic, grammatic, or pragmatic perspective.

In English linguistics, an idiom is a multiword expression that has a figurative meaning and is comprehended in regard to a common use of that expression that is separate from the literal meaning or definition of the words of which it is made, as is specified in *The Oxford Companion to the English Language* (McArthur 1992: 495): "an idiom is a phrase or a fixed expression that has a figurative, or sometimes literal, meaning. Categorized as formulaic language, an idiom's figurative meaning is different from the literal meaning." Therefore, the words that construct an idiom no longer keep their original meaning or popular sense, while in the process of its formation, it develops a specialized meaning as an entity whose sense is different from the literal meanings of the constituent elements. Thus, an idiom is a metaphor—a term requiring some historical background knowledge, contextual information, and cultural experience. Idioms are mostly used only within a particular

---

[1] Both idiomatic and habitual expressions will be referred to as *shuyu* in this chapter for convenience.

[2] 歇后语 *xiehouyu* is an idiomatic two-part double pun. Part one is akin to a riddle, while part two is usually a double pun based on part one and reveals the metaphorical meaning of part one.

language, where conversational parties must possess common cultural references, so idioms are considered not only part of the language but part of a nation's history, society, and culture.

From the analysis above, one can see that the concept of "idiom" in English is not equivalent to the Chinese *chengyu*, even though the Chinese language base has been called an "idiom knowledge base." Traditionally speaking, *chengyu* in Chinese includes both idioms and instances of *shuyu*. The criteria for distinguishing idioms and *shuyu* need to be both widely acknowledged and taxonomically correct. We defined a Chinese idiom from the following three linguistic perspectives. First, semantically, an idiom cannot be understood literally and must possess a metaphorical meaning; for instance, 狐假虎威 *hujiahuwei* "a fox borrowing the tiger's fierceness," "to bully people by flaunting one's powerful connections" is an idiom, whereas 自作主张 *zizuozhuzhang* "to self-assert" is an instance of *shuyu*.

Second, pragmatically, an idiom is "classic" (i.e., it has a source or origin). Zhou (1994: 29–35) posited that an important criterion to justify an idiom is its "classicality," and proposed that:

> Idioms should be originated from authoritative works such as *The Thirteen Classic Works*,[3] officially or privately written chronicles, masterpieces from Confucian works and collections; therefore they possess 'classicality'. Other idiomatic expressions, such as *shuyus*, proverbs, *xiehouyus*, most proverbs do not possess 'classicality' since they are not authorized and mostly created colloquially and casually from informal expressions.

This is rather important because phrases like 饮马长江 *yinmachangjiang* "to drink one's horse in the Yangtze River" (literally) and "to successfully invade Southern China" (metaphorically), and 斩钉截铁 *zhandingjietie* "to cut a nail and sever iron" (literally) and "to be resolute and decisive without hesitation" (metaphorically) have metaphorical meanings but are not regarded as idioms as well because of their lack of classic origins. Likewise, although phrases like 引首以望 *yinshouyiwang* "to stretch one's neck to look" and 未老先衰 *weilaoxianshuai* "be decrepit before one's age" are from *Mencius* and a well-known poet in the Tang Dynasty (618–907), respectively, they are not regarded as idioms because they lack metaphorical meaning. Wang et al. (2013: 564–571) investigated the "classicality" of Chinese idioms and concluded that the Han Dynasty (202 B.C.–220 A.D.) was the time when most Chinese idioms came into being. This also proves that notions such as the "Han Language" and "Han Nation" are from that period. From the perspective of idiom generation, *The Analects* ranks at the top in terms of "classicality" in Chinese literary history, followed by *Mencius*, *The Book of Songs*, and *Chuang-Tzu*, which confirms that Confucian tradition has a great influence on Chinese culture.

Third, grammatically, an idiom can only serve as a word but not an individual sentence or in parentheses. Therefore, 路遥知马力，日久见人心。 *lu yao zhi ma li,*

[3] *The Thirteen Classic Works* refer to the 13 Confucian works, including *The Book of Poems*, *The Analects*, *Mencius*, etc.

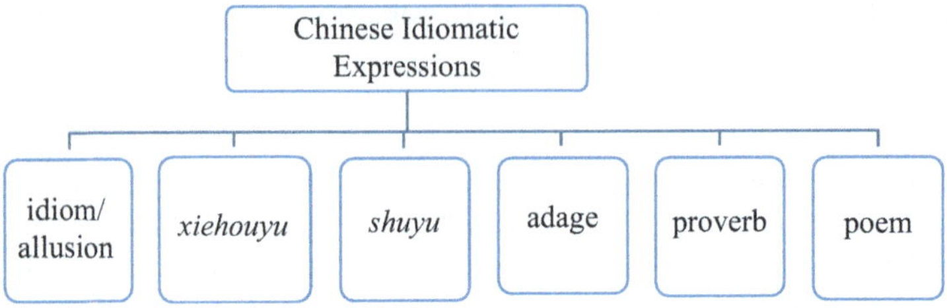

Fig. 8.1 Categories of Chinese idiomatic expressions

ri jiu jian ren xin "As a long road tests a horse's strength, so a long task proves the sincerity of a person" is not an idiom but an adage.

8.2 Construction, Structure, and Properties of the Knowledge Base for Chinese Idiomatic Expressions

In the past three decades, the Institute of Computational Linguistics at Peking University (ICL/PKU) has been dedicated to the construction of knowledge bases of Chinese set phrases, which commenced with building the Chinese Idiom Knowledge Base (CIKB) with the support of the 973 National Basic Research Program of China in 2004. With further progress on the CIKB and participation from other resources, the Knowledge Base for Chinese Idiomatic Expressions (CIEKB) was built in the following years as an expansion of the CIKB and is now being used as a comprehensive lexicon for Chinese idiomatic expressions.

Based on the importance of idiomatic expressions in the Chinese language and culture, an idiom bank with about 6790 entries was included in the most influential Chinese language knowledge base—the Grammatical Knowledge Base (GKB) of Contemporary Chinese—completed by the ICL/PKU, which has been working on language resources for over 30 years and building many knowledge bases of the Chinese language. The CIKB was constructed in 2004 and has collected more than 36,000 instances of *chengyu*, with various attributes added (Wang et al. 2012: 302–310). Later, the CIKB was expanded to include other fixed expressions, such as instances of *xiehouyu*, proverbs, adages, and poems, and has become a complete knowledge base of Chinese idiomatic expressions. The composition of the CIKB is shown in Fig. 8.1.

All the entries in the CIEKB make up a total of 281,830 characters, with 5621 different characters. The number of entries, characters used, and the average length of various Chinese idiomatic expressions are shown in Table 8.1.

Wang et al. (2012: 302–310) investigated the CIKB and found 34,709 instances of *chengyu* that had four characters, accounting for 95% of the total instances. This is in accordance with other linguists' notions, such as Lü and Zhu (1979), who

Table 8.1 Statistics of entries, characters, and average length

	Number of entries	Characters used	Average length
Idioms	5238	20,439	3.9
Xiyu	12,652	50,395	4.1
Proverbs	912	11,880	13.3
Xiehouyu	13,633	150,828	11.1
Adages	1251	15,232	12.4
Poem lines	2137	14,180	6.2

suggested that most Chinese idioms have four characters and are composed in a pattern of antithesis, such as 粗茶淡饭 *cuchadanfan* "coarse tea and plain rice." Wang et al. (2012: 302–310) also argued that in spite of the large number of four-character instances of *chengyu*, there are still some exceptions. The meaning of an idiom usually surpasses the sum of the meanings carried by the few characters, as Chinese idioms are often closely related to the fable, story, or historical account from which they were originally derived. As their constructs have remained stable through history, Chinese idioms do not follow the usual lexical pattern and syntax of the modern Chinese language, which has been reformed many times; they are instead highly compact and resemble Ancient Chinese in many linguistic features.

Basically, the properties of each entry in the CIKB are classified into four categories—lexical, semantic, syntactic, and pragmatic—each of which also includes several fields in its container, the SQL database. Li et al. (2006: 241–248) investigated the frequency and formation of idiom usage in the *People's Daily*, a newspaper that has the largest circulation in China. In most cases, an idiom was used with some intention of the writer or to express certain emotions or attitudes. Thus, by nature, idioms are exaggerative and descriptive and do not belong to the plain type of expression. Therefore, to classify idioms according to their emotional property or descriptive property is important for many practical applications. Wang et al. (2015) conducted experiments on the emotion classification of idioms using a machine learning method and the idioms were categorized into three types—"appreciative (A)," "derogatory (D)," and "neutral (N)."

As culture typically is localized, idioms often can only be understood within the same cultural background; nevertheless, this is not a definite rule because some idioms can overcome cultural barriers and can easily be translated across languages, and their metaphoric meanings can still be deduced. There are three fields of translation for an idiom in the CIKB. Although a literal translation of an idiom does not reflect its metaphorical meaning generally, it is still of value to those who expect to be familiar with the constituent characters and may want to connect its literal meaning with its metaphorical meaning, especially for learners of Chinese as a foreign language.

Syntactic features are also annotated in the CIKB, which were mostly transferred from the GKB, and according to the syntactic functions that they serve in a sentence, they are classified into seven categories, as shown in Table 8.2.

Table 8.2 Features of syntactic functions

ID	Syntactic function	Tag	Entries
1	As a noun	IN	537
2	As a verb	IV	429
3	As an adjective	IA	214
4	As a complement	IC	2560
5	As an adverbial	ID	1178
6	As a classifier	IB	41
7	As a modifier	IM	236

Table 8.3 Allusion attributes and their instances in the CIKB

	Attributes	Instances
Allusion	Entry	269
	Related allusion	58
	Reference allusion	11
	Dynasty	170
	Related characters	178
Origin	Book	269
	Essay	49
	Author	269
	Author's dynasty	269
Other	Quotation	269
	Variant	82

For their "classicality," idioms are closely related to 典故 *diangu* "allusion," which has been constantly referred to throughout Chinese literary history. Lo et al.'s (2013: 1–29) grant from the Chiang Ching-kuo Foundation for International Scholarly Exchange (2009) facilitated the CIKB to be mapped with the Chinese Allusion Knowledge Base (CAKB), and many idioms found their allusions demonstrated in various forms in Chinese classic literary works, such as essays, poems, and novels. Now an idiom entry has extra allusion attributes, as illustrated in Table 8.3.

Among all the idiomatic expressions, idioms and instances of *shuyu* in the CIEKB have relatively complete annotations due to the work done in its first stage of construction when funds were sufficient. Table 8.4 shows the details of their annotation and tagged attributes.

8.3 Nature, Living, History, Culture, and Idiomatic Expressions

A national language is raised in a national society, which is also cradled in its natural environment where geography, climate, transportation, and produce all exert significant influence on the birth and formation of idiomatic expressions. The Chinese people have long held the belief of 天人合一 *tianrenheyi* "the unity of heaven and

Table 8.4 Attributes annotated in the CIEKB

	Attributes			
Categories	Lexical	Semantic	Syntactic	Pragmatic
Idioms	Pinyin,[a] full pinyin,[b] *bianti*,[c] explanation, origin	Synonym, antonym, literal translation, free translation, English equivalent	Part-of-speech (POS), syntactic function	Frequency, emotion
Shuyu	Pinyin, full pinyin, *bianti*, explanation, origin	Synonym, antonym, literal translation, free translation, English equivalent	POS, syntactic function	Frequency, emotion
Proverbs	Pinyin, origin	Category, translation	NULL	NULL
Xiehouyu	Pinyin	Category, tenor, vehicle	NULL	NULL
Adages	Pinyin, author[d]	Translation	NULL	NULL
Poem lines	Pinyin, author, title, dynasty	Theme, translation[e]	NULL	NULL

[a]Pinyin (拼音 "phonetics," or more literally, "spelling sound," or "spelled sound"), or more formally, Hanyu Pinyin (汉语拼音 "Chinese Pinyin"), is currently the most commonly used Romanization system for standard Mandarin. The system is now used in Mainland China, Hong Kong, Macau, parts of Taiwan, Malaysia, and Singapore to teach Mandarin Chinese and to teach Mandarin internationally as a second language. It is also often used to spell Chinese names in foreign publications and can be used to enter Chinese characters on computers and cell phones
[b]Full pinyin is a form of pinyin that replaces the tone marks with numbers 1 to 5 to indicate the five tones of Chinese characters for the convenience of computer processing
[c]*Bianti* is a variant form of an idiom that was caused by random misuse, literary malapropism, etc.
[d]The authors of the adages collected are both Chinese and English
[e]Some of the translation is still in progress

human and that the universe consists of 五行 *wuxing* "the Five Elements." This cognition of nature is undoubtedly reflected in their way of thinking and everyday activities and, furthermore, the formation of their language. In southern China, where the climate is humid and rainfall is abundant, people used to resort to boats and rafts for transportation on rivers and lakes, whereas in the relatively dry north, the 车 *che* "carriage" was the most popular vehicle and appeared in many idiomatic expressions, together with parts of *che*. For instance, the idiom 刻舟求剑 *kezhouqiujian* "to mark the boat in order to find the lost sword" was used in the Zhou Kingdom (now Hubei Province, through which the Yangtze River winds), and the idiom 南辕北辙 *nanyuanbeizhe* "to try to go south by driving the chariot north" was used in the Wei Kingdom (now Shanxi Province and Hebei Province, where Mount Taihang is located). Many name entities, especially geographical locations, are mentioned in idioms. For instance, the two places in the idiom 得陇望蜀 *delongwangshu* "to long for Shu State though already owning Long State" refer to Zhuge Liang's ambition to occupy the whole of today's Sichuan Province after his army took over Long. The idiom 逼上梁山 *bishangliangshan* "to be forced to settle on Mount Liang" is from a popular novel from the Ming Dynasty (1368–1662), 水浒传 *shuihuzhuan* "*Outlaws of the Marsh*," and Mount Liang was the place where all the rebels in the Northern Song Dynasty (960–1127) gathered and fought against the government.

Most Chinese idioms are derived from ancient literature, especially Chinese Classics, and are widely used in written Chinese texts. Some idioms appear in spoken or vernacular Chinese. Usually, a Chinese idiom reflects the moral behind the story from which it was derived (Wang 2011). For instance, the idiom 指鹿为马 *zhiluweima* literally means "to call a stag a horse," and it was based on a historical story. In the late Qin Dynasty (221–207 B.C.), the powerful eunuch Zhao Gao forced the emperor's first son to commit suicide and crowned the second son, Hu Hai. Zhao also attempted to crown himself but was not sure whether the subjects would obey him. One day, he took a stag into the palace and told Hu it was a horse, but Hu said it was obviously a stag. Zhao allowed Hu to ask the subjects standing by whether it was a horse or a stag. Some of the subjects admitted that it was a horse out of fear of Zhao's power, while those who told the truth were persecuted by Zhao and put to death, so the idiom *zhiluweima* metaphorically means "deliberately confounding right and wrong." Another typical example is the idiom mentioned above, *bishangliangshan*. In the Northern Song Dynasty, the coach of the royal guards, Lin Chong, was exiled to Cangzhou, where he was assigned to manage the fodder site, for offending Premiere Gao Qiu. On a snowy night, two men sent by Premiere Gao intended to murder Lin via arson. After learning of their plot accidentally, Lin decided not to be tolerant anymore and resisted, killing the two men. He then went to Mount Liang to join the rebels led by Song Jiang. We conducted statistics on several subjects in the CIEKB and the results are shown in Table 8.5.

Xiehouyu represents metaphorical expressions that are vernacular, witty, and full of imagination. Oral communication embedded with instances of *xiehouyu* is crafty and vivid, which helps boost the language's expressive power. The rhetorical devices employed by instances of *xiehouyu* are metaphor, pun, partial tone, personification, hyperbole, character analysis, antithesis, etc., although many instances resort to combinations; for instance, 竹篮打水–一场空 *zhulan da shui–yi chang kong* "to fetch water with a basket–all in vain" uses an impossible activity to imply an utter disappointment. Pun is used in the *xiehouyu* 吃了秤砣–铁了心 *chi le chengtuo–tie le xin*, where the word *tie* has a double meaning: one indicates a "sliding weight made of iron" and the other means "one's heart has become as hard as iron–being very determined." Things and animals are often personified in instances of *xiehouyus* to embody them with thoughts and emotions. In 黄鼠狼给鸡拜年–没安好心 *huangshulang gei ji bainian–mei an hao xin*, the yellow weasel's bad intention is shown by a New Year's greeting to its prey—the hen—though its pretense poses as good will. For combinations of rhetorical devices, the *xiehouyu* 孔夫子搬家–净是书(输) *kongfuzi banjia–jing shi shu* "Confucius's moving–only books" uses both the partial tone of 书 "book" and 输 "to lose" and hyperbole to imply that one always loses in gambling and competition. Wang et al. (2013) also conducted statistics on the tenors and vehicles that are often used in instances of *xiehouyu*.

Proverbs and adages are meant to teach moral lessons and propagate wisdom, which is true in both Chinese and English. For instance, the English proverb "where there's a will there's a way" has the Chinese equivalent 有志者事竟成 *youzhizhe shi jing cheng*. During the language's long history, some Ancient Chinese proverbs have

Table 8.5 Statistics on natural objects in Chinese idioms

Categories	Meteorology and geography	Nature and climate	Clothing, food, shelter, transportation
Natural objects and their frequencies	日(*ri*, 'sun', 316)	金 (*jin*, 'gold', 313)	丝 (*si*, 'silk', 47)
	月(*yue*, 'moon', 38)	木 (*mu*, 'wood', 298)	棉 (*mian*, 'cotton', 54)
	星 (*xing*, 'star', 93)	水 (*shui*, 'water', 127)	酒 (*jiu*, 'wine', 65)
	天 (*tian*, 'sky', 531)	火 (*huo*, 'fire', 229)	果 (*guo*, 'fruit',18)
	地 (*di*, 'earth', 232)	土 (*tu*, 'soil', 67)	舟 (*zhou*, 'boat', 27)
	人 (*ren*, 'human', 281)	云 (*yun*, 'cloud', 63)	车 (*che*, 'carriage', 12)
	山 (*Shan*, 'mountain', 139)	雨 (*yu*, 'rain', 83)	马 (*ma*, 'horse', 28)
	川 (*chuan*, 'river', 28)	风 (*feng*, 'wind', 73)	辕 (*yuan*, 'bar', 3)
		雪 (*xue*, 'snow', 86)	屋 (*wu*, 'room', 21)
		雷 (*lei*, 'thunder', 27)	房 (*fang*, 'house', 14)
		电 (*dian*, 'lightening', 52)	
		霜 (*shuang*, 'frost', 61)	
		花 (*hua*, 'flower', 32)	

been condensed into instances of *chengyu* and the dividing line between the two has since become obscure; in addition, dedication to the four-character form and structural antithesis has further facilitated their integration. Proverbs that have retained their integrity are those about agriculture and meteorology (i.e., agro-meteorological proverbs), which have been summarized by farmers throughout the ages in observation of farming practices and experience. Concise and lyrical in form, they are easy to understand and memorize and have been passed down from generation to generation. Thus, it is significant to collect agro-meteorological proverbs to facilitate agricultural development in a practical sense. In terms of content, agro-meteorological proverbs can be categorized into (1) season, which is closely associated with the 二十四节气 *ershisi jieqi* "24 solar terms," for example, 立秋一场雨，遍地是黄金。 *liqiu yi chang yu, biandi shi huangjin* "a rainfall in the Autumn Begins will result in gold[4] in the fields"; (2) weather forecasts, for example, 五月南风涨大水。 *wuyue nanfeng zhang dashui* "a south wind in May will bring floods"; and (3) agro-meteorological disaster prevention, for example, 豌豆开花，最怕风

[4]Gold is a metaphor for the harvest color in the fall.

刮。*wandou kaihua, zuipa fenggua* “when the peas are in blossom, a farmer shall be cautious of strong winds.”

Most proverbs related to food acknowledge health and living, such as 饭后百步走, 活到九十九。*fanhou baibu zou, huo dao jiushijiu* “an after-dinner walk of a hundred paces will let you live to ninety-nine years old.” Nevertheless, most knowledge in this regard comes from an important Classic of Chinese medicine—本草纲目 *bencaogangmu, Compendium of Materia Medica*—a book on Chinese herbal medicine. One of the book’s basic principles is that “(herbal) medicine and food are actually the same to health.” For instance, garlic is one of the “five smelly vegetables” that should be eaten on the lunar-calendar date of the beginning of Spring. Ancient Chinese used garlic as an “antidote” to treat epidemic diseases such as typhoid, dysentery, enteritis, and malaria. The book states that garlic can “boost *yang*[5] energy,” and its strong smell can “reach the five inner organs and all the seven apertures in the human head, i.e. eyes, ears, nostrils and mouth, remove ‘cold and humidity’, eliminate pathogenic factors and reduce swelling and ease pain, help with digesting meat.” Thus, Chinese people believe that 大蒜是个宝, 常吃身体好。*dasuan shi ge bao, chang chi shenti hao* “garlic is a treasure and good for your health if you eat it often.” and 糖醋大蒜汤, 降压是秘方。 *tangcu dasuan tang, jiangya shi mifang* “garlic stewed with sugar and vinegar is the secret recipe for reducing blood pressure.” Some proverbs also offer potential hazards to health regarding certain foods or excess intake of certain foods. For instance, 鱼生火, 肉生痰, 青菜豆腐保平安。 *yu sheng huo, rou sheng tan, qingcai doufu bao pingan* “fish incurs inflammation and meat produces sputum, while vegetables and tofu will secure a good condition” and 西瓜祛暑, 多食伤气。 *xigua qu shu, duo shi shang qi* “watermelon is good for relieving summer heat, but too much may compromise your *Chi* (energy force).” The classification of six of the nine categories of proverbs is shown in Table 8.6.

8.4 Conclusion

An idiomatic expression can serve as a word, a phrase, or a sentence syntactically. This is mainly due to the fact that the rules of its composition are inherited historically from speakers’ or writers’ habits of expression rather than grammatically from reasonable analysis. Therefore, idiomatic expressions are usually regarded as the most difficult part of the formalization of a language and may not be identified and analyzed by the grammatical rules available. From a semantic perspective, for

[5] In Chinese philosophy, *yin yang* describes how opposite or contrary forces are actually complementary, interconnected, and interdependent in the natural world and how they give rise to each other as they interrelate to one another. Many tangible dualities (such as light and dark, fire and water, expanding and contracting) are thought of as physical manifestations of the duality symbolized by *yin yang*. This duality lies at the origins of many branches of classical Chinese science and philosophy, as well as its role as a primary guideline of traditional Chinese medicine.

Table 8.6 Proverbs classified into categories based on their pragmatic purposes

Categories	Example	No. of entries
Personal cultivation	家有黄金用斗量, 勿如送儿上学堂。 *jia you huangjin yong dou*[a] *liang, wu ru song er shang xuetang* "sending one's kids to school is better than having *dous* of gold at home"	174
Socialization	一个篱笆三个桩, 一个好汉三个帮。 *yi ge liba san ge zhuang, yi ge haohan san ge bang* "a fence has to be made with pegs. A bawcock has to be made with coagents"	293
Politics	兵宁可百年不用, 不可一日不备。 *bing ningke bainian bu yong, bu ke yi ri bu bei* "military forces of a country may not be used for a 100 years, but cannot be absent for even 1 day"	117
Family relation	知子莫若父 *zhi zi mo ruo fu* "a father knows his son best"	83
Business and trade	井要打深, 艺要学精。 *jing Yao da shen, yi yao xue jing* "a well needs to be deep, while a trade needs to be proficient"	120
Education	读万卷书不如行万里路。 *du wan juan shu bu ru xing wan li lu* "it's better to travel 10,000 miles than to read 10,000 books"	79

[a]*Dou* was a measure of volume for rice, grain, etc. in ancient China. One *dou* is approximately 10 L

each constituent in an idiomatic expression that does not reflect its meaning as a whole, the semantic role labeling of its constituents poses a great challenge to natural language processing (NLP) tasks (Fellbaum 2007). Moreover, because of the huge number of idiomatic expressions, few lexicons can include them completely. Contrary to common knowledge that language is a living thing, idioms do not readily change as time passes. Some idioms gain and lose favor in popular literature or speeches, but they rarely have any actual shift in their constructs as long as they do not become extinct. In real life, people also have a natural tendency to manipulate their way of expression by overexaggerating what they mean or overdescribing what they have seen or heard, and this in turn gives birth to new idioms.

Acknowledgments Our work was supported by the National High Technology Research and Development Program of China (863 Program) (No. 2015AA015402) and the National Natural Science Foundation (Grant No. 61772278).

References

Baldwin, Timothy, Colin Bannard, Takaaki Tanaka, and Dominic Widdows. 2003. An empirical model of multiword expression decomposability. In *Proceedings of the ACL 2003 Workshop on Multiword Expressions: Analysis, Acquisition and Treatment*, 89–96. Sapporo, Japan.

Fellbaum, Christiane. 2007. *Idioms and collocations: Corpus-based linguistic and lexicographic studies (Research in corpus and discourse)*. London: Continuum International Publishing Group Ltd.

Li, Yun, Huarui Zhang, Hongjun Wang, and Shiwen Yu. 2006. Investigation on the frequency and formation of idioms in the *People's Daily*. In *Proceedings of the 7th Chinese Lexicon and Semantics Workshop*, 241–248. Taiwan.

Lo, Feng-ju, Kazuko Saka, Binggui Jiang, Shiwen Yu, Lei Wang, and Baobao Chang. 2013. Phase-based pedagogical syllabus design of multi-lingual Chinese idiom knowledge base. *Chinese Teaching Research of Taiwan* 6(1):1–29.

Lü, Shuxiang, and Dexi Zhu. 吕叔湘, 朱德熙. 1979. *Speech on grammar and rhetoric 语法修辞讲话*. Beijing: China Youth Press.

McArthur, Tom. 1992. *The Oxford companion to the English language*. London: Oxford University Press.

Wang, Lei. 2011. *1,000 idioms for Chinese learners*. Beijing: Peking University Press.

Wang, Lei, Shiwen Yu, Xuefeng Zhu, and Yun Li. 2012. Chinese idiom knowledge base for Chinese information processing. Paper presented at the *13th Workshop, CLSW 2012*, 302–310. Wuhan, China.

Wang, Lei, Shujing Li, Weiguang Qu, and Shiwen Yu. 2013. Construction and application of the knowledge base of Chinese multiword expressions. Paper presented at the *14th Workshop, CLSW 2013*, 564–571. Zhengzhou, China.

Wang, Lei, Shiwen Yu, Zhimin Wang, Weiguang Qu, and Houfeng Wang. 2015. Emotional classification of Chinese idioms based on Chinese idiom knowledge base. Paper presented at the *16th Workshop, CLSW 2015*, 197–203. Beijing, China.

Xia, Zhengnong, Zhili Chen. 夏征农, 陈至立 (eds.). 2009. *Lexic Sea 辞海* (6th ed.). Shanghai: Shanghai Lexicographical Publishing House.

Zhou, Jian. 周荐. 1994. *On the classicality and nonclassicality of Shuyu 熟语的经典性与非经典性*. *Research on Chinese* 3:29–35.

Chapter 9
Lexical Knowledge Representation and Semantic Composition of E-HowNet

Yueh-Yin Shih, Wei-Yun Ma, and Keh-Jiann Chen

Abstract Extended HowNet (E-HowNet) is a frame-based entity-relation model extended from HowNet that defines lexical sense to achieve natural language understanding. The major extension features include the following: (a) word senses are defined by either primitives or any well-defined concepts and conceptual relations; (b) semantic relations are explicitly expressed; (c) uniform representation of content words, function words, and phrases; (d) semantic composition and decomposition capacities; and (e) near-canonical representations for lexical senses and phrasal senses. Adapted from the HowNet ontology, the framework of the E-HowNet ontology has demonstrated lexical representation and semantic composition. Strategies for semantic role labeling were also addressed since this is a crucial task for automatic semantic composition. The goal of achieving natural language understanding should be accomplished after future improvement and evolution of the current E-HowNet model.

Keywords Word sense · Ontology · Semantic composition · Sematic role labeling

9.1 Introduction

The purpose of designing a lexical semantic representation model, in this case Extended HowNet (E-HowNet) (Chen et al. 陳克健等 2004; Chen et al. 2005a; Chen et al. 陳怡君等 2005b; Chung et al. 2007; Huang et al. 2008; Ma and Shih 2018), is for natural language understanding, particularly mechanical natural language understanding. E-HowNet is a frame-based entity-relation model extended from HowNet (Dong 1999; Dong and Dong 2006) that defines lexical senses to achieve compositional semantics. When one says that a sentence is "understood," this means that the concepts and the conceptual relationships expressed by the sentence are unambiguously identified, and one can make correct inferences

Y.-Y. Shih (✉) · W.-Y. Ma · K.-J. Chen
Institute of Information Science, Taipei, Taiwan
e-mail: yuehyin@iis.sinica.edu.tw; ma@iis.sinica.edu.tw; kchen@iis.sinica.edu.tw

C.-R. Huang et al. (eds.), *Chinese Language Resources*, Text, Speech and Language Technology 49, https://doi.org/10.1007/978-3-031-38913-9_9

and/or responses. Therefore, computer systems should know the sense similarity and dissimilarity of words and sentences. Achieving the goal of natural language understanding will require the support of ontologies that can provide the following functions:

- Identifies synonymous concepts and measures the similarity distance between two concepts
- Knows the shared semantic features and feature differences between two concepts
- Provides unique indices for each concept, such that associated knowledge can be coded and accessed
- Provides logical inferences through the conceptual property inheritance system
- Provides dynamic concept decomposition and composition mechanisms

None of the currently available ontologies provide all of the above functions, and so far, there has been little research on applying HowNet to semantic composition. However, HowNet has established an online common-sense knowledge base that has revealed inter-conceptual relations and inter-attribute relations of concepts as connoted in Chinese lexicons and their English equivalents. Each concept is represented and understood by its definition and association links to other concepts. Compared with WordNet (Fellbaum 1998), HowNet's architecture provides richer information apart from hyponymy relations. It also enriches relational links between words via encoded feature relations. The advantages of HowNet are the inherent properties of concepts that are derived from encoded feature relations in addition to hypernym concepts, as well as information regarding conceptual differences between different concepts and morph-semantic structures, which are encoded. HowNet's advantages make it an effective electronic dictionary that partially achieves the abovementioned functions.

The function of identifying synonymous concepts and measuring similarity distance between two concepts is achieved by the conceptual expressions of lexical senses. The function of knowing the shared semantic features and feature differences between two concepts is achieved if all lexical senses are well defined and an associated common-sense knowledge base is available. The third function, providing unique indices for each concept, such that associated knowledge can be coded and accessed, is hardly achieved by HowNet, since all lexical senses are expressed by primitive concepts and not all concepts can be uniquely identifiable by lexical expressions, in particular, without compositional semantic capabilities. The fourth function of logical inferences is achieved by the taxonomy of concepts with inheritance properties and implicit/explicit relation expressions, which requires a great deal of knowledge-engineering work to achieve effective results. The last but most important function of providing dynamic concept decomposition and composition mechanisms is lacking in most of the current ontological systems, including HowNet, as there is no mechanism to decompose complex concepts into primitive expressions nor to compose phrasal senses from lexical senses. Nonetheless, HowNet has been applied to the researches of word similarity calculation (Liu and

Li 劉群, 李素建 2002), machine translation (Dong 1999), and information retrieval (Dorr et al. 2000).

We therefore proposed a framework extending HowNet called E-HowNet to achieve the above functions using our design. In Sect. 9.2, an overview of E-HowNet will be introduced. Section 9.3 will address the mechanisms that have achieved the major functions of language understanding. The related task of semantic role labeling will be discussed in Sect. 9.4. Section 9.5 will present the conclusion and future work.

9.2 Overview of E-HowNet

As mentioned, E-HowNet is a frame-based entity-relation model for representing lexical semantics, which intends to achieve the function of compositional semantics. In E-HowNet, all concepts are either primitive concepts or defined (expressed) by simpler concepts (i.e., either primitive concepts or basic concepts) in terms of an entity-relation model. A primitive concept has an English equivalent beside it (e.g., {read|讀}), whereas a basic concept is expressed by a Chinese word and its English translation pair, which is further defined by primitive concepts (e.g., {狗|dog} defined as {livestock|牲畜:telic = {TakeCare|照料:patient = {family|家庭, agent = {~}}}}).

The concepts form a hierarchical structure, and the associated property or knowledge regarding a particular concept can be directly accessed or encoded through its definition or indirectly inherited from its ancestors. Furthermore, the hierarchical taxonomy also indicates the semantic distance between two concepts. Unlike conventional taxonomies, which do not provide the exact semantic similarities and dissimilarities of two concepts, E-HowNet's definitions of concepts show not only the semantic similarities of two concepts but also the semantic differences between them. For instance, <teacher> and <student> are both <human> and hence inherit the properties of <human>. They also participate in the event of <teach>, but the semantic difference is that they are denoted by different semantic roles and therefore inherit different properties of their semantic relations. Thus, each definition is respectively expressed as 老師 *laoshi* "teacher" def = {human|人: telic = {teach|教:agent = {~}}} and 學生 *xuesheng* "student" def = {human|人: telic = {teach|教: target = {~}}}.

E-HowNet also accommodates existing ontologies, such as WordNet and Wikipedia. We established links between E-HowNet concepts and WordNet synsets; thus, WordNet synsets were used as an alternative intermediate representational language. In the future, we will link the events of E-HowNet to the event frames of FrameNet (Baker et al. 1998).

9.2.1 Ontology of Concepts

The E-HowNet ontology is formed by entity taxonomy and relation taxonomy, in which each word sense is a node of the taxonomy and is expressed by an E-HowNet expression, and synonyms or near synonyms are expressed by the same expression. Therefore, E-HowNet ontology was formed by all lexical senses as well as primitive and basic concepts in a hierarchical order. We adopted and extended approximately 2600 primitives from HowNet to form the top-level ontology of E-HowNet, which includes two types of subtrees: entities and relations. Entities indicate concepts that have substantial content. By contrast, relations play the role of linking semantic relations between entities. Any concept inherits all the fundamental features of its hypernym and must have at least one feature that its hypernym does not own. The top levels of the E-HowNet ontology are shown in Fig. 9.1, and a complete taxonomy can be found on our website.[1]

The entity subtree is formed by the event subtree and the object subtree. Events further branch out into acts and states. Objects include thing, time, space, and relation. Relation concepts such as color, shape, and size may also play the role of subject/object syntactically and are considered a subtype of object entities called relation-entities.

Relation-entities have the same expression patterns as other entities and are expressed as {color|顏色}, {shape|形狀}, {size|大小}, etc. They form a subtree of {relation|關聯} under the node of {object|物體}. The {relation|關聯} subtree and the relation subtree (i.e., semantic roles) correspond to each other but have different usages and are different subtrees in the E-HowNet ontology.

Some of the relation-entities also serve to describe the relations between two entities, which is a closed set and all major relations are included in this set. This set of relations also forms a hierarchical structure that includes attributes and functions. The attributes include the semantic roles of RoleForEntity, RoleForObject, and RoleForEvent. All semantic roles are binary relations rel(x,y), with the parameter x usually being the head of a constituent and y being the dependent daughter. The relation rel(x,y) is written as rel(x) = {y}, which means "rel of x is y." For instance, agent(eat) = {dog} means "agent of eating is a dog." The sense of the event "dog eats" is expressed as {eat: agent = {dog}}, where "agent = {dog}" is an abbreviation of agent(~) = {dog} and ~ denotes the head concept, which is "eat" in this example. A relation rel(x) = {y} is considered a mapping from domain(x) to range (y). The parameter types of domains and ranges depend on the relation type. The parameters of ranges are called relation-values. For instance, the color-values are {blue|藍}, {red|紅}, {green|綠}, and so forth. Participant roles of events are RoleForEvents, such as agent, theme, goal, etc. Their range values are determined by the head events.

A function is a special kind of relation that maps concept/concepts to a specific concept in the same domain. Functions are not like semantic roles used to establish

[1] http://ckip.iis.sinica.edu.tw/taxonomy/

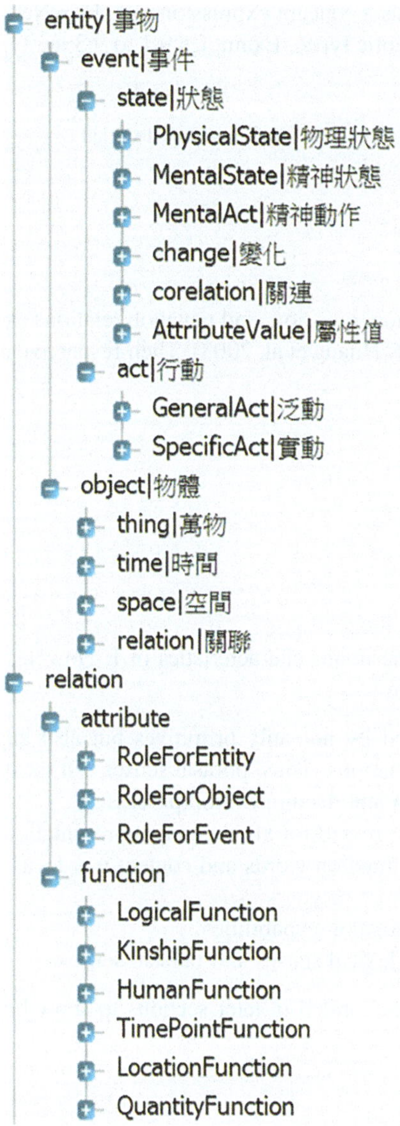

Fig. 9.1 Top levels of the E-HowNet ontology

the thematic relation or property attribute between two entities, but instead they transform a concept into a new concept. Functions have a compositional property. New functions can be constructed by the composition of many functions of the same type. For instance, the kinship function of father(father(x)) denotes "grandfather of x" and the direction function of {north({east({place|地方})})} denotes "the direction of north-east." Both are compositions of basic functions. Function expressions are written as function(x) and treated as a concept expression in E-HowNet. Different functions may have different semantic types. Examples 9.1 to 9.3 are typical:

(9.1)	車燈 *chedeng* "vehicle headlight"
	def: {part({LandVehicle|車}): telic={illuminate|照射: instrument={~}}}
(9.2)	岳父 *yuefu* "wife's father, father-in-law"
	def: {father({wife|妻子})}
(9.3)	東台灣 *dongtaiwan* "Eastern Taiwan"
	def: {EastPart({台灣|Taiwan})}

In E-HowNet, we also regarded union, question, and negation relations as logical functions (Chen et al. 陳怡君等 2005b; Huang et al. 2008). Their respective usage is shown in Examples 9.4 to 9.6.

(9.4)	進出*jinchu* "get in and out"
	def: {union({GoInto|進入},{GoOut|出去})}
(9.5)	為何*weihe* "why"
	def: cause={Ques|疑問}
(9.6)	不悅 *buyue* "be frown on"
	def: {not({joyful|喜悅})}

In conclusion, the following are the major characteristics of E-HowNet, which makes it different from other ontologies:

- Word senses (concepts) are defined by not only primitives but also any well-defined concepts and conceptual relations. Thus, phrasal senses can be similarly expressed by semantic composition and decomposition processes.
- Semantic relations are explicitly expressed for all meaning representations.
- Uniform representation model for function words and content words, as well as phrases.
- Semantic composition and decomposition capabilities.
- Near-canonical representations for lexical senses and phrasal senses.

The above characteristics will be elaborated in later sections to show how they were achieved.

9.3 Lexical Knowledge Representation and Semantic Composition

E-HowNet is an entity-relation model in which entities indicate objects or events and relations are semantic links between entities, as described above. Since concepts can be understood and represented from different angles and each annotator may focus on different aspects, guidelines for sense definitions will be provided in the following section to achieve near-canonical representations.

9.3.1 Principles of Sense Definitions

The meanings of a concept are supported by its associated concepts, including its formal properties, constituents, purposes, relations to other concepts, etc. However, for the sense definition of a concept, it is not possible to encode all its associated relations. The principles of sense definition are necessary and will be addressed as follows.

A concept is defined by its hypernym and prominent properties. *The Generative Lexicon* (Pustejovsky 1995) presents a novel and exciting theory of lexical semantics that addresses the problem of the "multiplicity of word meanings," that is, how we are able to give an infinite number of senses to words with finite meanings. The first formally elaborated theory of a generative approach to word meaning, it lays the foundation for an implemented computational treatment of word meanings that connects explicitly to compositional semantics.

Following the ideas in *The Generative Lexicon*, in E-HowNet a concept is defined, the immediate hypernym of that concept is the first to be identified, and then its most important features are encoded, which serves to differentiate this concept from other concepts. Pustejovsky (1995) defined the qualia structure as the modes of explanation associated with a word or phrase in language. The qualia of an object includes agentive, telic, constitutive, and formal properties. Agentive expresses the factors involved in the origin or "bringing about" of the object. Telic expresses the purpose and function of the object. Constitutive denotes the relations between the object and its constituents, such as its materials, parts, and components. Formal expresses the properties that distinguish the object within a larger domain, such as its shape, magnitude, and color. In E-HowNet, the qualia structure is used as the major feature of a nominal-type concept. Examples 9.7 to 9.10 respectively show the usage of agentive, telic, constitutive, and formal properties:

(9.7)	早產兒 *zaochaner* "premature baby"
	def: {human|人:age={child|少兒}, agentive={labour|臨產:TimeFeature={early|早}}}
(9.8)	狗食 *goushi* "dog food"
	def: {food|食品:telic={feed|餵:target={狗|dog}}}
(9.9)	木棍 *mugun* "wooden stick"
	def: {棍子|stick:material={wood|木}}
(9.10)	彩霞 *caixia* "rosy clouds"
	def: {CloudMist|雲霧:color={colored|彩}}

There are two different types of attribute features. One is the simplex attribute type and the other is the complex relative clause type. The simplex attribute is a feature-value type and the value is expressed by some discrete elements. The constitutive and formal properties can be represented by simple attribute-value pairs (i.e., the Relation = {Concept} pair, as in Examples 9.7 to 9.10). For the complex relative clause type, the attribute relation is an eventive feature. The telic and agentive properties are usually represented by eventive features, which are event frames. For instance, the concepts of 老師 *laoshi* "teacher" and 學生 *xuesheng* "student" may be defined and differentiated as 老師 *laoshi* "teacher" def = {human|人: telic = {teach|教:agent = {~}}} and 學生 *xuesheng* "student" def = {human|人: telic = {teach|教: target = {~}}}.

Event-type concepts are also defined by their hypernym event type, and brotherhood concepts are differentiated by their event frame elements, which include participant roles and adjuncts as well as their semantic restrictions. For instance, lexical entries such as 有勞 *youlao* "sorry to trouble you," 強求 *qiangqiu* "forcibly request," and 苛求 *keqiu* "make excessive demands" are all defined by the hypernym {request|要求} but differentiated by SpeakerAttitude, manner, and degree. Example 9.11a–c are their respective E-HowNet sense representations:

(9.11a)	有勞 *youlao* "sorry to trouble you"
	def: {request|要求:SpeakerAttitude={modest|謙}}
(9.11b)	強求*qiangqiu* "forcibly request"
	def: {request|要求:manner={force|強迫}}
(9.11c)	苛求*keqiu* "make excessive demands"
	def: {request|要求:degree={more|較}}

The above examples are all defined by the same head concept, so they share the same event frame of {request|要求}, which has the participant roles of agent, target, content, etc.

Primitives, basic concepts, and relations are used to define new concepts. HowNet uses a set of primitive semantic units called sememes to define concepts. For instance, 狗 *gou* "dog" is defined as def: {livestock|牲畜}. However, using primitives only to define concepts causes information to degrade and fails to establish some important ontological relations between concepts. For instance, HowNet defines 獅子狗 *shizigou* "Beijing dog" as def: {livestock|牲畜} as well, in which the hyponymy relation to "dog" is missing. Thus, following HowNet, we adopted an entity-relational model to define word senses. However, a concept defined by basic or simpler concepts instead of semantic primitives is allowed, and all attribute relations are explicitly expressed. The well-defined simpler concepts are called basic concepts, which consist of a Chinese word head followed by its English equivalent. For instance, in E-HowNet 獅子狗 *shizigou* "Beijing dog" is defined as def: {狗|dog:source = {北京|Beijing}}. With the basic concept "狗|dog" as the head sense, it denotes the hypernym-hyponym relation between "dog" and "Beijing dog." Hence, the definitions in E-HowNet are self-organized as an ontological network.

To achieve unambiguous and language-independent definitions, E-HowNet adopted WordNet synsets as an alternative vocabulary for conceptual indexing and representation, as shown in Example 9.12a–c.

(9.12) 證物 *zhengwu* "exhibit as evidence"

a. Original E-HowNet definition

def:{inanimate|無生物: domain={police|警},
telic={prove|證明: instrument={~}}}.

b. Definition in terms of WordNet Synset id-numbers

def: {[00010572N]: domain={[06093563N]},
telic={[00686544V+01816870V]: instrument={~}}}.

c. Definition in terms of WordNet Synset concepts

def: {<substance>: domain={<police>},
telic= {<testify+corroborate>:instrument={~}}}.

Multilevel representations: High-level representations can be decomposed into primitive representations. E-HowNet adopted the set of HowNet sememes (semantic primitives) for ground-level definitions. In E-HowNet, new concepts can be defined by any well-defined concepts and dynamically decomposed into lower-level representations until a ground-level definition is reached, in which all features in the definitions are sememes. For instance, the top-level definition of 文學系 *wenxuexi* "department of literature" is like Example 9.13a. Since the concept {科系|department} is a well-defined basic concept, as in Example 9.13b, the above definition can be further extended into a primitive-level definition, as in Example 9.13c. Note that the feature of "telic = {and({teach|教},{study|學習}): location = {~}}" in Example 9.13c is redundant and will be eliminated after the feature unification process.

(9.13) 文學系 *wenxuexi* "department of literature"

a. def: {科系|department: predication={and({teach|教},{study|學習}): location={~},
content={literature|文}}}

b. def: {part({InstitutePlace|場所:qualification={HighRank|高等},
telic={and({teach|教},{study|學習}):location={~},
domain={education|教育}}}))}

c. def: {part({InstitutePlace|場所:qualification={HighRank|高等},
telic={and({teach|教},{study|學習}):location={~},
domain={education|教育},content={literature|文}}}))}

Such a multilevel representational framework makes sense definitions more precise. It also retains the advantage of using semantic primitives to achieve canonical sense representation. Additional advantages of multilevel representations are listed below:

- All concepts are expressed by a limited number of basic concepts.
- More precise definitions can be achieved using high-level concepts to define complex concepts.
- Basic concepts are more concise for the human cognitive process.
- Higher-level representations can be dynamically decomposed into primitive representations.

Table 9.1 The sense spectrum for syntactic categories

Function words		Content words
Relational senses	←――――――――――――――――→	Content senses
de, prepositions, conjunctions, adverbs	………….,…………	adjectives, verbs, nouns

Table 9.2 Examples of E-HowNet representations

Word	PoS	Definition
因為*yinwei* 'because'	Cb(conjunction)	cause = {}
下雨*xiayu* 'rain'	VA(intransitive verb)	{下雨| ToRain}
衣服*yifu* 'clothes'	Na(common noun)	{clothing|衣物}
都*dou* 'all'	Da(adverb)	quantity = {complete|整}
濕*shi* 'wet'	VH(state verb)	{wet|濕}
了*le* 'ASP'	Ta(particle)	aspect = {Vachieve|達成}

- Higher-level representations are more readable as more information can be inherited from higher-level concepts than from lower-level concepts.
- Better and easier knowledge management.

9.3.2 Uniform Representation of Content Words and Function Words for Semantic Composition

The sense of a natural-language sentence is the result of the composition of the senses of constituents and their relations. Lexical senses are processing units for sense composition. Conventional linguistic theories classify words into content words and function words. Content words denote entities and function words mainly mark grammatical functions. However, there is no clear-cut distinction between the two classes, especially for the Chinese language.

In Chinese, to identify a word as a function word means it denotes more relational sense than content sense. For instance, 被 *bei* "by" is a preposition that introduces an agent role/relation without additional content sense. As well, the morpheme "-ly," in a word like "gently" establishes a "manner" relation between its content sense "gentle" and the action indicated by the sentential head. By contrast, content words, such as verbs and nouns, have more content senses and less (or underspecified) relational senses. A verb denotes an event as well as the senses of its event roles. A noun refers to objects while playing the role of verb arguments or modifiers of nouns. Therefore, E-HowNet treats both nouns and verbs as entities joined by relations of semantic roles. Thus, we claim that all word interpretations involve two types of senses: relation sense and content sense. However, different syntactic categories could well be said to have different degrees of these senses. A spectrum could be diagrammed as in Table 9.1 (Chen et al. 陳怡君等 2005b).

For a lexical knowledge representation system, it is necessary to encode both relation senses and content senses in a uniform framework. E-HowNet is an entity-relation model that achieves representations of content/function word senses and sentence/phrasal senses. Some E-HowNet representations of word senses are shown in Table 9.2, and their sense representations are elaborated in the following section:

9.3.3 Basic Composition Process

In a semantic composition process, if two constituents are syntactically dependent, their E-HowNet representations will be unified according to the following basic composition process:

If constituent *B* is a dependency daughter of constituent *A* (i.e., *B* is a modifier or an argument of *A*), then unify the semantic representation of *A* and *B* using the following steps:

Step 1: Disambiguate the senses of *A* and *B*.

Step 2: Identify the semantic relation between *A* and *B* to derive relation $(A) = \{B\}$.

Step 3: Unify the semantic representation of *A* and *B* by inserting relation $(A) = \{B\}$ as a sub-feature of *A*.

How the lexical concepts are combined into the sense representation of a sentence is demonstrated in Example 9.14.

(9.14)	因為下雨,	衣服都濕了。
	Yinwei__xiayu,	yifu__dou__shi__le.
	because__ rain,	cloth__all__wet__ASP.
	Because of raining,	*clothes are all wet*

Table 9.3 Examples of E-HowNet event frames

Event type	Prototypical semantic role
exist|存在	LOCATION{location},THEME: *thing exists*{theme} /*LOCATION有可能是topic, 但不視為argument*/
ComeToWorld|問世	THEME{theme},LOCATION{location}
appear|出現	LOCATION{location,source},THEME: *thing appearing*{theme}
enjoy|享受	ACTOR{experiencer}, GOAL{content}
happen|發生	THEME: *happing to*{theme}, GOAL: *accident,event*{content}
function|活動	THEME{theme}
pregnant|懷孕	ACTOR{agent,causer},THEME{theme}
GoOn|繼續 (dual)	ACT ACTOR{agent,causer},GOAL: *thing that continues*{content}
	STATE THEME{theme}
like|愛惜	ACTOR{experiencer},GOAL: *entity ACTOR cherishes*{content}

In the above sentence, 濕 *shi* "wet," 衣服 *yifu* "clothes," and 下雨 *xiayu* "rain" are content words, while 都 *dou* "all," 了 *le* "ASP," and 因為 "because" are function words. The E-HowNet sense representations of these words are shown in Table 9.3. The difference between their representation is that function words start with a relation, but content words have underspecified relations. If a content word plays the dependency daughter role of a head concept, the relation between the head concept and this content word will be established after the parsing process. Suppose that the following dependency structure and semantic relations are derived after parsing, as shown in the sentence in Example 9.15.

(9.15) S(reason:VP(Head:Cb:因為|dummy:VA:下雨)|theme:NP(Head:Na:衣服) | quantity: Da: 都 | Head:Vh:濕|particle:Ta:了)。

After the unification process, the following semantic composition result in Example 9.16 is derived. The representations of the dependency daughters became the feature attributes of the sentential head "wet|濕."

(9.16) def: {wet|濕: theme={clothing|衣物}, aspect={Vachieve|達成}, quantity={complete|整}, cause={下雨| ToRain }}.

In Example 9.15, the function word 因為 *yinwei* "because" links the relation of "cause" between the head concept 濕 *shi* "wet" and 下雨 *xiayu* "rain." The result of the composition is expressed as cause(wet|濕) = {下雨| ToRain}. For the sake of notational convenience, the head argument of the relation was omitted. Therefore, cause(wet|濕) = {下雨| ToRain} is expressed as cause = {下雨| ToRain}; theme (wet|濕) = {clothing|衣物} is expressed as theme = {clothing|衣物}, and so on.

The next section will address the issue regarding semantic role identification in more detail.

9.4 Semantic Role Labeling

As a matter of fact, there is an unlimited number of possible semantic relations between two constituents, from coarse-grained to fine-grained relations, and a constituent may have different relations with other constituents. However, practically, we needed a set of a limited number of semantic roles and unique labels for each constituent. Therefore, how to establish a reasonable set of semantic roles and determine the best role labeling were our major considerations.

9.4.1 Establishing a Reasonable Set of Semantic Roles

Dowty (1989) mentioned four characteristics of thematic roles for events and we adopted and extended them to include roles for adjuncts and object-related roles, as well as derived the following design criteria to better characterize sets of semantic roles.

- Completeness: Every constituent (dependent daughter) of every semantic head may be assigned some semantic roles to describe its semantic relations to its head.
- Uniqueness: Every constituent of every semantic head may have one semantic role that best describes its semantic relations to its head.
- Distinctness: Every constituent of every semantic head is distinguished from the other constituents by the role it is assigned, except adjuncts.
- Independence: Each role is given a consistent semantic definition that applies to all verbs and all situations.

We used two sets of semantic roles because of the different purposes of syntactic-major and semantic-major tree structure representations. The Sinica Treebank[2] performs skeletal parsing, showing syntactic structures and coarse-grained semantic information (i.e., each constituent of a tree structure is tagged with its part-of-speech and semantic role). There are 60 different semantic roles, including five object-related roles. E-HowNet consists of definitions for lexical senses, where more than 100 semantic roles are used to describe the sense relations. The mapping between the two sets of semantic roles was established to convert between coarse- and fine-grained semantic roles. For instance, the *theme* of Treebank can be mapped to a fine-grained role in E-HowNet like *possession*, *PatientProduct*, and *ContentProduct*. Conversely, these fined-grained relations can also be replaced with a coarse-grained Treebank role, *theme*, if necessary.

Semantic roles in E-HowNet are arranged from coarse-grained to fine-grained relations in a hierarchical way and are used to represent basic argument structures for more than 100,000 word senses in the CKIP dictionary, which justified the design criteria of completeness for semantic roles. Our corpus-based approach guaranteed the completeness and independence criteria empirically. This hierarchical approach resolved the uniqueness problem, since fine-grained semantic roles may better describe multiple semantic relations. As for distinctness, we adopted the thematic roles of major theories, which satisfied the criteria of distinctness and independence. Details of our definition of each semantic role can be found in our technical report (CKIP 2015).

[2]http://turing.iis.sinica.edu.tw/treesearch/

9.4.2 Guidelines for Pursuing Role Assignment

Four factors determined the semantic role of a constituent. The first factor was verb sense, from which the event frame was derived (i.e., the semantic roles of arguments were specified). Event frames were coded for all verb/event primitives, resulting in 1290 event frames created in E-HowNet. Every eventive lexical item followed the event frame of its hypernym event concept. Some examples of the E-HowNet event frames are shown in Table 9.3. For a complete version, please refer to technical report no. 15-01 (CKIP 2015).

The second factor was the major sense of the constituent. Many adjuncts' semantic roles or modifiers of semantic roles or modifiers of objects were self-describing, such as temporal, aspectual, color, weight, etc. Furthermore, in some cases the argument roles in an event frame were underspecified so they needed to be refined by the sense of arguments. As exemplified in Example 9.17, a noun with or without the [+volitive] feature could determine whether a role should be an agent or a causer.

(9.17)	聯合國 決定	vs.	天候狀況 決定
	lianheguo__jueding	vs.	tianhou__zhuangkuang_jueding
	UN__decide	vs.	climate__situation__decide
	the UN decides	vs.	*the condition of climate decides*
Semantic Role: agent[+volitive] head verb		vs. causer[-volitive] head verb	

The third factor was prepositions, a relation marker, as shown in Example 9.18, which specified the direction of a pronoun. Similarly, markers could specify the range of a location and transform an experiencer into a theme.

(9.18)	朝 我 看
	chao__wo__kan
	toward__me__look
	look toward me
Semantic Role: PP-direction head verb	

The fourth factor was the construction pattern. As a matter of fact, construction patterns specified the order of the semantic roles. As exemplified in Example 9.19, a deep semantic structure was determined by the construction patterns and surface word senses.

(9.19)	因為 工作 繁重 所致
	yinwei__gongzuo__fanzhong__suozhi
	because__workload__heavy__caused by
	caused by the heavy workloads
Syntactic Structure: reason theme head verb-VH	
Semantic Structure: cause={工作繁重}	

The guidelines for semantic role labeling are as follows. For each phrase, the syntactic head was determined and was assigned the semantic role head. Then, for each dependent daughter of the head, the semantic relations between the head and the dependent daughter was found by referring to the event frame of the head verb, the semantic type of the noun phrase, the semantic features of the prepositions, and additional framing provided by construction patterns.

9.4.3 Difficulties and Solutions

In real implementations of semantic composition, some semantic relations were indirect and hard to identify. Some difficulties that were noticed will be discussed as follows.

Filling semantic gaps by automatic deduction. Semantic elements were frequently omitted from surface sentences. Since we encoded the event frames and the object-attribute relations in the E-HowNet system, we were able to restore the sense omissions, as shown in Example 9.20. Because the semantic role "color" is an attribute of objects, this implies that an object was missing in Example 9.20, and thus it was known that the target "like" must be recovered from the context.

(9.20) 我喜歡紅的 *wo xihuan hong de* "I like the red (something)"
def: {FondOf|喜歡:experiencer={speaker|說話者}, target={object|物體:color={red|紅}}}

Setting roles to convert between the surface and deep semantic role labeling. We also encountered the difficulty of whether to determine a role from the viewpoint of the surface form or of deep sense. This usually took place in the sentences with the head verb of a static viewpoint of acts, such as 受害 *shouhai* "suffer," 睡著 *shuizhao* "fall asleep," etc. By identifying the verbs of the static viewpoints of acts in prototypical actions and markers/complements, we returned the static viewpoint of acts to actions while regaining their event frames. For instance, 受害 *shouhai* "suffer" can be analyzed as an intransitive state with the PoS of VH and an argument theme, or a transitive act joined with a passive marker, represented as [受 (passive marker) 害 (VC)], which has the event frame of agent and patient.

9.5 Conclusion and Future Work

HowNet proposed a new model to represent lexical knowledge, inspiring us to expand this framework to achieve the task of mechanical natural language understanding. E-HowNet confines each concept to a semantic type and defines the relation between these types. Hence, we created a consistent approach to representing concepts so that computers can process and relate meanings.

Semantic composition is a crucial component of language understanding. We proposed a uniform representation system for both function words and content words to achieve semantic compositions, such that meaning representations for morphemes, words, phrases, and sentences could be uniformly represented under the same framework. New concepts could be defined by previously known concepts and definitions could be dynamically decomposed into lower-level representations until the ground-level definition was reached. Near-canonical representation thus could be achieved at a suitable level of representation for synonyms or paraphrases. We also suggested compositional functions to extend the expression of new concepts and make word and phrase definitions more detailed and accurate. Since sense omission increases the potential for misunderstandings, we tried to fill semantic gaps by automatic inference through the framework of E-HowNet.

There are still many obstacles to achieving the goal of automatically extracting knowledge from language. Apart from sense disambiguation, discord between syntactic structures and their associated semantic representations is another critical problem. To reveal all fine-grained semantic relations for constituents at different levels of syntactic structure, we embarked on a new project called E-HowNet SemBank annotation. Gap filling processes, as discussed, need to be an integral part of the mechanism. The normalization of sense representation to achieve real canonical sense representation and fine-grained semantic representations are also indispensable. Our future research will continue to address these issues.

References

Baker, Colin F., Charles J. Fillmore, and John B. Lowe. 1998. The Berkeley FrameNet project. In *Proceedings of the 1998 COLING-ACL*, Université de Montréal, Montréal, Quebec, Canada, 86–90. Available at http://www.aclweb.org/anthology/P98-1013. Accessed 24 August 2018.

Chen, Keh-Jiann, Shu-Ling Huang, Yueh-Yin Shih, and Yi-Jun Chen 陳克健, 黃淑齡, 施悅音, 陳怡君. 2004. Multi-level definitions and complex relations in Extended-HowNet 多層次概念定義與複雜關係表達—繁體字知網的新增架構. Paper presented at the *Workshop on Chinese Lexical Semantics*, Beijing University, Beijing, China. Available at http://ckip.iis.sinica.edu.tw/CKIP/paper/Extended-HowNet_multi-level_concept_definition_and_complex_relation_description.pdf. Accessed 24 August 2018.

Chen, Keh-Jiann, Shu-Ling Huang, Yueh-Yin Shih, and Yi-Jun Chen. 2005a. Extended-HowNet—A representational framework for concepts. Paper presented at the *OntoLex 2005—Ontologies and Lexical Resources IJCNLP-05 Workshop*, Jeju Island, South Korea. Available at http://aclweb.org/anthology/I05-7001. Accessed 24 August 2018.

Chen, Yi-Jun, Shu-Ling Huang, Yueh-Yin Shih, and Keh-Jiann Chen 陳怡君, 黃淑齡, 施悅音, 陳克健. 2005b. Semantic representation and definitions for function words in Extended-HowNet 繁體字知網架構下之功能詞表達初探. Paper presented at the *Workshop on Chinese Lexical Semantics*, Xiamen University, Fujian, China. Available at http://ckip.iis.sinica.edu.tw/CKIP/paper/function_word_of_big5HN.pdf. Accessed 24 August 2018.

Chung, You-Shan, Shu-Ling Huang, and Keh-Jiann Chen. 2007. Modality and modal sense representation in E-HowNet. In *Proceedings of the 21st Pacific Asia Conference on Language, Information and Computation*, Seoul National University, Seoul, Korea, 136–145. Available at http://www.aclweb.org/anthology/Y07-1013. Accessed 24 August 2018.

CKIP. 2015. Semantic roles and semantic role labeling. Technical Report no.15-01. Available at http://ckip.iis.sinica.edu.tw:8080/report/. Accessed 7 September 2018.

Dong, Zhendong. 1999. Bigger context and better understanding—Expectation on future MT technology. In *Proceedings of the International Conference on Machine Translation & Computer Language Information Processing*, 17–25. Available at www.keenage.com/papers/mtfuturetech.doc. Accessed 24 August 2018.

Dong, Zhendong, and Qiang Dong. 2006. *HowNet and the computation of meaning*. Singapore: World Scientific Publishing Co. Pte. Ltd.

Dorr, Bonnie J., Gina-Anne Levow, and Dekang Lin. 2000. Construction of Chinese-English semantic hierarchy for information retrieval. Paper presented at the *Workshop on English-Chinese Cross Language Information Retrieval, International Conference on Chinese Language Computing*, Chicago, IL, 187–194. Available at http://users.umiacs.umd.edu/~bonnie/Publications/icclc-00.pdf. Accessed 24 August 2018.

Dowty, David R. 1989. On the semantic content of the notion "thematic role". *Properties, types and meanings* (Vol. II), ed. Barbara Partee, Gennaro Chierchia, and Ray Turner, 69–130. Dordrecht: Kluwer.

Fellbaum, Christiane. 1998. *WORDNET—An electronic lexical database*. Cambridge, MA: MIT Press.

Huang, Shu-Ling, You-Shan Chung, and Keh-Jiann Chen. 2008. E-HowNet: The expansion of HowNet. Paper presented at *The First National HowNet Workshop*, Beijing, China.

Liu, Qun, and Sujian Li 劉群, 李素建. 2002. Word similarity computing based on How-net 基於《知網》的辭彙語義相似度計算. *International Journal of Computational Linguistics and Chinese Language Processing* 7(2):59–76.

Ma, Wei-Yun, and Yueh-Yin Shih. 2018. Extended HowNet 2.0—An entity-relation commonsense representation model. In *Proceedings of LREC 2018*, Miyazaki, Japan. Available at http://www.iis.sinica.edu.tw/papers/ma/21291-F.pdf. Accessed 24 August 2018.

Pustejovsky, James. 1995. *The generative lexicon*. Cambridge, MA: The MIT Press.

Chapter 10
Sense Tagging Unknown Chinese Words with Word Embedding

Wenlei Bai, Tingxin Wei, Fuyong Meng, Min Gu, Xuri Tang, Yanhui Gu, and Weiguang Qu

Abstract This chapter will present our proposed new model to predict the senses of unknown Chinese words using a combination of word embedding, part-of-speech (POS) filtering, and suffix filtering. The model first utilized the external feature of contexts to find synonyms of unknown words by training the contexts with word embedding and then detected the semantic categories of these synonyms in *Tongyici Cilin*, a Chinese thesaurus. Internal features such as POS and suffixes were used to filter out the semantic categories that were inconsistent with the unknown words in terms of POS and suffixes. The model then used voting to select the best sense category. Our experiments showed that the model based on a combination of external features and internal features achieved good precision in sense tagging.

Keywords Unknown Chinese words · Sense tagging · Word embedding · Part-of-speech filtering · Suffix filtering

10.1 Introduction

Unknown words are words not present in the dictionary for word segmentation. According to the statistics of Academic Sinica in Taiwan, about 3.51% of the words in corpora are unknown words (Chen and Lin 2000). While unknown words make

W. Bai · M. Gu · Y. Gu
School of Computer Science and Technology, Nanjing Normal University, Nanjing, China

Information Security and Confidential Technology Engineering Research Center of Jiangsu Province, Nanjing, China

T. Wei
International College for Chinese Studies, Nanjing Normal University, Nanjing, China

F. Meng · X. Tang
School of Foreign Languages, Huazhong University of Science and Technology, Wuhan, China

W. Qu (✉)
School of Artificial Intelligence, Nanjing Normal University, Nanjing, China
e-mail: wgqu@njnu.edu.cn

C.-R. Huang et al. (eds.), *Chinese Language Resources*, Text, Speech and Language Technology 49, https://doi.org/10.1007/978-3-031-38913-9_10

up only a small proportion of the corpora, they play a key role in processing and understanding texts. Our research was mainly focused on the detection of and sense tagging these unknown words. Detection is a prerequisite step in sense tagging, which is very important in many natural language processing tasks such as text content and theme analysis, information retrieval, and machine translation. In the literature, sense tagging has mainly exploited the information of the internal features of unknown words. Our study proposed a new model that combined internal and external features and incorporated word embedding (external feature), part-of-speech (POS) filtering (internal feature), and suffix filtering (internal feature) (王洪君等 2005; 曾立英 2008) to guess the senses of unknown Chinese words. The validity of this model has been proven by our experiments.

10.2 Related Work

Research on unknown Chinese word sense guessing can be classified into three categories based on internal features, external features, and a combination of both features:

1. **Model Based on Internal Features.** Chen and Lin (2000), Lu (2006, 2007), and Shang 尚芬芬 (2015) attempted to determine the relationship between the components of unknown words and the semantic category of the whole word by computing their coefficient. Shang 尚芬芬 (2015) put forward an integrated model based on internal features to predict the semantics of unknown words. First, a rule-based model was used to predict the meaning of unknown words. For those that could not be predicted by the rule-based model, their semantic categories were obtained by voting using the reiterative model and the character-category association model, in which the category that receives the most votes wins.
2. **Model Based on External Features.** Chen and Lin (2000) focused on only the external features of unknown words to make semantic predictions using an English-Chinese dictionary and a corpus-based model, and the accuracy rate reached 34%. However, this method could only process words that were already included in the dictionary. In previous research on unknown Chinese word sense guessing, most of the studies used internal features to predict the senses of unknown Chinese words. Therefore, we attempted to use the external features of unknown Chinese words to prove that external features (contextual content) can also be helpful in unknown Chinese word sense guessing. However, the experimental results were not as expected.
3. **Model Based on Internal and External Features.** Lu (2007) first selected five candidate semantic categories based on internal features and then selected a category with the highest score as the final prediction with the help of external features. This method did not achieve a good performance, with an accuracy rate of only 37%. Qiu et al. (2009) and Qiu et al. (2011) proposed a new method

combining internal and external features and achieved a good performance, which showed that both internal and external features are useful in the semantic prediction of unknown Chinese words.

All the methods mentioned above have shortcomings. Shang 尚芬芬 (2015) only considered internal features, while Chen and Lin (2000) used external features only. Lu (2007) combined the internal and external features of the unknown words to select candidate semantic categories and sorted them based on external features only, which was not a close combination. Qiu et al. (2011) proposed a new method combining internal and external features and expressed the context of a word "w" as $<v_1, v_2 \ldots v_n>$, where v_i represents the weight of the i-th context word. Although the context-based methods used alone performed not as well as the structure-based methods, the combination of contextual and structural information performed much better than using them alone. However, this representation of context may lead to data sparsity as it cannot exploit the possible relationships between words when using external features to calculate the similarity between words.

10.3 Linguistic Features of Unknown Words

10.3.1 Paradigmatic Features of Words

In general linguistics, there are syntagmatic and paradigmatic relationships in languages. The paradigmatic relationship refers to the fact that language units with some common features can be replaced with each other in a particular construction. At the sentence level, these language units, which can appear in the same context, are words. They have the same syntactic function and certain relevance or similarity in semantics. This feature of words provided the idea of sense tagging unknown words. When the semantics of unknown words cannot be directly accessed, the category of relevant or similar words that appear in the same contexts can be used.

10.3.2 Features of Chinese Word Formation

Modern Chinese words are composed of simple words, composite words, and compound words, with compound words as the dominant type. Unknown words have a higher proportion of compound words due to their derivative feature. According to the research on disyllabic compound words in Chinese by Yuan and Huang 苑春法, 黄昌宁 (1998), the semantics of 87.8% nouns, 93.2% verbs, and 87.0% adjectives were all composed of their component morpheme meanings. It should be noted that the morphemes that participated in word formation did not weigh the same. Williams (1981) proposed the "center-right principle" of compound words (i.e., the center of the compound word is its rightmost component). In

Chinese, attribute-centered words are found most in disyllabic nouns, accounting for 80.6%, with joint words second, accounting for 9.3%. Verbs are mainly the verb-object structure, joint structure, and adverbial-centered structure, each accounting for 39.7%, 27.0%, and 23.3%, respectively. Adjectives are mainly joint words, with 62.5% (Yuan and Huang 苑春法, 黄昌宁 1998).

According to the research on the word formation of new words by Xu and Kang 徐艳华, 亢世勇 (2004), words with attribute-centered structures in new three-syllable words accounted for 64.7% of all three-syllable words. The rightmost character in the modifier-head structure carried most of the semantics of the word, while in the joint structure, suffixes (for the sake of convenience, in our study suffix refers to the rightmost character in a word, so the term is not used strictly in its traditional sense) can also basically represent the meaning of the word since the meanings of the components are usually mutually manifested or complemented. The suffixes of Chinese compound words are loaded with much semantic information. If words with the same part-of-speech tags happen to have the same suffixes, they tend to have the same core meanings and differ in limited meanings, such as 咖啡色 *kafeise* "brown" and 绿色 *lvse* "green," 海军 *haijun* "navy" and 陆军 *lujun* "army," and so on.

10.4 Introduction of the Semantic Resource

The extended version of *Tongyici Cilin* (梅家驹等, 1983) is a semantic dictionary compiled by Mei and other researchers and updated by HIT-CIR. It contains a collection of more than 70,000 words and is a widely used semantic dictionary, which is why we chose it as the basis for sense tagging.

The extended version of *Tongyici Cilin* (hereafter referred to as *Cilin*) is a dictionary arranged according to meanings. It follows the characteristics of Chinese language, arranging words with close semantic relationships into one category or neighboring categories and polysemous words into different word clusters. The semantic system is composed of 12 major categories, 94 medium categories, and 1428 small categories, and each small category is divided into clusters according to the principle of synonyms. Each cluster is titled with a headword. Therefore, when classifying the semantic category of an unknown word, we found another word with the most similar meaning to it and marked the semantic category of that word as the semantic category of the unknown word.

Cilin uses five-level coding. The first level uses capital English letters, including 12 major categories from A to L, in which A to D are major categories for nouns, E is mostly for adjectives, and F to J is mostly for verbs. Medium categories are represented by lowercase letters and minor categories by two decimal integers. The fourth- and fifth-level coding are represented as capital letters and two decimal integers, respectively. For instance, the complete five-level code for 渔民 *yumin* "fisherman" is Ae07C01. According to Liu et al. 刘丹丹等 (2014), when using the semantic information in *Cilin* to extract information, performance is best if the semantic information granularity is a minor category. Our study used three-level coding (i.e., minor category tagging), for example, we classified the unknown word 运算量 *yunsuanliang* "computation amount" as Dn03 in *Cilin*.

10.5 Model Construction

10.5.1 Model Based on Word Embedding

A word needs to be represented by a set of vectors for computers to understand it. One of the simplest methods is one-hot representation. If the current word appeared in the lexicon, we set it at 1; if it did not appear, we set it at 0. There are two problems with this type of representation: one is the dimensionality curse; and the other is that it is difficult to describe the similarity between words. To solve these problems, scholars have designed a dense representation of word vectors in low-dimensional space that can express the words as low-dimensional continuous real vectors and map them into a new space. This method is called word embedding (Chen et al. 2014). The more similar the words are, the nearer their word vectors are. We used word embedding to find the words with the most similar semantics of unknown words to predict the senses of unknown words.

Word2vec is an open-source word vector tool released by Google. It mainly transforms the words in the text corpus into vector forms. Our study used word2vec with the skip-gram model to train the text corpus, as shown in Fig. 10.1. Assuming

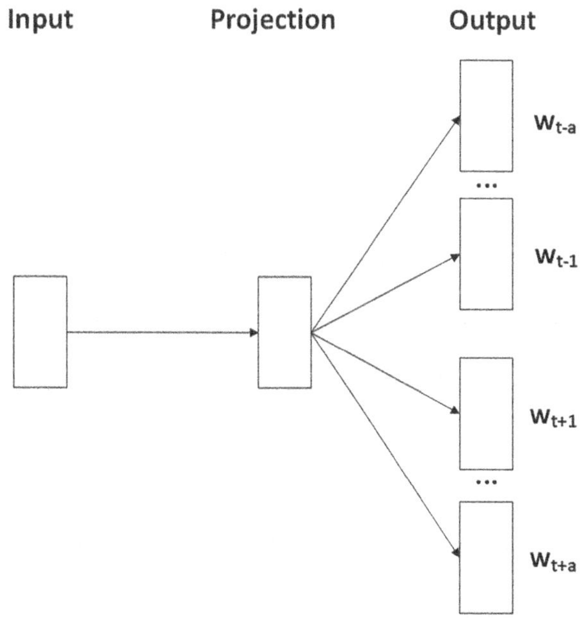

Fig. 10.1 Skip-gram model in word2vec

that there is a sequence of words in the corpus, the objective function (Mikolov et al. 2013) is shown in Eq. (10.1):

$$F = \frac{1}{T}\sum_{t=1}^{T}\sum_{-a \le i \le a,\, i \ne 0} \log P(w_{t+i}|w_t) \tag{10.1}$$

In the equation, “a” is a constant that determines the context window size.

We utilized word2vec to train the text corpus and obtain the corresponding word vector training model. After inputting the target words, we found words related or similar to the target words. The procedure of word embedding model was as follows:

1. We first used word embedding to obtain the first K words with the highest similarity to the unknown word and then found the semantic categories of these words in *Cilin*.
2. The semantic category with the most votes was the final prediction in the word embedding model.

For instance, consider the unknown word 钢铁厂 *gangtiechang* “steel plant.” Assuming $K = 20$, we used word embedding to predict the top 20 Chinese words that are related or similar to the unknown word and then mapped them to their semantic categories in *Cilin*. The results are shown in Table 10.1. Bm02 had 1 vote, Ee12 had 1 vote, Dm03 had 4 votes, and Bo19 had 1 vote. The semantic category with the most votes was Dm03, so the model predicted that the semantic category of the unknown word 钢铁厂 *gangtiechang* “steel plant” was Dm03. The headword of this category was 工厂 *gongchang* “factory,” 工场 *gongchang* “plant.” Thus, the prediction was consistent with manual labeling.

10.5.2 Combined Model Based on Word Embedding and POS Filtering

Compared with the model using only internal features, the word embedding model introduced and utilized the external features of a word, but it had a problem with semantic prediction: word embedding training produced not only similar words according to the unknown words but also a large number of related words. These related words often co-existed with the unknown words in the training corpus but differed greatly in semantics. For instance, the candidate words of the unknown word 案发地 *anfadi* “incident” obtained by word embedding were 作案 *zuoan* “offense,” 自首 *zishou* “surrender,” 抢劫 *qiangjie* “rob,” 杀人 *sharen* “homicide,” 嫌犯 *xianfan* “suspect,” 关押 *guanya* “imprison,” 刑讯 *xingxun* “torture,” 法院 *fayuan* “court,” etc. Therefore, to reduce the noise and to find more accurate candidate words, we added POS filtering to the model to retain only the candidates with the same POS tags of the unknown words.

Table 10.1 Top 20 words that are most similar to 钢铁厂 *gangtiechang* "steel plant"

Related words	Semantic category	Related words	Semantic category
钢厂 *gangchang* "steel plant"	Null	轧钢厂 *zhagangchang* "steel rolling mill"	Dm03
钢铁公司 *gangtiegongsi* "iron and steel companies"	Null	济钢 *jigang* "Jinan Iron & Steel Co Ltd"	Dm03
沙钢 *shagang* "Shagang-steel"	Null	本钢 *bengang* "BXSTEEL"	Null
国丰 *guofeng* "Guoman"	Null	上海宝钢集团 *shanghaibaogangjituan* "Shanghai Baosteel Group"	Null
钢铁 *gangtie* "iron and steel"	Bm02, Ee12	唐钢 *tanggang* "Tangshan steel"	Null
高炉 *gaolu* "blast furnace"	Bo19	鞍钢 *angang* "Anshan Steel & Iron"	Dm03
文丰 *wenfeng* "WHENFOR"	Null	硫酸厂 *suanliuchang* "sulfuric acid plant"	Null
钢铁集团 *gangtiejituan* "Iron & Steel Group"	Null	烧结厂 *shaojiechang* "sintering machine"	Null
亚通 *yatong* "ATON"	Null	湘钢 *xianggang* "Xiangtan steel company"	Null
京唐 *jingtang* "Jingtang"	Null	炼铁厂 *liangangchang* "iron-making plant"	Dm03

According to *Cilin*, A to D categories are mainly nouns, the E category is mostly adjectives, and the F to J categories are mostly verbs. In our study, we proposed a POS filtering method for the semantic predictions of unknown words: first, we used the word embedding technique to find related words of unknown words and then found the categories of these related words in *Cilin*. If the unknown word was a noun and the category of the related word was not in the A to D categories, then the category was filtered out. Similarly, if the unknown word was an adjective and the category of the related word was not in the E category, the category was filtered out. If the unknown word was a verb and the category of the related word was not in the F to J categories, the category was filtered out. The procedure for the combined model based on word embedding and POS filtering was as follows:

1. We first used word embedding to obtain the first K words with the highest similarity to the unknown word and then found the semantic categories of these words in *Cilin*.
2. If the unknown word was a noun, if and only if the category of the candidate word fell under the A to D categories, it counted as one vote. Similarly, when the unknown word was an adjective, if and only if the category of the candidate word fell under the E category, it counted as one vote. When the unknown word was a verb, if and only if the category of the candidate word fell under the F to J categories, it counted as one vote.
3. The category that received the most votes was the semantic category predicted for the unknown word.

For instance, consider the unknown word 作案者 *zuoanzhe* "perpetrator," assuming $K = 20$. We used word embedding to predict the top 20 words related or similar to the unknown word and then mapped these words to the semantic categories in *Cilin*. The results are shown in Table 10.2. The Hn01 category had one vote, the An02 category had three votes, the Hh05 category had three votes, and the Hh03 category had one vote. The semantic categories with the largest number of votes were An02 and Hh05, so the prediction of semantic category could not be made. If we used the model based on word embedding and POS filtering, since 作案者 *zuoanzhe* "perpetrator" is a noun, semantic categories not in the A to D categories (i.e., Hn01, Hh05, and Hh03) were filtered out. The An02 category thus had the most votes, so it was predicted that the semantic category of the unknown word 作案者 *zuoanzhe* "perpetrator" was An02. The headword of this category was "criminal," making this prediction consistent with manual labeling.

10.5.3 Model Based on Word Embedding, POS Filtering, and Suffix Filtering

The combination of word embedding and POS filtering provided a partial solution when the semantic difference between candidate words and unknown words was too big. However, the filtered candidate words were still noisy, such as the 13 words remaining after filtering out non-nouns in the case of 案发地 *anfadi* "incident": 嫌疑犯 *xianyifan* "suspects," 嫌犯 *xianfan* "suspects," 警方 *jingfang* "police," 嫌疑人 *xianyiren* "suspects," 报案人 *baoanren* "informants," 麻永东 *mayongdong* "Ma Yongdong, person name," 彭阳县 *pengyangxian* "Peng Yangxian," 作案动机 *zuoandongji* "motives," 疑犯 *yifan* "suspects," 案发地点 *anfadidian* "the location of the crime," 民警 *minjing* "the police," 在逃犯 *zaitaofan* "fugitives," and 邓某 *dengmou* "Dengmou, person name." It was clear that the semantic category of 罪犯 *zuifan* "suspects" would win the voting even though it was wrong, because even with

Table 10.2 Top 20 words that are most similar to 作案者 *zuoanzhe* "perpetrator"

Related words	Semantic category	Related words	Semantic category
丙说	Null	杀人	Hn05
bingshuo		*sharen*	
"Bing said"		"murder"	
丁说	Null	王说	Null
dingshuo		*wangshuo*	
"Ding said"		"Wang said"	
乙说	Null	案均	Null
yishuo		*anjun*	
"Yi said"		"bad word segmentation"	
作案	Hn01	告破	Null
zuoan		*gaopo*	
"offense"		"solved"	
同案犯	An02	还性	Null
tonganfan		*Huanxing*	
"accomplice"		"bad word segmentation"	
作案动机	Null	收脏	Null
zuoandongji		*shouzang*	
"motive"		"receiving stolen property"	
做案	Null	杀害	Hn05
zuoan		*shahai*	
"offense"		"homicide"	
邓某	Null	分尸案	Null
dengmou		*fenshian*	
"Deng"		"dismemberment case"	
嫌犯	An02	凶杀	Hn05
xianfan		*xiongsha*	
"suspect"		"murder"	
抢劫	Hn03	惯犯	An02
qiangjie		*guanfan*	
"rob"		"habitual offender"	

the same POS tag, there were still many candidates semantically related while not close to the unknown word. Since the semantic focus of Chinese words, especially nouns, usually falls under the last character (i.e., suffixes), better sense tagging can be achieved by choosing candidate words with the same suffixes. We added suffix filtering to the model, making it a joint model based on word embedding, POS filtering, and suffix filtering. The model thus consisted of the following steps:

1. We first used word embedding to obtain the first K words with the highest similarity to the unknown word, and then found the semantic categories of these words in *Cilin*.
2. If the unknown word was a noun, if and only if the related words' semantic categories fell under the A to D categories and had the same suffix as the

unknown word, it counted as one vote. Similarly, when the unknown word was an adjective, if and only if the related words' semantic categories fell under the E category and had the same suffix as the unknown word, it counted as one vote. If the unknown word was a verb, if and only if the related words' semantic categories fell under the F to J categories and had the same suffix as the unknown word, it counted as one vote.

3. The category that received the most votes was the predicted semantic category in this model.

Take the unknown word 柿树 *shishu* "persimmon tree" as an example and assume $K = 20$. We used word embedding to predict the top 20 Chinese words that were related or similar to the unknown word and then mapped these related words to the semantic categories in *Cilin*. The results are shown in Table 10.3. The model based on word embedding and POS filtering filtered out the semantic categories that did not fall under the A to D categories. Of the candidates remaining, Bh07 had three votes, Bh01 had two votes, and Bh12, Bh13, and Da14 each had one vote. Bh07 was the predicted category since it received the most votes. After adding suffix filtering, the model filtered out candidates whose suffixes were not 树 *shu* "tree." As a result, Bh07, Bh12, Bh13, and Da14 were filtered out. Then, we examined the remaining candidates and found that Bh01 had two votes. Since it was the category with the most votes, the semantic category of the unknown word 柿树 *shishu* "persimmon tree" was predicted as Bh01. The headword of this category was 树木 *shumu* "tree," 竹子 *zhuzi* "bamboo." Thus, the prediction was consistent with manual labeling.

10.6 Experiments

10.6.1 Evaluation Metrics

The sense tagging of unknown Chinese words task is regarded as a classification problem, which generally uses the metrics of precision, recall, and F-Score. Our study also adopted these metrics. Precision is the fraction of the number of correctly predicted unknown words to the number of all the predicted unknown words, as shown in Eq. (10.2).

$$P = \frac{\text{The number of correctly predicted unknown words}}{\text{The number of all the predicted unknown words}} \tag{10.2}$$

Recall is the fraction of the number of correctly predicted unknown words to the number of all the unknown words, as shown in Eq. (10.3).

Table 10.3 Top 20 words that were most similar to 柿树 *shishu* "persimmon tree"

Related words	Semantic category	Related words	Semantic category
柿子树 *shizishu* "persimmon tree"	Null	嫁接 *jiajie* "inoculation"	Hd22
芽接 *yajie* "bud grafting"	Hd22	软枣 *ruanzao* "dateplum persimmon"	Bh07
油桐树 *youtongshu* "Aluerites fordii Hemsi"	Null	栽培 *zaipei* "cultivation"	Hc23, Hd20, Hg07
油柿 *youshi* "wild kaki persimmon"	Bh07	实生苗 *shishengmiao* "seeding"	Bh12
石榴树 *shiliushu* "pomegranate tree"	Null	果树 *guoshu* "fruit tree"	Bh01
冬剪 *dongjian* "winter pruning"	Null	栽种 *zaizhong* "planting"	Hd20
柿属 *shishu* "diospyros"	Null	雷竹 *leizhu* "phyllostachys praecox"	Null
果实 *guoshi* "fruits"	Bh13, Da14	君迁子 *junqianzi* "dateplum persimmon"	Null
桃树 *taoshu* "peach tree"	Bh01	耐寒 *naihan* "drought tolerance"	Null
花椒树 *huajiaoshu* "zanthoxylum bungeanum"	Null	柿子 *shizi* "persimmon"	Bh07

$$R = \frac{\text{The number of correctly predicted words}}{\text{The number of all the unknown words}} \tag{10.3}$$

F-Score is the harmonic mean of precision and recall, as shown in Eq. (10.4).

$$F_1 = \frac{2 \times P \times R}{P + R} \tag{10.4}$$

10.6.2 Experimental Setting

The unknown words selected and the corpus used here were different from Qiu et al. (2009) and Qiu et al. (2011), so no contrast could be made. This experiment was based on Shang 尚芬芬 (2015), with an aim to improve the prediction performance of the sense tagging of unknown Chinese words. The contrast experiment used the test data and the integrated model from Shang 尚芬芬 (2015) as the baseline model. All 3000 unknown words used in the experiment were from Shang 尚芬芬 (2015) and were manually annotated with the correct semantic categories. The semantic categories predicted by the prediction model were compared with the annotations to find precision. The annotation work was conducted by doctoral students and post-graduates in linguistics. The corpus used to train the word embedding model included sentences obtained by searching for unknown words at www.baidu.com. Take the unknown word 柿树 *shishu* "persimmon tree" as an example. The following sentence was extracted from www.baidu.com:

于1985和1987两年对柿树叶片和果实中主要营养元素含量的年周期变化进行了研究。 yu__1985__he__1987__liangnian__dui__shishu__yepian__he__guoshizhong__zhuyao__ yinyangyuansu__hanliangde__nianzhouqi__bianhua__jinxingle__yanjiu.
in__1985__and__1987__ two years__to__persimmon tree__blade__and in the fruit__ main__nutrient element__content__annual cycle__change__carried out__research.
Annual variation in the contents of the main nutrient elements in the leaves and the fruits of persimmon trees were carried out in 1985 and 1987

We extracted the top 75 search pages containing sentences with unknown words at www.baidu.com. When calculating precision, if the test unknown word had multiple meanings and multiple semantic categories in *Cilin*, it was accepted as a correct prediction if it matched any one of them.

10.6.3 Experiments and Analysis

Setting the Size of Related Words" K Values

In the experiments, the K value was set at 50, 100, 200, 250, 300, and 400, respectively, in the model based on word embedding, POS filtering, and suffix filtering. The test data of the unknown words contained 2370 nouns, 56 adjectives, and 574 verbs. The results are shown in Tables 10.4, 10.5, and 10.6. The number returned represents the number of semantics returned. We used some examples from the next section so that the notions of "number returned" and "correct number" of "semantics" are more clearly explained. Take the unknown word 运算量 *yunsuanliang* "computation" as an example. We classified the unknown word 运算量 *yunsuanliang* "computation amount" as Dn03 in *Cilin* using a cascade model. Therefore, the returned number added 1. If the model's prediction semantic category

Table 10.4 Prediction of 2370 nouns with different *K* values

K value	50	100	150	200	250	300	350	400
Number returned	1103	1275	1360	1411	1466	1502	1525	1563
Correct number	988	1147	1225	1274	1301	1325	1336	1362
Precision	0.896	0.900	0.901	**0.903**	0.887	0.882	0.876	0.871

Table 10.5 Prediction of 56 adjectives with different *K* values

K value	50	100	150	200	250	300	350	400
Number returned	8	10	13	14	15	17	17	16
Correct number	6	7	9	9	9	9	9	8
Precision	**0.750**	0.700	0.692	0.643	0.600	0.529	0.529	0.563

Table 10.6 Prediction of 574 verbs with different *K* values

K value	50	100	150	200	250	300	350	400
Number returned	146	176	185	195	205	210	220	230
Correct number	109	131	146	154	157	160	160	166
Precision	0.735	0.744	0.789	**0.790**	0.766	0.762	0.727	0.722

matched the manually annotated semantic category, the correct number added 1. Another example is the unknown word 头孢三嗪 *toubaosanqin* "ceftriaxone sodium." We could not predict its semantic category using the cascade model, so the cascade model did not return any values in that case. Table 10.4 shows that when $K = 200$, precision was the highest for the nouns, at 0.903, using the model based on word embedding, POS filtering, and suffix filtering.

Table 10.5 shows that when $K = 50$, precision was the highest for the adjectives, at 0.750, using the model based on word embedding, POS filtering, and suffix filtering.

Table 10.6 shows that when $K = 200$, precision was the highest for the verbs, at 0.790, using the model based on word embedding, POS filtering, and suffix filtering:

In the 3000 unknown words tested, the proportion of adjectives was small compared with nouns and verbs. Because precision for nouns and verbs reached the highest rate when $K = 200$, the K value for adjectives was also set at 200.

Results and Analysis

The results of using the three models to process the sense tagging of unknown words are shown in Tables 10.7, 10.8, and 10.9. Apparently, recall of the model proposed by our study was lower than that of the baseline model, while precision was higher. In the contrast experiment, we used the baseline model to predict the semantics of the words and the results are shown in the "Baseline Model ☆" row. For instance, of the 2370 unknown nouns, there were 1411 words with semantics returned in our model

Table 10.7 Semantic prediction of 2370 nouns using the three models

	Number of returned word predictions	Correct number	Precision
Baseline model	2353	1690	0.718
Word embedding (WE) model	1936	672	0.347
WE + POS model	1941	701	0.361
WE + POS + suffix model	1411	1274	**0.903**
Baseline model☆	1411	1090	0.773

Table 10.8 Semantic prediction of 56 adjectives using the three models

	Number of returned word predictions	Correct number	Precision
Baseline model	55	30	0.545
Word embedding (WE) model	44	3	0.068
WE + POS model	30	2	0.066
WE + POS + suffix model	14	9	**0.643**
Baseline model☆	14	7	0.500

Table 10.9 Semantic prediction of 574 verbs using the three models

	Number of returned word predictions	Correct number	Precision
Baseline model	563	320	0.568
Word embedding (WE) model	436	66	0.151
WE + POS model	368	107	0.291
WE + POS + suffix model	195	154	**0.790**
Baseline model☆	195	113	0.579

and 1274 of them were correctly predicted, with 0.903 precision. The results for the baseline model were 1090 correctly predicted out of 1411 words, with 0.773 precision.

Comparing and analyzing the experimental results of the three models, we reached the following conclusions:

1. For the unknown nouns, adjectives, and verbs, precision increased when internal features such as POS and suffix were added to the model, particularly the use of suffix filtering, which resulted in a great increase in precision. These findings show that in the sense tagging of unknown Chinese words, with the combination of internal and external features (i.e., word embedding + POS filtering + suffix filtering), the model's precision largely improved compared with the model using only external features (i.e., word embedding). This suggests that internal features are important in the sense tagging task.

2. Comparing the results of the word embedding model and the baseline model ☆, it was concluded that the word embedding + POS filtering + suffix filtering model achieved higher precision than the baseline model ☆ (using only internal features) and that external features are also useful in the sense tagging task.
3. The word embedding + POS filtering + suffix filtering model achieved the best performance with nouns, with precision larger than 90%. Verbs came in second while the performance of adjectives was poor. This suggests that the suffix filtering in this model actually predicted the meaning of suffixes, which applied well to modifier-head words. Moreover, since nouns are mostly modifier-head words, this model achieved the best performance with nouns.

In addition, we examined the words that the word embedding + POS filtering + suffix filtering model could not predict for the following reasons:

1. There were some nonrational and irregular words in the unknown words whose meanings could not be obtained from the component morphemes, such as human names, place names, plant names, and other named entities, transliterated words, dialect words, etc. The meanings of these words' suffixes were not involved in the meaning of the whole word. For instance, in the word 桑拿 *sangna* "sauna," the suffix 拿 *na* "take" has nothing to do with the meaning of 桑拿 *sangna* "sauna." Thus, our model could not predict these kinds of words.
2. There were also classical Chinese words and terminologies in the unknown words. On the one hand, their frequency was low, so word embedding training could not obtain highly relevant words for them. On the other hand, due to their distinctiveness, their suffixes were rarely found in other words, so they could not be predicted by our model. Examples of these words are 粉黛 *fendai* "makeup," 夕曛 *xixun* "dusk," and 氧哌嗪 *yangpaiqin* "oxygen piperazine."
3. There were many idioms in the unknown words whose semantic transparency was low, so the performance of these words was poor.
4. There were some problems in the semantic classification system of *Cilin*, which made it difficult to classify semantic categories. There are 12 categories and 97 medium categories in *Cilin*, but these categories are not balanced. Categories regarding persons are mainly distributed in the A category, including 14 medium categories: 泛称 *fancheng* "general term," 男女老少 *nannvlaoshao* "people of all ages and both sexes," 体态 *titai* "posture," 籍属 *jishu* "birthplace," 职业 *zhiye* "profession," 身份 *shenfen* "identity," 状况 *zhuangkuang* "status," 亲人 *qinren* "relatives," 辈次 *peici* "seniority in the family," 关系 *guanxi* "relationship," 品性 *pinxing* "moral character," 才识 *caishi* "ability," 信仰 *xinyang* "faith," and 丑类 *choulei* "evil person.". This taxonomy was too detailed in that some concepts overlapped with each other, thus causing prediction errors. Furthermore, there were words not in the categories above like 持卡者 *chikazhe* "card holders" and 归还者 *guihuanzhe* "person who returns things"; since they did not involve a certain attribute of the persons they referred to, this could have led to the failure of predicting them. Third, each medium and small category within this category had plenty of words with the suffixes 者 *zhe* "-er" and 人 *ren* "human," which were important in distinguishing meanings in other categories but had little effect in

this one. Therefore, the word embedding + POS filtering + suffix filtering model did not perform well when predicting words of persons.

5. *Cilin* was compiled mainly according to semantics, also taking into account lexical categories, so nouns and verbs, or verbs and adjectives, can co-exist under the same category. By default, our model treated words in the A to D categories as nouns, words in the E category as adjectives, and words in the F to J categories as verbs. Words with supplementary POS tags in these categories were excluded. In addition, there are many words that can be either verbs or nouns in Chinese, which similarly could not be well predicted using our model.

Some examples of the unknown words and predictions are shown in Table 10.10 so that readers can have a better idea about how we evaluated the performance of the model proposed in our study.

Table 10.10 Examples of unknown Chinese words and predictions

Word	Predicted semantic category	Manually annotated semantic category	Word	Predicted semantic category	Manually annotated semantic category
运算量	Dn03	Dn03	体育局	Dm01	Dm01
yunsuanliang			*tiyuju*		
"computation"			"sports bureau"		
修心养性	Hg03	Hg03	调压	Ha05	Hc03
xiushengyangxing			*tiaoya*		
"cultivate one"s original nature"			"pressure regulating"		
申请权	Di21	Di21	泥污	Bg08	Bg08
shenqingquan			*niwu*		
"application right"			"muddiness"		
计分器	Ba05	Ba05	吟哦	Null	Hg10
jifenqi			*yine*		
"score indicator"			"chant"		
甜酒药	Br11	Br11	头孢三嗪	Null	Br13
tianjiuyao			*toubaosanqin*		
"sweet Chinese yeast"			"ceftriaxone sodium"		
柿树	Bh01	Bh01	作案者	An02	An02
shishu			*zuoanzhe*		
"persimmon tree"			"perpetrator"		

Table 10.11 Results of comparison between the cascade model and the baseline model

	Number of returned word predictions	Correct number	Precision	Recall	F-score
Baseline model	2972	2040	0.686	0.680	0.683
Cascade model	2976	2267	**0.762**	**0.756**	**0.759**

10.7 Multimodel Cascade

The word embedding + POS filtering + suffix filtering model achieved high precision and low recall, while the baseline model performed oppositely. We combined the merits of these two models into a cascade model to predict the meanings of unknown words, as follows:

1. We performed sense tagging on 3000 unknown words with the word embedding + POS filtering + suffix filtering model.
2. We used the baseline model to predict those words that could not be predicted with the word embedding + POS filtering + suffix filtering model.

The results are shown in Table 10.11.

Compared with the baseline model, the cascade model improved the precision by 7.8%, recall by 7.6%, and F-score by 7.6%. The baseline model predicted the 3000 unknown words and 28 of them did not return predictions. The word embedding + POS filtering + suffix filtering model provided four words of the 28 words with predictions, which were 太田痣 *taitianzhi* “nevus of ota,” 瓷埙 *cixun* “porcelain Xun,” 藏獒 *zangao* “Tibetan mastiff,” and 除祛 *chuqu* “removal.”

10.8 Conclusion

Our study proposed a new strategy for sense tagging unknown Chinese words, which combined internal and external features, incorporating word embedding, POS filtering, and suffix filtering to create a new model, and applied it to the work of sense tagging unknown words. A rather good performance was achieved. In future work, we will continue to explore the improvement of the Chinese semantic prediction model and try to apply the cascade model to other types of lexicons.

Acknowledgments This work was partially supported by the Chinese National Fund of Natural Science under Grants 61772278, 61472191, and 41571382 and the Chinese National Fund of Social Science under Grant 18BYY127.

References

Chen, Hsin His, and Chi Ching Lin. 2000. Sense-tagging Chinese corpus. In *Proceedings of the ACL-2000 Workshop on Chinese Language*, 7–14. Hong Kong.

Chen, En Hong, Siyu Qiu, Chang Xu, Fei Tian, and Tieyan Liu. 陈恩红, 邱思语, 许畅, 田飞, 刘铁岩. 2014. Word embedding: Continuous space representation for natural language 单词嵌入——自然语言的连续空间表示. *Journal of Data Acquisition and Processing 数据采集与处理 19–29.*

Liu, Dandan, Cheng Peng, Longhua Qian, and Guodong Zhou 刘丹丹, 彭成, 钱龙华, 周国栋. 2014. The effect of *Tongyici Cilin* in Chinese entity relation extraction 《同义词词林》在中文实体关系抽取中的作用. *Journal of Chinese Information Processing 中文信息学报 28(2): 91–99.*

Lu, Xiaofei. 2006. *Hybrid model for Chinese unknown word resolution*. Columbus, OH: The Ohio State University.

Lu, Xiaofei. 2007. Hybrid model for semantic classification of Chinese unknown words. In *Proceedings of the North American Chapter of the Association for Computational Linguistics: Human Language Technologies*, 188–195. Rochester, NY.

Mei, JiaJu, Yiming Zhu, Yunqi Gao, and Hongxiang Yin. 梅家驹, 竺一鸣, 高蕴奇, 殷鸿翔. 1983. *Tongyici Cilin* 同义词词林. Shanghai: Shanghai Lexicographical Publishing House 上海: 上海辞书出版社.

Mikolov, Tomas, Kai Chen, Greg Corrado, and Jeffrey Dean. 2013. Efficient estimation of word representations in vector space. *Computer Science* 1–12. arXiv preprint arXiv:1301.3781.

Qiu, Likun, Kai Zhao, and ChangJian Hu. 2009. A hybrid model for sense guessing of Chinese unknown words. In *Proceedings of the 23rd Pacific Asia Conference on Language, Information and Computation (PACLIC)*, 464–473. Hong Kong.

Qiu, Likun, Yunfang Wu, and Yanqiu Shao. 2011. Combining contextual and structural information for supersense tagging of Chinese unknown words. In *Proceedings of the International Conference on Computational Linguistics and Intelligent Text Processing*, 15–28. Tokyo, Japan.

Shang, Fenfen 尚芬芬. 2015. *Research on the sense guessing of Chinese unknown words 汉语未登录词语义预测研究. Nanjing Normal University 南京师范大学.*

Wang, Hongjun, and Li Fu 王洪君, 富丽. 2005. A research on the semi-affix of Mandarin Chinese 试论现代汉语的类词缀. *Linguistic Sciences 语言科学 5:3–17.*

Williams, Edwin. 1981. On the notions "lexically related" and "head of a word". *Linguistic Inquiry* 12(2):245–274.

Xu, Yanhua, and Shiyong Kang 徐艳华, 亢世勇. 2004. A research on the formation of new words based on corpus 基于语料库的新词语识别规则研究. *Journal of Ludong University (Philosophy and Social Sciences Edition) 鲁东大学学报 (哲学社会科学版) 21(4):286–291.*

Yuan, Chunfa, and Changning Huang 苑春法, 黄昌宁. 1998. A research on Chinese morphemes and word formation based on morpheme database 基于语素数据库的汉语语素及构词研究. *Chinese Teaching In The World 世界汉语教学 2:8–13.*

Zeng, Liying. 曾立英. 2008. On the semi-affixes of three-character phrases 三字词中的类词缀. *Applied Linguistics* 语言文字应用 2:32–40.

Chapter 11
PKUSenseCor: A Large-Scale Word Sense Annotated Chinese Corpus

Peng Jin, Yunfang Wu, Xuefeng Zhu, Diana McCarthy, Weiguang Qu, and Shiwen Yu

Abstract Word ambiguity is ubiquitous in texts and computational systems address this with word sense disambiguation. To develop such systems, it is crucial to have high-quality word sense annotated corpora to test the systems. For many top-performing systems, such data is also required for training. For the English language, there are several word sense-tagged corpora in which all content words are tagged, the largest example being SemCor. To the best of our knowledge, such a word sense-tagged corpus is lacking for the Chinese language. In response, a corpus called PKUSenseCor has been constructed, the details of which will be described in this chapter.

Keywords Word sense disambiguation · Word sense annotated corpus · Inter-annotator agreement

---

P. Jin (✉)
Sichuan Provincial Key Laboratory of Philosophy and Social Science for Language Intelligence in Special Education, Leshan Normal University, Leshan, China
e-mail: jandp@pku.edu.cn

Y. Wu · X. Zhu · S. Yu
Institute of Computational Linguistics, Peking University, Beijing, China

Key Laboratory of Computational Linguistics, Peking University, Ministry of Education, Beijing, China
e-mail: wuyf@pku.edu.cn

D. McCarthy
Department of Theoretical and Applied Linguistics, University of Cambridge, Cambridge, UK
e-mail: diana@dianamccarthy.co.uk

W. Qu
School of Artificial Intelligence, Nanjing Normal University, Nanjing, China
e-mail: wgqu@njnu.edu.cn

C.-R. Huang et al. (eds.), *Chinese Language Resources*, Text, Speech and Language Technology 49, https://doi.org/10.1007/978-3-031-38913-9_11

11.1 Introduction

Word ambiguity is ubiquitous in natural language. Computational linguistics systems, which aim at more than a superficial understanding of texts, handle it with a process known as word sense disambiguation (WSD) (Agirre and Edmonds 2006; McCarthy 2009; Navigli 2009). A crucial requirement for this process is data for testing such systems. This gold-standard data usually takes the form of corpus texts that have been tagged with senses. This data is also essential for supervised systems that need it for training. Word sense annotated corpus texts are either texts with only a fixed sample of target lemmas with sense tags, which are referred to as "lexical sample" sense-tagged corpora, or they have all lemmas of a particular type (such as all content words) tagged, in which case they are referred to as "all-word" sense-tagged corpora. Data of either type is critical for developing WSD systems, and all-words corpora are particularly useful to ensure that the systems being developed are capable of scaling up to handle a wider variety of texts.

There are many English word sense-tagged corpora, such as DSO (Ng and Lee 1996), SemCor (Miller et al. 1994), and MASC (Ide et al. 2008). Many of these have been tagged with WordNet senses (Fellbaum 1998; Miller et al. 1990), but other sense inventories have also been used (Kilgarriff and Rosenzweig 2000). Since SENSEVAL[1] (Kilgarriff 1998), WSD international evaluation events have been a major catalyst for the development of further corpora. Word sense-tagged corpora are now available for many different languages, some using a translation approach (Bond et al. 2012) and others annotating from scratch such as the OntoNotes project (Hovy et al. 2006), which also provides a sense inventory along with annotations of dependency structures. One aim of the OntoNotes sense-tagging process was to focus on producing coarse-grained senses, which resulted in good inter-tagger agreement in the consequent sense tagging task. The iterative process of OntoNotes allows for the reconsideration of the inventory whenever good agreement cannot be reached; however, this process is easier for some words than others (Chen and Palmer 2009).

This chapter will describe the construction of an all-word sense-tagged corpus of Mandarin Chinese (mainland Mandarin, with simplified characters). This corpus is important since Mandarin is the most widely spoken of the world's languages, yet there are no Mandarin Chinese all-word sense-tagged corpora. The OntoNotes project has produced valuable sense annotations in Mandarin for a lexical sample of some 761 nouns and verbs. This has provided a very valuable resource for Mandarin, with an excess of 84,000 annotated tokens from this sample of 761 words in its current release (Weischedel et al. 2013).[2] Of these annotations,

[1] Now called SemEval.

[2] There were no further plans to expand the sense tagging data. After the second or third year, work focused on the predicate-argument structure.

82,720 are attributed to words that have more than one sense in the inventory.[3] There are also 1423 monosemous sense tags and 921 cases where the annotators noted that a token for the target word did not match any of the listed senses.

The all-word sense-tagged corpus described in this chapter covers all the words, with more than one coarse-grained sense, in a sample of over 13 million words from the *People's Daily* newspaper, which has been word-segmented and POS-tagged in prior work (Duan et al. 2003; Zhan et al. 2006). The sense-tagged corpus described here is called PKUSenseCor. It covers a wider range of markables compared to OntoNotes in that it includes some function words as well as open class words. In addition, all of the tokens have been double annotated.

11.2 Corpus and Knowledge Base Selection

11.2.1 Corpus

The PKUSenseCor corpus was built using data from an existing resource, the PKU Chinese Word Segmentation Corpus, which has been described in Zhan et al. (2006) and referred to as the PKU-ICL-PD-Corpus, while the segmentation process has been described by Duan et al. (2003). The PKUSenseCor has word segmentation as well as part-of-speech (POS) tags with pinyin tags to disambiguate polyphonic words. The processing was performed automatically and then manually verified. The PKUSenseCor corpus consists of data from the PKU-ICL-PD-Corpus including all the texts from the *People's Daily* newspaper (PDN) published in 2000, along with additional data from PDN written in January 1998.[4] PKU-ICL-PD-Corpus comprises more than 50 million Chinese characters. An example sentence is shown below:

咱们/rr 中国/ns 这么/rz 大 {da4}/a 的 {de5}/ud 一个/mq 多/a 民族/n 的{de5}/ud 国家/n 如果/c 不/df 团结/a , /wd 就/d 不/df 可能/vu 发展/v 经济/n , /wd 人民/n 生活/n 水平/n 也/d 就/d 不/df 可能/vu 得到/v 改善/vn 和{he2}/c 提高

/vn 。/wj

(Gloss: *We in China are such a large multi-ethnic nation, if we do not show solidarity then we cannot develop the economy and the people's living standard cannot be improved*)

Part-of-speech tags were assigned to every word and punctuation tokens and pinyin tags were supplied for all polyphonic words. For instance, the word "和" can be pronounced as *he2*, *he4*, *hu2*, *huo*, *huo2*, and *huo4*, but in the sentence above, *he2* is the intended pronunciation. The POS inventory has been described by Zhan

[3]Not all are for ambiguous words because the sense inventory was produced in an iterative process alongside the development of the corpora.

[4]The January 1998 sub-corpus of the PKU-ICL-PD-Corpus was provided on the ICL website for free download, and we therefore decided to include it in the PKUSenseCor corpus.

et al. (2006).[5] PKUSenseCor, the subset of PKU-ICL-PD-Corpus to which word sense tagging was applied, consists of 23 million Chinese characters (nearly 14 million words).

For the sense inventory, the grammatical knowledge base (GKB) of contemporary Chinese was used (Yu et al. 2003). This knowledge base contains a coarse-grained inventory, which allows for the specification of grammatical information together with word meaning. For every word in the GKB that has more than one meaning for a given word in a given part-of-speech, all the tokens for these target words were tagged in all the PDN texts from the year 2000 and January 1998 PKU-ICL-PD-Corpus data, giving a total of more than 840,000 word sense tokens. This is the largest amount of sense-tagged Mandarin data and, to the best of our knowledge, the only existing all-word sense-tagged Mandarin corpus.

11.2.2 Sense Inventory: The Grammatical Knowledge Base of Contemporary Chinese

The knowledge base that we used for our sense inventory in this project was the GKB (Yu et al. 2003), which is a rich lexical resource with wide coverage. One of its main features is the detailed descriptions of the syntactic attributes of Chinese words in the database. The GKB was constructed in 1991 by many computational linguistics researchers, and it has been continually refined and updated.

Table 11.1 below provides some example verb entries for just a few attributes that are applicable out of 46 attributes in total. Only the subset of those shown in Table 11.1 will be described since the focus is on the sense inventory. Most of the attribute values are binary, for example, auxiliary and intransitive. Some attributes are enumerated types, for instance, for the tense auxiliary attribute "着了过": "着" denotes present tense, "了" denotes past tense, and "过" denotes perfect tense. "单作谓语" indicates whether the word can be used as a standalone predicate (i.e., a "lexical" verb rather than an auxiliary or modal verb) and "单作补语" specifies whether the word can act as a complement. For these two attributes (谓语 and 补语), "可" is a positive value, whereas a blank is interpreted as a verb lacking this property. "兼 类" indicates that this word has more than one POS and the other POS categories are provided.

There are 78,947 word types (word and POS combinations) in this database, which is organized by POS. That is to say, each POS has its own table. The 18 main POS types include nouns, time words, location words, localizers, numerals, measure words, distinguishing words, pronouns, verbs, adjectives, state words, adverbs, prepositions, conjunctions, auxiliary words, modal particles, onomatopoeias, and interjections. Besides these word classes, there are another eight POS categories,

[5] Available at http://icl.pku.edu.cn/icl_res/segtag98/catetkset.html with a translated version at http://www.dianamccarthy.co.uk/downloads/GKBCCPoSinfo.pdf

Table 11.1 Some entries for a subset of attributes in the verb sub-database

词语 (Word)	同形 (Homograph)	义项 (Glosses)	助动 (Auxiliary)	外内 (Intransitive)	着了过	单作谓语	单作补语	兼类
理发 (hair cut)				1	了过	可		
会 (meet with)	A	见面			着了过			n
会 (master)	B1	理解				可	可	
会 (will)	B2	可能	Yes			可		
会 (pay bill)	C	付帐				可		
会 (be able to)	D	能够	Yes			可		
保管 (take care of)	1	保存			着了过	可		
帮 (help)		帮助			着了过	可		q
冒险 (risk)				1	过			a

Table 11.2 A sample of a homograph

Word	Pinyin	Homograph	Glosses	Sentences	English trans.	More grammatical info.
笔记本	bi3ji4ben3	1	本子	软皮~	Notebook	...
笔记本	bi3ji4ben3	2	笔记本式计 算机	大容量~	Laptop	...

such as enclitics, idioms, and punctuation, which were treated as further POS types even though they are not word classes.

The GKB has been used in nearly all fields of Mandarin natural language processing, such as event nouns (Wang and Huang 2011), machine translation (Chang et al. 2010), WSD (Che and Zhang 2011), and parsing (Drábek and Zhou 2001). Besides the syntactic information, coarse granularity semantic distinctions (akin to distinctions at the homograph level) are also provided in this huge knowledge base. Table 11.2 provides an example of a homograph for the word 笔记本, which has two senses: a paper notebook and a laptop. This homograph, of course, also has detailed grammatical information, but for the sake of brevity, it will not be provided here.

Table 11.3 Statistics for the GKB and the PKUSenseCor

POS	#Word types	#Homograph	#Sense	#Word tokens	#Homograph tokens
Noun (n)	37,637	287	575	4,461,150	36,108
Verb (v)	15,405	415	958	3,451,763	651,155
Adjective (a)	3153	18	36	651,990	900
Adverb (d)	1234	2	4	707,269	481
Preposition (p)	111	2	5	591,147	33,661
Conjunction (c)	246	9	20	388,167	30,798
Numeral (m)	161	1	2	548,048	2120
Measure words (q)	476	43	96	310,651	22,481
Total	58,423	777	1696	11,110,185	777,704

In producing the PKUSenseCor, we annotated any occurrences of the homographs identified as such in the GKB in a sample of over 13 million words from the PDN in 2000 and in January 1998.

11.3 Corpus Annotation

In the PKUSenseCor, there are 13,719,918 words.[6] All the homographs described by the GKB were tagged. Within our corpus of over 13 million words,[7] more than 840,000 word tokens were assigned a word sense. In what follows, the tags applied to all homographs, except those listed as pronouns, interjections, modal particles, onomatopoeias, location words, localizers, and time words, will be described. Details for all the content words (i.e., nouns, verbs, and adjectives) and some function words (i.e., adverbs, prepositions, conjunctions, numerals, and measures words) are shown in Table 11.3.

Table 11.3 provides statistics from the application of the GKB to the PKUSenseCor. The second, third, and fourth columns relate to the GKB, whereas the final two columns relate to the statistics of the tagged senses in the PKUSenseCor. Column 2 shows the number of word types from the GKB for the respective POS; column 3 shows the number of homographs; column 4 shows the number of senses for the homographs; column 5 shows the number of word tokens in the corpus, regardless of whether they were tagged or not; and column 6 shows the number of tokens that were tagged with the homograph senses in the PKUSenseCor. Table 11.3 shows that 7% of the markable tokens are homographs in the PDN in 2000, although only 1.33% of the word types in the dictionary for these specified POS categories are homographs.

[6]There are also 2,434,875 punctuations.

[7]11 million words were tagged with POS.

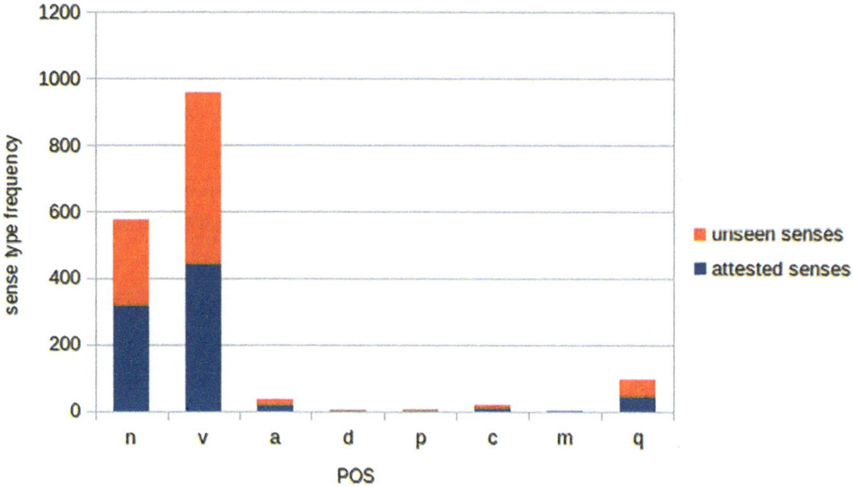

Fig. 11.1 Sense type frequency from the GKB attested or unattested in the PKUSenseCor

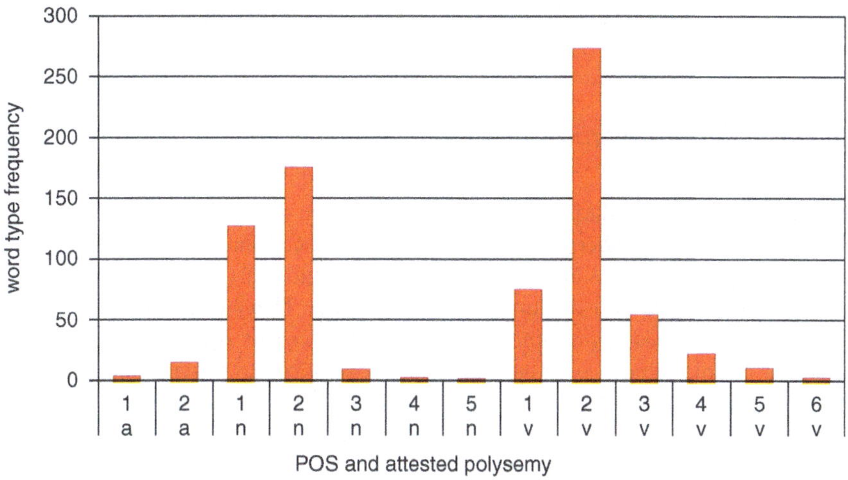

Fig. 11.2 Word type frequency by POS and attested polysemy in the PKUSenseCor for nouns, verbs, and adjectives

Although many tokens in the PKUSenseCor are homographs, many senses of the homographs in the GKB do not appear in the corpus due to the Zipfian distribution of words and the skewed nature of word sense distributions. Thus, some words are not attested in the corpus and, furthermore, many of words that do appear do not occur in all their senses (Agirre and Edmonds 2006). This is illustrated in Fig. 11.1, which shows the number of senses attested (seen) in the PKUSenseCor compared to those unseen (i.e., the total for each POS gives the total number of homograph senses, as in the fourth column—#Sense—in Table 11.3). Figure 11.2, meanwhile, shows the

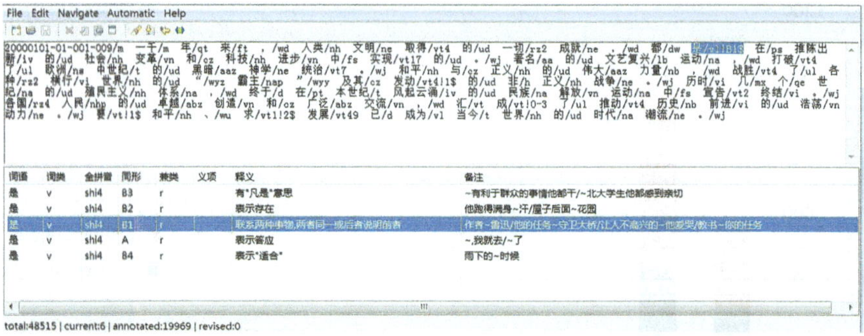

Fig. 11.3 The annotation tool

number of different word types with the number of attested senses (attested polysemy) for the noun, verb, and adjective[8] homographs that appear in the PKUSenseCor. All of these are homographs in the GKB, but many are shown with only one sense in the PKUSenseCor; nevertheless, as can be seen in Fig. 11.2, there is plenty of ambiguity still attested in the PKUSenseCor, as the majority of nouns, verbs, and adjectives appear with at least two of their senses:

11.3.1 The Annotation Process

In all, 20 native Mandarin speakers were involved in the annotation. Of these annotators, 18 were undergraduates (computer science) and the remaining 2 were doctors in computational linguists (two of the co-authors). The 18 undergraduates were trained by the two doctors before annotating. They were divided into nine groups and assigned equal amounts of data. The corpus data were tagged in a standard double-blind way. The annotators were asked to provide one sense tag for each markable homograph token. Figure 11.3 shows the annotation tool. The upper part shows the context surrounding an occurrence of the homograph, while the lower part displays all the relevant information from the GKB. The annotators could easily annotate the intended sense by clicking the entry from the GKB that best reflected the sense of the word in the context shown.

Whenever two junior annotators disagreed, the two senior academics conferred and used a tool to check the annotations (see Fig. 11.4), and one was in charge of making the final decision. The upper part of the interface in Fig. 11.4 shows the running text of cases where there was a homograph with a discrepancy in the annotation arising from the two junior annotators. The middle section displays the details of the disagreement, with columns marked 1 and 2 displaying the choices from each of the two junior annotators. The bottom part of the screen provides the

[8]The data were restricted to these types for the sake of brevity.

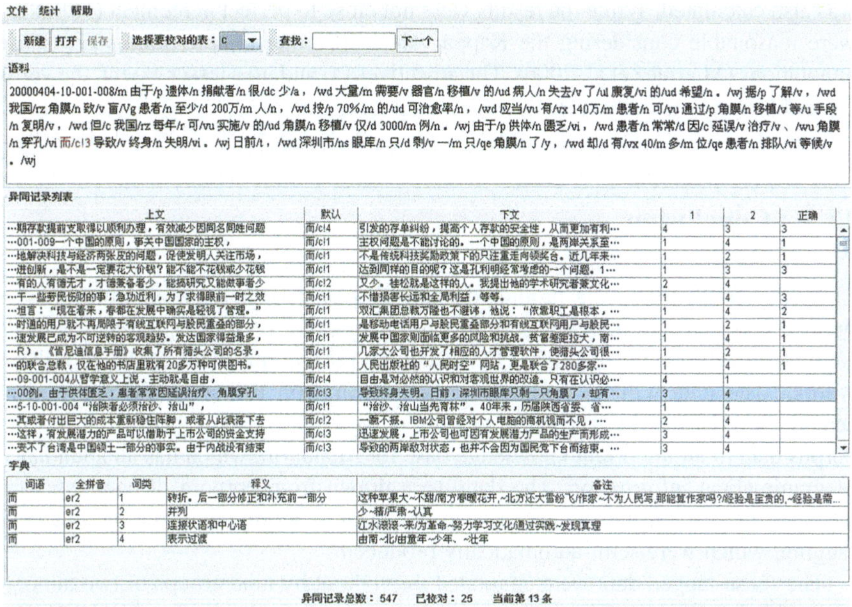

Fig. 11.4 The adjudication tool

Table 11.4 Inter-annotator agreement

POS	KAPPA	Number of annotated tokens	Annotated tokens with the same tag	IAA
a	0.24	40	24	0.60
c	0.54	1870	1568	0.84
d	0.59	36	33	0.92
m	0.47	90	67	0.74
n	0.48	1854	1593	0.86
p	0.57	1882	1532	0.81
q	0.60	1254	1091	0.87
v	0.25	36,297	28,204	0.78

relevant information from the GKB, and the adjudicating annotator selected the correct entry from the list of senses.

11.4 Inter-annotator Agreement

A portion of the data, from the first 20 days of June 2000, contained the original sense annotations from two independent annotators to calculate inter-tagger agreement. The results showed that the overall inter-tagger agreement was 0.787, and the results by POS are provided in Table 11.4. Cohen's Kappa (Bruce and Wiebe 1998) was also calculated. While the results were not close to perfect agreement (1.0), they were reasonable considering the Kappa values for other double-blind word sense annotations (Màrquez et al. 2006). The adjectives (a) and, to a lesser extent, the verbs (v) had lower agreement rates than the nouns (n).

11.5 Conclusion

This chapter described the production and data of a large-scale all-word coarse-grained sense-tagged Mandarin corpus comprising in excess of 840,000 sense tokens (more than 777,000 for the main POS categories) in a corpus with nearly 14 million words.[9] The data will be useful to those working on the computational lexical semantics of Mandarin. The sense tagging is particularly useful because it ties the corpus data to an important knowledge base for Mandarin, which has an abundance of grammatical information. The data were drawn from corpora of contemporary Chinese that had further annotations in the form of word segmentation and POS tagging, which were semi-automatically produced.

The sense-tagged data were annotated throughout by nine groups of two annotators, with adjudication by another two. The data have already been used for the evaluation of computational linguistic systems in the task of finding infrequent word senses (Jin and Wu 2010), which is an important task in the application of text-to-speech production. In the future, we plan to add further layers of annotation to the PKUSenseCor corpus. We also intend to apply fine-grained sense tagging to all the words that have been tagged with the coarse-grained senses in this project. We have started the process of applying a dependency parser to a 3-month portion of the PDN data (January to March 2000) and are also in the process of tagging syntactic relationships between sub-sentences.

Acknowledgments We would like to acknowledge Nianwen Xue for his advice on OntoNotes. This work was partly supported by the National Natural Science Foundation of China (61373056, 61272221, 61772278).

References

Agirre, Eneko, and Philip Edmonds. 2006. *Word sense disambiguation: Algorithms and applications*. Springer Press.

Bond, Francis, Timothy Baldwin, Richard Fothergill, and Kiyotaka Uchimoto. 2012. Japanese SemCor: A sense-tagged corpus of Japanese. In *Proceedings of the 6th International Conference of the Global WordNet Association*, Matsue, Japan.

[9]Readers who are interested in obtaining the data can contact the first and second authors.

Bruce, Rebecca, and Janyce Wiebe. 1998. Word-sense distinguishability and inter-coder agreement. In *Proceedings of the third Conference on Empirical Methods for Natural Language Processing*, 53–60, Granada, Spain.

Chang, Baobao, Byeong Kwu Kang, and Shiwen Yu. 2010. Developing CAT tools for translating Chinese scientific monographs. *Journal of Translation Studies* (13)2:165–179.

Che, Ling, and Yangsen Zhang. 2011. Study on word sense disambiguation knowledge base based on multi-sources. In *Proceedings of the 3rd International Workshop on Intelligent Systems and Applications*, Wuhan, China.

Chen, Jinying, and Martha Palmer. 2009. Improving English verb sense disambiguation performance with linguistically motivated features and clear sense distinction boundaries. *Journal of Language Resources and Evaluation* (43)2:181–208.

Drábek, Franco Elliot, and Qiang Zhou. 2001. Use of a lexical feature database for partial parsing of Chinese. In *Proceedings of the 6th Natural Language Processing Pacific Rim Symposium*, Tokyo, Japan.

Duan, Huiming, Xiaojing Bai, Baobao Chang, and Shiwen Yu. 2003. Chinese word segmentation at Peking University. In *Proceedings of the 2nd SIGHAN Workshop on Chinese Language Processing*, Sapporo, Japan.

Fellbaum, Christiane (ed). 1998. *WordNet: An electronic database*. Cambridge, MA: The MIT Press.

Hovy, Eduard, Mitch Marcus, Martha Palmer, Lance Ramshaw, and Ralph Weischedel. 2006. OntoNotes: The 90% solution. In *Proceedings of the HLT-NAACL*. New York, USA.

Ide, Nancy, Baker Colin, Christiane Fellbaum, Charles Fillmore, and Rebecca Passonneau. 2008. MASC: The manually annotated sub-corpus of American English. In *Proceedings of the 6th LREC*, Marrakech, Morocco.

Jin, Peng, and Yungfan Wu. 2010. SemEval-2 Task 15: Infrequent sense identification for Mandarin text to speech systems. In *Proceedings of the 5th International Workshop on Semantic Evaluation*, Upsala, Sweden.

Kilgarriff, Adam. 1998. SENSEVAL: An exercise in evaluating word sense disambiguation programs. In *Proceedings of the 8th EURALEX International Congress*, Liège, Belgium.

Kilgarriff, Adam, and Joseph Rosenzweig. 2000. English SENSEVAL: Framework and results. In *Proceedings of the 2nd LREC*, Athens, Greece.

Màrquez, Lluís, Gerard Escudero, David Martínez, and German Rigau. 2006. Supervised corpus-based methods for word sense disambiguation. In *Word sense disambiguation. Algorithms and applications*, eds. Eneko Agirre and Philip Edmonds. Springer Press.

McCarthy, Diana. 2009. Word sense disambiguation: An overview. *Language and Linguistics Compass* (3)2:537–558.

Miller, A. George, Richard Beckwith, Christiane Fellbaum, Derek Gross, and Katherine J. Miller. 1990. WordNet: An online lexical database. *Journal of Lexicography* (3)4:235–244.

Miller, A. George, Martin Chodorow, Shari Landes, Claudia Leacock, and Robert G. Thomas. 1994. Using a semantic concordance for sense identification. In *Proceedings of the 3th ARPA Human Language Technology Workshop*, Plainsboro, New Jersey.

Navigli, Roberto. 2009. Word sense disambiguation: A survey. *ACM Computer Survey* (41)2.

Ng, Hwee Tou, and Hian Beng Lee. 1996. Integrating multiple knowledge sources to disambiguate word senses: An exemplar-based approach. In *Proceedings of the 34th ACL*, Santa Cruz, California.

Wang, Shan, and Chu-Ren Huang. 2011. Compound event nouns of the "modifier-head" type in Mandarin Chinese. In *Proceedings of the 25th Pacific Asia Conference on Language, Information and Computation*, Singapore.

Weischedel, Ralph, Martha Palmer, Mitchell Marcus, Eduard Hovy, Sameer Pradhan, Lance Ramshaw, Nianwen Xue, Ann Taylor, Jeff Kaufman, Michelle Franchini, Mohammed El-Bachouti, Robert Belvin, and Ann Houston. 2013. OntoNotes Release 5.0 LDC2013T19. Web download. Philadelphia, PA: Linguistic Data Consortium. Available at https://catalog.ldc.upenn.edu/LDC2013T19. Accessed 5 June 2017.

Yu, Shiwen, Xuefeng Zhu, Hui Wang, Huarui Zhang, Yunyun Zhang, Dexi Zhu, Jianming Lu, and Rui Guo. 2003. *Grammatical knowledge-base of contemporary Chinese—A complete specification* (2nd ed.). Beijing: Tsinghua University Press.

Zhan, Weidong, Baobao Chang, Huiming Duan and Huarui Zhang. 2006. Recent developments in Chinese corpus research. In *Proceedings of the 13th NIJL International Symposium, Language Corpora: Their Compilation and Application*, Tokyo, Japan.

Chapter 12
Semantic Annotation and Mandarin VerbNet

Meichun Liu

Abstract This chapter will examine the challenging issues in the semantic annotation of verbal information in Mandarin Chinese. It will also probe into the unique array of semantic properties encoded in the Mandarin verbal lexicon and propose a frame-based constructional approach that is aligned with linguistic premises in functional theories, including frame semantics, construction grammar, and cognitive grammar. Given that semantic processing pertains to cognitive mechanisms in general, the semantic transfer and profile of base schemas in event chains should be considered for verbal categorization and representation. The proposed approach has been adopted in the development of Mandarin VerbNet, which was designed to provide the lexical semantic information of the major classes of Mandarin verbs in an attempt to offer a linguistically valid and application useful representation of the Mandarin verbal lexicon.

Keywords Lexical annotation · Mandarin VerbNet · Verbal semantics · Mandarin verb lexicon · Frame-based constructional approach

12.1 Introduction

Natural language processing (NLP) research of the Chinese language[1] has achieved a fairly good performance rate on a number of tasks, such as word segmentation, POS tagging, and even syntactic parsing. However, semantic annotation has always been a tougher issue since "meaning" involves a vast and complex system of conceptual structures that may be encoded at various levels of linguistic realization. It is thus difficult to create an exhaustive and all-applicable set of tags that can fully represent semantic relations. Efforts in semantic tagging that have focused on a

[1] In this chapter, "Mandarin" refers to Putonghua (or Guoyu ""national language"") and "Chinese" refers to the Chinese language, which includes Mandarin and other Chinese dialects.

M. Liu (✉)
Department of Linguistics and Translation, City University of Hong Kong, Hong Kong, China
e-mail: meichliu@cityu.edu.hk

C.-R. Huang et al. (eds.), *Chinese Language Resources*, Text, Speech and Language Technology 49, https://doi.org/10.1007/978-3-031-38913-9_12

"generic" set of semantic roles centered on verbs (cf. Sinica Treebank [Chen et al. 1996] and PKU Project [Wang et al. 王惠等 2003]) have encountered problems because the predetermined tagsets were not flexible and accurate enough to be applied to the whole inventory of verb senses. On the other hand, semantic annotation based on verb frames (cf. PropBank [Palmer et al. 2005] and FrameNet [Ruppenhofer et al. 2016]) has encountered problems in the distinction and classification of frames, which may not be easily detectable and definable. No matter how broad or fine-grained the semantic tags are, semantic annotation remains a challenge because it is closely related to the human cognitive ability of conceptualization as well as semantic transfer, from concrete to abstract domains, from human to non-human experiences, and from prototypical to peripheral members. This chapter will present some of the major problems in semantic role annotation in an attempt to find a suitable annotation framework for the Mandarin verbal lexicon. It will also review the design of Mandarin VerbNet,[2] which adopted a hybrid approach to frame-based semantic roles and construction-based syntactic criteria (Liu and Chang 2016). This chapter will show that a frame-based constructional approach to the analysis of Mandarin verbs and verb classes is linguistically well-motivated and methodologically well-founded. Moreover, a language-specific comprehensive work is in great need as the Mandarin verbal lexicon may encode different frame taxonomies from those in English.

One of the major problems in using general semantic tags is that a specific tag may not be applicable to all possible candidates occurring in the same position. For instance, the semantic role of Agents is normally defined as deliberately acting initiators of an action, and thus Agents are most commonly instantiated by a human subject, but when the action involves a non-human subject, it is not so intuitively appropriate to mark it as an Agent, as illustrated in Example (9.1).

(9.1)	Different Agent-subjects of the action verb "hit":
(a)	**The boy** hit her hard. → human Agent
(b)	**The wind** hit her hard. → non-human, physical Agent (?)
(c)	**His words** hit her hard. → non-human, non-physical Agent (??)

The solution may be twofold: either redefine the semantic roles or redefine the verb senses. However, both solutions are costly and result in further complications in sense distinction. A more cognitively and linguistically sound approach is to re-examine the meaning of verbs with their supporting roles within a conceptually viable system that simulates the way the human mind works. Human beings cognize the world by categorization (Harnad 2005), and verbs provide a means to categorize events (Croft 1990; Croft and Cruse 2004). Each event category is a distinct event type depicting a conceptually salient schema, which is best represented by the prototypical members (i.e., verbs) of the category. This line of research has been advocated by cognitive linguists and partially implemented into FrameNet based on

[2] http://verbnet.lt.cityu.edu.hk

the theory of frame semantics (Fillmore 1982, 1985), with the premise that verb meanings are embedded in a conceptual background that serves as a semantic prerequisite for verb behavior. This semantic background, however, is depicted mainly by a set of frame-specific elements. While syntactic templates are given, they are only used to illustrate the range of semantic roles. Moreover, no explicit constructional information is given to highlight the grammatical distinctions associated with different types of verbs. When applying a frame-based semantic annotation system to Mandarin in the current study, several issues were found that needed to be resolved, given the unique characteristics of Chinese.

12.2 Issues in the Annotation of Chinese Verbs

While it is debatable whether Chinese verbs or even "words" can be clearly defined (cf. Dai 1992; Duanmu 1998; Feng 馮勝利 2001; Huang 1984; Huang et al. 黃居仁等 1998; Lü 呂叔湘 1981; Packard 2000), it may be helpful to discuss some common issues arising from morphological flexibility in the Chinese verbal lexicon. Chinese verbs are highly compositional in morphological structures, which results in an open class of partially filled semi-lexical templates that generate possible bimorphemic or multimorphemic verbs. While PropBank allows some phrasal verbs such as "go off" and "blow up" (cf. Palmer et al. 2005), they are relatively limited in English. However, Chinese verbs are morphologically productive in combination with other morphemes. For instance, monomorphemic verbs in Mandarin are commonly combined with an adverbial or manner verb to form manner-verb (M-V) compounds, and different frames of verbs may prefer different manner adverbials. In the communication domain, verbs such as 喊 *han* "yell" and 叫 *jiao* "shout" commonly co-occur with volume-related adverbials such as 高/大/猛 *gao/da/meng* "high/big/strong." These types of verbs then form an open and semi-lexicalized class of bimorphemic M-V compounds as the manner component can be filled with various elements indicating the manner of yelling or shouting, such as 狂喊/猛喊/大喊/亂喊/高喊 *kuang-han/meng-han/da-han/luan-han/gao-han* "to yell wildly/fiercely/loudly/randomly/loudly." This results in a productive set of co-lexemes (Hilpert 2008), or the so-called host-class expansion (Himmelmann 2004). In the annotation of verbal information, it is essential to decide whether the productive M-V compound should be taken as one lexical entity or as having a manner argument criticized to the verb. It is perceivable that the compound M-*han* "M-shout" is semantically and syntactically different from the single verb *han* since manner has been added, which will result in certain grammatical consequences (no separate manner will then be used in the clause). Yet this manner component is almost obligatory in some cases where bimorphemic verbs are preferred, which favors the treatment of the M-V compound as one unitary item rather than two separate components juxtaposed for semantic annotation. This preference is exemplified in Example (9.2), in which the sentence would be less acceptable if manner was omitted, which shows that M-*han* cannot be replaced by the single verb *han*:

(9.2a)	第三球進了之後, 全場狂喊/??喊 (Huang 2009)	
	disan__qiu__jin__le__zhihou__quanchang__**kuang-han/??han**	
	third__ball__enter__PERF__after__audience__**madly-yell/shout**	
	After the third shot was made, the audience yelled out madly.	
(9.2b)	數百名技師聚集立法院前, 高喊/??喊「歐晉德下台」(Huang 2009)	
	shubai-ming__jishi__juji__lifayuan__qian__**gao-han/??han**__Oujinde__xiatai	
	thousands-CL__technician__gather__ Legislative Yuan__front__	
	loudly.yell/??yell__Oujinde__step down	
	Thousands of technicians gathered in front of the Legislative Yuan, shouted loudly	
	"Oujinde step down"	

On the other hand, the verb *han* in an M-*han* compound may be replaced by other similar verbs in the communication domain, which may be equally well formed in structure and meaning. For instance, *han* can be replaced by another yelling verb like *jiao* to form M-*jiao* compounds (e.g., 狂叫/大叫/亂叫 *kuang-jiao/da-jiao/luan-jiao* "to yell wildly/loudly/randomly") or 吼 *hou* "roar" to form M-*hou* compounds (e.g., 狂吼/大吼/亂吼 *kuang-hou/da-hou/luan-hou* "to roar wildly/loudly/randomly"). Thus, the three variants of M-Vs can be generalized as "M-$V_{yelling}$" (*han/jiao/hou* in the yelling frame), which can be listed as a semi-lexicalized, open-class verb in the communication domain.

Another issue regarding productive compounding in a semantic frame is that the prototypical or default verb in the frame can normally form combinations with other semantically more specified lemma to produce new verb compounds. For instance, the three commonly used verbs for hanging—掛/懸/吊 *gua/xuan/diao* "hang"—can be combined into verb-verb (V-V) compounds that belong to the same semantic frame (e.g., 懸掛/懸吊/吊掛 *xuan-gua/xuan-diao/diao-gua* "hang") or with verbs from other classes to form compounds in different frames (e.g., 掛慮/懸疑/吊念 *gua-lü/xuan-yi/diao-nian* "worry/suspect/condole").

It is also common to find collocates of verb-object (V-O) compounds that are semi-lexicalized in a specific frame (e.g., 掛心/懸賞/吊球 *gua-xin/xuan-shang/diao-qiu* "worry/bounty-offer/lob"). Given the frequent use of bare nouns in Chinese, some V-O compounds in each domain may be used as either one consolidated lexical entity or two separate words. A gradation in terms of lexical status can occur as in the combination of 吊球 *diao-qiu* "lob," for example. The compound *diao-qiu* is semantically fixed as the meaning unit "lob" in English; however, when *diao-qiu* is used to portray the event of lobbing, there are three different ways to use the compound and they vary, not just in separability but also in morphoconstructional patterns, as shown in Example (9.3).

(9.3a)	*diao* with inverted *qiu*
	後衛從左翼將球吊到球門前
	houwei__cong__zuoyi__jiang__qiu__**diao**__dao__qiumenqian
	back__from__left-wing__JIANG__ball__**lob**__to__goalmouth *The back lobbed the ball to the goalmouth from the left wing.*

(continued)

(9.3b)	As one unit: *diao-qiu*
	後衛從左翼吊球到球門前
	houwei__cong__zuoyi__**diao-qiu**__dao__qiumenqian
	back__from__left-wing__**lob-ball**__to__goalmouth
	The back lobbed the ball to the goalmouth from the left wing.
(9.3c)	With an inserted element: *diao*-X-*qiu*
	後衛從左翼吊高球到球門前
	houwei__cong__zuoyi__**diao-gao-qiu**__dao__qiumenqian
	back__from__left-wing__**lob-high-ball**__to__goalmouth
	The back lobbed the ball highly to the goalmouth from the left wing.

The morphological flexibility in forming various V-V and V-O compounds needs to be dealt with as the initial task of identifying verb entities. It has been found that available word segmentation systems may not be fine-tuned enough to cover frame-specific compounding patterns, which may vary with their semantic specificities from verb to verb and from frame to frame. Thus, a set of semi-lexicalized compounding templates needs to be included in each frame that can accommodate the productive process. Finding the best strategy to accurately identify and predict the morphologically specified verb templates in each frame is still a challenging and empirical issue.

One consequence of the compositional flexibility of Chinese verbs discussed above is that monomorphemic verbs can often be combined with other monomorphemic components to form bimorphemic verbs of various sorts that may affect the classification of verbs. As a result, monomorphemic verbs are potentially polysemous as they may be combined into bimorphemic verbs to render different meanings. Take the verb 放 *fang* as an example, as defined in Example (9.4a–g).

(9.4)	Polysemous nature of monomorphemic verbs in Chinese:
(a)	放置 ***fang*** *zhi*: put or place
(b)	放棄 ***fang*** *qi*: give up
(c)	放任 ***fang*** *ren*: let go
(d)	釋放 *shi* ***fang***: release, set free
(e)	解放 *jie* ***fang***: liberate
(f)	流放 *liu* ***fang***: exile
(g)	裝放 *zhuang* ***fang***: load

This leads to the issue that is commonly addressed as sense disambiguation. Given the high frequency of homonyms and polysemes in Chinese, the issue of how many distinct senses a verb may have or how many frames a verb may belong to is especially challenging. Besides polysemous combinations of verbs, another source of sense extension originates from the cognitive mechanism of conceptual transfer. In Example (9.5a–c), the uses of *fang* are interrelated, as the more abstract, nonspatial sense is extended from the prototypically concrete and spatial sense:

(9.5a)	Spatial-motional *fang*	
	他把書放在桌子上	
	ta__ba__shu__fang__zai__zhuozi-shang	
	3rd.sg__BA__book__put__at__table-above	
	He put the books on the table	
(9.5b)	Less spatial-motional *fang*	
	他把文章放在他的部落格上	
	ta__ba__wenzhang__fang__zai__ta__de__buluoge-shang	
	3rd.sg__BA__article__put__at__3rd.sg__GEN__blog-above	
	He posted the articles on his blog	
(9.5c)	Non-spatial-motional	
	他把心思放在孩子身上	
	ta__ba__xinsi__fang__zai__haizi__shen-shang	
	3rd.sg__BA__mind__put__at__child__body-above	
	He put his mind on the children	

In the three uses of *fang* in Example (9.5a–c), there is a gradation of concreteness, spatiality, and motionness, which are identical in their syntactic forms but vary in semantic frames: (9.5a) describes placement; (9.5b) describes publishing; and (9.5c) describes caring about children. Can they all be categorized into one sense according to their shared syntactic structure? One possible approach to answering this question is to define each semantic frame with a set of defining constructions but also allow a general set of metaphorical principles to be applied to all Mandarin verbs, such as the following Example (9.6a–c).

(9.6)	General metaphorical principles for verbal sense extension:
(a)	motional to nonmotional
(b)	spatial to nonspatial
(c)	concrete to nonconcrete

Conceptual transfer allows verbs to have many various uses. In Chinese WordNet (Huang et al. 黃居仁等 2010),[3] *fang* has 37 distinctive senses and thus inevitably raises the question of how a verb can be used so diversely and how it is possible to annotate all the senses. Using a different measure for sense distinction, Hwang and Chen 黃郁純, 陳薌宇 (2005) proposed eight distinct senses of *fang* based on the frequency of its collocations compared with 擺 *bai* "set." However, it was not clear how the proposed senses were syntactically motivated and in what ways they were interrelated. In a further attempt to consolidate the senses of *fang*, Luo 羅云普 (2011) suggested that the different uses of *fang* can be generalized into two polar meanings, namely, "to put" and "to release," as exemplified in Example (9.7a–b). But again, there was no account provided for the determining criteria and interconnection between the two postulated meanings.

[3] http://lope.linguistics.ntu.edu.tw/cwn2

(9.7) Two senses of *fang*: "put" vs. "release"

(a) Placement frame

她把畫放出來展示

ta__ba__hua__fang__chu-lai__zhanshi

3rd.sg__BA__painting__put__out __display

She put out the painting for display

(b) Releasing Frame

她把貓放出來展示

ta__ba__mao__fang__chulai__zhanshi

3rd.sg__BA__cat__release__out__display

She let the cat out for display

Potentially, the sentences in Example (9.7a–b) are ambiguous since they share exactly the same surface forms. How can a semantic annotation framework detect differences? While Levin's (1993) work on English verb classes made it clear that semantic analysis should be rooted in syntactic evidence such as diathesis alternations, it is equally important to maintain that syntactic criteria also need to be selected and guided by semantic frameworks so that the surface forms can be made sense of. For a non-inflectional language like Chinese, the eminent issue is how to identify the range of morphosyntactic features that are most salient for annotating Mandarin verbal semantics.

This leads to yet another issue about the definition and scope of verb frames. How should verb-anchoring frames be defined and related to each other? At first sight, the senses of "put" and "release" seem to be unrelated, but if taking into consideration the natural progression of motion, there is a clear eventive inference between the two: an entity must be released from its source location before it can be put into an endpoint location. The releasing of an entity may naturally implicate a progression of a path, with the entity landing at an endpoint location. Thus, "releasing" may be viewed as a motional prerequisite in the event of "putting." The two distinguished senses of *fang* simply highlight or "profile" the two ends of a motional event chain. This explains why the two distinct senses are semantically related and formally encoded by the same verb. It also indicates a semantic link between the seemingly unrelated verb frames (releasing and placement frames) as they represent two separable but related stages in an event chain. All in all, semantic annotation must take note of the way events are conceptualized and cross-referenced, as reflected in the specific inventory of verbs and verb senses in a given language.

12.3 Frame-Based Constructional Approach to Semantic Annotation

To accommodate the unique features of Chinese, a hybrid approach was adopted in annotating the Mandarin verbal lexicon, which incorporated the tenets of frame semantics (Fillmore 1982, 1985), construction grammar (Goldberg 1995, 2002), and cognitive grammar (Langacker 1987). From a cognitive semantic perspective, great emphasis has been placed on the conceptual framework as a prerequisite to defining meaning. According to frame semantics, the meaning of a verb can be defined only in relation to a structured background of eventive knowledge and experiences. The Background Frame is shared by semantically related lemmas that can be best described and unified within a set of frame-specific participant roles (i.e., Frame Elements). On the other hand, a commonly held belief in lexical semantic studies is that the meaning of a verb is manifested in syntactic realizations (Levin 1993). Under this premise, verbal meanings can only be distinguished if they are syntactically detectable.

Expanding on frame-verb relations by integrating the syntactic-to-semantic notion that verbal meanings can be distinguished with the help of their formal behaviors,[4] the proposed approach is a hybrid that refines the semantic notion of frames with the aid of syntactic constraints from construction grammar. A construction is defined as a basic form-meaning mapping template that can be instantiated with a semantically compatible verb as an instance of construction realization. Constructions and verbs, which are meaning-bearing units, go hand in hand in defining the semantics of argument realizations characteristic of a given Background Frame. The construction-based approach is powerful in its account of the idiosyncratic uses of a verb in a nontypical syntactic frame (e.g., *He sneezed the napkin off the table.*). By shifting the point of interest from verb-based to construction-based, the constructional approach is useful in defining the form-meaning mapping relations uniquely associated with verb classes, but it needs to be constrained by a deeper consideration and incorporation of lexical specificities to capture finer lexical distinctions. As Boas (2003, p. 14) suggested, "[e]ach sense of a verb forms a mini-construction containing frame semantic as well as syntactic information. . . ."

In view of the theoretical concerns, a frame-based lexical-constructional approach has been applied to the analysis of Mandarin verbs (cf. Boas 2003; Iwata 2008). With this approach, lexical senses are analyzed initially via Eventive Frames, and the profiling specifications of individual verbs or verb classes are then identified with lexical-constructional variations that serve as formal indicators of semantic distinctions. As exemplified in Example (9.8a–d), using the placement verb 放 *fang* "to put/place," the semantic annotation of verbs is realized by two main categories of

[4] It should be noted that this approach adopted just the notion that verbal meanings could be distinguished by syntactic variants, but not the generative viewpoint.

information[5]: Frame Elements and Construction Markers (marked with an asterisk [*]). Frame Elements are verb-specific core and non-core elements (participant roles) that profile the verb meaning based on Fillmore's (1982, 1985) theory that verb senses are anchored in frames, while Construction Markers are salient syntactic indicators that are closely associated with verbs based on Levin's (1993) alternation-based approach, indicating the close relation between verb classes and syntactic constructions.

(9.8) Defining the placement verb *fang*:

(a) Frame: placement frame

(b) Core Frame Elements: Placer, Figure, Ground[6]

(c) Construction markers: *BA, *Locative_Marker, *Aspect_Zhe

(d) Basic constructional patterns (selected):

(i) Transitive *BA*-construction

[她$_{\text{Placer}}$] [把$_{\text{*BA}}$] [玩具$_{\text{Figure}}$] 放 [在$_{\text{*Locative_Marker}}$] [房間裡$_{\text{Ground}}$]

ta__ba__wanju__fang__zai__fangjian-li

3rd.sg__BA__toy__put__in__room-inside

She put the toys in the room

(ii) Figure-prominent intransitive:

[玩具$_{\text{Figure}}$] 放 [在$_{\text{*Locative_Marker}}$] [房間裡$_{\text{Ground}}$]

wanju__fang__zai__fangjian-li

toy__put__in__room-inside

The toys were put in the room

(iii) Ground-prominent locative inversion:

[房間裡$_{\text{Ground}}$] 放 [著$_{\text{*Aspect_Zhe}}$] [玩具$_{\text{Figure}}$]

fangjian-li__fang__zhe__wanju

room-inside__put__DUR__toy

In the room was put toys

The constructions within a frame are not randomly selected but are cognitively motivated in defining and representing the meaning of the frame. As for the three basic constructions of *fang* in Example (9.8d), they are different profiles of a semantic base (i.e., the placement event [cf. Langacker 1987]). For the placement event, one can profile the event where "someone placed something in somewhere" or profile the spatial-configuration state between the figure and ground, with either a figure- or ground-prominent viewpoint.

From this perspective, the applicational goal was to build a verbal database, called Mandarin VerbNet, which aimed to provide salient lexical semantic information uniquely presented by the Mandarin verb lexicon. What follows is a brief introduction of the infrastructure and design principles of Mandarin VerbNet (http://ct001.cityu.edu.hk/home). With the frame-based constructional approach outlined above,

[5]The remainder of this paragraph is in response to one of the reviewer's concerns about the form of the semantic annotation in Mandarin VerbNet.

[6]Figure refers to the moved entity and ground refers to the location or endpoint (Talmy 1975).

Mandarin VerbNet recognizes that there are different scopes of meaning lexicalized in verbs, indicating different scopes of frames. Since meaning is defined and anchored within a frame, it observes the "ONE frame, ONE meaning" hypothesis in the analysis and classification of verbs. The database was built consistently and systematically with the following principles (i.e., the introduction of Mandarin VerbNet; see also Liu and Chiang 2008 for a discussion):

1. Frames are identified with a descriptive definition and a set of Frame Elements, which depict the semantic property characteristics of event categories. Conceptually, frames are also represented by an eventive schematic, which serves as the conceptual motivation that characterizes the cognitive basis.
2. The framework is hierarchically structured with a potentially four-layered working taxonomy to capture the varied scopes of frames: archi-frame > (primary frame) > basic frame > (micro-frame). The lower-layered frames can be viewed as the subframes of higher-layered frames (Liu and Chang 2005). That is to say, the hierarchical structure embeds top-down inheritance and using relations. Archi-frames and basic frames are required, while primary frames and micro-frames are optionally provided when necessary.
3. Basic frames are basic-level frames that are supposed to be cognitively salient and acquired earlier. They are the most constructionally sensitive, specified with a descriptive definition, representative lemmas, a set of core Frame Elements defining constructional patterns (the grammatical expression of Frame Elements and Construction Markers), and semi-lexicalized collocates to capture morphological flexibility in certain frames.
4. Archi-frames are broad semantic domains of superordinate event categories distinguished by a self-containing conceptual schema with the most relevant Frame Elements; basic frames are distinguished according to syntactically expressed constructions, defined as form-meaning mapping constructs, which may foreground or background certain Frame Elements inherited from the archi-frame. When necessary, primary frames are provided to capture a higher-level generalization of semantic and syntactic correlation (e.g., the emotion archi-frame has five primary frames that are distinguished according to their different profiles of subject roles and transitivity). For certain frequently occurring near synonym sets under a basic frame, a micro-frame will be given to anchor their semantic common ground. For instance, the verbs for hanging (e.g., 懸/掛/吊) share a micro-frame under the basic frame of placement, which helps further distinguish the fine-tuned semantic distinctions of the near-synonyms.
5. All semantic classifications of verbs are made according to syntactic distinctions in constructional patterns realized by Frame Elements and Construction Markers.
6. The sense distinction of polysemy follows the "ONE sense, ONE frame" principle. Therefore, verbs with multiple senses belong to multiple frames.
7. Semantic inheritance exists from top to bottom in the hierarchical structure. There are basically two types of frame relations: inheritance and using. Multiple inheritance relations may occur at all levels under the archi-frame.
8. Verbs are annotated with Frame Elements and Construction Markers.

Since the first introduction of the framework, 20 major domains of Mandarin verbs have been analyzed and the prototypical members of each domain have been annotated accordingly.[7] It was found that each class of Mandarin verbs demonstrated some significant differences from their English counterparts. Taking emotion verbs as an example, Liu (2016) showed that Mandarin emotion predicates lexicalize an additional set of semantic roles that are implicit and non-lexical in English. Distinct from traditionally proposed roles (e.g., experiencer vs. stimulus), the affector-affectee relation is lexically realized in a subclass of Mandarin verbs to encode a more dynamic and eventive emotional impact. Next, examples of emotion and motion domains will demonstrate how the Mandarin VerbNet framework works.

12.3.1 Emotion Archi-frames

The emotion archi-frame involves five primary frames (Liu 2016). While all describe the status between the stimulus (Stim) and the experiencer (Exp), they have various focuses and profiles, as briefly introduced in Example (9.9a–e).

(9.9) Five primary frames under the emotion archi-frame:
(a) Exp-subj verbs with intransitive S
• Lexical meaning: internal state of the experiencer
• Profile: experiencer
• Defining pattern: Exp + *hen* + V
• Representative lemmas: 高興 *gaoxing* "happy," 生氣 *shengqi* "angry"
(b) Exp-subj verbs with transitive A
• Lexical meaning: internal state of the experiencer
• Profile: both experiencer and stimulus
• Defining pattern: Exp + *hen* + V + Stim
• Representative lemmas: 羨慕 *xianmu* "envy," 愛 *ai* "love"
(c) Stim-subj verbs with intransitive S
• Lexical meaning: property of the stimulus
• Profile: stimulus
• Defining pattern: Stim + *hen* + V
• Representative lemmas: 恐怖 *kongbu* "scared," 有趣 *youqu* "interesting"
(d) Stim-subj Verbs with Transitive A
• Lexical meaning: property of the stimulus
• Profile: both stimulus and experiencer
• Defining pattern: Stim + *hen* + V + Exp
• Representative lemmas: 困擾 *kunrao* "obsess", 吸引 *xiyin* "attract"
(e) Affector-subj Verb with Transitive A

(continued)

[7] The seven domains are communication, cognition, perception, emotion, judgment, social interaction, and motion.

- Lexical meaning: impact by the affector
- Profile: affector and affectee
- Defining pattern: Affector + V + *le* + Affectee
- Representative lemmas: 激怒 *jinu* "anger", 打動 *dadong* "move (one"s heart)"

Take the "exp-subj verbs with Intransitive S" frame for further demonstration, as shown in Example (9.10a–e).

(9.10) Defining the exp-subj verbs with intransitive S frame:

(a) Definition: This frame describes an emotional status between the stimulus and the experiencer

(b) Core frame elements: stimulus, experiencer

(c) Frequently collocated construction markers: *degree, *causative[8]

(d) Basic constructional patterns (selected):

(i) Experiencer-prominent intransitive

[我$_{\text{Experiencer}}$] [非常$_{\text{*Degree}}$] 生氣

wo__feichang__shenqi

1st.sg__very__angry

I am very angry

(ii) Stimulus-prominent causative construction

[你的行為$_{\text{Stimulus}}$] [令$_{\text{*Causative}}$] [我$_{\text{Experiencer}}$] [很$_{\text{*Degree}}$] 生氣

ni__de__xingwei__ling__wo__hen__shenqi

2nd.sg__GEN__behavior__cause__1st.sg__very__angry

Your behavior makes me very angry

(e) Associated lemmas (selected): 高興 *gaoxing* "happy," 快樂 *kuaile* "happy," 生氣 *shengqi* "angry," 遺憾 *yihan* "regret," 煩 *fan* "annoy," etc.

The "exp-subj verbs with intransitive S" frame is distinguished from other frames based on a different set of core Frame Elements. Moreover, constructional patterns serve as important criteria. For instance, 愛 *ai* "love" and 討厭 *taoyan* "hate" are differentiated from the experiencer-oriented frame as they cannot participate in the intransitive construction, as exemplified in Example (9.11a–b).

(9.11a) ??我很愛

wo__hen__ai

1st.sg__very__love

(9.11b) ??我很討厭

wo__hen__taoyan

1st.sg__very__hate

[8]Construction Markers are marked with an asterisk (*) to separate them from Frame Elements.

12.3.2 Motion Archi-frames

Motion is another major class of verbs. The motion domain describes events whereby a figure moves to a ground along a path (cf. Talmy 1975), and it primarily involves two event prototypes, or two primary frames: the self-motion frame, in which the figure moves itself, and the caused-motion frame, in which the figure is moved by a causer. Take the caused-motion frame as an example for further demonstration. Several basic frames can be defined under the caused-motion frame based on various profiling and syntactic expressions, such as the releasing frame, caused-to-move frame, and placement frame. Information on each frame is exemplified, respectively, in Examples (9.12) to (9.14).

(9.12) Defining the releasing frame:
(a) Definition: a caused-motion process whereby a releaser causes a figure to move away from the confinement source
(b) Core frame elements: releaser, figure, (source)[9]
(c) Frequently collocated Construction Markers: *Path.out, (*Source_Marker)
(d) Basic constructional patterns (selected):
(i) Releaser-prominent transitive
[他$_{\text{Releaser}}$] [從$_{\text{*Source_Marker}}$] [鳥籠裡$_{\text{Source}}$] 放 [出$_{\text{*Path.out}}$] [一隻鴿子$_{\text{Figure}}$]
ta__cong__ niaolong-li __fang-chu__yi-zhi__gezi
3rd.sg__from__ birdcage-inside__release-out__one-CL__dove
He releases a dove from the birdcage.
(ii) Figure-prominent inchoative
[內部儲存的能量 $_{\text{Figure}}$] 突然放 [出 $_{\text{*Path.out}}$]
neibu__chucun__de__nengliang__turan__fang-chu
inside __store__GEN__power__suddenly__release.out
The power stored inside suddenly released
(e) Associated lemmas (selected): 放 *fang* "release," 釋 *shi* "release," 釋放 *shifang* "release," etc.
(9.13) Defining the caused-to-move frame
(a) Definition: a caused-motion process whereby a causer causes a figure to move to an endpoint ground
(b) Core frame elements: causer, figure, End.Ground
(c) Frequently collocated Construction Markers: *Path
(d) Basic constructional patterns (selected):
(i) Agent-prominent transitive *BA*-construction
[我$_{\text{Causer}}$] [把$_{\text{*BA}}$] [兩張桌子$_{\text{Figure}}$] 搬 [到$_{\text{*Path}}$] [教室裡$_{\text{End.Ground}}$]
wo__ba__liang-zhang__zhuozi__ban-dao__jiaoshi-li
1st.sg__BA__two-CL__table__move-to__classroom-inside
We moved two tables to the classroom

(continued)

[9] Source is commonly unexpressed in syntax due to the cognition bias of human beings (Regier and Zheng 2007).

(ii) Theme-prominent inchoative

[桌子$_{\text{Figure}}$] 搬 [到$_{\text{*Path}}$] [教室裡$_{\text{End.Ground}}$] (了)

zhuozi__ban-dao__jiaoshi-li__ (le)

table__move-to__classroom-inside__(PERF)

The tables were moved to the classroom

(e) Associated lemmas (selected): 搬 *ban* "move," 帶 *dai* "bring," 推 *tui* "push," 投 *tou* "pitch/shoot," 搬遷 *banqian* "move," 搬移 *banyi* "move," 挪 *nuo* "move," 投擲 *touzhi* "pitch/shoot," etc.

(9.14) Defining the placement frame:

(a) Definition: a caused-motion process whereby a placer causes a figure to be placed in a locative ground

(b) Core frame elements: causer, figure, Loc.Ground

(c) Frequently collocated Construction Markers: *Locative_Marker[10], *Aspect_Zhe

(d) Basic constructional patterns (selected):

(i) Placer-prominent transitive *BA*-construction

[我$_{\text{Placer}}$] [把$_{\text{*BA}}$] [紙條$_{\text{Figure}}$] 放 [在$_{\text{*Locative_Marker}}$] [口袋裡$_{\text{Loc.Ground}}$]

wo__ba__zhitiao__fang-zai__koudai-li

1st.sg__BA__note__put-in__pocket-inside

I put the note in the pocket

(ii) Figure-prominent inchoative

[紙條$_{\text{Figure}}$] 放 [在$_{\text{*Locative_Marker}}$] [口袋裡$_{\text{Loc.Ground}}$] (了)

zhitiao__fang-zai__koudai-li__ (le)

note__put.in__pocket.inside__(PERF)

The note was put in the pocket

(iii) Ground-prominent locative inversion

[口袋裡$_{\text{Loc.Ground}}$] 放 [著$_{\text{*Aspect_Zhe}}$] [一張紙條$_{\text{Figure}}$]

koudai-li__fang__zhe__yi-zhang__zhitiao

pocket-inside__put__DUR__one-CL__note

In the pocket was put a note

(e) Associated lemmas (selected): 放 *fang* "put," 懸 *xuan* "hang," 掛 *gua* "hang," 裝 *zhuang* "load," 塗 *tu* "spread," 擺放 *baifang* "put/set," 懸掛 *xuangua* "hang," etc.

The releasing versus caused-to-move versus placement frames are distinguished based on different sets of core Frame Elements as well as different constructional behaviors. In terms of the ambiguous issue exemplified in Example (9.7a–b), the constructional patterns serve as criteria to differentiate the meanings of *fang*. Which frame *fang* belongs to can be determined on the basis of its constructional pattern. If *fang* belongs to the Releasing Frame instead of the placement frame, it must not be compatible with the constructional variations given in (9.14d), especially with the locative inversion, which is essential to placement verbs (Liu and Chang 2015), as exemplified in Example (9.15).

[10] "Locative_Marker" refers to the locative co-verb *zai* 在, which is semantically different from other path co-verbs such as *jìn* 進 and *dao* 到.

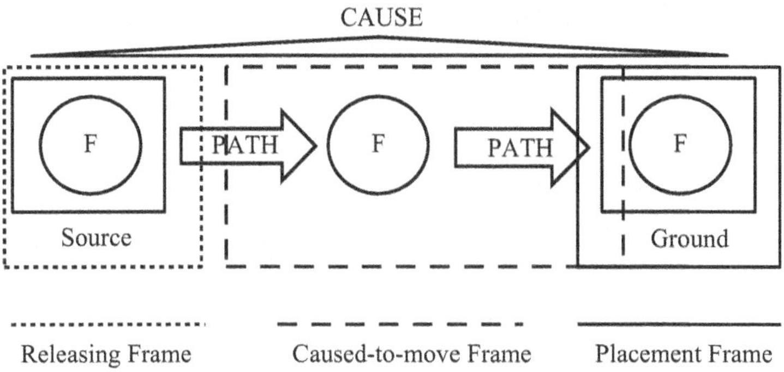

Fig. 12.1 Semantic base and profile of the caused-motion frame

(9.15)	房間裡放著一隻貓給大家欣賞
	fangjian-li__fang__zhe__yi-zhi__mao__gei__dajia__xinshang
	room-inside__put__DUR__one-CL__cat__for__everyone__enjoy
	In the room was put a cat for display

While these frames can be differentiated, they can also be interrelated. Cognitively speaking, these three events are various subevents of a caused-motion causal chain (cf. Croft 1990) that serves as the cognitive base for different semantic profiles (cf. Langacker 1987). These three types of verbs—releasing, caused-to-move, and placement—profile different subparts of the semantic base, as illustrated in Fig. 12.1.

In analyzing placement verbs, a major difference was found between English and Mandarin. The prototypical placement verb 放 *fang* in Mandarin lexicalizes a broader semantic range than the English "put" (cf. Levin 1993): *fang* can denote the notion of caused-to-move collocating with Path coverbs such as 進/到 *jin/dao* "into/to," but "put" is compatible only with the locative, not goal, preposition; *fang* can also be expressed by various constructions to show different profiles of the semantic base, but "put" is only involved in prototypical constructions, as exemplified in Example (9.16a–c). In short, the placement event is encoded differently by Mandarin *fang* and English "put."

(9.16)	The constructional constraints of English "put" (cf. Levin 1993, p. 111):
(a)	I put the book on/under/near/*to/?onto the table.
(b)	*The books put on the table. (causative alternation)
(c)	*On the table put the books. (locative inversion)

12.4 Advantages of the Approach

In terms of the advantages of the cognitively motivated, frame-based, and constructionally defined annotation approach, there are three features worth mentioning. First, the hierarchically structured frame taxonomy is potentially viable, with ontological knowledge that is linguistically and conceptually testable. In the motion domain, higher-level verbs such as 移動 *yidong* "move" are semantically underspecified and syntactically flexible, while more basic-level terms such as 搬 *ban* "move" and 放 *fang* "put" are basic-level categories that are cognitively more fundamental, semantically more specified, and syntactically more restricted.

Second, frame-relevant annotation allows conceptual and metaphorical transfers by grouping a diverse range of functionally similar arguments into the same frame-specific role in a syntactically designated position, as shown in Example (9.17a–c).

(9.17)	Frame-relevant role assignment:
(a)	[我 $_{\text{Placer}}$] 把 [書 $_{\text{Figure}}$] 放在 [桌上 $_{\text{Loc.Ground}}$]
	Wo__ba__shu__fang-zai__zhuo-shang
	1st.sg__BA__book__put-in__table-top
	I put the book on the table
(b)	[那家企業 $_{\text{Placer}}$] 把 [廢棄物 $_{\text{Figure}}$] 放在 [山裡面 $_{\text{Loc-Ground}}$]
	najia__qiye__ba__feiqiwu__fang-zai__shan-limian
	that.CL__enterprise__BA__waste__put-in__mountain-inside
	The enterprise put the waste in the mountain
(c)	[她 $_{\text{Placer}}$] 把 [老師的話 $_{\text{Figure}}$] 放在 [心上 $_{\text{Loc.Ground}}$]
	ta__ba__laoshi__de__hua__fang-zai__xin-shang
	3rd.sg__BA__teacher__GEN__word__put-in__heart-inside
	She put the teacher's words in her heart

Using the event frame as a semantic filter for role assignment may help solve the problem of overgeneralized, class-independent semantic annotation (e.g., Agent and Patient) that may not be applicable to conceptual transfers constantly at work (e.g., from human to non-human and from concrete to abstract). For instance, the Agent role, according to its definition, may not be suitable for describing non-human and non-physical subjects, as shown in Example (9.1a–c) and repeated here in Example (9.18a–c).

(9.18)	Different Agent subjects of the action verb "hit":
(a)	**The boy** hit her hard. → human Agent
(b)	**The wind** hit her hard. → non-human physical Agent (?)
(c)	**His words** hit her hard. → non-human, non-physical Agent (??)

To solve this, one way is to overgeneralize the semantic range of Agent to make the Agent neutral. However, this may void the semantic role of Agent, as it contains no semantic properties and no longer falls under frame semantics, as meanings are defined in relation to the Background Frame. Another solution is to undergeneralize the element. In the placing frame in FrameNet,[11] there are two core elements of placer—Agent and Cause—which refer to the non-Agent Placer, as illustrated in Example (9.19).

(9.19) Grass. . .is another plant which PUTS nitrogen into the soil.[12]

Since the plant ("grass") in (9.19) is the subject, the role of the Agent may not be applicable to it, and thus it is tagged as another element (Cause). At first sight, this seems to be reasonable. However, Agent entails Cause, which means that Agent and Cause are conceptually implicative and metaphorically transferrable, and they are essentially similar in semantic function. Therefore, using the two labels as two separate roles may lead to the problem of undergeneralization, which can result in redundant annotation. The third solution is to redefine the Agent as a more frame-relevant element, which was adopted in the present study, as exemplified in (9.17a–c), using Placer instead of Agent. With frame-relevant annotation, the frame-specific role tags can help capture the semantic nature of the participant in the particular frame and strengthen its semantic flexibility to include conceptual or metaphorical transfers. Frame-based semantic tagging that is specific enough to profile features of the frame and broad enough to include relevant subclasses may thus have the advantage of being semantically revealing and adequate without over- or undergeneralization.

Third, constructional criteria are incorporated in the definition of frames. Constructions are form-meaning mapping entities that help to encode semantic profiles in a given event schema. Collo-constructional patterns are reliable "formal criteria" that differentiates related but distinct verb senses based on overt syntactic marking. For instance, the moving frame and placement frame, though both related to caused motion, are syntactically differentiable with a choice of locative markers: 放到/搬到 *fang dao/ban dao* "put to/move to" signals a moving Path, while 放在/*搬在 *fang zai/*ban zai* "put in/*move in" signals a placing endpoint in which *ban* is not allowed. The range of constructional uses allowed by a verb defines its range of frame membership. While the verb *ban* "move" is semantically restricted to the moving frame, the verb *fang* "put" is semantically broader and includes a wider range of related frames in a perceivable event chain.

As illustrated in (9.20a–e) below, the senses of *fang* extend along eventive inferences of a caused-motion schema that naturally goes from "caused-to-move" to "caused-to-be" and to "spatial configuration." If motional progression is a default semantic base, then different constructions may help highlight different stages of the event schema, which may involve the formal coding of an agentive motion (把X 放到Y), an agentive placement (把X 放在Y), a dynamic change (X 放到Y 了), a location-prominent placement (在Y 放X), and a theme-prominent locative state

[11] The Placement Frame in Mandarin is quite similar to the English Placing Frame in FrameNet in terms of their semantic and syntactic behavior, and thus they can be compared.

[12] The source for the example is https://framenet2.icsi.berkeley.edu/fnReports/data/frameIndex.xml?frame=Placing

(locative construction: X放在Y) to a location-prominent spatial state (i.e., locative inversion: Y 放著X). A caused-motion event will eventually lead to a ground-figure spatial configuration as the end result. The causally related event ramp provides a semantic base to anchor the multiple uses of 放 *fang* "put," which may lexically profile various facets of the event schema. On the other hand, the constructional patterns associated with different semantic profiles may, in turn, provide syntactic criteria to identify the distinct frames with associated verb members. Thus, the prototypical placement verbs, such as *fang* and *gua*, display a full range of constructional uses (see 20a–e), showing a clear departure from pure caused-motion verbs in the moving frame, such as *ban* "to move," which only allows the dynamic path marker *dao* "to" + LocNP, as shown in Example (9.20a) and (9.20c). Placement verbs also differ from pure spatial configuration verbs, such as 站 *zhan* "to stand," which do not allow agentive-transitive uses.

(9.20)	Constructional variation with semantic profiles[13]:
(a)	Caused-to-move:
	[我 $_{\text{Mover}}$] 把 [書 $_{\text{Figure}}$] 放 [到 $_{\mathbf{*Path}}$] [桌上 $_{\text{Ground}}$]
	wo__ba__shu__fang-**dao**__zhuo-shang
	1^{st}sg__BA__book__put-**to**__table-above
	I put a book to the table
(b)	Placement:
	[我 $_{\text{Mover}}$] 把 [書 $_{\text{Figure}}$] 放 [在 $_{\mathbf{*Locative\_Marker}}$] [桌上 $_{\text{Ground}}$]
	wo__ba__shu__fang-**zai**__zhuo-shang
	1^{st}sg__BA__book__put-**in**__table-above
	I put a book on the table
(c)	Dynamic result:
	[書 $_{\text{Figure}}$] 放 [到 $_{\mathbf{*Path}}$] [桌上 $_{\text{Ground}}$] 了
	shu__fang-**dao**__zhuo-shang__le
	book__put-to__table-above__PERF
	The book was put to the table
(d)	Locative state:
	[書 $_{\text{Figure}}$] 放 [在 $_{\mathbf{*Locative\_Marker}}$] [桌上 $_{\text{Ground}}$]
	shu__fang-**zai**__zhuo-shang
	book__put-in__table-above
	The book was put on the table
(e)	Spatial configuration:
	[桌上 $_{\text{Ground}}$] 放 [了/著 $_{\mathbf{*Aspect}}$] [一本書 $_{\text{Figure}}$]
	zhuo-shang__fang__le/zhe__yi-ben__shu
	table-above__put__PERF/DUR__one-CL__book
	On the table was put a book

[13] The more general element tags are used here to show the cross-categorial properties of *fang* 放 using [mover] and [ground] instead of [placer] and [Loc.Ground]/[End.Ground] (cf. [8] and [9]).

With the frame shift from caused motion to spatial configuration, the semantic relation between the arguments also shifts. Spatial configuration profiles a static spatial relation between ground and figurse, instead of a dynamic path relation. The unique range of grammatical distributions exemplified above in (9.20a–e) shows how constructional patterns are associated with different constructional meanings or semantic profiles, which may be the key to differentiating verb classes.

In addition, with the constructional approach, the semantic variations between similar and related expressions of a verb can be clearly annotated and presented. For instance, consider the following sentences that consist of the placement 放 *fang* "put" in Example (9.21a–c).[14]

(9.21a)	那本書放在桌子上
	na-ben__shu__fang__zai__zhuo-shang
	that-CL__book__put__at__table-above
	The book was put on the table
(9.21b)	那本書我放在桌上
	na-ben__shu__wo__fang__zai__zhuo-shang
	that-CL__book__1stsg__put__at__table-above
	The book, I put it on the table
(9.21c)	那本書被我放在桌上
	na-ben__shu__bei__wo__fang__zai__zhuo-shang
	that-CL__book__passive__1stsg__put__at__table-above
	The book was put on the table by me

These expressions are related because they are all figure prominent, they all predicate the spatial state of the figure, and they are constructional variants of the figure-prominent family. However, it should be noted that, while related, they are different constructions with varied surface forms and are associated with different meanings. That is to say, they are not paraphrases nor interchangeable expressions, but formally and semantically distinct constructions. Example (9.21a) is not simply derived from Example (9.21b) or (9.21c) with the Agent (placer) omitted, or vice versa. Example (9.21a) represents the so-called locative construction, which denotes the locative state (i.e., the spatial-location of a figure), and it takes only two semantic components: Example (9.21b) is a double-NP construction, with the figure topicalized, and Example (9.21c) is clearly a *bei*-marked passive construction in which the Agent (placer) is marked by the Construction Marker *bei*. Therefore, Example (9.21a–c) is annotated differently, as shown in Example (9.22a–c). This illustrates exactly what the constructional approach can provide: a clear picture of the constructional distribution of each verb or frame. Distinct verbs and frames may select distinct constructional patterns that best match their distinct lexical meanings. As verbs and constructions are both form-meaning mapping entities, they are equally sensitive to semantic components (or Frame Elements) and syntactic patterns with

[14]This paragraph and following example are in response to one of the reviewer's concerns about the constructional differences among the three sentences in Example 21.

Construction Markers. As such, the subtle differences between related sentences can be clearly annotated.

(9.22a)	[那本書$_{\text{Figure}}$] 放 [在$_{\text{*Locative_Marker}}$] [桌子上$_{\text{Ground}}$]
(9.22b)	[那本書$_{\text{Figure}}$] [我$_{\text{Placer}}$] 放 [在$_{\text{*Locative_Marker}}$] [桌子上$_{\text{Ground}}$]
(9.22c)	[那本書$_{\text{Figure}}$] [被$_{\text{*Passive-}bei}$] [我$_{\text{Placer}}$] 放 [在$_{\text{*Locative_Marker}}$] [桌子上$_{\text{Ground}}$]

Verbs and constructions are mutually dependent, reciprocally definable, and semantically and syntactically complementary to each other in a gestalt-like relationship (Liu and Chang 2015). Given the frame-based constructional criteria, finer distinctions of subframes can be made with clearly defined collo-constructional criteria.

Finally,[15] semantic annotation using a frame-based constructional approach provides a useful knowledge base for foreseeable applications in several semantically demanding NLP tasks and challenges, such as automatic semantic role labeling, word sense detection, word sense disambiguation, automatic verb classification, semantic inferencing, and information retrieval. For instance, the carefully annotated semantic information of verbs and verb frames in Mandarin VerbNet is believed to be more discriminative than unstructured features (e.g., bag-of-words [BOW]) for training machine learning (ML) models (e.g., Naïve Bayes, support vector machines, J48 decision trees, etc.) to predict word senses, classify word classes, or label semantic roles in applicational uses.

Take word sense disambiguation (WSD)[16] as an example. Past studies relied heavily on surface contextual features (e.g., BOW or word-to-vectors) from unstructured data and often encountered dissatisfactory labeling performance due to low recall and precision rates. Part of the reason is that unstructured features are fairly blind (noisy) and computationally demanding. As for structured data, even though the preprocessing of texts with deep annotation is time-consuming, linguistic encoding provides more reliable and intelligent training data for ML models to learn and predict the senses in a more precise and algorithmic-easy way. This advantage in WSD is well illustrated with the case of the polysemous verb 煩 *fan* "to annoy/be annoying/be annoyed" illustrated in Example (9.23).

(9.23)	他好煩啊!	
	ta__hao__fan__a	
	3rdsg__DEG__annoy__final particle	
(a)	Sense 1: He is very annoying!	
(b)	Sense 2: He feels so annoyed!"	

[15]This paragraph is in response to one of the reviewer's concerns about how annotated information can potentially improve present Chinese NLP tasks.

[16]WSD is a practical NLP task that aims at resolving lexical semantic ambiguity automatically by disambiguating the sense of a polysemous word based on its contextual information.

The sentences in (9.23) above, while remaining lexically and syntactically identical, may render two possible meanings. Training on lexical context features will not help ML models to predict the sense of the verb, but if such sentences were deep annotated with semantic information as in Example (9.24a–b), the sense of the verb 煩 *fan* can be clearly inferred by the core element.

(9.24a)	[他$_{\text{Stimulus}}$] [好$_{\text{*Degree}}$] 煩啊!
	Sense 1: He is very annoying!
(9.24b)	[他$_{\text{Experiencer}}$] [好$_{\text{*Degree}}$] 煩啊!
	Sense 2: He feels so annoyed!

Semantic annotation helps to differentiate a stimulus-oriented reading in (9.24a) from an experiencer-oriented reading in (9.24b). Example (9.24a–b) indicates a simple contribution of the potential usefulness of applying a linguistically enriched database to major NLP tasks and challenges. More analytical and annotational work will be conducted to augment the database of Mandarin VerbNet, and continued upgrades will be accomplished to further attest and evaluate the applicational merits of Mandarin VerbNet. As a linguist, I firmly believe that by incorporating fine-grained linguistic knowledge in understanding and processing languages, the future of NLP applications may be carried out with more productive and fruitful results. The task of analyzing and representing Mandarin verbal information is academically significant and applicational needed to advance Chinese NLP technologies, which require a systematic, comprehensive, fine-grained, linguistically motivated, and Chinese-specific database, like Mandarin VerbNet.

12.5 Conclusion

The proposed frame-based constructional approach was adopted to provide lexical information of Mandarin verbs and verb classes in the systematic representation of the Mandarin verbal lexicon. While there are still challenges and difficulties in semantic annotation in Mandarin and other Chinese dialects yet to be solved, as mentioned in Sect. 12.2, it is believed that the frame-based constructional approach can provide a well-motivated and application-oriented linguistic resource for verb categorization and semantic annotation. The ultimate goal of the continuous efforts in constructing Mandarin VerbNet is to establish a language-specific lexical database with well-annotated linguistic knowledge for teaching and learning Mandarin verbs to facilitate further research in Mandarin verbal semantics. Furthermore, the accumulated linguistic knowledge base of the Chinese verbal lexicon can serve as a gold standard for training ML models with deep linguistic features in many NLP application tasks, such as automatic semantic role labeling, word sense detection, word sense disambiguation, automatic verb classification, semantic inferencing, and information retrieval. The delicate linguistic interpretations provided by Mandarin VerbNet are deemed to be more useful and discriminative document features for

ML models to predict the correct verb class, verb sense, and semantic roles in such NLP technologies. Following the construction and augmentation of Mandarin VerbNet, it has completed the investigation and annotation of some major categories of verbs, including "communication," "cognition," "perception," "emotion," "judgment," "social interaction," "emotion," "self-motion," and "caused motion." It currently has moved on to a comprehensive and in-depth analysis of spatial configuration verbs, which will lead to new discoveries of spatially embedded frames that are lexically significant in Chinese. Although semantic annotation is time-consuming and labor-intensive, it is believed that the deep annotation of semantic information is theoretically nurturing and practically rewarding and hence is crucial for advancing both lexical semantic studies and relevant NLP research and applications.

Acknowledgments The database presented in this chapter was made possible with the support of research grants from the Taiwan Ministry of Science and Technology (MOST) in earlier years and Strategic Research Grants from City University of Hong Kong since 2015. I would like to thank my research assistant, Mr. Jui-Ching Chang, for his valuable and diligent help in preparing the preliminary materials for the study and Dr. Mingyu Wan for her valuable assistance in reviewing and editing the information for this chapter. My hearty thanks also go to Dr. Tianqi He for her lead in the semantic annotation of verb frames. Any errors in the chapter are mine alone.

References

Boas, Hans. 2003. Towards a lexical-constructional account of the locative alternation. In *Proceedings of the 13th Western Conference on Linguistics*, ed. Lesley Charmichael, Chia-Hui Huang, and Vida Samiian, 27–42. Fresno: Department of Linguistics at California State University, Fresno. Available at http://sites.la.utexas.edu/hcb/files/2011/02/Boas2003a_Locative_Alternation.pdf. Accessed 11 March 2019.

Chen, Keh-Jiann, Chu-Ren Huang, Li-ping Chang, and Hui-Li Hsu. 1996. Sinica corpus: Design methodology for balanced corpora. In *Proceedings of the 11th Pacific Asia Conference on Language, Information and Computation*, ed. Byung-Soo Park and Jong-Bok Kim, 167–176. Seoul: Kyung Hee University. Available at http://www.aclweb.org/anthology/Y96-1018. Accessed 11 March 2019.

Croft, William. 1990. Possible verbs and the structure of events. In *Meanings and prototypes: Studies in linguistic categorization*, ed. Savas L. Tsohatzidis, 48–73. London: Routledge Publishing Co.

Croft, William, and Alan Cruse. 2004. *Cognitive linguistics*. Cambridge, UK: Cambridge University Press.

Dai, Xiang-ling. 1992. *Chinese morphology and its interface with the syntax*. Ph.D. dissertation. Columbus, OH: The Ohio State University.

Duanmu, San. 1998. Wordhood in Chinese. In *New approaches to Chinese word formation: Morphology, phonology and the lexicon in modern and ancient Chinese*, ed. Jerome L. Packard, 135–196. Berlin and NewYork: Mouton de Gruyter.

Feng, Shengli 馮勝利. 2001. The multidimensional properties of "word" in Chinese 論漢語"詞"的多維性. *Contemporary Linguistics 當代語言學* 3(3):161–174.

Fillmore, Charles J. 1982. Frame semantics. In *Linguistics in the morning calm*, ed. The Linguistic Society of Korean, 111–137. Seoul: Hanshin Publishing Co.

Fillmore, Charles J. 1985. Frames and the semantics of understanding. *Quaderni di Semantica* 6(2): 222–254.

Goldberg, Adele E. 1995. *Constructions: A construction grammar approach to argument structure*. Chicago, IL: University of Chicago Press.

Goldberg, Adele E. 2002. Verbs, frames and constructions. In *Syntax, lexical, semantics and event structure*, ed. Malka Rappaport Hovav, Edit Doron, and Ivy Sichel, 39–58. Oxford: Oxford University Press.

Harnad, Stevan. 2005. To cognize is to categorize: Cognition is categorization. In *Handbook of categorization in cognitive science*, ed. Henri Cohen and Claire Lefebvre, 19–43. Elsevier.

Hilpert, Martin. 2008. *Germanic future constructions: A usage-based approach to language change*. John Banjamins Publishing Company.

Himmelmann, Nikolaus P. 2004. Lexicalization and grammaticization: Opposite or orthogonal? In *What makes grammaticalization? A look from its fringes and its compoments*, ed. Walter Bisang, Nikolaus P. Himmelmann, and Björn Wiemer, 21–42. Berlin and New York: Mouton de Gruyter.

Huang, James C. T. 1984. Phrase structure, lexical integrity, and Chinese compounds. *Journal of the Chinese Language Teachers Association* 19(2):53–78.

Huang, Chu-Ren. 2009. Tagged Chinese Gigaword version 2.0. Philadelphia, PA: Linguistic Data Consortium. Available at http://www.ldc.upenn.edu/Catalog/catalogEntry.jsp?catalogId=LDC2009T14. Accessed 20 September 2018.

Huang, Chu-Ren, Kathleen Ahrens, and Keh-jiann Chen 黃居仁, 安可思, 陳克健. 1998. A data-driven approach to the mental lexicon: Two studies on Chinese corpus linguistics 由語料出發驗證心理詞庫–漢語語料庫語言學研究二例. *Bulletin of the Institute of History and Philology 中央研究院歷史語言研究所集刊* 69(1):151–179.

Huang, Chu-Ren, Shu-Kai Hsieh, Jia-Fei Hong, Yun-Zhu Chen, I-Li Su, Yong-Xiang Chen, and Seng-Wei Huang 黃居仁, 謝舒凱, 洪嘉馡, 陳韵竹, 蘇依莉, 陳永祥, 黃勝偉. 2010. Chinese Wordnet: Design, implementation, and application of an infracture for cross-lingual knowledge processing 中文詞彙網路: 跨語言知識處理基礎架構的設計理念與實踐. *Journal of Chinese Information Processing 中文信息學報* 24(2):14–23.

Hwang, Yu-chun, and Xiang-yu Chen 黃郁純, 陳薌宇. 2005. Relation between lexical collocation and near-synonymy: A corpus-based study 以語料庫為本分析詞語搭配及近義關係. *Chinese Teaching Research 華語文教學研究* 2(2):57–71.

Iwata, Seizi. 2008. *Locative alternation: A lexical-constructional approach*. John Benjamins Publishing Company.

Langacker, Ronald W. 1987. *Foundations of cognitive grammar: Theoretical prerequisites* (Vol. 2). Stanford, CA: Stanford University Press.

Levin, Beth. 1993. *English classes and alternations: A preliminary investigation*. Chicago, IL: University of Chicago Press.

Liu, Meichun. 2016. Emotion in lexicon and grammar: Lexical-constructional interface of Mandarin emotional predicates. *Lingua Sinica*, (2016)2:4. doi: https://doi.org/10.1186/s4065501600130.

Liu, Meichun and Chun Edison Chang. 2005. From frame to subframe: Collocational asymmetry in Mandarin verbs of conversation. *International Journal of Computational Linguistics and Chinese Language Processing* 10(4): 431–444.

Liu, Meichun, and Jui-ching Chang. 2015. Redefining locative inversion in Mandarin: A lexical-constructional approach. In *Proceedings of the 27th North American Conference on Chinese Linguistics (NACCL-27), 2015, Vol. 2,* ed. Hongyin Tao et al., 439–461. Los Angeles: University of California, Los Angeles. Available at https://naccl.osu.edu/proceedings/naccl-27. Accessed 20 September 2018.

Liu, Meichun, and Jui-ching Chang. 2016. Semantic annotation for Mandarin verbal lexicon. Paper presented at the *International Conference on Asian Language Processing (IALP)*, 30–36. Tainan, Taiwan. Available at https://ieeexplore.ieee.org/document/7875928. Accessed 20 September 2018. doi: https://doi.org/10.1109/IALP.2016.7875928.

Liu, Meichun, and Ting-yi Chiang. 2008. The construction of Mandarin VerbNet: A frame-based approach to the classification of statement verbs. *Language and Linguistics* 9(2):239–270.
Lü, Shu-Xiang 呂叔湘. 1981. *"Talking about language" 語文常談*. Hong Kong: Joint Publishing.
Luo, Yun-Pu 羅云普. 2011. *The study of the polysemous verb "fang4" in Mandarin Chinese 漢語多義動詞「放」的研究*. M.A. thesis. Hsinchu, Taiwan: Institute of Linguistics, National Tsing Hua University.
Packard, Jerome L. 2000. *The morphology of Chinese: A linguistic and cognitive approach.* Cambridge, UK: Cambridge University Press.
Palmer, Martha, Daniel Gildea, and Paul Kingsbury. 2005. The proposition bank: An annotated corpus of semantic roles. *Computational Linguistics* 31(1):71–106.
Regier, Terry, and Mingyu Zheng. 2007. Attention to endpoints: A cross-linguistic constraint on spatial meaning. *Cognitive Science* 31(4):705–719.
Ruppenhofer, Josef, Michael Ellsworth, Miriam R. L. Petruck, Christopher R. Johnson, Collin F. Baker, and Jan Scheffczyk. 2016. *FrameNet II: Extended theory and practice*. Institut für Deutsche Sprache, Bibliothek.
Talmy, Leonard. 1975. Semantics and syntax of motion. In *Syntax and semantics* (Vol. 4), ed. John P. Kimball, 181–238. New York: Academic Press.
Wang, Hui, Weidong Zhan, and Shiwen Yu 王惠, 詹衛東, 俞士汶. 2003. The specification of the semantic knowledge-base of comtemporary Chinese 現代漢語語義詞典規格說明書. *Journal of Chinese Language and Computing*, 13(2):159–176.

Chapter 13
The Construction of a Chinese Semantic Dependency Graph Bank

Yanqiu Shao, Wanxiang Che, Ting Liu, and Yu Ding

Abstract Semantic dependency parsing is a deep semantic analysis task based on large-scale and canonically annotated corpora. This chapter will present a new Chinese semantic dependency scheme using solid linguistic knowledge of Chinese. Chinese is a meaning-combined language with flexible syntactic structures and complex modifying relations among words. Thus, we used dependency graphs instead of dependency trees as target representations to allow nodes to have more than one incoming arc and crosses among dependency arcs. We annotated the dependency structures of 30,161 sentences, with 570,403 words, using this scheme. This chapter will describe the semantic dependency scheme in detail, including its specifications and the process involved in creating the corpus. Using Fleiss' kappa, the inner-annotated agreement evaluation results were 0.835 for non-labeled arcs and 0.686 for labeled arcs as assignments. This chapter will also provide the statistics of the annotated corpus.

Keywords Semantic analysis · Dependency tree · Dependency graph · Semantic corpus

13.1 Introduction

Sentence analysis based on dependency grammar has recently become a hot issue in natural language processing. This task has been extensively studied and has proven to be useful in several applications, including question answering (Cui et al. 2005; Punyakanok et al. 2004), semantic structure extraction (Johansson and Nugues 2007), and semantic role labeling (Hacioglu 2004; Pradhan et al. 2005).

Y. Shao (✉)
College of Information Sciences, Beijing Language and Culture University, Beijing, China
e-mail: shaoyanqiu@blcu.edu.cn

W. Che · T. Liu · Y. Ding
Computer Science and Technology College, Harbin Institute of Technology, Harbin, China
e-mail: car@ir.hit.edu.cn; tliu@ir.hit.edu.cn; yding@ir.hit.edu.cn

C.-R. Huang et al. (eds.), *Chinese Language Resources*, Text, Speech and Language Technology 49, https://doi.org/10.1007/978-3-031-38913-9_13

Much work has focused on constructing dependency parsers. So far, all the dependency parsing technologies have been data driven, and large-scale corpora have been annotated to construct automatic dependency parsers. The Prague Dependency Treebank (Böhmová et al. 2003), the first dependency structure annotation work, has been influential. Dependency treebanks have been built for at least 30 languages, on a large or small scale, by hand or via algorithms to automatically convert available phrase structure treebanks to dependency structure notations (Marimon and Bel 2014), such as Chatterji et al. (2014), Haverinen et al. (2014), and Marneffe and Manning (2008). Liu et al. (2006) created a Chinese syntactic dependency treebank (CDT) consisting of 60,000 sentences from the *People's Daily* in the 1990s. Several studies have been conducted on Chinese dependency parsing using this corpus, such as Niu et al. (2009) and Li et al. (2012). Most studies on dependency analysis have been syntax-oriented. Semantic dependencies were seldom studied until the share tasks in the SemEval-2012 (Che et al. 2012) and SemEval-2014 (Oepen et al. 2014), where semantic dependencies annotated in Chinese and English were provided for participants to build dependency parsing systems.

Distinct from English, Chinese is an ideographic language belonging to the Sino-Tibetan family (Lu 2001) that organizes sentences based on logical connections among lexical meanings and the semantics of sub-sentences, so no formal meanings or fixed syntactic structures are available. Because rich latent information is hidden in facial words, the semantic analysis of Chinese is specialized. Conversely, English is a hypotaxis language that organizes sentences by linguistically formal meanings, wherein grammar prioritizes syntax and even disengages from semantics.

Semantic dependency parsing aims to determine all the word pairs with exact semantic relations and connect each word pair to a dependency arc with a relation label, indicating their semantic relations. Semantic dependency has similarities with and differences from syntactic dependency. Both are based on dependency grammar (Robinson 1970) and annotate each word in a sentence. Syntactic dependency gives a transparent encoding of the predicate-argument structure, while semantic dependency explicitly displays semantics hidden behind predicate-argument structures.

The number of semantic dependency labels is more than five times higher than syntactic dependency labels[1], which allows them to express different information of sentences. Syntactic dependency analyzes syntactic functions from the perspective of grammar systems (e.g., subjective, predicate, and objective), and for this task, dependency tree structures are sufficient. By contrast, semantic dependency involves semantic relations (e.g., agent, patient, and experiencer) between each pair of words. According to the above analysis of the Chinese language, semantic relations between word pairs do not always generate tree structures, and graphs describe semantics

[1]CDT and Malt syntactic dependency have 13 and 12 labels, respectively. The Malt dependency corpus was acquired via automatic conversion from Penn Chinese Treebank phrase structure trees using Penn2Malt. Semantic dependency labels exceed 50, including those produced by Li et al. (2003) and Chen et al. (1999). Hundreds of labels are available in our BLCU-HIT Semantic Dependency Parsing (BH-SDP) system.

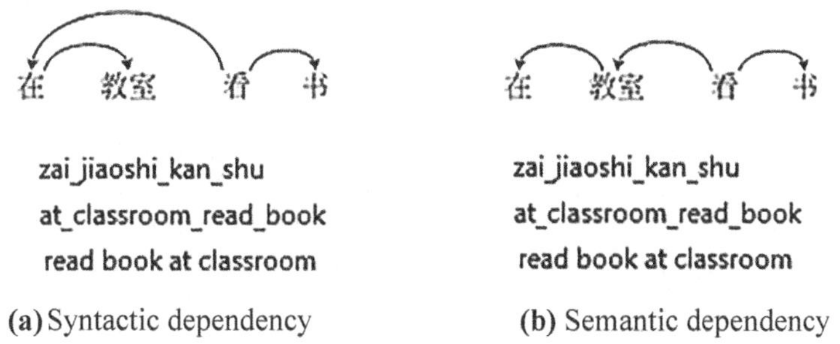

Fig. 13.1 Difference between syntactic and semantic dependency for prepositions. (**a**) Syntactic dependency. (**b**) Semantic dependency

better than trees. These findings coincide with the meaning-text theory (MTT), a theoretical framework for the description of natural languages (Žolkovskij and Mel'čuk 1967). MTT considered that trees are not sufficient to express the complete meaning of sentences in some cases, which has been proven undoubted in our practice of corpus annotation.

Comparing word pairs connected by dependency arcs, semantic dependency seeks to depict the relations among content words, whereas syntactic dependency mostly relies on functional words (e.g., coordinating conjunctions and prepositions). Figure 13.1 presents an example of this difference. In the prepositional phrase 在教室 *zai jiaoshi* "at the classroom," the preposition 在 *zai* "at" is the head word in (a), whereas the headword in (b) is the content word 教室 *jiaoshi* "classroom."

The rest of this chapter is organized as follows. Section 13.2 will describe the details of our dependency scheme, while Sect. 13.3 will introduce the origin of our corpus and the design of our annotation tool. Then, an evaluation of the inner-annotator agreement of our annotated corpus will be given, concretely describing the assessment method, in Sect. 13.4. Section 13.5 will present some statistics of our annotated corpus, followed by the conclusion in Sect. 13.6.

13.2 Annotation Scheme of the Semantic Dependency Graph

Dependency tree structures are traditionally prerequisites for syntactic dependency analysis. However, dependency trees are not suited for meaning representation because of some distortion in or omission of the dependency arcs needed to preserve a legal dependency structure. According to large-scale real corpus and parataxis characteristics, a word may be the argument of more than one predicate, resulting in multiple incoming arcs. Therefore, we extended dependency tree structures to graphs.

13.2.1 Graph Structure of Semantic Dependency

Semantic dependency graphs (SDGs) are directed acyclic graphs. Nodes refer to words, while edges refer to semantic relations between labeled words. There is only one node without a head, which is the root of the entire graph. Graphs overcome the limitations of dependency trees by allowing more than one head on certain nodes and crosses of arcs. Figure 13.2 shows that the node 杯子 *beizi* "cup" has semantic relations with both 打 *da* "break" and 破 *po* "damaged," which means that 杯子 *beizi* "cup" has two heads, and the arcs connecting 杯子 *beizi* "cup" and 破 *po* "damaged" as well as 他 *ta* "he" and 打 *da* "break" cross.

The dependency structure in traditional dependency grammar must be single-headed, connective, acyclic, and projective. Since dependency graphs do not include single-headed and projective relations, only connective and acyclic relations, they are considered extensions of dependency grammar.

13.2.2 Semantic Relation Set

Lu (2001) explained the parataxis network of Chinese grammar. We applied this semantic unit classification and semantic combination, as well as integrated the semantic characteristics, to construct a clear semantic relation scheme. At the same time, we also considered some of the semantic relation tags in HowNet (Dong and Dong 2006).

Semantic units are divided from high to low into event chains, events, arguments, concepts, and marks. Arguments refer to noun phrases related to certain predicates. Concepts are simple elements in basic human thought or content words in syntax. Marks represent the meaning attached to the entity information conveyed by speakers (e.g., speakers' tones or moods). These semantic units correspond to compound sentences, simple sentences, chunks, content words, and function words. The meanings of sentences are expressed by event chains, which consist of multiple simple sentences. The meanings of simple sentences are expressed by arguments, while arguments are reflected by predicate, referential, or defining concepts. Marks are attached to concepts.

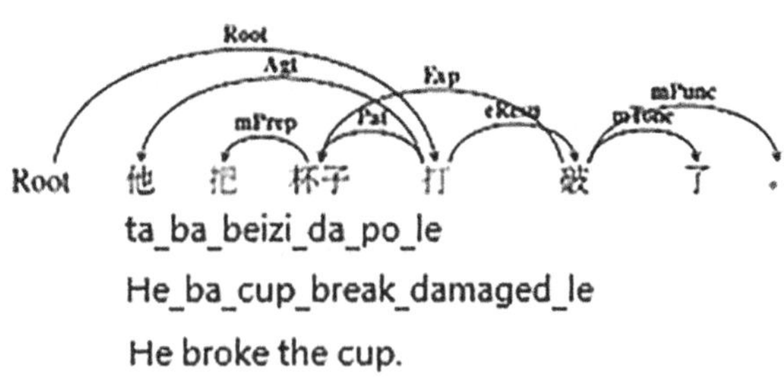

Fig. 13.2 Sample sentence annotated with the SDG scheme

Table 13.1 Label set of semantic relations

Semantic roles	
Subject roles	Agt (agent), Exp (experiencer), Aft (affection), Poss (possessor)
Object roles	Pat (patient), Cont (content), Prod (product), Orig (origin), Datv (dative), Comp (comparison)
Copula roles	Belg (belongings), Clas (classification), Accd (according)
Cause roles	Reas (reason), Int (intention), Cons (consequence)
Condition roles	Mann (manner), tool, Matl (material)
Space-time roles	Time, Loc (location), Dir (direction), Proc (process), Sco (scope)
Measurement roles	Quan (quantity), Qp (quantity phrase), Freq (frequency), Seq (sequence)
Special attribute roles	Desc (description), host, Nmod (name modifier), Tmod (time modifier)
Reverse relations	r + semantic roles, e.g., r-Agt, r-pat, etc.
Nested relations	d + semantic roles, e.g., d-Agt, d-pat, etc.
Event relations	
Symmetric relations	eCoo (coordination), eSelt (selection), eEqu (equivalent)
Consecutive relations	ePrec (precedent), eSucc (successor), eProg (progression), eCau (cause), eAdvt (adversative), eResueResu (Resutl), eInf (inference), eCond (condition), eSupp (supposition), eConc (concession), eSum (summary), eRect (recount)
Semantic marks	
Relation marks	mConj (conjection), mAux (auxiliary), mPrep (preposition)
Attachment marks	mTone, mTime, mRang (range), mDegr (degree), mMod (modal), mFreq (frequency), mDir (directon), mPars (parenthesis), mNeg (negation)
Auxiliary marks	mMaj (majority), mSepa (separation), mRept (repetition), mVain, mPunc (punctuation)

The meaning of a sentence consists of the meanings of the semantic units and their combinations, including semantic relations and attachments. Semantic attachments refer to marks on semantic units which are listed in Table 13.1 as "semantic marks" such as prepositions, mood words, punctuations, and so on. Semantic relations are classified into symmetric and asymmetric types. Symmetric relations include coordination, selection, and equivalence relations, while asymmetric relations include the following:

1. Cooperative relations occur between core and non-core roles. For example, in 工人修理管道 *gongren_xiuli_guandao* "workers repair the pipeline," 管道 *guandao* "pipeline" serves as a non-core role and is the patient of 修理 *xiuli* "repair," which is a verb that serves as a core role. Relations between predicates and nouns belong to cooperative relations. Semantic roles usually refer to cooperative relations. Table 13.1 presents the 32 semantic roles we defined, divided into 8 small categories.

2. Additional relations refer to the modifying relations among concepts within an argument, in which all semantic roles are available; for example, in 地下的管道 *dixia_de_guandao* "underground pipeline," 地下 *dixia* "underground" is the modifier of 管道 *guandao* "pipeline," which refers to a location relation.
3. Connectional relations are bridging relations between two events that are neither symmetric nor nested relations. For example, for the sentence "如果天气好, 我会去颐和园 *ruguo_tianqi_hao, wo_hui_qu_yiheyuan* 'If the weather is good, I will go to the Summer Palace'," the former event is the hypothesis of the latter. Fifteen event relations were defined by our scheme.

We analyzed how the elements of each sentence constitute the entire meaning of the sentence and used the results as the theoretical basis in designing the SDG corpus. Table 13.1 shows the entire semantic relations set, which includes five types of semantic relations, i.e., semantic roles, reverse relations, nested relations, event relations, and semantic marks.

13.2.3 Special Situations

1. Reverse relations. When a verb modifies a noun, a reverse relation is applied with the label r-XX (XX refers to a single-level semantic relation). A reverse relation is generated when a word pair with the same semantic relation appears in different sentences with different modifying orders. A reverse relation distinguishes different modifying orders (i.e., they have arcs with reverse directions in the two situations). For example, the semantic relation between the head word 男孩 *nanhai* "boy" and the kernel word 打 *da* "play" in Fig. 13.3 is the r-agent, and the label agent is labeled the kernel word 打 *da* "play" and its modifier 男孩 *nanhai* "boy." The expression of the semantic tri-tuple of this pair of words in Fig. 13.3a is 男孩 *nanhai* "boy," 打 *da* "play," r-agent, and in Fig. 13.3b, it is 打 *da* "play," 男孩 *nanhai* "boy," agent. Here, the first word in the tri-tuple is the head word, and the second one is a modified or dependency word, while the last one has asemantic role.

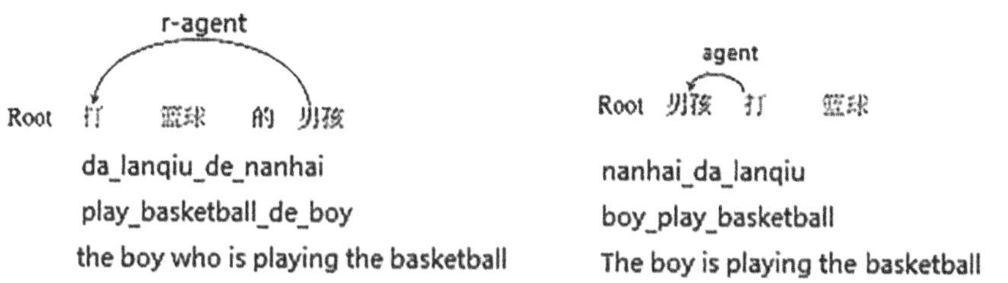

(a) The verb phrase is a modifier **(b)** The verb is the kernel word

Fig. 13.3 Sample of reverse relations. (**a**) The verb phrase is a modifier. (**b**) The verb is the kernel word

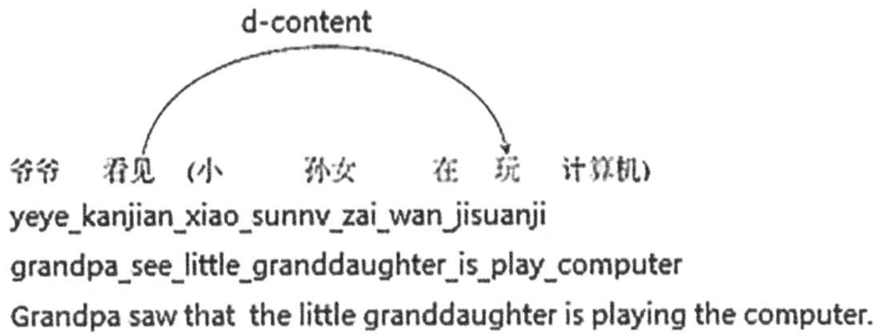

Fig. 13.4 Sample nested relation; the event within the round bracket serves as a nested constituent

2. Nested events. Two events have a nested relation (i.e., one event is regarded as a grammatical item of the other), which belongs to two semantic hierarchies. For example, in the sentence in Fig. 13.4, the event 小孙女在玩计算机 *xiao_sunnv_zai_wan_jisuanji* "little granddaughter is playing the computer" is regarded as the content of the action 看见 *kanjian* "see." A prefix "d" is added to single-level semantic relations as a "distinctive" label. The tri-tuple of this sentence is labeled 看见 *kanjian* "see," 玩 *wan* "play," d-content.
3. Quantitative phrases. There are no English quantifiers such as 个 *ge*, 本 *ben*, 只 *zhi*, etc. in Chinese. Here, a "quantitative word" refers to the combination of one numeral and one quantifier, such as 十个 *shi_ge* "ten," and a "quantitative phrase" represents the combination of a quantitative word and a noun, such as 十个人 *shi_ge_ren* "ten persons." In our scheme, considering that sometimes numerals can be omitted, such as 这本书 *zhe_ben_shu* "this book," the quantifier of the quantitative word was labeled the head word, and the numeral was the dependency word, while the semantic relation between them was labeled "Quan" (quantity), a measurement role. When a quantitative word modified a noun, the noun was labeled the head word of the whole quantitative phrase, and the quantifier was the dependency word. The semantic relation between the noun and the quantitative word was labeled "Qp" (quantity phrase). For example, for the quantitative phrase 五本书 *wubenshu* "five books," the semantic tri-tuples were 本 *ben* "ben," 五 *wu* "five," Quan and 书 *shu* "book," 本 *ben* "ben," Qp.
4. Serial verb sentences. When several verbs occur in one sentence and there is neither a pause punctuation nor a conjunction sub-sentence, these kinds of sentences are called serial verb sentences or compressed sentences, which in fact includes more than two events in one sentence. Mostly, the front verb of the serial verb sentence is selected as the head word, and in rare cases such as manner serial verb sentences, the head word is the rear verb. According to the relations between different verbs, the semantic relations of serial verb sentences are classified as succession, purpose, manner, result, and soon. For instance, the head word of the Chinese sentence "他穿衣服走了。 *ta_chuan_yifu_zou_le* 'He wore his cloth and left'." is the front verb 穿 *chuan* "wear," and the relation between the two events is labeled "eSucc" (successor event). The tri-tuple of the two verbs in this sentence is 穿 *chuan* "wear," 走 *zou* "leave," eSucc. In fact, the

subject word 他 *ta* "he" has two parent nodes—one is the verb 穿 *chuan* "wear" and the other is the verb 走 *zou* "leave."

5. "De" structures with the omission of the head word. The Chinese word 的 *de* "De" is always used as an auxiliary word, and it is often taken as a dependency mark. However, sometimes the head word of the De structure is omitted. In this head word deletion situation, 的 *de* "De" was labeled the head word in our scheme. For example, in the Chinese sentence "卖菜的走了。*mai_cai_de_zou_le* 'The man who sold vegetables left'.", the head word 人 *ren* "person" of the De structure was omitted. Different from the Abstract Meaning Representation (AMR) semantic labeling system (Li et al. 2016), our scheme did not add the omitted component to the sentence, so the auxiliary word 的 *de* "De" was considered the head word of the De structure, and the tri-tuples were expressed as 走 *zou* "leave," 的 *de* "De," agent and 的 *de* "De," 卖 *mai* "sell," r-agent. Because 的 *de* "De" is often labeled as an auxiliary mark, if it is not annotated as a mark, it will mean that the situation of omission has occurred.
6. Predicate-complement structures. The semantic relations between verbs in verb serial sentences can also be applied to the predicate-complement structure. For example, for the Chinese sentence "他走累了。 ta_zou_lei_le 'He got tired of walking'.", the semantic relation between the predicate 走 zou "walk" and the complement 累 lei "tired" was labeled "eResu" (result event), which means that the complement was the "result" of the verb.
7. Separable words. In Chinese, some words can be separated into two parts, which are called "separable words." For example, the word 洗澡 *xizao* "take a bath" can be split into 洗个澡 *xi_ge_zao* "take a bath" by inserting the Chinese quantifier word 个 *ge* "Ge" into the word 洗澡 *xizao* "take a bath." In this case, the semantic relation between the two Chinese characters 洗 *xi* "take" and 澡 zao "bath" can be labeled "mSepa" (separation mark).

13.3 Corpus

13.3.1 Corpus Origin

Our corpus contained more than 30,000 sentences. The sentences were chosen from newspapers, spoken sentences, and Sina Weibo microblogs. We selected 10,068 newspaper sentences and labeled the word segmentation and part-of-speech (POS) information using Chinese PropBank 6.01 (Xue and Palmer 2003). Of the remaining sentences, 10,038 spoken and 10,055 Sina Weibo sentences had no annotated tags. Thus, we annotated the morphological information first before annotating semantic dependency. Chinese Treebank (CTB)-style POS tags were derived from the Penn English Treebank, which belongs to the Indo-European word class system that includes 33 POS tags.

Table 13.2 Raw corpus details

	Sentence number	Word number	Average length
News sentences	10,068	308,383	30.63
Spoken sentences	10,038	101,140	13.44
Microblog sentences	10,055	160,880	16.00

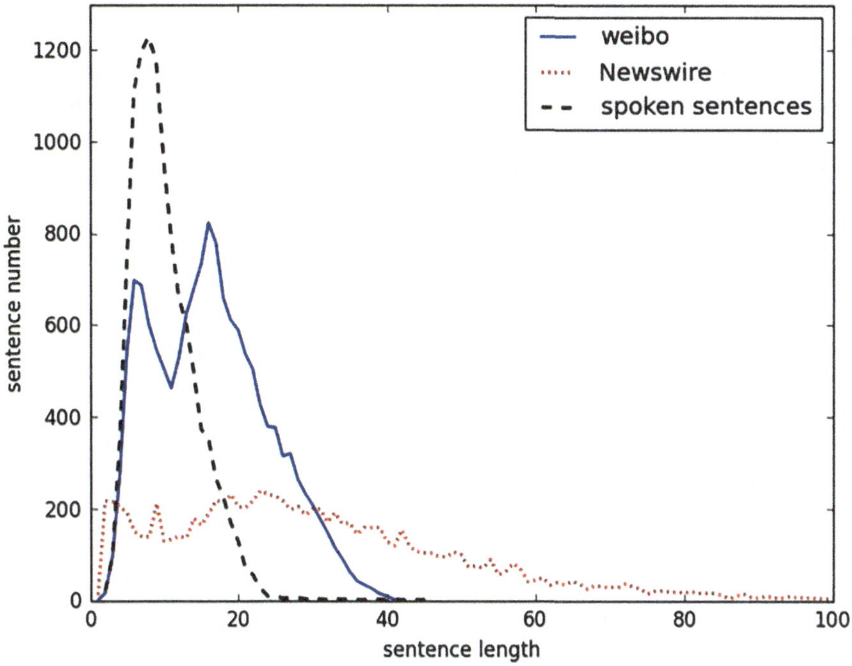

Fig. 13.5 Number of sentences relative to sentence length

Table 13.2 presents additional details on our annotated corpus, while Fig. 13.5 shows the curve of the number of sentences relative to sentence lengths. Spoken sentences refer to sentences with rich expressions (e.g., dialogues, dialogue sentences, Chinese-English bilingual sentences, and primary school texts). The sentences in the primary school texts were not all colloquial, as some of them exploited luxuriant expressions. Differences and the diversification of resources resulted in rich linguistic phenomena. Fan (1998) and Huang and Liao (2003) reduced sentence patterns into single and compound sentences from a linguistic perspective. In our annotated corpus, single sentences were categorized into 8 patterns, while compound sentences were categorized into 12 patterns, and each sentence pattern had corresponding sentences.

13.3.2 Annotation Tool

We developed an online annotation tool to enable annotators to conveniently search, annotate, and revise. Figure 13.6 shows the annotation interface of the tool. On the annotation page, two buttons are used to switch to the word segmentation and POS tagging sub-pages. On the history page, sentences are displayed with dependency labels and relations. Annotators can click on a sentence, which will take them to a page to revise the annotation. On the search page, different keywords and their combinations can be used to search for sentences and corresponding annotation results. When annotators are confused about certain words or relations, they can search and learn from other labeling results. This online tool provides helpful functions for those involved in the annotation process.

13.4 Evaluation of the Corpus

The quality of an annotated corpus is crucial for automatic dependency parsing. We measured the consistency degree of the inner-annotators' agreement to evaluate the quality of our annotated corpus, wherein the same linguistic phenomena were labeled with the same dependency structures and relation labels. We employed three linguistics master's students to annotate the same smaller corpus blindly. The smaller corpus included 422 randomly selected sentences from the 30,000 sentences collected. We evaluated the agreements on the dependency arcs level and both the arc and relation levels, respectively. The average agreements among the three pairs of annotators were 88.78% for arcs only and 72.15% for both arcs and relations. The latter result was lower than the former because only when both the

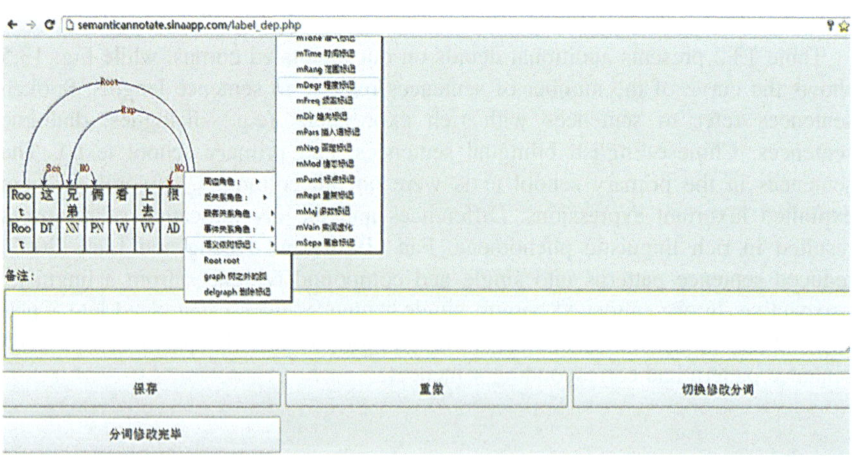

Fig. 13.6 Interface of the online annotation tool

Table 13.3 Agreement results of three separate annotator pairs

	A1 and A2 (%)	A1 and A3 (%)	A2 and A3 (%)	Average (%)
Arcs only	87.48	91.14	87.71	88.78
Both arcs and relations	69.45	74.78	72.21	72.15

dependency arcs and corresponding relations were consistent could an agreement item be obtained. Hundreds of relations were defined, so this low result was conceivable. Table 13.3 shows the agreement results.

In addition, we evaluated the agreement using Fleiss' kappa discussed in Fleiss (1971). The degree of agreement between all annotators was computed in terms of Fleiss' kappa (κ), as shown in Eq. (13.1):

$$\kappa = \frac{\overline{P} - \overline{P}_e}{1 - \overline{P}_e} \tag{13.1}$$

The proportion of all assignments used for assigning the *jth* assignment was defined using Eq. (13.2), where N is the total number of words, n is the number of annotators for our resource building work, K is the total number of assignment types conducted by the annotators, and $N \times n$ is the total number of assignments made by all the annotators, while the mean proportion of assignments for all assignments was defined using Eq. (13.3):

$$P_j = \frac{1}{N \times n} \sum_{i=1}^{N} n_{ij} \tag{13.2}$$

$$\overline{P}_e = \sum_{j=1}^{K} P_j^2 \tag{13.3}$$

The extent of the annotator pairs' agreement for the *ith* word was defined using Eq. (13.4), where subscript i (1, …, N) represents the words and subscript j (1, …, K) represents the assignments; thus, nij is the number of annotators who assigned the *ith* word to the *jth* assignment, and $n(n - 1)/2$ represents the pairs of annotators, while the mean of agreements for all words was defined using Eq. (13.5):

$$P_i = \frac{1}{n(n-1)} \sum_{j=1}^{K} n_{ij}(n_{ij} - 1) \tag{13.4}$$

$$\overline{P} = \frac{1}{N} \sum_{i=1}^{N} P_i \tag{13.5}$$

In this case, n is equal to 3 (i.e., the three annotators that participated in this experiment). The total number of sentences annotated was 422, which included 6634 words. We calculated two Fleiss' kappa scores, one using arcs as assignments and the other using both arc and relation labels. For the two criteria, we had 48 and 1638 assignments, respectively. We achieved kappa scores of 0.835 and 0.686, respectively, for the two criteria. If all three annotators agreed on all the assignments, then the kappa score would be 1. Generally, when the kappa score is above 0.7, agreement is good, and when the kappa score is below 0.7 but above 0.4, agreement is reasonable. The kappa scores indicated that the three annotators mostly agreed when annotating the semantic dependency graph corpus.

13.5 Corpus Statistics

We performed statistics on our annotated corpus. Table 13.4 illustrates the highest and lowest frequent labels in the annotated corpus. The bottom five labels with the least occurrence were reverse or nested relations, which are uncommon kinds of linguistic phenomena. By contrast, the labels with the most frequent appearances are shown in the third and fourth columns. The mPunc (punctuation) label was excluded. Each sentence had at least one punctuation mark, and the total occurrence of mPunc exceeded 30,161. Both Exp (experiencer) and Agt (agent) appeared in the top 5 label list because they belong to the subject-predicate structure, which frequently appears in languages, at the syntactic level. Two relation marks—mAux (auxiliary mark) and mMod (modal mark)—had the highest frequencies. Desc (description) appeared the most frequently as it was used between most adjectives and nouns.

Figure 13.7 shows the relation numbers and frequencies by relation groups. The frequencies of each group were added. We recorded 27 nested relations and 28 reverse relations in our annotated corpus. Reverse relations appeared the least among all groups, followed by nested relations. These two kinds of linguistic phenomena are not common in the Chinese language. The occurrence of event relations was directly related to the number of sub-sentences.

Table 13.5 shows the arc proportions that caused crossed arcs and nodes with multiple heads. Statistical analysis was performed on the entire annotated corpus, including 30,161 sentences. The proportion of sentences with cross arcs was 24.31%, while sentences with multiple heads accounted for 30.59%. Figure 13.8a shows an example of the sentence with crossed arcs, and Fig. 13.8b is an example of

Table 13.4 Sample of semantic relations with the least and most occurrences

No. of occurrence	Bottom labels	No. of occurrence	Top labels
1	dQuan, dAft	22,585	Desc
1	rComp, rMalt, rSco, rSeq	22,273	mAux
3	dFreq, rQp	20,529	Exp
4	rAccd	18,151	Agt
6	rInt	15,189	mMod

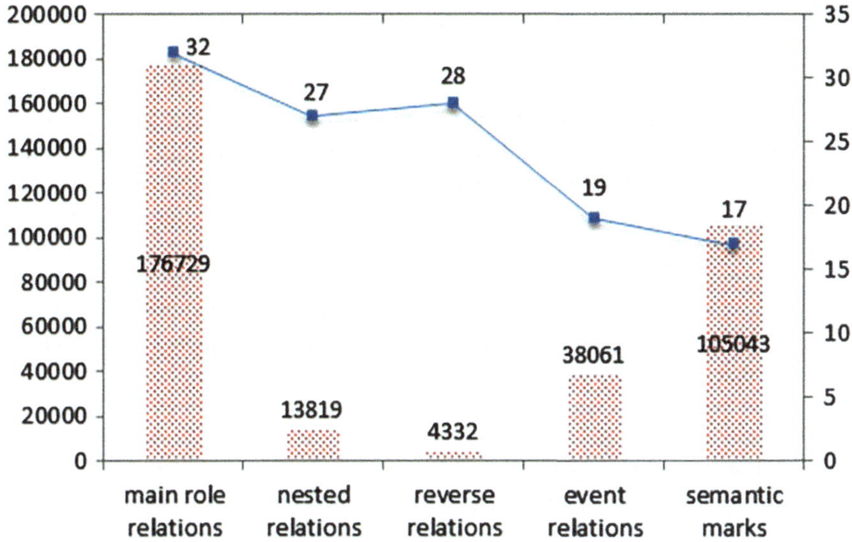

Fig. 13.7 The number and occurrence of labels in each relation category

Table 13.5 Proportion of crossed arcs and sentences, including nodes with multiple heads

	Number	Proportion
Sentences with crossed arcs	7332	24.31%
Sentences with multiple heads	9226	30.59%
Total sentences	30,161	–

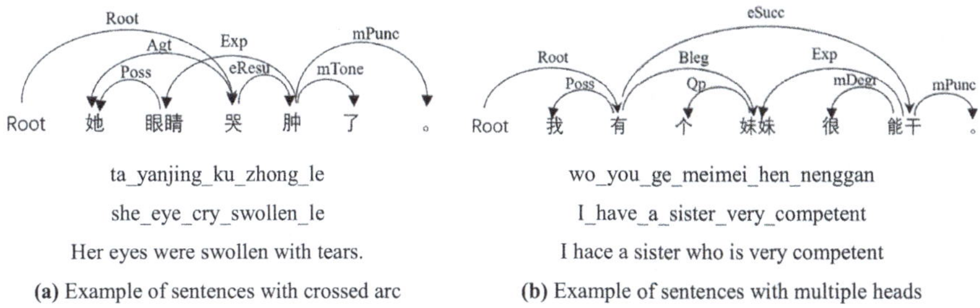

Fig. 13.8 Examples of crossed arcs and nodes with multiple heads. (**a**) Example of sentences with crossed arcs. (**b**) Example of sentences with multiple heads

sentence with multiple heads. Example (a) shows the Agt arc from 哭 *ku* "cry," 她 *ta* "she," and the Exp arc from 肿 *Zhong* "swollen," to 眼睛 *yanjing* "eye" cross, while (b) shows the node 妹妹 *meimei* "sister," which has two parent nodes—有 *you* "have" and 能干 *nenggan* "competent." As can be seen, the structure of quite a few sentences in Chinese highlights the limitations of dependency trees, so using semantic dependency graphs to describe semantic structures is quite necessary.

13.6 Conclusion

The current chapter proposed a scheme for Chinese semantic dependency, and each label in this scheme reflected concrete semantic information. The SDG is a human-understandable semantic representation both visually and logically. The semantic relations were designed from the perspective of linguistics to adapt to the characteristics of the Chinese language. Very little abstraction of semantic information exists, which distinguishes this proposed scheme from existing dependency schemes. Inducing semantics directly, we employed more relation labels than syntactic dependencies. To clarify the boundaries of relation labels, we classified them into several hierarchies that represented different types of information, namely, main semantic roles, event relations, and semantic marks.

We annotated more than 30,000 sentences based on this scheme. The sentences were chosen from spoken sentences, newswires, and Sina Weibo microblogs, covering both the common core of the language and more specialized domains. In the process of constructing this corpus, we obtained the utmost out of other gold standard information labeled in the sentences to generate pre-annotation results by rules or by machine learning tools. Triple-blinded annotation experiments were conducted to measure the inner-annotators' agreement by calculating the widely used Fleiss' kappa. We achieved kappa scores of 0.835 and 0.686 for non-labeled arcs and labeled arcs as assignments, respectively. These results indicate that the three annotators had a great majority of agreements while annotating the corpus, although the semantic dependency scheme was slightly complicated.

According to the statistics and analysis of the annotated corpus, we arrived at the conclusion that although most sentences constitute projective dependency trees in Chinese, non-projective trees and dependency graphs do exist but in a smaller proportion. Thus, using semantic dependency graphs to describe semantic information is quite necessary and reasonable.

Acknowledgments We appreciatively acknowledge the support of the National Natural Science Foundation of China (61872402), the Humanities and Social Science Project of the Ministry of Education (17YJAZH068), and the Science Foundation of Beijing Language and Culture University (supported by the Fundamental Research Funds for the Central Universities, 18ZDJ03).

References

Böhmová, Alena, Jan Hajič, Eva Hajičová, and Barbora Hladká. 2003. The Prague dependency treebank: A three-level annotation scenario. In *Treebanks: Building and using parsed corpora*, ed. Anne Abeillé, Amsterdam: Kluwer, 103–127.

Chatterji, Sanjay, Tanaya Mukherjee Sarkar, Pragati Dhang, Samhita Deb, Sudeshna Sarkar, Jayshree Chakraborty, Anupam Basu. 2014. A dependency annotation scheme for Bangla treebank. *Language Resources and Evaluation* 48:443–477.

Che, Wanxiang, Meishan Zhang, Yanqiu Shao, and Ting Liu. 2012. SemEval-2012 task 5: Chinese semantic dependency parsing. In *Proceedings of the First Joint Conference on Lexical and*

Computational Semantics (Vol. 1): *Proceedings of the main conference and the shared task*; (Vol. 2): *Proceedings of the sixth international workshop on semantic evaluation*, Montréal, Canada, 378–384. Available at https://aclanthology.info/papers/S12-1050/s12-1050. Accessed 8 March 2019.

Chen, Feng-Yi, Pi-Fang Tsai, Keh-jiann Chen, and Chu-Ren Huang 陈凤仪, 蔡碧芳, 陈克健, 黄居仁. 1999. Project Report: Sinica Treebank 中文句结构树资料库的构建. *Computational Linguistics and Chinese Language Processing 中文计算语言学期刊* 4(2):87–104.

Cui, Hang, Renxu Sun, Keya Li, Min-Yen Kan, and Tat-Seng Chua. 2005. Question answering passage retrieval using dependency relations. In *Proceedings of the 28th Annual International ACM SIGIR Conference on Research and Development in Information Retrieval—SIGIR'05, ACM Press*, New York, NY, 400–407. Available at https://www.researchgate.net/publication/221300315_Question_answering_passage_retrieval_using_dependency_relations. Accessed 8 March 2019.

De Marneffe, Marie-Catherine, and Christopher D. Manning. 2008. The Stanford typed dependencies representation. In *Proceedings of the COLING 2008 Workshop on Cross-framework and Cross-domain Parser Evaluation*, Manchester, United Kingdom, 1–8. Available at https://nlp.stanford.edu/pubs/dependencies-coling08.pdf. Accessed 8 March 2019.

Dong, Qiang, and Zhendong Dong. 2006. *HowNet and computation of meaning*. World Scientific Publishing Company.

Fan, Xiao 范晓. 1998. *The sentence types of Chinese 汉语的句子类型*. Shuhai Publishing House.

Fleiss, Joseph L. 1971. Measuring nominal scale agreement among many raters. *Psychological Bulletin* 76(5):378–382.

Hacioglu, Kadri. 2004. Semantic role labeling using dependency trees. In *Proceedings of the 20th International Conference on Computational Linguistics—COLING '04*, Geneva, Switzerland, Article number 1273. 1–4. Available at https://dl.acm.org/citation.cfm?doid=|1220355.1220541 . Accessed 8 March 2019.

Haverinen, Katri, Jenna Nyblom, Timo Viljanen, Veronika Laippala, Samuel Kohonen, Anna Missilä, Stina Ojala, Tapio Salakoski, Filip Ginter. 2014. Building the essential resources for Finnish: The Turku dependency treebank. *Language Resources and Evaluation* 48:493–531.

Huang, Bo-rong, and Xu-dong Liao 黄伯荣, 廖旭东. 2003. *Contemporary Chinese language 现代汉语*. Higher Education Press.

Johansson, Richard, and Pierre Nugues. 2007. LTH: Semantic structure extraction using nonprojective dependency trees. In *Proceedings of the 4th International Workshop on Semantic Evaluations*, Prague, Czech Republic, 227–230. Available at https://dl.acm.org/citation.cfm?id=1621522. Accessed 8 March 2019.

Li, Mingqin, Juanzi Li, Zhendong Dong, Zuoying Wang, and Dajin Lu. 2003. Building a large Chinese corpus annotated with semantic dependency. In *Proceedings of the Second SIGHAN Workshop on Chinese Language Processing* (Vol. 17), Sapporo, Japan, 84–91. Available at http://aclweb.org/anthology/W03-1712. Accessed 8 March 2019.

Li, Zhenghua, Ting Liu, and Wanxiang Che. 2012. Exploiting multiple treebanks for parsing with quasi synchronous grammars. In *Proceedings of the 50th Annual Meeting of the Association for Computational Linguistics: Long Papers* (Vol. 1), Jeju Island, Korea, 675–684. Available at http://ir.hit.edu.cn/~lzh/papers/zhenghua-P12-multi-treebanks.pdf. Accessed 8 March 2019.

Li, Bin, Lijun Wen, Weiguang Qu, Lijun Bu, and Nianwen Xue. 2016. Annotating the Little Prince with Chinese AMRs. In *Proceedings of the 10th Linguistic Annotation Workshop held in conjunction with ACL 2016 (LAW-X 2016)*, Berlin, Germany, 7–15. Available at http://aclweb.org/anthology/W16-1702. Accessed 8 March 2019.

Liu, Ting, Jinshan Ma, and Sheng Li 刘挺, 马金山, 李生. 2006. Chinese dependency parsing model based on lexical governing degree 基于词汇支配度的汉语依存分析模型. *Journal of Software 软件学报* 17(9):1876–1883.

Lu, Chuan 鲁川. 2001. *The parataxis network of the Chinese grammar 汉语语法的意合网络*. The Commercial Press.

Marimon, Montserrat, and Núria Bel. 2014. Dependency structure annotation in the IULA Spanish LSP treebank. *Language Resources and Evaluation* 49(2):433–454.

Niu, Zheng-Yu, Haifeng Wang, and Hua Wu. 2009. Exploiting heterogeneous treebanks for parsing. In *Proceedings of the Joint Conference of the 47th Annual Meeting of the ACL and the 4th International Joint Conference on Natural Language Processing of the AFNLP: Volume 1-Volume 1, Association for Computational Linguistics*, Suntec, Singapore, 46–54. Available at http://www.aclweb.org/anthology/P09-1006. Accessed 8 March 2019.

Oepen, Stephan, Marco Kuhlmann, Daniel Zeman, Yusuke Miyao, Dan Flickinger, Jan Hajič, Angelina Ivanova, and Yi Zhang. 2014. SemEval-2014 task 8: Broad-coverage semantic dependency parsing. In *Proceedings of the Eighth International Workshop on Semantic Evaluation (SemEval-2014)*, Dublin City University, Dublin, Ireland, 63–72. Available at http://aclweb.org/anthology/S14-2008. Accessed 8 March 2019.

Pradhan, Sameer, Wayne Ward, Kadri Hacioglu, James H. Martin, Daniel Jurafsky. 2005. Semantic Role Labeling Using Different Syntactic Views. In *Proceedings of the 43rd Annual Meeting on Association for Computational Linguistics*, Ann Arbor, Michigan, 581–588. Available at http://cemantix.org/papers/pradhan-acl-2005.pdf. Accessed 8 March 2019.

Punyakanok, Vasin, Dan Roth, and Wen-tau Yih. 2004. Mapping dependencies trees: An application to question answering. In *Proceedings of International Symposium on Artificial Intelligence & Mathematics Fort*, 1–10. Available at http://l2r.cs.uiuc.edu/~danr/Papers/PunyakanokRoYi04a.pdf. Accessed 8 March 2019.

Robinson, Jane J. 1970. Dependency structures and transformational rules. *Language* 46:259–285.

Xue, Nianwen, and Martha Palmer. 2003. Annotating the propositions in the Penn Chinese treebank. In *Proceedings of the Second SIGHAN Workshop on Chinese Language Processing*, Sapporo, Japan, 47–54. Available at http://www.aclweb.org/anthology/W03-1707. Accessed 8 March 2019.

Žolkovskij, Aleksandr, and Igor A. Mel'čuk. 1967. O sistemesemantiˇceskogosinteza. II: Pravilapreobrazovanija [On a system of semantic synthesis (of texts). II: Paraphrasing rules]. *Nauˇcno-texniˇceskaja informacija 2, Informacionnye processy I sistemy*, 17–27.

Chapter 14
A Chinese Dialogue Corpus Annotated with Dialogue Act

Shida Li, Wenjie Zhou, and Yunfang Wu

Abstract This chapter will introduce a Chinese dialogue corpus with annotated dialogue acts and users' intent, which contains 5026 multi-turn and multiplayer dialogue messages with an average of 13 utterances per round. This dataset will provide a unique resource of Chinese dialogue corpora as well as a baseline for research on Chinese dialogue act classification and dialogue intent prediction. We proposed a detailed annotation scheme and annotation specification using three dimensions and manually annotated the dataset. We also implemented the conditional random field (CRF) model and the recurrent neural network (RNN) model to predict dialogue acts and dialogue intent. The experimental results of the baseline methods will be presented in Section "Experimental Results," followed by the conclusion of this chapter.

Keywords Dialogue corpus · Dialogue act · Group chat

14.1 Introduction

A computer's ability to converse with a human in a natural and coherent manner has long been held as one of the primary objectives of artificial intelligence (AI). Dialogue systems are very practical and widely used, involving a large number of intelligent customer services, chat robots, and other services and entertainment applications. The annotation of dialogue act is a basic but important work in research on Chinese dialogue, and the data quality and annotation effects have a direct impact on the development of Chinese dialogue systems. At present, many public English benchmark datasets for dialogue state tracking have been used in scientific research,

S. Li
School of Computer Science, Peking University, Beijing, China
e-mail: lishidaup@pku.edu.cn

W. Zhou · Y. Wu (✉)
Key Laboratory of Computational Linguistics, Peking University, Ministry of Education, Beijing, China
e-mail: wjzhou013@pku.edu.cn; wuyf@pku.edu.cn

C.-R. Huang et al. (eds.), *Chinese Language Resources*, Text, Speech and Language Technology 49, https://doi.org/10.1007/978-3-031-38913-9_14

such as the Dialog State Tracking Challenges (DSTCs) including DSTC1, DSTC2, DSTC3, and DSTC4 (Henderson et al. 2013, 2014; Kim et al. 2015; Williams et al. 2013). Although there are many methods to draw lessons from, resources of public Chinese dialogue corpora are very scarce. This chapter will discuss the multi-turn and multiplayer Chinese dialogue corpus that we constructed, which contains the human annotation of dialogue acts and topic changes.

To evaluate the task's difficulty and the quality of the data, we implement a conditional random field (CRF) model to extract multiple features, as well as a recurrent neural network (RNN) model. The experimental results show that the same feature sets in the CRF model had great different impact on predicting different dimensions of dialogue intent. The performance of our baseline methods was far behind human performance, leaving much room for improvement.

14.2 Related Work

14.2.1 Existing Datasets

Currently, there are many data recordings of human dialogue that can be used to train dialogue systems after preprocessing. These corpora contain human-to-human and human-to-machine conversations in the form of spoken or written language. There are more datasets available for human-to-human dialogue than for human-to-machine dialogue. From a linguistic viewpoint, there are key differences between written and spoken language (Serban et al. 2015). Spoken language tends to be less formal and contains fewer pronouns than written language (we found it after counting the number of pronouns used in spoken and written text). In addition, logic is usually poor in spoken language. However, in writing, users can think about content before sending messages, which usually comes out with a better logic. Written dialogue may also include spelling errors, which are not recorded in spoken dialogue corpora.

Many written dialogue corpora have been constructed according to the topics of the dialogues. For example, the Settlers of Catan Corpus (Afantenos et al. 2012) contains logs of 40 games, and the Internet Argument Corpus (IAC) (Walker et al. 2012) is a forum-based corpus in which each topic is controversial in nature. Another source of constrained text-based corpora is chat-room environments. The Multi-Party Chat (MPC) Corpus (Shaikh et al. 2010) consists of 14 multi-party dialogue sessions. The Ubuntu Dialogue Corpus (Lowe et al. 2015) contains Ubuntu Internet Relay Chat (IRC) channel logs, where users can log in and ask questions about Ubuntu and can be answered by other users. The IRC Corpus (Elsner and Charniak 2008) contains approximately 50 h occasional social chats from Linux IRC channel logs, which consist of similar technical conversations as the Ubuntu IRC channel logs.

14.2.2 Traditional Methods

A basic but important step in analyzing, understanding, and generating a dialogue with computer is dialogue act annotation, whose task is labeling appropriate dialogue act tags for each dialogue unit. Dialogue acts contain much information considering the sentences spoken or written, such as sentence patterns, the speaker's intention, etc. Research on English dialogue systems is advanced, as annotation standards and tagging systems have already been established. However, the annotation of Chinese dialogue acts got a late start, resulting in less research experience.

The Dialog Act Markup in Several Layers (DAMSL) framework proposed by Allen and Core (1997) has been used in many English dialogue annotation systems (Dhillon et al. 2004; Jurafsky et al. 1997). The classification of sentences using DAMSL is based on the speaker's intention. In terms of a semantic annotation framework, Bunt et al. (2012) focused on the annotation standards of conversational behavior.

In research on the automatic annotation of dialogue acts, Jurafsky et al. (1998) proposed that dialogue acts are related to the grammatical, lexical, and prosodic features of utterances, and they investigated the contributions of these three types of features to the recognition of dialogue acts. With the newly released Switchboard (SWBD) tag set, a new attempt has been made to automatically label dialogue acts. Stolcke et al. (2000) proposed a method to use grammatical and lexical features, which regarded dialogue as an independent sentence stream, and established an implicit Markov model to accomplish the task of classifying dialogue acts. Kim et al. (2010) proposed that incorporating the structure of dialogue and the dependency between words could improve the performance of the model which was based on grammatical lexical features and used the conditional random field (CRF) model for sequence labeling. To solve the problem caused by low-frequency tags, Omuya et al. (2013) proposed level classification using label frequency rather than simple classification based on confidence, which achieved significant improvements in the classification of low-frequency tags.

Combining n-grams, decision trees, and neural networks to generate effective features, the work of Stolcke et al. (2000) achieved 65% accuracy in the SWBD Corpus. Ang et al. (2005) applied the decision tree model to the segmentation of dialogue act units and achieved 44% accuracy. Takechi et al. (2007) proposed a conditional random field algorithm for sentence segmentation, which used the unigram and bigram characteristics of word to examine different window sizes, and achieved 47% accuracy. Wang et al. (2010) used a graph algorithm that regarded each clause as a vertex of a graph and reached 74% accuracy based on the machine learning method.

Research on dialogue acts was a comprehensive study with many aspects. Besides sentence segmentation, research on question recognition has also been integrated. Studies on question recognition began with rule-based methods and then gradually used word features to distinguish the questions. Cong and Wang

(2008) used the labeled sequential pattern (LSP) sequencing method to identify questions.

14.2.3 Deep Learning Models

Deep learning frameworks have been applied to deal with natural language processing (NLP) tasks. Collobert and Weston (2007, 2008) and Collobert et al. (2011) constructed deep neural network structures for NLP tasks, which projected one-hot word representations into distributed representations and built either a feedforward or convolutional neural network upon them. These models have been adopted for different tasks, which has resulted in reduced workloads compared with feature engineering. Hu et al. (2013) proposed generating text and non-text features, respectively, by using a deep neural network, and then the generated features of the deep neural network were used as features of a linear classifier to recognize dialogue acts, and this method obtained a good performance. Kim (2014) proposed a convolutional neural network (CNN) model with just one convolution and pooling layer used with multi-channel word embeddings, followed by a softmax classifier, which succeeded in many NLP tasks, such as sentence classification, sentiment analysis, and so on.

The RNN model, originally proposed by Elman (1990), aims to remember previous information and process sequence data. Hochreiter and Schmidhuber (1997) proposed long short-term memory (LSTM), which used a cell with input, forget, and output gates to prevent the vanishing gradient problem in the RNN model. Palangi et al. (2015) proposed taking each word in a sentence sequentially, extracting its information, and embedding it into a semantic vector to access the sentence-level vector and using it to deal with other tasks such as information retrieval. Shen and Lee (2016) introduced a type of attention mechanism for sentence modeling based on LSTM, optimizing the model by highlighting important information in long sentences.

However, it is not long sentences that hinder dialogue act annotation but rather the large proportion of short sentences in corpora. Lee and Dernoncourt (2016) regarded this problem as a sequential short-text classification problem, which is a good direction to follow; however, although they tried to capture historical information, the capability of the feedforward neural network was too limited to seize long-distance information in a conversation.

14.3 Annotation of a Group Chat Corpus

14.3.1 Data Collection and Preprocessing

To obtain high-quality dialogue data, we collected a total of 85 group chats, with more than 31 million messages. These group chats involved a wide range of topics, including novels, campus recruitment, students, academic exchange, and so on. The dialogue messages were diverse, including:

Text messages, the main dialog content

URL of a website

Action messages, such as [打手鼓 *dǎshǒugǔ* "strike the tambourine"]

System messages, such as "***加入了群聊 *jiārùlequnliáo* 'joined the group chat'"

Pictures, shown as [图片 *túpiàn* "picture"]

Expressions without meaning, such as [表情 *biǎoqíng* "expression"]

Expressive expressions, such as [哈哈 *haha* "Aha"], [鄙视 *bǐshì* "disdainful"], [no]

Punctuation strings or number strings, such as "!!!", "。。。", "???", "666", "2333"

In the preprocessing stage, in order to protect the speakers' privacy, we replaced their personal information with an ID number. We also deleted system messages, expressions without content, and redundant or meaningless dialogues. There were long time spans, uneven time distributions, and different activities in the group chats. We segmented the chat records into 24 h to make a rough segmentation of a conversation by topic. When the time interval between two messages in a record exceeded the threshold, the chat record was cut and saved as a new file. To ensure the number of rounds in a multi-turn conversation, we retained the segmentation data with more than ten messages as a candidate set. A sample of 5026 dialogues was used for manual annotation, involving 5 groups, with a total of 37 segmentation files.

14.3.2 Annotation Specification

We defined the annotation scheme and annotation specification in detail and annotated all the data manually. We chose two annotators who had experience in labeling and annotating data and fully explained the annotation sets and annotation specification. For each sentence in a dialogue, we defined the dialogue act labels using the following three dimensions.

Dimension 1 (D1): Semantic Information

The tags of this dimension indicated the semantic information of an individual sentence without considering the context.

<S>: expresses statements
For example, 我要回家了
wǒ__yào__huí__jiā__le
I__want__go__home__yet
I want to go home.

<O>: expresses opinions about somebody or something
For example, 估计这个岗位竞争激烈
gūji__zhègè__gǎngwèi__jìngzhēng__jīliè
guess__this__job__compete__fierce
It is estimated that the job is highly competitive.

<E>: expresses emotions or feelings of the speaker
For example, 今天太开心了
jīntiān__tài__kāixīn__le
Today__too__happy__yet
I am so happy today.

<P>: polite expression
For example, 好的, 谢谢
hǎode,__xièxie
okay,__thanks
Okay, thanks.

<QYN>: yes-no question
For example, 有武汉的岗位?
yǒu__wǔhàn__de__gǎngwèi?
have__Wuhan__of__job?
Is there a job in Wuhan?

<Q>: open question
For example, 怎么做?
zěnme_zuò?
How__do?
How to do?

<U>: unknown message
For example, http://sohustaff.kuaizhan.com/

If a sentence was ambiguous, or if a sentence could not be categorized under any of the proposed labels, it was marked as "<U>". In addition, the speakers in the group chats sent diverse messages. Besides pure text, there were expressions, symbols, pictures, URLs, and so on. If this kind of information (such as URLs, pictures, etc.) did not have a specific meaning or it was too simple or too vague to be assigned a label, it was also marked as "<U>".

Dimension 2 (D2): Reaction to Context

The tags of this dimension took context into account, indicating a reaction to the context of a sentence in the current topic. According to responses or complements to the previous sentence as well as the meaning of the previous sentence, the labels were set as follows:

<**RS**>: response to the last sentence that expressed statements.

<**RO**>: response to the last sentence that expressed opinions.

<**RE**>: response to the last sentence that expressed emotions or feelings.

<**RP**>: response to the last polite expressions.

<**AYN**>: answer to the last yes-no question.

<**AQ**>: answer to the last open question.

<**RU**>: response to the last unknown message.

<**ADD**>: supplement or extend the last sentence.

<**B**>: void. If a message can't be assigned to other labels, it should be marked as "<B>".

We regarded the current sentence as a response to the last sentence as a default setting; otherwise, we marked the line number of the sentence being responded to.

Dimension 3 (D3): Effect of Turn-Taking on Topic

The following tags were created to address the effect of turn-taking on a topic:

<**ST**>: open a new topic.

<**B**>: void, continue the original topic.

Multiple topics often occurred in the group chats. If someone did not continue the original topic and opened a new topic, the message was labeled <ST>. If there were several meanings and labels available for one message in a single dimension, the annotator selected the most prominent tag according to his or her comprehension.

14.3.3 Annotated Example

We selected an example from the group chat data, as shown in Table 14.1, to display the annotated dialogue act information, which consisted of the line number, time, speaker ID, and content. The results of the annotation are represented by the D1 tag, D2 tag, D3 tag, and the line number of the cross-line reply.

Table 14.1 An annotated example containing dialogue messages

Line number	Time	Speaker ID	Content	Tag of D1	Tag of D2	Tag of D3	Line number of cross-line reply
51	18: 55:05	id2	我们今天选课结果出来了	<S>		<ST>	
			wǒmen__jīntiān__xǔan__kè__jiéguǒ__chūlái__le				
			we__today__select__course__result__out__yet				
			The results of course selection came out today				
52	18: 55:49	id5	怎么样	<Q>	<RS>		
			Zěnmeyàng				
			How				
			How				
53	18: 56:38	id2	掉了两门	<S>	<AQ>		
			diào__le__liǎng__mén				
			drop__yet__two__gate				
			Missed two subjects				
54	18: 58:53	id2	我们还有人掉了必修课	<S>	<ADD>		
			wǒmen__háiyǒu__rén__diàole__bìxiū__kè				
			we__have__people__drop__obligatory__course				
			Someone even missed two required courses				
55	18: 59:34	id1	怎么这么快考试。。	<Q>	<RS>		
			zěnme__zhème__kuài__kǎoshì. . .				
			how__so__fast__test. . .				
			Why are you taking a test so soon. . .				
56	19: 11:02	id2	超胜要考试?	<QYN>			
			chāoshèng__yào__kǎoshì?				
			chaosheng__want__test?				
			Is Chaosheng going to take a test?				

57	19: 18:13	id1	不是啊我说你们 bùshì__a__wǒ__shuō__nǐmen no__ah__I__say__you *No, I mean you*	<S>	<AYN>		
58	19: 18:23	id1	什么叫掉了2门 shénme__jiào__diào__le__2__mén what__call__drop__yet__two__gate What's the meaning of missing two courses	<Q>	<RS>		54
59	19: 18:57	id5	我也不知道 wǒ__yě__bù__zhīdào I__also__no__know I don't know either	<S>	<AQ>		
60	19: 19:07	id5	求解释 qiú__jiěshi beg__explain Please explain	<S>	<ADD>		

14.3.4 Consistency Check

We sampled 1012 messages from the corpus for double-blind annotation, consistency check, confusion matrix analysis, and human performance evaluation. We calculated the kappa value (Carletta 1996) of the annotation results and checked their consistency. If the consistency check passed, the annotation set and annotation specification proved reasonable without ambiguity from the annotators, as well as validated the consistency of the two annotators and ensured the reliability of the data. The results of the consistency check are shown in Table 14.2, where the observation consistency is the percentage of consistent instances in the double-blind annotated data and the kappa value is the statistic calculated by the observation consistency and expected consistency (i.e., the rate of consistency caused by chance).

The statistical results showed that the kappa values of the three dimensions were within the range of 0.60–0.80, indicating a high degree of consistency. This demonstrated that the annotation set and annotation specification were reasonable and the annotated data was reliable.

14.3.5 Dataset Statistics

Based on the annotated data, we calculated the distribution information of the dialogue act tags, which is shown in Table 14.3.

According to the statistical results, <S> and <O> accounted for the largest amount of semantics information among the Dimension 1 tags; <B> and <ADD> accounted for the largest amount of reaction to context among the Dimension 2 tags; and the ratio of the number of <ST> to the number of <B> that represented topic changes was about 12:1 for the two Dimension 3 tags, meaning that each dialogue had an average of 13 messages. The uneven distribution of tags showed the characteristics of our multi-turn corpus.

Table 14.2 Kappa values in the double-blind annotated data

	Observation consistency	Kappa value
D1	0.7796	0.6998
D2	0.6887	0.6058
D3	0.9447	0.7833

Table 14.3 Distribution of tags

D1	<S>, 0.5546; <O>, 0.1211; <QYN>, 0.1016; <Q>, 0.0923; <E>, 0.0536; <U>, 0.0455; <P>, 0.0314
D2	<B>, 0.3581; <ADD>, 0.2366; <RS>, 0.2197; <AYN>, 0.0625; <AQ>, 0.0542; <RO>, 0.0399; <RE>, 0.0139; <RU>, 0.0093; <RP>, 0.0058
D3	<B>, 0.9258; <ST>, 0.0742

14.3.6 Confusion Matrix

There may have been inconsistencies due to the annotators' different understanding of each sentence. We highlighted the labels that could have been easily confused in the process of annotation to observe this inconsistency phenomenon by analyzing 1000 double-blind annotated messages and generated a confusion matrix for all 3 dimensions. The confusion matrixes for the Dimension 1 and Dimension 2 tags are shown in Tables 14.4 and 14.5, respectively. The confusion matrixes show that the <S> and <O>, <S> and <U>, <S> and <E>, <Q> and <QYN>, and <U> and <E> tags tended to be confused in Dimension 1 and the <RS> and <RO>, <RS> and <AYN>, <RS> and <ADD>, and <AQ> and <AYN> tags tended to be confused in Dimension 2.

14.4 Baseline Methods

To perform dialogue act classification, we implemented the CRF model and the RNN model as the baseline methods.

Table 14.4 Confusion matrix for the Dimension 1 tags

	Labeler A	<S>	<Q>	<QYN>	<O>	<E>	<P>	<U>
Labeler B	<S>	386	3	3	15	5	7	28
	<Q>	4	115	9	0	0	0	2
	<QYN>	10	15	82	0	0	0	1
	<O>	41	0	1	81	7	3	2
	<E>	20	0	0	7	12	0	6
	<P>	2	1	0	0	1	59	0
	<U>	8	3	0	3	12	1	45

Table 14.5 Confusion matrix for the Dimension 2 tags

	<RS>	<RO>	<RE>	<RU>	<RP>	<ADD>	<AQ>	<AYN>
<RS>	127	8	2	3	1	4	6	7
<RO>	11	14	1	1	0	0	0	0
<RE>	4	1	3	0	0	1	0	1
<RU>	1	1	1	12	0	0	0	0
<RP>	0	0	0	0	5	1	0	0
<ADD>	9	4	1	0	1	195	2	1
<AQ>	3	0	0	0	0	1	70	5
<AYN>	5	0	0	0	0	2	8	45

14.4.1 Dataset

We sampled 1000 messages from the double-blind annotated data to form a test set and a human performance reference set. The remaining 4026 messages served as the training set. The ratio of training data to test data was about 4:1.

14.4.2 Evaluation Metrics

We used three different metrics to evaluate model performance.

Metric 1: Exact match (EM) – the ratio of the number of correct predictions to the total number.

Metric 2: Weighted F1 (W-F1) – this metric measured the weighted average of different classes. First, the F1 values were computed for each class, and then the weighted average of the F1 values was computed.

Metric 3: Macro-averaged F1 (Ma-F1) – this metric measured the arithmetic mean of different classes. First, the F1 values were computed for each class, and then the arithmetic mean of the F1 values was computed.

14.4.3 Conditional Random Field (CRF) Model

The CRF model is a discriminant probabilistic undirected graphical model proposed by Lafferty et al. (2001), which is based on the maximum entropy model together with the hidden Markov model and can be used to label and segment sequential data. In the most commonly used CRF model, $x = \{x_1, x_2, x_n\}$ represents an observation sequence, while $y = \{y_1, y_2, y_n\}$ is a collection of finite states, and the prediction probability of tag y was obtained using Formulas (14.1) and (14.2):

$$p(y|x, \lambda) = \frac{1}{Z(x)} \exp\left(\sum_{i=1}^{n} \sum_{j} \lambda_j f_j(y_{i-1}, y_i, x, i)\right) \tag{14.1}$$

$$Z(x) = \sum_{j} \exp\left(\sum_{i=1}^{n} \sum_{j} \lambda_j f_j(y_{i-1}, y_i, x, i)\right) \tag{14.2}$$

We extracted ten kinds of basic features for each message in our task:

Feature 1: The number of words (filter spaces)

Feature 2: The ratio of the number of verbs to the number of words

Feature 3: The ratio of the number of nouns to the number of words

Feature 4: The ratio of the number of pronouns to the number of words

Feature 5: The ratio of the number of conjunctions to the number of words

Feature 6: The ratio of the number of punctuation marks to the number of words

Feature 7: The ratio of the number of overlapped words between previous message and current message to the number of words in current message

Feature 8: The ratio of the number of overlapped words between following message and current message to the number of words in current message

Feature 9: The sum of the term frequency-inverse document frequency (TF-IDF) of overlapped words between previous message and current message

Feature 10: The position where the first verb appears in the message

14.4.4 Recurrent Neural Networks (RNN)

The recurrent neural network model (Medsker and Jain 2001) consists of input layers, hidden layers, and output layers. Inputs of the hidden layers not only rely on current input layers but also the last hidden layer, which stores contextual information. The output y(t) was calculated by Formulas (14.3) and (14.4), where $w(t)$ is the current word vector, $s(t-1)$ is the output of the last hidden layer, $s(t)$ is the output of the current hidden layer, and w, u, and v represent the weight matrix. $f(z)$ and $g(z)$ represent the sigmoid function and the softmax activation function, respectively, and for the softmax activation function, the outputs represent the probability distribution. Please refer to Formulas (14.5) and (14.6) for functions' details:

$$\mathrm{s(t)} = f(u \cdot w(t) + w \cdot s(t-1)) \tag{14.3}$$

$$\mathrm{y(t)} = g(v \cdot s(t)) \tag{14.4}$$

$$\mathrm{f(z)} = \frac{1}{1+e^{-z}} \tag{14.5}$$

$$\mathrm{g}(z_m) = \frac{e^{z_m}}{\sum_k e^{z_k}} \tag{14.6}$$

14.5 Experimental Results

14.5.1 Human Performance

We generated a test set and a human performance reference set using the method in Sect. 14.4.1 and then compared these two sets (the human performance reference set was regarded as human predictions) to evaluate human performance. The results were shown in Table 14.6.

Table 14.6 Human performance

Dimension	EM	W-F1	Ma-F1
D1	0.78	0.7765	0.7056
D2	0.69	0.6885	0.5949
D3	0.944	0.9437	0.8908
D1 + D2 + D3	0.524	0.5167	0.3836

Table 14.7 Results of random selection

Dimension	EM	W-F1	Ma-F1
D1	0.1275	0.149	0.1035
D2	0.1107	0.1368	0.0834
D3	0.4912	0.5596	0.4252
D1 + D2 + D3	0.0089	0.0124	0.0045

Table 14.8 Performance of the CRF model in Dimension 1

Feature	EM	W-F1	Ma-F1
Feature 1	0.449	0.278	0.089
+Feature 2	0.419	0.289	0.108
+Feature 3	0.422	0.301	0.127
+Feature 4	0.427	0.320	0.159
+Feature 5	0.439	0.331	0.172
+Feature 6	0.438	0.336	0.186
+Feature 7	**0.446**	**0.353**	**0.210**
+Feature 8	0.434	0.341	0.201
+Feature 9	0.431	0.334	0.190
+Feature 10	0.432	0.334	0.190

14.5.2 Model Performance

Random Selection

We randomly selected tags by computer simulations to facilitate the evaluation of the model's performance. The results are shown in Table 14.7.

CRF Model

After word segmentation for each message, we extracted ten features from Sect. 14.4.3 to train the model, using CRF++ (http://crfpp.googlecode.com/svn/trunk/doc/index.html). The experimental results were shown in Tables 14.8, 14.9, 14.10, and 14.11, respectively.

Table 14.8 indicates that the CRF model obtains optimal performance after adding Feature 7, on which W-F1 achieved 0.353. Feature 4 worked the most. The performance of the model decreased with Feature 8, Feature 9, and Feature 10.

Table 14.9 indicates that the CRF model obtains optimal performance after adding Feature 6, on which W-F1 achieved 0.258. Feature 3 worked the most. The

Table 14.9 Performance of the CRF model in Dimension 2

Feature	EM	W-F1	Ma-F1
Feature 1	0.331	0.165	0.055
+Feature 2	0.332	0.180	0.063
+Feature 3	0.331	0.223	0.088
+Feature 4	0.330	0.237	0.100
+Feature 5	0.329	0.234	0.100
+Feature 6	**0.334**	**0.258**	**0.114**
+Feature 7	0.324	0.255	0.118
+Feature 8	0.305	0.236	0.103
+Feature 9	0.306	0.238	0.105
+Feature 10	0.311	0.241	0.108

Table 14.10 Performance of the CRF model in Dimension 3

Feature	EM	W-F1	Ma-F1
Feature 1	0.848	0.778	0.459
+Feature 2	0.848	0.778	0.465
+Feature 3	0.848	0.780	0.466
+Feature 4	0.847	0.778	0.459
+Feature 5	**0.848**	**0.778**	**0.459**
+Feature 6	0.847	0.778	0.459
+Feature 7	0.848	0.780	0.465
+Feature 8	0.846	0.776	0.458
+Feature 9	0.846	0.776	0.458
+Feature 10	0.846	0.776	0.458

Table 14.11 Performance of the CRF model in Dimension 1 + 2+ 3

Feature	EM	W-F1	Ma-F1
Feature 1	0.082	0.014	0.003
+Feature 2	0.086	0.052	0.012
+Feature 3	0.098	0.070	0.024
+Feature 4	0.089	0.073	0.026
+Feature 5	0.107	0.074	0.023
+Feature 6	**0.103**	**0.075**	**0.026**
+Feature 7	0.099	0.069	0.026
+Feature 8	0.088	0.059	0.017
+Feature 9	0.093	0.064	0.018
+Feature 10	0.09	0.061	0.018

performance of the model decreased with Feature 7, Feature 8, Feature 9, and Feature 10.

Table 14.10 indicates that the CRF model obtains optimal performance after adding Feature 5, on which W-F1 achieved 0.778. Feature 3 worked the most. The performance of the model decreased with Feature 9 and Feature 10.

Table 14.11 indicates that the CRF model obtains optimal performance after adding Feature 6, on which W-F1 achieved 0.075. Feature 3 worked the most. The performance of the model decreased with Feature 7, Feature 8, Feature 9, and Feature 10.

RNN Model

We generated word vectors using Word2Vector (Mikolov et al. 2013; https://code.google.com/archive/p/word2vec/); after word segmentation, we created a fully connected layer containing a hidden layer with 128 nodes and trained the RNN model using TensorFlow (https://www.tensorflow.org). The learning rate was set to 0.001, the number of iterations was set to 100,000, and the batch value was set to 100. Table 14.12 shows the performance of the RNN model.

The results indicate that the RNN model was effective on this task, and its performance was better than that of the CRF model with a few features but worse than that of the optimal CRF model. These results suggest that increasing the CRF model's features facilitates mining more information from texts and that the current RNN model is relatively naive in nature.

14.6 Conclusions

The scarcity of data is a big challenge in understanding Chinese dialogue acts and developing dialogue system. To help computers understand Chinese dialogue better, we created a dialogue corpus with group chats, which contained more than 5000 multi-turn and multiplayer dialogue messages. We described in detail the tag sets and labeling procedure using different dimensions, the human-annotated dataset, and the statistical analysis of the annotation results. In addition, this study implemented a CRF model and a RNN model as baseline methods to automatically predict dialogue acts, which can provide references for further research. At present, the baseline models' performance was far beyond human performance in all three dimensions, suggesting that there is ample opportunity for further improvements. We intend to make our dataset freely available to encourage exploration and research on Chinese dialogue systems.

Based on the above research, we anticipate further work in the following aspects to expand and improve the existing corpus resources. First, we aim to expand the size of the corpus, since the current dataset represented only a small part of our collection of group chats, and we expect to add more data to cover more topics and crowds.

Table 14.12 Performance of the RNN model

Dimension	EM	W-F1	Ma-F1
D1	0.447	0.311	0.167
D2	0.334	0.167	0.099
D3	0.846	0.776	0.458
D1 + D2 + D3	0.05	0.062	0.021

Second, we will annotate more dialogue messages; in addition to the tags of the three dimensions and the line numbers of the cross-line replies, we intend to mine more information from the corpus. Third, we aim to provide better baseline methods to promote Chinese dialogue act prediction.

Acknowledgment This work was supported by the National Natural Science Foundation of China (61371129, 61773026).

References

Afantenos, Stergos, Nicholas Asher, Farah Benamara, Anaïs Cadilhac, Cédric Dégremont, Pascal Denis, Markus Guhe, Simon Keizer, Alex Lascarides, Oliver Lemon, Philippe Muller, Saumya Paul, Verena Reieser, and Laure Vieu. 2012. Developing a corpus of strategic conversation in the Settlers of Catan. In *SeineDial 2012—The 16th Workshop on the Semantics and Pragmatics of Dialogue*, Paris, France, September 20, 2012. Available at https://hal.inria.fr/hal-00750618/ Accessed 28 July 2017

Allen, J., & Core, M. 1997. DAMSL: Dialogue act markup in several layers. *National Conference on Artificial Intelligence*. Available at https://www.researchgate.net/publication/245831225_DAMSL_Dialogue_act_markup_in_several_layers

Ang, Jeremy, Yang Liu, and Elizabeth Shriberg. 2005. Automatic dialog act segmentation and classification in multiparty meetings. In *Proceedings of IEEE International Conference on Acoustics, Speech, and Signal Processing*, 2005:46–51. Available at https://ieeexplore.ieee.org/stamp/stamp.jsp?arnumber=1415300. Accessed 28 July 2017

Bunt, Harry, Jan Alexandersson, Jae-Woong Choe, Alex Chengyu Fang, Koiti Hasida, Volha Petukhova, Andrei Popescu-Belis, and David R. Traum. 2012. Iso 24617-2: A semantically-based standard for dialogue annotation. *Language Resources and Evaluation Conference*, Istanbul, Turkey, May 23–25, 2012:430–437. Available at https://pdfs.semanticscholar.org/75cf/b9ec8ec951637f376cce771c0531bf05409d.pdf

Carletta, Jean. 1996. Assessing agreement on classification tasks: The kappa statistic. *Computational Linguistics* 22:2249–2254. Available at https://dl.acm.org/citation.cfm?id=230390

Collobert, Ronan, and Jason Weston. 2007. Fast semantic extraction using a novel neural network architecture. In *Annual Meeting—Association for Computational Linguistics* (Vol. 45):560. Available at http://www.anthology.aclweb.org/P/P07/P07-1.pdf#page=598. Accessed 28 July 2017

Collobert, Ronan, and Jason Weston. 2008. A unified architecture for natural language processing: Deep neural networks with multitask learning. In *Proceedings of the 25th International Conference on Machine Learning*, New York, July 5–9, 2008:160–167. Available at https://dl.acm.org/citation.cfm?id=1390177. Accessed 28 July 2017

Collobert, Ronan, Jason Weston, Léon Bottou, Michael Karlen, Koray Kavukcuoglu, and Pavel Kuksa. 2011. Natural language processing (almost) from scratch. *Journal of Machine Learning Research* 12:2493–2537. Available at http://www.jmlr.org/papers/v12/collobert11a.html

Cong, Gao, and Long Wang. 2008. Finding question-answer pairs from online forums. In *Proceedings of the 31st Annual International ACM SIGIR Conference on Research and Development in Information Retrieval*, Singapore, July 20–24, 2008:467–474. Available at https://dl.acm.org/citation.cfm?id=1390415. Accessed 28 July 2017

Dhillon, Rajdip, Sonali Bhagat, Hannah Carvey, and Elizabeth Shriberg. 2004. Meeting recorder project: Dialog act labeling guide. Technical report, DTIC Document. Available at http://www1.icsi.berkeley.edu/ftp/pub/speech/papers/MRDA-manual.pdf. Accessed 28 July 2017

Elman, Jeffrey L. 1990. Finding structure in time. *Cognitive Science* 14(2):179–211. Available at http://onlinelibrary.wiley.com/doi/10.1207/s15516709cog1402_1/full

Elsner, Micha, and Eugene Charniak. 2008. You talking to me? A corpus and algorithm for conversation disentanglement. *Association for Computational Linguistics (ACL).* Available at https://pdfs.semanticscholar.org/99e2/f311b08b17ecc048be387386b487c146ca96.pdf

Henderson, Matthew, Blaise Thomson, and Jason Williams. 2013. Dialog state tracking challenge 2 & 3. *DSTC Handbook* (2013):23–30. Available at http://camdial.org/~mh521/dstc/downloads/handbook.pdf

Henderson, Matthew, Blaise Thomson, and Jason D. Williams. 2014. The second dialog state tracking challenge. In *Proceedings of the SIGDIAL 2014 Conference—Special Interest Group on Discourse and Dialogue*, Philadelphia, Pennsylvania, June 18–20, 2014:263–272. Available at http://www.sigdial.org/workshops/conference15/proceedings/pdf/W14-4337.pdf

Hochreiter, Sepp, and Jürgen Schmidhuber. 1997. Long short-term memory. *Neural Computation* 9(8):1735–1780. Available at http://www.mitpressjournals.org/doi/abs/10.1162/neco.1997.9.8.1735

Hu, Haifeng, Bingquan Liu, Baoxun Wang, Ming Liu, and Xiaolong Wang. 2013. Multimodal DBN for predicting high-quality answers in cQA portals. In *Proceedings of the 51st Annual Meeting of the Association for Computational Linguistics*, Sofia, Bulgaria, August 2013: 843–847. Available at http://www.aclweb.org/old_anthology/P/P13/P13-2.pdf#page=891. Accessed 28 July 2017

Jurafsky, Dan, Elizabeth Shriberg, and Debra Biasca. 1997. Switchboard SWBD-DAMSL shallow-discourse-function annotation coders manual. *Institute of Cognitive Science Technical Report* 97–102. Available at http://ci.nii.ac.jp/naid/10022006083/. Accessed 28 July 2017

Jurafsky, Daniel, Elizabeth Shriberg, and Barbara Fox. 1998. Lexical, prosodic, and syntactic cues for dialog acts.In *Proceedings of the ACL/CoLING-98 Workshop on Discourse Relations and Discourse Markers*, 1998:114–120. Available at http://web5.cs.columbia.edu/~julia/courses/old/cs6998-02/jurafsky98.pdf. Accessed 28 July 2017

Kim, Yoon. 2014. Convolutional neural networks for sentence classification. *arXiv:1408.5882.* Available at https://code.google.com/p/word2vec/. Accessed 28 July 2017

Kim, Su Nam, Lawrence Cavedon, and Timothy Baldwin. 2010. Classifying dialogue acts in one-on-one live chats. In *Proceeding of the 2012 Conference on Empirical Methods in Natural Language Processing*, Cambridge, Massachusetts, October 9–11, 2010:862–871. Available at http://www.mitpressjournals.org/doi/abs/10.1162/089120100561737. Accessed 28 July 2017

Kim, Seokhwan, Luis Fernando D'Haro, Rafael E. Banchs, Jason Williams, and Matthew Henderson. 2015. Dialog state tracking challenge 4. Available at http://www.colips.org/workshop/dstc4/DSTC4_pilot_tasks.pdf

Lafferty, John, Andrew McCallum, and Fernando C. N. Pereira. 2001. Conditional random fields: Probabilistic models for segmenting and labeling sequence data. In *Proceedings of the 18th International Conference on Machine Learning 2001 (ICML 2001)*:282–289. Available at http://repository.upenn.edu/cis_papers/159/. Accessed 28 July 2017

Lee, Ji Young, and Franck Dernoncourt. 2016. Sequential short-text classification with recurrent and convolutional neural networks. *arXiv:1603.03827.* Available at https://arxiv.org/pdf/1603.03827

Lowe, Ryan, Nissan Pow, Iulian Serban, and Joelle Pineau. 2015. The Ubuntu dialogue corpus: A large dataset for research in unstructured multi-turn dialogue systems. In *Proceedings of the SIGDIAL 2015 Conference—Special Interest Group on Discourse and Dialogue (SIGDIAL)*, Prague, Czech Republic, 2015a:285–294. Available at https://arxiv.org/abs/1506.08909. Accessed 28 July 2017

Larry R. Medsker, and Lakhmi C. Jain (ed.). 2001. *Recurrent neural networks. Design and applications.* Boca Raton, Florida: CRC Press. Available at http://citeseerx.ist.psu.edu/viewdoc/download?doi=10.1.1.375.5562&rep=rep1&type=pdf

Mikolov, Tomas, Kai Chen, Greg Corrado, and Jeffrey Dean. 2013. Efficient estimation of word representations in vector space. *arXiv:1301.3781.* Available at https://arxiv.org/pdf/1301.3781

Omuya, Adinoyi, Vinodkumar Prabhakaran, and Owen Rambow. 2013. Improving the quality of minority class identification in dialog act tagging.In *Proceedings of the 2013 Conference of the North American Chapter of the Association for Computational Linguistics: Human Language Technologies*, Atlanta, Georgia, June 2013:802–807. Available at http://www.aclweb.org/anthology/N13-1099. Accessed 28 July 2017

Palangi, Hamid, Li Deng, Yelong Shen, and Jianfeng Gao. 2015. Deep sentence embedding using long short-term memory networks: Analysis and application to information retrieval. *IEEE/ACM Transactions on Audio Speech & Language Processing* 24(4):694–707. Available at https://dl.acm.org/citation.cfm?id=2992457

Serban, Iulian Vlad, Ryan Lowe, Peter Henderson, Laurent Charlin, and Joelle Pineau. 2015. A survey of available corpora for building data-driven dialogue systems. *arXiv:1512.05742*. Available at https://arxiv.org/abs/1512.05742

Shaikh, Samira, Tomek Strzalkowski, Aaron Broadwell, Jennifer Stromer-Galley, Sarah Taylor, and Nick Webb. 2010. MPC: A multi-party chat corpus for modeling social phenomena in discourse. In *The International Conference on Language Resources and Evaluation (LREC)*, Malta, May 19–21, 2010. Available at https://webpages.uncc.edu/sshaikh2/pubs/c3.pdf. Accessed 28 July 2017

Shen, Sheng-syun, and Hung-yi Lee. 2016. Neural attention models for sequence classification: Analysis and application to key term extraction and dialogue act detection. *arXiv:1604.00077*. Available at https://arxiv.org/pdf/1604.00077

Stolcke, Andreas, Klaus Ries, and Noah Coccaro. 2000. Dialogue act modeling for automatic tagging and recognition of conversational speech. *Computational Linguistics* 26(2000): 339–373. Available at http://www.mitpressjournals.org/doi/abs/10.1162/089120100561737

Takechi, Mineki, Takenobu Tokunaga, and Yuji Matsumoto. 2007. Chunking-based question type identification for multi-sentence queries. *SIGIR 2007 Workshop on Focused Retrieval*, Amsterdam, Netherlands, July 27, 2007:41–48. Available at http://www.cs.otago.ac.nz/homepages/andrew/involvement/2007-SIGIR-FR.pdf#page=46. Accessed 28 July 2017

Walker, Marilyn A., Pranav Anand, Jean E. Fox Tree, Rob Abbott, and Joseph King. 2012. A corpus for research on deliberation and debate. *International Conference on Language Resources and Evaluation (LREC)*, Istanbul, Turkey, May 23–25, 2012b:812–817. Available at https://pdfs.semanticscholar.org/6d4b/244deee49cd1bf8d28e2df9a08afb8828fb2.pdf

Wang, Kai, Zhao-Yan Ming, Xia Hu, and Tat-Seng Chun. 2010. Segmentation of multi-sentence questions: Towards effective question retrieval in cQA services. *33th Annual International ACM SIGIR Conference on Research & Development on Information Retrieval*, Geneva, Switzerland, July 18–23, 2010:387–394. Available at https://dl.acm.org/citation.cfm?id=1835515

Williams, Jason, Antoine Raux, Deepak Ramachandran, and Alan Black. 2013. The dialog state tracking challenge. In The *14th Annual Meeting of the Special Interest Group on Discourse and Dialogue—Special Interest Group on Discourse and Dialogue (SIGDIAL)*, Metz, France, August 22–24, 2013. Available at http://www.sigdial.org/node/1818 Accessed 28 July 2017

Chapter 15
Automatic Construction of Parallel Dialogue Corpora with Rich Information

Xiaojun Zhang, Longyue Wang, Andy Way, and Qun Liu

Abstract Due to the lack of ideal resources, few researchers have investigated how to improve the machine translation (MT) of conversational materials by exploiting their internal structure. In this chapter, we will propose a novel strategy to automatically construct a parallel dialogue corpus by bridging two kinds of resources: movie subtitles and movie scripts. First, we collected parallel subtitles and their corresponding monolingual scripts from the Internet. After sentence alignment, we then projected all useful information from the script side to its corresponding subtitle side. Finally, we automatically built a Chinese-English dialogue corpus, which contains bilingual subtitle utterances, speaker names and actions, scene descriptions and boundaries, and script sentences. To demonstrate the usefulness of our data, we used speaker name tags to improve the translation performance. Our experiments showed that our approach achieved 81.79% accuracy in speaker name annotation, and the speaker-based model adaptation obtained around a 0.5 BLEU (bilingual evaluation understudy) point improvement in translation quality. We believe that our resources will benefit various tasks, such as dialogue systems, image/movie descriptions, and MT.

Keywords Dialogue · Machine translation · Parallel corpus · Movie script · Movie subtitle · Discourse information

X. Zhang (✉)
Xi'an Jiaotong-Liverpool University, Suzhou, China
e-mail: xiaojun.zhang01@xjtlu.edu.cn

L. Wang
Tencent AI Lab, Shenzhen, China
e-mail: vinnylywang@tencent.com

A. Way
ADAPT Centre, Dublin City University, Dublin, Ireland
e-mail: andy.way@adaptcentre.ie

Q. Liu
Huawei Noah's Ark Lab, Hong Kong, China
e-mail: qun.liu@huawei.com

C.-R. Huang et al. (eds.), *Chinese Language Resources*, Text, Speech and Language Technology 49, https://doi.org/10.1007/978-3-031-38913-9_15

15.1 Introduction

Dialogue is an essential component of social behavior as it expresses human emotions, moods, attitudes, and personalities. To date, few researchers have investigated how to improve the machine translation (MT) of conversational materials by exploiting their internal structure. This lack of research on dialogue MT is surprising, since dialogue exhibits more cohesiveness than single sentences and at least as much as textual discourse. There are currently no resources that contain both bilingual sentences and discourse-related information.

Although there are a number of papers on corpus construction for various natural language processing (NLP) tasks, dialogue corpora are still scarce for MT. Some work regarding bilingual subtitles as parallel corpora exists, but it lacks rich information between utterances (e.g., a sentence-level corpus) (Itamar and Itai 2008; Lavecchia et al. 2007; Tiedemann 2007a, 2008, 2012; Xiao and Wang 2009; Zhang et al. 2014). Other work has focused on mining the internal structure of dialogue data from movie scripts. However, these monolingual data cannot be used for MT (Banchs 2012; Danescu-Niculescu-Mizil and Lee 2011; Schmitt et al. 2012; Walker et al. 2012). In general, bilingual subtitles are ideal resources from which to extract parallel sentence-level utterances, and movie scripts contain rich discourse information such as dialogue boundaries and speaker tags. However, these two fields have so far developed in relative isolation.

Inspired by these facts, we first proposed a novel strategy to build a dialogue corpus by bridging the information in scripts and subtitles (Wang et al. 2016c). The new corpus is expected to be parallel and contextual, as well as contain dialogue information. First, we extracted parallel sentences from bilingual subtitles and mined dialogue information from monolingual movie scripts. For the subtitle script document alignment, we applied the Internet Movie Database (IMDb) identifier to determine whether a subtitle and a script were from the same movie (Lison and Tiedemann 2016). For sentence alignment, we employed the information retrieval (IR) approach. After these two steps, we projected dialogue information from script utterances to the corresponding parallel subtitle sentences and built the new corpus. To evaluate the mapping performance, we manually annotated the dialogue boundaries and speaker tags of about 200,000 sentence pairs. To validate the effect of the proposed approach, we carried out experiments on our generated corpus. The results showed that the automatic annotation approach achieved around 82% and 98% accuracy in speaker tags and dialogue boundaries annotation, respectively. Furthermore, we explored the integration of speaker information into MT via domain adaptation techniques. The results showed that we improved translation performance by around 0.5 BLEU (bilingual evaluation understudy) points compared to the baseline system. Generally, the contributions of our study include the following:

- We proposed an automatic method to build parallel dialogue corpora with useful information.
- By exploring dialogue information with MT, we showed that speaker information is very helpful for dialogue translation.

- We also manually annotated about 200,000 sentences from our dialogue corpus. This gold standard dataset[1] can be further used to search for coherence and consistency clues in discourse structures to implement a dialogue MT system.
- We showed that this corpus improved the performance of dialogue machine translation and will also benefit a number of works, such as movie/image descriptions (Rohrbach et al. 2016) and dialogue systems (Lison and Meena 2016).

The rest of this chapter is organized as follows. In Sect. 15.2, we will describe related work, while Sect. 15.3 will present in detail our approaches to building a dialogue corpus as well as the structure of the generated database. The experimental results for both corpus annotation and translation will be reported in Sect. 15.4. Finally, Sect. 15.5 will present our conclusion and future work.

15.2 Related Work

In the specific case of dialogue MT systems, data acquisition can impose challenges, including data scarcity, translation quality, and scalability. The release of the Penn Discourse Treebank[2] (PDTB) (Prasad et al. 2008) helped bring about a new sense of maturity in discourse analysis, finally providing a high-quality large-scale resource for training discourse parsers for English. Based on the PDTB, some have applied the insights to MT (Meyer and Popescu-Belis 2012). A resource like the PDTB is extremely valuable, and it would be desirable to have a similar resource for dialogue and conversation as well.

There are two directions of work related to dialogue corpus construction. One is parallel corpora construction for dialogue and conversation MT (Itamar and Itai 2008; Lavecchia et al. 2007; Tiedemann 2007a, 2007b, 2008, 2012; Xiao and Wang 2009). Because of the effects of crowdsourcing and fan translation in audiovisual translation (O'Hagan 2012), subtitles can be regarded as parallel corpora. Zhang et al. (2014) leveraged the existence of bilingual subtitles as a source of parallel data for Chinese-English language pairs to improve the MT systems in the movie domain; however, their work only considered sentence-level data instead of extracting more useful information for dialogue. Moreover, Japanese researchers constructed a speech dialogue corpus for a machine interpretation system by collecting speech dialogue corpora for machine interpretation research via recording and transcribing Japanese/English interpreters' consecutive/simultaneous interpreting in the booth (Aizawa et al. 2000; Matsubara et al. 2002; Takezawa and Kikui 2003). The German VERBMOBIL speech-to-speech translation program (Wahlster 2013) also collected and transcribed task-oriented dialogue data. This related work focused on speech-to-

[1] We released our DCU-Huawei Chinese-English Dialogue Corpus 1.0 at http://computing.dcu.ie/~lwang/resource.html.

[2] Available at https://www.seas.upenn.edu/~pdtb. Accessed 23 May 2018

speech translation, including three modules of automatic speech recognition (ASR), MT, and text-to-speech (TTS).

The other direction is mining rich information from other resources such as movie scripts. Danescu-Niculescu-Mizil and Lee (2011) created a conversation corpus containing large metadata-rich collections of fictional conversations extracted from raw movie scripts. Both Banchs (2012) and Carnegie Mellon University (CMU) released dialogue corpora extracted from the Internet Movie Script Database (IMSDb).[3] Based on IMSDb, Walker et al. (2012) annotated 862 film scripts to learn and characterize the character style for an interactive story system, and Schmitt et al. (2012) annotated 347 dialogues to explore a spoken dialogue system. Resources for movie scripts, such as IMSDb, are good enough to generate conversational discourse for dialogue processing. However, monolingual movie scripts are not enough for MT, which requires a large-scale bilingual dialogue corpus to train and tune translation models.

15.3 Building a Parallel Dialogue Corpus

As shown in Fig. 15.1, our method can be described as a pipeline:

1. Given a monolingual movie/episode script, we identified dialogue information such as scene boundaries and speaker tags using clues such as format and story structure tags in the script.
2. For a bilingual subtitle, we aligned each sentence with its translation using clues such as format and time information.
3. We used the IMDb identifier to process the movie alignment between subtitles and scripts.
4. For each aligned subtitle script, we applied IR techniques to sentence alignment, matching utterances in the subtitle with the sentences in the scripts.
5. We projected the annotation, such as speaker names and dialogue boundaries, on the script side to the matched line(s) on the subtitle side.

15.3.1 Script and Subtitle

Figure 15.2 depicts a browser snapshot illustrating an episode script layout of the sitcom Friends. There are three kinds of information in the script: speaker names, scene descriptions, and actions. The speaker element (red ellipses) contains the corresponding character who says the utterance(s). The scene tags (e.g., "SCENE," "SHOT," "CUT INTO:", "CUT TO:", etc.) are regarded as the boundaries of the

[3] Available at http://www.imsdb.com. Accessed 23 May 2018

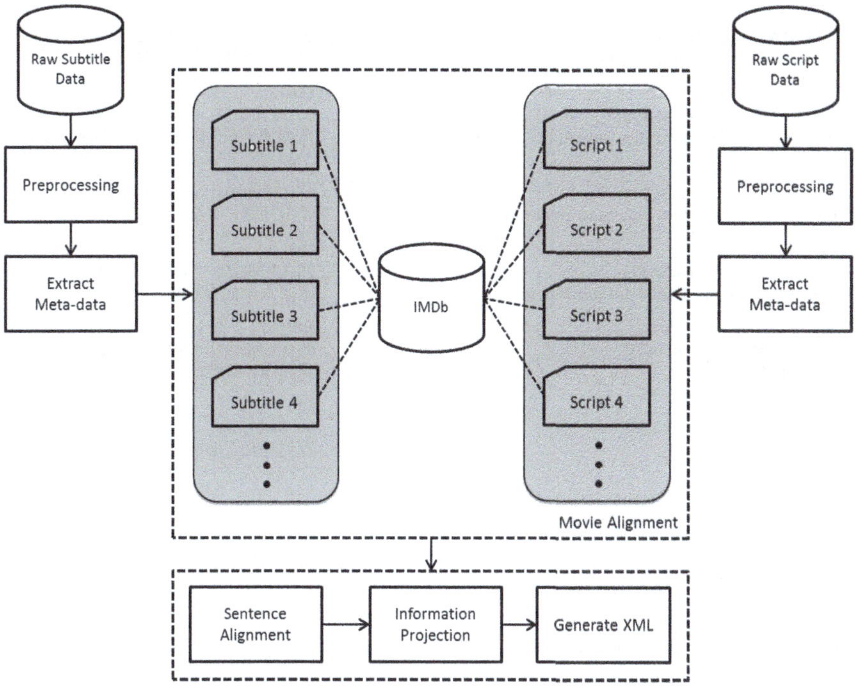

Fig. 15.1 Processing workflow for building the new corpus

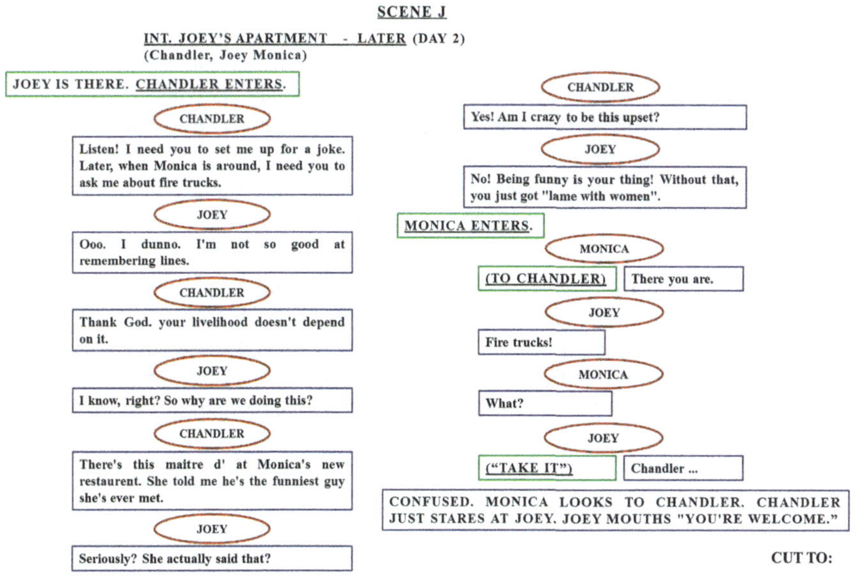

Fig. 15.2 Example of a script from the sitcom Friends in English

195
00:13:43,823 --> 00:13:45,484
I need you to set me up for a joke.

196
00:13:45,658 --> 00:13:48,126
When Monica's around, ask me about fire trucks.

197
00:13:49,195 --> 00:13:53,291
I don't know, Chandler. I'm not so good with remembering lines.

198
00:13:55,701 --> 00:13:58,226
Thank God your livelihood doesn't depend on it.

199
00:13:58,404 --> 00:14:00,235
I know, right?

200
00:14:01,373 --> 00:14:02,738
Why are we doing this?

… …

206
00:14:19,892 --> 00:14:21,154
Fire trucks!

(a)

195
00:13:43,522 --> 00:13:45,149
我需要你帮忙让我讲笑话...

196
00:13:45,357 --> 00:13:47,791
当莫妮卡在的时候，问我消防车怎样

197
00:13:48,894 --> 00:13:52,955
我不知道，钱德，我不是很会记台词的

198
00:13:55,434 --> 00:13:57,925
感谢上帝你不是靠记台词吃饭的

199
00:13:58,137 --> 00:13:59,934
我知道，棒吧?

200
00:14:01,106 --> 00:14:02,437
我们为什么要这样做呢?

… …

206
00:14:19,592 --> 00:14:20,820
消防车!

(b)

Fig. 15.3 Example of bilingual subtitles (SRT) in a script from the sitcom Friends in English and Chinese

dialogues. For instance, the tags "SCENE J" and "CUT TO:" refer to the beginning and end of a dialogue, respectively. The action (green frames) contains all additional information of a narrative nature and explains what is happening in the scene.

Figure 15.3 is the corresponding bilingual subtitle of the script shown in Fig. 15.2. Subtitles are often organized in two formats: Advanced SubStation Alpha (ASS) and SubRip Text (SRT). As most lines were one-to-one aligned on the two language sides, it was easy to process them into a parallel corpus. We also used line ID and timeline information to deal with one-to-many or mismatching cases.

First, we applied a series of preprocessing steps to raw subtitles and scripts, including full/half-width conversion, Unicode conversation, simplified/traditional Chinese conversion, punctuation normalization, English/Chinese tokenization and sentence segmentation, letter casing, word stemming, etc. We then extracted information from the subtitles and scripts according to their formats. Finally, we obtained the processed subtitle and script data in JavaScript Object Notation (JSON) format.

15.3.2 Movie Alignment

The IMDb[4] is an online database of information related to films, television programs, and video games, including cast, production crew, etc. As IMDb assigns a unique identifier to each movie, we aligned subtitles and scripts with the same IMDb identifier (Lison and Meena 2016; Lison and Tiedemann 2016).

First, we extracted metadata from subtitles and scripts. For the scripts, the metadata included the movie title, completion date, and writers' names. For the subtitles, it was much easier to extract the metadata because some resources already provided the IMDb identifier. Finally, we went to the IMDb website to search for the IMDb code associated with a given script and then proceeded with the alignment of the subtitle associated with that code.

15.3.3 Sentence Alignment

Comparing the examples in Figs. 15.2 and 15.3, we found that the script and the subtitle shared the same language (i.e., English). However, the subtitle lines were not always the same as the utterances in a script because the actors may have changed their lines on site, either slightly or to a greater extent. For example, the first utterance in the script is "Later, when Monica's around, I want you to ask me about fire trucks," while the corresponding line in the subtitle is "When Monica's around, ask me about fire trucks." Another phenomenon is that one utterance on the script side may be split into several lines on the subtitle side. This change was made to accommodate the size of the TV screen. It was a big challenge to deal with these changed, missing, or duplicated terms during matching. All of these problems made the task a complex N-to-N matching, where $N \geq 0$.

Therefore, we regarded the matching and projection as an IR task (Wang, Wong and Chao 2012b). The vector space model (VSM) (Salton et al. 1975) is a state-of-the-art IR model in which each document is represented as a vector of identifiers (here, we describe each identifier as a term). The ith utterance D_i in the script is represented as the vector $D_i = [w_{1,i}, w_{2,i}, \ldots w_{k,i}]$, in which k is the size of the term vocabulary. Many similarity functions can be employed to calculate the similarity between two utterance vectors (Cha 2007). We applied cosine distance as shown in Eq. (15.1):

[4] Available at http://www.imdb.com. Accessed 23 May 2018

$$\mathrm{sim}\left(d_i, d_j\right) = \sum_{k=1}^{N} w_{i,k} \cdot w_{j,k} \sqrt{\sum_{k=1}^{N} w_{i,k}} \cdot \sqrt{\sum_{k=1}^{N} w_{j,k}} \tag{15.1}$$

where N is the number of terms in an utterance vector and $w_{i,k}$ and $w_{j,k}$ represent the weight of the *i*th/*j*th term in the utterance D_i/D_j, respectively. Technically, the distance between documents in the VSM is calculated by comparing the deviation of angles between vectors. The Boolean retrieval model sets a term weight to be either 0 or 1, while an alternative solution is calculating the term weights according to the appearance of a term within the document collection. To calculate the term weights according to the appearance of a term within the document collection, we applied term frequency-inverse document frequency (TF-IDF) (Ramos 2003) as one term-weighting model. The weight w of each term t is determined by its own term frequency $tf(t, d)$ in a document d and its inverse document frequency $idf(t, d, D)$ within the search collection. The definition of term weight $w_{t,d}$ is shown in Eqs. (15.2) and (15.3).

$$w_{t,d} = tf(t,d) \cdot idf(t,d,D) \tag{15.2}$$

$$idf(t,d,D) = \log\left(\frac{|D|}{|\{d \in D | t \in d\}|}\right) \tag{15.3}$$

where D is the total number of documents in the document collection.

In practice, we regarded each utterance as a document and built an index for each movie script. Then, we used each subtitle sentence as a query to search for target-related utterances. To deal with inconsistency problems, we employed several strategies:

- For better indexing and searching, we split the sentences/utterances into the smallest units using a sentence splitter.
- Except for punctuation marks, we did not remove any stop words. Furthermore, we lowercased each word.
- Each original query was split into n subqueries. For each subquery, we applied a 1-best search. The search results of the subqueries were combined to vote for the best candidate for the original query.
- Since a query may be similar to several utterances in different lines of a script, the candidate closest to the last matched term was more likely to be correct. Thus, we imposed a dynamic window for subspace searching.

After the scripts and the subtitles were bridged, we projected speaker tags and dialogue boundaries in the scripts to their corresponding lines in the subtitles. Finally, we preserved the results in Extensible Markup Language (XML) format, which is illustrated in Fig. 15.4.

```xml
<dialogue id="4884" n_utterances="12">
    <context id="1" action= "JOEY IS THERE. CHANDLER ENTERS" >
        <utterance id="1" speaker="CHANDLER">
            <EN>I need you to set me up for a joke.</EN> <ZH>我需要你帮忙让我讲笑话...</ZH>
        </utterance>
        <utterance id="2" speaker="CHANDLER">
            <EN>When Monica's around, ask me about fire trucks.</EN> <ZH>当莫妮卡在的时候，问我消防车怎样</ZH>
        </utterance>
        <utterance id="3" speaker="JOEY">
            <EN>I don't know, Chandler. I'm not so good with remembering lines.</EN> <ZH>我不知道，钱德，我不是很会记台词的</ZH>
        </utterance>
        <utterance id="4" speaker="CHANDLER">
            <EN>Thank God your livelihood doesn't depend on it.</EN> <ZH>感谢上帝你不是靠记台词吃饭的</ZH>
        </utterance>
        <utterance id="5" speaker="JOEY">
            <EN>I know, right?</EN> <ZH>我知道，棒吧?</ZH>
        </utterance>
        <utterance id="5" speaker=" JOEY ">
            <EN>Why are we doing this?</EN> <ZH>我们为什么要这样做呢?</ZH>
        </utterance>
            … …
    </context>
    <context id="2" action= "MONICA ENTERS. TO CHANDLER" >
        … …
        <utterance id="12" speaker="JOEY">
            <EN>Fire trucks!</EN> <ZH>消防车!</ZH>
        </utterance>
    </context>
        … …
    <context id="3" action= "CONFUSED. MONICA LOOKS TO CHANDLER… …" >NULL</context>
</dialogue>
```

Fig. 15.4 A sample of generated dialogue in an episode script in XML format

15.4 Experiments and Results

In this section, we will describe how we built the parallel dialogue corpus and then conducted MT experiments using the data collected.

15.4.1 Parallel Dialogue Corpus Construction

We applied our methods to the ten-season sitcom Friends and obtained our new corpus in the format shown in Fig. 15.4. For data processing, we employed a sentence splitter and the English tokenizer in the Moses toolkit as well as our in-house Chinese segmenter (Wang et al. 2012a, 2012c). Furthermore, we employed Apache Lucene[5] for indexing and search tasks. Our new corpus was built based on two existing corpora: OpenSubtitles2016[6] (a subtitle corpus) and IMSDb[7] (a script corpus).

Table 15.1 presents the main statistics of the resulting bilingual dialogue corpus. We obtained 5428 bilingual dialogues with annotated speaker and dialogue boundary information. To verify the validity of our methods (described in Sect. 15.3), we conducted an evaluation of the matching accuracy of speaker tags and dialogue

[5] Available at https://lucene.apache.org. Accessed 23 May 2018

[6] Available at http://opus.lingfil.uu.se/OpenSubtitles2016.php. Accessed 23 May 2018

[7] Internet Movie Script Database, available at http://www.imsdb.com. Accessed 23 May 2018

Table 15.1 Statistics of the generated parallel dialogue corpus

Item	Size
Total number of scripts processed	236
Total number of dialogues	5428
Total number of speakers	42
Total number of utterances	109,268
Average amount of dialogues per script	23
Average amount of speakers per dialogue	3.5
Average amount of utterances per dialogue	20

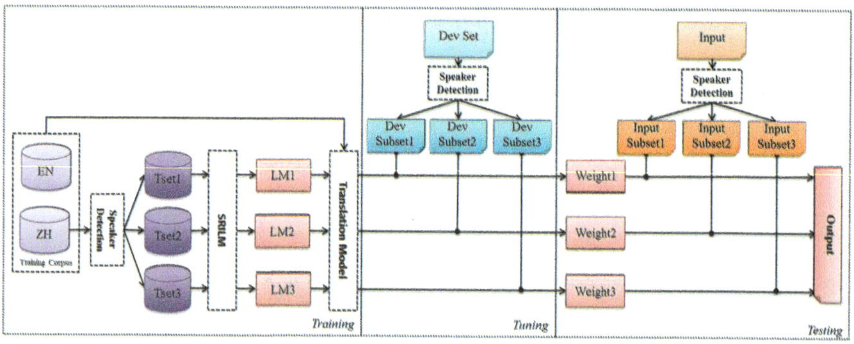

Fig. 15.5 The architecture of the personalized MT system

boundaries in the generated corpus. To generate gold standard references, we also manually annotated the dialogue information based on the generated parallel dialogue corpus. The agreements between automatic labels and manual labels were 81.79% for speaker tags and 98.64% for dialogue boundaries, respectively. This indicated that the proposed automatic annotation strategy through mapping was reasonably trustworthy.

15.4.2 *Improved Translation with Speaker Information*

As shown in Fig. 15.5, we conducted a personalized MT experiment to explore the effects of speaker tags on dialogue MT. We first built a baseline MT engine using Moses (Koehn et al. 2007) for our generated parallel corpus (described in Table 15.1). We trained a 5-gram language model (LM) using the SRI Language Toolkit (Stolcke 2002) on the target side of the parallel corpus. In addition, we used GIZA++ (Och and Ney 2003) for word alignment and minimum error rate training (Och 2003) to optimize feature weights. Based on the hypothesis that different types of speakers have specific speaking styles, we employed a language model adaptation method to boost the MT system (Wang et al. 2014). Instead of building an LM based on all the data, we split the data into two separate parts based on the speakers' sex and then built two separate LMs. As Moses supports multiple LM integrations, we

Table 15.2 Translation results of speaker-based language model adaption

Systems	Language	Development set	Test set
ZH-EN	Baseline	20.32	16.33
	Speaker *LM*	21.05	16.83 (+0.50)
EN-ZH	Baseline	16.78	14.11
	Speaker *LM*	17.23	14.54 (+0.43)

directly fed into Moses the two LMs. The translation results are listed in Table 15.2. For Chinese-to-English (i.e., "ZH-EN"), the baseline system achieved BLEU scores of 20.32 and 16.33 for development and test data, respectively, while for English-to-Chinese (i.e., "EN-ZH"), the BLEU scores were 16.78 and 14.11, respectively. The BLEU scores were relatively low because we had only one reference, the training corpus was small, and dialogue MT is a challenging task. Using LM adaptation, we improved the performance of the test data by +0.50 and +0.43 BLEU points in the Chinese-to-English and English-to-Chinese tasks, respectively.

15.5 Conclusion and Future Work

We proposed a novel approach to building a parallel dialogue discourse corpus from monolingual scripts and their corresponding bilingual subtitles. We identified the dialogue boundaries according to the scene tags in the script to segment the monolingual dialogue and then mapped the matched monolingual dialogues to the source part of the bilingual subtitles with the speaker and utterance elements to obtain the bilingual discourse dialogues. Finally, we aligned the bilingual dialogue subtitle lines to produce suitable MT training materials.

We expanded the current dialogue generation resources from movie scripts to movie/episode scripts and specified the current parallel corpus construction to the bilingual dialogue corpus built based on bilingual subtitles. We piloted this approach on the ten-season sitcom Friends and automatically generated 5428 bilingual parallel dialogue discourses. This was a quick way to generate a bilingual dialogue corpus.

To validate the effect of the proposed approach, we annotated the speaker tags and dialogue boundaries manually in the fourth season of Friends and compared the manual results with our automatic findings. Our experimental results showed that the automatic annotation approach achieved around 81.79% and 98.64% for dialogue boundaries and speaker tags, respectively. Furthermore, we explored the integration of speaker tags into MT using domain adaptation techniques. The experiments showed that we improved translation performance compared with the baseline system.

As far as future work is concerned, we intend to explore dialogue corpus construction for low-resource language pairs such as Chinese-Portuguese (Liu et al. 2018) and investigate other discourse-aware MT models, such as dropped-pronoun-aware statistical MT (SMT) (Wang et al. 2016a, 2016b, 2017b), cross-sentence neural MT (NMT) (Wang et al. 2017a), and reconstructor-augmented NMT (Wang et al. 2018).

Acknowledgments This work was most done while the authors were working in ADAPT Centre, Dublin City University. This work is supported by the Science Foundation Ireland (SFI) ADAPT project (grant no. 13/RC/2106) and partly supported by the XJTLU KSF Project (grant no. KSF-E-24) and the Open Projects Program of GDFS Translation Studies Centre (grant no. TSC201501).

References

Aizawa, Yasuyuki, Shigeki Matsubara, Nobuo Kawaguchi, Katsuhiko Toyama, and Yasuyoshi Inagaki. 2000. Spoken language corpus for machine interpretation research. In *Proceedings of the 6th International Conference on Spoken Language Processing* (Vol. 3), 398–401. Beijing, China.

Banchs, Rafael E. 2012. Movie-dic: A movie dialogue corpus for research and development. In *Proceedings of the 50th Annual Meeting of the Association for Computational Linguistics*: Short Papers (Vol. 2), 203–207. Jeju, Republic of Korea.

Cha, Sung-Hyuk. 2007. Comprehensive survey on distance/similarity measures between probability density functions. *International Journal of Mathematical Models and Methods in Applied Sciences* 1:300–307.

Danescu-Niculescu-Mizil, Cristian, and Lillian Lee. 2011. Chameleons in imagined conversations: A new approach to understanding coordination of linguistic style in dialogs. In *Proceedings of the 2nd Workshop on Cognitive Modeling and Computational Linguistics, 76–87.* Portland, Oregon.

Itamar, Einav, and Alon Itai. 2008. Using movie subtitles for creating a large-scale bilingual corpora. In *Proceedings of the 6th International Conference on Language Resources and Evaluation*, 269–272. Marrakech, Morocco.

Koehn, Philipp, Hieu Hoang, Alexandra Birch, Chris Callison-Burch, Marcello Federico, Nicola Bertoldi, Brooke Cowan, Wade Shen, Christine Moran, Richard Zens, Chris Dyer, Ondrej Bojar, Alexandra Constantin, and Evan Herbst. 2007. Moses: Open source toolkit for statistical machine translation. In *Proceedings of the 45th Annual Meeting of the Association for Computational Linguistics Companion Volume Proceedings of the Demo and Poster Sessions*, 177–180. Prague, Czech Republic.

Lavecchia, Caroline, Kamel Smaïli, and David Langlois. 2007. Building parallel corpora from movies. In *Proceedings of the 4th International Workshop on Natural Language Processing and Cognitive Science*, 201–210. Funchal, Madeira, Portugal.

Lison, Pierre, and Raveesh Meena. 2016. Automatic turn segmentation for movie & TV subtitles. Paper presented at *the Spoken Language Technology Workshop (SLT)*, 245–252. San Diego, California.

Lison, Pierre, and Jörg Tiedemann. 2016. Opensubtitles2016: Extracting large parallel corpora from movie and TV subtitles. In *Proceedings of the 10th Language Resources and Evaluation Conference*. Portorož, Slovenia.

Liu, Siyou, Longyue Wang, and Chao-Hong Liu. 2018. Chinese-Portuguese machine translation: A study on building parallel corpora from comparable texts. arXiv preprint: arXiv:1804.01768.

Matsubara, Shigeki, Akira Takagi, Nobuo Kawaguchi, and Yasuyoshi Inagaki. 2002. Bilingual spoken monologue corpus for simultaneous machine interpretation research. In *Proceedings of the Third International Conference on Language Resources and Evaluation*, 153–159. Las Palmas, Canary Islands, Spain.

Meyer, Thomas, and Andrei Popescu-Belis, A. 2012. Using sense-labeled discourse connectives for statistical machine translation. In *Proceedings of the Joint Workshop on Exploiting Synergies between Information Retrieval and Machine Translation and Hybrid Approaches to Machine Translation*, 129–138. Avignon, France.

O'Hagan, Minako. 2012. From fan translation to crowdsourcing: Consequences of web 2.0 user empowerment in audiovisual translation. *Approaches to Translation Studies* 36:25–41.

Och, Franz Josef. 2003. Minimum error rate training in statistical machine translation. *In Proceedings of the 41st Annual Meeting on Association for Computational Linguistics* (Vol 1), 160–167. Sapporo, Japan.

Och, Franz Josef, and Hermann Ney. 2003. A systematic comparison of various statistical alignment models. *Computational Linguistics* 29(1):19–51.

Prasad, Rashmi, Nikhil Dinesh, Alan Lee, Eleni Miltsakaki, Livio Robaldo, Aravind Joshi, and Bonnie Webber. 2008. The Penn discourse treebank 2.0. In *Proceedings of the 6th International Conference on Language Resources and Evaluation*. Marrakech, Morocco.

Ramos, Juan. 2003. Using tf-idf to determine word relevance in document queries. In *Proceedings of the 1st Instructional Conference on Machine Learning*. Piscataway, New Jersey.

Rohrbach, Anna, Atousa Torabi, Marcus Rohrbach, Niket Tandon, Christopher Pal, Hugo Larochelle, Aaron Courville, and Bernt Schiele. 2016. Movie description. In arXiv:1605.03705v1.

Salton, Gerard, Alec Wong, and Chung-shu Yang. 1975. A vector space model for automatic indexing. *Communications of the ACM* 18:613–620.

Schmitt, Alexander, Stefan Ultes, and Wolfgang Minker. 2012. A parameterized and annotated spoken dialog corpus of the cmu let's go bus information system. In *Proceedings of the 8th International Conference on Language Resources and Evaluation*, 3369–3373. Istanbul, Turkey.

Stolcke, Andreas. 2002. Srilm—An extensible language modeling toolkit. In *Proceedings of the 7th International Conference on Spoken Language Processing*, 901–904. Denver, Colorado.

Takezawa, Toshiyuki, and Gen-ichiro Kikui. 2003. Collecting machine-translation-aided bilingual dialogues for corpus-based speech translation. In *Proceedings of the 8th European Conference on Speech Communication and Technology*, 2757–2760. Geneva, Switzerland.

Tiedemann, Jörg. 2007a. Building a multilingual parallel subtitle corpus. In *Proceedings of the 17th Conference on Computational Linguistics in the Netherlands*, 1–14. Leuven, Netherlands.

Tiedemann, Jörg. 2007b. Improved sentence alignment for movie subtitles. In *Proceedings of the 3rd Conference on Recent Advances in Natural Language Processing* (Vol. 7), 582–588. Borovets, Bulgaria.

Tiedemann, Jörg 2008. Synchronizing translated movie subtitles. In *Proceedings of the 6th International Conference on Language Resources and Evaluation*, 1902–1906. Marrakech, Morocco.

Tiedemann, Jörg. 2012. Parallel data, tools and interfaces in opus. In *Proceedings of the 8th International Conference on Language Resources and Evaluation*, 2214–2218. Istanbul, Turkey.

Wahlster, Wolfgang (ed.). 2013. Verbmobil: Foundations of speech-to-speech translation. Springer Science & Business Media.

Walker, Marilyn A., Grace I. Lin, and Jennifer E. Sawyer. 2012. An annotated corpus of film dialogue for learning and characterizing character style. In *Proceedings of the 8th International Conference on Language Resources and Evaluation*, 1373–1378. Istanbul, Turkey.

Wang, Longyue, Shuo Li, Derek F. Wong, and Lidia S. Chao. 2012a. A joint Chinese named entity recognition and disambiguation system. In *Proceedings of the Second CIPS-SIGHAN Joint Conference on Chinese Language Processing*, 146–151. Tianjin, China.

Wang, Long-Yue, Derek F. Wong, and Lidia S. Chao. 2012b. An improvement in cross-language document retrieval based on statistical models. In *Proceedings of the 24th Conference on Computational Linguistics and Speech Processing*, 144–155. Chung-Li, Taiwan.

Wang, Longyue, Derek F. Wong, Lidia S. Chao, and Junwen Xing. 2012c. Crfs-based Chinese word segmentation for micro-blog with small-scale data. In *Proceedings of The Second CIPS-SIGHAN Joint Conference on Chinese Language Processing*, 51–57. Tianjin, China.

Wang, Longyue, Yi Lu, Derek F. Wong, Lidia S. Chao, Yiming Wang, and Francisco Oliveira. 2014. Combining domain adaptation approaches for medical text translation. In *Proceedings of the 9th Workshop on Statistical Machine Translation*, 254–259. Baltimore, Maryland.
Wang, Longyue, Zhaopeng Tu, Xiaojun Zhang, Hang Li, Andy Way, and Qun Liu. 2016a. A novel approach for dropped pronoun translation. In *Proceedings of the 2016 Conference of the North American Chapter of the Association for Computational Linguistics: Human Language Technologies*, 983–993. San Diego, California.
Wang, Longyue, Xiaojun Zhang, Zhaopeng Tu, Hang Li, and Qun Liu. 2016b. Dropped pronoun generation for dialogue machine translation. In *Proceedings of the 41st IEEE International Conference on Acoustics, Speech and Signal Processing*, 6110–6114. Shanghai, China.
Wang, Longyue, Xiaojun Zhang, Zhaopeng Tu, Andy Way, and Qun Liu. 2016c. Automatic construction of discourse corpus for dialogue translation. In *Proceedings of the 10th Language Resources and Evaluation Conference*. Portorož, Slovenia.
Wang, Longyue, Zhaopeng Tu, Andy Way, and Qun Liu. 2017a. Exploiting cross-sentence context for neural machine translation. In *Proceedings of the 2017 Conference on Empirical Methods in Natural Language Processing*, 2816–2821. Copenhagen, Denmark.
Wang, Longyue, Zhaopeng Tu, Xiaojun Zhang, Siyou Liu, Hang Li, Andy Way, and Qun Liu. 2017b. A novel and robust approach for pro-drop language translation. *Machine Translation* 1–23.
Wang, Longyue, Zhaopeng Tu, Shuming Shi, Tong Zhang, Yvette Graham, and Qun Liu. 2018. Translating pro-drop languages with reconstruction models. In *Proceedings of the Thirty-Second AAAI Conference on Artificial Intelligence. New Orleans*, Louisiana.
Xiao, Han, and Xiaojie Wang. 2009. Constructing parallel corpus from movie subtitles. In *Proceedings of the 22nd International Conference on Computer Processing of Oriental Languages. Language Technology for the Knowledge-based Economy*, 329–336. Hong Kong.
Zhang, Shikun, Wang Ling, and Chris Dyer. 2014. Dual subtitles as parallel corpora. In *Proceedings of the Nineth International Conference on Language Resources and Evaluation*, 1869–1874. Reykjavik, Iceland.

Chapter 16
A Chinese Event-Based Emotion Corpus: Emotion Cause Detection

Sophia Yat Mei Lee, Shoushan Li, and Chu-Ren Huang

Abstract This chapter will introduce a Chinese event-based emotion corpus and explore an important task in emotion analysis—emotion cause detection. The corpus design and the data collection and annotation procedures will be described, as will the emotion cause detection task, which aims to detect the triggering cause of an emotion automatically. We regard the detection task as a sequence labeling issue and determined whether a clause contained an emotion cause, accordingly. In concrete terms, the conditional random field (CRF) model was adopted with various features taken into consideration for the detection task, such as lexical features, part-of-speech features, contextual features, and linguistic features. The experiments demonstrated that all these features were effective in recognizing emotion causes, in particular, the contextual features. In addition, the sequence labeling model yielded better performance than the multi-label classification model when similar features were employed.

Keywords Emotion corpus · Emotion cause event · Sequence labeling model · CRF · Chinese

16.1 Introduction

Emotion is basic to human experience and communication and at the same time very abstract and complex in nature. It is commonly defined as the bodily reaction to actual external stimuli, which in turn leads to potential consequences. For example, the emotion of fear can be evoked by a threatening situation, which in turn motivates potential actions to remove fear, as shown in (16.1) below:

S. Y. M. Lee (✉) · C.-R. Huang
Department of Chinese and Bilingual Studies, The Hong Kong Polytechnic University, Hong Kong, China
e-mail: ym.lee@polyu.edu.hk; churen.huang@polyu.edu.hk

S. Li
Natural Language Processing Lab, Soochow University, Suzhou, China
e-mail: lishoushan@suda.edu.cn

C.-R. Huang et al. (eds.), *Chinese Language Resources*, Text, Speech and Language Technology 49, https://doi.org/10.1007/978-3-031-38913-9_16

(16.1) 他看了這種現象, 感到非常害怕, 於是也趕快逃跑了。

ta__kan__le__zhe__zhong__xianxiang, gandao__feichang__haipa,

he__see__LE__this__CL__phenomenon, feel__very__frightened

yushi__ye__ gankuai__taopao__ le.

then__also__quickly__run away__LE.

[When] he saw such a thing, he was frightened. Then [he] ran away very quickly.

Example (16.1) shows the context of the emotion of fear (害怕 *hàipà* "fear"), in which the event 他看了這種現象 *tā kàn le zhè zhǒng xiànxiàng* "he saw such a thing" triggered the emotion, which in turn led to another event 趕快逃跑 *gǎnkuài táopǎo* "[he] ran away very quickly." Although the connection of the various events is logically assumed to be true, the linguistic analysis of emotion-event interaction is underexplored. From a linguistic and psychological perspective, most emotion theories treat recognition of a triggering cause event as an integral part of emotional processing (Descartes 1649; James 1884; Wierzbicka 1999). Therefore, knowing the cause of an emotion is a stepping stone to understanding how emotions are elicited and what mechanisms are involved in the linguistic expression of emotions. However, most previous research has focused on emotion detection and classification in an attempt to detect emotions (e.g., HAPPINESS, SADNESS, SURPRISE, etc.) in text automatically (Alm et al. 2005; Tokuhisa et al. 2008), yet little work has been done to examine emotion cause events.

Lee and colleagues (Chen et al. 2010; Lee 2010; Lee et al. 2009, 2010, 2013), who pioneered early research in this field, conducted a series of studies on emotion cause detection based on the assumption that the cause event is one of the crucial clues in classifying emotion. Lee et al. (2010, 2013) proposed a rule-based approach to emotion cause detection, while Chen et al. (2010) proposed a multi-label classification approach, and both approaches achieved satisfactory results. There are, however, some limitations regarding these approaches. In particular, the rule-based approach requires specialists of the discipline to set up a large number of rules, which is rather labor intensive and time-consuming. It is relatively easier to construct a multi-label classification model; moreover, this model has achieved an even better performance than the rule-based approach for emotion cause detection. However, the multi-label classification model treats each clause within the text separately, and it does not capture the correlations among clauses in the text. In fact, the correlations among clauses play a central role in emotion cause detection. Consider (16.2) below:

(16.2) 林依晨在「十八歲的約定」飾演癡情種子, 因為[*01e] 感情失意[*02e], 所以有不少<emo id=0>傷心</emo>流淚的鏡頭。

Linyichen__zai__Shibasuideyueding__shiyan__chiqing__zhongzi,

Ariel Lin__in__True Love__play__lovestruck__girl,

yinwei[*01e]__ganqing__shiyi[*02e], suoyi__you__bushao__

because[*01e]__love__loss[*02e], so__have__many__

<emo id=0>shangxin</emo>__liulei__de__jingtou.

<emo id=0>heartbreak</emo>__tear__DE__scene.

(continued)

	In the drama "True Love," Ariel Lin played a lovestruck girl, who, due to loss of love,
	had many scenes portraying her in a state of heartbreak and tears.

In (16.2), 因為 *yīnwèi* "because" is a function word that marks 感情失意 *gǎnqíng shīyì* "loss of love" as the cause of the emotion 傷心 *shāngxīn* "sad." After identifying a sentence that contains an emotion, there is little likelihood of the cause occurring in the preceding or the subsequent sentences. Treating emotion cause detection as a sequence labeling issue, our study proposed a detection model using the conditional random field (CRF) model, which incorporates morphological, distance, grammatical, and contextual features.

This chapter will first introduce a Chinese event-based emotion corpus, with a focus on the corpus design and the data collection and annotation procedures. It will also account for the linguistic interactions between triggering events (i.e., cause events) and caused emotions, as well as the correlations between the emotions and events induced (i.e., post-events) in texts. In addition, we will present the development of our automatic emotion cause detection system, which we used to mine crucial deep-level information (i.e., emotion cause). Taking (16.3) below as an example, our objective was to identify 你遺棄我 *nǐ yíqì wǒ* "you abandoned me" as the cause event of the emotion 傷心欲絕 *shāngxīnyùjué* "sad." (Note: Contents in between [*01e] and [*02e] represent the cause event, and contents encased by <emo id = 0> and </emo> represent the emotion keyword). The recognition of cause events has laid the groundwork for future research on automatic classification and analysis of emotion-related events, which can be further applied to other tasks such as emergency monitoring and opinion summarization.

(16.3)	[*01e] 你遺棄我 [*02e]後, 我<emo id=0>傷心欲絕</emo> 。
	[*01e]ni__yiqi__wo[*02e]__hou, wo__<emo id=0>shangxinyujue</emo>.
	[*01e]you__abandon__me[*02e]__after, I__<emo id=0>heartbreak</emo>.
	After you abandoned me, I am heartbroken.

The organization of this chapter is as follows. Section 16.2 will present contemporary studies related to emotion analysis, while Sect. 16.3 will introduce the construction of the Chinese emotion corpus, including the data collection, annotation scheme, and corpus analysis. In Sect. 16.4, the emotion cause detection task and the emotion cause corpus will be described. Section 16.5 will propose the sequence labeling approach and related features. In Sect. 16.6, the performance of the proposed model compared with previous approaches will be discussed. Finally, Sect. 16.7 will highlight the contributions of this work and possible future work.

16.2 Related Work

The earliest research on emotion focused on the representation and processing of emotion in facial expressions and body language (Andrew 1963; Ekman and Friesen 1978). More recently, there has been mounting research on the neurobiological basis of emotion (Craig 2009; Hervé et al. 2012; Messina et al. 2016; Olson et al. 2007) and how emotion is linked with other aspects of human cognition (Bridge et al. 2010; Power and Dalgleish 2015; Smith and Kirby 2001; Smith and Lazarus 1993). Previous work has also reported on the close link between types of emotions and various prosodic features. Kehrein (2002) showed that the type of emotion resulted in different intensity and rate of speech. For example, ANGER is closely related to higher intensity and faster speech than FRUSTRATION. Abelin and Allwood (2000), on the other hand, suggested that speech duration varies with emotion types, for example, FEAR and SADNESS are more connected to speeches with shorter duration compared to HAPPINESS and SURPRISE.

This line of research has been extended to cover emotion in verbal language as well. It has been shown that when humans encounter emotional language, the processing of language and the processing of emotion are highly intertwined (Hervé et al. 2012). The language processing part of the brain is responsible for extracting linguistic cues for emotion, while the emotion processing part makes inferences about emotional content based on linguistic meanings. Emotion has also been well studied in natural language processing (Dellaert et al. 1996; Ortony et al. 1990; Picard 1995). Recent research has begun to place more emphasis on automatic emotion detection and classification from textual input (Ahmad 2008; Li et al. 2013; Mihalcea and Liu 2006; Yuan and Purver 2015; Zhou et al. 2016). Most of the previous studies have focused on classifying descriptive emotions given a known emotion context, such as a sentence or a document, using either rule-based (Chaumartin 2007) or statistical learning (Mihalcea and Liu 2006) approaches.

Some works have begun to explore both emotion detection and classification. Tokuhisa et al. (2008) created a Japanese emotion cause corpus using an unsupervised approach, whereas Chen et al. (2009) developed a Chinese emotion corpus and an English emotion corpus using a semi-unsupervised approach. Li and Xu (2014) proposed and implemented a new method of emotion classification in micro-blog posts that attempted to import knowledge and theories from other disciplines, such as sociology, to infer and extract emotion causes. Rao et al. (2014) proposed two sentiment topic models, and both models were applied to classify social emotions and generate both explicit and implicit social emotion lexicons.

Other studies have explored different approaches to emotion cause detection. Gao et al. (2015) proposed a rule-based approach to emotion cause detection in Chinese micro-blogs to extract the corresponding cause components in fine-grained emotions, and an emotion lexicon was constructed automatically and manually from the corpus. Russo et al. (2011) proposed a method for emotion cause detection based on the interaction between linguistic patterns and common-sense knowledge. Ghazi

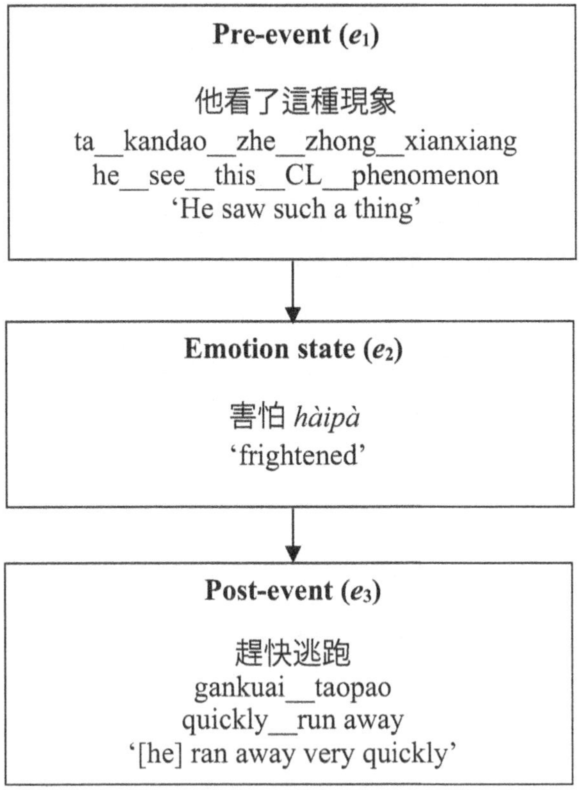

Fig. 16.1 Emotion-event interaction

et al. (2015) framed emotion cause detection using CRFs. Finally, Gui et al. (2016) designed a convolution kernel-based learning method to identify emotion cause events, while Gui et al. (2017) proposed a question answering (QA) approach to extract emotion cause.

16.3 An Event-Based Emotion Corpus in Chinese

16.3.1 Emotion-Associated Events and Corpus Data

Based on the assumption that emotion is a sub-type of event that interacts with other associating events, namely, pre-events and post-events (Lee 2010), we constructed an event-based emotion corpus. The interaction between the emotion and the two types of events presented in (16.1) is shown in Fig. 16.1.

A pre-event (e_1) refers to the event that is triggered by or highly linked with the presence of the corresponding emotion (e_2). A post-event (e_3) is an event triggered by the emotion (e_2), which shows a clear cause-effect relation. Both types of events are usually linguistically represented in the form of verbs, as in (16.4); nominals, as in (16.5); and nominalizations, as in (16.6) below, respectively:

(16.4)	他非常**傷心**, 於是哭了一場 。 (e_3: verb)
	ta__feichang__shangxin, yushi__ku__le__yi__chang.
	he__very__heartbreak, so__cry__LE__one__CL.
	He was terribly heartbroken, and so cried many tears.
(16.5)	對於未來, 老實說我很**害怕** 。 (e_1: nominal)
	duiyu__weilai, laoshishuo___wo__hen__haipa.
	regarding__future, honestly__I__quite__scared.
	Regarding the future, I'm honestly quite scared.
(16.6)	剛剛你那副爬不起來的样子, 是有點叫我**害怕** 。 (e_1: nominalization)
	ganggang__ni__na__fu__pa__bu__qilai__de__yangzi,
	just now__you__that__CL__get__NEG__up__de__look,
	shi__youdian__jiao__wo__haipa.
	is__a little bit__let__I__frightened.
	That you couldn't get up frightened me.

Although we argue that emotion is treated as a pivot event that links pre-events and post-events as described in Fig. 16.1, it is not assumed that the two events always exist in every instance of emotion. All the following combinations of the various events in (16.7) below were found in the corpus:

(16.7a)	Pre-event(s) + emotion + post-event(s)
(16.7b)	Pre-event(s) + emotion
(16.7d)	Emotion + post-event(s)
(16.7d)	Emotion (without any associating event)

The corpus data were extracted from the Sinica Corpus, a tagged balanced corpus of Mandarin Chinese containing ten million words, using a pattern-based method. Based on the list of 91 Chinese primary emotion keywords identified in Chen et al. (2009), we extracted 8973 instances of sentences from the Sinica Corpus by keyword matching. Each instance contained a focus sentence with an emotion keyword "<FocusSentence>," plus the sentence before "<PrefixSentence>" and after "<SuffixSentence>" it. A sample instance is given in Fig. 16.2. The emotion is indicated as <emo id = 0> 生氣 *shēngqì* "anger"</emo>, whereas the pre-event is marked with "[[...]]" and the post-event "{{...}}."

16.3.2 Event Annotation

An annotation tool was designed to facilitate the annotation process, which allowed better consistency. Four annotators were recruited for the annotation task. Two annotators annotated the pre-events and post-events of the same set of emotion

snc_11417 Y 0/生氣/Anger
<PrefixSentence> 過些時候，[[魯班的妻子懷孕了]]，肚子一天比一天大。
</PrefixSentence>

<FocusSentence>魯班的父親很<emo id=0>生氣</emo>，就{{她}}說：我兒子在涼州做事，離家那麼遠，很久没有回來過，你竟然懷孕了，真是可耻 ！
</FocusSentence>

<SuffixSentence>魯班的妻子受了冤枉，很不甘心，就把魯班每晚乘木⊠回来的情形告訴他父親。</SuffixSentence>

snc_11417 Y 0/生氣/Anger
<PrefixSentence>After some time, [[Luban’s wife became with child]]. Her pregnant belly grew with each day. </PrefixSentence>
<FocusSentence>Luban’s father was <emo id=0>furious</emo>, {{scolding her}}: “My son works in faraway Liangzhou and has not come back for so long. Yet you have conceived. What a shameful act!” </FocusSentence>
<SuffixSentence>Luban’s wife could not bear the wrongful accusation, and told her father-in-law of how Luban had returned home each night by riding a wooden kite to be with her. </SuffixSentence>

Fig. 16.2 An example of an event-annotated instance

instances. Figure 16.3 shows an example instance annotated with the corresponding pre-event and post-event using our annotation tool. For each identified event, annotators marked whether it was a pre-event or a post-event, together with other information, including event type and event subject. Event type refers to a verbal or nominal event. A verbal event is a linguistic expression denoting an event that involves a verb or nominalization (indicated as “event” in the annotation tool), whereas a nominal event is simply a noun (indicated as “nominal” in the annotation tool). Event subject suggests whether the subject of the pre-event or post-event is the experiencer of the emotion.

For the event annotating unit, we marked the shortest meaningful pre-events and post-events that were closest to the emotion keywords. Some guidelines for marking the events are given in the following.

Determining the Event Boundaries

I. Only the immediate pre-events or post-events were annotated. For example, in (16.8) below, 身體僵硬 *shēntǐ jiāngyìng* “body stiff” is considered the direct reaction to fear (i.e., the post-event). The follow-up action, such as 痛哭求饒 *tòngkū qiú ráo* “broke down in tears and begged for mercy,” was marked as the post-event.

(16.8)	一動也不動的站著, 因**恐懼**而<u>身體僵硬</u>。 最後甚至痛哭求饒 。
	yi__dong__ye__bu__dong__de__zhan__zhe, yin__kongju__er__

(continued)

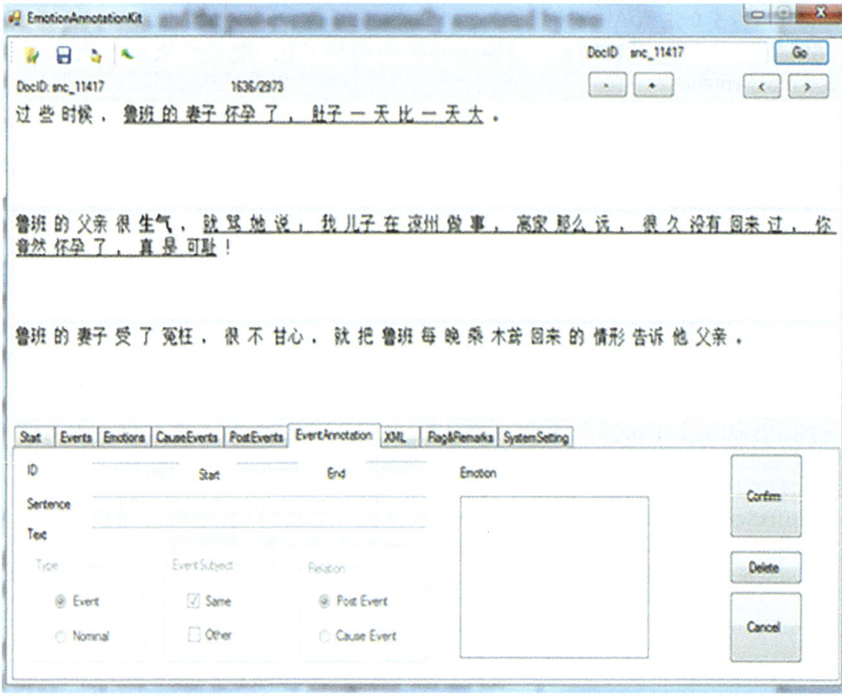

Fig. 16.3 An example of event annotation using the annotation tool

	one__move__also__NEG__move__DE__stand__ZHE, because__fear__and__
	shenti__jiangying. zuihou__shenzhi__tongku__qiu__rao.
	body__stiff. at last__even__cry__beg__mercy.
	(He) stood still, unmoved, body stiff from fear. At last, (he) broke down in tears and begged for mercy.

II. When two events were closely tied, both events were marked as the pre-events or post-events. For example, in (16.9) below, "he fell ill" and "[he] passed away" are closely tied both syntactically and semantically. Hence, they were both marked as the post-events of the SADNESS emotion.

(16.9)	那少年很**傷心**, 生了一場病便死了。
	na__shaonian__hen__shangxin, sheng__le__yi__chang__bing__bian__si__le.
	that__youth__very__sad, have__LE__one__CL__sick__and__pass away__LE.
	The youth was deeply heartbroken; he fell ill and passed away.

III. A pre-event can trigger different emotions. Similarly, a post-event can be triggered by different emotion keywords. In (16.10) below, the underlined characters represent the post-event of the two events of 害怕 *hàipà* "fear," as shown in the corresponding text:

(16.10) 娼妓會成為「人類最古老的行業」, 主要原因就是社會為了保全家庭, **害怕**亂倫及不正常的婚外性關係, **害怕**性苦悶沒有合法的解決管道, 所以藉開放周邊價值來保全中心價值 。

changji__hui__chengwei__renlei__zui__gulao__de__hangye,
prostitution__can__become__human being__most__old__DE__profession,
zhuyao__yuanyin__jiu__shi__shehui__weile__baoquan__jiating,
main__reason__JIU__is__society__for__protect__family,
haipa__luanlun__ji__bu__zhengchang__de__hunwai__xing__guanxi,
fear__incest__and__NEG__normal__DE__extramarital__sex__relationship,
haipa__xing__kumen__meiyou__hefa__de__jiejue__guandao,
fear__sex__boredom__NEG__appropriate__DE__release__channel,
suoyi__jie__kaifang__zhoubian__jiazhi__lai__baoquan__zhongxin__jiazhi.
so__via__concede__marginal__values__LAI__preserve__core__values.
Prostitution became "the world's oldest profession" primarily because of society's need to protect the family. As [it] ***feared*** *the existence of incest and abnormal extramarital relationships, and [it]* ***feared*** *that sexual boredom could not find release through appropriate channels, [it] conceded on marginal values to preserve its core ones.*

IV. The subject of the pre-event or post-event was marked when it was present in the context. For example, 辛巴 *Xīnba* "Simba" in (16.11) below was marked as part of the post-event:

(16.11) 當辛巴聽到父親死去的消息後, **傷心**的不得了, 認為是自己害死了父親, 再加上刀疤的慫恿, 辛巴便離開家園 。

dang__Xinba__tingdao__fuqin__siqu__de__xiaoxi__hou,
when__Simba__hear__father__pass away__DE__news__after,
shangxin__de__budeliao, renwei__shi__ziji__haisi__le__fuqin,
hearbreak__DE__terribly, think__is__self__kill__LE__father,
zai__jiashang__daoba__de__songyong, Xinba__bian__likai__jiayuan.
and__add__Scare__DE__influence, Xinba__then__leave__home.
When Simba heard the news of his father's passing, he became terribly heartbroken. Under the impression he had caused his father's death, and the influence of Scar, Simba left his home.

V. The action of saying was considered part of a pre-event or post-event. The "say" verb and the content were both marked in (16.12) below:

(16.12) 蘭妮公主聽到自己永遠不能恢復人形, 傷心極了 。 只好對王子說:「忘了我吧!」

Lanni__gongzhu__tingdao__ziji__yongyuan__bu__neng__huifu__renxing,
Lanni__princess__hear__self__forever__NEG__can__return__human being
shangxin__ji__le. zhihao__dui__wangzi__shuo__wang__le__wo__ba!
sad__very__LE. have to__toward__prince__say__forget__me__BA!
Princess Lanny was very sad to hear that she would never be returned to a human being. She then told the Prince, "Please forget me!"

VI. Some peripheral information was not marked as part of the pre-events or post-events, which included:

(a) Reported verbs (e.g., 談到 *tándào* and 說到 *shuōdào* "speaking of"), as in (16.13) below:

(16.13) 談到「寶來國際金融機場」, 寶來證券集團董事長白文正難掩**興奮**之情。
tandao__Baolaiguojijinrongjichang, Baolai__zhengquan__
speaking of__The Polaris International Financial Airport, Polaris__security
jituan__dongshizhang__Baiwenzheng__nan__yan__xingfenzhiqing.
group__chairman__Baiwenzheng __hard__conceal__excitement.
Speaking of "The Polaris International Financial Airport," the chairman of the board of Polaris Securities, Bai Wenzheng, could barely contain his excitement.

(b) Prepositions (e.g., 對於 *duìyú* and 關於 *guānyú* "regarding"), as in (16.14) below:

(16.14) 對於未來, 老實說我很**害怕**。
duiyu__weilai, laoshishuo__wo__hen__haipa.
regarding__future, honestly__I__quite__scared.
Regarding the future, I'm honestly quite scared.

(c) Conjunctions (e.g., 於是 *yúshì* and 所以 *suǒyǐ* "and so"), as in (16.15) below:

(16.15) 他非常**傷心**, 於是哭了一場。
ta__feichang__shangxin, yushi__ku__le__yi__chang.
he__very__heartbreak, so__cry__LE__one__CL.
He was terribly heartbroken, and so cried many tears.

(d) Adverbs (e.g., 也 yě "also" and 就 jiù "then"), as in (16.16) below, unless they were in the middle of the pre-event or post-event:

(16.16) **傷心**的醜小鴨, 也就離開美麗的大池塘了。
shangxin__de __chouxiaoya,
sad__DE__ugly duckling,
ye__jiu__likai__meili__de__da__chitang__le.
also__then__leave__beautiful__DE__big__lake__LE.
The sad ugly duckling, then left the beautiful lake.

(e) Sentence final particles (e.g., 了 *le* "LE"), as in (16.16) above

(f) Unnecessary punctuation marks (e.g., commas and full stops; necessary marks were question marks, exclamation marks, and opening and closing quotation marks)

Determining the Appropriate Events

In Chinese, the usage of the three particles 得 *de*, 的 *de*, and 地 *de* "DE" can be confusing. It was found that the three particles were used interchangeably in the corpus data, which was rather misleading. To determine the appropriate events to annotate, we set the following guidelines:

I. The structure "emotion word + 得 de 'DE' + verb" denoted a cause-effect relation. For instance, in (16.17) below, 說不出話來 *shuō bu chū huà lái* "[he] could not bear to speak" is the effect of 傷心 *shāngxīn* "sadness." In this case, 說不出話來 *shuō bu chū huà lái* "[he] could not bear to speak" was considered a post-event.

(16.17)	尼奧**傷心**得說不出話來。
	Ni'ao__shangxin__de__shuo__bu__chu__hua__lai.
	Leo__heartbreak__DE__say__NEG__out__word__LAI.
	Leo was so heartbroken that [he] could hardly speak.

II. The structure "emotion word + 的/地 de/de 'DE' + verb" mostly denoted two simultaneous actions, as shown in (16.18) and (16.19) below. For example, in (16.18), the state of sadness and the action of bringing back the body of the deceased are not a cause-effect relation.

(16.18)	一行人**哀傷**的將屍體運回。
	yixingren__aishang__de__jiang__shiti__yunhui.
	a group__grieving__DE__JIANG__corpse__bringback.
	The grieving party brought back the body of the deceased.
(16.19)	談到保養心得, 黃嘉千**心虛**地說:「其實我很愛漂亮, 可是又有點懶……」
	tandao__baoyang__xinde, Huangjiaqian__xinxu__de__shuo__
	speaking of__anti-aging__secrets, Huang Jiaqian__diffident__DE__say__
	qishi__wo__hen__ai__piaoliang, keshi__you__youdian__lan……
	actually__I__very__love__beauty, but__also__a bit__lazy……
	On the topic of anti-aging secrets, Huang Jiaqian said diffidently, "I actually love
	beauty, but I'm also a bit lazy…"

III. Since the three particles were sometimes used interchangeably in the corpus data, it was suggested that the event be rewritten as the double-conjunction structure 因為… 所以… *yīnwèi… suǒyǐ* "because…therefore…," which denotes a clear causal relation, for example:

(a)	因為傷心所以哭, as in (16.17)
	yinwei__shangxin__suoyi__ku
	because__heartbreak__so__cry
	(because [he was] heartbroken, [therefore] he could hardly speak)
(b)	*因為哀傷所以把屍體運回, as in (16.18)
	yinwei__aishang__suoyi__ba__shiti__yunhui
	because__sad__so__BA__corpse__bring back
	(because [they were] sad, therefore [they] brought back the deceased body)
(c)	*因為心虛所以說…, as in (16.19)
	yinwei__xinxu__suoyi__shuo
	because__diffident__so__say
	(because [she felt] diffident, [therefore] (she) said)

IV. When the event involved a bodily reaction (e.g., "cry" and "tremble"), it was considered a pre-event or post-event, as in (16.20) below.

(16.20)	小寶一邊傷心的哭著
	Xiaobao__yibian__shangxin__de__ku__zhe

(continued)

Xiaobao__while__sad__DE__cry__ZHE
Xiao Bao was cried sadly

Corpus Analysis

Out of the 8973 instances of emotion in the corpus, 73.9% contained a pre-event and 15.3% contained a post-event in context. We also noticed that pre-events tended to occur before the emotion keyword (64.1%), while post-events mostly occurred after the emotion keyword (94.5%). Details are summarized in Table 16.1. This finding is in line with the assumption that there is a sequential ordering among various events. Of the 35.9% of the pre-events that appeared after the emotion keyword, most were represented in the form of "…emotion word + 的是 *deshì* 'is' + pre-event" in that the pre-events were explicitly expressed as the reason for the emergence of that particular emotion.

In terms of linguistic representation, both pre-events and post-events were mostly expressed as verbs, which were 83.6% and 97.9%, respectively. Nominal pre-events were more likely to appear as the topic of the sentence. In addition, the pre-events and post-events tended to be introduced by a list of linguistic cues, as shown in Tables 16.2 and 16.3, respectively.

As for post-events, it was also observed that there was a close association between the emotion and the event type. For instance, the emotion of anger often triggers shouting events that are expressed as 罵 *mà* "to scold," 大吼 *dàhǒu* "to yell," 咆哮

Table 16.1 Analysis of pre-events and post-events found in the corpus

	Pre-events (%)	Post-events (%)
Total	73.9	15.3
Before emotion keyword	64.1	94.5
After emotion keyword	35.9	5.5
Verb	83.6	97.9
Nominal	16.4	2.1

Table 16.2 Linguistic cues associated with pre-events

Types	Cue words
Causative verbs	讓 *ràng*, 令 *lìng*, 使 *shǐ* "to cause"
Reported verbs	說到 *shuōdào*, 談到 *tándào* "speaking of"
Epistemic markers	看到 *kàndào* "to see," 聽到 *tīngdào* "to hear"
Say verbs	的說 *deshuō* "to say"
Prepositions	為了 *wèile*, 對於 *duìyú* "for"
Conjunctions	因為 *yīnwèi*, 由於 *yóuyú* "because"
Others	的是 *deshì* "is"

With a larger set of data in our study, we also found similar linguistic cues identified in Lee et al. (2013). For a full version of the list of linguistic cues, please refer to Lee et al. (2013)

Table 16.3 Linguistic cues associated with post-events

Types	Cue words
Causative verbs	讓 *ràng*, 令 *lìng* "to cause"
Particles	得 *de*, 的 *de* "to the extent that"
Adverbs	也 *yě* "also," 就 *jiù* "then," 起來 *qǐlái* "start to," 之後 *zhīhòu* "afterwards," 不禁 *bùjīn* "can't help"
Conjunctions	於是 *yúshì*, 因此 *yīncǐ*, 而 *ér* "so," 結果 *jié guǒ* ("as a result")

Table 16.4 Emotion-event association

Emotions	Event types
Happiness	笑 *xiào* "to laugh," 擁抱 *yōngbào* "to hug," 跑 *pǎo* "to run," 大叫 *dàjiào* "to shout"
Sadness	哭 *kū* "to cry," 死 *sǐ* "to die," 離開 *líkāi* "to leave,"下定決心 *xiàdìng juéxīn* "to determine"
Fear	不敢 *bùgǎn* "not dare," 躲 *duǒ* "to hide," 逃 *táo* "to flee"
Anger	罵 *mà* "to scold," 大吼 *dàhǒu* "to yell," 咆哮 *páoxiào* "to roar," 破壞 *pòhuaì* "to destroy," 殺 *shā* "to kill"

páoxiào "to roar," etc. More examples of emotion-post-event association are shown in Table 16.4.

The corpus data indicated that emotions interacted with pre-events and post-events in various ways, including syntactic representations, linguistic markers, and event types. We believe that emotion as a pivot event underlies an innovative approach toward a linguistic model of emotion/event, as well as automatic emotion detection and classification. As will be discussed in the next section, our study focused on how pre-events (emotion cause) could be recognized automatically, with consideration of lexical features, part-of-speech features, contextual features, and linguistic features.

16.4 Emotion Cause Detection

Research on emotion cause detection is at an early stage. As mentioned in Sect. 16.1, Lee et al. (2010) and Chen et al. (2010) were pioneers in emotion cause detection in proposing a rule-based approach and a multi-label classification approach, respectively. Unlike those studies, our study employed a sequence labeling approach for emotion cause detection. We argue that the proposed method helped construct a better model for the detection task and thereby achieved a better performance.

Given that emotion causes often occur close to their corresponding emotions, Chen et al. (2010) suggested that more than 80% of emotion cause events occur either two clauses before or after the emotion keyword. Thus, we annotated the surrounding sentences of each emotion keyword. As shown in Table 16.5, we determined whether a clause contained an emotion cause of a particular emotion,

Table 16.5 Emotion cause annotation of Example (21)

Position	Example	Tag
Left2	陸陸續續的 *lùlùxùxù de* "over time"	0
Left1	我又聽到幾位同事也因這位主管的口不擇言 *wǒ yòu tīngdào jǐ wèi tóngshì yě yīn zhè wèi zhǔguǎn de kǒubùzéyán* "I discovered other colleagues. . .by this manager's careless speech"	1
Left0	感到受挫 *gǎndào shòucuò* "felt frustrated"	0
Right0	甚至消極好一陣子 *shènzhì xiāojí hǎo yí zhènzi* "even depressed"	0
Right1	這位主管做事果斷有決心 *zhè wèi zhǔguǎn zuò shì guǒduàn yǒu juéxīn* "He was assertive and determined in his manner of work"	0

such as the emotion keyword "傷心 *shāngxīn* 'sad'" in (16.21) below, within the surrounding sentences (i.e., Left2, Left1, Left0, Right0, and Right1). If a cause was found in a clause, the clause was tagged "1"; otherwise, it was marked "0." Table 16.5 shows the annotated results of (16.21).

(16.21)	<PrefixSentence>只為了澄清謠言中不實的部分, 而並非強辯他對我批評, 於是私底下與他溝通, 最後他向我道歉了事。 </PrefixSentence> <FocusSentence>陸陸續續的, 我又聽到幾位同事也因[*01e]這位主管的口不擇言[*02e], 感到受挫、 <emo id=0>傷心</emo>, 甚至消極好一陣子。 </FocusSentence><SuffixSentence>這位主管做事果斷有決心, 但是喜歡批評別 人, 而且經常斷章取義的搬弄是非, 弄得同事們心裡不快。 </SuffixSentence>
	<PrefixSentence>zhi__weile__chengqing__yaoyan__zhong__bu__shi__de__
	<PrefixSentence>only__for__clarify__rumor__in__NEG__real__DE
	bufen, er__bingfei__qiangbian__ta__dui__wo__piping,
	part, and__NEG__make excuse__he__toward__me__criticism,
	yushi__sidixia__yu__ta__goutong, zuihou__ta__xiang__wo__
	thus__in private__with__him__communicate, finally__he__toward__me__
	daoqian__liaoshi. </PrefixSentence>luluxuxu_de, wo__you__tingdao__
	apologize__get over. </PrefixSentence>over time__DE, I__again__hear__
	ji__wei__tongshi__ye__yin__[*01e]zhe__wei__zhuguan__
	several__CL__colleague__also__because__[*01e]this__CL__manager__
	de__koubuzeyan, [*02e]gandao__shoucuo__<emo id=0>shangxin</emo>,
	DE__careless speech, [*02e]feel__frustrated__<emo id=0>sad</emo>,
	shenzhi__xiaoji__hao__yizhenzi.
	even__depressed__long__a period of time.
	</FocusSentence><SuffixSentence>zhe__wei__zhuguan__zuoshi__
	</FocusSentence><SuffixSentence>this__CL__manager__work__
	guoduan__you__juexin, danshi__xihuan__piping__bieren,
	assertive__have__determined, but__like__criticize__others,
	erqie__jingchang__duanzhangquyi__de__bannongshifei,
	and__often__jump to conclusion__DE__gossip,
	nong__de__tongshi__men__xinli__bu__kuai.
	cause__DE__colleague__PL__heart__NEG__happy.
	I only wished to clarify the falsehoods in the rumors, and not make excuses for his

(continued)

Table 16.6 Summary and examples of corpus data in Lee (2010)

	Number of instances	Example(s)
Instances	5964	Sentences (1), (2), and (3)
Instances with emotion	4260	<emo id = 0> 傷心</emo>
Instances with emotion causes	3460	[*01e]這位主管的口不擇言[*02e]
Instances with verbal cause event	2941	[*01e]這位主管的口不擇言[*02e]，感到受挫、<emo id = 0> 傷心</emo>
Instances with nominal cause event	519	提到[*01n]球場[*02n]，就很 <emo id = 0> 傷心</emo>

*criticism toward me. Thus, I communicated with him in private, and he eventually apologized to me. Over time, I discovered other colleagues who had felt frustrated, <emo id=0>sad</emo>, and even depressed by [*01e] this manager's careless speech [*02e]. He was assertive and determined in his manner of work, but enjoyed criticizing others, and often jumped to conclusions when gossiping, causing much grief and distress to his colleagues.*

With a view to investigating emotion causes and constructing a corresponding rule-based system for emotion cause detection, Lee et al. (2010) collected and annotated 5964 emotion instances from the Sinica Corpus. In the corpus, cause events were categorized into two types: verbal events and nominal events. A verbal event referred to a triggering event that involved a verb or a nominalization, whereas a nominal event was simply a noun. Example (16.21) above is an actual example taken from the corpus, in which the cause event occurs between [*01e] and [*02e]. In particular, the "0" shows which index of emotion keyword it refers to, "1" marks the beginning of the cause event, "2" marks the end of the cause event, "e" refers to a verbal event, and "n" denotes a nominal event. A summary and examples of the emotion cause corpus data are illustrated in Table 16.6.

As shown in Table 16.6, emotion causes were very likely to occur in emotional entries, as 81% of the emotion keywords appeared with a corresponding cause that was more often expressed by a verbal event than a nominal one.

16.5 Sequence Labeling Model for Emotion Cause Detection

Previous work regarding emotion cause detection has suggested that it is a classification issue. As mentioned in the introduction, the multi-label classification model failed to capture the correlations among clauses in a text. To make good use of the correlations among clauses, our study treated emotion cause detection as a sequence

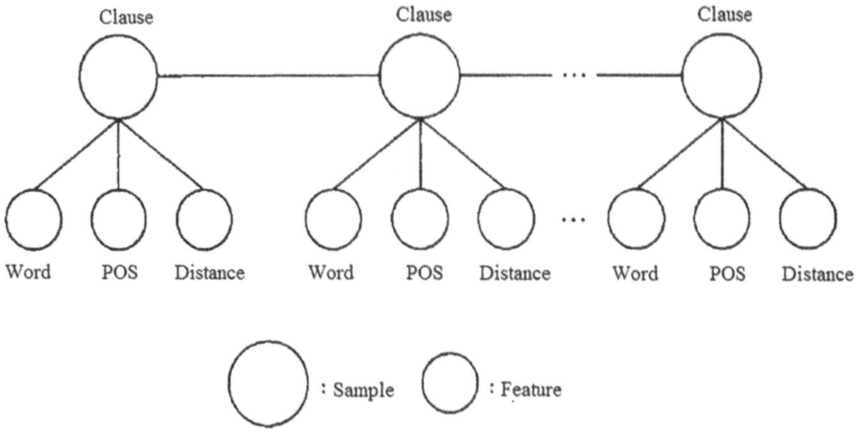

Fig. 16.4 Sequence labeling model for emotion cause detection

labeling issue and thus constructed another model for the detection task. The sequence labeling model is demonstrated in Fig. 16.4. The major difference between the sequence labeling model and existing models is the inclusion of correlations among clauses, which improved the performance of cause recognition. Apart from that, the proposed model also incorporated certain features of the clause, such as lexical features and part-of-speech (POS) features, into the model for machine learning and classification.

Among the models used for sequence labeling, CRFs perform relatively better. Developed by Lafferty et al. (2001) based on maximum entropy (MaxEnt) models and hidden Markov models (HMMs), CRFs are an undirected graphical and conditional probability model used for labeling and segmenting sequence data. The CRF model optimizes the entire sequence using the following formula:

$$p_{\lambda}(Y|W) = \frac{1}{Z(W)} \exp\left(\sum_{t \in T} \sum_{k} \lambda_k f_k(y_{t-1}, W, t.)\right)$$

where $Y = \{y_t\}$ is the corresponding output label sequence set and $y_t \in \{1, 0\}$ indicates whether the corresponding clause contains an emotion cause or is one of the clauses of an emotion cause. When referring to the testing clauses, $Z(W)$ is a normalization factor, f_k is a characteristic function, and t is the subscript of the corresponding feature.

The feature sets consist of the description of the basic features of the current object and the description of contextual information, as illustrated in Tables 16.7 and 16.8, respectively. Basic features refer to the nouns, the verbs, and the number of nouns and verbs of the current clause. The reason we chose only nouns and verbs is because emotion causes are mainly of two kinds—nouns referring to causes with nominal events and verbs mapping onto causes with verbal events. The distance feature is another important positional feature. Generally speaking, emotion causes

Table 16.7 Basic features: lexical features and distance feature in the current clause

Feature	Description
Noun	Noun(s) in the current clause. If no, marked as "NULL"
Verb	Verb(s) in the current clause. If no, marked as "NULL"
No. of nouns	The number of nouns in the current clause
No. of verbs	The number of verbs in the current clause
Distance	The distance between the current clause and the clause containing an emotion keyword

Table 16.8 Contextual features

Feature	Description
Verb(s) of the previous clause	Verb(s) found in the previous clause. If no, marked as "NULL"
Noun(s) of the previous clause	Noun(s) found in the previous clause. If no, marked as "NULL"
Tag(s) of the previous clause	The classification tag marked in the previous clause. If no, marked as "NULL"
Verb(s) of the subsequent clause	Verb(s) found in the subsequent clause. If no, marked as "NULL"
Noun(s) of the subsequent clause	Noun(s) found in the subsequent clause

tend to occur at the position to the left of the emotion keyword, which can be fully captured by the distance feature. Contextual features mainly include the lexical features of the preceding and following sentences. In addition, the classification label of the preceding sentence provides sufficient information in sequence labeling, as mentioned in the introduction. Therefore, we included the classification tag of the previous sentence as one of the features as well.

In addition to the abovementioned features, we also added the linguistic rule-based features proposed in Lee et al. (2013). The patterns of rules are exemplified in Table 16.9. These rules were used to locate the clause positions of an emotion cause, in which I/II/III/IV/V/VI are the groups of linguistic cue words.

The abbreviations C, K, B, F, and A used in the rules are defined as follows: C represents the emotion cause; K is the emotion keyword; F is the focus clause that contains the emotion keyword; B is the clause before the focus clause (left side of F); and A is the clause after the focus clause (right side of F).

- I = {"為 *wèi* 'for'," "為了 *wèile* 'for'," "對 *dùi* 'for'," "對於 *dùiyú* 'for'," "以 *yǐ* 'for'"}
- II = {"因 *yīn* 'because'," "因為 *yīnwèi* 'because'," "由於 *yóuyú* 'because'," "於是 *yúshì* 'so'," "所以 *suǒyǐ* 'so'," "因而 *yīnér* 'so'," "可是 *kěshì* 'but'"}
- III = {"讓 *ràng* 'to cause'," "令 *lìng* 'to cause'," "使 *shǐ* 'to cause'"}

Table 16.9 Linguistic rules for emotion cause detection

Rules	Patterns
1	(i) C(B/F) + III(F) + K(F)
	(ii) C = the nearest N/V before III in F/B
2	(i) IV/V/I/II(B/F) + C(B/F) + K(F)
	(ii) C = the nearest N/V before K in F
3	(i) I/II/IV/V(B) + C(B) + K(F)
	(ii) C = the nearest N/V after I/II/IV/V in B
4	(i) K(F) + V/VI(F) + C(F/A)
	(ii) C = the nearest N/V after V/VI in F/A
5	(i) K(F) + II(A) + C(A)
	(ii) C = the nearest N/V after II in A
6	(i) III(F) + K(F) + C(F/A)
	(ii) C = the nearest N/V after K in F or A
7	(i) *yuè* C *yuè* K "the more C, the more K" (F)
	(ii) C = the V in between the two instances of yuè in F
8	(i) K(F) + C(F)
	(ii) C = the nearest N/V after K in F
9	(i) IV(B) + C(B) + K(F)
	(ii) C = the nearest N/V after IV in B
10	(i) C(B) + K(F)
	(ii) C = the nearest N/V before K in B

- IV = {"想到 *xiǎngdào* 'to think'," "想起 *xiǎngqǐ* 'to think'," "想來 *xiǎnglái* 'to think'," "說道 *shuōdào* 'speaking of'," "說起 *shuōqǐ* 'speaking of'," "講到 *jiǎngdào* 'speaking of'" 等}
- V = {"聽 *tīng* 'to hear'," "聽到 *tīngdào* 'to hear'," "聽說 *tīngshuō* 'hear about'," "看 *kàn* 'to see'," "看到 *kàndào* 'to see'," "看見 *kànjiàn* 'to see'," "見到 *jiàndào* 'to see'" 等}
- VI = {"的是 *deshì* 'is'," "的說 *deshuō* 'is'," "於 *yú* 'with regard to'," "能 *néng* 'can'"}

16.6 Experiments

16.6.1 Experimental Setting

Our study adopted the emotion cause corpus constructed by Lee (2010). For the emotion cause corpus, we reserved 80% as the training data and used 20% as the testing data. The part-of-speech tagging was produced by the Stanford Parsing Tool/ Stanford Parser.[1] The evaluation scores were based on precision, recall, and F-score. Given that there were two types of tasks involved (i.e., with the presence of emotion

[1] https://nlp.stanford.edu/software/lex-parser.shtml

Table 16.10 Performance of the sequence labeling model with different features

Evaluation feature(s)	Precision-P	Recall-P	Fscore-P	Precision-N	Recall-N	Fscore-N
Lexical	0.506	0.207	0.294	0.833	0.951	0.888
+ Contextual	0.519	0.344	0.414	0.854	0.923	0.887
+ Distance	0.523	0.364	0.429	0.858	0.920	0.888
+ Linguistic rules	0.520	0.377	0.437	0.860	0.917	0.888

cause and without the presence of emotion cause), they were evaluated separately. For example, Precision-P indicated the precision degree of the clause with the presence of the emotion cause; on the contrary, Precision-N indicated the same without an emotion cause. In the experiments, the sequence labeling model was used with the help of the CRF++ tool to create the default parameters. All the features mentioned in Sect. 16.5 were added to the feature template using the current features of unigram and the contextual features of bigram, etc.

16.6.2 Results and Discussion

Table 16.10 shows the performance of the sequence labeling model for emotion cause detection with various features. The lexical features were composed of the nouns, the verbs, and the number of verbs and nouns in the clause; the distance feature considered the distance between the clause and the clause that contained the emotion keyword as the feature; and the linguistic features were the corresponding features of the rules listed in Table 16.9. Due to the setting of the emotion cause detection task, the number of clauses without an emotion cause (N) was considerably larger than those with an emotion cause (P). This imbalance resulted in significantly higher scores of Fscore-N compared with Fscore-P. The following observations were suggested by the statistics shown in Table 16.10:

(i) Although Fscore-N was already high when we simply employed the lexical features, Fscore-P only achieved 0.294. This indicates that the lexical features failed to cater to our needs.
(ii) Combining both the lexical and contextual features, Fscore-P reached a significantly better value. This proves that contextual features play an important role in emotion cause detection.
(iii) Incorporating the lexical, contextual, and distance features, Fscore-P increased slightly. This suggests that the distance feature was of some use in the detection task.
(iv) Merging the linguistic rule-based features with the model mentioned in (16.21), the performance of Fscore-P was further improved. This result demonstrates the effectiveness of the linguistic rule-based features in recognizing emotion causes. However, the improvement was not a marked one. This may be because

Table 16.11 Performance of the multi-label classification model and the sequence labeling model

Evaluation model	Precision-P	Recall-P	Fscore-P	Precision-N	Recall-N	Fscore-N
Multi-label classification model	0.312	0.500	0.384	0.900	0.803	0.849
Sequence labeling model	0.537	0.364	0.434	0.858	0.924	0.890

Fscore-N already reached its maximum value, and no further improvement could therefore be obtained.

Table 16.11 shows the performance of the sequence labeling model and the multi-label classification model. The multi-label classification model employed the maximum entropy classifier and made use of lexical, distance, and linguistic features. As illustrated in Table 16.10, the sequence labeling model obviously outperformed the multi-label classification model. In comparison with the multi-label classification model, Fscore-P and Fscore-N of the sequence labeling model were ~5% and ~4.1% higher, respectively. The major difference between the two models is that the sequence labeling model took contextual features into account, which is an advantage over the multi-label classification model. That explains the importance of the contextual features in the detection task. It is worth mentioning that the results proposed in Chen et al. (2010) are different from ours since the part-of-speech tags in Chen et al. (2010) were manually annotated, while the tags were classified by a part-of-speech parser in our study. Thus, performance could not be significantly enhanced as the accuracy of the rules was affected.

16.6.3 Error Analysis

Although the sequence labeling model yielded a promising performance, emotion cause detection in some exceptional cases still requires more effort for improvement mainly due to the following reasons:

(i) When the clause denoting the cause of the emotion was far away from the emotion keyword, as in (16.22) below, the CRF model mistakenly took the closest clause next to the emotion keyword as the clause denoting the emotion cause; thus, the CRF model mistakenly identified the clause "老公公一點也不覺得痛 *lǎoggōngōng yìdiǎn yě bù juéde tòng* 'the old man did not feel any pain'" as the emotion cause.

(16.22)	小精靈的領袖說完, [*01e] 紅色的精靈馬上伸手摸摸老公公臉頰上的大瘤 。 那個瘤立刻被摘下來 [*02e] 。 可是, 老公公一點也不覺得痛 。 老公公<emo id=0>高興</emo>極了, 用手摸摸突然變輕的臉頰, 笑嘻嘻的走下山, 回到家裡 。
	xiaojingling__de__lingxiu__shuo__wan, [*01e]hongse__de__jingling__
	elf__DE__leader__say__finish, [*01e]red__DE__elf__

(continued)

mashang__shen__shou__momo__laogonggong__lianjia__shang__de__
immediately__reach out__hand__touch__old man__forehead__on__DE__
da__liu. na__ge__liu__like__bei__zhaixialai[*02e]. keshi,
big__tumor. that__CL__tumor__right away__BEI__come off[*02e]. but,
laogonggong__yidian__ye__bu__juede__tong. Laogonggong__<emo id=0>
old man__a bit__also__NEG__feel__pain. old man__<emo id=0>
gaoxing</emo>__ji__le, yong__shou__momo__turan__bian__qing__
vhappy__</emo>__very__LE, use__hand__touch__sudden__change__light__
de__lianjia, xiaoxixi__de__zou__xia__shan, huidao__jia__li.
DE__forehead, laugh__DE__walk__down__mountain, back__home__LI.
*The leader of the elves finished talking. [*01e] The red elf immediately reached out and touched the tumor on the old man's forehead. It came off right away[*02e]. However, the old man did not feel any pain. He was extremely <emo id=0>happy</emo> and felt his now tumor-free forehead with his hand, laughing and making his way down the mountain and back home.*

(ii) When no emotion cause was found in the emotion entries, as in (16.23) below, the CRF model sometimes misclassified a cause; (16.23) is a rare example that contains only the emotion but not the corresponding emotion cause. As the clause denoting an emotion cause usually occurs adjacent to its corresponding emotion, the CRF model recognized the clause "就載著滿船的鵝 *jiù zài zhe mǎn chuán de é* 'he loaded his boat full of geese'" as the emotion cause, leading to the misclassification.

(16.23) 王羲之大喜過望, 道士也趕緊把早就準備好的筆墨跟絹拿出來請他寫。 王羲之寫完了道德經, 就載著滿船的鵝, <emo id=0>高高興興</emo>的回去了。
Wangxizhi__daxiguowang, daoshi__ye__ganjin__ba__zao__jiu__
Wangxizhi__happy, Taoist priest__also__hurry up__BA__long__JIU__
zhunbei__hao__de __bi__mo__ gen__juan__na__chulai__qing__ta__xie.
prepare__well__DE__pen__ink__and__silk__take__out__invite__he__write.
Wangxizhi__xie__wan__le__Daodejing, jiu__zai__zhe__man__
Wangxizhi__write__finish__LE__Tao Te Ching, then__load__ZHE__full__
chuan__de__e, <emo id=0> gaogaoxingxing</emo>de__huiqu__le.
boat__DE__goose, <emo id=0> happy</emo>DE__back__LE.
Wang Xizhi was feeling happy. The Taoist priest also took out the pen, ink and silk he had prepared for him to write with. After Wang had finished writing the Tao Te Ching, he loaded his boat full of geese, and went home <emo id=0>happily</emo>.

(iii) When a cause occurred across clauses, the CRF model could only identify one of the clauses, as illustrated in (16.24) below. In (16.24), the two clauses denoting emotion cause are "他們只知道學成後, 我依然可以當老師 *tāmen zhǐ zhīdào xué chéng hòu, wǒ yīrán kěyǐ dāng lǎoshī* 'They only knew that after completing the studies, I could still be a teacher'," yet the CRF model simply considered "我依然可以當老師 *wǒ yīrán kěyǐ dāng lǎoshī* 'I could still be a teacher'" as the target clause and neglected the previous clause.

(16.24) 老畫家范洪甲回憶當初自台南師範學校畢業後, 要繼續到東京美術學校深造時父母並沒有反對 。 「[*01e] 他們只知道學成後, 我依然可以當老師 [*02e], 就十分<emo id = 0> 高興</emo>, 很少出門的祖父還到港口來送我, 」范洪甲回憶 。

lao__huajia__Fanhongjia__huiyi__dangchu__zi__
old__painter__Fan Hongjia__recall__before__from__
Tainanshifanxuexiao__biye__hou, yao__jixu__
the National University of Tainan__graduate__after, want__continue__
dao__Dongjingmeishuxuexiao__shenzao__shi__fumu__bing__meiyou__
come__the Tokyo Fine Arts School__study__when__parents__and__NEG__
fandui. [*01e]tamen__zhi__zhidao__xue__cheng__hou, wo__yiran__keyi__
object. [*01e]they__only__know__study__complete__after, I__still__can__
dang__laoshi[*02e], jiu__shifen__<emo id = 0> gaoxing</emo>,
be__teacher[*02e], JIU__very__<emo id = 0> happy</emo>,
hen__shao__chumen__de__zufu__hai__dao__gangkou__lai__
very__little__leave home__DE__grandfather__also__come__port__LAI__
song__wo, Fanhongjia__huiyi.
see off__me__, Fan Hongjia__recall.

*Old painter Fan Hongjia recalled the fact that his parents had not objected to him wanting to continue his studies at the Tokyo Fine Arts School after graduating from the National University of Tainan. "[*01e] They only knew that after completing the studies, I could still be a teacher[*02e] and were very <emo id=0>happy</emo>. Even my grandfather, who never left home, went to the port to see me off," Fan Hongjia recalls.*

16.7 Conclusion

There were two major aims of this chapter. The first one was to introduce a Chinese event-based emotion corpus with annotation analysis results; the annotation scheme was proposed to annotate emotion-associated events consistently. The second aim was to detect emotion causes automatically by treating the detection task as a sequence labeling issue. The detection task was performed with the help of the conditional random field (CRF) model. In the learning process, various features were taken into account for emotion cause recognition, namely, lexical features, part-of-speech features, distance features, contextual features, and linguistic features. The experiments in our study showed that these features were of value to emotion cause detection, in particular, the contextual features. In addition, the proposed model outperformed the multi-label classification model when similar features were employed.

As indicated by the results, emotion cause detection is still a very challenging task. The performance of the existing approaches is far from satisfactory, as the F-score performance of the clauses with an emotion clause was relatively low (~45%). In future work, we will specifically find solutions to the detection errors mentioned in this chapter (i.e., entries without emotion causes and emotion causes occurring across causes). We will then conduct a thorough investigation and modify the proposed model with a view to further improving the performance of emotion cause detection.

References

Abelin, Åsa, and Jens Allwood. 2000. Cross linguistic interpretation of emotional prosody. In *Proceedings of the ISCA ITRW on Speech and Emotion*, 110–113. Newcastle, Northern Ireland, United Kingdom.

Ahmad, Khurshid. (ed.). 2008. *Proceedings of the LREC workshop on sentiment analysis: Emotion, metaphor, ontology and terminology*. In Association with LREC-08.

Alm, Cecilia Ovesdotter, Dan Roth, and Richard Sproat. 2005. Emotions from text: Machine learning for text-based emotion prediction. In *Proceedings of EMNLP-05*, 579–586. Vancouver, Canada.

Andrew, Richard John. 1963. Evolution of facial expressions. *Science* 142:1034–1041.

Bridge, Donna J., Joan Y. Chian, and Ken A. Paller. 2010. Emotional context at learning systematically biases memory for facial information. *Memory & Cognition* 38:125–133.

Chaumartin, François-Régis. 2007. A knowledge-based system for headline sentiment tagging. In *Proceedings of the 4th International Workshop on Semantic Evaluations*, 422–425. Prague, Czech Republic.

Chen, Ying, Sophia Yat Mei Lee, and Chu-Ren Huang. 2009. A cognitive-based annotation system for emotion computing. In *Proceedings of the Third Linguistic Annotation Workshop (The LAW III)*, 1–9. Singapore.

Chen, Ying, Sophia Yat Mei Lee, Shoushan Li, and Chu-Ren Huang. 2010. Emotion cause detection with linguistic constructions. In *Proceeding of COLING-10*, 179–187. Beijing, China.

Craig, Arthur D. 2009. How do you feel now? The anterior insula and human awareness. *Nature Reviews Neuroscience* 10(1):59–70.

Dellaert, Frank, Thomas Polzin, and Alex Waibel. 1996. Recognizing emotion in speech. In *Proceedings of the Fourth International Conference on Spoken Language Processing (ICSLP-96),* 1970–1973. Philadelphia, Pennsylvania.

Descartes, René. 1649. The passions of the soul. In *The philosophical writings of Descartes*. (Vol. 1), ed. John Cottingha, Robert Stoothoff, and Dugald Murdoch, 325–404. London: Cambridge University Press.

Ekman, Paul, and Wallace V. Friesen. 1978. *Facial action coding system*. Palo Alto, CA: Consulting Psychology Press.

Gao, Kai, Hua Xu, and Jiushuo Wang. 2015. A rule-based approach to emotion cause detection for Chinese micro-blogs. *Expert Systems with Applications* 42(9):4517–4528.

Ghazi, Diman, Diana Inkpen, and Stan Szpakowicz. 2015. Detecting emotion stimuli in emotion-bearing sentences. In *Computational linguistics and intelligent text processing*, ed. Alexander Gelbukh, 152–165. Springer.

Gui, Lin, Dongyin Wu, Ruifeng Xu, Qin Lu, and Yu Zhou. 2016. Event-driven emotion cause extraction with corpus construction. In *Proceedings of the 2016 Conference on Empirical Methods in Natural Language Processing*, 1639–1649. Austin, Texas.

Gui, Lin, Jiannan Hu, Yulan He, Ruifeng Xu, Qin Lu, and Jiachen Du. 2017. A question answering approach to emotion cause extraction. In *Proceedings of the 2017 Conference on Empirical Methods in Natural Language Processing*, 1593–1602. Copenhagen, Denmark

Hervé, Pierre-Yves, Annick Razafimandimby, Mathieu Vigneau, Bernard Mazoyer, and Nathalie Tzourio-Mazoyer. 2012. Disentangling the brain networks supporting affective speech comprehension. *NeuroImage* 61(4):1255–67.

James, William. 1884. What is an emotion? *Mind* 9(34):188–205.

Kehrein, Roland. 2002. The prosody of authentic emotions. In *Proceedings of Speech Prosody 2002*, 423–426. Aix-en-Provence, France.

Lafferty, John, Andrew McCallum, and Fernando C.N. Pereira. 2001. Conditional random fields: Probabilistic models for segmenting and labeling sequence data. In *Proceedings of the Eighteenth International Conference on Machine Learning (ICML-2001)*, 282–289. Williamstown, Massachusetts.

Lee, Sophia Yat Mei. 2010. *A linguistic approach to emotion detection and classification*. Ph.D. dissertation. The Hong Kong Polytechnic University, Hong Kong.

Lee, Sophia Yat Mei, Ying Chen, and Chu-Ren Huang. 2009. Cause event representations for happiness and surprise. In *Proceedings of the 23rd Pacific Asia Conference on Language, Information and Computation (PACLIC 23)*, 345–354. Hong Kong.

Lee, Sophia Yat Mei, Ying Chen, and Chu-Ren Huang. 2010. A text-driven rule-based system for emotion cause detection. In *Proceedings of NAACL-HLT 2010 Workshop on Computational Approaches to Analysis and Generation of Emotion in Text*, 45–53. Los Angeles, California.

Lee, Sophia Yat Mei, Ying Chen, Chu-Ren Huang, and Shoushan Li. 2013. Detecting emotion causes with a linguistic rule-based approach. *Computational Intelligence* 29(3):390–416.

Li, Weiyuan, and Hua Xu. 2014. Text-based emotion classification using emotion cause extraction. *Expert Systems with Applications* 41(4):1742–1749.

Li, Shoushan, Lei Huang, Rong Wang, and Guodong Zhou. 2013. Sentence-level emotion classification with label and context dependence. In *Proceedings of the 53rd Annual Meeting of the Association for Computational Linguistics and the 7th International Joint Conference on Natural Language Processing*, 1045–1053. Beijing, China.

Messina, Irene, Marco Sambin, Petra Beschoner, and Roberto Viviani. 2016. Changing views of emotion regulation and neurobiological models of the mechanism of action of psychotherapy. *Cognitive, Affective, & Behavioral Neuroscience* 16(4):571–587.

Mihalcea, Rada, and Hugo Liu. 2006. A corpus-based approach to finding happiness. In *Proceedings of the AAAI Spring Symposium on Computational Approaches to Weblogs*, 139–144. Palo Alto, California.

Olson, Ingrid R., Alan Plotzker, and Youssef Ezzyat. 2007. The enigmatic temporal poles: A review of findings on social and emotional processing. *Brain* 130(7):1718–1731.

Ortony, Andrew, Gerald L. Clore, and Allan Collins. 1990. *The cognitive structure of emotions*. Cambridge University Press.

Picard, Rosalind Wright. 1995. *Affective computing*. Cambridge, MA: The MIT Press.

Power, Mick, and Tim Dalgleish. 2015. *Cognition and emotion: From order to disorder*. New York: Psychology Press.

Rao, Yanghui, Qing Li, Xudong Mao, and Liu Wenyin. 2014. Sentiment topic models for social emotion mining. *Information Sciences* 266:90–100.

Russo, Irene, Tommaso Caselli, Francesco Rubino, Ester Boldrini, and Patricio Martínez-Barco. 2011. Emocause: An easy-adaptable approach to emotion cause contexts. In *Proceedings of the 2nd Workshop on Computational Approaches to Subjectivity and Sentiment Analysis*, 153–160. Portland, Oregon.

Smith, Craig A., and Leslie D. Kirby. 2001. Toward delivering on the promise of appraisal theory. In *Appraisal processes in emotion: Theory, methods, research*, ed. Klaus R. Scherer, Angela Schorr, and Tom Johnstone, 121–138. Oxford: Oxford University Press.

Smith, Craig A., and Richard S. Lazarus. 1993. Appraisal components, core relational themes, and the emotions. *Cognition and Emotion* 7:233–269.

Tokuhisa, Ryoko, Kentaro Inui, and Yuji Matsumoto. 2008. Emotion recognition using massive examples extracted from the web. In *Proceedings of COLING*, 881–888. Manchester, United Kingdom.

Wierzbicka, Anna. 1999. *Emotions across languages and cultures: Diversity and universals*. Cambridge: Cambridge University Press.

Yuan, Zheng, and Matthew Purver. 2015. Predicting emotion labels for Chinese microblog texts. In *Proceedings of the 1st International Workshop on Sentiment Discovery from Affective Data*, 129–149. Bristol, United Kingdom.

Zhou, Deyu, Xuan Zhang, Yin Zhou, Quan Zhao, and Xin Geng. 2016. Emotion distribution learning from texts. In *Proceedings of the 2016 Conference on Empirical Methods in Natural Language Processing*, 638–647. Austin, Texas.

Part III
Language Resources and Linguistic Analysis

Chapter 17
Using Forced Alignment for Phonetics Research

Jiahong Yuan, Wei Lai, Christopher Cieri, and Mark Liberman

Abstract Forced alignment has been at the core of speech recognition technology since the 1970s, and it was first used in phonetics research in the 1990s. Progress in digital multimedia, networking, and mass storage has created enormous and growing volumes of transcribed speech, which forced alignment can turn into vast phonetic databases. However, speech science has so far taken relatively little advantage of this opportunity, because it requires tools and methods that are now difficult for most speech researchers to access. Moreover, these tools have not been completely developed and tested for many applications. These technologies are leading the study of human speech into a revolutionary new era—a movement from the study of small, private, and mostly artificial datasets to the analysis of published collections of natural speech that are thousands or even millions of times larger. In this chapter, we will illustrate some of the ways that forced alignment can be used as a tool in speech science and discuss directions for improvement.

Keywords Forced alignment · Corpus phonetics · Phonetic segmentation

17.1 Introduction

In the last 25 years, an enormous and growing body of digital speech has become available, such as archived broadcasts of news reports, interviews, speeches, and debates; oral histories; court recordings; podcasts; audiobooks; and so on. A small

J. Yuan (✉)
Interdisciplinary Research Center for Linguistic Sciences, School of Humanities and Social Sciences, University of Science and Technology of China, Hefei, China
e-mail: jiahongyuan@ustc.edu.cn

W. Lai
Department of Psychology and Human Development, Vanderbilt University, Nashville, TN, USA

C. Cieri · M. Liberman
Linguistic Data Consortium, University of Pennsylvania, Philadelphia, PA, USA
e-mail: ccieri@ldc.upenn.edu; myl@cis.upenn.edu

C.-R. Huang et al. (eds.), *Chinese Language Resources*, Text, Speech and Language Technology 49, https://doi.org/10.1007/978-3-031-38913-9_17

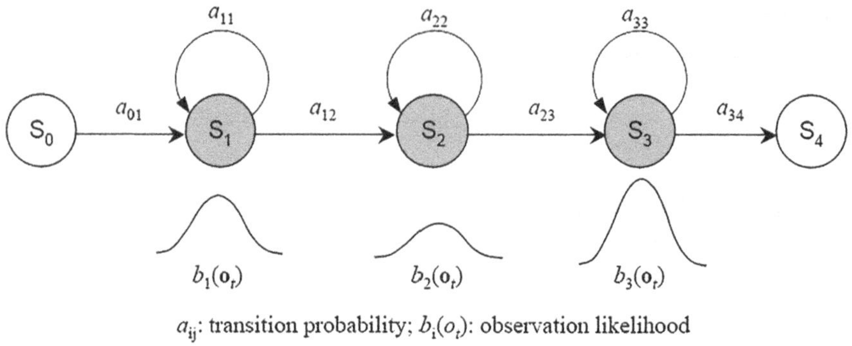

Fig. 17.1 Hidden Markov Model with three non-skipping states

fraction of this material—comprising many thousands of hours—has been collected and published in the form of corpora for speech technology research. These very-large-scale bodies of data make it possible to use natural speech in developing and testing hypotheses across many types of individual, social, regional, temporal, and contextual variations, as well as across languages. However, in contrast to speech technology research, speech science has so far taken relatively little advantage of this opportunity. This is partly because most researchers lack the knowledge and skills required to access the needed tools and methods and partly because the tools and methods themselves are incomplete and untested.

Given only digital audio, researchers can study the distribution of speech and silence segments as well as purely acoustic-phonetic features such as fundamental frequency. For most kinds of speech science, however, researchers need to know which words were said when and how they were pronounced, which entails the availability of phonetic segmentation and transcription. Relatively few speech corpora include such annotations, because manual phonetic segmentation is time-consuming, expensive, and inconsistent, with much less than perfect inter-annotator agreement (Cucchiarini 1993; Godfrey et al. 1992; Leung and Zue 1984). Automatic phonetic segmentation is, therefore, necessary for corpus-based phonetics research. Fortunately, automatic phonetic segmentation is the essential result of forced alignment, a technique developed to train automatic speech recognition systems (Jelinek 1976) and to extract acoustic units for speech synthesis systems (Wightman et al. 1997).

Automatic phonetic segmentation normally requires two inputs: recorded audio and conventional (orthographic) transcription. In this task, the transcribed words are mapped into a phone sequence or a lattice of possible phone sequences using a pronouncing dictionary and/or grapheme-to-phoneme rules. Phone boundaries are determined by comparing the observed speech signal with pre-trained Hidden Markov Model (HMM)-based acoustic models. Typically, every phone in the acoustic models is represented as an HMM that consists of three left-to-right non-skipping states (as shown in Fig. 17.1), the beginning (s_1), middle (s_2), and ending (s_3) parts of the phone, plus empty start (s_0) and end states (s_4) for entering and exiting the phone. From the training data, an acoustic model (e.g., a Gaussian mixture model) is built for each state (except s_0 and s_4), as well as the transition probabilities between pairs of states (see Fig. 17.1). The speech signal is then analyzed as a successive set of frames (e.g., every 10 ms). The alignment of frames with phones is determined by finding the most likely sequence of hidden states (which are constrained by the known sequence of phones derived from transcription), given the observed data and the acoustic models represented by the HMMs. The reported performances of state-of-the-art HMM-based forced alignment systems range from 80% to 93% agreement (of all boundaries) within 20 ms compared with manual segmentation (Hosom 2009; Yuan et al. 2013) in the TIMIT Corpus (Garofolo et al. 1993). Human labelers have an average agreement of 93% within 20 ms, with a maximum of 96% within 20 ms for highly trained specialists (Hosom 2000).

With the availability of automatic speech recognition toolkits such as the Hidden Markov Model Toolkit (HTK) and Kaldi, forced alignment techniques for speech researchers are more easily accessible. In recent years, automatic speech analysis with the use of forced alignment has been developed in phonetic and sociolinguistic research, for example, automatic measurement of vowel formants (Evanini et al. 2009; Labov et al. 2013), voice onset time (Sonderegger and Keshet 2012), and speech variation in general (Fox 2006).

This chapter will describe the use of forced alignment in corpus-based phonetics research, particularly the case of two very different kinds of speech data—recordings of a Mandarin proficiency test and collections of Mandarin broadcast news speech—and efforts to improve forced alignment for phonetics research. In this context, we will present the following three areas of research work based on the studies of Yuan et al. (2016), Yuan and Liberman (2015), and Yuan et al. (2013) and Yuan et al. (2014), respectively: using forced alignment as a method to produce phonetic segmentation, using forced alignment as a method to investigate allophonic variation, and efforts to improve the performance of forced alignment itself.

17.2 Using Forced Alignment for Phonetic Segmentation

Yuan et al. (2016) investigated the use of pauses and pause fillers (such as 嗯 and 呃) in Mandarin Chinese. They focused on two factors—speaker sex and proficiency—and their analysis was based on 13 h of monologue speech from 267 speakers.

17.2.1 Corpus

The Putonghua Shuiping Ceshi (PSC) is the national standard Mandarin proficiency test in China. The test consists of four parts: the first two parts involve reading 100 monosyllabic and 50 disyllabic words; the third part requires reading an article of 300 characters, randomly selected from a pool of 60 articles; and the last part

Table 17.1 Frequencies and relative frequencies of pauses and pause fillers

	Female	Male	L1	L2	L3	L4
No. of *e*	671	521	384	403	352	53
No. of *en*	1287	579	568	655	478	165
No. of pauses	17,828	9057	7231	11,165	6591	1898
No. of words	68,331	31,881	29,514	42,461	22,695	5542
e/(e + en)	***0.343***	***0.474***	0.403	0.381	0.424	0.243
e/words	***0.010***	***0.016***	0.013	0.010	0.016	0.010
en/words	0.019	0.018	0.019	0.015	0.021	0.030
(e + en)/words	0.029	0.035	0.032	0.025	0.037	0.039
Pauses/words	***0.261***	***0.284***	***0.245***	***0.263***	***0.290***	***0.343***

entails speaking freely on a given topic for 3 min. The four parts are graded separately and numerically, and the total score out of 100 points is converted to one of six categorical proficiency levels, ranging from high to low: 一级甲等 (Class 1 Level 1), 一级乙等 (Class 1 Level 2), 二级甲等 (Class 2 Level 1), 二级乙等 (Class 2 Level 2), 三级甲等 (Class 3 Level 1), and 三级乙等 (Class 3 Level 2). To qualify for teaching K-12, for example, candidates must achieve at least 二级乙等 (Class 2 Level 2).

Yuan et al.'s (2016) dataset consisted of recordings of college students at Beijing Normal University who took the PSC test in 2011. They used the spoken monologues (the last part of the test) from 267 speakers (178 female and 89 male), which contained approximately 13 h of speech. The proficiency levels of the speakers ranged across four levels, from 一级乙等 (Class 1 Level 2) to 三级甲等 (Class 3 Level 1) (classified as L1 to L4, respectively, in Table 17.1).

17.2.2 Transcription and Forced Alignment

The spoken monologues were first transcribed by a professional transcriptionist and then proofed for errors and pause fillers, which were ignored in the first pass but then added. The pause fillers were categorized into two types via transcription: one without nasalization (transcribed as *e*) and one with nasalization (transcribed as *en*). Yuan et al. (2016) then employed forced alignment to determine the boundaries of the transcribed words, including pause fillers.

Pauses are usually not transcribed. To automatically identify pauses in speech using forced alignment, a special HMM called a "tee-model" can be inserted at word boundaries. A "tee-model" has a direct transition from the entry to the exit node. Therefore, it can be either aligned to a true pause if there is a silence in speech or completely skipped if there is no silence. Through forced alignment with a "tee-model" to identify inter-word pauses, Yuan et al. (2016) located 26,885 pauses in the 267 monologues in their dataset. The dataset also contained 100,212 words and 3058 pause fillers, of which 1192 were *e* and 1866 were *en*.

17.2.3 *Effect of Speaker Sex and Proficiency Level on Pauses and Pause Fillers*

The total number of pause fillers, pauses, and words for males and females and for different proficiency levels are listed in the top part of Table 17.1.

For each speaker, Yuan et al. (2016) computed five relative frequencies:

1. *e*/(*e* + *en*): the proportion of *e* in pause fillers
2. *e/words*: the number of *e* per word
3. *en/words*: the number of *en* per word
4. *(e + en)/words*: the number of pause fillers per word
5. *pauses/words:* the number of pauses (including all silent intervals) per word

Mixed-effects logistic regression models (Bates et al. 2015) were used to assess the effects of sex and proficiency level on the relative frequencies of pauses and pause fillers, in which "speaker" was treated as a random factor. The results are shown in the bottom part of Table 17.1, where the mean values of the five relative frequency measures are listed, with bold-italic numbers representing statistical significance at $p < 0.05$. Males used *e* more than females did, but there was no difference between them regarding the frequency of *en*. Therefore, the proportion of nasal-final pause fillers was higher in female than in male speakers, as was also found in a study on Germanic languages (Wieling et al. 2016). Proficiency did not appear to have affected the frequency of either *e* or *en*. With respect to the use of pauses, both sex and proficiency were a significant factor—males used more pauses than females did, and less proficient speakers also used more pauses.

17.3 Using Forced Alignment to Investigate Speech Variation

Yuan and Liberman (2015) employed skip-state HMMs to adapt forced alignment to the investigation of phonetic reduction and deletion. With the improved forced alignment method, they investigated the reduction of plosives and affricates in terms of duration in Mandarin broadcast news speech.

17.3.1 *Corpus*

The 1997 Mandarin Broadcast News Speech (HUB4-NE, LDC98S73) Corpus was used (Huang et al. 1997). Yuan and Liberman (2015) extracted "utterances" (defined as between-pause units that were manually time-stamped) from the corpus and listened to each to exclude those with background noise or music. Utterances from speakers whose names were not tagged in the corpus or from speakers with accented speech were also excluded. The final dataset consisted of 7849 utterances from 20 speakers.

17.3.2 Forced Alignment with Skip-State HMMs

Phonetic reduction is pervasive in natural speech (Johnson 2004). This is not only an important topic in linguistic research but also presents a great challenge in forced alignment and other speech technologies. Figure 17.2 shows three examples of the phoneme /j/ (which is /tɕ/ in IPA, an alveolo-palatal affricate) from the same speaker in the corpus. From both the waveforms and spectrograms, one can see that the first example is a full phonetic realization of the phoneme, which contains a complete closure followed by a portion of frication noise. The second example contains only an incomplete closure but no frication. The third example does not show any consonantal features, suggesting that the phoneme was deleted.

Apparently, non-skipping three-state HMMs (see Fig. 17.1) cannot handle severe reduction and deletion in natural speech. Yuan and Liberman (2015) modeled phonetic reduction and deletion by employing skip-state HMMs (as shown in Fig. 17.3), in which every state could be skipped. If all the states were skipped, the result would be a phone with zero duration (i.e., a phone that is deleted in the surface form but is still preserved in the lexicon or pronunciation model). In many cases, coarticulation and phonetic transitions remain even after a phone is "deleted," as can be seen in the third example of /j/ in Fig. 17.2.

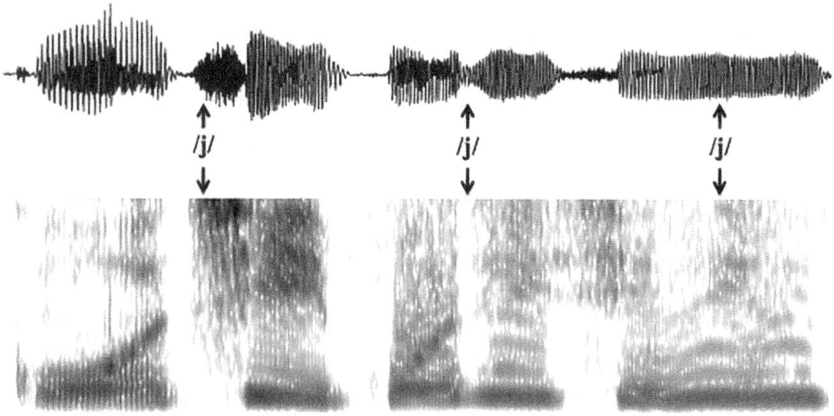

Fig. 17.2 Examples of variation in the phonetic realization of /j/: full, reduction, and deletion

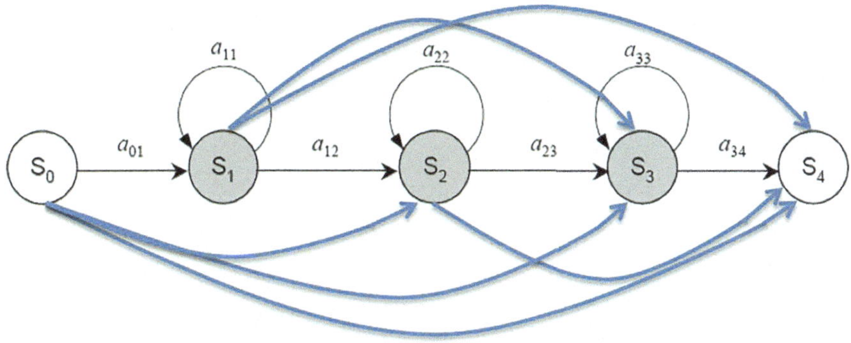

Fig. 17.3 HMM with skip-state transitions

Table 17.2 Mean durations of the four types of plosives and affricates

Consonant type	Aspiration	Frication	Duration (ms)
Unaspirated stops	–	–	50.2
/b, d, g/			Base
Unaspirated affricates	–	+	65.7
/z, zh, j/			≈ Base +15 (F)
Aspirated stops	+	–	85.4
/p, t, k/			≈ Base +35 (A)
Aspirated affricates	+	+	98.1
/c, ch, q/			≈ Base +15 (F) + 35 (A)

17.3.3 Reduction of Plosives and Affricates in Mandarin Broadcast News Speech

Resulting from forced alignment with skip-state HMMs for plosives and affricates, the mean durations of the four types of plosives and affricates are listed in Table 17.2, which shows the inherent durations of the four consonant types in ascending order: unaspirated stops (~50 ms), unaspirated affricates (~65 ms), aspirated stops (~85 ms), and aspirated affricates (~100 ms). Table 17.2 also shows that the two dimensions—aspiration and frication—in the production of these consonants are additive in terms of segment duration: the base duration (unaspirated stops) is ~50 ms; frication adds ~15 ms; and aspiration adds ~35 ms.

Figure 17.4 shows the duration distributions (cumulative percentages) of the four consonant types. For any given duration of 30 ms or longer, an inherently longer plosive/affricate is unlikely to be shorter than that duration than an inherently shorter one. This result suggests that the four types of plosives and fricatives had similar patterns of reduction (and strengthening) in terms of duration. However, at 10 and 20 ms (which represents a severe reduction or deletion), the cumulative percentages did not correlate with the inherent durations of the consonant types. The aspirated stops had higher cumulative percentages than the unaspirated affricates at 10 ms

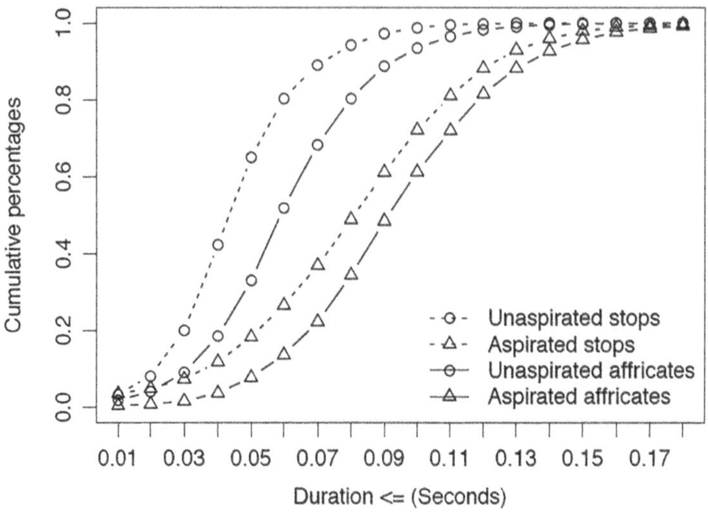

Fig. 17.4 Duration distributions of the four types of plosives and affricates

(3.5% vs. 1.9%) and 20 ms (4.9% vs. 4.1%), although the inherent duration of the aspirated stops was longer than that of the unaspirated affricates (and therefore less likely to be reduced if the correlation held). This result suggests that stops are more likely to be deleted than affricates in Mandarin broadcast news speech. It also suggests that reduction and deletion may result from different phonetic processes, rather than a continuum of the same process.

17.4 Improving Forced Alignment for Phonetics Research

17.4.1 Phone Boundary Models for Forced Alignment

A main drawback of the HMM-based forced alignment for phonetic segmentation is that phone boundaries are not represented in the model. The boundaries are simply derived from the alignment of phone states with frames. This is different from the manual phonetic segmentation process, in which the acoustic landmarks at phone boundaries (Stevens 2002), for example, an abrupt spectral change, are used to determine the location of a boundary. In an effort to overcome this drawback and improve forced alignment, Yuan et al. (2013) and Yuan et al. (2014) employed explicit phone boundary models within the HMM framework. The idea was to treat phones and phone boundaries as independent HMMs. A boundary was determined by the alignment of its own state with frames. The phone boundary models were a special one-state HMM (as shown in Fig. 17.5), in which the state could not repeat itself.

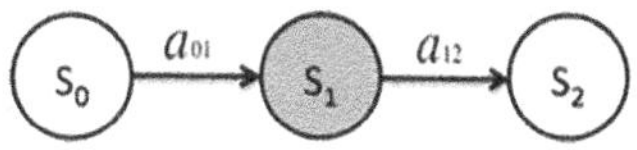

Fig. 17.5 Special one-state HMM for phone boundaries with transition probabilities $a_{01} = a_{12} = 1$

The special one-state phone boundary HMMs were combined with three-state phone HMMs. Given a phonetic transcription, phone boundaries were inserted between phones. For example, "*sil i g e sil*" became "*sil sil_i i i_g g g_e e e_sil sil*". The boundary states were tied through decision tree-based clustering, similar to triphone state tying in speech recognition (Young et al. 1994). The results demonstrated that using special one-state HMMs for phone boundaries significantly improved forced alignment accuracy in both the English TIMIT Corpus (~25% relative error reduction) (Yuan et al. 2013) and the Mandarin Hub-4 Broadcast News Speech Corpus (~40% relative error reduction) (Yuan et al. 2014).

17.4.2 Phone Boundary Models for Automatic Scoring of Mandarin Proficiency

It is well known that some phonetic contrasts are more difficult in language learning. The retroflex consonants (/zh, ch, sh, r/) in Mandarin Chinese, for example, are difficult to learn for many speakers whose first language does not have retroflex sounds. The pronunciation of these consonants is a prominent cue for native speakers to perceive accent. Phone boundaries may also contain useful information about a speaker's language proficiency. The timing of voicing in stop consonants, which is measured by voice onset time (VOT), is a boundary-bound phonetic feature that has been extensively studied in linguistics (Cho and Ladefoged 1999; Lisker and Abramson 1964). The VOT of stops varies across languages, for example, individuals who learn a second language (L2) later in life often fail to produce consonants with authentic VOT values in L2 (Flege 1991).

In this study, having both phone and phone boundary models in forced alignment, we compared the "goodness" of different phones and phone boundaries in the automatic scoring of Mandarin proficiency. Following the method in Witt and Young (2000), we computed a goodness of pronunciation score for every phone and phone boundary in the Putonghua Shuiping Ceshi Corpus. The idea was to find the posterior probability of a phone p given its acoustic segment $O^{(p)}$, $P(p|O^{(p)})$, which was approximated by the likelihood of $O^{(p)}$corresponding to phone p, divided by the maximum likelihood of $O^{(p)}$, as shown in the equation below:

$$\text{GOP}_{(p)} = \log \frac{p\left(o^{(p)}|p\right)}{\max p_{q \in Q}\left(o^{(p)}|q\right)}$$

where Q is the set of all phone and boundary models trained in "standard" Mandarin speech. The acoustic segment boundaries of $O^{(p)}$ and the corresponding likelihood (the numerator) were determined by forced alignment. To compute the maximum likelihood of $O^{(p)}$ (the denominator), all utterances were recognized using the acoustic models and an unconstrained phone and boundary loop. The likelihood of $O^{(p)}$ corresponding to the best hypothesis within its boundaries (as it may contain more than one phone or boundary) was used to approximate its maximum likelihood. The goodness of the pronunciation scores was expected to have a positive correlation with human scores—a lower goodness of pronunciation score suggested that the phone or boundary fit the "standard" models less well and hence should have received a lower proficiency score.

For every speaker in the dataset, in this study, we calculated his/her mean goodness of pronunciation score on every phoneme. The phone boundaries were grouped into two types—within-syllable (i.e., boundaries between an initial and a final) and cross-syllable (i.e., boundaries between a final and an initial)—and a mean goodness of pronunciation score was calculated for each type. For each phone and boundary type, we then computed the correlation between all speakers' mean goodness of pronunciation scores and their proficiency scores. The results are listed in Table 17.3.

As can be seen from Table 17.3, correlation varied greatly across phonemes. The two boundary types had the highest correlations, suggesting that phone boundaries are more helpful than phonemes in automatic proficiency scoring. Within-syllable boundaries worked better than cross-syllable boundaries. Among the phonemes, the retroflex consonants, /zh, ch, sh/, and the vowel following these consonants, /iii/, were better than the others. The vowel /e/ was the only phoneme that had a negative correlation, although the correlation was not significant. The vowel /e/ appears in the possessive particle (~s) 的 *de0* in Mandarin Chinese, which is the most frequent character in the language. In the dataset of this work, there were 23,501 /e/ tokens, and 15,919 (64.7%) of the tokens were with the character 的 *de0*.

17.5 Conclusion

In this chapter, we illustrated the integration of forced alignment, a technique developed in automatic speech recognition, into corpus-based phonetics research. We discussed three aspects of this research: forced alignment as a tool for phonetic segmentation, forced alignment as a method for investigating speech variation, and efforts to improve the technique of forced alignment itself. The integration of techniques from speech technology is helping the field of phonetics to enter a new era—a movement from the study of small, mostly artificial datasets to the analysis of published corpora of natural speech that are thousands of times larger.

Much remains to be done. In particular, researchers need to do a better job of bridging the gap between standard orthographic transcriptions and phonetic representations. Because natural speech is so highly variable, simple word-to-phoneme

Table 17.3 Correlations between goodness of pronunciation and proficiency scores

Phone or boundary	Correlation (Pearson's r)	Phone or boundary	Correlation (Pearson's r)
within-syl	**0.472**	G	0.157
cross-syl	**0.445**	R	0.144
iii	**0.422**	B	0.141
sh	**0.383**	uan	0.126
zh	**0.327**	M	0.125
s	0.277	iao	0.120
a	0.271	iu	0.114
ch	**0.269**	I	0.114
ian	0.256	ei	0.112
i	0.245	N	0.111
ing	0.238	eng	0.110
d	0.225	en	0.102
h	0.225	ie	0.100
an	0.224	K	0.060
l	0.214	ong	0.054
z	0.210	uo	0.052
q	0.202	ao	0.045
t	0.194	iang	0.041
j	0.192	U	0.036
f	0.190	ang	0.029
in	0.182	V	0.019
x	0.179	ii	0.007
ui	0.174	***E***	***−0.004***

Correlations lower than 0.120 were not significant

mapping (either using a pronouncing dictionary or grapheme-to-phoneme rules) may not always generate phone sequences that contain the correct pronunciation. Moreover, orthographic transcriptions are often inaccurate or incomplete, typically omitting most disfluencies and self-corrections. Future research needs to do a better job of modeling pronunciation variation (e.g., deletion, reduction, and insertion), disfluencies, and imperfect transcription in forced alignment.

References

Bates, Douglas, Martin Mächler, Ben Bolker, and Steve Walker. 2015. Fitting linear mixed-effects models using lme4. *Journal of Statistical Software* 67:1–48.

Cho, Taehong, and Peter Ladefoged. 1999. Variation and universals in VOT: Evidence from 18 languages. *Journal of Phonetics* 27:207–229.

Cucchiarini, Catia. 1993. Phonetic transcription: A methodological and empirical study, Ph.D. thesis. University of Nijmegen, Netherlands.

Evanini, Keelan, Stephen Isard, and Mark Liberman 2009. Automatic formant extraction for sociolinguistic analysis of large corpora. *Interspeech* 2009:1655–1658.

Flege, James Emil. 1991. Age of learning affects the authenticity of voice-onset time (VOT) in stop consonants produced in a second language. *Journal of the Acoustical Society of America* 89: 395–411.

Fox, Michelle Annette Minnick. 2006. Usage-based effects in Latin American Spanish syllable-final/s/lenition. Doctoral dissertation. University of Pennsylvania, Philadelphia, PA.

Garofolo, John S., Lori F. Lamel, William M. Fisher, Jonathan G. Fiscus, David S. Pallett, Nancy L. Dahlgren, and Victor Zue. 1993. TIMIT acoustic-phonetic continuous speech corpus LDC93S1. Philadelphia, PA: Linguistic Data Consortium. Available at https://catalog.ldc.upenn.edu/LDC93S1. Accessed 2 April 2019.

Godfrey, John J., Edward C. Holliman, and Jane McDaniel. 1992. SWITCHBOARD: Telephone speech corpus for research and development. In *Proceedings of ICASSP 1992*, 517–520. San Francisco, California. Available at https://ieeexplore.ieee.org/stamp/stamp.jsp?tp=&arnumber=225858. Accessed 2 April 2019.

Hosom, John-Paul. 2000. *Automatic time alignment of phonemes using acoustic-phonetic information*. Ph.D. thesis. Oregon Graduate Institute of Science and Technology, Beaverton, OR.

Hosom, John-Paul. 2009. Speaker-independent phoneme alignment using transition-dependent states. *Speech Communication* 51:352–368.

Huang, Shudong, Jing Liu, Xuling Wu, Lei Wu, Yongmin Yan, and Zhoakai Qin. 1997. Mandarin broadcast news speech (HUB4-NE) LDC98S73. Philadelphia, PA: Linguistic Data Consortium. Available at https://catalog.ldc.upenn.edu/LDC98S73. Accessed 2 April 2019.

Jelinek, Frederick. 1976. Continuous speech recognition by statistical methods. In *Proceedings of the IEEE* 64(4):532–556. Available at https://ieeexplore.ieee.org/stamp/stamp.jsp?tp=&arnumber=1454428. Accessed 2 April 2019.

Johnson, Keith. 2004. Massive reduction in conversational American English. In *Spontaneous speech: Data and analysis*, ed. Kiyoko Yoneyama and Kikuo Maekawa. In *Proceedings of the 1st Session of the 10th International Symposium*, 29–54. Tokyo, Japan. Available at http://citeseerx.ist.psu.edu/viewdoc/download?doi=10.1.1.142.5012&rep=rep1&type=pdf. Accessed 2 April 2019.

Labov, William, Ingrid Rosenfelder, and Josef Fruehwald. 2013. One hundred years of sound change in Philadelphia: Linear incrementation, reversal, and reanalysis. *Language* 89:30–65.

Leung, Hong C., and Victor W. Zue. 1984. A procedure for automatic alignment of phonetic transcription with continuous speech. In *Proceedings of ICASSP 1984*, 73–76. San Diego, California. Available at https://ieeexplore.ieee.org/stamp/stamp.jsp?tp=&arnumber=1172426. Accessed 2 April 2019.

Lisker, Leigh, and Arthur Abramson. 1964. A cross-language study of voicing in initial stops: Acoustical measurements. *Word* 20:384–422.

Sonderegger, Morgan, and Joseph Keshet. 2012. Automatic measurement of voice onset time using discriminative structured prediction. *Journal of the Acoustical Society of America* 132:3965–3979.

Stevens, Kenneth N. 2002. Toward a model for lexical access based on acoustic landmarks and distinctive features. *Journal of the Acoustical Society of America* 111:1872–1891.

Wieling, Martijn, Jack Grieve, Gosse Bouma, Josef Fruehwald, John Coleman, and Mark Liberman. 2016. Variation and change in the use of hesitation markers in Germanic languages. *Language Dynamics and Change* 199–234.

Wightman, Colin W., and David T. Talkin, D. 1997. The aligner: Text to speech alignment using Markov Models. In *Progress in speech synthesis*, ed. Jan P. H. van Santen, Richard W. Sproat, Joseph P. Olive, and Julia Hirschberg, 313–323. New York: Springer Verlag.

Witt, Silke M., and Steve J. Young. 2000. Phone-level pronunciation scoring and assessment for interactive language learning. *Speech Communication* 30:95–108.

Young, Steve J., J. J. Odell, and Philip C. Woodland. 1994. Tree-based state tying for high accuracy acoustic modeling. In *Proceedings of the ARPA Workshop on Human Language Technology*, 307–312. Plainsboro, New Jersey. Available at https://www.aclweb.org/anthology/H94-1062. Accessed 2 April 2019.

Yuan, Jiahong, and Mark Liberman. 2015. Investigating consonant reduction in Mandarin Chinese with improved forced alignment. In *Proceedings of Interspeech 2015*, 2675–2678. Dresden, Germany. Available at http://languagelog.ldc.upenn.edu/myl/MandarinConsonantReduction.pdf. Accessed 2 April 2019.

Yuan, Jiahong, Neville Ryant, Mark Liberman, Andreas Stolcke, Vikramjit Mitra, and Wen Wang. 2013. Automatic phonetic segmentation using boundary models. In *Proceedings of Interspeech 2013*: 2306–2310. Lyon, France. Available at https://www.researchgate.net/publication/286363369_Automatic_phonetic_segmentation_using_boundary_models. Accessed 2 April 2019.

Yuan, Jiahong, Neville Ryant, and Mark Liberman. 2014. Automatic phonetic segmentation in Mandarin Chinese: Boundary models, glottal features and tone. In *Proceedings of ICASSP 2014*: 2539–2543. Florence, Italy. Available at https://ieeexplore.ieee.org/stamp/stamp.jsp?tp=&arnumber=6854058. Accessed 2 April 2019.

Yuan, Jiahong, Xiaoying Xu, Wei Lai, and Mark Liberman. 2016. Pauses and pause fillers in Mandarin monologue speech: The effects of sex and proficiency. In *Proceedings of Speech Prosody 2016*, 1167–1170. Boston, Massachusetts. Available at https://pdfs.semanticscholar.org/7f15/be1f4954ec9f9e7600264666bcae2119e5bb.pdf. Accessed 2 April 2019.

Chapter 18
The Extraction of Linguistic Knowledge and Construction of Linguistic Resources

Yulin Yuan, Qiang Li, Guoxiang Wu, and Ren Zhou

Abstract In recent years, our research team has completed a series of studies and established a cognition-based, computation-oriented linguistic approach and practical technology roadmap. In one of these studies, a paraphrasing template library for Chinese noun-noun compounds (NNCs) was constructed to reveal implicit predicates, and an automatic paraphrasing system was developed to explain the meaning of the whole construction. Another study focused on the automatic paraphrasing of *ba*-constructions in Chinese, classified into different types based on the sentence patterns they can be transformed into. A pattern recognition-based program was then developed to automatically paraphrase the construction and transform the syntactic formation of *ba*-constructions. This chapter will introduce the structure of a lexical knowledge base and the construction of a Chinese verbal and adjectival valency dictionary, as well as a nominal qualia dictionary and a semantic role system for Chinese. Finally, a discussion on how the lexical knowledge base can be employed to make inferences and facilitate the computing of content in natural language processing will be presented.

Keywords Computational linguistics · Implicit predicate · Noun-noun compound (NNC) · *Ba*-sentence · Lexical knowledge base

---

Y. Yuan (✉)
Department of Chinese Language and Literature, Faculty of Arts and Humanities, University of Macau, Macau, China

Department of Chinese Language and Literature, Peking University, Beijing, China
e-mail: yuanyl@pku.edu.cn

Q. Li
College of Liberal Arts, Shanghai University, Shanghai, China

G. Wu
College of Foreign Languages, Huaqiao University, Quanzhou, China
e-mail: wugx@hqu.edu.cn

R. Zhou
Department of Chinese Language and Literature, Peking University, Beijing, China

C.-R. Huang et al. (eds.), *Chinese Language Resources*, Text, Speech and Language Technology 49, https://doi.org/10.1007/978-3-031-38913-9_18

18.1 Cognition-Based Computational Linguistic Research

Classic cognitive science is loyal to the basic belief that the computer can serve as a model of the human brain, which can in turn be used to simulate the human cognitive process. Just as the human mental process can be interpreted as a computational process in which symbols are manipulated, the process of human language understanding can be regarded as a computational process in which knowledge is presented. This cognitive point of view is fully manifested in Winograd (1983), who posited that the use of language is a knowledge-based communicative process. When people speak or understand an utterance, mental images related to the objects described or events in the external world are constructed in their brains. These mental images can be referred to as internal language. With this as the starting point, Yuan et al. 袁毓林等 (2010) proposed the following technology roadmap for computational linguistic research:

- **Cognitive modeling.** The aim of cognitive modeling is to establish a cognitive model for semantic situations, which involves events, relations, or states denoted by words or phrases.
- **Logical modeling.** The aim of logical modeling is to formulate logical expressions to reflect the relations between situational elements. In addition, semantic axioms are created to express the relations among these logical expressions.
- **Linguistic modeling.** Linguistic modeling aims to construct a lexico-grammatical knowledge base, which stores the lexical meaning and syntactic information of words and sentences, especially the descriptions of predicates and arguments, with examples showing their lineal configuration. Such a knowledge base is connected not only to the network of situations but also to instances (e.g., sentences) that illustrate the events (or relations or states) in real texts.
- **Computational modeling.** After proper algorithms are used and computer programming is complete in computational modeling, a computational knowledge platform is built and applied to specific natural language processing (NLP) systems and problem-solution systems.

The general purpose of the technology roadmap is, on the one hand, to establish a cognitive research paradigm for the use of human language; on the other hand, such a paradigm can be translated into specific algorithmic rules and formal expressions by the computer, with the aim of simulating the cognitive process of the human brain. In so doing, studies in cognitive linguistics are closely integrated with NLP applications. It is believed that linguistic research and computer science will continually benefit each other with this roadmap.

In recent years, we have put into practice the above mentioned cognition-based, computation-oriented linguistic approach and completed a number of studies on Chinese grammar. In Sects. 18.2 and 18.3, two case studies will be presented, respectively.

18.2 Understanding Chinese NNCs

18.2.1 Implicit Predicates in NNCs

The features of modifier-head noun-noun compounds (NNCs) are "strong productivity, simple compositionality, and high ambiguity" (Wang et al. 王萌等 2010: 3). It is because of these features that NNCs draw much attention from both theoretical and computational linguists. According to Wang et al. 王萌等 (2010: 4), studies on how to interpret the meaning of NNCs have been conducive to a number of NLP tasks, including information retrieval, question answering systems, and machine translation.

To properly analyze NNCs, Yuan 袁毓林 (1995) proposed the concept of "implicit predicate," which is a predicate that can be inserted in an NNC to provide a full and correct understanding of the meaning of the NNC, as shown in (18.1) and (18.2) below:

(18.1)	红木家具	
	hóngmù__jiājù	
	rose wood__furniture	
	rose wood furniture	
	→	红木制造的家具
		Hóngmù__**zhìzào**__de__jiājù
		rose wood__**made**__PART__furniture
		the furniture made of rose wood
(18.2)	摩托妈妈	
	mótuō__māmā	
	motorcycle__mother	
	the motorcycle mother	
	→	骑/坐/造/修摩托的妈妈
		qí/zuò/zào/xiū__mótuō__de__māmā
		ride/take/make/repair__motorcycle__PART__mother
		the mother who rides/takes/makes/repairs the motorcycle

To understand the ambiguous 摩托妈妈 *mótuō māmā* "motorcycle mother," different implicit predicates, such as 骑/坐/造/修 *qí/zuò/zào/xiū* "ride/take/make/repair," can be inserted for disambiguation.

The remaining problem is how to determine the implicit predicate in an NNC automatically without personal subjectiveness. Can an implicit predicate be generated by a rule-based mechanism? If not, the concept of implicit predicates may be thought of as redundant, unnatural, or much too arbitrary. The next section will introduce a computer program capable of automatically discovering and presenting the implicit predicates of NNCs.

18.2.2 GLT as a Solution to Finding the Implicit Predicates of NNCs

The Generative Lexicon Theory (GLT) provides an intelligent solution to determining implicit predicates in NNCs. The GLT was formally put forward by Pustejovsky (1991, 1995), and since then, it has drawn considerable attention in the fields of linguistics and NLP. The theory takes qualia structure (QS) as one of its core components. For a lexical item, its QS is used as a method for expressing its semantic structure, demonstrating "the essential attributes of an object as defined by the lexical item" (Pustejovsky 1991, p. 419), including the constituents of the object, the forms it takes, the way it is created, and the function it serves.

The concept of QS originated from Aristotle's four causes of knowledge—the material cause, the formal cause, the efficient cause, and the final cause. On this basis, the GLT established four qualia roles in the QS—formal (FOR), constitutive (CON), telic (TEL), and agentive (AGE) (Pustejovsky 1995, pp. 85–86). The formal role "distinguishes the object within a larger domain," including orientation, magnitude, shape, and dimensionality (Pustejovsky 1995, p. 85). The constitutive role is used to describe "the relation between an object and its constituents, or proper parts," including material, weight, parts, and component elements (ibid). The telic role describes purposes and functions of the object (Pustejovsky 1995, p. 86). The agentive role is used to describe "factors involved in the origin or 'bringing about' of an object," including creators and causal relations (Pustejovsky 1995). The QS of a lexical item actually presents the knowledge of relevant objects, events, and relations. In this sense, the QS provides a conceptual structure for and a formal solution to the description and prediction of the meaning of an NNC.

According to our analysis, the implicit predicate between the two nouns basically belongs to the telic or agentive role of N1 or N2. For example, the meaning of 摩托妈妈 *mótuō māmā* "motorcycle mother" may be paraphrased as 骑/坐/造/修摩托的妈妈 *qí/zuò/zào/xiū mótuō de māmā* "the mother who rides/takes/makes/repairs a motorcycle." In this paraphrase, *qí/zuò* "ride/take" is the telic role of *mótuō* "motorcycle" and *zào/xiū* "make/repair" is the agentive role.

18.2.3 Automatic Paraphrasing System for Chinese NNCs

Wei and Yuan 魏雪, 袁毓林 (2013) examined and analyzed 850 Chinese NNCs (N1 + N2), in which N1 was the modifier of N2. These 850 instances were handled by 2 major steps:

1. All semantic categories of N1s and N2s were annotated according to the SKCC[1] and their qualia roles to construct a noun-verb collocation database, which also included some other syntactic, semantic, and phonological information (see Table 18.1).
2. Based on the paraphrasing verbs and the semantic category of N1 and N2, a noun-noun collocation database, which included paraphrasing templates, was built for NNCs (see Table 18.2).

From the analysis of the 850 NNC instances, 326 patterns of semantic categories (hereafter semantic patterns) and 208 paraphrasing templates were acquired. Some new random data samples were introduced to test the predicting power and the performance of the patterns and templates.

Wei and Yuan 魏雪, 袁毓林 (2014) designed an automatic program to paraphrase Chinese NNCs. The program includes five functional modules and respective algorithms. The process involves the following steps:

1. For each NNC, word segmentation and parts-of-speech (POS) tagging are conducted to acquire N1 + N2 instances.
2. The semantic categories of N1 and N2, namely, S1 and S2, are retrieved from the noun-verb collocation database.
3. The paraphrasing template(s) specific to the semantic pattern S1 + S2 is(are) collected from the noun-noun collocation database.
4. According to the requirement of the paraphrasing template(s), the verb and its qualia roles of the related nouns are also collected.
5. The verb, N1, and N2 are then inserted into the paraphrasing template to generate the paraphrase.

Take 农民专家 *nóngmín zhuānjiā* "farmer expert" as an example. The automatic paraphrasing of the NNC is described as follows:

1. After word segmentation and POS tagging, the returned word string is "*nóngmín*/n *zhuānjiā*/n."
2. The program examines the noun-verb collocation database and returns the results: the semantic category of *nóngmín* is 身份 *shēnfèn* "identity" and that of *zhuānjiā* is also *shēnfèn*.
3. The program examines the noun-noun collocation database and returns the semantic pattern "*shēnfèn* + *shēnfèn*," under which there are two paraphrasing templates: (1) "*shēnfèn* + *shì* + N1 + *De* + N2" (identity + is + N1 + *De* + N2) and (2) "V2 + N1 + *De* + N2" (V2 + N1 + *De* + N2), in which V2 is the telic role of N2.
4. The program consults the noun-verb collocation database and returns the telic role 研究 *yánjiū* "research" of N2 *zhuānjiā*.

[1]The Semantic Knowledge-base of Contemporary Chinese (SKCC), developed by the Institute of Computational Linguistics at Peking University, is a large-scale Chinese semantic database that stores massive amounts of paradigmatic and syntactic information on 66,539 Chinese words.

Table 18.1 Noun-verb collocation database

Noun-verb							
Noun	POS	Pinyin	Semantic	Semantic category	Telic role	Agentive role	Is a content noun
哀荣 (posthumous honor)	N	*ai1rong2*		抽象事物 (abstraction)			No
哀思 (sorrow)	N	*ai1si1*		意识 (cognition)	怀念 (miss)	表达、传达 (express, convey)	No
癌 (cancer)	N	*ai2*	也叫癌瘤或癌肿 (also called *ailiu* or *aizhong*)	生理 (physiological_state)	控制 (control)	罹患 (suffer)	No
矮凳 (low stool)	N	*ai3deng4*		家具 (furniture)	坐、蹲 (sit, squat)	制作 (make)	No
暗号 (secret code)	N	*an4hao4*		信息 (information)	传递 (express)	编辑、写 (edit, write)	Yes

Table 18.2 Noun-noun collocation database

Noun_Noun				
Noun 1	Noun 2	Number of template	Template	Type of verb
处所 (location)	地表物 (land)	1	位于 + N1 + 的 + N2 (located in + N1 + *De* + N2)	
材料 (material)	处所 (location)	1	V2 + N1 + 的 + N2	功用角色 (telic)
创作物 (works)	个人 (individual)	1	V1 + N1 + 的 + N2	施成角色 (agentive)
草 (grass)	身份 (identity)	2	V1 + N1 + 的 + N2	施成角色|功用角色/功用角色 (agentive | telic/ telic)
			V2 + N1 + 的 + N2	
建筑物 (building)	身份 (identity)	3	V1 + N1 + 的 + N2	施成角色/功用角色 (agentive/telic)
			V2 + N1 + 的 + N2	
			从事 + 跟N1有关的行业 + 的 + N2 (engaged in + N1-related business + *De* + N2)	

5. The program inserts V2, N1, and N2 into the two paraphrasing templates, and two paraphrases with the least ambiguity were generated accordingly: (1) "*shēnfèn* + *shì* + *nóngmín* + *De* + *zhuānjiā*" (the expert whose identity is a farmer) and (2) "*yánjiū* + *nóngmín* + *De* + *zhuānjiā*" (the expert who researches the farmer). The program then terminates.

Such a knowledge-based processing module can effectively analyze Internet users' queries and capture their searching intentions.

18.3 Understanding Chinese *ba*-Constructions

18.3.1 Transformation-Based Analysis of ba-*Constructions*

Chinese *ba*-constructions are notorious for their semantic complexity and configurational diversity. In addition, their transformation from related subject-verb-object (SVO) sentences, passive *bei*-sentences, verb-copy sentences, and causative sentences is particularly irregular. Obviously, understanding *ba*-constructions is a challenging task in NLP.

Wang and Yuan 王璐璐, 袁毓林 (2015) developed an auto-paraphrasing method for transforming *ba*-constructions into related sentence patterns, rendering them easier to process, with their basic sentential proposition meanings maintained. Wang and Yuan 王璐璐, 袁毓林 (2015) decomposed Chinese *ba*-constructions into three parts, the predicate (VP) and the pre- and post-*ba* constituents (X and

Y), as in X + *Ba*-Y + VP. In this formula, X can either serve as an argument of VP, be an additional constituent, or be absent. Y is a compulsory constituent, commonly serving as an argument of VP. VP cannot be a bare verb and is usually a predicate-aspect,[2] adverbial-head, predicate-object, or predicate-complement construction.

The inner structures and semantic features of X, Y, and VP provide certain useful clues to predict the possibility of transforming *ba*-constructions into other sentence patterns. For example, if the VP of a *ba*-sentence has the semantic feature of [+ strong action], and the subject X has the feature of [+ high animacy], then the *ba*-sentence could be transformed into a corresponding SVO sentence, passive sentence, and patient-subject sentence (a kind of topic sentence), as shown in (18.3) below:

(18.3) 他把杯子打破了。
tā__bǎ __bēizi__dǎ-pò__le.
he__BA__cup__hit-broken__PERF
He broke the cup.
→ (a) 他打破了杯子。
tā__dǎ-pò__le__bēizi. (SVO sentence)
he__hit-broken__ PERF__cup
He broke the cup.
(b) 杯子被他打破了。
bēizi__bèi__tā__dǎ-pò__le. (passive sentence)
cup__BEI__he__hit-broken__PERF
The cup was broken by him.
(c) 杯子他打破了。
bēizi__tā__dǎ-pò__le. (patient-subject sentence)
cup__he__hit-broken__PERF
It is the cup that he broke.

If the VP of a *ba*-sentence has the semantic feature of [+ adhesion], then the *ba*-sentence can only be transformed into a passive sentence, not a patient-subject sentence or an SVO sentence, as shown in (18.4) below:

(18.4) 他把照片挂在了墙上。
tā__bǎ__zhàopiān__guà__zài__le__qiáng__shàng.
he__BA__photo__hang__on__PERF__wall__PART
He hung the painting on the wall.
→ (a) 照片被他挂在了墙上。
zhàopiān__bèi__tā__guà__zài__le__qiáng__shàng.
photo__BEI__he__hang__on__ PERF__wall__PART
The photo was hung on the wall by him.
(b) ? 照片他挂在了墙上。

(continued)

[2] If the predicate takes an aspectual marker, it is referred to as a predicate-aspect structure, for example, 他把房子卖了 *tā bǎ fángzǐ mài le* "he sold the house," in which 卖 *mài* "sell" is the predicate and 了 *le* is the (perfective) aspect.

? zhàopiān_tā_guà_zài_le_qiáng_shàng. (topic sentence)
? photo_he_hang_on_ASP_wall_PART
(c) *他挂照片在墙上。
* tā_guà_zhàopiān_zài_qiáng_shàng.
* he_hang_photo_on_wall_PART

Wang and Yuan 王璐璐, 袁毓林 (2015) classified Chinese *ba*-constructions into 37 subtypes. Based on this classification and the description of its syntactic-semantic features, a linguistic and computational model was constructed, and an operable system was developed for the computer to distinguish different types of *ba*-constructions.

18.3.2 *Formal Research-Based System to Paraphrase and Transform* ba-*Constructions*

Based on the classification of Wang and Yuan 王璐璐, 袁毓林 (2015), Wang et al. 王璐璐等 (2015) designed a program that automatically paraphrases and transforms *ba*-constructions, as follows:

1. A *ba*-sentence is input into the text box of the system.
2. The system identifies and classifies the *ba*-sentence automatically and stores the results in a temporary file.
3. According to the classification, the system searches for the paraphrasing template (PT) and syntactic transformation template(s) (STT) for relevant types of *ba*-sentences, inserts the identified elements into the corresponding PT and STT, and paraphrases the *ba*-sentence and transforms it into alternative expressions.
4. The system presents the paraphrase(s) and the transformational expression(s) in the corresponding text boxes.
5. Finally, the system presents the results of the syntactic analysis in a tree form.

For example, the *ba*-sentence 老干部把经验传授给新干部 *lǎo gànbù bǎ jīngyàn chuánshòu gěi xīn gànbù* "old cadres taught their experience to new cadres" can be paraphrased and transformed using the following steps:

1. The system first identifies the sentence and makes a syntactic analysis of it, thus being informed of its syntactic and semantic structure. The syntactic information includes NP1 = 老干部 *lǎo gànbù* "senior cadres," NP2 = 经验 *jīngyàn* "experience," NP3 = 新干部 *xīn gànbù* "new cadres," and ROOT = 传授 *chuánshòu* "teach." The semantic information includes A (agent) = *lǎo gànbù*, P (patent) = *jīngyàn*, D (dative) = *xīn gànbù*, and ROOT = *chuánshòu*.
2. The system maps the syntactic-semantic information onto different types of *ba*-constructions, automatically identifies the current sentence as the first type, and annotates *ba* as "Ba1." This annotation will be used to facilitate later syntactic analysis.

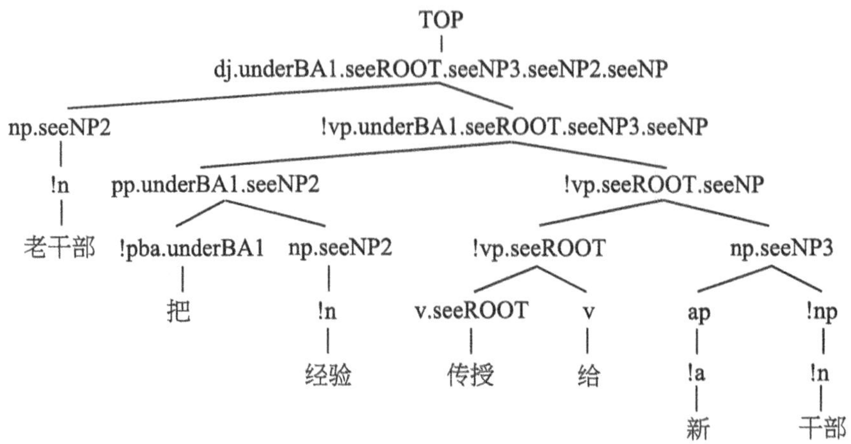

Fig. 18.1 Results of the computer program

3. According to the PT(s) and the STT(s) of "Ba1," the syntactic-semantic information is inserted into the corresponding slots. In this case, the PT is "NP1 + VP + NP2, *shǐ de* (so that) + NP3 + *huòxī* (be informed of) + NP2," and the output is 老干部传授经验, 使得新干部获悉经验 *lǎo gànbù chuánshòu jīngyàn, shǐ de xīn gànbù huòxī jīngyàn* "senior cadres taught experiences, so that new cadres are informed of experiences"; the STTs include "NP1 + VP + NP2 + *Gei* + NP3; NP2 + Bei + NP1 + VP + *Gei* + NP3; NP2, NP1 + VP + *Gei* + NP3," and the output is a set of transformational expressions, including those in (18.5) below:

(18.5a)	老干部传授经验给新干部。
	lǎo gànbù__chuánshòu__jīngyàn__gěi__xīn gànbù.
	senior cadres(NP1)__teach(VP)__experience(NP2)__give(Gei)__new cadres(NP3)
	Senior cadres taught experiences to new cadres.
(18.5b)	经验被老干部传授给新干部。
	jīngyàn__bèi__lǎo gànbù__chuánshòu__gěi__xīn gànbù.
	experience(NP2)__BEI__senior cadres(NP1)__teach(VP)__give(Gei)__new cadres(NP3)
	Experiences were taught to new cadres by senior cadres.
(18.5c)	经验, 老干部传授给新干部。
	jīngyàn,__lǎo gànbù__chuánshòu__gěi__xīn gànbù.
	experience(NP2),__senior cadres(NP1)__teach(VP)__give(Gei)__new cadres(NP3)
	Experiences, senior cadres taught to new cadres.

The input, the output and their transformational expressions are summed up as follows (Fig. 18.1):

系统输入 (input sentence):	老干部把经验传授给新干部
释义输出 (output paraphrase):	老干部传授经验, 使得新干部获悉经验

(continued)

变换输出 (transformation):	老干部传授经验给新干部;
	经验被老干部传授给新干部;
	经验，老干部传授给新干部

Wang et al.'s 王璐璐等 (2015) program reduces the complexity in identifying different types of *ba*-sentences and provides a fine pre-treatment for a machine translation system.

18.4 Lexical Valency, Semantic Roles, and Construction of Lexical Knowledge Resources

18.4.1 Chinese Valency Grammar

"Valency," which was originally a chemical term, refers to the number of nominal constituent(s) that a predicate can govern in a linguistic field. With regard to the valency of the Chinese predicate verb, in-depth research has been carried out by numerous scholars in the last three decades. Moreover, Okuda 奥田宽 (1982), Liu 刘丹青 (1987), and Tan 谭景春 (1992) conducted research on the valency of Chinese adjectives and relevant syntactic transformation, while Yuan 袁毓林 (1992) discussed the ambiguity caused by the valency of some Chinese nouns.

Despite the controversies among different scholars over issues about the nature, criteria, and testing methods of verbal valency, as well as the syntactic frame in which the valent value is judged, Yuan 袁毓林 (1998/2010) integrated predicate logic, dependency grammar, and the argument structure theory into valency grammar; investigated the valent structure of the Chinese verb and the ways to allocate valency; and studied how argument roles can be classified, conflated, and transformed. On this basis, Yuan 袁毓林 (2010) proposed the concept of "valence hierarchy," in which the following four categories are identified—link, item, position, and argument:

1. Link refers to the number of nominal constituent(s) (playing different semantic roles) to which a verb relates in various sentences.
2. Item refers to the number of nominal constituent(s) to which a verb relates in one sentence (including the nominal constituent[s] introduced by a preposition).
3. Position refers to the number of nominal constituent(s) to which a verb relates in one sentence without the use of a preposition.
4. Argument refers to the number of nominal constituent(s) to which a verb relates in a simple sentence.

In addition, Yuan 袁毓林 (2007) annotated a number of news texts and identified necessary or optional arguments, so as to propose the following hierarchical classification for arguments (see Fig. 18.2). This hierarchical system of semantic roles

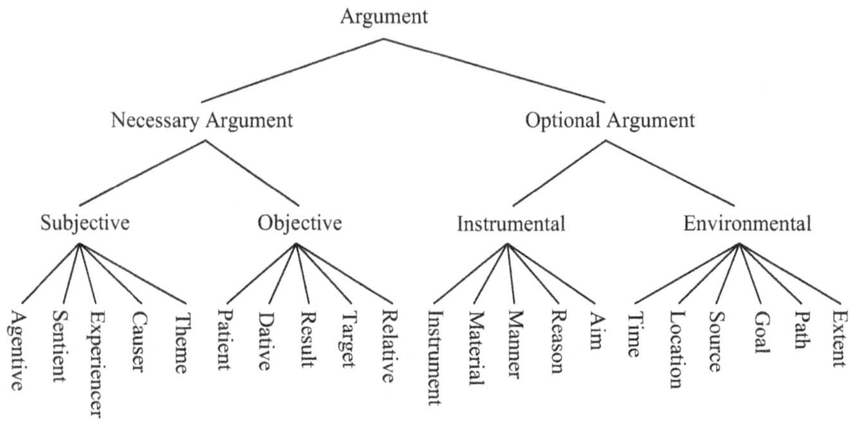

Fig. 18.2 Hierarchical system of semantic roles

finely demonstrates the relationship between the predicate and its arguments. With this hierarchy, arguments can be clearly distinguished and defined according to the roles they play in a sentence. For the computer to understand the meaning of a sentence, this instantialized knowledge of argument roles is an important resource, especially when it is used to make inferences based on natural language understanding.

18.4.2 Chinese Predicate Valency Dictionaries

Based on valency research and the system of semantic roles, Yuan 袁毓林 (2013) proposed a consistent, unified framework to describe the semantic structure of Chinese predicates (including verbs and adjectives). The framework is composed of two major parts:

1. A set of semantic roles played by various arguments governed by a given sense of a predicate (one lexical item may have two or more senses)
2. A set of syntactic formats that configure the predicate and its arguments

For example, the verb 吃 *chī* "eat" can be described as follows:

吃 *chī* "eat" <a verb taking a nominal object, neutral>
To have food; to chew food in the mouth and then swallow
[1] Semantic roles
Agent A: the person or animal who eats something
Patient P: the thing that the agent eats
Dative D: the person for (or related to) whom the agent eats something
Instrument I: the tool used to eat something, including 碗 *wǎn* "bowl" and 筷子

(continued)

kuàizi "chopstick"
Manner M: the way of eating something or the standard for the diet, e.g., 包伙 *bāohuǒ* "table board" and 小灶 *xiǎozào* "special kitchen"
Location L: the place where someone eats something
Goal GO: the place in which the patient is located after it is eaten, generally a body part, e.g., 肚子 [中] *dùzi* [*zhōng*] "[in] the stomach" and 嘴 [里] *zuǐ* [*lǐ*] "[in] the mouth"
[2] Syntactic formats
S1: A + __ + P
For example, (a) 弟弟~了一个苹果。
dìdi__~__le__yī__ge__píngguǒ.
younger brother__~__PERF__one__CL__apple
My younger brother ate an apple.
(b) 咱们~烤鸭吧!
zánmen__~__kǎoyā__ba!
we__~__roast duck__MOD
Let's eat roast duck!
S2: P + A + __ -le
For example, (a) 苹果我~了。
píngguǒ__wǒ__~__le.
apple__I__~__PERF
The apple was eaten by me.
(b) 蛋糕大家都~了。
dàngāo__dàjiā__dū__~__le.
cake__we__all__~__PERF
We all eat the cake.
S3: A + __ + D + P
For example, (a) 他~了小李一个苹果。
tā__~__le__Xiǎo Lǐ__yī__ge__píngguǒ.
he__~__PERF__Xiao Li__one__CL__apple
He ate one of Xiao Li's apples.
(b) 弟弟~了我一包巧克力。
dìdi__~__le__wǒ__yī__bāo__qiǎokèlì.
younger brother__~__PEFT__I__one__CL__chocolate
My younger brother ate one package of my chocolate.
S4: A + 用 *yòng* "use" + __ + P
For example, (a) 长工们都用大碗~饭。
chánggōngmen__dū__yòng__dàwǎn__~__fàn.
long-term worker__all__use__big bowl__~__rice
All long-term workers eat with big bowls.
(b) 他正用刀叉~牛排呢。
tā__zhèng__yòng__dāochā__~__niúpái__ne.
he__just__use__fork and knife__~__steak__MOD
He is eating steak with a fork and knife.
S5: I + (A +) __ + P

(continued)

For example, (a) 这副刀叉~牛排。	
zhè__fù__dāochā__~__niúpái.	
this__CL__fork and knife__~__steak	
This fork and knife is used to eat steak.	
(b) 这个碗我~面条。	
zhè__ge__wǎn__wǒ__~__miàntiáo.	
this__CL__bowl__I__~__noodle	
With this bowl I eat noodles.	
S6: A + __ + I/M	
For example, (a) 男人们~大碗, 孩子们~小碗。	
nánrénmen__~__dàwǎn,__háizimen__~__xiǎowǎn.	
men__~__big bowl__kids__~__small bowl	
Men eat with big bowls and kids eat with small bowls.	
(b) 他一直~小灶。	
tā__yīzhí__~__xiǎozào.	
he__always__~__small stove	
He always prepares special food for himself.	
(c) 工人们都~包伙。	
gōngrénmen__ dōu __~__bāohuǒ.	
workers__all__~__table board	
All workers eat in a table-board manner.	
S7: A + 在 *zài* "in" L + __ + P	
For example, (a) 学生们都在食堂~午饭。	
xuéshēngmen__dōu__zài__shítáng__~__wǔfàn.	
student__all__in__canteen__~__lunch	
All students have lunch in the canteen.	
(b) 他们在全聚德~晚饭。	
tāmen__zài__Quánjùdé__~__wǎnfàn.	
they__in__Quanjude__~__supper	
They all have dinner in the Quanjude restaurant.	
S8: P + A + 在 *zài* "in" L + __	
For example, (a) 午饭他在食堂~。	
wǔfàn__tā__zài__shítáng__~.	
lunch__he__in__canteen__~	
He has lunch in the canteen.	
(b) 早饭孩子们都在家里~。	
zǎofàn__háizimen__dū__zài__jiā__lǐ__~.	
breakfast__children__all__at__home__inside__~	
All children have breakfast at home.	
S9: (P +) A + __+ L	
For example, (a) 他经常~食堂。	
tā__jīngcháng__~__shítáng.	
he__often__~__canteen	
He often eats in the canteen.	

(continued)

(b) 晚饭咱们~馆子吧。

wǎnfàn__zánmen__~__guǎnzi__ba.

supper__we__~__restaurant__MOD

Let's have the dinner in a restaurant.

S10: A + *bǎ* P + __ -le

For example, (a) 你快把面条~了。

nǐ__kuài__bǎ__miàntiáo__~__le.

you__quickly__BA__noodle__~__PERF

You eat the noodles as quickly as you can.

(b) 弟弟把整块蛋糕都~了。

dìdi__bǎ__zhěng__kuài__dàngāo__dū__~__le.

younger brother__BA__whole__CL__cake__all__~__PERF

My younger brother ate the whole cake.

S11: A + *bǎ* P + __ + (到 *dào* "to"/在 *zài* "in") GO

For example, (a) 犯人把纸团~到肚子里了。

fànrén__bǎ__zhǐtuán__~__dào__dùzi__lǐ__le.

prisoner__BA__paper ball__~__to__stomach__inside__PERF

The prisoner swallowed the paper into this stomach.

(b) 小猴子已经把果仁~到嘴里了。

xiǎo hóuzi__yǐjīng__bǎ__guǒrén__~__dào__zuǐ__lǐ__le.

little monkey__already__BA__nut__~__in__mouth__inside__PERF

The little monkey has put the nut into its mouth.

S12: P + *bèi* A + __-le

For example, (a) 面条被他~了。

miàntiáo__bèi__tā__~__le.

noodle__BEI__he__~__PERF

The noodle has been eaten by him.

(b) 生日蛋糕被邻居的孩子~了。

shēngrì__dàngāo__bèi__línjū__de__háizi__~__le.

birthday__cake__BEI__neighbor__PART__child__~__PERF

The birthday cake was eaten by children of our neighbor.

S13: P + *bèi* A + __ + (到 *dào* "to") GO

For example, (a) 孙悟空被铁扇公主~肚子里了。

Sūn Wùkōng__bèi__tiěshàn__gōngzhǔ__~__dùzi__lǐ__le.

Sun Wukong__BEI__iron fan__princess__~__stomach__inside__PERF

Sun Wukong was eaten by Princess Tieshan into her stomach.

(b) 果仁已经被小猴子~到嘴里了。

guǒrén__yǐjīng__bèi__xiǎo hóuzi__~__dào__zuǐ__lǐ__le.

nut__already__BEI__little monkey__~__into__stomach__inside__PERF

The little monkey has already put the nuts into his mouth.

This syntactic-semantic descriptive system demonstrates the semantic structure and the syntactic configuration of verbs and adjectives (i.e., predicates). Both the semantic roles and the syntactic formats are instantialized with examples. This instantialized knowledge is an important resource for natural language

形容词句法语义功能检索系统

A Retrieval System for the Syntactic-Semantic Functions for Adjeictves

检索词 (Input Word) 乌黑 检索 (Retrieve)

词目 (lexical item):	乌黑 (dark-black)
汉语拼音 (Chinese Pinyin):	wūhēi
词类属性 (Word Class):	状态词 (descriptive)
词义解释 (Word Meaning):	颜色深黑 (the color of deep black)。
近义词 (Synonym):	黢黑 (deep-black)
反义词 (Antonym):	雪白 (snow-white)
语义角色 (Semantic Role):	主事 (Theme, TH): the object that appear to be deep black; 范围 (Range, RA): the specific aspect in the object that has the color of deep black.
句法格式 (Syntactic Format):	S1: TH + (一片+) __ E.g., 天空一片～。(The whole sky is in ~.) S2: __ + 的 + RA E.g., ～的颜色 (the color of ~) | ～的脸色 (~ face) S3: (RA +) __ + 的 + TH E.g., ～的颜色 (~ eyeball) | 脸色～～的山里人 (a hillman with very ~ face)

Fig. 18.3 Interface of the syntactic-semantic knowledge base for Chinese adjectives

understanding and automatic reasoning. On this basis, the descriptive system serves as an interface of the syntactic-semantic knowledge base where the predicate (verbs and adjectives) and its arguments are readily connected. It is therefore regarded as a concise conceptual and linguistic model that abstracts the syntactic-semantic knowledge of verbs and adjectives as a whole. Currently, over 6000 verbs and over 3000 adjectives have been described within this framework, and 2 dictionaries have been compiled (i.e., *Chinese Verb-Based Sentence Dictionary* and *Chinese Adjective-Based Sentence Dictionary*), which will be published by The Commercial Press, providing 2 additional reference books for researchers in linguistics and NLP.

Correspondingly, an electronic version of the knowledge base—a network platform—was developed. Figure 18.3 shows a screenshot of the interface of the syntactic-semantic knowledge base for adjectives, including the Chinese phonetic transcription, POS, word meaning, and synonyms. A syntactic-semantic knowledge base for verbs is also under construction. This platform will serve as a reference for language learners and provide valuable resources of semantic knowledge for NLP researchers. It is hoped that this platform of syntactic-semantic knowledge will eventually support cross-searches among Chinese nouns, verbs, and adjectives. The platform will eventually be transformed into an object-oriented semantic knowledge base with nouns (entities) as the core search words.

18.4.3 Qualia Structure of Chinese Nouns Dictionary

The qualia structure proposed in the GLT explains the nature of the object denoted by a noun and how this object is related to other objects and events. With the concept of QS, the conceptual relation between different objects is eventually realized as collocations among different words (i.e., as the relation between a noun and other nouns, verbs, or adjectives).

As mentioned in Sect. 18.2, Pustejovsky (1991, 1995) proposed four qualia roles—formal, constitutive, telic, and agentive. According to the collocations of nouns in real Chinese contexts, Yuan 袁毓林 (2013, 2014) expanded the four-role system to a ten-role system. The six newly added roles include unit, evaluation, material, action, handle, and orientation. They are defined as follows:

- **Unit (UNI):** Unit is used to reflect the measurement of the object denoted by a noun. It follows the numeral of the noun, for example, 张 [纸] *zhāng* [*zhǐ*] "[a] piece [of paper]," 双 [筷子] *shuāng* [*kuàizi*] "[a] pair [of chopsticks]," 斤 *jīn* [*báijiǔ*] "[a] jin (a unit of weight, equal to 1/2 kilogram) [liquor]," etc.
- **Evaluation (EVA):** Evaluation is used to reflect people's subjective evaluation of and emotion to the object denoted by a noun. For example, the evaluation of 月亮 *yuèliàng* "moon" includes 洁白 *jiébái* "purely white," 皎洁 *jiǎojié* "brightly pure and clear," 明亮 *míngliàng* "bright," 明朗 *mínglǎng* "clear," 朦胧 *ménglóng* "hazy," 圆圆 *yuányuán* "round," 圆润 *yuánrùn* "mellow and full," 弯弯 *wānwān* "curved," etc.
- **Material (MAT):** Material is used to reflect the things used to create the object denoted by a noun. For example, the material of 书 *shū* "book" includes 帛 *bó* "silk," 竹 *zhú* "bamboo," 纸草 *zhǐcǎo* "papyrus," 羊皮 *yángpí* "sheepskin," 竹皮 *zhúpí* "bamboo veneer," 树叶 *shùyè* "leaf," 纸板 *zhǐbǎn* "paper," 电子 *diànzǐ* "digit," etc.
- **Action (ACT):** Action is used to reflect the conventional movement, behavior, or activity of the object denoted by a noun. For example, the action of 细菌 *xìjūn* "bacterial" includes 繁殖 *fánzhí* "reproduce," 生长 *shēngzhǎng* "grow," 死亡 *sǐwáng* "die," 吞噬 *túnshì* "annex," 传播 *chuánbō* "spread," 散布 *sànbù* "scatter," 感染 *gǎnrǎn* "infect," 侵染 *qīnrǎn* "invade," 进入 *jìnrù* "enter," 分解 *fēnjiě* "decompose," 腐蚀 *fǔshé* "corrode," etc.
- **Handle (HAN):** The handle role reflects one object or person's conventional movement, behavior, or influence on another object denoted by a noun. For example, the handle role of 眼泪 *yǎnlèi* "tear" includes 抹 *mǒ* "wipe," 含着 *hánzhe* "full of," 噙着 *qínzhe* "be filled with," 忍着 *rěnzhe* "hold back," 充满 *chōngmǎn* "brim with," 擦 *cā* "clean," 弹 *tán* "flip," etc.
- **Orientation (ORI):** This is the space, time, or direction to which one object denoted by a noun is located in relation to another object or person. For example, the orientation of 今天 *jīntiān* "today" includes 在 *zài* "at," 到 *dào* "to," 从 *cóng* "from," 过了 *guò le* "over," etc.

In addition to qualia roles, the descriptive framework also includes syntactic formats, which capture the way nouns and various qualia roles are configured in real contexts. Qualia roles and syntactic formats complement each other to serve as an interface of the syntactic-semantic knowledge base for Chinese nouns. For example, the syntactic-semantic knowledge of the noun 食品 *shípǐn* "food" can be framed as shown below:

食品 *shípǐn* "food" <noun, positive> the processed diet being sold in shops

[1] Qualia roles

FOR: substance, commodity, edible substance, diet

CON: food, with nutrition, heat, etc. as its constituents, can be classified according to its source, function, manner of processing or packaging, or timeline as follows: fish, meat, poultry, chicken, milk, plant, animal, sugar; imported, healthy, nutritious, medicinal, convenient, fast, emergent, raw, cooked, fresh, salted, smoked, fortified, puffing, freezing, frozen, canned, bagged; acidic, green, environment-friendly, organic, genetically modified, flavored, Muslim; baby, elderly, animal, army, field, festival, expired, overnight, polluted, etc.

UNI: collective, batch, package, kind, part, etc.; measure, ton, kilogram, etc.; indefinite, a bit, some, etc.; container, box, pocket, table, house, basket, etc.

EVA: fresh, metamorphic, corruptive, delicious, precious, cheap, traditional, novel, special, fine, advanced, high-quality, short, rich (diverse), adequate, deficient, etc.

AGE: process, produce, etc.

TEL: eat, swallow, enjoy, taste, consume, etc.

HAN: sell, purchase, store, freeze, pack, transport, distribute, disinfect, etc.

[2] Syntactic formats

S1: __ + 有 *yǒu* "have"/*De* + CON

For example, ~有营养 *~yíngyǎng* "~ have nutrition" |~有热量 *~yǒu rèliàng* "~ have heat" |~的营养 *~de yíngyǎng* "nutrition of ~"|~的热量 *~de rèliàng* "the heat of ~"

S2: NUM + UNI + __

For example, 一批~ *yī pī~* "a batch of ~"|一包~ *yī bāo~* "a bag of ~"|一种~ *yī zhǒng~* "a kind of ~"|一部分~ *yī bùfèn~* "a part of ~"|一顿~ *yī dūn~* "a ton of ~"|一点儿~ *yī diǎnr~* "a bit of ~"|一些~ *yī xiē~* "some of ~"|一箱~ *yī xiāng~* "a box of ~"|一口袋~ *yī kǒudài~* "a pocket of ~"|一桌子 ~ *yī zhuōzi~* "a table of ~"|一屋子~ *yī wūzi~* "a house of ~"|一篮子~ *yī lánzi~* "a basket of ~"

S3: EVA + (*De*+) __

For example, 新鲜(的)~ *xīnxiān (de)~* "fresh ~"|变质[的]~ *biànzhì (de)~* "deteriorate ~"|腐败[的]~ *fǔbài (de)~* "corruptive ~"|美味[的]~ *měiwèi (de) ~* "delicious ~"|珍贵[的]~ *zhēnguì (de)~* "precious ~"|廉价[的]~ *liánjià (de)~* "cheap ~"|传统~ *chuántǒng~* "traditional ~"|新颖[的]~ *xīnyǐng (de)~* "novel ~"|特殊~ *tèshū~* "special ~"|精细~ *jīngxì~* "delicate ~"|高级~ *gāojí~* "advanced ~"|优质~ *yōuzhì~* "superior ~"

S4: __ + EVA

For example, ~[严重]短缺 ~ *(yánzhòng) duǎnquē* "~ is [badly] inadequate"|~丰富[多样] ~ *fēngfù (duōyàng)* "~ is rich [and diverse]"|~充足 ~ *chōngzú* "~ is enough"|~匮乏 ~ *kuìfá* "short of ~"

S5: AGE + __

For example, 加工~ *jiāgōng~* "process ~"|制作~ *zhìzuò~* "produce ~"|作~ *zuò~* "make ~"

S6: TEL + __

For example, 吃~ *chī~* "eat ~"|吞噬~ *tūnshí* "swallow ~"|下咽~ *xiàyàn~* "devour ~"|享用~ *xiǎngyòng~* "enjoy ~"|品味~ *pǐnwèi~* "taste ~"|尝~ *cháng~* "try ~"|品尝~ *pǐncháng~* "taste ~"

(continued)

S7: HAN + __
For example, 出售~ *chūshòu~* "offer ~ for sale"|卖~ *mài~* "sell ~"|销售~ *xiāoshòu ~* "market ~"|买~ *mǎi~* "buy ~"|购买~ *gòumǎi~* "purchase ~"|存放~ *cúnfàng~* "store ~"|冷藏~ *lěngcáng~* "package ~"|运输~ *yùnshū~* "transport ~"

This QS-based descriptive system presents the syntactic-semantic knowledge of nouns along with qualia roles and syntactic formats. On the one hand, qualia roles conceptualize the basic property of the object denoted by a noun and how the object is related to other objects. On the other hand, syntactic formats describe the selective constraints under which a noun is collocated with other nouns, verbs, and adjectives. This system serves as an interface of the syntactic-semantic knowledge base for nouns. In this sense, the QS-based descriptive system can be seen as a concise conceptual and linguistic model that abstracts the syntactic-semantic information of the nouns. So far, the framework includes descriptions of over 1500 frequently used nouns. In the future, all nouns listed in the glossary of the HSK (test of Chinese language ability for foreigners) will be described, with a total number of over 20,000. Similar to that of verbs and adjectives, an online syntactic-semantic knowledge base for nouns, including basic lexical information (such as the phonetic transcription, sentiment polarity, and word meaning), qualia roles, and syntactic formats illustrated with examples, as shown in Fig. 18.4, has also been developed. These resources are expected to be applicable to international Chinese education and NLP tasks.

18.5 Conclusion: The Use of Knowledge Bases for Default Reasoning

The two lexical knowledge bases presented in this chapter will be employed to achieve the following goal: to mutually connect the semantic roles of predicates and the qualia roles of nouns to solve NLP problems (e.g., "the tennis problem"). Because connections among nouns, verbs, and adjectives create a lexical network, which conceptualizes and expresses world knowledge about the relation between objects (denoted by nouns) and events (denoted by verbs) or states (denoted by adjectives), this should lead to the building of an object-oriented semantic knowledge base that takes nouns (entities) as the primary search words, presented as a visualized knowledge graph capable of zooming in and out. Our ultimate goal is to provide necessary knowledge resources for default reasoning based on situational association. Furthermore, from the lexical knowledge bases presented in this chapter, seeds and training sets can be extracted to facilitate the statistical mining and deep learning of linguistic knowledge. Hopefully, the resources we have constructed can be effectively applied in NLP and other related fields.

词条信息 (Lexical Informaton)

词语 (Lexical Item)	大家
拼音 (Pinyin)	da4jia1
情感色彩 (Sentiment Polarity)	Positive
词典释义 (Word Meaning)	Famous expert.

物性角色 (Qualia Role)

形式 (Formal)	人、个人、身份；
构成 (Constitutive)	书法、魔术、作曲、提琴、同行，等等；
材料 (Material)	
单位 (Unit)	个、名、位、代；部分；些；
评价 (Evaluative)	伟大、著名、知名、杰出、优秀、（第）一流，等
施成 (Agentive)	被称为、当、成为、作为，等等；
功用 (Telic)	传授弟子、传播知识或技术、做贡献，等等；
行为 (Action)	研究、提倡、从事、发现、发言、认为，等等；
处置 (Handle)	邀请、寻找、咨询、尊敬、相信、批评，等等；
定位 (Orientation)	

句法格式 (Syntactic Format)

格式 1 (S1)	CON + (的) + __
示例 (Example)	书法(的)～ | 魔术(的)～ | 作曲(的)～

Fig. 18.4 Interface of the syntactic-semantic knowledge base for Chinese nouns

Acknowledgments Our research was supported by the Major Project of the Ministry of Education Key Research Base of Humanities and Social Sciences *Research on the Representation and Computation System for Lexico-Semantic Knowledge in the Framework of Chinese Paratactic Grammar* 汉语意合语法框架下的词汇语义知识表示及其计算系统研究 and the Key Project of Chinese National Program for Fundamental Research and Development (973 Program) *The Neuro-Mechanism of Linguistic Cognition* 语言认知的神经机制 (2014CB340502). We extend our special thanks to these two foundations, and we sincerely thank professor Liang Mao-Cheng 梁茂成 for his polishing of the language in this chapter.

References

Liu, Dan-Qing 刘丹青. 1987. Adjective-noun co-occurrence and the dimensions of the adjective 形名同现及形容词的向. *Journal of Nanjing Normal University 南京师范大学学报 3:56–61.*

Okuda, Hiroshi 奥田宽. 1982. On compulsory and optional connections of the Mandarin Chinese adjective 论现代汉语形容词的强制性联系和非强制性联系. *Nankai Journal南开学报3:67–74.*

Pustejovsky, James. 1991. The generative lexicon. *Computational Linguistics* 17(4):409–441.

Pustejovsky, James. 1995. *The generative lexicon*. Cambridge, MA: The MIT Press.

Tan, Jing-Chun 谭景春. 1992. Bidirectional and multi-referential adjectives and relevant syntactic relations 双向和多指形容词及相关的句法关系. *Studies of the Chinese Language 中国语文 2.*

Wang, Lu-Lu, and Yuan Yu-Lin 王璐璐, 袁毓林. 2015. A transformation-based grammatical classification and linguistic modelling of the *ba*-sentence 基于变换的"把"字句的分类研究和语言建模. *Journal of Sino-Tibetan Languages 汉藏语学报 8:181–195.*

Wang, Meng, Huang Chu-Ren, Yu Shi-Wen, and Li Bin 王萌, 黄居仁, 俞士汶, 李斌. 2010. A verb-based study on the paraphrase of the Chinese compound-noun phrase 基于动词的汉语复合名词短语释义研究. *Journal of Chinese Information Processing 中文信息学报 24:3–9.*

Wang, Lu-Lu, Sun Wei-Wei, and Yuan Yu-Lin 王璐璐, 孙薇薇, 袁毓林. 2015. A study on the automatic paraphrase and syntactic transformation of the *ba*-sentence "把"字句的自动释义与句式变换研究. *Computer Engineering and Applications 计算机工程与应用 19:129–137.*

Wei, Xue, and Yuan Yu-Lin 魏雪, 袁毓林. 2013. Constructing paraphrase templates for the noun-noun group based on semantic categories and qualia structure 基于语义类和物性角色构建名名组合的释义模板. *Chinese Teaching in the World 世界汉语教学 2:172–181.*

Wei, Xue, and Yuan Yu-Lin 魏雪, 袁毓林. 2014. A rule-based study on the automatic paraphrase of the Chinese noun-noun group 基于规则的汉语名名组合的自动释义研究. *Journal of Chinese Information Processing 中文信息学报 3:1–10.*

Winograd, T. 1983. *Language as a cognitive process*. London: Addison-Wesley Publishing Company.

Yuan, Yu-Lin 袁毓林. 1992. A study on nominal valency in Mandarin Chinese 现代汉语名词的配价研究. *Social Sciences in China 中国社会科学 3:205–223.*

Yuan, Yu-Lin 袁毓林. 1995. The implicit predicate and its syntactic consequence: The referential rules of *de*-construction, the grammatical functions of *de* and its semantic functions 谓词隐含及其句法后果——"的"字结构的称代规则和"的"的语法、语义功能. *Studies of the Chinese Language 中国语文 4:241–255.*

Yuan, Yu-Lin 袁毓林. 1998/2010. *Studies on Chinese verbal valency 汉语动词的配价研究. Nanchang: Jiangxi Education Publishing House.*

Yuan, Yu-Lin 袁毓林. 2007. Granularity of semantic roles and their applications in information processing 语义角色的精细等级及其在信息处理中的应用. *Journal of Chinese Information Processing 中文信息学报 4:10–20.*

Yuan, Yu-Lin 袁毓林. 2010. *Studies on Chinese valency grammar 汉语配价语法研究. Beijing: The Commercial Press.*

Yuan, Yu-Lin 袁毓林. 2013. Towards a semantic knowledge system: With the generative lexicon theory and the argument structure theory as its theoretical basis 基于生成词库论和论元结构的语义知识体系研究. *Journal of Chinese Information Processing 中文信息学报 6:23–30.*

Yuan, Yu-Lin 袁毓林. 2014. A qualia-structure-based descriptive system for the Chinese noun and application cases 汉语名词物性结构的描写体系和应用案例. *Contemporary Linguistics 当代语言学 1:31–48.*

Yuan, Yu-Lin, Chen Zhen-Yu, Zhang Xiu-Song, Li Xiang, Zhou Qiang, and Gao Song 袁毓林, 陈振宇, 张秀松, 李湘, 周强, 高嵩. 2010. From cognitive assumption to computational analysis and programming: A computational paradigm and technical route to cognitive linguistic studies 从认知假设到计算分析和程序实现——一种认知语言学研究的计算范式与技术路线. *Contemporary Linguistics 当代语言学 2:97–114.*

Chapter 19
Toward an Empirical Theory of Sense: A Corpus-Based Study of Mandarin Conceptual Lexicalization

Jia-Fei Hong, Kathleen Ahrens, and Chu-Ren Huang

Abstract The empirical theory of sense is one of the most challenging and least studied topics in computational lexical semantics. Previous studies have focused on disambiguation and sense tagging, both of which rely on prior knowledge of the inventory of possible senses of a word. However, because prior lexical knowledge cannot be assumed, and linguistic behavior is the only information available for determining both the number and the definition of senses of any given word, the study presented in this chapter proposed predicting sense clusters for each target word based on distributional information from corpora. In addition, the study intended to find all possible linguistic information and lexical senses of words automatically by employing distributional information. Using collocational information from the Chinese Gigaword Corpus, usage examples of four target words—*chi1* "eat," *wan2* "play," *huan4* "change," and *shao1* "burn"—were clustered into different sense divisions. These automatically discovered senses were then compared with the manually analyzed senses of these words in Chinese WordNet and *Xiandai Hanyu Cidian* (*The Contemporary Chinese Dictionary*) to evaluate their accuracy and coverage. Finally, the automatically discovered sense divisions were tested against an offline psycholinguistic experiment using multiple-choice tasks (Burton et al. 1991).

J.-F. Hong (✉)
Department of Chinese as a Second Language, National Taiwan Normal University, Taipei, Taiwan
e-mail: jiafeihong@ntnu.edu.tw

K. Ahrens
Department of English and Communication, The Hong Kong Polytechnic University, Hong Kong, China
e-mail: kathleen.ahrens@polyu.edu.hk

C.-R. Huang
Department of Chinese and Bilingual Studies, The Hong Kong Polytechnic University, Hong Kong, China
e-mail: churen.huang@polyu.edu.hk

C.-R. Huang et al. (eds.), *Chinese Language Resources*, Text, Speech and Language Technology 49, https://doi.org/10.1007/978-3-031-38913-9_19

Keywords Empirical theory of sense · Corpus-based approach · Character similarity clustering analysis · Concept similarity clustering analysis · Mandarin conceptual lexicalization division

19.1 Introduction

Conceptual lexicalization is one of the most important research topics in lexical semantics (Cruse 1986; Levin and Pinker 1992). Establishing lexical semantic systems and the correlation between conceptual systems and lexical semantic systems are two crucial issues in conceptual lexicalization studies (Pustejovsky 1995). Previous studies on lexical semantic systems have focused on presenting lexical semantic relations, such as the establishment of WordNet (Fellbaum 1998), sense divisions, sense relations, and basic sense exploration (Wierzbicka 1996). These previous studies, in particular, the computational and corpus-based ones, assumed that lexical senses were already known and assigned (Hong 2015). However, there are few, if any, studies on how senses can be detected without presumed conceptual segmentation or semantic primitives. Therefore, our study took a corpus-based and computational approach to the discovery of conceptual lexicalization and the empirical theory of sense.

Lexical ambiguity poses theoretical and computational problems in lexical semantic studies (cf. Ravin and Leacock 2000). Recent computational linguistic research on conceptual lexicalization has produced prolific studies on lexical ambiguity, especially disambiguation that often involved verbs. These studies include mental processing comprehension (Klepousniotou 2002), lexicon and WordNet interpretations (Buscaldi et al. 2007; McRoy 1992; Wu 2003), context-based analysis (Prior et al. 2011; Van Petten and Luka 2006; Wong and Mooney 2006), information retrieval and machine translation (Buscaldi et al. 2007; Li et al. 2003; Prior et al. 2011; Wong and Mooney 2006; Zhou et al. 2006), conceptual lexicalization representation (Agirre et al. 2006; Ten Hacken and Thomas 2013), and lexical semantic knowledge representation and the frame-based approach (Bolette 1997; Hsu and Liu 2004; Lien 2000; Liu et al. 2005).

These studies on lexical ambiguity can be divided into two categories: the corpus-based and computational approach and the conceptual comprehension perspective (Hong 2015). All related studies that used the corpus-based and computational approach involved adaptive systems that were based on context to divide the senses of lexically ambiguous words and find all possible senses of a word (Canas et al. 2003; Chen et al. 2005; Chen and Palmer 2009; Ramakrishnan et al. 2004; Gries 2012; Jin et al. 2007; Ker and Chen 2004; Kipper et al. 2008; Martinez et al. 2006; Moldovan and Novischi 2004; Pitler et al. 2009; Resnik and Yarowsky 2000; Véronis and Ide 1990; Xue et al. 2006; Zhang et al. 2005). Previous studies that employed the conceptual comprehension perspective were all based on reaction time approaches that determined literal bias meanings and metaphorical bias meanings, and they demonstrated that context does not influence automatic lexical access (Ahrens 1998, 2001, 2006; Lin and Ahrens 2000), but conceptual domains involving a linguistic context do influence lexical access, although it may not be automatic (Li 1998a, 1998b; Li and Yip 1996; Tabossi and Zardon 1993). In addition, related studies have examined the comprehension of different senses in lexically ambiguous words, processed ambiguous words that can occur both as nouns and as verbs, and lexical ambiguity comprehension to determine the meanings of literal bias and metaphorical bias (Angwin et al. 2017; Elston-Guttler and Friederici 2006; Gunter et al. 2003; Li et al. 2004; Mason and Just 2007; Zempleni et al. 2007).

Although automatic lexical classification research has a long history (e.g., Zempleni et al. 2007), very little has been done on this topic using Chinese. Research on the automatic discovery of linguistic classes in Chinese using distributional information from corpora can be traced back to Redington et al. (1995), who were able to automatically classify words into syntactic category clusters based on distributional information from the Sinica Corpus. Huang et al. (1998) later attempted to automatically identify the semantic classes of nouns based on classifier noun collocation information from the Sinica Corpus. Considering these recent developments in distributional models for semantics, distributional memory (Baroni and Lenci 2010) and whether distributional information is adequate in predicting lexical senses have become even more important.

Our study examined four target words, assuming no prior knowledge of lexically assigned senses, in an attempt to discover the division of senses for each word. Adopting the most fundamental tenet of (corpus) linguistics (i.e., that linguistic generalization can be discovered through the similarity of linguistic behaviors), we hypothesized that the senses of a word form can be discovered by examining the distributional patterns of that word form in a corpus. In particular, we utilized different methods to cluster and detect distributional patterns that are significant for sense division based on the composition of characters, semantic features, and conceptual primitives. The language resources used in our study include the Chinese Gigaword Corpus, HowNet, Chinese WordNet (CWN), and *Xiandai Hanyu Cidian* (*Xian Han*).

Our study focused on four highly polysemous word forms in Mandarin Chinese: *chi1* "eat," *wan2* "play," *huan4* "change," and *shao1* "burn." Based on previous lexicographic analysis, the four target words have transitive verb usages, and they each have far more than two senses. Collocation was realized to determine these senses. To collect a large amount of data concerning all possible senses of the four target words, the Chinese Gigaword Corpus was chosen as the database. Although the Chinese Gigaword Corpus contains three different newspaper sources, the sole source used for our study was Taiwan's Central News Agency.

When conducting the character similarity clustering analysis, we employed identical morphemes of some of the collocation words to cluster them into the same cluster. In addition, when conducting the concept similarity clustering analysis, we plugged these identical morphemes into HowNet to map different concepts of the collocation words in the same sense cluster. Therefore, the two main strategies adopted in our study were character similarity clustering analysis and concept similarity clustering analysis, which are based on HowNet's (a) similarity between sememes and (b) similarity between concepts, respectively. Moreover, the performances of the character similarity clustering analysis and the concept similarity clustering analysis of the four target words were evaluated by comparing the results with CWN and *Xian Han* to verify the felicity of these automatically discovered senses and to evaluate the study's computational approach.

Finally, in addition to evaluating the results by comparing them with an expert lexicographic account, we verified whether these sense divisions were psychologically felicitous and recognized by native speakers using an offline experiment that consisted of multiple-choice tasks to test the participants' comprehension (Burton et al. 1991). Our study concluded with a summary of the results and a discussion on the significance of corpus-based studies on the empirical theory of sense.

19.2 Research Method

Following related research and questions about lexical ambiguity, our study proposed three research questions: (i) How can the word senses of a lexically ambiguous word be predicted to present different interpretations in different contexts or domains? (ii) How can more than two corpora be used as the database in the study? (iii) Can other approaches be used to verify the analysis of the study's corpus-based and computational approach?

19.2.1 Corpora and Tools

In our study, we explored all possible senses of four target words—*chi1* "eat," *wan2* "play," *huan4* "change," and *shao1* "burn." Because it was necessary to collect a large amount of data to analyze and examine these target words objectively, the Chinese Gigaword Corpus was chosen for the collection of this data. In addition, in the concept similarity clustering analysis, the four target words were mapped and assigned all related collocation words using HowNet as the knowledge base. Finally, to evaluate the four target words, CWN and *Xian Han* were used as the criteria for this evaluation.

Chinese Gigaword Corpus

The second version of the Chinese Gigaword Corpus contains about 1.4 billion Chinese characters, including about 800 million characters from Taiwan's Central News Agency (from 1991 to 2004), nearly 500 million characters from China's Xinhua News Agency, and approximately 30 million characters from Singapore's newspaper *Zaobao*. Before loading Chinese Gigaword into Sketch Engine, all of the simplified characters were converted to traditional characters, and the texts were segmented and POS-tagged using the Academia Sinica segmentation and tagging system (Huang et al. 1998). The segmentation and tagging functions were performed automatically, with both automatic and manual post-checking. The precision accuracy was estimated to be over 96.5% (Ma and Huang 2006).

Sketch Engine (also known as the Word Sketch Engine [Kilgarriff et al. 2004]) is a novel corpus query system that incorporates word sketches, grammatical relations, and a distributional thesaurus. The advantage of using Sketch Engine as a query tool is that it focuses on the grammatical context of a word, instead of returning an arbitrary number of adjacent words. All the components of Sketch Engine were implemented, including Concordance, Word Sketch, Thesaurus, and Sketch Difference. Because our study explored all possible language usages in the Taiwan region only, Taiwan's Central News Agency was the sole source used to predict all possible senses. Using the Word Sketch function in Sketch Engine, we obtained all possible collocations representing all possible senses of the four target words.

HowNet

HowNet is an online common-sense knowledge base that reveals the inter-conceptual and inter-attribute relations of concepts as connoted in the Chinese lexicon and that of their English equivalents. HowNet, which is a semantic knowledge dictionary system, not a semantic dictionary, includes an abundance of both semantic and world knowledge and thus is an important resource for natural language processing and knowledge mining (Dong and Dong 2000). In addition, there are several information features in HowNet: (i) Main Features of Concepts; (ii) Secondary Features of Concepts; (iii) Synonymous, Antonymous and Converse Relations (SACR); and (iv) Event Relatedness and Role-shifting (ERRS). These are the fundamental components of the system, not merely coding specifications, and they were used in conjunction with the knowledge dictionary.

There are two important notations in HowNet. The first notation is polysemy, a phenomenon whereby a concept describes a semantic sense of words. In natural language, one word may have several concepts. The second notation is sememes. In HowNet, concepts are described by Knowledge Description Language (KDL), and the basic element of KDL is a sememe, which is the basic unit used to describe concepts. It is important to point out that HowNet does not put all of the concepts into a tree directly but, rather, describes them by a set of sememes. The exception is that in HowNet, the hypernym-hyponym relation organizes sememes into several trees. Therefore, not all senses of all collocation words can be mapped to all concepts in HowNet. That is to say, not all possible concepts of all words in HowNet can be obtained.

Chinese WordNet

Some of the collocation words of the four target words collected through Taiwan's Central News Agency were clustered to predict different senses in a character similarity clustering analysis and in a concept similarity clustering analysis. It was very important and necessary to consider their accuracy and recall. For this reason, CWN was used to estimate the evaluations of the four target words in our study.

The architecture of CWN follows the standard established by Princeton's WordNet (WN, Fellbaum 1998), which has two unique design features. First, WordNet aims to maintain the balance between the universality of cross-lingual synset-based sense mapping and the felicity of the language-specific lexicalization of concepts. Second, it aims to represent sense at the level of lexical conventionalization, as well as meaning facets at the level of conceptual specification (Ahrens et al. 2003). In CWN, each entry includes phonetic symbols (Pinyin and National Phonetic Alphabets), a sense definition, a corresponding synset, the part of speech (POS), example sentences, and explanatory notes. There are 10,363 lemmas in CWN.

Xiandai Hanyu Cidian (Xian Han)

To estimate the evaluations and observe the accuracy and recall of the four target words, it was not enough to use only CWN to evaluate them. Therefore, *Xian Han* (Chinese Academy of Social Sciences 2005) was used concurrently with CWN for this purpose. The results from both CWN and *Xian Han* were then compared to point out crucial differences.

Created in 1956, *Xian Han* is a modern Chinese dictionary, the first of its kind, published by The Commercial Press, now in its seventh edition (2016). This newest edition contains 70,000 entries, and throughout its publication history, over 2000 obsolete, regional, or rarely used terms have been removed. In *Xian Han*, lemmas include their phonetic transcriptions (*han4 yu3 pin1 yin1*), POS, definitions, examples, and simple sentences.

19.2.2 Data Collection

There were two main reasons for choosing the four target words: they are all transitive verbs and they each have more than two senses (Hong 2015). These two reasons may not fully explain why they were selected from the many transitive verbs available in the corpora. Therefore, to further clarify our reasoning in selecting the four target words, we employed the Module-Attribute Representation of Verbal Semantics (MARVS) theory (Huang et al. 2000). Since the MARVS theory presents verbal event structures and shows their logical primary units and entailments, each verb is interpreted by its verifiable entailment. The MARVS theory is based on Mandarin Chinese data (Huang et al. 2000) and contains two types of modules: the Event Structure Module and the Role Module. There are also two types of attributes, Event-Internal Attributes and Role-Internal Attributes, which are linked to the Event Structure Module and the Role Module, respectively.

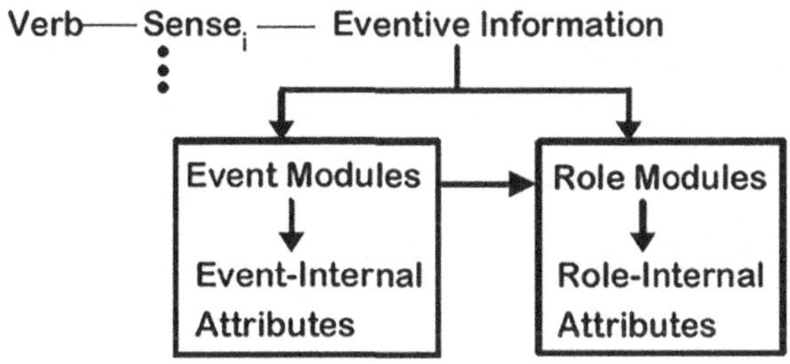

Fig. 19.1 Module-Attribute Representation of Verbal Semantics (MARVS)

In the MARVS theory, Huang et al. (2000) mentioned that lexical knowledge is classified into two types: (1) structural information, which is represented by means of the composition of atomic modules, and (2) content information, which is represented by means of attributes attached to these modules. In addition, the roles that participate in the events are represented in the Role Module. The semantic attributes pertaining to the complete event are called Event-Internal Attributes, which are attached to the Event Structure Module. In addition, Event-Internal Attributes refer to the semantics of the event itself. Moreover, the semantic attributes pertaining to each role are termed Role-Internal Attributes, which are attached to the appropriate role within the Role Module. The overall shape of the Event Structure Module is defined by the composition of five event modules. It is important to note that eventive information is attached to the sense of a verb. Verbs with different senses will have different eventive information. A representation of the MARVS theory is shown in Fig. 19.1.

Referring to the MARVS theory, the Event-Internal Attributes of the Event Structure Module and the Role-Internal Attributes of the Role Module for the four target words used in our study will be explained. In addition, their common points and constructions, as well as their different internal attributes, will be presented. Finally, following the verb module attribute representation in the MARVS theory, we were able to determine and explain that *chi1* "eat," *wan2* "play," *huan4* "change," and *shao1* "burn" belonged to the same verbal category, even though they displayed slight differences, and they could be used as a set of words for further study.

In Taiwan's Central News Agency (Chinese Gigaword Corpus), there are 33,385 sentences with the target word *chi1* "eat"; 10,319 sentences with the target word *wan2* "play"; 20,345 sentences with the target word *huan4* "change"; and 5165 sentences with the target word *shao1* "burn." Since the target words are all transitive verbs, their object positions must be nouns; in other words, these nouns are regarded as important related collocation words. Therefore, we employed these nouns to predict all possible senses of the four target words.

In Chinese, the main object (noun) usually appears after the transitive verb, but sometimes the main object (noun) appears before the transitive verb. Following the rules for structural construction in Chinese, five criteria were used: (1) the noun after the target word (e.g., 「吃」魚 *chi1 yu2* "eat more fish"); (2) the head noun of the first noun phrase after the target word (e.g., 「玩」電腦遊戲 *wan2 dian4 nao3 you2*

Table 19.1 The number of sentences and collocation words for the target words *chi1* "eat," *wan2* "play," *huan4* "change," and *shao1* "burn"

Target word	Number of sentences formed in the corpus	Sentences that have one of the five collocation patterns	Collocation words
chi1 "eat"	33,385	29,421	3961
wan2 "play"	10,319	8833	2086
huan4 "change"	20,345	19,394	3003
shao1 "burn"	5165	4668	1565

xi4 "play computer games"); (3) the head noun of the last noun phrase before the first punctuation mark of the target word (e.g., 「吃」豬內臟與豬腳筋 *chi1 zhu1 nei4 zang4 yu3 zhu1 jiao3 jin1* "eat pig viscera and pig-foot tendons"); (4) the noun before the first punctuation mark of the target word (e.g., 「換」點清淡的新口味 *huan4 dian3 qing1 dan4 de5 xin1 kou3 wei4* "change the eating pattern and try a light new flavor"); and (5) the noun nearest the punctuation mark before the target word (e.g., 沒有足夠垃圾可「燒」 *mei2 you3 zu2 gou4 le4 se4 ke3 shao1* "not have enough rubbish to burn").

From the 5 collocation selection criteria, there were 29,421 sentences for the collocation words of *chi1* "eat"; 8833 sentences for the collocation words of *wan2* "play"; 19,394 sentences for the collocation words of *huan4* "change"; and 4668 sentences for the collocation words of *shao1* "burn." From these sentences, there were 3961 collocation words for *chi1* "eat"; 2086 collocation words for *wan2* "play"; 3003 collocation words for *huan4* "change"; and 1565 collocation words for *shao1* "burn." The distribution of the four target words is shown in Table 19.1.

The collocation words of the four target words were very useful, and they played an important role in our study. When conducting the character similarity clustering analysis, we used the same morphemes of some of the collocation words to cluster them into the same cluster. In addition, when conducting the concept similarity clustering analysis, we plugged these identical morphemes into HowNet to map different concepts of the collocation words in the same sense cluster. Therefore, not only were we able to predict all possible senses of the four target words but we were also able to compare the accuracy of the two different analyses using the corpus-based and computational approach.

19.2.3 Predictions

The empirical data consisting of the sentences and collocation words collected were used to explore all possible senses of the four target words—*chi1* "eat," *wan2* "play," *huan4* "change," and *shao1* "burn"—in different contexts or discourses. Then, the four target words were evaluated via CWN and *Xian Han*.

Next, we predicted that different clusters could represent different senses using automatic computational programming for the character similarity clustering analysis and concept similarity clustering analysis, and we examined the accuracy rates of the four target words via our own intuition. We used multiple-choice tasks for the experimental evaluation of the four target words to examine which words belonged to the same sense cluster and whether some related words were regarded as being in the same cluster by concept via native speakers' intuition.

Finally, we demonstrated that using offline tasks to test native speakers' intuition supported the notion that different clusters that have been divided using a corpus-based and computational approach represent different senses. Moreover, different collocation words affected the interpretations of the four target words. If we could demonstrate that there were several clusters of related collocation words for *chi1* "eat," *wan2* "play," *huan4* "change," and *shao1* "burn" via the offline tasks, we could predict several different senses for these four target words.

19.3 Analysis

The two main strategies of automatic computational programming used in our study were character similarity clustering analysis and concept similarity clustering analysis, which encompassed similarity between sememes and similarity between concepts, respectively, via HowNet. Even though we could ensure better performances and obtain better accuracy rates utilizing these analyses, it was still necessary to perform sense prediction evaluations in our study. Therefore, we evaluated the four target words via CWN and *Xian Han*.

19.3.1 Character Similarity Clustering Analysis

Fujii and Croft (1993) observed that a document in Japanese is likely to be relevant if it contains an index term that has a morpheme (Kanji) in common with a query term. Kanji words frequently consist of long compounds. Fujii and Croft (1993) also discussed Kanji in terms of an ideogram, postulating that if two words shared a Kanji character, some shared conceptual elements were observed between them. They called this phenomenon the thesaurus effect of Kanji. Following Fujii and Croft's (1993) study, we used character similarity to cluster related collocations to predict possible senses of the four target words, although by a different method. In our study, we first used the corpus-based and computational approach to deal with the character similarities of all possible senses and to determine which target words (*chi1* "eat," *wan2* "play," *huan4* "change," and *shao1* "burn") in the different sentences belonged to the same sense.

Similar features in Chinese characters are often synonymous compounds that share a common morpheme (Hong 2015). For instance, [飯 *fan4* "rice," 米飯 *mi3 fan4* "rice"] and [案 *an4* "case," 案件 *an4 jian4* "case"], respectively, share the common morphemes [飯 *fan4* "rice"] and [案 *an4* "case"]. In the character similarity clustering analysis, two steps were employed, namely, character similarity comparison between words and group similarity comparison between words. The two corresponding formulas for these steps are presented in Eqs. (19.1) and (19.2) below:

$$\text{dice}(x, y) = \frac{2|x \cap y|}{|x| + |y|} \tag{19.1}$$

Character similarity comparison between words

In Eq. (19.1), x and y represent two words: $|x \cap y|$ is the simultaneous length of these two words, $|x|$ and $|y|$ individually represent the length of x and y, and $dice(x, y)$ shows the similarity of x and y.

In the first step, the main goal was to collect the collocation words of the four target words and cluster them. Using the Dice coefficient (Dice 1945) in Eq. (19.1), we calculated and compared the similarity between different words by identifying their collocation words and assigning these collocation words to their appropriate clusters. For example, 藥 *yao4* "medicine," 減肥藥 *jian3 fei2 yao4* "reducing weight medicine," and 中藥 *zhong1 yao4* "traditional Chinese medicine" can be clustered in the same cluster, and 飯 *fan4* "rice," 年夜飯 *nian2 ye4 fan4* "dinner on lunar New Year's Eve," and 米飯 *mi3 fan4* "rice" can be clustered in the same cluster.

After comparing the character similarity between different words using Eq. (19.1), the second step involved grouping the clustered words in their appropriate clusters, as shown in Eq. (19.2) below:

$$\text{sim}(x, Y) = \frac{\sum_{y \in Y} \text{dice}(x, y)}{|Y|} \tag{19.2}$$

Group similarity comparison between words

In Eq. (19.2), x represents one undefined word (no lexically assigned senses), while y represents each word of Y, where Y indicates a particular cluster. To determine which words belong in which clusters, first, one undefined word (x) must be compared with another word (y), and then their average similarity must be calculated to gain the maximum similarity. Finally, this undefined word (x) is placed into a particular cluster (Y).

After finishing the two steps for the character similarity clustering analysis, we used another automatic computational programming strategy to achieve more precise sense clusters by averaging the similarity of two different clusters, as shown in Eq. (19.3) below:

Step 1: Select all sentences that include the target word *w* from the corpus; all sentences, respectively, belong to initial clusters clu_1, clu_2...clu_n, and then to the collective *S*.
Step 2: Establish the number of clusters.
Step 3: Calculate the similarity between two initial clusters for all the clusters in the collective *S*:

$$sim(clu_1, clu_2) = \frac{\sum_{s \in clu_1} \sum_{t \in clu_2} (dice(s,t))}{|clu_1| \times |clu_2|}$$

Using this algorithm, the similarity between two words is represented by the following:

$$dice(x, y) = \frac{2|x \cap y|}{|x| + |y|}$$

Step 4: Combine two clusters with the highest similarity into a new cluster.
Step 5: Repeat Step 3 and Step 4 until the final default target, which has been set previously for the four target words, is achieved.

Fig. 19.2 Steps and algorithms for the character similarity clustering process

$$\mathrm{sim}(clu_1, clu_2) = \frac{\sum_{s \in clu_1} \sum_{t \in clu_2} (\mathrm{dice}(s,t))}{|clu_1| \times |clu_1|} \tag{19.3}$$

Average similarity of two different clusters

In Eq. (19.3), clu_1 and clu_2 represent different clusters, *s* and *t* are the word members in clu_1 and clu_2, and $|clu_1|$ and $|clu_2|$ represent the number of clusters in clu_1 and clu_2, respectively. Hence, each word is placed into a cluster, the similarity between the two clusters is calculated, and then the two clusters that have the highest similarity are combined into a new cluster until all the clusters have been combined or they achieve the default target that was set previously. The entire process, including the steps and algorithms, is shown in Fig. 19.2.

Before averaging the similarity of two different clusters using Eq. (19.3), which will automatically predict the senses of lexically ambiguous words, the number of clusters must be determined and then set as the default targets. This step in the character similarity clustering analysis is necessary, as generalized clusters, which will most likely include unrelated, unpredictable, or irrelevant words, will be formed first. Concerning the number of clusters of the four target words, they were predicted using words with lexically assigned senses in CWN and word frequencies in Taiwan's Central News Agency corpus.

In addition, utilizing the two steps in the character similarity clustering analysis—character similarity comparison (Eq. 19.1) and group similarity comparison (Eq. 19.2)—and calculating the average similarity of two different clusters (Eq. 19.3), the results can be further categorized into two subgroups, the physical sense group and the metaphorical sense group, as shown in Examples (19.1) to (19.4) below:

(19.1a)	一名女子<吃>減肥藥吃到被判刑, 想減肥的民眾要特別注意服用的減肥藥成分
	Yi1_ming2_nu3zi3_<**chi1**>**_jian3fei2yao4_**chi1dao4_bei4_pan4xing2, xiang3_jian3fei2_de5_min2zhong4_yao4_te4bie2_zhu4yi4_fu2yong4_de5_jian3fei2yao4_cheng2fen4
	A woman took diet pills to lose weight. People who want to reduce their weight must pay special attention to what is in diet pills.
(19.1b)	柯林頓說, 巴格達自從一九九一年在波斯灣戰爭<吃>敗仗以來, 這是首次同意開放所有地點
	Ke1lin2dun4_shuo1, ba1ge2da2_zi4cong2_1991_nian2_zai4_po1si1wan1_zhan4zheng1_<**chi1**>**_bai4zhang4**_yi3lai2, zhe4shi4_shou3ci4_tong2yi4_kai1fang4_suo3you3_di4dian3
	Clinton said that after Baghdad's defeat in the Gulf War in 1991, it was the first time they agreed to open all locations to inspectors.
(19.2a)	在大街小巷隨處均可見到民眾<玩>足球
	Zai4_da4jie1_xiao3xiang4_sui2chu4_jun1ke3_jian4dao4_min2zhong4_<**wan2**>**_zu2qiu2**
	We can see people playing soccer everywhere.
(19.2b)	年輕人愛賺錢, 敢花錢, <玩>網路, 拼流行, 每個都是個性一族
	Nian2qing1ren2_ai4_zhuan4qian2, gan3_hua1qian2, <**wan2**>**_wang3lu4**、pin1_liu2xing2, mei3ge4_dou1shi4_ge4xing4_yi1zu2
	Young people like to make money and dare to spend it on unique fashion. Everyone is an individual.
(19.3a)	美國準備對「以石油<換>糧食」的方式進行「適度調整」的檢討。
	Mei3guo2_zhun3bei4_dui4_「yi3_shi2you2_<**huan4**>**_liang2shi2**」de5_fang1shi4_jin4xing2_「shi4du4_diao2zheng3」_de5_jian3tao3
	Americans will review whether it is appropriate to exchange food for oil.
(19.3b)	她即將<換>跑道, 接受一家英國公司聘請, 出任財務長
	Ta1_ji2jiang1_<**huan4**>**_pao3dao4**, jie1shou4_yi1jia1_ying1guo2_gong1si1_pin4qing4, chu1ren4_cai2wu4zhang3
	She could change tracks by accepting an invitation from a British company and occupying the position of chair of financial affairs.
(19.4a)	農政單位呼籲農民勿<燒>稻草。
	Nong2zheng4_dan1wei4_hu1yu4_nong2min2_wu4_<**shao1**>**_dao4cao3**
	The agricultural authority appealed to farmers not to burn straw.
(19.4b)	這些投資就好似在<燒>錢一樣, 但與實際營運所得卻不成比例。
	Zhe4xie1_tou2zi1_jiu4_hao3si4_zai4_<**shao1**>**_qian2**_yi1yang4, dan4_yu3_shi2ji4_ying2yun4_suo3de2_que4_bu4cheng2_bi3li4。
	These investments are similar to spending, but the incomes of actual operations are not proportionate.

We checked all the clusters of the four target words in Examples (19.1) to (19.4) using our intuition, based on the sense divisions in CWN, to determine whether they were regarded as physical senses or metaphorical senses. Therefore, not only did we

Table 19.2 The accuracy rate of the four target words in the character similarity clustering analysis

Target word	Accuracy rate (%)
chi1 "eat"	76.08
wan2 "play"	84.77
huan4 "change"	74.98
shao1 "burn"	77.95
Average	**78.45**

discover some clusters for physical senses but we also discovered some clusters for metaphorical senses, even before we performed any sense division work.

As stated before, without determining the number of clusters and the default targets of the four target words, the empirical theory of sense via automatic computational programming is without value. The key then is to determine the number of clusters set as the default targets to eliminate unrelated, unpredictable, and irrelevant words. By doing so, the default targets can be utilized to predict and assign senses to the four target words. Therefore, before placing collocation words into clusters, collocation words with frequencies that were less than or equal to two (≦2) were cut from the manually examined data. Then, the character similarity clustering analysis utilized automatic computational programming to process sense discovery and their collocation types.

By examining the partial testing data of the four target words using intuition, we were able to calculate the accuracy rate of the correct sentences, as shown in Table 19.2.

In sum, the character similarity clustering analysis of the four target words by sentence achieved an average accuracy rate of 78.45%.

Regarding the cluster determination from the character similarity clustering analysis, we concentrated on the same morpheme of all the collocation words in each cluster. However, if we focused only on the morpheme, then many non-related collocation words might be assigned to the same cluster or, alternatively, many related collocation words might be assigned to different clusters. Even though we were able to categorize appropriate words in the same cluster via the character similarity clustering analysis of the four lexically ambiguous target words in our study, some words still wound up in the wrong clusters. For example, 山藥 *shan1 yao4* "Chinese yam" and 藥 *yao4* "medicine" were in the same cluster, which is incorrect. In addition, 漢堡肉 *han4 bao3 rou4* "hamburger meat" was categorized in the 漢堡 *han4 bao3* "hamburger" cluster rather than in the 肉 *rou4* "meat" cluster.

Therefore, we further employed concept similarity clustering analysis to observe sense predictions, which should have yielded better results with higher accuracy rates. As will be seen in the next section, these default targets were used to evaluate the sense predictions of the four target words via CWN and *Xian Han*.

19.3.2 Concept Similarity Clustering Analysis

In the character similarity clustering analysis, we concentrated only on the collocation characters to obtain clusters with words that have the same characters and similar meanings. However, as mentioned above, some words that had the same characters, but dissimilar senses, were categorized into the same cluster—for example, 山藥 *shan1 yao4* "Chinese yam" and 藥 *yao4* "medicine." Consequently, this condition should be avoided; to achieve this, we first assigned all the words' lexical concepts via HowNet and then calculated the concept similarities to cluster these words. Since HowNet can provide more definite semantic elements and semantic features for all words, we utilized it to examine and ensure feature and concept determination. Moreover, we categorized the same semantic features of the collocation words of the four target words in the same cluster to aid in the empirical theory of sense. In addition, some collocation words were categorized into the same cluster, while other collocation words were categorized into a different cluster. Therefore, it was necessary to focus on the relationship between the concepts of the words by calculating the concepts' similarities and the distances between the words to predict some senses of lexically ambiguous words using HowNet.

The corpus-based and computational approach finds information via words, such as word collocation frequencies, and then calculates similarity using a complex statistics model (Jiang and Conrath 1997; Li et al. 2003; Lin 1998; Resnik 1999). As for the semantic distance-based approach, similarity is measured according to the distance between the locations of two words in a sense-based tree structure, such as in thesauri. Referring to previous studies (Ahrens et al. 2003; Dai et al. 2008; Mei et al. 1984; Miller et al. 1990), more than one approach was available to calculate concept similarity for different words in our study. We utilized a similarity calculation as the basis for clustering, which allowed us to extract the sememes of the concept for each collocation word using HowNet and further analyze their sememes.

Owing to more words being mapped to the same concept, these are usually regarded as synonymous words to some degree; for instance, the concepts of *xi1 gua1* "watermelon," *shi4 zi5* "persimmon," *ping2 guo3* "apple," and *pu2 tao2* "grapes" are regarded as synonyms of fruit. Therefore, they are categorized in the same cluster. In this way, we calculated the similarities of the concepts in our sense prediction study.

The two main strategies employed in the concept similarity clustering analysis were similarity between sememes and similarity between concepts via HowNet. First, we identified lexically ambiguous words. Next, we transformed all of the collocation words into concepts that might also be composed of several sememes. Finally, the senses of the most overlapping sememes were regarded as the senses of the lexically ambiguous words.

Similarity Between Sememes

Concerning distance-based approaches, Dai et al. (2008) mentioned that these approaches measure the semantic similarity between two words using the distance defined in a lexicon or knowledge base. Because HowNet does not organize words directly into a tree, Dai et al. (2008) were not able to measure similarity between words directly; instead, they measured the semantic similarity between sememes. For example, the distance between *beast* and *animal* is the same as that between *thing* and *entity*; however, the latter sememe pair is more abstract, so the similarity between *beast* and *animal* would be higher than that between *thing* and *entity* (Dai et al. 2008).

HowNet organizes all the sememes into several trees, and each sememe is considered a node of a tree. In this way, the distance between any two sememes can be calculated (Dai et al. 2008). In addition, the distance between the sememes can be defined as the length of the path between them, as shown in Eq. (19.4) below:

$$\text{sim\_seme}(S_1, S_2) = \frac{\min(d(S_1), d(S_2))}{\text{dis}(S_1, S_2) + \min(d(S_1), d(S_2))} \tag{19.4}$$

Similarity between sememes

In Eq. (19.4), $d(S_1)$ and $d(S_2)$ represent the level of sememes S_1 and S_2, respectively, in the semantic concept tree, while dis(S_1, S_2) represents the distance between sememes S_1 and S_2 in the semantic concept tree. We then employed the strategy of similarity between sememes to proceed to the next step—similarity between concepts in the concept similarity clustering analysis.

Similarity Between Concepts

Liu and Li (2002) defined word similarity as two words that can be substituted for each other in the same context and still keep the sentence syntactically and semantically consistent, meaning two similar words can be used in place of each other in certain contexts. Li et al. (2005) used similarity functions—bi-gram collocation extraction, construct synonym set, and synonym collocation—to deal with the synonym collocation extraction study by Liu and Li (2002).

In our study, we followed Dai et al. (2008), Liu and Li (2002), and Li et al. (2005) when trying to find the similarity between two concepts; however, we used three different dimensions to calculate them, summed the three amounts by their weight, and then obtained their similarity. Our schema is expressed in Eq. (19.5) below:

Table 19.3 Average accuracy rate of the four target words using the concept similarity clustering analysis

Target word	Accuracy rate (%)
chi1 "eat"	85.59
wan2 "play"	87.21
huan4 "change"	85.98
shao1 "burn"	84.81
Average	85.90

$$\underbrace{\mathrm{sim}_{\mathrm{def}(m,n)} = \alpha \times \mathrm{sim}_{\mathrm{seme}(pm,pn)} + \beta \times \frac{\sum_i \min\left(\mathrm{sim}_{\mathrm{seme}\left(m_i,n_j\right)}\right)}{|m|} + \gamma \times \frac{|m \cap n|}{|m| + |n|}}_{\text{Similarity between concepts}} \tag{19.5}$$

In Eq. (19.5), *pm* and *pn* represent the primary sememes of concept *m* and concept *n*, respectively. We then calculated the similarity, which is *sim_seme(pm, pn)*, between the main sememes of two concepts. Finally, we gained the final average similarity via Eq. (19.5) to determine the sense clusters. Further, *m* and *n* are two concepts that are regarded as a set of sememes, and *mp* and *np* are the main sememes of the two concepts. Separately, $|m \cap n|$ represents the sememe numbers for the two concepts $|m|$ and $|y|$. Since collocation words with frequencies that were less than or equal to two (≦2) were removed in the character similarity clustering analysis, following the same condition, collocation words with frequencies that were less than or equal to two (≦2) were also cut in the concept similarity clustering analysis.

Because the concepts were revealed by the collocation words in all the sentences with the four target words, where one cluster should have expressed one sense, it was reasonable to select clusters to examine their accuracy both randomly and directly. From these selected clusters, using our intuition, we examined the mapping concepts of the collocation words by focusing on the sentences in each cluster. Finally, after examining these clusters, their accuracy rates were obtained by examining their sentences. In this case, the accuracy rate of the clusters was over 84% for all clusters, with an average accuracy rate of 85.90%, as can be seen in Table 19.3.

Comparing the average accuracy rate found in the character similarity clustering analysis with the accuracy rate found in the concept similarity clustering analysis, the latter (see Table 19.3) produced a higher accuracy rate than the former (see Table 19.2), even when comparing the individual accuracy rates of the four target words. Next, the sense discoveries of the four target words were evaluated via Chinese WordNet and *Xian Han*.

19.3.3 Evaluation via CWN and Xian Han

Even though we could ensure better performances and obtain better accuracy rates utilizing the character similarity clustering and concept similarity clustering analyses, it was still necessary to perform evaluations of the empirical theory of sense in our study. To examine the accuracies of the sense discoveries of the four target words and certify their lexical senses, we evaluated the four target words via CWN and *Xian Han*.

Using CWN and *Xian Han*, the four target words were analyzed and assigned appropriate senses. Because we focused only on transitive verbs in this study, we needed to remove the noun usage senses and non-transitive verb usage senses in CWN and *Xian Han*. In addition, because we concentrated on modern Chinese only, we also needed to remove early period vernacular usage senses. Therefore, in CWN, there were 28 senses for *chi1* "eat," 9 senses for *wan2* "play," 5 senses for *huan4* "change," and 13 senses for *shao1* "burn," and in *Xian Han*, there were 7 senses for *chi1* "eat," 3 senses for *wan2* "play," 3 senses for *huan4* "change," and 5 senses for *shao1* "burn."

Next, we evaluated the sense discoveries of the four target words and examined their accuracy and recall based on the character similarity clustering analysis and the concept similarity clustering analysis using a corpus-based and computational approach.

Empirical Theory of Sense Based on Character Similarity Clustering Analysis

Although in the character similarity clustering analysis the main goal was character similarity, we were able to collect collocation words that had the same morpheme, place them into a particular cluster, and regard them as having the same sense before evaluating the sense discoveries of the four target words.

Based on the character similarity clustering analysis, we obtained the following results: 22 predicted senses out of 28 senses in CWN and 7 predicted senses out of 8 senses in *Xian Han* for *chi1* "eat"; 8 predicted senses out of 9 senses in CWN and 3 predicted senses out of 3 senses in *Xian Han* for *wan2* "play"; 5 predicted senses out of 5 senses in CWN and 3 predicted senses out of 3 senses in *Xian Han* for *huan4* "change"; and 8 predicted senses out of 13 senses in CWN and 4 predicted senses out of 8 senses in *Xian Han* for *shao1* "burn." Table 19.4 shows the results of the CWN and predicted senses.

Table 19.4 Evaluations in CWN based on the character similarity clustering analysis

Target word	CWN sense	Predicted sense	Recall (%)
chi1 "eat"	28	22	78.57
wan2 "play"	9	8	88.89
huan4 "change"	5	5	100.00
shao1 "burn"	13	8	61.54
Average			**82.25**

We found that when we tagged senses to the selected character similarity clusters based on sense division in CWN, for *chi1* "eat," only 22 senses could be predicted by intuition. At the same time, we also calculated the recall rate. Checking the evaluations made by intuition for *wan2* "play," only one sense could not be predicted in CWN, which was "沒有特定目的用手撥弄後述對象 (toy with something by hand purposelessly)." For *huan4* "change," we observed all five senses by intuition, while for *shao1* "burn," we observed only eight senses.

Under the same condition, based on the character similarity clustering analysis, we removed the noun usage senses, the non-transitive verb usage senses, and the early period vernacular usage senses in *Xian Han* for the evaluation of the target words. We did not find the sense "被多見於早期白話 (passive)" for *chi1* "eat" by intuition or four out of the eight senses for *shao1* "burn," such as "發燒 (fever)," "比正常體溫高的體溫 (the temperature is higher than normal)," and so on. However, we observed all of the *Xian Han* senses in the evaluations of *wan2* "play" and *huan4* "change" by intuition.

For *chi1* "eat," we found that when we tagged senses to these selected character similarity clusters based on sense division in CWN, only 22 senses could be predicted by intuition. For example, we observed the CWN sense "使食物經過口中吞入體內 (to take food through the mouth and swallow into the body)," but we did not observe the CWN sense "比喻取得對方棋子或牌 (to capture other chess pieces or playing cards)." At the same time, we also calculated the recall rate. Checking the evaluations made by intuition in *wan2* "play," we observed that only one CWN sense could not be predicted, which was "沒有特定目的用手撥弄後述對象 (toy with something by hand purposelessly)." For the evaluation of *huan4* "change," we observed all five CWN senses by intuition, while for the evaluation of *shao1* "burn," we observed only eight senses in CWN.

Empirical Theory of Sense Based on Concept Similarity Clustering Analysis

In Sect. 19.3.2, we discussed how we used three different dimensions to calculate the similarity between two concepts of the words in the same cluster in the concept similarity clustering analysis via HowNet as our knowledge base. These concepts became the features used to calculate concept similarities in our study. That is to say, each cluster represented one sense.

Similar to the evaluations based on the character similarity clustering analysis, the clusters for the target words found in the concept similarity clustering analysis were examined and evaluated using CWN and *Xian Han*. In the concept similarity clustering analysis, we tagged 24 senses from 28 senses for *chi1* "eat," 9 senses from 9 senses for *wan2* "play," 5 senses from 5 senses for *huan4* "change," and 10 senses from 13 senses for *shao1* "burn" in CWN. In *Xian Han*, we tagged seven senses from seven senses for *chi1* "eat," three senses from three senses for *wan2* "play," three senses from three senses for *huan4* "change," and four senses from five senses for *shao1* "burn." We then calculated their recalls.

In comparison to the evaluations of the four target words in the character similarity clustering analysis, the average accuracy rate in the concept similarity clustering analysis was higher than that in the character similarity clustering analysis. Following this inference, we expected the recalls of the four target words in the concept similarity clustering analysis to be higher as well. However, for the predicted clusters in the concept similarity clustering analysis, we did not obtain a higher average recall rate compared to that in the character similarity clustering analysis.

Concerning the evaluations of the predicted clusters based on the concept similarity clustering analysis in CWN, we predicted *wan2* "play" and *huan4* "change" completely, while we predicted 24 senses from 28 senses for *chi1* "eat" and 10 senses from 13 senses for *shao1* "burn." The missing senses included "比喻佔便宜 (to gain extra advantage)" for *chi1* "eat" and "形容超過正常的較高體溫 (the temperature is higher than normal)" for *shao1* "burn."

Comparisons of the Four Target Words in CWN and in *Xian Han*

It is worth noting that for both the character similarity clustering analysis and the concept similarity clustering analysis, we tagged less senses than the CWN senses for *chi1* "eat," *wan2* "play," *huan4* "change," and *shao1* "burn." The comparisons of the recalls between the character similarity clustering analysis and the concept similarity clustering analysis in CWN and in *Xian Han* are presented in Tables 19.5 and 19.6, respectively.

The divided senses included colloquial or slang usages in both CWN and *Xian Han*, but we did not find colloquial usages in Taiwan's Central News Agency (Chinese Gigaword Corpus). Concerning CWN and *Xian Han*, there were more senses of the four target words in CWN than in *Xian Han*, which means that the

Table 19.5 Comparisons of the recalls between the character similarity clustering analysis and the concept similarity clustering analysis in CWN

Target word	CWN sense	Character similarity	Concept similarity
chi1 "eat"	28	22	24
wan2 "play"	9	8	9
huan4 "change"	5	5	5
shao1 "burn"	13	8	10

Table 19.6 Comparisons of the recalls between the character similarity clustering analysis and the concept similarity clustering analysis in *Xian Han*

Target word	*Xian Han* sense	Character similarity	Concept similarity
chi1 "eat"	7	7	7
wan2 "play"	3	3	3
huan4 "change"	3	3	3
shao1 "burn"	5	4	4

CWN sense divisions were more detailed than the *Xian Han* sense divisions. That is to say, in CWN, the senses were used extensively; on the contrary, in *Xian Han*, the senses used were more common.

Therefore, if we could provide more semantic features or concepts when presenting the collocation words of the four target words in detail, their evaluations and their recalls could also be improved based on both the character similarity clustering analysis and the concept similarity clustering analysis (see Table 19.5). Regarding *Xian Han*, the evaluations of the four target words were the same for both the character similarity clustering analysis and the concept similarity clustering analysis, even though we set up two different cluster numbers to evaluate them (see Table 19.6).

Finally, regarding another interesting finding, because there were more senses in CWN than in *Xian Han*, we observed some senses that appeared only in CWN. The senses in CWN were richer and more varied, thus representing detailed senses in different contexts or discourses. On the contrary, the senses in *Xian Han* were simpler, and they represented only common senses in different contexts, for instance, for *chi1* "eat," 吃奶嘴 *chi1 nai3 zui3* "to keep pacifiers," 吃好處 *chi1 hao3 chu4* "to gain benefits," 吃宴會 *chi1 yan4 hui4* "to dine at a banquet," 吃案 *chi1 an4* "to cover cases," and 吃銅板 *chi1 tong3 ban3* "to accept coins"; for *wan2* "play," 玩打火機 *wan2 da3 huo3 ji1* "to toy with a lighter" and 玩專案 *wan2 zhuan1 an4* "to play a game"; and for *shao1* "burn," 燒數據 *shao1 shu4 ju4* "to copy data," 燒時間 *shao1 shi2 jian1* "to expend time," and 燒稅金 *shao1 shui4 jin1* "to expend taxes."

19.4 Experimental Evaluation

In this section, we will demonstrate that using offline tasks to test native speakers' intuition supports the notion that different clusters that have been divided using a corpus-based and computational approach represent different senses. To examine the related collocation words of the lexically ambiguous target words, we employed multiple-choice tasks. Moreover, we obtained experimental data from and designed the multiple-choice tasks based on the related collocation words of *chi1* "eat," *wan2* "play," *huan4* "change," and *shao1* "burn" in the character similarity clustering analysis using the corpus-based and computational approach. In the first multiple-choice task, which was independent of context, there were four alternatives for each question. The participants were asked to choose one word/item that was different from the other three words/items presented. In other words, the concept of the selected word/item was obviously different from the concept of the other three words/items.

The experimental evaluation also included four main multiple-choice tasks to test the four target words and the four different clusters (four different head nouns of collocation types) of each target word from the character similarity clustering analysis using the corpus-based and computational approach. Based on questionnaires that contained 60 questions (15 items per suffix for each target word), 80 students were divided into 4 groups of 20 participants to examine 8 different lists of the 4 target words (2 lists for each target word), and each group of participants was assigned to 2 different lists. We then ran the four main multiple-choice tasks to test the four target words, respectively. After obtaining the results, we analyzed the two lists for each main multiple-choice task.

19.4.1 Participants

A separate group of 20 participants (mean age = 20.6, SD = 1.5 years, ranging from 18 to 23 years old) took part in the offline multiple-choice tasks for each target word. There were 11 females and 9 males, all right-handed and all with no linguistic background knowledge. These participants were all undergraduate students at National Taiwan University, had lived in Taiwan since birth, and were native speakers of Mandarin, such as Taiwanese, Hakka, or an Austronesian language. None of the students had participated in any of the pretests, nor had they participated in the *chi1* "eat" task. All of the participants were paid NT$100 (equivalent to US$3.14) for their participation, which took about 30 min.

19.4.2 Stimuli

Discussing all the stimuli from the related collocation words for *chi1* "eat" in the character similarity clustering analysis using the corpus-based and computational approach, we focused on four different sense clusters: 藥 *yao4* "medicine," 飯 *fan4* "rice," 餐 *can1* "meal," and 肉 *rou4* "meat."

There were 60 different collocation items for *chi1* "eat" in Mandarin Chinese, such as 中藥 *zhong1 yao4* "traditional Chinese medicine," 米飯 *mi3 fan4* "rice," 早餐 *zao3 can1* "breakfast," 豬肉 *zhu1 rou4* "pork," and so on. In other words, among the 4 sense clusters—藥 *yao4* "medicine," 飯 *fan4* "rice," 餐 *can1* "meal," and 肉 *rou4* "meat"—there were 15 collocation items in each sense cluster, which were all nouns, had the same suffix, and had 2 or 3 respective characters, such as 止痛藥 *zhi3 tong4 yao4* "anodyne," 八寶飯 *ba1 bao3 fan4* "Chinese rice pudding," and 早餐 *zao3 can1* "breakfast" versus 自助餐 *zi4 zhu4 can1* "buffet" and 豬肉 *zhu1 rou4* "pork." In addition, all of the collocation items occurred in the Chinese Gigaword Corpus.

Regarding the fillers, they were all nouns with the same suffix for the 藥 *yao4* "medicine," 飯 *fan4* "rice," 餐 *can1* "meal," and 肉 *rou4* "meat" clusters in the *chi1* "eat" task based on the new dictionary mandated by the Ministry of Education, R.O.C. (http://140.111.34.46/newDict/dict/index.html), and they all appeared in the Chinese Gigaword Corpus—for example, 山藥 *shan1 yao4* "Chinese yam," 牢飯 *lao2 fan4* "imprisonment," 誤餐 *wu4 can1* "missing meal," and 椰肉 *ye2 rou4* "coconut." We did this to control their frequencies and to make sure that they all appeared in the same corpus as our stimuli.

19.4.3 Procedure

In the multiple-choice tasks for the experimental evaluation of the 4 target words, we designed offline questionnaires containing 60 questions and used the same stimuli and fillers to create 2 different lists for each target word. Moreover, the construction and content of the offline questionnaires were similar to the previously used materials: 2 different lists for each target word, 60 questions for each questionnaire, 8 random questions per page, and a suffix that occurred 2 times per page. For example, the completed questionnaires for *chi1* "eat" are shown in List 1 and List 2 below:

List 1. The offline multiple-choice task for *chi1* "eat"

(1) Which concept of the selected word/item is obviously different from the concepts of the other three words/items?

a) *Zhi3 tong4 yao4*；b) *Shan1 yao4*；c) *Xie4 yao4*；d) *Cheng2 yao4*

(2) Which concept of the selected word/item is obviously different from the concepts of the other three words/items?

a) *Xi1 can1*；b) *Zhong1 can1*；c) *Xheng4 can1*；d) *Bian4 can1*

(3) Which concept of the selected word/item is obviously different from the concepts of the other three words/items?

a) *Gan1 fan4*；b) *Ba1 bao3 fan4*；c) *Bai2 fan4*；d) *Dan4* fan4

(4) Which concept of the selected word/item is obviously different from the concepts of the other three words/items?

a) *Guo3 rou4*；b) *Lu4 rou4*；c) *Jing1 rou4*；d) *Fei2 rou4*

List 2. The offline multiple-choice task for *chi1* "eat"

(1) Which concept of the selected word/item is obviously different from the concepts of the other three words/items?

a) *Huo3 yao4*；b) *Zhong1 yao4*；c) *An1 mian2 yao4*；d) *Nong2 yao4*

(2) Which concept of the selected word/item is obviously different from the concepts of the other three words/items?

a) *Kuai4 can1*；b) *Dai4 can1*；c) *He2 can1*；d) *Su4 can1*

(3) Which concept of the selected word/item is obviously different from the concepts of the other three words/items?

a) *Zhu1 rou4*；b) *Guo3 rou4*；c) *Pi2 rou4*；d) *Ji1 rou4*

(4) Which concept of the selected word/item is obviously different from the concepts of the other three words/items?

a) *Du2 yao4*；b) *Ma2 yao4*；c) *Zha3 yao4*；d) *Jian3 fei2 yao4*

After running the multiple-choice tasks for the 4 target words, we analyzed the 60 questions/answers from the questionnaires of each participant and placed them into either the YES group or the NO group. In the YES group, items that represented

Table 19.7 Multiple-choice task for *chi1* "eat" by subject

	Yes	No
Average	48.95	11.05
Percentage	81.58%	18.42%

Table 19.8 Multiple-choice task for *wan2* "play" by subject

	Yes	No
Average	49.50	10.50
Percentage	82.50%	17.50%

Table 19.9 Multiple-choice task for *huan4* "change" by subject

	Yes	No
Average	52.15	7.85
Percentage	86.92%	13.08%

Table 19.10 Multiple-choice task for *shao1* "burn" by subject

	Yes	No
Average	46.65	13.35
Percentage	77.75%	22.25%

Table 19.11 Multiple-choice task for *chi1* "eat" by item

	Yes	No
Average	16.32	3.68
Percentage	81.58%	18.42%
Chi-squared	$p = 1.43293\text{E-}30$ ($p < 0.05$), significant	

stimuli were collected from the collocation words of the four target words based on the character similarity clustering analysis. In the NO group, items that were fillers were collected from the new dictionary mandated by the Ministry of Education, R.O.C. Although the stimuli and fillers had the same suffix, more words with different concepts were observed; for example, in the *chi1* "eat" task, 眼球 *yan3 qiu2* "eyeball" was different from 球 *qiu2* "ball" in concept, 盾牌 *dun4 pai2* "shield" was different from 牌 *pai2* "playing card" in concept, 焊槍 *han4 qiang1* "welding torch" was different from 槍 *qiang1* "gun" in concept, and 吊車 *diao4 che1* "hoisting machine" was different from 車 *che1* "car" in concept.

While we distinguished and analyzed the YES group and the NO group based on the participants' answers, the multiple-choice tasks containing the four target words also demonstrated other related analysis based on each item. If the participants chose items that were collected from the collocation words of the four target words based on the character similarity clustering analysis, we regarded these answers as belonging to the YES group; otherwise, the answers were regarded as belonging to the NO group. We then manually calculated the numbers in the YES group and the NO group by subject. Some findings are presented in Tables 19.7, 19.8, 19.9, and 19.10.

Concerning the calculation of the multiple-choice tasks containing the four target words, we found that it was more important to calculate by item than by subject. Therefore, we used a chi-squared test to compare the YES group with the NO group.

Table 19.12 Multiple-choice task for *wan2* "play" by item

	Yes	No
Average	16.50	3.50
Percentage	82.50%	17.50%
Chi-squared	$p = 7.60103E\text{-}41$ ($p < 0.05$), significant	

Table 19.13 Multiple-choice task for *huan4* "change" by item

	Yes	No
Average	17.38	2.62
Percentage	86.92%	13.08%
Chi-squared	$p = 6.45069E\text{-}26$ ($p < 0.05$), significant	

Table 19.14 Multiple-choice task for *shao1* "burn" by item

	Yes	No
Average	15.55	4.45
Percentage	77.75%	22.25%
Chi-squared	$p = 1.48997E\text{-}35$ ($p < 0.05$), significant	

We found that the *p* values were obviously significant, which means that we controlled all the stimuli and fillers for the YES group and the NO group. The distributions are shown in Tables 19.11, 19.12, 19.13, and 19.14.

Therefore, whether by subject or by item, we knew which words belonged to the same sense cluster of the four target words via the multiple-choice tasks for experimental evaluation. In addition, we observed not only a higher percentage by subject via these multiple-choice tasks but also a higher percentage and significance by item.

19.4.4 Analysis

We analyzed the four main tasks, respectively, and calculated the accuracy rates for the YES group using intuition. We found that the highest accuracy rate was for *huan4* "change," while the lowest accuracy rate was for *shao1* "burn." In addition, because the stimuli were collected from the character similarity clustering analysis using the corpus-based and computational approach, we demonstrated the viability of this approach by the results presented in our study.

When we analyzed the questionnaires, we found that the participants chose items consistently. In other words, the participants understood the items and consistently chose the appropriate items as the answers in the questionnaires. For example, in the *shao1* "burn" task, the participants chose "雪車" as the answer for different questions.

Moreover, among all 60 items in the *chi1* "eat" task, we observed that the 2 items with the lowest accuracy rates were in the 飯 *fan4* "rice" cluster and the 餐 *can1* "meal" cluster, which clearly affected the accuracy rates of these 2 clusters. Some other findings concluded that the two items with the lowest accuracy rates were in the 槍 *qiang1* "gun" cluster in the *wan2* "play" task, the item with the lowest accuracy rate in the *huan4* "change" task was in the 車 *che1* "car" cluster, and the item with the lowest accuracy rate in the *shao1* "burn" task was in the 菜 *cai4* "vegetable" cluster.

In analyzing the lower accuracy rates in these multiple-choice tasks for the experimental evaluation of the *chi1* "eat," *wan2* "play," *huan4* "change," and *shao1* "burn" tasks, we extracted their fillers, for example, 會飯 *hui4 fan4* "millet" and 素餐 *su4 can1* "having official's salary without contribution" in the *chi1* "eat" task; 焊槍 *han4 qiang1* "welding torch" and 銲槍 *han4 qiang1* "welding torch" in the *wan2* "play" task; 雪車 *xue3 che1* "vehicle for sliding in the snow" and 吊車 *diao4 che1* "hoisting machine" in the *huan4* "change" task; and 燕菜 *yan4 cai4* "edible nest of cliff swallows" and 洋菜 *yang2 cai4* "agar" in the *shao1* "burn" task. We also found that they all appeared in the Chinese Gigaword Corpus; however, their frequencies were lower in general, meaning it was more difficult for all of the participants to comprehend and recognize the interpretation of the concepts properly.

Following these offline multiple-choice tasks for the experimental evaluation of *chi1* "eat," *wan2* "play," *huan4* "change," and *shao1* "burn," we demonstrated that some of the words we examined were the same in concept and were regarded as having the same sense by native speakers' intuition, such as by using the corpus-based and computational approach.

19.5 Comparison

In our study, we first discussed two methods using the corpus-based and computational approach: character similarity clustering analysis and concept similarity clustering analysis. We then ran offline multiple-choice tasks for the experimental evaluation of *chi1* "eat," *wan2* "play," *huan4* "change," and *shao1* "burn," one based on automatic computational programming and one based on human comprehension. Compared with the results of the experimental evaluation of the four target words, their accuracy rates were over 77%, while the average accuracy rate was over 82%. The previous results of the accuracy rates of the four target words were combined and are shown in Table 19.15.

Table 19.15 Three main average accuracy rates of the four target words

Target word	Character similarity (%)	Concept similarity (%)	Experimental evaluation (%)
chi1 "eat"	76.08	85.59	81.58
wan2 "play"	84.77	87.21	82.50
huan4 "change"	74.98	85.98	86.92
shao1 "burn"	77.95	84.81	77.75
Average	**78.45**	**85.90**	**82.19**
Note	**Over 78**	**Over 85**	**Over 82**

The three main average accuracy rates of the four target words in our study shown in Table 19.15 do not display differences that are far from what is considered normal. Because we focused only on their similar morphemes, clustered them into the same cluster, and regarded them as having the same sense in the character similarity clustering analysis, we were able to concentrate on the concepts of all the collocations of the four target words to calculate their similarities. We then selected several stimuli from the character similarity clustering analysis to run offline multiple-choice tasks for the experimental evaluation of the four target words, selecting only the same head nouns for the tasks. As a result, we discovered that the conditions that focused on the concept similarities of the collocations of the four target words in the concept similarity clustering analysis were stricter than the conditions that focused only on the morpheme similarities in the collocations of the four target words in the character similarity clustering analysis; hence, the average accuracy rate is 85% versus 78%. Moreover, when we selected words that had the same head nouns as the stimuli, we obtained better performances and higher accuracy rates in the offline multiple-choice tasks for the experimental evaluation of the four target words; hence, the average accuracy rate is 82% versus 78%.

19.6 Conclusion

In our study, we explored conceptual lexicalization divisions by automatically predicting all possible senses for a given word. We took four target words—*chi1* "eat," *wan2* "play," *huan4* "change," and *shao1* "burn"—and used a large-scale corpus as empirical data to compute their clusters to demonstrate all possible senses in an attempt to verify the schemas of conceptual lexicalization processing.

The goal of our study aimed to find appropriate approaches to exploring all possible senses of the four target words, which had no lexically assigned senses. Although the fundamental strategies were corpus-based linguistic approaches to the empirical theory of sense, two important perspectives that include the corpus-based and computational approach and experimental evaluation were also discussed.

In the corpus-based and computational approach, character similarity clustering analysis and concept similarity clustering analysis were the main strategies employed. We obtained better performances and higher accuracy rates in the concept similarity clustering analysis. To demonstrate the significant meaning and value of these two approaches, not only did we focus on their accuracy rates but we also observed the evaluations of *chi1* "eat," *wan2* "play," *huan4* "change," and *shao1* "burn" via Chinese WordNet (CWN) and *Xiandai Hanyu Cidian* (*Xian Han*). In doing so, we were able to present significant results for the character similarity clustering analysis and the concept similarity clustering analysis and evaluate their performances, respectively.

In our study, according to these discussions, comparisons, and results, we found that it was useful to employ both the character similarity clustering analysis and the concept similarity clustering analysis using the corpus-based and computational approach. It was also helpful to run offline multiple-choice tasks for the experimental evaluation of the four target words to support this study regarding the empirical theory of sense. Future challenges include explaining and demonstrating regular patterns of conceptual lexicalization divisions in lexical semantic studies.

References

Agirre, Eneko, Izaskun Aldezabal, and Eli Pociello. 2006. Lexicalization and multiword expressions in the Basque WordNet. Paper presented at the *Third International WordNet Conference*. Jeju Island, Korea. Available at http://citeseerx.ist.psu.edu/viewdoc/download?doi=10.1.1.302.9214&rep=rep1&type=pdf. Accessed 13 March 2019.

Ahrens, Kathleen. 1998. Lexical ambiguity resolution: Languages, tasks and timing. In *Sentence processing: A cross-linguistic perspective*, ed. Dieter Hillert, 11–31. San Diego: Academic Press.

Ahrens, Kathleen. 2001. On-line sentence comprehension of ambiguous verbs in Mandarin. *Journal of East Asian Linguistics* 10(4):337–358.

Ahrens, Kathleen. 2006. The effect of visual target presentation times on lexical ambiguity resolution. *Language and Linguistics* 7(3):677–696.

Ahrens, Kathleen, Chu-Ren Huang, and Shirley Chuang. 2003. Sense and meaning facets in verbal semantics: A MARVS perspective. *Language and Linguistics* 4(3):468–484.

Angwin, Anthony J., Nadeeka N. W. Dissanayaka, Katie L. McMahon, Peter A. Silburn, and David A. Copland. 2017. Lexical ambiguity resolution during sentence processing in Parkinson's disease: An event-related potential study. *PLoS ONE* 12(5):e0176281. Available at https://doi.org/10.1371/journal.pone.0176281. Accessed 5 October 2017.

Baroni, Marco, and Alessandro Lenci. 2010. Distributional memory: A general framework for corpus-based semantics. *Computational Linguistics* 36(4):673–721.

Bolette, Sandford Pedersen. 1997. Lexical ambiguity in machine translation: Using frame semantics for expressing regularities in polysemy. In *Recent advances in natural language processing II*, ed. Nicolas Nicolov and Ruslan Mitkov, 207–220. Amsterdam/Philadelphia: John Benjamins Publishing Company.

Burton, Steven J., Richard R. Sudweeks, Paul F. Merrill, and Bud Wood. 1991. *How to prepare better multiple-choice test items: Guidelines for university faculty*. Doctoral dissertation, Brigham Young University. Department of Instructional Science.

Buscaldi, Davide, Paolo Rosso, and Emilio Sanchis. 2007. A WordNet-based indexing technique for geographical information retrieval. In Evaluation of Multilingual and Multi-modal Information Retrieval of *Lecture notes in computer science (LNCS) 4730*, ed. Carol Peters, Paul Clough, Fredric C. Gey, Jussi Karlgren Bernardo Magnini, Douglas W. Oard, Maarten de Rijke, and Maximilian Stempfhuber, 954–957. Berlin: Springer.

Canas, Alberto J., Alejandro Valerio, Juan Lalinde-Pulido, Marco Carvalho, and Marco Arguedas. 2003. Using WordNet for word sense disambiguation to support concept map construction. In *Proceedings of SPIRE 2003—10th International Symposium on String Processing and Information Retrieval*, 350–359. Manaus, Brazil. Available at https://link.springer.com/chapter/10.1007/978-3-540-39984-1_27. Accessed 13 March 2019.

Chen, Jinying, and Martha Palmer. 2009. Improving English verb sense disambiguation performance with linguistically motivated features and clear sense distinction boundaries. *Language Resources and Evaluation* 43(2):181–208.

Chen, Hao, Tingting He, Donghong Ji, and Changqin Quan. 2005. An unsupervised approach to Chinese word sense disambiguation based on Hownet. *Computational Linguistics and Chinese Language Processing* 10(4):473–482.

Chinese Academy of Social Sciences. 2005. *The Contemporary Chinese Dictionary* 现代汉语词典 (5th ed.). Beijing: The Commercial Press.

Cruse, D. Alan. 1986. *Lexical semantics*. Cambridge, UK: Cambridge University Press.

Dai, Liu-Ling, Bin Liu, Yuning Xia, and Shi-Kun Wu. 2008. Measuring semantic similarity between words using HowNet. In *Proceedings of the International Conference on Computer Science and Information Technology*, 601–605. Singapore. Available at https://ieeexplore.ieee.org/abstract/document/4624938. Accessed 13 March 2019.

Dice, Lee R. 1945. Measures of the amount of ecologic association between species. *Journal of Ecology* 26:297–302.

Dong, Zhen-Dong, and Qiang Dong. 2000. HowNet knowledge database 知网. Available at http://www.keenage.com. Accessed 5 October 2017.

Elston-Guttler, Kerrie E., and Angela D. Friederici. 2006. Ambiguous words in sentences: Brain indices for native and non-native disambiguation. *Neuroscience Letters* 414:85–89.

Fellbaum, Christiane (ed.). 1998. *WordNet: An electronic lexical database*. Cambridge, MA: MIT Press.

Fujii, Hideo, and Bruce W. Croft. 1993. A comparison of indexing techniques for Japanese text retrieval. In *Proceedings of the Sixteenth Annual International ACM SIGIR Conference on Research and Development in Information Retrieval*, 237–246. Pittsburgh, PA. Available at https://dl.acm.org/citation.cfm?id=160728. Accessed 13 March 2019.

Gries, Stefan Th. 2012. Behavioral profiles: A fine-grained and quantitative approach in corpus-based lexical semantics. In *Methodological and analytic frontiers in lexical research*, ed. Gonia Jarema, Gary Libben, and Chris Westbury, 57–80. Amsterdam and Philadelphia: John Benjamins.

Gunter, Thomas C., Susanne Wagner, and Angela D. Friederici. 2003. Working memory and lexical ambiguity resolution as revealed by ERPs: A difficult case for activation theories. *Journal of Cognitive Neuroscience* 15(5):643–657.

Hong, Jia-Fei. 2015. *Verb sense discovery in Mandarin Chinese—A corpus based knowledge-intensive approach*. Berlin: Springer.

Hsu, Ya-Ling, and Mei-chun Liu. 2004. A resolution for polysemy: the case of Mandarin verb *ZOU* (走). Paper presented at the *Conference on Computational Linguistics and Speech Processing: ROCLING XVI*. Howard Pacific Green Bay, Taipei, Taiwan, R.O.C. Available at http://www.aclweb.org/anthology/O04-1016. Accessed 13 March 2019.

Huang, Chu-Ren, Keh-Jiann Chen, and Zhao-Ming Gao. 1998. Noun class extraction from a corpus-based collocation dictionary: An integration of computational and qualitative approaches. In *Quantitative and computational studies of Chinese linguistics*, ed. Benjamin Tsou, Tom Lai, Samuel Chan, and William S.-Y. Wang, 339–352. Hong Kong: City University of Hong Kong.

Huang, Chu-Ren, Kathleen Ahrens, Li-Li Chang, Keh-Jiann Chen, Mei-Chun Liu, and Mei-Chih Tsai. 2000. The module-attribute representation of verbal semantics: From semantics to argument structure. In *Computational Linguistics and Chinese Language Processing* [Special issue], ed. Yung-O Biq 5(1):19–46.

Jiang, Jay J., and David W. Conrath. 1997. Semantic similarity based on corpus statistics and lexical taxonomy. In *Proceedings of the International Conference Research on Computational Linguistics (ROCLING X)*. Taipei, Taiwan. Available at https://arxiv.org/abs/cmp-lg/9709008. Accessed 13 March 2019.

Jin, Peng, Xu Sun, Yunfang Wu, and Shiwen Yu. 2007. Word clustering for collocation-based word sense disambiguation. In *Proceedings of the Eighth International Conference on Intelligent Text Processing and Computational Linguistics (CICLing 2007), LNCS 4394*, 267–274. Mexico City, Mexico. Available at https://link.springer.com/chapter/10.1007/978-3-540-70939-8_24. Accessed 13 March 2019.

Ker, Sue-Jin, and Jen-Nan Chen. 2004. Adaptive word sense tagging on Chinese corpus. In *Proceedings of PACLIC 18*, 267–273. Waseda University, Tokyo. Available at http://www.aclweb.org/anthology/Y04-1028. Accessed 13 March 2019.

Kilgarriff, Adam, Pavel Rychlý, Pavel Smrz, and David Tugwell. 2004. The Sketch Engine. In *Proceedings of EURALEX*. Lorient, France. Available at https://pdfs.semanticscholar.org/00ab/8d58aef326267a47d1d724f6ed9bf1f6561f.pdf. Accessed 13 March 2019.

Kipper, Karin, Anna Korhonen, Neville Ryant, and Martha Palmer. 2008. A large-scale classification of English verbs. *Language Resources and Evaluation Journal* 42(1):21–40.

Klepousniotou, Ekaterini. 2002. The processing of lexical ambiguity: Homonymy and polysemy in the mental lexicon. *Brain and Language* 81(1–3):205–223.

Levin, Beth, and Steven Pinker (eds.). 1992. *Lexical and conceptual semantics. A special issue of cognition*. Oxford: Blackwell.

Li, Ping. 1998a Crosslinguistic variation and sentence processing: The case of Chinese. In *Sentence processing: A cross-linguistic perspective*, ed. Dieter Hillert. San Diego, CA: Academic Press.

Li, Ping. 1998bContext effects and processing of spoken homophones. In *Reading and writing: An interdisciplinary journal* (Vol. 10), ed. Che Kan Leong and Katsuo Tamaoka, 223–243. Dordrecht: Kluwer Academic Publishers.

Li, Ping, and Michael Yip. 1996. Lexical ambiguity and context effects in spoken word recognition: Evidence from Chinese. In *Proceedings of the 18th Annual Meeting of the Cognitive Science Society*, ed. G. Cottrell, 228–232. Hillsdale, NJ: Lawrence Earlbaum Associates. Available at http://blclab.org/wp-content/uploads/2013/02/cogsci96-1.pdf. Accessed 13 March 2019.

Li, Yu-Hua, Zuhair A. Bandar, and David McLean. 2003. An approach for measuring semantic similarity between words using multiple information sources. *IEEE Transactions on Knowledge and Data Engineering* 15:871–182.

Li, Ping, Zhen Jin, and Li Hai Tan. 2004. Neural representations of nouns and verbs in Chinese: An fMRI study. *Neuroimage* 21:1533–1541.

Li, Wanyin, Qin Lu, and Ruifeng Xu. 2005. Similarity based Chinese synonym collocation extraction. *Computational Linguistics and Chinese Language Processing* 10(1):123–144.

Lien, Chinfa. 2000. A frame-based account of lexical polysemy in Taiwanese. *Language and Linguistics* 1(1):119–138.

Lin, Dekang. 1998. Automatic retrieval and clustering of similar words. In *Proceedings of the 36th Annual Meeting of the Association for Computational Linguistics*, 768–774. Montréal, Québec, Canada. Available at http://www.aclweb.org/anthology/C98-2122. Accessed 13 March 2019.

Lin, Charles, and Kathleen Ahrens. 2000. Calculating the number of senses: Implications for ambiguity advantage effect during lexical access. In *Proceedings of the Seventh International Symposium on Chinese Languages and Linguistics*, ed. Hao-Yi Tai and Yungli. Chang, 141–155. Chai-yi: National Chung-Cheng University. Available at http://www.u.arizona.edu/~clin/professional/papers/00iscll7.pdf. Accessed 13 March 2019.

Liu, Qun, and Su-Jian Li. 2002. The word similarity calculation on <<HowNet>>. In *Proceedings of the 3rd Conference on Chinese Lexicography*. Taipei, Taiwan.

Liu, Mei-chun, Ting-Yi Chaing, and Ming-hui Chou. 2005. A Frame-based approach to polysemous near-synonymy: The case with Mandarin verbs of expression. *Journal of Chinese Language and Computing* 15(3): 137–148.

Ma, Wei-yun, and Chu-Ren Huang. 2006. Uniform and effective tagging of a heterogeneous Gigaword corpus. Paper presented at the *5th International Conference on Language Resources and Evaluation (LREC2006)*. Genoa, Italy. Available at http://cwn.ling.sinica.edu.tw/churen/C06_Uniform.pdf. Accessed 13 March 2019.

Martinez, David, Eneko Agirre, and Xinglong Wang. 2006. Word relatives in context for word sense disambiguation. In *Proceedings of the 2006 Australasian Language Technology Workshop (ALTW2006)*, 42–50. Sydney, Australia. http://www.aclweb.org/anthology/U06-1008. Accessed 13 March 2019.

Mason, Robert A., and Marcel Adam Just. 2007. Lexical ambiguity in sentence comprehension. *Brain Research* 1146:115–127.

McRoy, Susan. 1992. Using multiple knowledge sources for word sense disambiguation. *Computational Linguistics* 18(1):1–30.

Mei, Jiaju 梅家驹, Yiming Zhu 竺一鸣, Yunqi Gao 高蕴琦, and Hongxiang Yin 殷鸿翔. 1984. *Dictionary of Synonymous Words* 同义词词林. *Shanghai*. Shanghai Lexicographical Publishing House.

Miller, George A., Richard Beckwith, Christiane Fellbaum, Derek Gross, and Katherine Miller. 1990. Introduction to WordNet: An on-line lexical database. *International Journal of Lexicography* 3(4): 235–244.

Moldovan, Dan, and Adrian Novischi. 2004. Word sense disambiguation of WordNet glosses. *Computer Speech and Language* 18:301–317.

Pitler, Emily, Annie Louis, and Ani Nenkova. 2009. Automatic sense prediction for implicit discourse relations in text. In *Proceedings of the 47th Annual Meeting of the ACL and the 4th IJCNCLP of the AFNLP*, 683–691. Suntec, Singapore. Available at https://dl.acm.org/citation.cfm?id=1690241. Accessed 13 March 2019.

Prior, Anat, Shuly Wintner, Brian MacWhinney, and Alon Lavie. 2011. Translation ambiguity in and out of context. *Applied Psycholinguistics* 32:93–111.

Pustejovsky, James. 1995. *The generative lexicon*. Cambridge, MA: MIT Press.

Ramakrishnan, Ganesh, Bhattacharya Pushpak Prithviraj, A. Deepa, Pushpak Bhattacharyya, and Soumen Chakrabarti. 2004. Soft word sense disambiguation. In *Proceedings of the Second Global Wordnet Conference 2004*, 291–298. Brno, Czech Republic. Available at https://www.researchgate.net/profile/Zhihui_Jin/publication/2936910_Statistical_Overview_of_WordNet_from_16_to_20/links/561db42908aef097132b2719/Statistical-Overview-of-WordNet-from-16-to-20.pdf#page=303. Accessed 13 March 2019.

Ravin, Yael, and Claudia Leacock. 2000. Polysemy: An overview. In *Polysemy: Theoretical and computational approaches*, ed. Yael Ravin and Claudia Leacock, 1–29. New York: Oxford University Press.

Redington, Martin, Nick Chater, Chu-Ren Huang, Li-Ping Chang, Steve Finch, and Keh-Jiann Chen. 1995. The universality of simple distributional methods: Identifying syntactic categories in Mandarin Chinese. In *Proceedings of the International Conference on Cognitive Science and Natural Language Processing*. Dublin City University, Ireland. Available at https://www.dectech.co.uk/publications/LinksNick/Language/universality%20of%20simple%20distributional%20methods.pdf. Accessed 13 March 2019.

Resnik, Philip. 1999. Semantic similarity in a taxonomy: An information-based measure and its application to problems of ambiguity in natural language. *Artificial Intelligence Research* 11: 95–130.

Resnik, Philip, and David Yarowsky. 2000. Distinguishing systems and distinguishing senses: New evaluation methods for word sense disambiguation. *Natural Language Engineering* 5(3): 113–133.

Tabossi, Patrizia, and Francesco Zardon. 1993. Processing ambiguous words in context. *Journal of Memory and Language* 32:359–372.

Ten Hacken, Pius, and Claire Thomas. 2013. *The semantics of word formation and lexicalization*. Edinburgh University Press.

Van Petten, Cyma, and Barbara Luka. 2006. Neural localization of semantic context effects in electromagnetic and hemodynamic studies. *Brain and Language* 97:279–293.

Véronis, Jean, and Nancy M. Ide. 1990. Word sense disambiguation with very large neural networks extracted from machine readable dictionaries. In *Proceedings of the 13th Conference on Computational Linguistics*, 389–394. Helsinki, Finland. Available at https://dl.acm.org/citation.cfm?id=998006. Accessed 13 March 2019.

Wierzbicka, Anna. 1996. *Semantics: Primes and universals*. Oxford: Oxford University Press.

Wong, YukWah, and Raymond J. Mooney. 2006. Learning for semantic parsing with statistical machine translation. In *Proceedings of the Human Language Technology Conference of the North American Chapter of the Association for Computational Linguistics (HLT/NAACL–2006)*, 439–446. New York City. Available at https://dl.acm.org/citation.cfm?id=1220891. Accessed 13 March 2019.

Wu, Hsiao-Ching. 2003. A case study on the grammaticalization of GUO in Mandarin Chinese—Polysemy of the motion verb with respect to semantic changes. *Language and Linguistics* 4: 857–885.

Xue, Nianwen, Jinying Chen, and Martha Palmer. 2006. Aligning features with sense distinction dimensions. In *Proceedings of the COLING/ACL Main Conference Poster Sessions*, 921–928. Sydney, Australia. Available at https://dl.acm.org/citation.cfm?id=1273191. Accessed 13 March 2019.

Zempleni, Monika-Zita, Remco Renken, John C. J. Hoeks, Johannes M. Hoogduin, and Laurie A. Stowe. 2007. Semantic ambiguity processing in sentence context: Evidence from event-related fMRI. *Neuroimage* 34:1270–1279.

Zhang, Yuntao, Ling Gong, and Yongcheng Wang. 2005. Chinese word sense disambiguation using HowNet. In *ICNC 2005, LNCS 3610*. Lipo Wang, Ke Chen, and Yew-Soon Ong (eds), 925–932.

Zhou Guodong, Jian Su, and Min Zhang. 2006. Modeling commonality among related classes in relation extraction. In *Proceedings of COLING-ACL'2006*, 121–128. Sydney, Australia. Available at https://dl.acm.org/citation.cfm?id=1220191. Accessed 13 March 2019.

Chapter 20
Chinese Locative Expressions: Prepositions and Localizers

Hui-Ju Hsiung

Abstract In Chinese locative expressions, the spatial relation between Figure and Ground is encoded not only by prepositions but also by localizers. Within prepositional phrases (PPs), prepositions and localizers have distinct functions: prepositions, which are either static or dynamic, denote the path of Figure, whereas localizers denote the region or dimension of Figure with respect to Ground and encode topological or projective relations between them. There are two locative constructions in Chinese—[P + NP] and [P + [NP + L]]—which indicate that localizers in locative expressions may be obligatory, not allowed, or optional. The distribution of localizers is generally determined by three factors: the types of localizers, the properties of noun phrases (NPs), and the number of syllables in NPs. Among the three distribution patterns—obligatory, not allowed, and optional—the optional use of localizers is the most complicated, which is closely related to the semantic interpretation of a locative expression. The theory of degree of explicitness provides a good explanation for the presence of localizers, and the theory of *routine sociale* "social routine" adequately accounts for the absence of localizers.

Keywords Chinese locative expressions · Prepositions · Localizers · Distribution of localizers · Degree of explicitness · Routine sociale (social routine)

20.1 Introduction

Spatial relations between a located object and a reference object are expressed in many languages by prepositions or postpositions that take a noun phrase (NP) as their complement. Following Talmy (1975, 2000) and Herskovits (1985, 2009), the located object and the reference object is referred to as the "Figure" object and the "Ground" object, respectively. According to Talmy's definitions (2000: 184), the Figure object is "a moving or conceptually movable entity whose path, site or

H.-J. Hsiung (✉)
Department of English, National University of Tainan, Tainan, Taiwan
e-mail: hjhsiung@mail.nutn.edu.tw

C.-R. Huang et al. (eds.), *Chinese Language Resources*, Text, Speech and Language Technology 49, https://doi.org/10.1007/978-3-031-38913-9_20

orientation is conceived as a variable, the particular value of which is the relevant issue," and the Ground object is "a reference entity, one that has a stationary setting relative to a reference frame, with respect to which the Figure's path, site or orientation is characterized." In brief, the Figure's location is determined and specified in relation to Ground, and the Figure-Ground relation in locative expressions is often denoted by spatial adpositions.

Herskovits (1985) referred to a locative expression as any spatial expression that involves a preposition, its complement, and whatever the prepositional phrase modifies, for example, *The mouse is in the hole* in English. The meaning of "in" might be X is "in" Y if and only if a part of X is spatially included in Y, that is, "the meaning of a locative expression is a proposition predicating the relation denoted by the preposition of the objects referred to by the noun phrases" (Herskovits 1985: 342).

In Mandarin Chinese, the Figure's locations are generally also encoded by spatial prepositional phrases (PPs). However, unlike in English, the structure of the PPs in Chinese locative expressions has two alternatives. First, there are locative expressions in which the complement of the preposition consists of an NP alone, as shown in (12.1) below:

(12.1)	飛機降落在戴高樂機場.
	fēijī_jiàngluò_zài_dàigāolè_jīchǎng
	airplane_land_at_Charles de Gaulle_airport
	The airplane came down at Charles de Gaulle Airport.

The location of the airplane (Figure) is specified by the airport (Ground), which functions as the NP complement of the PP headed by the spatial preposition 在 *zài* "at, in, on."

Second, there are also locative expressions in which the complement in the PP consists of an NP followed by a localizer, as shown in (12.2) below:

(12.2)	把書放到抽屜裡.
	bǎ_shū_fàng_dào_chōutì_lǐ
	object-marker_book_put_to_drawer_inside
	Put the book in the drawer.

In the spatial PP headed by 到 *dào* "to," the NP 抽屜 *chōutì* "drawer" and its ensuing localizer 裡 *lǐ* "inside" together describe the location of the Figure 書 *shū* "book."

Both types of spatial PPs[1] can occur either in the post-verbal position, as shown in examples (12.1) and (12.2), or in the pre-verbal position, as shown in the following sentences in (12.3) and (12.4) below:

[1]The existence of an entity in a location can also be expressed by a complement that occurs in the initial position of a sentence and functions as a locative subject, for example, 桌子上有一杯水 zhuōzi_shàng_yǒu_yībēi_shuǐ (table_up_there-is_one_CL_water) *There is a glass of water on the*

(12.3)	我們在餐廳吃飯.
	women_zài_cāntīng_chīfàn
	we_at_restaurant_dine
	We dined in a restaurant.
(12.4)	群眾在市政府前集合.
	qúnzhòng_zài_shìzhèngfǔ_qián_jíhé
	crowd_at_city-hall_front_gather
	The crowd gathered in front of the City Hall.

In summary, the basic structure of a locative construction includes a spatial preposition and an NP complement, which may sometimes be followed by a localizer. According to the elements involved in a spatial PP, there are two locative constructions in Mandarin Chinese, illustrated in (12.5) and (12.6) below:

(12.5) [P + NP]
(12.6) [P + [NP + L]][2]

As the two locative constructions in (12.5) and (12.6) show, Mandarin Chinese is very different from most other languages that use either prepositions or localizers to describe a location in space in that it sometimes uses prepositions alone and at other times uses prepositions together with localizers. Hsieh (1989) pointed out that Chinese uses a two-step strategy to describe spatial relations between the Figure object and the Ground object. In the first step, prepositions are used to indicate that the relation in question is a spatial relation of some kind. In the second step, localizers are used to further indicate the dimension of the relation, for example, whether the Figure object is on the surface or inside of the Ground object.

This raises some questions about the employment of the two types of function words: What information is provided by prepositions and what information is provided by localizers? Are the constructions in (12.5) and (12.6) completely equivalent in their expression of spatial relation? If they are not completely equivalent, then what are the differences between them? When are localizers obligatory and when are they not allowed? Can they be optional in certain cases? Are there any regularities to be found in the distribution of localizers?

The study presented in this chapter aimed to answer the questions above from multidisciplinary points of view. This chapter is organized into four sections. Section 20.1 presented the introduction of this chapter. Section 20.2 will elaborate the functions of the prepositions and localizers and will divide them into

table. This type of construction is generally called an "existential" or "presentative" construction in Chinese linguistics. Since this is not the focus of this chapter, it will not be discussed further.

[2]This type of structure is called "circumposition" by some linguists, for example, Liu 劉丹青 (2003), among others. However, there are also linguists who do not agree with this circumpositional treatment. For example, Sun (2008: 200) claimed that there are neither postpositions nor circumpositions in Chinese. A detailed discussion of this issue will not be given because the debate is beyond the scope of this chapter.

subcategories according to their functional characteristics. In Sect. 20.3, the three distribution patterns of localizers with syntactic properties, the phonological constraints of NP complements, and the types of localizers will be discussed, and further explanations of the tendency of the optional use of localizers from semantic perspectives will also be provided. The conclusion of the chapter will be presented in Sect. 20.4.

20.2 Functions of Prepositions and Localizers in Chinese Locative Constructions

There are more than 150 prepositions, including monosyllabic and dissyllabic ones, in Mandarin Chinese (Chen 陳昌來 2002). Spatial prepositions are among the most numerous, which consist of about 45 members, including, for example, 在 *zài* "at, in, on," 從 *cóng* "from," 經由 *jīngyóu* "through," 向 *xiàng* "toward," and 到 *dào* "to, at." In Chinese locative constructions, the spatial PPs headed by the spatial prepositions 在 *zài* "at, in, on" and 到 *dào* "to, at" are the most common (Chao 1968). This is the reason why in this chapter a large part of the examples used to illustrate locative expressions involve PPs headed by these two prepositions.

As for localizers derived from nouns through the process of grammaticalization (Chappell and Peyraube 2008; Li 李崇興 1992; Wang and Zhang 王文麗, 張長永 2011), they are, according to Chao (1968: 620–621), "a special category of words with a preceding subordinated substantive," which "usually express the location of things." Due to their controversial syntactic status, there is often disagreement among linguists as to which syntactic category localizers belong to. In related studies dealing with this problem in the literature, localizers are regarded as locative particles (Li and Thompson 1981), nouns (Li 1990), NP enclitics (Liu 1998; Sun 2008), and postpositions (Chappell and Peyraube 2008; Djamouri et al. 2013; Ernst 1988). As the main purpose of the current study did not involve addressing this issue, the less controversial term "localizer" will be used in this chapter to refer to the category in question.

Localizers, just like prepositions, are either monosyllabic or disyllabic. However, their number is relatively small in comparison with the large amount of prepositions. There are only 16 monosyllabic localizers: 上 *shàng* "up," 下 *xià* "down," 前 *qián* "front," 後 *hòu* "back," 左 *zuǒ* "left," 右 *yòu* "right," 裡 *lǐ* "inside," 外 *wài* "outside," 內 *nèi* "inside," 中 *zhōng* "middle," 間 *jiān* "middle," 旁 *páng* "side," 東 *dōng* "east," 西 *xī* "west," 南 *nán* "south," and 北 *běi* "north." Disyllabic localizers are formed by attaching a suffix to monosyllabic localizers, such as 邊 *biān* "side," 面 *miàn* "face," and 頭 *tóu* "head" (e.g., 上面 *shàngmiàn* "on top of" and 後頭 *hòutóu* "behind, back"), or a prefix, such as 以 *yǐ* "of" and 之 *zhī* "of" (Peyraube 2003) (e.g., 以東 *yǐdōng* "east of" and 之內 *zhīnèi* "inside of"). It is generally recognized that disyllabic localizers are nouns, while monosyllabic localizers are bound forms that cannot appear alone without immediately following an ordinary noun (Chappell and Peyraube 2008: 17). The discussion of localizers in this chapter will mainly focus on monosyllabic localizers.

Prepositions and localizers both denote spatial relations within prepositional phrases, but they play different roles that are functionally distinguishable. The following sections will discuss the differences between prepositions and localizers in locative expressions based on their semantic functions, which will clarify the distribution of localizers and may explain why there are two locative constructions in Mandarin Chinese as shown in (12.5) and (12.6).

20.2.1 Division of Labor Between Prepositions and Localizers

In Talmy's (2000: 25) definition, the basic motion event "consists of one object (the Figure) moving or located with respect to another object (the reference object or Ground)." Apart from remaining motionless, when a figure in a motion event takes a trajectory to travel from one location to another, the trajectory may include some particular parts, such as source, route, direction, or goal, which are referred to as "path" in the motion event. As Zwarts (2008: 81) put it, "most of the prepositions can be defined in terms of locative conditions they impose on particular parts of the path."

In many European languages, a spatial preposition may convey at least two separate kinds of information as to whether the preposition indicates a static or moving object and whether the location of an object has one, two, or three dimensions. In Mandarin Chinese, however, these two kinds of information are separately coded by two different elements—prepositions and localizers. Compare the same spatial relationships expressed in English and in Chinese in (12.7) to (12.10) below:

(12.7)	The book is on the table.
(12.8)	The ball rolled into the cave.
(12.9)	書放在桌子上.
	shū_fàng_zài_zhuōzi_shàng
	book_put_at_table_up
	The book is on the table.
(12.10)	球滾到洞穴裡.
	qiú_gǔn_dào_dòngxuè_lǐ
	ball_roll_to_cave_inside
	The ball rolled into the cave.

In (12.7) and (12.8), the location of Figure (the book/the ball, respectively) is restricted within the boundary of Ground (the table/the cave, respectively) by the spatial relation simply denoted by the preposition (on/into, respectively). However, in the Chinese counterparts shown in (12.9) and (12.10), the spatial relation between Figure and Ground is denoted by both the prepositions 在 *zài* "at" and 到 *dào* "to" and the localizers 上 *shàng* "up" and 裡 *lǐ* "inside," respectively. In contrast to prepositions that denote a pure spatial relation (Zhang 2017), as suggested by Hsieh (1989), localizers are used to indicate the dimension of the spatial relation between Figure and Ground. Many other researchers have similar opinions and have remarked that localizers are used to denote locations, such as Chu 儲澤祥 (2004: 114), Guo 郭銳 (2002: 207), and Djamouri et al. (2013). Moreover, Qiu 邱斌 (2008: 50) noted that localizers are used to indicate the direction and region of an object, as shown in (12.11) below:

(12.11)	貓跳到桌子上.
	māo_tiào_dào_zhuōzi_shàng
	cat_jump_to_desk_up
	The cat jumped on the desk.

In (12.11), the preposition 到 *dào* "to" encodes the path relation between Figure (the cat) and Ground (the table), whereas the localizer 上 *shàng* "up" specifies the region of Ground where Figure is located.

In summary, unlike in English, where path and region are conflated and expressed by prepositions, they are denoted by different elements in Chinese locative expressions: prepositions generally denote a path, while localizers denote a region, direction, or dimension. Sections 20.2.2 and 20.2.3 will elaborate the semantic functions of prepositions and localizers and subcategorize them into different types.

20.2.2 Classification of Spatial Prepositions

Spatial prepositions can be subcategorized in different ways. They are traditionally divided into static prepositions and dynamic prepositions depending on whether they are used in descriptions of static or dynamic spatial events. Static prepositions, such as "in," "on," and "at" in English, primarily denote the location of an object, while dynamic prepositions, such as "to," "from," and "across," primarily denote the path of an object (Herskovits 1985; Jackendoff 1983). Examples in English are shown in (12.12) and (12.13) below:

(12.12)	The book is on the table. [static]
(12.13)	The dog ran across the street. [dynamic]

Within Chinese spatial prepositions, a distinction can likewise be made between static and dynamic prepositions, as shown in (12.14a–b) below:

(12.14a)	**Static prepositions**: 在 *zài* "in, on, at," 於 *yú* "in, on, at"
(12.14b)	**Dynamic prepositions**: 從 *cóng* "from," 由 *yóu* "from, through," 經由 *jīngyóu* "through," 經過 *jīngguò* "through," 順著 *shùnzhe* "along," 沿著 *yánzhe* "along," 往 *wǎng* "toward," 朝 *cháo* "toward," 向 *xiàng* "toward," 到 *dào* "to," etc.

Except for the preposition 於 (also written as 于) *yú* "in, on, at," which was mainly used in Ancient Chinese or Classical Chinese, 在 *zài* "in, on, at" is the only generic preposition in Modern Mandarin Chinese, which indicates the stative position of an entity relative to another entity (Müller and Lipenkova 2013). Hence, the PPs headed by 在 *zài* "in, on, at" refer to a spatial relation that describes a static position, as shown in (12.15) below:

(12.15)	他在房間看書.
	tā_zài_fángjiān_kànshū
	he_at_bedroom_read_book
	He reads in the bedroom.

Compared with static prepositions, there are many more dynamic prepositions in Mandarin Chinese. For example, the dynamic preposition 到 *dào* "to" in (12.16) below denotes the goal of Figure, and 往 *wǎng* "toward" in (12.17) below denotes its direction:

(12.16)	樹葉落到地上.
	shùyè_luò_dào_dì_shàng
	leaf_fall_to_ground_up
	The leaves fell to the ground.
(12.17)	火車開往倫敦.
	huǒchē_kāi_wǎng_lúndūn
	train_drive_toward_London
	The train is bound for London.

Static prepositions in many languages can be further subcategorized according to the viewer's perspective; they can also generally be divided into two classes—topological prepositions and projective prepositions (Frawley 1992). Topological prepositions refer to spatial positions that are independent of a viewer, whereas projective prepositions designate locations that are projected from the major dimensional axes of the Ground object, and sometimes the determination of the principal axes of an object depends on the frame of reference that is adopted (Kemmerer and Tranel 2000: 394). Thus, topological locations are invariant with respect to changes in Ground, as can be seen in (12.18) below:

(12.18)	The cat is lying on the chair.

The relation between Figure and Ground in (12.18) remains the same no matter whose perspective is adopted or from which angle Figure is perceived.

On the contrary, projective locations depend on the perspective of the speaker or the properties of Ground, as shown in (12.19) below:

(12.19)	The ball is in front of the table.

The preposition "in front of" specifies the relation of anteriority defined in terms of the horizontal axis of Ground, the table. This front-back relation may vary from one viewer to another because a table is not an object that has an intrinsic front and back. Hence, the ball may be in front of the table from one perspective and behind the table from another perspective.

However, it is noteworthy that the distinction between topological and projective relations in Chinese locative expressions is not determined by spatial prepositions. Instead, it is localizers that indicate these two types of relations between Figure and Ground. Further discussion is provided in the following section.

20.2.3 Classification of Localizers

The differences between the functions of prepositions and localizers are especially clear when sentences (12.18) and (12.19) above are translated into their Chinese counterparts in (12.20) and (12.21) below:

(12.20)	貓躺在椅子上.
	māo_tǎng_zài_yǐzi_shàng
	cat_lie_at_chair_up
	The cat is lying on the chair.
(12.21)	球放在桌子前.
	qiú_fàng_zài_zhuōzi_qián
	ball_put_at_table_front
	The ball is in front of the table.

In both examples, the projective or non-projective relation is not specified by the preposition 在 *zài* "at" but rather by localizers. In (12.20), the topological relation between the cat and the chair is expressed by the localizer 上 *shàng* "up." Likewise, in (12.21), the projective relation between the ball and the table is expressed by the localizer 前 *qián* "front."

The 16 monosyllabic localizers in Mandarin Chinese can be divided into topological localizers and projective localizers. Within the set of topological localizers, three subcategories further express three basic topological locations based on Frawley's (1992) approach, which are coincidence, interiority, and exteriority. The relation of coincidence refers to "the near or total spatial overlap of the located object and the reference object" (Frawley 1992: 255). Consider the following in (12.22) below:

(12.22)	小貓躺在鋼琴上.
	xiǎo_māo_tǎng_zài_gāngqín_shàng
	little_cat_lie_at_piano_up
	The cat lies on the piano.

In (12.22), 上 *shàng* "up" indicates that the cat has contact with the piano. According to Frawley (1992), contact entails spatial overlap, so an expression of coincidence appears in this sentence.

Interiority, the second type of topological location, is defined as the inclusion or containment of a Figure object in a Ground object, as shown in (12.23) below:

(12.23)	流浪漢睡在公園裡.
	liúlànghàn_shuì_zài_gōngyuán_lǐ
	vagrant_sleep_in_park_inside
	The vagrant slept in the park.

In (12.23), 裡 *lǐ* "inside" indicates that the vagrant is located somewhere in the area of the park and hence denotes the relation of interiority between the two objects.

Finally, the third type of topological location is exteriority, which, according to Frawley's (1992) definition, denotes the relation whereby Figure is external to or outside of Ground, as can be seen in (12.24) below:

(12.24)	他站在房間外偷聽.
	tā_zhàn_zài_fángjiān_wài_tōu_tīng
	he_stand_at_room_outside_furtive_listen
	He stood outside the room and eavesdropped.

Frawley (1992: 261) mentioned that exteriority is actually the converse of interiority. Thus, to be the converse of 裡 *lǐ* "inside" in (12.23), the localizer 外 *wài* "outside" in (12.24) indicates the relation of exteriority between the eavesdropping man and the room.

An example of a localizer that denotes a projective location was presented in (12.21), 前 *qián* "front." Consider another example illustrating a different projective relation in (12.25) below:

(12.25)	梯子立在電線杆後.
	tīzi_lì_zài_diànxiàngān_hòu
	ladder_stand_at_electricity-pole_back
	The ladder stands behind the electricity pole.

Normally, there is no intrinsic front and back of an electricity pole. The meaning of 後*hòu* "back" in (12.25) is therefore determined by "the frame of reference inherent to the viewer" (Frawley 1992: 263), that is, the viewer is facing the electricity pole, which is located between the ladder and the viewer.

Monosyllabic localizers with spatial use in Mandarin Chinese can be classified into different categories according to the relation they denote, as shown in (12.26a–b) below:

(12.26)	Classification of localizers
	(a) Topological relation

(continued)

(1)	Coincidence: 上 *shàng* "up" and 下 *xià*[3] "down"
(2)	Interiority: 上 *shàng* "up," 內 *nèi* "inside," 裡 *lǐ* "inside," and 中 *zhōng* "middle"
(3)	Exteriority: 外 *wài* "outside," 旁 *páng* "side," 間 *jiān* "middle," 東 *dōng* "east," 西 *xī* "west," 南 *nán* "south," and 北 *běi* "north"
(b)	**Projective relation**
	上 *shàng* "up," 下 *xià* "down," 前 *qián* "front," 後 *hòu* "back," 左 *zuǒ* "left," and 右 *yòu* "right"

As the lists in (12.26a–b) indicate, a few localizers, such as 上 *shàng* "up" and 下 *xià* "down," can be assigned to more than one category. This is because such localizers have meanings that are both topological and projective in nature due to their polysemous senses. Take 上 *shàng* "up" as an example, as it denotes both coincidence and interiority as a topological location as well as denotes a projective location. The three types of relations indicated by 上 *shàng* "up" are exemplified in (12.27), (12.28), and (12.29), respectively, below:

(12.27)	貓在屋頂上睡覺.
	māo_zài_wūdǐng_shàng_shuìjiào
	cat_at_roof_up_sleep
	The cat is sleeping on the roof.
(12.28)	乘客在火車上聊天.
	chéngkè_zài_huǒchē_shàng_liáotiān
	passenger_at_train_up_chat
	Passengers chat on the train.
(12.29)	白雲浮在屋頂上.
	bái_yún_fú_zài_wūdǐng_shàng
	white_cloud_drift_at_roof_up
	The white clouds drift over the roof.

In Fig. 20.1, the construction of full-fledged locative expressions in Mandarin Chinese contains a preposition, an NP, and a localizer. Although both prepositions and localizers are likely to be the most important way to denote spatial relations between two objects, their syntactic and semantic functions do not overlap as each category is completely different.

[3] Although the localizer 下 xià "down" denotes that the coincident relation is not common, such as 口香糖黏在桌子下 kǒuxiāngtáng_nián_zài_zhuōzi_xià (chewing-gum_stick_at_table_down) *The chewing gum is stuck underneath the table*, it should still be distinguished from 下 xià "down," which denotes a projective relation, as in 貓躺在桌子下 māo_tǎng_zài_zhuōzi_xià (cat_lie_at_table_down) *The cat is lying under the table.*

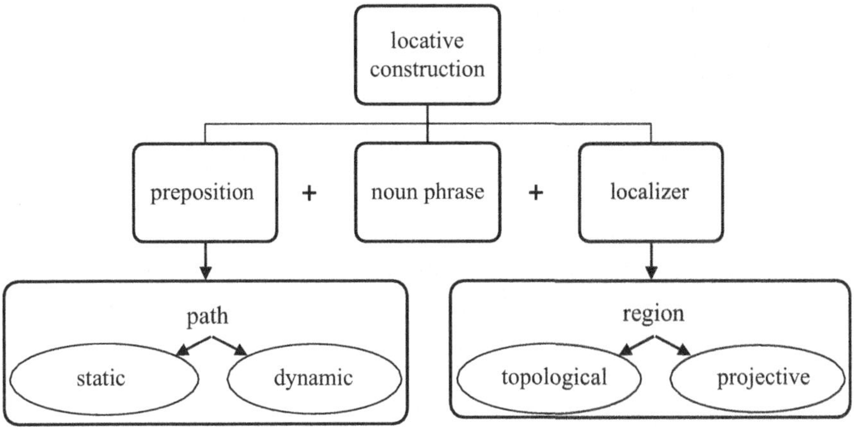

Fig. 20.1 Structure of Chinese locative construction

20.3 Distribution of Localizers

It has been shown, as discussed in the introduction, that there are two constructions in Chinese locative expressions—one with a localizer and the other without a localizer. In other words, there are three patterns for the use of localizers: (i) not allowed, (ii) obligatory, and (iii) optional. It has long been a challenge for researchers to explain the regularity of the distribution of localizers. Among the small number of studies related to this issue, the works of Chu 儲澤祥 (2004, 2010) and Sun (2008) are worthy of special mention.

Chu 儲澤祥 (2004, 2010) discussed the mechanisms in the omission of localizers in "*zài* + locative phrases" from six aspects: the properties of the NPs, the properties of the localizers, the types of spatial relation between the located objects and the reference objects, the prosodic structure of the NPs, the semantic requirement, and the pragmatic view of the locative expressions. In Chu's 儲澤祥 (2004, 2010) analysis, he tried to list all the conditions for localizers that can and cannot be omitted but did not mention the optional use of a set of words, which seems to be the most complicated pattern.

Sun (2008: 208) proposed a selectional condition and a multisyllabic constraint on the non-directional nominal after the generic preposition 在 *zài* "at" to account for the omission of localizers, arguing that "a non-spatial nominal after the underspecified 在 *zài* 'at' is acceptable only if it is explicitly marked as definite by a demonstrative, an ordinal marker, or a relative clause." Sentences (12.30) and (12.31) below are two examples offered by Sun (2008: 207):

(12.30)	我在這本書(上)加了很多插圖.
	wǒ_zài_zhè_běn_shū_(shàng)_jiā_le_hěn_duō_chātú
	1st_at_this_CL_book_(up)_add_LE_very_many_illustration
	I added to this book many illustrations.

(continued)

(12.31)	*我在書加了很多插圖
	wǒ_zài_shū_jiā_le_hěn_duō_chātú
	1st_at _book_add_LE_very_many_illustration

Sun (2008) argued that the localizer 上 *shàng* "up" in (12.30) is optional because the demonstrative quantifier phrase 這本 *zhè-běn* marks the NP as definite. On the contrary, sentence (12.31) is not acceptable because 上 *shàng* "up" cannot be omitted due to the lack of an explicit definite marking.

However, (12.32) and (12.33) below show that the selectional condition proposed by Sun (2008) does not always hold true. In these two examples, the sentences are still acceptable despite the absence of a localizer after the indefinite NPs 封面 *fēngmiàn* "cover" and 牆壁 *qiángbì* "wall."

(12.32)	我在封面加了很多插圖.
	wǒ_zài_fēngmiàn_jiā_le_hěn_duō_chātú
	1st_at_cover_up_add_LE_very_many_illustration
	I added many illustrations to the covers of books.
(12.33)	小孩喜歡在牆壁塗鴉.
	xiǎohái_xǐhuān_zài_qiángbì_túyā
	child_like_at_wall_scrawl
	Children like to scrawl on the wall.

The second part of this chapter was motivated by the wide variety of observations in the literature that have tried to account for the presence or absence of localizers. However, instead of reforming the exhaustive descriptions and rules in previous studies, the aim here is to discuss the key principles that underlie the distribution of localizers from phonological and syntactic perspectives and emphasize the functions of localizers from semantic aspects.

20.3.1 Syntactic and Phonological Constraints

Three important factors that determine the three distribution patterns of localizers were identified in the current study. These factors relate to the syntactic and phonological constraints on the elements that constitute locative constructions, which are (i) the properties of NPs, (ii) the types of localizers, and (iii) the number of syllables in NPs.

Properties of NPs

The first factor that affects the distribution of localizers is the properties of the NP complements in the spatial PPs. According to Chao (1968: 519–520), substantives that are not place words usually cannot be the objects of verbs or prepositions of place or movement. That is, the objects of prepositions of place or movement are usually place words, which constitute a special category in the Chinese lexicon called *chùsuǒcí* (處所詞) or *dìfāngcí* (地方詞) "place words." Based on Chao's (1968: 520–531) classification, Chappell and Peyraube (2008: 16) distinguished five types of place words according to their syntactic and semantic properties, which are listed below:

(a) Place names or geographical locations, such as 中國 *Zhōngguó* "China" and 巴黎 *Bālí* "Paris"
(b) Nouns with an inherently locative value, such as 學校 *xuéxiào* "school" and 圖書館 *túshūguǎn* "library"
(c) Disyllabic localizers expressing spatial deixis, such as 裡頭 *lǐtou* "inside" and 旁邊兒 *pángbiānr* "side, beside"
(d) Common nouns followed by monosyllabic or disyllabic localizers, such as 桌子上 *zhuōzi shàng* "on the table" and 房子背後 *fángzi bèihòu* "back of the house"
(e) Demonstrative locative pronouns, such as 這兒 *zhèr* "here" and 那兒 *nàr* "there"

The PPs in examples (12.34) to (12.38) below are formed by spatial prepositions and the different types of their ensuing place words:

(12.34) 到歐洲旅行 Type (a)
dào_ōuzhōu_lǚxíng
to_Europe_travel
to travel to Europe
(12.35) 在圖書館(裡)看書 Type (b)
zài_túshūguǎn_(lǐ)_kànshū
in_library_(inside)_read
to read in the library
(12.36) 從旁邊走過 Type (c)
cóng_pángbiān_zǒu_guò
from_side_walk_across
to walk across from the side
(12.37) 放在桌子上 Type (d)
fàng_zài_zhuōzi_shàng
put_at_table_up
to put (something) on the table
(12.38) 走到那兒去 Type (e)
zǒu_dào_nàr_qù
walk_to_there_go
to walk there

In the examples above, the NP complements can be a single place word as in the locative construction shown in (12.5), for instance, (12.34), (12.35), (12.36), and (12.38). Alternatively, they can be a place word followed by a monosyllabic localizer as in the locative construction shown in (12.6), such as (12.35) and (12.37).

One of the important functions of localizers is to convert common nouns into place nouns; therefore, they are obligatory in locative expressions when the place words are common nouns such as those in Type (d). For example, in (12.37), if the localizer 上 *shàng* "up" is omitted, the NP 桌子 *zhuōzi* "table" cannot obtain a locative value, and the sentence becomes unacceptable, as illustrated in (12.39) below:

(12.39)	*放在桌子.
	fang_zài_zhuōzi
	put_at_table
	Put (something) on the table.

By contrast, localizers are not allowed when the NP complements are (i) place names or geographical locations such as those in Type (a), (ii) disyllabic localizers expressing spatial deixis such as those in Type (c), and (iii) demonstrative locative pronouns such as those in Type (e). These distributions are exemplified by (12.34), (12.36), and (12.38), respectively.

In addition, localizers are often optional when the NPs are place words with an inherently locative value such as those in Type (b), as shown in (12.40) below:

(12.40)	在客廳(裡)看電視
	zài_kètīng_(lǐ)_kàn_diànshì
	at_living-room_(inside)_watch_television
	to watch television in the living room

When someone is watching TV in a living room, the audience and the TV set should both be located inside the living room, so the use of the localizer 裡 *lǐ* "inside" gives a more informative description of the Figure's location. On the other hand, if 裡 *lǐ* "inside" is not present, the sentence is still correct and does not change in meaning because the event of watching TV is supposed to take place inside the living room rather than outside the room, so the occurrence of 裡 *lǐ* "inside" here seems to be redundant in such a circumstance.

There is an exception for Type (a) place words. If one wants to specify the direction or dimension of a geographical location, topological localizers that denote the relation of exteriority cannot be omitted, such as 旁 *páng* "side," 東 *dōng* "east," 西 *xī* "west," 南 *nán* "south," and 北 *běi* "north." Consider (12.41) below, which is an example of the localizer 南 *nán* "south":

(12.41)	七月丙寅, 治兵于邾南 (左傳昭公 13).
	qīyuè_bǐngyín, zhì_bīng_yú_zhū_nán
	July_29th_inspect_troop_in_Zhu_south
	The troops were inspected in southern Zhu on 29th July.

In (12.41), the localizer is normally not necessary after the country name, Zhu, except when it is a topological localizer that denotes a relation of exteriority between Figure and Ground.

Types of Localizers

The distribution of localizers has a close relation with their types of classification, that is, whether the localizers are topological ones or projective ones. All the projective localizers are obligatory for Type (b) and Type (d) place words because they are crucial for indicating the direction or the dimensional axes of Figure with respect to Ground. As discussed in Sect. 20.2.3, the localizer 上 *shàng* "up" in (12.29) is a projective localizer that conveys information about the direction of the cloud (Figure) related to the roof (Ground). The cloud does not have direct contact with the roof, and neither is it located within the boundary of the roof for containment; rather, the relation between the two objects depends on which projected viewpoint is taken. Thus, if the projective localizer 上 *shàng* "up" is omitted, the sentence will no longer be acceptable:

(12.42)	*白雲浮在屋頂.
	bái_yún_fú_zài_wūdǐng
	white_cloud_drift_at_roof
	The white clouds drift over the roof.

On the contrary, the distribution of topological localizers is much more variable since they are not necessarily obligatory, especially for those that denote coincident and interior relations expressing the spatial overlap or containment of Figure and Ground in certain conditions, such as in (12.43) below:

(12.43)	貓在屋頂(上)睡覺.
	māo_zài_wūdǐng_(shàng)_shuìjiào
	cat_at_roof_(up)_sleep
	The cat is sleeping on the roof.

In (12.43), the situation is such that there is direct contact between the cat and the roof. The relation of coincidence between the two objects is denoted by 上 *shàng* "up," which refers to the surface of the roof where the cat slept. Thus, the topological localizer 上 *shàng* "up" in this sentence is optional.

However, this is not the case in (12.28) shown earlier. The topological localizer 上 *shàng* "up" in that sentence was used to indicate a relation of interiority between the passengers and the train, as it expressed a meaning equivalent to that of 內 *nèi* "inside, within" or 裡 *lǐ* "inside, within." The use of the topological localizer was therefore obligatory, and its absence, shown in (12.44) below, makes the sentence unacceptable:

(12.44)	*乘客在火車聊天.
	chéngkè_zài_huǒchē_liáotiān
	passenger_at_train_chat
	Passengers chatted on the train.

In addition, topological localizers are also obligatory when Figure is external to Ground. If the exterior relation between two objects is not explicitly described by localizers, the exact dimensional location of Figure relative to Ground cannot be identified, as in (12.45) below, for instance:

(12.45)	小貓睡在火爐*(旁).
	xiǎo_māo_shuì_zài_huǒlú_*(páng)
	little_cat_sleep_at_chimney_(side)
	The little cat slept by the fire.

It is noteworthy that, for phonological reasons, dissyllabic topological localizers that express a relation of exteriority such as 東邊 *dōngbian* "east (of)," 之西 *zhīxī* "west (of)," 以南 *yǐnán* "south (of)," and 以北 *yǐběi* "north (of)" are generally preferred to their counterparts in monosyllabic forms (i.e., 東 *dōng* "east," 西 *xī* "west," 南 *nán* "south," and 北 *běi* "north") when they are used in multisyllabic place names. Since place names are overwhelmingly multisyllabic in Modern Mandarin Chinese, dissyllabic topological localizers are therefore used much more frequently. Most of all, whether topological localizers that denote an exterior relation are monosyllabic or dissyllabic, their occurrence after a place name or geographical location is obligatory, as illustrated in (12.46) below:

(12.46)	降雨集中在新竹以北.
	jiàngyǔ_jízhōng_zài_xīnzhú_yǐběi
	rainfall_center_at_Xinzhu_north
	The rainfall centered on the north side of Xinzhu.

Number of Syllables in NPs

The use of localizers is also subject to the number of syllables in NP complements. Localizers are usually obligatory when place words are monosyllabic nouns with locative value such as those in Type (b). Compare the two sentences in (12.47) and (12.48) below:

(12.47)	郵輪停泊在港*(內).
	yóulún_tíngbó _zài_gǎng_*(nèi)
	cruise-liner_dock_at_harbor_(inside)
	The cruise liner docked at the harbor.
(12.48)	郵輪停泊在港口(內).

(continued)

Table 20.1 Distribution of localizers in Chinese locative expressions

Types of localizers		Topological			
Types of NPs		Coincidence	Interiority	Exteriority	Projective
Type (a)	Monosyllabic	NA	NA	OB	NA
	Multisyllabic	NA	NA	OB	NA
Type (b)	Monosyllabic	OB	OB	OB	OB
	Multisyllabic	OP	OP	OB	OB
Type (c)		NA	NA	NA	NA
Type (d)	Monosyllabic	OB	OB	OB	OB
	Multisyllabic	OB	OB	OB	OB
Type (e)	Monosyllabic	NA	NA	NA	NA
	Multisyllabic	NA	NA	NA	NA

yóulún_tíngbó _zài_gǎngkǒu_(nèi)
cruise-liner_dock_at_harbor_(inside)
The cruise liner docked at the harbor.

Example (12.47) will not be acceptable if the localizer 内 *nèi* "inside" is omitted. However, if the noun with inherently locative value is multisyllabic, its ensuing localizer is not necessarily obligatory. As can be seen in (12.48), if 内 *nèi* "inside" does not occur after the disyllabic noun 港口 *gǎngkǒu* "harbor," the sentence is still acceptable.

Summary

The distribution of localizers, as discussed above, is summarized in Table 20.1, in which **NA** means not allowed, **OB** means obligatory, and **OP** means optional.

20.3.2 Semantic Considerations

As discussed in the previous sections, localizers that indicate the relation of coincidence and interiority are optional only when they are preceded by multisyllabic place words with an inherently locative value. This type of distribution is much more complicated than the other two types because it is difficult to find regularities or tendencies when choosing between two options, namely, to use or not to use localizers.

In fact, the choice between the two options, PPs with or without localizers, reflects a speaker's cognitive process toward the semantic functions of localizers. Taking into consideration the cognitive dimension, the current study aimed to find regularities and tendencies in the optional use of localizers and account for the subtle differences between the two constructions. A discussion of this issue will be carried out based on two theories: the degree of explicitness proposed by Svorou (1993) and the social routine (translated from the French *routine sociale*) proposed by Vandeloise (1987). The first theory provides a good explanation for the presence of localizers and the second theory that for the absence of localizers.

Degree of Explicitness: Tendency to Use Localizers

According to Svorou (1993: 6–7), "explicitness incorporates the weighted relevance of various conceived elements of the situation with respect to the communicative intent of the speaker." Svorou (1993) exemplified this viewpoint with the English locative adverb "here" and argued that "here" has the lowest degree of explicitness than other expressions, such as *in front of the TV* and *the back door*. Svorou (1993: 6) also noted that each expression "carries a different degree of explicitness in the encodings of referents in the world."

Based on Svorou's (1993) concept of explicitness, the current study proposed that an important difference between the two locative constructions consists in the degree of explicitness of Figure's location with respect to Ground. In Mandarin Chinese, for those locative expressions in which the localizers are optional, the expressions without localizers have a lower degree of explicitness than those with localizers. In the following examples shown in (12.49a–b) to (12.52a–b) below, the sentences in each pair differ in their degree of explicitness—the sentences in (b) impart a higher degree of explicitness than the sentences in (a):

(12.49a) 他在圖書館看書.
tā_zài_túshūguǎn_kàn_shū
he_in_library_see_book
He is reading at the library.
(12.49b) 他在圖書館裡看書.
tā_zài_túshūguǎn_lǐ_kàn_shū
he_in_library_inside_see_book
He is reading inside the library.
(12.50a) 我們約在公園碰面.
women_yuē_zài_gōngyuán_pèngmiàn
we_make-an-appointment_at_park_meet
We have made an appointment to meet at the park.
(12.50b) 我們約在公園裡碰面.
women_yuē_zài_gōngyuán_lǐ_pèngmiàn
we_make-an-appointment_at_park_inside_meet
We have made an appointment to meet inside the park.
(12.51a) 船隻停靠在港口躲避颱風.
chuánzhī_tíngkào _zài_gǎngkǒu_duǒbì_táifēng
ship_anchor_in_harbor_avoid_typhoon
Ships are anchored at the harbor to avoid the typhoon.

(continued)

(12.51b) 船隻停靠在港口內躲避颱風.
chuánzhī_tíngkào_zài_gǎngkǒu_nèi_duǒbì_táifēng
ship_anchor_in_harbor_inside_avoid_typhoon
Ships are anchored inside the harbor to avoid the typhoon.
(12.52a) 學生在操場做運動.
xuéshēng_zài_cāochǎng_zuò_yùndòng
student_at_sports-ground_do_sports
The students are doing sports at the sports ground.
(12.52b) 學生在操場上做運動.
xuéshēng_zài_cāochǎng_shàng_zuò_yùndòng
student_at_sports-ground_up_do_sports
The students are doing sports in (or on the surface of) the sports ground.

All of the sentences in (a) designate only a general location of Figure that is already adequate, while the sentences in (b) further specify the details related to the locations. As Svorou (1993: 6–7) mentioned, "the degrees of explicitness with which speakers decide to talk about the location of entities depends on their intentions, the addressee, and the communicative context they are in."

In the examples above, although the locations where the events take place in the two sentences of each pair are identical, speakers have different intentions when choosing between the sentences in (a) and (b). First, speakers can choose to give more precise information in describing scenes or giving instructions. Take the sentences in (12.49a–b) as an example: *to read inside the library building* in (12.49b) is more explicit than *to read at the library* in (12.49a) because (12.49b) refers only to the library building, whereas (12.49a) refers to a larger location that includes the building and **its surrounding** area. Second, speakers can provide, with the two alternatives, a contrast between an interior space and an exterior environment and hence can give more precise information about the location. For instance, (12.50b) has a higher degree of explicitness than (12.50a) and is expected to produce a contrast in location: the meeting place is *inside the park* rather than *outside the park*.

"Routine Sociale" and Telic Qualia: Tendency to Not Use Localizers

In certain circumstances, locative expressions not only indicate a location but also evoke a "telic reading" of the NP complements in the PPs. In other words, some locative expressions exhibit a duality of interpretations: one is an interpretation of spatial localization and the other is a telic interpretation (Aurnague 2012; Corblin 2013). A telic reading can be seen as an enrichment of a locative reading; the key point of identifying a telic reading is that the human subject is conceived as the argument of the telic qualia[4] associated with the noun (Asic and Corblin 2014; Corblin 2011). For example, in *Pierre goes to school* (the example cited in Asic and Corblin 2014), it is not merely a matter of describing Pierre's location; rather, the telic reading of the sentence implies that Pierre is a schoolboy.

The topic of "telic reading" has been widely discussed in the literature on French, which was inspired by the notion of *routine sociale* "social routine" proposed by Vandeloise (1987). According to Asic and Corblin (2014), the emergence of social routine reading in French is composed of four ingredients: (i) a telic qualia associated with the head of the NP; (ii) a functional interpretation of the definite NP taking an animate subject as its argument; (iii) the use of the propositions *à* ("at," "on," and "in" in English); and (iv) the use of a semantically underspecified verb of movement or location, such as *être* ("to be") and *aller* ("to go").

Locative expressions in Chinese can also evoke a telic reading even though they are not entirely performed by the same constructions as in the case of French. There are three conditions that license a telic reading as a preferred alternative to a mere spatial reading:

(a) The typical locative expressions that evoke a telic reading are manifested in two constructions: (i) S + 在 *zài* "at, on" + NP + VP and (ii) S + 到 *dào* "to" + NP + VP. They indicate a static localization and a dynamic localization, respectively.
(b) The subject of the sentence associated with the social institution noun is animate.
(c) The action of the verb is directly associated with the telic function of the social institution noun.

These conditions can be paraphrased as someone (S) is at/goes to a social institution (NP) and performs an action expressed by the verb phrase (VP) associated with this social institution. When these conditions are fulfilled, the telic reading is the preferred reading of the sentence.

Once a telic reading emerges, localizers tend to be eliminated. This tendency is clear in the comparison of the pair of sentences in (12.53a–b) below:

(12.53a) 他到學校上課.
tā_dào_xuéxiào_shàngkè
he_to_school_attend-classes/give-classes
He attended classes/gave classes at school.
(12.53b) ?他到學校裡上課.
tā_dào_xuéxiào_lǐ_shàngkè
he_to_school_inside_attend-classes/give-classes
He attended classes/gave classes inside school.

[4]Qualia structure, defined by Pustejovsky (1998: 289), is a framework that deals with "how words can have different meanings in different contexts, how new senses can emerge compositionally, and how semantic types predictably map to syntactic forms in language." A telic qualia is one of the four basic roles that encode "information on purpose and function" (Pustejovsky and Zezek 2016: 7).

A school (學校 *xuéxiào*) is a social institution where teachers teach and students learn; both activities are encoded in Chinese by the verb 上課 *shàngkè*. When the spatial meaning is weakened, the localizer that indicates the dimension or region of Figure is not indispensable anymore. Therefore, if the localizer is not eliminated, the sentence will sound odd, though it will not be ungrammatical, as shown in (12.53b).

It is noteworthy that the emergence of the telic reading not only indicates the social routine function of a given location or place but also implies the social identity of the human subject, for instance, his/her occupation. Consider again (12.53a): the social function of a school, as mentioned above, has a strong relation with the polysemous verb 上課 *shàngkè*, which means either attending classes (as a student) or giving classes (as a teacher). When someone regularly goes to school as a routine activity, he or she could be a student or a teacher.

The implication of an occupation is usually triggered by VPs that denote an action performed by a human subject in a certain location. Compare the following two sentences in (12.54a–b):

(12.54a) 老張在火車站上班.
lǎo-zhāng_zài_huǒchē_zhàn_shàngbān
Lao-Zhang_at_train_station_work
Lao-Zhang works at a train station.
(12.54b) ?老張在火車站裡上班
lǎo-zhāng_zài_huǒchē_zhàn_lǐ_shàngbān
Lao-Zhang_at_train_station_inside_work

Since the telic reading of (12.54a) implies that the human subject, Lao-Zhang, is a railway station employee, the emphasis here is on his job rather than on the location where he is employed. As an employee, his work place is not necessarily restricted only to a fixed place; he could work inside or outside the station building. Thus, if the localizer 裡 *lǐ* "inside" occurs, the sentence will sound awkward as shown in (12.54b).

Spatial-telic constructions can exert an effect on the distribution of localizers, and the reverse is also true. The distribution of localizers can also differentiate expressions with a mere spatial reading from those with a telic reading. Compare the two sentences in (12.55a–b) below:

(12.55a) 老張在火車站賣口香糖.
lǎo-zhāng_zài_huǒchē_zhàn_mài_kǒuxiāngtáng
Lao-Zhang_at_train_station_sell_chewing-gums
Lao-Zhang sells chewing gums at a train station.
(12.55b) 老張在火車站裡賣口香糖.
lǎo-zhāng_zài_huǒchē_zhàn_lǐ_mài_kǒuxiāngtáng
Lao-Zhang_at_train_station_inside_sell_chewing-gums
Lao-Zhang sells chewing gums inside a train station.

Both sentences in (12.55) are acceptable, but there is a subtle difference between them. The selling of chewing gums is neither one of the social routine functions provided by the railway station nor is it an activity that has a constant and permanent relation with the social institution. It seems, at first sight, that there is only a locative reading for these expressions since the VP does not trigger a telic function of the location. However, the distribution of the localizer helps to capture the nuance between expressions with a locative reading and those with a telic reading.

In (12.55b), the use of the localizer 裡 *lǐ* "inside" confirms the spatial reading of the expression, so Lao-Zhang could be a peddler who sells chewing gums somewhere inside the station building. In (12.55a), on the contrary, the locative reading is much less salient due to the lack of a localizer. This sentence thus puts emphasis on the occupation of the human subject rather than on the location. Instead of being a peddler, Lao-Zhang is more like a station employee who sells chewing gums at the shop located in the railway station.

The optional use of localizers in regard to the social routine reading of locative expressions is not governed by syntactic rules but rather influenced by a tendency that would be associated with one's cognitive process. This distribution tendency can be confirmed by examining the frequency of expressions with a localizer and that of expressions without a localizer. Compare the following pairs of sentences in (12.56a–b) to (12.63a–b)[5] that were taken from the Peking University CCL Online Corpus. As the human subjects of the sentences did not affect the results of the comparison, they are ignored in these examples. The number given in the right column shows the frequency of the expressions in the CCL Corpus.

Frequency
(12.56a) 在圖書館看書 10
zài_túshūguǎn_kàn_shū
at_library_see_book
to read in the library
(12.56b) 在圖書館裡看書 2
zài_túshūguǎn_lǐ_kàn_shū
at_library_inside_see_book
(12.57a) 在廚房做飯 12
zài_chúfáng_zuò-fàn
at_kitchen_cook
to cook in the kitchen
(12.57b) 在廚房裡做飯 7
zài_chúfáng_lǐ_zuò-fàn
at_kitchen_inside_cook
(12.58a) 在餐廳吃飯 14
zài_cāntīng_chīfàn

(continued)

[5]Noting that the list is not exhaustive, only some examples that show tendency are listed due to the space constraints of this chapter.

at_restaurant_dine
to dine in the restaurant
(12.58b) 在餐廳裡吃飯 2
zài_cāntīng_lǐ_chīfàn
at_restaurant_inside_dine
(12.59a) 到食堂就餐 8
dào_shítáng _jiùcān
to_canteen_eat
to eat in the canteen
(12.59b) 到食堂裡就餐 0
dào_shítáng_lǐ_jiùcān
to_canteen_inside_eat
(12.60a) 到菜市場買菜 12
dào_cài_shìchǎng_mǎi_cài
to_vegetable_market_buy_vegetables
to buy food at a market
(12.60b) 到菜市場裡買菜 0
dào_cài_shìchǎng_lǐ_mǎi_cài
to_vegetable_market_inside_buy_vegetables
(12.61a) 到學校上課 28
dào_xuéxiào_shàngkè
to_school_attend-classes/give-classes
to attend classes/give classes at school
(12.61b) 到學校裡上課 0
dào_xuéxiào_lǐ_shàngkè
to_school_inside_attend-classes/give-classes
(12.62a) 到醫院看病 43
dào_yīyuàn_kànbìng
to_hospital_see-a-patient/see-a-doctor
to go to the hospital to see a patient/see a doctor
(12.62b) 到醫院裡看病 1
dào_yīyuàn_lǐ_kànbìng
to_hospital_inside_see-a-patient/see-a-doctor
(12.63a) 到電影院看電影 10
dào_diànyǐngyuàn_kàn_diànyǐng
to_cinema_see_movie
to go to the cinema to see a movie
(12.63b) 到電影院裡看電影 0
dào_diànyǐngyuàn_lǐ_kàn_diànyǐng
to_cinema_inside_see_movie

In each pair, the localizer is absent in the first sentence and present in the second sentence. In comparison with the frequency of the expressions in (a), the frequency of the expressions in (b) is significantly lower or even zero in the CCL Corpus. This difference of frequency confirms the analysis that localizers are not obligatory when a telic reading is evoked in locative expressions. In other words, if a telic reading is the preferred reading in a locative expression, the occurrence of localizers usually turns out to be semantically unnecessary.

20.4 Conclusion

Mandarin Chinese has long been noted for its two-step strategy in locative expressions, where the spatial relation between Figure and Ground is encoded not only by prepositions but also by localizers. Based on the study presented in this chapter, some concluding remarks can be made.

Although both denote a spatial relation within prepositional phrases, prepositions and localizers have distinct functions: prepositions denote the path of Figure, which are either static or dynamic, whereas localizers denote the region or dimension of Figure with respect to Ground and encode topological or projective relations between them.

In Chinese locative expressions, localizers may be obligatory, not allowed, or optional. The distribution of localizers is generally subject to three major factors: the properties of NPs, the types of localizers, and the number of syllables in NPs. Localizers are obligatory when their preceding NPs are common nouns as well as monosyllabic nouns with an inherently locative value. Moreover, when localizers denote a relation of exteriority between two objects, they are also always present when their preceding NPs are a place name or geographical location or multisyllabic nouns with an inherently locative value. On the contrary, localizers are always not allowed when the NP complements in the PPs are demonstrative locative pronouns or disyllabic localizers expressing spatial deixis. In addition, if the NPs are place names or geographical locations, the projective localizers and the localizers that denote a relation of coincidence and interiority are also not allowed. Finally, the localizers that denote a relation of coincidence and interiority tend to be optional when their preceding place words are multisyllabic nouns with an inherently locative value.

The optional use of localizers is closely related to the semantic interpretation of the locative expressions. Expressions with localizers show a higher degree of explicitness of the Figure's location with respect to Ground than those without localizers. Another subtle and important distinction between expressions with and without localizers is related to the different readings of the expressions in question. When place words are associated with an activity that evokes a social routine function, locative expressions have a telic reading in addition to a mere locative reading. In such circumstances, the use of localizers is unfavorable.

Acknowledgments The findings reported in this chapter are partially based on a research project sponsored by the Ministry of Science and Technology of Taiwan under grant number NSC 99-2410-H-024-027. I would also like to express my gratitude to the anonymous reviewers for their insightful comments on the original paper.

References

Asic, Tijana, and Francis Corblin. 2014. Telic definite and their prepositions. French and Serbian. In *Weak referentiality*,ed. Ana Aguilar-Guevara, Bert Le Bruyn, and Joost Zwarts, 183–212. Amsterdam: Benjamins.

Aurnague, Michel. 2012. Quand la routine s'installe: Remarques sur les emplois de 'à' de type "routine sociale". *Revue Romane* 47(2):189–218.

Chao, Yuen-ren. 1968. *A grammar of spoken Chinese*. Berkeley and Los Angeles: University of California Press.

Chappell, Hilary, and Alain Peyraube. 2008. Chinese localizers: Diachrony and some typological considerations. In *Space in languages of China: Cross-linguistic, synchronic and diachronic perspectives*, ed. Xu Dan, 15–37. Dordrecht: Springer.

Chen, Changlai 陳昌來. 2002. *Prepositions and their introductory functions 介詞與介引功能. Hefei: Anhui Education Press.*

Chu, Zexiang 儲澤祥. 2004. The mechanisms responsible for the deletion of locative particles in 'zài' + locative phrases 漢語'在+方位短語'裡的隱現機制. *Chinese Language 中國語文 299(2):112–122.*

Chu, Zexiang 儲澤祥. 2010. *A study on spatial phrases in Chinese 漢語空間短語研究. Beijing: Peking University Press.*

Corblin, Francis. 2011. Des définis para-intensionnels: être à l'hôpital, aller à l'école. *Langue Française* 171(3):55–76.

Corblin, Francis. 2013. Locus et telos: aller à l'école, être à la plage. In *Corela 11, numéro thématique 'Langue, espace, cognition'*, ed. Benjamin Fagard and Dejan Stosic. Available at http://corela.edel.univ-poitiers.fr/index.php?id=2722. Accessed 14 August 2014.

Djamouri, Redouane, Waltraud Paul, and John Whitman. 2013. Postpositions vs. prepositions in Mandarin Chinese: The articulation of disharmony. In *Theoretical approaches to disharmonic word orders*, ed. Theresa Biberauer and Michelle Sheehan, 74–105. Oxford: Oxford University Press.

Ernst, Thomas. 1988. Chinese postpositions—Again. *Journal of Chinese Linguistics* 16(2): 219–244.

Frawley, William. 1992. *Linguistic semantics*. Hillsdale, NJ, Hove, and London: Lawrence Erlbaum.

Guo, Rui 郭銳. 2002. *A study on parts of speech in contemporary Chinese 現代漢語詞類研究. Beijing: The Commercial Press.*

Herskovits, Annette. 1985. Semantics and pragmatics of locative expressions. *Cognitive Science* 9(3):341–378.

Herskovits, Annette. 2009. *Language and spatial cognition: An interdisciplinary study of the prepositions in English*. Cambridge [Cambridgeshire] and New York: Cambridge University Press.

Hsieh, Hsin-I. 1989. Time and imagery in Chinese. In *Functionalism and Chinese grammar*, ed. James Tai and Frank Hsueh, 45–94. Chinese Language Teachers Association. Monograph Series Number 1.

Jackendoff, Ray. 1983. *Semantics and cognition*. Cambridge, MA: MIT Press.

Kemmerer, David, and Daniel Tranel. 2000. A double dissociation between linguistic and perceptual representations of spatial relationships. *Cognitive Neuropsychology* 17(5):393–414.

Li, Yen-hui Audrey. 1990. *Order and constituency in Mandarin Chinese*. Dordrecht: Kluwer.

Li, Chongxing 李崇興. 1992. A preliminary study on the historical development of place words 處所詞發展歷史的初步考察. In *The study of modern Chinese 近代漢語研究, ed. Zhuan Hu, Naisi Yang, and Shaoyu Jiang 胡竹安, 楊耐思, 蔣紹愚, 243–263. Beijing: The Commercial Press.*

Li, Charles N. and Sandra A. Thompson.1981. *Mandarin Chinese: a Functional Reference Grammar*. Berkeley: University of California Press.

Liu, Feng-Hsi. 1998. A clitic analysis of locative particles. *Journal of Chinese Linguistics* 28(1): 48–70.

Liu, Danqing 劉丹青. 2003. *Word order typology and a theory of adpositions 語序類型學與介詞理論. Beijing: The Commercial Press.*

Müller, Stefan, and Janna Lipenkova. 2013. ChinGram: A TRALE implementation of an HPSG fragment of Mandarin Chinese. In *Proceedings of PACLIC 2013*, 240–249. Taipei, Taiwan. Available at https://www.aclweb.org/anthology/Y13-1023. Accessed 1 April 2019.

Peyraube, Alain. 2003. On the history of place words and localizers in Chinese: A cognitive approach. In *Functional structure(s): Form and interpretation,* ed. Yen-hui, Audrey Li, and Andrew Simpson, 180–198. London and New York: Routledge Curzon.

Pustejovsky, James. 1998. Generativity and explanation in semantics: A reply to Fodor and Lepore. *Linguistic Inquiry* 29(2):289–311.

Pustejovsky, James, and Elisabetta Jezek. 2016. *A guide to generative lexicon theory.* Cambridge, UK: Oxford University Press.

Qiu, Bin 邱斌. 2008. *Studies on issues related to Chinese locative words 漢語方位類詞相關問題研究. Shanghai: Xuelin Press.*

Sun, Chaofen. 2008. Two conditions and grammaticalization of the Chinese locative. In *Space in languages of China: Cross-linguistic, synchronic and diachronic perspectives*, ed. Xu Dan, 199–227. Dordrecht: Springer.

Svorou, Soteria. 1993. *The grammar of space*. Amsterdam: Benjamins.

Talmy, Leonard. 1975. Figure and ground in complex sentences. In *Proceedings of the First Annual Meeting of the Berkeley Linguistics Society*, 419–430. Berkeley, CA. Available at https://journals.linguisticsociety.org/proceedings/index.php/BLS/article/viewFile/2322/2092. Accessed 1 April 2019.

Talmy, Leonard. 2000. *Toward a cognitive semantics. Volume 1: Concept structuring systems*. Cambridge, MA: MIT Press.

Vandeloise, Claude. 1987. La préposition à et le principe d'anticipation. *Langue française* 76:77–111.

Wang, Wenli, and Changyong Zhang 王文麗, 張長永. 2011. The origin of localizers and the development of locative adpositional phrases 方位詞的產生與處所介詞詞組語序的演變. *Modern Chinese 現代語文 10:50–53.*

Zhang, N. 2017. Adpositions. In *Encyclopedia of Chinese language and linguistics* (Vol. 1), ed. Rint Sybesma, Wolfgang Behr, Yueguo Gu, Zev Handel, C.-T. James Huang, and James Myers, 116–122. Leiden: Brill.

Zwarts, Joost. 2008. Aspects of a typology of direction. In *Theoretical and crosslinguistic approaches to the semantics of aspect*, ed. Susan Rothstein, 79–106. Amsterdam: John Benjamins.

Corpus

CCL Online Corpus: Provided by the Center for Chinese Linguistics at the University of Peking. Available at http://ccl.pku.edu.cn:8080/ccl_corpus/. Accessed 6 November 2017.

Chapter 21
Verb Polysemy and Compounding Productivity in Chinese: A Quantitative Study

Chao-Jan Chen

Abstract In Mandarin Chinese, monosyllabic verbs (V characters) are particularly rich in polysemy and morphologically productive in compounding. The senses of V characters are usually associated with their related compounds. This chapter will examine the relationship between the polysemy and compounding productivity of V characters both qualitatively and quantitatively. A morphological phenomenon called "compounding-abbreviation loop" has been proposed as a way to enrich the polysemy of V characters. It has been argued that the compounding-abbreviation loop accounts for the strong semantic ties between V characters and their related compounds. Supporting this view, this chapter will present a quantitative study that examined the association between the polysemy and compounding productivity of V characters. The data on the characters, compounds, and word senses used in the study were collected from the Academia Sinica Balanced Corpus, *Thesaurus of Chinese Words* 同義詞詞林 *Tóngyìcí Cílín*, and the Chinese dictionary 漢語大詞典 *Hanyu Da Cidian*. The results showed a positive correlation between the mean number of senses and the number of related compounds.

Keywords Polysemy · Abbreviation · Compounding · Morphological productivity · Power law distribution · Frequency effect

21.1 Introduction

As the basic semantic units in Chinese morphology, monosyllabic morphemes, or *zì* in Chinese (simply termed "character" in this chapter), are often highly polysemous, whether they are free or bound. The study that will be presented in this chapter examined the polysemy of words collected from *Thesaurus of Chinese Words* 同義詞詞林 *Tóngyìcí Cílín* (henceforth, CILIN) (Mei et al. 梅家駒等 1984), which is one of the most frequently used thesauruses in Chinese natural language processing, and used their semantic classes in CILIN as rough word senses for simple statistical

C.-J. Chen (✉)
Department of Foreign Languages and Literature, National Chi Nan University, Puli, Taiwan

C.-R. Huang et al. (eds.), *Chinese Language Resources*, Text, Speech and Language Technology 49, https://doi.org/10.1007/978-3-031-38913-9_21

analysis. The results showed that the average number of senses of one-character words was 2.15, which was about twice that of multi-character words, 1.14 (the average number of senses of two-character words, three-character words, and four-character words were 1.16, 1.04, and 1.12, respectively). Moreover, among all the characters, verb characters, or one-character verbs (henceforth, V characters), were particularly highly polysemous. Comparing V characters and N characters (noun characters), the two major lexical categories in Chinese, the statistics based on the data from CILIN showed that the average number of senses of N characters was 2.30, while that of the V characters was 2.70, which was larger than the former. Focusing on the most polysemous characters, the difference in the average richness of polysemy between the two categories of characters was even more pronounced. For example, counting only the top 100 most polysemous V characters and the top 100 most polysemous N characters, the average number of senses of the 100 V characters was 7.47, while that of the 100 N characters was 5.06.

Viewing the above statistical data, why are Chinese V characters particularly rich in polysemy? To answer this question, the study examined the senses of such highly polysemous V characters and found that they were usually associated with the senses of their related compounds. In the study, a related compound of a V character was defined as a two-character compound verb in the form of X-V or V-Y, which represented a compound that contained the V character as one of its two components. For example, 攻打 *gōng-dǎ* "attack" and 打擊 *dǎ-jí* "strike" were both regarded as related compounds of the V character 打 *da* "hit." Furthermore, according to a simple preliminary observation, the more polysemous a V character was, the more related compounds it had and vice versa. This led to the question of whether the polysemy of V characters and their morphological productivity in forming related compounds (henceforth, compounding productivity) somehow influenced each other or even reinforced each other, as well as whether any quantitative evidence could be found to explain the phenomenon. Relevant research on polysemy and compounding in Chinese, however, has rarely focused on the quantitative relationship between the polysemy richness of a character and its compounding productivity. The study thus aimed to fill this gap by examining the relationship between the polysemy and compounding productivity of V characters as well as finding a qualitative account for this relationship.

The remainder of this chapter is structured as follows. Section 21.2 will provide a brief sketch of the semantic ties between V characters and their related compounds in light of paraphrasing. Section 21.3 will explore the interaction between compounding and abbreviation, the two morphological processes involved in the rich polysemy of V characters and the semantic ties between V characters and their related compounds. The concept "compounding-abbreviation loop" will also be introduced to account for the semantic ties. In Sect. 21.4, the quantitative study that explored the association between the compounding productivity and polysemy of V characters will be presented, while Sect. 21.5 will provide a summary of the chapter as well as some concluding remarks.

21.2 Paraphrasing V Characters

In Mandarin Chinese, there are strong links between the senses of a polysemous V character and those of its related compounds. More specifically, a polysemous V character can usually be paraphrased by some of its related compounds. Take the V character 拋 *pāo*, for example, which has at least three different senses, "to bring up," "to throw," and "to abandon," as in the phrasal expressions 拋議題 *pāo yìtí* "to bring up an issue," 拋鉛球 *pāo qiānqiú* "to throw a shot put," and 拋垃圾 *pāo lèsè* "to abandon trash." The character 拋 pāo in these phrasal expressions can, respectively, be paraphrased by its synonymous related compounds, 拋出 *pāo-chū* "to bring up," 拋擲 *pāo-zhì* "to throw," and 拋棄 *pāo-qì* "to abandon." As a V character, 拋 *pāo* is not a particular case of such paraphrasing. In fact, most V characters can be paraphrased with their related compounds in this way. Based on data from the Chinese thesaurus CILIN, the study explored the phenomenon of such paraphrasing for V characters by examining whether their related compounds could be found in the same semantic class, which would mean that they were synonymous (or at least near-synonymous) in a rough sense. With this method, the study found that 65% of the V characters in CILIN could be paraphrased by at least one of their related compounds.

In fact, paraphrasing a polysemous character with one of its related compounds is a frequent way of explaining a character's senses in Chinese. For example, in Chinese dictionaries, the meanings of a word are usually concisely explained by sets of synonyms instead of rigorous definitions with lengthy descriptions. Therefore, the polysemy of a V character is usually illustrated in a simple way by its different related compounds, as in the case of 拋 *pāo*. According to the results of the statistical analysis based on the data from 漢語大詞典 *Hanyu Da Cidian* (a prestigious Chinese dictionary that contains about 375,000 entries), 52% of the V characters were explained by at least one of its related compounds, and 9% of them were explained by more than five of its related compounds. Take the entry for the V character 追 *zhuī* in *Hanyu Da Cidian* (henceforth, HDC), for example. As shown in Table 21.1, among the 18 senses of the V character 追 *zhuī* listed in HDC, 15 senses are explained with two-character compound verbs, and 6 senses of the V character are explained with at least one of its synonymous related compounds.

Such paraphrasing is also a conventional and preferable way to disambiguate the sense of a polysemous character in a sentence when explaining the meaning of a

Table 21.1 The senses of 追 *zhuī* in HDC

1. 追逐；追趕。	2. 追兵。	3. 跟隨；追隨。
4. 趕得上；比配。	5. 回溯；追念。	6. 追悔；後悔。
7. 補救；挽回。	8. 事後補行。	9. 尋求；追求。
10. (向異性) 求愛。	11. 查問；追究。	12. 拘捕；傳拿。
13. 催逼；索取。	14. 削奪；收繳。	15. 驅除；消除。
16. 送行。	17. 招引；徵召。	18. (中醫) 補益。

passage written in Classical Chinese (文言文 *wényánwén*) or "translating" the passage into vernacular Chinese (白話文 *báihuàwén*). This approach is exemplified in the following sentences in (21.1) and (21.2) below, which are in Classical and vernacular Chinese, respectively. Example (21.1), which is from the Ancient Chinese text 戰國策 *Zhànguó cè* (*The Strategies of the Warring States*), is paraphrased in Example (21.2) with the three V characters 攻 *gōng*, 取 *qǔ*, and 賀 *hè* paraphrased by one of their related compounds, as in 攻打 *gong-dǎ*, 取得 *qǔ-dé*, and 恭賀 *gōng-hè*, respectively:

(21.1)	秦攻魏, 取寧邑, 諸侯皆賀。 (戰國策 *Zhànguó cè*)
	qín_gōng_wèi, qǔ_níng_yì, zhūhóu_jiē_hè
	Qin_attack_Wei_seize_NingYi_vassal_all_congratulate
	The Kingdom of Qin attacked the Kingdom of Wei and seized Ning Town; the vassals all congratulated (the Kingdom of Qin).
(21.2)	秦國攻打趙國, 取得了寧邑, 諸侯都恭賀(秦國)。
	qín_guó_gōng-dǎ_zhào_guó, qǔ-dé_le_níng_yì, zhūhóu_dōu_gōng-hè (qín_guó)
	Qin_kingdom_attack_Wei_kingdom_seize_LE_NingYi_vassal_all_congratulate (Qin_kingdom)
	The Kingdom of Qin attacked the Kingdom of Wei and seized Ning Town; the vassals all congratulated (the Kingdom of Qin).

21.3 Compounding Versus Abbreviation

The richness of a V character's polysemy and its richness in synonymous related compounds (i.e., V-X or X-V) are in fact highly linked to each other. Suppose that for a V character in a Chinese lexicon, nowadays, there is a (near-)synonymous related compound in the form of V-X or X-V (X as another character), as in the case of X-V, for example. Theoretically, there are two probable ways to derive the sense between the V character and the related compound V-X, either by compounding (from V to V-X; V is used to form the compound V-X), which means V-X is derived from V as a compound word roughly with a sense of V, or abbreviation (from V-X to V; V-X is abbreviated to V while keeping the same meaning), which means that V acquires a new sense from the existing compound V-X through abbreviation.

The ties between characters and their synonymous related compounds are so strong that a pertinent prosodic requirement has been argued to exist in Mandarin Chinese by Pan 潘文國 (2002: 246), who argued that in Chinese "幾乎每一個概念都可以有兩種說法，一種用單音字，一種用複音(主要是雙音)辭。原本是單音的，有辦法造一個雙音的臨時用；原本雙音的，也有辦法只用其中一個字，使用時完全靠文章節奏韻律的需要。

> almost every concept can be expressed in two ways: one with a mono-syllabic word (that is one-character word), the other with a multi-syllabic (mainly bi-syllabic) word. A mono-syllabic word can be replaced by a bi-syllabic word, which is formed to serve the temporary

usage; a bi-syllabic word can be reduced to one of its component characters. The application of such replacements depends totally on the prosodic requirement. (Translation mine)"

As a natural consequence, the frequently applied prosodic requirement in language usage facilitates and strengthens the two-way morphological link formed by compounding and abbreviation. Moreover, abbreviation can also serve as a productive way to extend meaning, which again strengthens the semantic link between compounding and abbreviation. As Jiang 蔣紹愚 (2005) remarked, if a word X-Y can be reduced to the abbreviated form X, and when such a form is frequently used, it can gain a new sense that originally belonged only to the word X-Y.

It is not always easy, however, to know which one of the two ways actually occurs in the course of polysemy development for a V character that possesses a sense that is the same as or close to that of its related compound. In fact, it is often extremely difficult to tell whether the sense of X-V or V-X contributes to the polysemy of V through abbreviation or one of V's senses contributes to the sense of its synonymous compound X-V or V-X through compounding. The reason is partly that, as Packard (2000: 268) remarked, "it is difficult to make a clear distinction between the two [compounding and abbreviation]. This is because almost every word formed by [compounding] can be paraphrased with longer words or phrases and may therefore 'masquerade' as an abbreviation."

Looking back at the example 拋 *pāo*, do "to bring up," "to throw," and "to abandon," as senses already possessed by the character 拋 *pāo*, contribute to the meanings of the related compounds 拋出 *pāo-chū*, 拋擲 *pāo-zhì*, and 拋棄 *pāo-qì*? Or, on the contrary, does the abbreviation of the related compounds contribute to the senses "to bring up," "to throw," and "to abandon" of 拋 *pāo*? It is not always easy to trace the historical development of meaning extension for a certain character and its related compounds to see whether the senses of the compounds contribute to the senses of the character in question by abbreviation.

However, considering some compounds among modern technology terms, the question might be much easier to answer. Take 掃瞄 *sǎo-miáo* "to scan (by machine)," for example. Both 掃瞄 *sǎo-miáo* and 掃 *sǎo* can be used to mean "to scan," as shown in Example (21.3) below. In this case, the sense "to scan (by machine)" of the V character 掃 *sǎo* obviously should appear after the coinage of its related compound word 掃瞄 *sǎo-miáo*. The sense of the compound 掃瞄 *sǎo-miáo* should be fed back to its component character 掃 *sǎo*, while it is probably the core sense "to sweep" of the character 掃 *sǎo* that is evoked to create the compound 掃瞄 *sǎo-miáo*, meaning "to scan" (due to its manner of movement similar to that of "to sweep"). That is to say, in (21.3), the sense S_1 of 掃 *sǎo* "to sweep" should contribute its meaning to form the compound 掃瞄 *sǎo-miáo* "to scan" first and have the sense "to scan" fed back to the character 掃 *sǎo* as the sense S_2 by abbreviation later, as the following schema shows:

掃 (S_1) → compounding → 掃瞄 (S_2) → abbreviation → 掃 (S_2)	
(21.3)	這台掃瞄器{掃瞄/掃}一張圖只要一秒鐘。
	Zhè_tái_sǎomiáoqì_{sǎo miáo/sǎo}_yī_zhāng_tú_zhǐ_yào_yī_miǎozhōng

(continued)

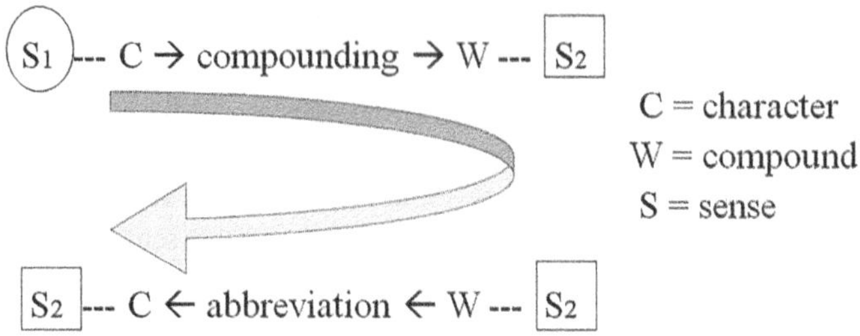

Fig. 21.1 Compounding-abbreviation loop

Fig. 21.2 Sense extension through repeated compounding-abbreviation loops

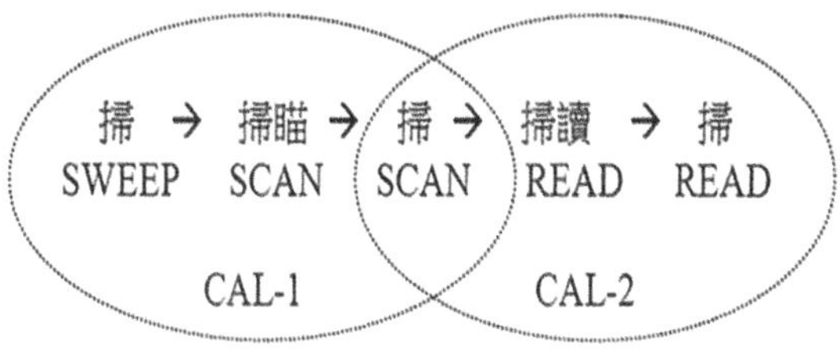

this_CL_scanner_scan_one_CL_picture_only_need_one_second
It takes only one second for this scanner to scan a picture.

In view of the interaction between a V character and its related compounds through compounding and abbreviation, the study proposed that a process of compounding followed by a process of abbreviation involving the same V character would form a loop of morphological processes called compounding-abbreviation loop (also abbreviated as CAL in this chapter). A compounding-abbreviation loop serves as a potential way to extend the senses of a V character. Figure 21.1 shows how character C, originally possessing the sense S_1, acquires a new sense S_2 through a loop consisting of the process of compounding (from C to its related compound W) and the process of abbreviation (reduced in form from its related compound W back to C). Theoretically, such loops can be repeated again and again so that a V character can acquire more and more related senses, enriching its polysemy.

Take, again, the case of 掃 *sǎo*, for example. As Fig. 21.1 shows, 掃 *sǎo* might possibly gain the sense S_3 of the new compound 掃讀 *sǎo-dú* "to read by scanning" in the future through a potential compounding-abbreviation loop, which is shown in the following schemas:

掃 (S_2) → compounding → 掃讀 (S_3) → abbreviation → 掃 (S_3)				
掃 →	掃瞄 →	掃 →	掃讀 →	掃 → ……. 掃 -X
S_1	S_2	S_2	S_3	S_3 S_n
SWEEP	SCAN	SWEEP	READ	READ?

Therefore, a V character like 掃 *sǎo* can potentially acquire new senses continuously through a series of compounding-abbreviation loops, as shown in Fig. 21.2.

From what has been discussed above, theoretically, every V-V compound can potentially contribute, by abbreviation, its sense to one of its component V characters. Such a potential sense of character C can actually be transferred from the compound word W to character C when abbreviation in the CAL is accomplished. Hence, each time a new related compound V-X or X-V is coined, a potential sense of the V character is produced. When a permanent abbreviation occurs constantly, the potential sense waits for the opportunity to become conventionally accepted by native speakers as an actual sense of the V character.

21.4 A Quantitative Study: Association Between Polysemy and Compounding Productivity

Following the discussions in Sect. 21.3, if the phenomenon of compounding-abbreviation loops is active enough in Chinese morphology, this crucial factor should contribute to enriching the polysemy of V characters. In this case, V characters with more related compounds should potentially be more apt to acquire new senses and hence become more polysemous. Accordingly, one should be able to perceive, quantitatively, a positive correlation between the degree of polysemy and the degree of compounding productivity of V characters. Thus, a statistical analysis was carried out to examine such an association between the richness of polysemy and compounding productivity.

In the research database of the quantitative study, V characters and their related compounds were collected from the Academia Sinica Balanced Corpus of Modern Chinese (ASBC) (http://asbc.iis.sinica.edu.tw/) version 3.0, which contains about five million word tokens. To make this quantitative study statistically significant as well as reasonably affordable on the part of indispensable manual work, the target set of V characters preferably had to be limited to a certain category of verbs with a size of about 1000 types. Therefore, it was desirable to choose one-character verbs syntactically tagged as VC, meaning 動作及物動詞 *dòngzuò jí-wù dòngcí* "transitive verb of action," in the ASBC, since the VC is the most numerous and active subcategory of verbs in the corpus. These types of V characters were counted as well as their related compounds in the ASBC and the number of their senses listed in HDC. After manually filtering out some data noise, the research database contained 1164 V characters along with their number of senses and number of related compounds.

Tables 21.2 and 21.3 present the quantitative correlation between the number of senses (S) and the number of related compounds (C), respectively, of the 20 most polysemous V characters and the 20 most compounding-productive V characters.

The two histograms in Figs. 21.3 and 21.4 show the distribution of the number of related compounds and the distribution of the number of senses of the V characters, respectively.

Table 21.2 Number of senses (S) and number of related compounds (C) of the top 20 most polysemous V characters

Rank	S(no. of sense)	C(no. of comp.)	Rank	S(no. of sense)	C(no. of comp.)
1	81	302	11	44	168
2	64	264	12	43	143
3	55	199	13	43	90
4	51	84	14	42	222
5	49	69	15	40	667
6	48	82	16	40	227
7	47	206	17	40	102
8	47	21	18	40	75
9	47	382	19	40	43
10	45	8	20	40	55

Table 21.3 Number of related compounds (C) and number of senses (S) of the top 20 most compounding-productive V characters

Rank	C(no. of comp.)	S(no. of sense)	Rank	C(no. of comp.)	S(no. of sense)
1	667	40	11	264	64
2	414	13	12	261	27
3	399	26	13	256	16
4	382	47	14	252	16
5	368	33	15	236	37
6	361	27	16	230	20
7	310	26	17	227	40
8	302	81	18	222	42
9	281	22	19	222	28
10	279	29	20	216	17

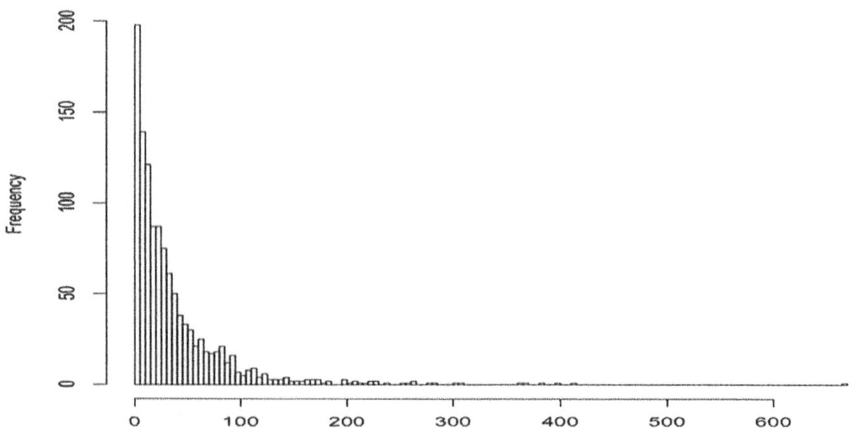

Fig. 21.3 Distribution of number of related compounds of V characters

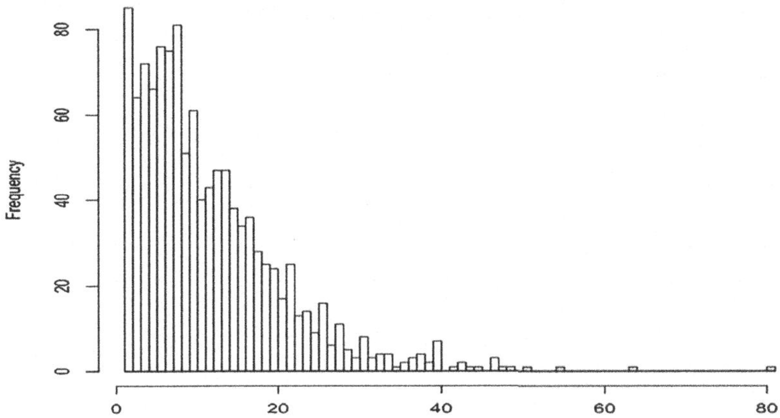

Fig. 21.4 Distribution of number of senses of V characters

Figure 21.3 shows that the distribution of the number of V characters' related compounds has the shape of a power law distribution, just as Chen (2012) found in the morphological productivity of characters in Chinese compounding. This power law distribution has been found in many kinds of real and virtual scale-free networks (e.g., see Barabási 2003; Newman et al. 2006). Based on the phenomenon of preferential attachment and incremental growth in network structures mainly found by Barabási's research (e.g., Barabási and Albert 1999), Chen (2012) proposed that such a power law distribution in Chinese compounding can be regarded as the signature of a "rich-get-richer" effect caused by a positive feedback loop in V characters' morphological productivity in compounding: the more related compounds a V character has (which reflects "past productivity" in Chen's terms), the more likely it is to be used to form new compound verbs in the future (which is "future productivity" in Chen's terms). This is, in fact, a kind of frequency effect that is often observed in language, especially in morphology (see Bybee 1985, 2007, 2010; Bybee and Hopper 2001; Chen 2013).

With the compounding-abbreviation loop as a means of sense extension, the probability of a V character acquiring a new sense depends on its opportunity to form new compounds and the opportunity of its related compounds to be abbreviated and then conventionalized as common word usage. Suppose that the realization of such abbreviation for a compound, which is under the contextual prosodic requirement, is a purely stochastic event; the probability of any abbreviation involving a V character should be roughly proportional to the number of its already coined related compounds. Likewise, as Chen's (2012, 2013) frequency effect research has shown, the probability of a V character forming a new compound is also proportional to the number of its already coined related compounds. Therefore, it is naturally expected that the more related compounds a V character has, the higher chance it has of gaining a new sense through a compounding-abbreviation loop. If this is the case, one should be able to observe, quantitatively, a positive correlation between the number of senses and the number of related compounds of V characters.

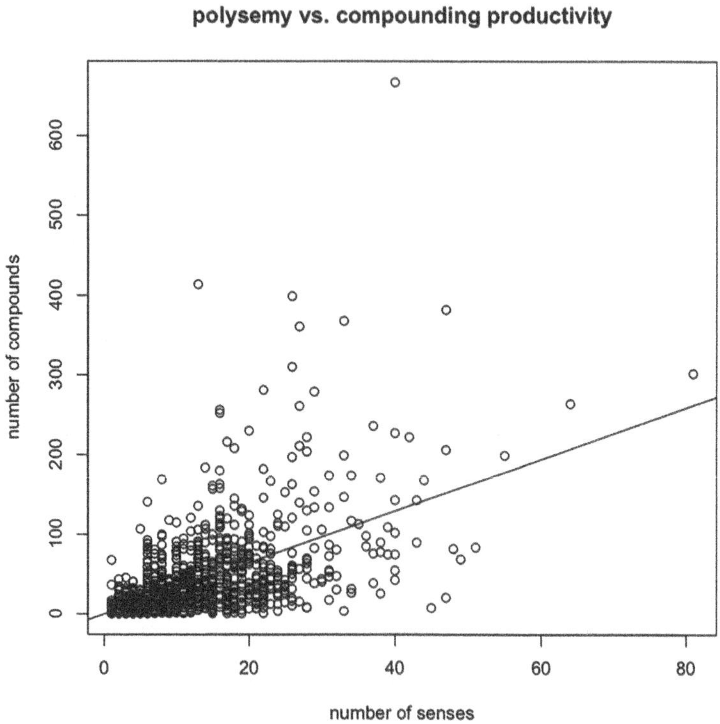

Fig. 21.5 Number of related compounds (y) of V characters with x senses

The scatter plot (with the regression line at $y = 3.24x - 0.13$) in Fig. 21.5 shows that there is indeed a positive correlation between the number of related compounds (y) of a V character and the number of its senses (x). More specifically, the correlation coefficient r_{xy} is 0.56 (with an R^2 of 0.3144). The statistical results show that the polysemy and compounding productivity of a V character are associated with each other by a remarkable degree. As the compounding-abbreviation loop is not the only factor that contributes to the increase in a V character's polysemous senses, the value of R^2 here is rather significant.

Focusing on the "rich" sides of the two distributions, one can see an even more clear association between the highly polysemous V characters and the highly compounding-productive V characters. For the top 100 polysemous V characters, their mean number of related compounds was 115.6, which was in contrast with 9.25 for the 100 least polysemous V characters, while the average for all V characters was 38.8. Likewise, for the top 100 compounding-productive V characters, their mean number of senses was 24.4, which was in contrast with 5.24 for the 100 least compounding-productive V characters, while the average for all V characters was 12.0.

When observing the mean number of related compounds (y) for V characters with x senses, the scatter plot for the two variables x and y in Fig. 21.6 shows that the

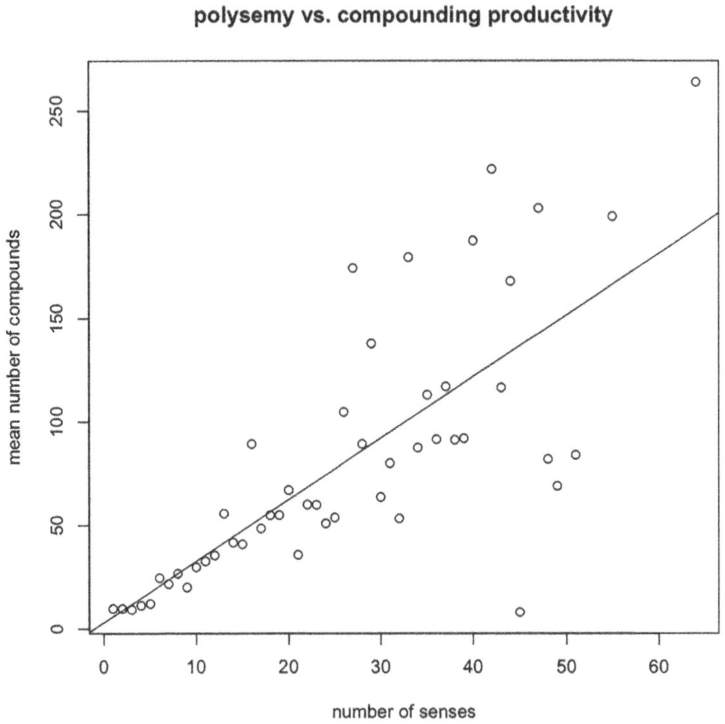

Fig. 21.6 Mean number of related compounds (y) of V characters with x senses

regression line is at $y = 2.97x + 2.96$, of which the correlation coefficient r_{xy} is 0.75 and the R^2 is 0.564. This scatter plot shows that the mean number of related compounds is even more strongly associated with the number of related compounds of a V character.

21.5 Summary and Concluding Remarks

In this chapter, the relationship between the polysemy and compounding productivity of V characters in Chinese was explored from three aspects: (1) the rich synonymy relations between V characters and their related compounds; (2) compounding and abbreviation—the morphological source of the synonymy relations between V characters and their related compounds; and (3) the quantitative correlation between the number of senses of V characters and the number of their related compounds.

The rich synonymy relations between V characters and their related compounds have been demonstrated by abundant usage of paraphrasing in the word meaning explanations in Chinese dictionaries and the translation of Classical Chinese texts from a literary style to a colloquial style. It is usually the case that a polysemous V character has several synonymous related compounds that can paraphrase it using different senses.

The productive application of two morphological processes—compounding and abbreviation—in Mandarin Chinese was the source of rich synonymy relations between V characters and their related compounds. The morphological phenomenon of the compounding-abbreviation loop was demonstrated as being able to serve as a special means of potential meaning extension of a V character. Consequently, the richness of polysemous senses of a V character and its abundance of related compounds were, in fact, linked to each other.

Finally, in the quantitative study presented in this chapter, a positive correlation between the number of senses of V characters and the number of their related compounds was found. The positive correlation confirmed the association between the polysemy and compounding productivity of V characters, which was naturally expected as a consequence of the active morphological and semantic interaction between characters and compounds through compounding and abbreviation in Mandarin Chinese. More specifically, the results of this quantitative study provide evidence for the effect produced by the compounding-abbreviation loop over the course of time.

Dynamically, the positive correlation also suggests that in one direction, the more related compounds a V character has, the more new senses the V character tends to acquire over the course of time. Likewise, in the other direction, it also suggests that the more senses a V character has, the more opportunities it has to result in new compounds and thus will have more related compounds in the future. The two directions of dynamic reinforcement—more compounds causing more senses and more senses causing more compounds—together form a loop of positive feedback. This loop of positive feedback can thus bring about the power law distribution of V characters' morphological productivity in compounding that Chen (2012, 2013) has shown. This suggests that the phenomenon of the compounding-abbreviation loop might be able to provide a possible linguistic explanation for the type frequency effect in Chinese verb compounding, although further detailed exploration still needs to be carried out in the future.

Acknowledgments The findings reported in this chapter were partially based on the research projects sponsored by grants NSC 99-2410-H-260-059, NSC 101-2410-H-260-043, and NSC 102-2410-H-260-034-MY2. I would also like to thank the anonymous reviewers for their valuable suggestions for the original paper.

References

Barabási, Albert-Lászl6. 2003. *Linked: How everything is connected to everything else and what it means*. New York: Plume.

Barabási, Albert-Laszlo, and Reka Albert. 1999. Emergence of scaling in random networks. *Science* 286:509–512.

Bybee, Joan L. 1985. *Morphology: A study of the relation between meaning and form*. Amsterdam and Philadelphia: John Benjamins.

Bybee, Joan L. 2007. *Frequency of use and the organization of language*. Oxford and New York: Oxford University Press.

Bybee, Joan L. 2010. *Language, usage and cognition*. Cambridge, UK, and New York: Cambridge University Press.

Bybee, Joan L., and Paul Hopper (eds.). 2001. *Frequency and the emergence of linguistic structure*. Amsterdam and Philadelphia: John Benjamins.

Chen, Chao-Jan. 2012. Power-law distribution in morphological productivity: A statistical analysis of Chinese compounds. In *In search of grammar: Experimental and corpus-based studies*, ed. James Myers, 97–118. Taipei: Institute of Linguistics, Academia Sinica.

Chen, Chao-Jan. 2013. Frequency effect in Chinese morphology: Diachronic evidence from a synchronic corpus. In *Breaking down the barriers: Interdisciplinary studies in Chinese linguistics and beyond*, ed. Cao Guangshun, Hilary Chappell, Redouane Djamouri, and Thekla Wiebusch, 371–381. Taipei: Institute of Linguistics, Academia Sinica.

Jiang, Shao-Yu 蔣紹愚. 2005. *The outline of Ancient Chinese vocabulary 古漢語詞彙綱要. Beijing: Peking University Press.*

Mei, Jia-Ju, Yi-Min Zhu, Yun-Qi Gao, and Hong-Xiang Yin 梅家駒,竺一鳴,高蘊琦,殷鴻翔. 1984. *Thesaurus of Chinese words 同義詞詞林. Hong Kong: The Commercial Press.*

Newman, Mark, Albert-Laszlo Barabási, and Duncan J. Watts (eds.). 2006. *The structure and dynamics of networks*. Princeton, NJ: Princeton University Press.

Packard, Jerome L. 2000. *The morphology of Chinese: A linguistic and cognitive approach*. New York: Cambridge University Press.

Pan, Wen-Guo 潘文國. 2002. *Character-centered theory and Chinese language studies 字本位與漢語研究. Shanghai: Huadong Normal University Press.*

Lexical Resources

Hanyu Da Cidian version 3 漢語大詞典 *3.0* 版. 2007. Hong Kong: The Commercial Press (H.K.) Ltd. 3.0 CD-ROM version, 光碟繁體單機 3.0 版.

Chapter 22
Audience Awareness and Lexical Frequency Patterns in Political Speeches

Kathleen Ahrens and Paul Yu-Chun Chang

Abstract Previous studies have used lexical frequency patterns to understand how conceptual models reflect ideology. Ahrens and Lee (2009) and Ahrens (2011) examined lexical frequency patterns in US senatorial speeches and presidential speeches, respectively, and argued that these patterns provide evidence for Lakoff's (2002) idea that the two major US political parties have conceptualized government as if it were a family leader, either as a "Strict Father" or as a "Nurturant Parent." In this chapter, we will extend these two models by applying them to the cross-strait relationship between Mainland China and Taiwan. Using Ahrens' (2011) and Ahrens and Lee's (2009) methodology, we found that the lexical frequency patterns in speeches made by an official office of the People's Republic of China (PRC) suggest audience awareness regarding how PRC ideology was construed: while the language appeared more hardline in speeches addressing Taiwan authorities and Mainland Chinese people, a more balanced approach was taken in speeches that directly addressed Taiwanese people. In addition, the findings were supported by the collocational patterns found in the data. This chapter will reveal how PRC representatives have modulated their language and tone to advance their political goals for the reunification of China.

Keywords Conceptual mapping model · Lexical frequency patterns · Political communication · Corpus linguistics

K. Ahrens (✉)
Department of English and Communication, The Hong Kong Polytechnic University, Hong Kong, China
e-mail: kathleen.ahrens@polyu.edu.hk

P. Y.-C. Chang
AppliedAI Initiative GmbH, Munich, Germany
e-mail: y.chang@lipp.lmu.de

C.-R. Huang et al. (eds.), *Chinese Language Resources*, Text, Speech and Language Technology 49, https://doi.org/10.1007/978-3-031-38913-9_22

22.1 Introduction

A driving issue in the study of political discourse is the identification and examination of ideology in written and spoken language. The analysis of political language has often focused on the language of individual political leaders (Ahrens 2011; Ahrens and Lee 2009; Charteris-Black 2011; Lim 2002), with less attention paid to governmental language—that is, the official language of a government in press releases or position papers. One reason for this is that in governmental language, there is no clear identifier for the creator of the document; it may have been created by a committee or by individual, unidentified speech writers with no clear ownership taken of the end result. But an interesting possibility arises if this question is viewed from a different angle: what about official government language that is created for the purpose of speaking to or influencing a particular audience? That is, the province of the remarks or text may belong to various speakers, or unidentified speakers, and be attributed to only the government organization itself, but the audience to whom the government officials are talking could vary. Seen from this angle, there may be certain features in the text that reflect a government's view toward a given audience (Echterhoff et al. 2013; Jing-Schmidt and Peng 2017; Menegatti and Rubini 2013).

To test this possibility, we examined the language used in official statements by the Taiwan Affairs Office of the State Council (TAOSC). This office is an official office of the People's Republic of China (PRC). Its function is to manage affairs related to Taiwan, including promoting the PRC's cross-strait policy as well as cross-strait business investments and academic/cultural exchanges. Because its functions vary, it can be seen as communicating with three different audiences: Taiwan authorities, the people of Taiwan, and the people of Mainland China.[1] As the speeches found on the website of this office (http://www.gwytb.gov.cn/) contain those that address these three groups, we downloaded these texts and examined whether the textual features of the speeches to these different groups varied.

There are a variety of features that can be examined. Le (2004), for example, looked at how editors used various metadiscursive strategies (including the use of evidentials, person markers, and/or relational markers) to present themselves as either respected journalists, public opinion representatives, or intellectuals in the French cultural tradition. Our study, however, focused on the discursive features that indicated ideological biases. Newspaper pundits are often attuned to these biases, noting that hardline language is a strategy used by the PRC to shoot down the advocacy of Taiwan independence in speeches addressed to Taiwan authorities (Huang 2011; Lin 2007; Tu 2008; Zeng 2012). One case in point is when the PRC severely condemned Taiwan's 2008 referendum (on whether Taiwan should seek membership in the United Nations) as a dangerous act designed to impede cross-

[1]Because we aimed to examine the language used by an official organization of the People's Republic of China in our study, we used the Xinhua News Agency as a reference corpus and followed the Xinhua News Agency's translations for relevant terms, such as 台灣當局, which is translated as "Taiwan authority(ies)."

strait peace. This type of hardline language is in line with the PRC's goals for the reunification of China, as it views the Taiwan authority's request for UN membership as counter-productive to its goals. However, other pundits have noted that the PRC has adopted a softer tone in speeches addressing Taiwanese people. This type of speech occurs at events such as the opening words at reception sessions addressing Taiwanese businesspeople who are attending commercial exchange forums, with the implicit goal of gaining their support (Lin 2007). This softened language use is not paradoxical if the audience is different; for example, the PRC may want to pressure Taiwan authorities while offering reassurance to the people of Taiwan. Both efforts, in fact, could be construed as different means to the same end: the reunification of China and Taiwan.

This use of hardline versus softened language in politics has been proposed to be related to the conceptual model of a family (Lakoff 2002), with the government understood as a parent and the parent type being one of two kinds: a Strict Father or a Nurturant Parent. In these two models, morality is understood as either "strength" and "authority" (STRICT FATHER) or "nurturance" and "empathy" (NURTURANT PARENT), respectively.[2] A number of studies have examined these two models in terms of their potential instantiation in the language and gestures of the Republican George W. Bush and the Democrat Al Gore during the US presidential debates in 2000 (Cienki 2004), as well as in the way political conservatives and liberals narrate their lives (McAdams et al. 2008). In addition, Ahrens and Lee (2009) and Ahrens (2011) examined US senatorial speeches and presidential speeches, respectively, and demonstrated that by analyzing the frequency of lexemes related to the STRICT FATHER/NURTURANT PARENT models, potentially contrastive patterns could be found and the language could be evaluated. In addition, Flowerdew and Leong (2007) conducted a content analysis of the reports and opinions regarding constitutional reform in Hong Kong in two local newspapers in post-colonial Hong Kong. They found that in the debates between the pro-(Hong Kong) democracy and pro-PRC newspapers, the nation was often metaphorically construed as a family and the government was construed as a parent. Notably, they claimed that the pro-PRC newspaper reflected the PRC's hybrid Communist/Confucianist ideology that emphasizes the importance of the family, but they did not analyze whether the "parental" language used was based on the STRICT FATHER or the NURTURANT PARENT model of parenting.

Given that the family metaphor is also used in Chinese discourse, our study took the next step and examined whether STRICT FATHER/NURTURANT PARENT patterns could be found in the official statements made by the PRC's TAOSC and, furthermore, examined whether these patterns were adjusted for a particular audience. Previous corpus-based analysis on the lexical patterns observed in US presidential speeches found that US President George W. Bush, for example, modulated his language when speaking to listeners highly in favor of his ideological worldview during his

[2]In this chapter, the terms "strict father" and "nurturant parent" are formatted in small capital letters when denoting conceptual models and they are simply capitalized elsewhere following standard practice.

Radio Addresses (using more Strict Father words in those cases) (Ahrens 2011). However, the same study found that he used both Strict Father and Nurturant Parent lexemes when speaking to all Americans in his State of the Union Addresses. This may be one reason pundits billed him as a "compassionate conservative," with the "conservative" ideology promoting a STRICT FATHER worldview and the "compassionate" aspect promoting a NURTURANT PARENT worldview.

Presidents Ronald Reagan and Bill Clinton, however, did not modulate their language, with Republican Ronald Reagan consistently (in a variety of addresses) using lexemes that prioritized a STRICT FATHER worldview, while Democrat Bill Clinton consistently used lexemes that emphasized a NURTURANT PARENT worldview (Ahrens 2011). In addition, Ahrens and Lee (2009) found that US senators, regardless of gender or political party, consistently used more lexemes related to a NURTURANT PARENT ideology than a STRICT FATHER one. Given that these senators were speaking only to other senators on the senate floor in the corpus that Ahrens and Lee used, the senators may not have found it necessary or effective to modulate their language to persuade their colleagues as found in the presidential addresses.

In what follows, we utilized the methodology used by both Ahrens (2011) and Ahrens and Lee (2009) as a starting point for the analyses of the Chinese data in our study, since this approach allowed us to compare our findings with previous work on these two conceptual models in English.[3] We proposed that evidence for a STRICT FATHER model would be found in the PRC political discourse to authorities in Taiwan, but that evidence for a NURTURANT PARENT model would be found when PRC officials addressed Taiwanese people. In particular, we hypothesized that (1) PRC speeches addressing Taiwan authorities would contain more Strict Father lexemes than Nurturant Parent lexemes and a similar tendency would be observed in speeches directed toward people in Mainland China, as the PRC has aimed to ensure that their citizens, especially in regions such as Tibet, do not consider independence or autonomous rule; (2) the proportion of Nurturant Parent lexemes compared with Strict Father lexemes would be greater in speeches addressing Taiwanese people; and (3) there would be the fewest Strict Father lexemes in speeches addressing Taiwanese people, while there would be the fewest Nurturant Parent lexemes in speeches addressing Taiwan authorities.

[3]Following the line of literature investigating the ideological contrast between the STRICT FATHER and NURTURANT PARENT models, our study was limited to the analysis of these two conceptual models to ease the comparison with results from similar studies. An alternative way to explore the underlying ideology in the political speeches would be to perform a more open search of all possible metaphors used in the speeches and comprehensively examine the messages intended to be conveyed.

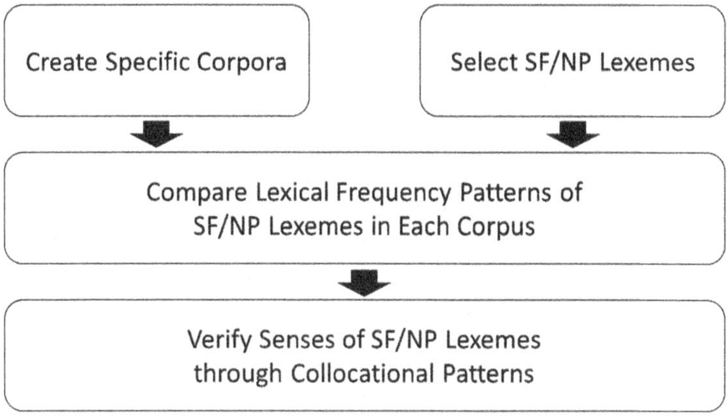

Fig. 22.1 Overview of the methodological procedure in our study

22.2 Methodology

Figure 22.1 provides an overview of the methodological procedure in our study. In the first stage, corpora were built and lexemes were selected; in the second stage, lexical frequency patterns were compared; and in the final stage, the senses of the lexemes were verified by examining collocational patterns.

These steps were in line with the methodology used in Ahrens (2011), who examined the lexical frequency patterns in US presidential speeches by selecting lexemes related to Lakoff's STRICT FATHER and NURTURANT PARENT models. As the top 2 metaphors listed in the two models were *morality is strength/authority* (STRICT FATHER) and *morality is nurturance/empathy* (NURTURANT PARENT), respectively, Ahrens (2011) searched for four related keywords—strength, authority, nurturance, and empathy—as well as their hypernyms, in WordNet 3.0. By selecting all the content words in the WordNet definitions, lexemes related to the STRICT FATHER/NURTURANT PARENT models were obtained and the frequencies of different groups of lexemes were compared. Ahrens (2011) then verified the results by examining the collocational patterns related to these lexemes. Our study essentially adopted this methodological procedure, although certain modifications were needed to handle the Chinese data, as explained below.

22.2.1 *Corpora Creation*

Among other organizations established by the PRC to communicate with Taiwan authorities, the TAOSC generally represents the official stance of the PRC on matters pertaining to Taiwan (Kan 2014). To create corpora for our study, therefore, we downloaded all full-text speech transcriptions from the website of the TAOSC (http://www.gwytb.gov.cn/) between 2003 and 2008.[4] The speeches were then manually categorized into three sub-corpora based on the second author's judgment. These three sub-corpora included (1) speeches addressing Taiwan authorities (TA) (the TA sub-corpus is listed in Table 22.1, e.g., a public statement expressing the PRC's displeasure toward Taiwan authorities for holding a referendum in Taiwan); (2) speeches addressing Mainland Chinese (MC) people (the MC sub-corpus is listed in Table 22.2, e.g., a televised speech delivered at a meeting of the National Committee of the Chinese People's Political Consultative Conference, CPPCC, to launch an appeal to the people for further efforts toward the reunification of China); and (3) speeches addressing Taiwanese (TW) people (the TW sub-corpus is listed in Table 22.3, e.g., an opening speech addressing Taiwanese scholars during an academic conference).

These files were subsequently imported into Microsoft Notepad to remove hidden formatting settings after they were copied from the webpages. They were then divided among three meta files according to their grouping, with headings, introductory paragraphs (stating the content or the time and place of the speeches), and editor's indications (e.g., 完 *wan2* "finished") removed, following Ahrens' (2011) methodology. We then took a further step by importing these files into the Chinese Word Segmentation System with Unknown Word Identification (http://ckipsvr.iis.sinica.edu.tw/) for later corpus analysis. This word segmentation system automatically processes continuous Chinese texts, inserts a space between recognized Chinese word units, and labels the words with their parts of speech. This facilitated the tally of word token frequencies and analysis of collocational patterns. The preprocessed data were then manually examined again to rectify word segmentation errors, for example, due to unknown words or neologisms that could not be handled by the automatic word recognition algorithm. In our study, we used R 3.1.0 as our corpus tool to analyze the data. A summary of the three sub-corpora is provided in Table 22.4.

22.2.2 Lexeme Choice

The first task was to identify STRICT FATHER/NURTURANT PARENT-related lexemes in Chinese based on WordNet and related lexical resources. We searched for the keywords used in Ahrens (2011), namely, strength and authority (Strict Father lexemes) and nurturance and empathy (Nurturant Parent lexemes), in Sinica BOW (the Academia Sinica Bilingual Ontological WordNet; http://bow.sinica.edu.tw/), an

[4]Note that this period represented a relatively cool period in cross-strait relations. Furthermore, this website was accessed during February and March in 2008, right before Chen Shui-bian was about to finish his term in office. After that, with the warming of cross-strait relations when Ma Ying-jeou began his term in office, the TAOSC website as well as its content was redesigned. We considered the data accessed in February and March 2008 a reflection of the views of the TAOSC during the period of Chen Shui-bian's term in office.

Table 22.1 List of speeches in the TA sub-corpus (PRC speeches addressing Taiwan authorities)

No.	Title	Speaker(s)	Post Date	Word Count
TA1	The Taiwan Affairs Office of the State Council was authorized to make a statement regarding the current cross-strait relationship 中臺辦、國臺辦受權就當前兩岸關係發表聲明	Taiwan Affairs Office of the State Council	17 May 2004	567
TA2	The spokesperson of the Taiwan Affairs Office of the State Council delivered a speech regarding the announcement of the organization for electoral affairs in Taiwan 國務院臺辦發言人就台灣選務機構發佈公告發表談話	The spokesperson of the Taiwan Affairs Office of the State Council (unidentified, possibly Wei-I Lee 李維 or Mingqing Zhang 張銘清)	26 March 2004	145
TA3	The Taiwan Affairs Office of the State Council of PRC made a statement regarding the referendum held by Taiwan authorities 中共中央臺辦、國務院臺辦就台灣當局舉辦公民投票發表聲明	Taiwan Affairs Office of the State Council	20 March 2004	41
TA4	The Taiwan Affairs Office of the State Council solemnly advised Taiwan authorities to stop divisive activities through "legislation for referendum" 國臺辦正告臺當局停止借"公投立法"搞分裂	Principal of the Taiwan Affairs Office of the State Council 國務院台灣事務辦公室負責人 (unidentified, possibly Yulin Chen 陳雲林)	17 November 2003	349
TA5	The spokesperson of the Taiwan Affairs Office of the State Council spoke about the march for "constitutional referendum" in Taiwan: "Taiwan Independence" is a disaster for Taiwan 國臺辦發言人談臺"公投制憲"遊行:"台獨"是台灣之災	The spokesperson of the Taiwan Affairs Office of the State Council (unidentified, possibly Wei-I Lee 李維 or Mingqing Zhang 張銘清)	27 October 2003	106
TA6	The Taiwan Affairs Office of the State Council made an authorized announcement regarding the announcement of the Chen Shui-bian authorities about holding the "Taiwanese United Nations membership referendums" 中	Taiwan Affairs Office of the State Council	2 February 2008	216

(continued)

Table 22.1 (continued)

No.	Title	Speaker(s)	Post Date	Word Count
	臺辦、國臺辦就陳水扁當局公告舉辦"入聯公投"發表受權聲明			
TA7	The principal of the Taiwan Affairs Office of the State Council delivered a speech regarding the approval of the "Resolution on a Normal Country" of DPP 中共中央台灣工作辦公室負責人就民進黨通過所謂"正常國家決議文"發表談話	Principal of the Taiwan Affairs Office of the State Council 中共中央臺灣工作辦公室負責人 (unidentified, possibly Yunlin Chen 陳雲林)	1 October 2007	231
TA8	The principal of the Taiwan Affairs Office of the State Council delivered a speech regarding the rejection of the application under the name Taiwan for membership in the UN through Chen Shui-bian to the Secretary-General of the UN 中臺辦、國臺辦負責人就陳水扁向聯合國秘書長提交所謂以台灣名義加入聯合國申請書遭退回發表談話	Principal of the Taiwan Affairs Office of the State Council 中台辦、國台辦負責人 (unidentified, possibly Yunlin Chen 陳雲林)	24 July 2007	583
TA9	The principal of the Taiwan Affairs Office of the State Council delivered a speech regarding Chen Shui-bian's divisive proposal for "Taiwan Independence" 中共中央臺辦、國務院臺辦負責人就陳水扁拋出"台獨"分裂主張發表談話	Principal of the Taiwan Affairs Office of the State Council 中共中央台灣工作辦公室、國務院台灣事務辦公室負責人 (unidentified, possibly Yunlin Chen 陳雲林)	5 March 2007	235
TA10	The Taiwan Affairs Office of the State Council was authorized to make a statement regarding the decision of Chen Shui-bian to terminate "National Unification Council" and "Guidelines for National Unification" 中臺辦國臺辦受權就陳水扁決定終止"國統會"和"國統綱領"發表聲明	Taiwan Affairs Office of the State Council	28 February 2006	441
TA11	The Taiwan Affairs Office of the State Council delivered a speech regarding Chen Shui-	Taiwan Affairs Office of the State Council	26 February 2006	492

(continued)

Table 22.1 (continued)

No.	Title	Speaker(s)	Post Date	Word Count
	bian's promotion of "abolition of unification" 中臺辦、國臺辦就陳水扁推動"廢統"發表談話			
TA12	Junjiu Zhang delivered a speech regarding Taiwan Affairs Office of the State Council's "May-17 Authorized Statement" 張俊九就中臺辦、國臺辦 "5·17受權聲明" 發表談話	Junjiu Zhang, the Vice Chairperson of All-China Federation of Trade Unions 中華全國總工會副主席張俊九	20 May 2004	376
TA13	Luli He delivered a speech regarding Taiwan Affairs Office of the State Council's "May-17 Authorized Statement" 何魯麗就中臺辦、國臺辦 "5·17受權聲明" 發表談話	Luli He 何魯麗	20 May 2004	572
TA14	Wenyi Lin delivered a speech regarding Taiwan Affairs Office of the State Council's "May-17 Authorized Statement" 林文漪就中臺辦、國臺辦 5·17 受權聲明發表談話	Wenyi Lin, Executive Vice Chairperson of the Central Committee of the Taiwan Democratic Self-Government League 臺灣民主自治同盟中央委員會常務副主席林文漪	19 May 2004	528
TA15	Qingyi Huang, Vice Chairperson of All-China Women's Federation, delivered a speech regarding Taiwan Affairs Office of the State Council's "May-17 Authorized Statement" 全國婦聯副主席黃晴宜就中臺辦、國臺辦 "5·17受權聲明" 發表談話	Qingyi Huang, Vice Chairperson of All-China Women's Federation 全國婦聯副主席黃晴宜	21 May 2004	459
TA16	Yong Zhao, Chairperson of All-China Youth Federation, delivered a speech regarding Taiwan Affairs Office of the State Council's "May-17 Authorized Statement" 全國青聯主席趙勇就中臺辦、國臺辦 "5·17受權聲明" 發表談話	Yong Zhao, Chairperson of All-China Youth Federation 中華全國青年聯合會主席趙勇	21 May 2004	561
TA17	Zhaoshu Lin, Chairperson of All-China Federation of Returned Overseas Chinese, delivered a speech regarding	Zhaoshu Lin, Chairperson of All-China Federation of Returned Overseas Chinese 中國僑聯主席林兆樞	21 May 2004	387

(continued)

Table 22.1 (continued)

No.	Title	Speaker(s)	Post Date	Word Count
	TAOSC's "May-17 Authorized Statement" 僑聯主席林兆樞就中臺辦、國臺辦聲明發表談話			
Total				6289

Table 22.2 List of speeches in the MC sub-corpus (PRC speeches addressing Mainland China people)

No.	Title	Speaker	Post Date	Word Count
MC1	Jiaxuan Tang: Let the compatriots on both sides of the Taiwan Strait be united to work diligently together for the reunification of the motherland 唐家璇:兩岸同胞團結起來,共同為祖國統一而努力奮鬥	Jiaxuan Tang, State Councilor 國務委員唐家璇	20 January 2004	1432
MC2	The speech of Qinglin Jia on the Commemoration of the 60th Anniversary of Taiwan's Recovery 賈慶林在紀念台灣光復 60週年大會上的講話	Qinglin Jia, a member of the Politburo Standing Committee and the Chairperson of the National Committee of the People's Political Consultative Conference 中共中央政治局常委、全國政協主席賈慶林	26 October 2005	2482
MC3	Guozhen Wu, the Vice Chairperson of the Central Committee of the Taiwan Democratic Self-Autonomy League: The mainland has always been frank and kind in developing the cross-strait relationship 臺盟中央副主席吳國禎:大陸一貫坦誠善意務實地發展兩岸關係	Guozhen Wu, the Vice Chairperson of the Central Committee of the Taiwan Democratic Self-Autonomy League 臺盟中央副主席吳國禎	11 March 2005	1039
Total				4953

online resource that provides translated Chinese equivalents of English WordNet (version 1.6/1.7.1). Whereas Ahrens (2011) selected all the content words from the WordNet definitions, we were unable to do so because Sinica BOW does not provide a Chinese translation of the WordNet sense definitions (e.g., the full Chinese translation of the definition of sense 2 of nurturance, i.e., "physical and emotional care and nourishment"); instead, it only provides Chinese equivalents of the lexemes in individual words (i.e., Chinese words carrying the same sense, e.g., 撫育 *fu3 yang3* "nurturance," which also has the sense "physical and emotional care and nourishment"). Hence, we selected the senses related to the STRICT FATHER/NURTURANT

Table 22.3 List of speeches in the TW sub-corpus (PRC speeches addressing Taiwan people)

No.	Title	Speaker	Post Date	Word Count
TW1	Bingcai Li, Executive Deputy Director of Taiwan Affairs Office of the State Council, delivered a speech at the "Seminar on the Listing of Taiwan-funded Enterprises on the Market of the Mainland" 國臺辦常務副主任李炳才在"台資企業在祖國大陸上市研討會"上致辭	Bingcai Li, Executive Deputy Director of Taiwan Affairs Office of the State Council 國臺辦常務副主任李炳才	26 February 2004	710
TW2	Zaixi Wang, Deputy Director of Taiwan Affairs Office of the State Council, delivered a speech at the closing ceremony of the Cross-Strait Relationship Forum 國臺辦副主任王在希在兩岸關係論壇閉幕式上發表講話	Wang Zaixi, the Deputy Director of Taiwan Affairs Office of the State Council 國臺辦副主任王在希	18 July 2003	1692
TW3	Shubei Tang: Exchange will eventually overcome confrontation, and cooperation will definitely resolve differences 唐樹備:交流終將戰勝對抗, 合作一定會化解分歧	Shubei Tang 唐樹備	18 July 2003	1467
TW4	Qinglin Jia proposed four views on promoting cross-strait exchanges 賈慶林就促進兩岸交流提出四點看法	Qinglin Jia 賈慶林	28 April 2007	2271
TW5	Qinglin Jia's speech at the opening ceremony of the first Cross-Strait Folk Elite Forum 賈慶林在第一屆兩岸民間菁英論壇開幕式上的演講	Qinglin Jia 賈慶林	15 September 2005	2568
TW6	Bingcai Li, Executive Deputy Director of Taiwan Affairs Office of the State Council, gave a speech at the 7th "Beijing-Taiwan Science and Technology Forum" 國臺辦常務副主任李炳才在第七屆"京臺科技論壇"上致辭	Li Bingcai, the Executive Deputy Director of Taiwan Affairs Office of the State Council 國臺辦常務副主任李炳才	10 September 2004	618
TW7	The speech of Zaixi Wang at the opening ceremony of the 2004 Cross-Strait Relationship Forum 王在希在 2004	Zaixi Wang 王在希	29 July 2004	1366

(continued)

Table 22.3 (continued)

No.	Title	Speaker	Post Date	Word Count
	兩岸關係論壇開幕式上的講話.			
TW8	Yunlin Chen was authorized to declare 15 policies and measures to benefit Taiwan compatriots 陳雲林受權宣佈 15項惠及台灣同胞的政策措施	Yunlin Chen 陳雲林	17 April 2006	1440
TW9	Deputy Director Mingwei Zhou gave a speech at the press conference for Taiwanese journalists covering "Lianghui" 周明偉副主任在採訪"兩會"台灣記者招待會上致辭	Mingwei Zhou, Deputy Director of Taiwan Affairs Office of the State Council 國臺辦副主任周明偉	13 March 2003	540
TW10	Yunlin Chen seeing off the visiting mission of the People First Party: An instant may create history 陳雲林為親民黨訪問團送行:瞬間可以創造歷史	Yunlin Chen 陳雲林	13 May 2005	295
TW11	The welcome address of Jintao Hu when he met Lien Chan in the Great Hall of the People 胡錦濤在人民大會堂會見連戰歡迎辭	Jintao Hu 胡錦濤	29 April 2005	643
Total				13,610

Table 22.4 Word count and number of speeches in the TA sub-corpus, the MC sub-corpus, and the TW sub-corpus

TAOSC sub-corpora	Number of speeches	Word count	Average number of words per speech
TA sub-corpus	17	6289	370
MC sub-corpus	3	4953	1651
TW sub-corpus	11	13,610	1237
Total	31	24,852	802

PARENT models that were selected also in Ahrens (2011) and directly used the corresponding Chinese translated equivalents of the lexemes as one source of the Strict Father/Nurturant Parent lexemes. The results are shown in the first three columns in Table 22.5. For example, for the lexeme nurturance, we selected its

Table 22.5 Selected senses, hypernyms, and translated equivalents

Lexeme	WordNet definition	Translation/ synset	Hypernyms and selected senses	Hypernyms' translations
Strength	Sense 3 (N): physical energy or intensity	氣力	**Intensity**	強烈
		qi4 li4	Sense 3 (N): high level or degree; the property of being intense	*qiang2 lie4*
		力量	**Intensiveness**	強力
		li4 liang4	Sense 1 (N): same as above	*qiang2 li4*
		力 *li4*		強度
				qiang2 du4
Authority	Sense 4 (N): the power to exercise authoritative or dominating control or influence over	權力	**Control**	控制
		quan2 li4	Sense 13 (N): power to direct or determine—"- under control"	*kong 4 zhi4*
Nurturance	Sense 2 (N): physical and emotional care and nourishment (1.7.1)	撫育	**Attention**	照料
		fu3 yu4	Sense 1 (N): the work of caring for or attending to someone or something	*zhao4 liao4* (from "attention" sense 1)
		養育	**Tending**	幫忙
		yang3 yu4	Sense 1 (N): same as attention	*bang1 mang2*
		培養	**Care**	幫助
		pei2 yang3	Sense 2 (N): same as attention	*bang1 zhu4* (from "aid" sense 3)
			Aid	
			Sense 2 (N): same as attention	
			Sense 3 (N): the activity of contributing to the fulfillment of a need or furtherance of an effort or purpose	
Empathy	Sense 1 (N): understanding and entering into another's feelings	憐憫	**Sympathy**	有同感
		lian2 min3	Sense 2 (N): sharing the feelings of others (especially feelings of sorrow or anguish)	*you3 tong2 gan3*
		同情	**Fellow feeling**	共鳴
		tong2 qing2	Sense 1 (N): same as sympathy	*gong4 ming2*

WordNet sense 2, "physical and emotional care and nourishment," thus obtaining three corresponding Chinese translated equivalents of the lexeme nurturance. These three Chinese translated equivalents—撫育 *fu3 yu4* "nurturance," 養育 *yang3 yu4* "nurturance," and 培養 *pei2 yang3* "development/nurturance"—all carried the sense "physical and emotional care and nourishment."

In the second step, we further investigated the four key lexemes' corresponding hypernyms and their Chinese translated equivalents (see the last two columns in Table 22.5). In this step, we were unable to select content words from the hypernyms' definitions as Ahrens (2011) did, as no full translations of the English WordNet definitions were provided in Sinica BOW. Moreover, for all the English hypernyms of a sense, sometimes only one single Chinese translated equivalent was found in Sinica BOW, which hindered us from obtaining adequate lexemes for later analysis. Therefore, we took a slightly different approach. Instead of simply looking at the hypernyms' translated equivalents, when only one Chinese translated equivalent was provided for the multiple hypernyms of a particular sense, we further selected one of the topmost related nominal senses in the hypernyms in order to obtain more related Chinese translated equivalents.[5] For example, for WordNet sense 2 of nurturance, four hypernyms were provided in Sinica BOW—attention, tending, care, and aid—but only one Chinese translated equivalent was provided for these four hypernyms: 照料 *zhao4 liao4* "tending." In this case, we further selected sense 3 of aid, "the activity of contributing to the fulfillment of a need or furtherance of an effort or purpose," which we considered the closest nominal sense to sense 2 above. By looking up the Chinese translated equivalent of aid in sense 3, we obtained two additional Chinese translated equivalents, namely, 幫忙 *bang1 mang2* "help" and 幫助 *bang1 zhu4* "help."

The third step involved obtaining further synonyms for the Chinese translated equivalents found earlier by employing the Thesaurus function in Chinese Word Sketch. This system incorporates Sketch Engine, a corpus query system developed by Kilgarriff et al. (2004), and the Chinese Gigaword corpus. Here, we selected the top 3 synonyms nearest to our query lexemes in the thesaurus (see Fig. 22.2).[6]

As shown in Fig. 22.2, the top 3 nearest synonyms for 撫育 *fu3 yang3* "nurturance" are 養育 *yang3 yu4* "nurturance," 撫養 *fu3 yang3* "nurturance," and 哺育 *fu3 yu4* "feeding/nurturance."

The final step involved screening out inappropriate candidates[7] and determining the final list of lexemes for analysis. We controlled for word length by using only disyllabic words, and we controlled for the number of words in the Strict Father

[5]In our study, only the hypernyms of nurturance needed such supplementation.

[6]As will be noted later, in our study, we controlled for word length by using only disyllabic words, the dominant type of words in Chinese, as queries. This criterion was established due to practical reasons: monosyllabic words (力 *li4* in this case) tend to be highly ambiguous in Chinese, and three-character sequences may not always be regarded as "words" (有同感 *you3 tong2 gan3* is a translated equivalent of "sympathy" and "fellow feeling" but is not recognized as a word in Chinese Word Sketch).

[7]These involved words repeatedly appearing, monosyllabic words or words with more than three syllables (see footnote 6), and clearly irrelevant words (i.e., 同樣 *tong2 yang4* "the same," 相同 *xiang1 tong2* "the same," and 特別 *te4 bie2* "special").

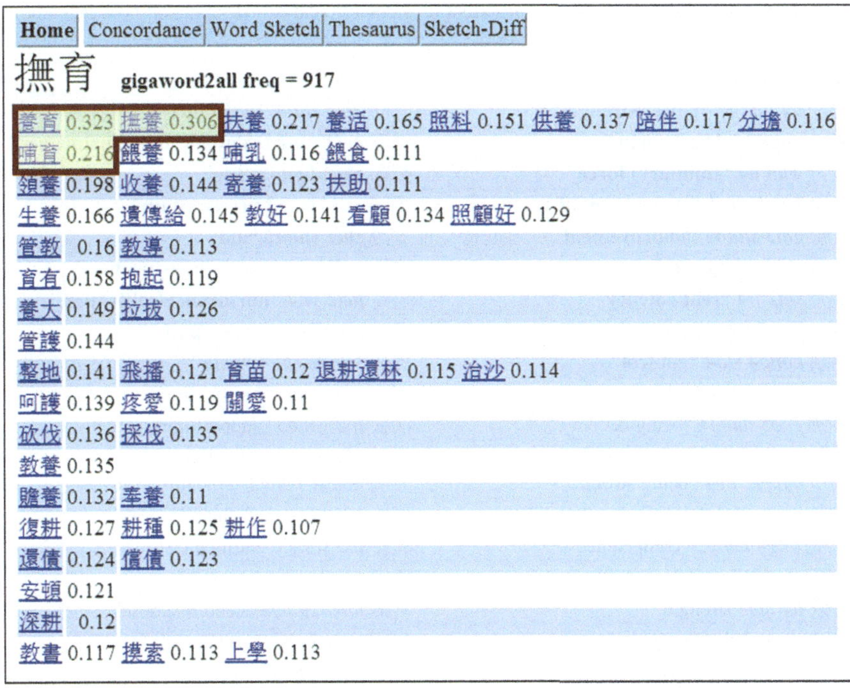

Fig. 22.2 The interface of results from the Thesaurus tool in Chinese Word Sketch

(STRICT FATHER)/Nurturant Parent (NURTURANT PARENT) lists (23 lexemes in each list). The results are shown in Table 22.6.

We used R 3.1.0 to search for all the Strict Father/Nurturant Parent lexemes listed in Table 22.6 in each sub-corpus. Nine lexemes from the Strict Father group occurred in these speeches, as did nine lexemes from the Nurturant Parent group. These lexemes are indicated in bold and listed above the dotted line in Table 22.6.

22.3 Results and Data Analyses

22.3.1 Lexical Frequency Patterns

Frequencies for each of the 18 lexemes found were determined. We next calculated the normalized ratios for the lexemes by representing language use in the PRC, multiplying their frequency in each corpus by 10,000. We compared the frequencies of Strict Father/Nurturant Parent lexemes in the three sub-corpora using an adjusted z-score test, where the proportion of the Strict Father/Nurturant Parent lexeme usage in a general reference corpus was taken into account (Scott and Seber 1983). This was necessary to avoid any bias in interpreting the statistical results, as the Strict

Table 22.6 Strict Father and Nurturant Parent lexemes for analyses (lexemes in bold face above the dotted line occurred in the sub-corpora)

Strict Father lexemes	Nurturant Parent lexemes
力量 ***li4 liang4*** **"power/strength"***	協助 ***xie2 zhu4*** **"assistance"**
權力 ***quan2 li4*** **"authority"**	培養 ***pei2 yang3*** **"development/nurturance"**
武力 ***wu3 li4*** **"(military) force"**	照顧 ***zhao4 gu4*** **"care"**
立場 ***li4 chang3*** **"stance/ground"**	認同 ***ren4 tong2*** **"recognition"**
改善 ***gai3 shan4*** **"improvement"**	支援 ***zhi1 yuan2*** **"aid"**
勢力 ***shi4 li4*** **"power"**	培訓 ***pei2 xun4*** **"training/education"**
實力 ***shi2 li4*** **"real potency"**	培育 ***pei2 yu4*** **"nurturance/cultivation"**
精力 ***jing1 li4*** **"energy"**	同情 ***tong2 qing2*** **"sympathy"**
控制 ***kong4 zhi4*** **"control"**	幫助 ***bang1 zhu4*** **"help"**
氣力 *qi4 li4* "strength"	撫育 *fu3 yang3* "nurturance"
果斷 *guo3 duan4* "being decisive"	扶養 *fu2 yang3* "support/nurturance"
掌握 *zhang3 kong4* "hold/control"	照料 *zhao4 liao4* "tending"
強烈 *qiang2 lie4* "being strong"	共鳴 *gong4 ming2* "empathy"
工夫 *gong1 fu1* "effort"	幫忙 *bang1 mang2* "help"
性能 *xing4 neng2* "competence"	撫養 *fu3 yang3* "nurturance"
能量 *neng2 liang4* "energy"	憐憫 *lian2 min3* "mercy"
力氣 *li4 qi4* "strength"	反響 *fan3 xiang3* "echo/response"
強度 *qiang2 du4* "intensity"	養育 *yang3 yu4* "nurturance"
權利 *quan2 li4* "right"	養活 *yang3 huo2* "support"
掌控 *zhang3 wo4* "manipulation/control"	陪伴 *pei2 ban4* "accompany"
強力 *qiang2 li4* "force"	迴響 *hui2 xiang3* "echo"
戰力 *zhan4 li4* "military competence"	哺育 *fu3 yu4* "feeding/nurturance"
職權 *zhi2 quan2* "authority (in business)"	喝采 *he4 cai3* "acclamation"

Translations provided do not follow Sinica BOW translations

Father lexemes may inherently be used more frequently than the Nurturant Parent lexemes, or vice versa, even when compared in the general corpus. Our study used the Xinhua News Agency of Beijing corpus as the general reference corpus. This corpus is embedded in the Chinese Gigaword corpus in the Chinese Word Sketch system (Kilgarriff et al. 2004) and contains 304.4 million words from past records of the Xinhua News Agency, the official newswire of the PRC. Based on the summed frequencies of the Strict Father/Nurturant Parent lexemes in the corpus (SF, 330,127 vs. NP, 241,638), we determined the proportion of Strict Father/Nurturant Parent lexeme usage in general language use to be 1 to 0.73.

Table 22.7 provides the normalized ratios of the Strict Father/Nurturant Parent lexemes in the three sub-corpora and the results of the adjusted *z*-score tests. As we hypothesized, Strict Father lexemes were used significantly more often in PRC speeches addressing Taiwan authorities, indicating strong, hardline language in those speeches. In addition, the difference between the use of Strict Father and Nurturant Parent lexemes in PRC speeches addressing Chinese people was also significant.

Table 22.7 Comparisons of Strict Father/Nurturant Parent lexemes in the TA sub-corpus, the MC sub-corpus, and the TW sub-corpus; normalized ratio (NR): $\alpha = 0.05$

TAOSC		Strict Father lexemes		Nurturant Parent lexemes			
sub-corpora	Word count	Raw frequency	NR	Raw frequency	NR	z	p
TA sub-corpus	6289	37	58.83	6	9.54	4.15	1.631E-05***
MC sub-corpus	4953	27	54.51	10	20.19	1.97	0.02*
TW sub-corpus	13,610	31	22.78	24	17.63	−0.21	0.42

***$p < 0.001$, *$p < 0.05$

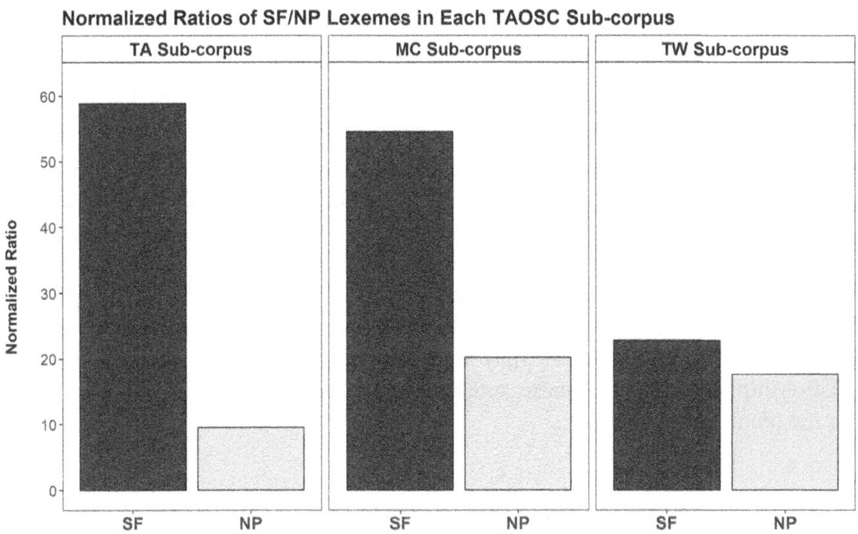

Fig. 22.3 Normalized ratios of Strict Father (SF)/Nurturant Parent (NP) lexemes in the TA sub-corpus, the MC sub-corpus, and the TW sub-corpus

Moreover, as we hypothesized, when comparing the normalized ratios, we found that the proportion of Nurturant Parent lexemes compared with the Strict Father lexemes within each sub-corpus varied: the speeches addressing Taiwan authorities represented the largest difference between the ratio of NP and SF lexemes, with a smaller difference for speeches addressing a Mainland Chinese audience and a much smaller difference for speeches addressing a primarily Taiwanese audience (see Fig. 22.3).

The results indicated that the language used in the speeches varied depending on the intended audience. When PRC officials addressed Taiwan authorities, the language was the most strident, and when PRC officials addressed Chinese people, the language also appeared to be authoritative, with comparatively more Strict Father than Nurturant Parent lexemes being used. However, in speeches addressing Taiwanese people, the lexical choices for the Strict Father and Nurturant Parent lexemes were more balanced. This was accompanied by the fact that among all the speeches, we found the fewest Strict Father lexemes (in terms of normalized ratios) used in speeches addressing Taiwanese people, while Strict Father lexemes in speeches addressing Taiwan authorities and Chinese people had roughly similar normalized ratios. Moreover, we found the fewest Nurturant Parent lexemes (in terms of normalized ratios) in speeches addressing Taiwan authorities, while Nurturant Parent lexemes in speeches addressing Chinese people and Taiwanese people had roughly similar normalized ratios. These facts taken together indicate that the PRC has emphasized a hardline with Taiwan authorities and a relatively hardline with its citizens in Mainland Chinese but that they want to appear less strident to the people of Taiwan.

The results suggest the possibility that, due to the PRC's goals for the reunification of China, PRC officials have generally adopted a STRICT FATHER model, where authority and rule of law are the prevailing values, when speaking to Taiwan authorities and Mainland Chinese people. In fact, this type of strident language might also be used to indicate to the Chinese people the PRC's determination concerning this issue, which may, in turn, serve to unify their opposition toward the notion of Taiwan independence. The results also indicate that PRC officials, whether consciously or unconsciously, adjusted their language when they were addressing different audiences; this can be seen most clearly in the speeches addressing Taiwanese people, as Strict Father lexemes were used comparatively less frequently. The PRC officials may be doing this to establish a more amicable relationship with the Taiwanese audience, which might also facilitate their goals for the reunification of China.

22.3.2 Collocational Patterns

As lexical frequency patterns are simply numerical data, the lexemes we selected, being polysemous, may not have been related to the STRICT FATHER/NURTURANT PARENT models in context. Therefore, it was necessary to verify the lexical frequency patterns we obtained to ensure that the results supported our hypotheses. We followed Ahrens' (2011) method by examining the collocational patterns of the Strict Father/Nurturant Parent lexemes to ascertain lexical meanings in context.[8] In

[8] Admittedly, in comparison to a full discourse analysis, collocational patterns are limited in providing complete linguistic evidence regarding the derivation of specific metaphorical

Table 22.8 Collocates one to the left of the keyword 勢力 *shi4 li4* "power" and *t*-scores

TA sub-corpus			MC sub-corpus			TW sub-corpus		
Freq.	T	Collocate	Freq.	T	Collocate	Freq.	T	Collocate
10	3.11	分裂 *fen1 lie4* "division"	12	3.44	分裂 *fen1 lie4* "division"	9	2.99	分裂 *fen1 lie4* "division"
2	1.27	台獨 *tai2 du2* "Taiwan Independence"	1	1.00	右翼 *you4 yi4* "right-winged"	3	1.71	台獨 *tai2 du2* "Taiwan Independence"
			1	1.00	外國 *wai4 guo2* "foreign"			
			1	0.99	軍國主義 *jun1 guo2 zhu3 yi4* "militarism"			
			1	0.89	台獨 *tai2 du2* "Taiwan Independence"			

doing so, we searched for collocates that were immediately to the left of the lexemes, ranking them according to *t*-score values, and examined up to five top collocates using R 3.1.0. Due to limited space, we exemplified the results by presenting only collocates one to the left (1L) of the most frequent Strict Father lexeme in our corpora (i.e., 勢力 *shi4 li4* "power"), as shown in Table 22.8.

As can be seen in Table 22.8, the collocates of 勢力 *shi4 li4* "power" suggest that these lexemes generally mean "power," as in 分裂勢力 *fen1 lie4 shi4 li4* "divisive power" or 台獨勢力 *tai2 du2 shi4 li4* "power of Taiwan Independence," in addition to the fact that they may be related to the issue of reunification/independence.

Although we could not present all the collocate data, we generally found similar results for other Strict Father/Nurturant Parent lexemes. That is, the collocational patterns of these Strict Father/Nurturant Parent lexemes and their collocates one to the left of the keyword suggest that their meanings are generally related to either the STRICT FATHER or NURTURANT PARENT models, as we hypothesized.[9] We therefore argue

interpretations. However, in accordance with Ahrens' (2011) original intention in developing this set of methods, collocational patterns may be particularly helpful when the amount of data massively grows and hinders a rapid recognition of the ideological bias or the conceptual models underlying the speeches based on manual discourse analyses. As our study aimed to test the replicability of the original methods in Ahrens (2011) in different political contexts, we chose to limit the current scope and leave a full discourse analysis for future studies.

[9] Among all of the 135 collocates one to the left of the Strict Father/Nurturant Parent lexemes in our study, only one case, 騙取 *pian4 qu3* "deceive," to the left of 同情 *tong2 qing2* "sympathy,"

that the collocational patterns supported the results of the lexical frequency patterns, which indicated the preference for using a strong STRICT FATHER model when PRC officials directed their speech to Taiwan authorities and to Mainland Chinese people, but a more nuanced approach was taken when speaking directly to the people of Taiwan.

22.4 Conclusion

Our study opened with two proposals: first, to examine whether there was cross-linguistic evidence for the STRICT FATHER/NURTURANT PARENT models in Chinese and, second, to examine whether there was evidence of a political entity (and not just a political speaker) modulating lexical choices in speeches to different audiences. We chose to investigate the speeches from the Taiwan Affairs Office of the State Council of the People's Republic of China, as these speeches were promulgated by the office and not by any single person. In addition, we chose the period between 2003 and 2008, which was a time when cross-strait relations were relatively cool. Following Ahrens and Lee (2009) and Ahrens (2011), we extracted lexical frequency patterns from three sub-corpora and indeed found evidence that there was lexical patterning used related to these two conceptual models of family. We also found that the sub-corpora differed in the ratio of Strict Father lexemes compared with Nurturant Parent lexemes after controlling for the frequency of these lexemes in a general corpus. In addition, the sub-corpus containing speeches to the people of Taiwan used comparatively fewer Strict Father lexemes compared with the TAOSC speeches to Taiwan authorities and to the people of Mainland China.

However, because our study focused on lexical frequency patterns, it did not shed light on whether these two models would be better thought of as two models within one conceptual metaphor (i.e., NATION IS A FAMILY) or whether it would be more useful to follow Musolff (2006, 2016) and view the source domain instead as a scenario, which includes narrative and evaluative perspectives. To evaluate this proposal, it would be necessary to examine specific examples of metaphors in the speeches and not just the lexical frequency patterns. But viewing these models as scenarios has an advantage in that it would allow for the postulation of "a particular set of presuppositions that are chosen for specific argumentative purposes" (Musolff 2016: 31). Given that the data shown in this chapter demonstrates that the TAOSC appears to be modulating its political language when speaking to Taiwanese people, Musolff's (2016) proposal acknowledges the "argumentative" purposes of this scenario selection, as these lexical frequency patterns suggest an implicit or explicit understanding of the needs and views of the audience being spoken to. It would also be useful in future work to examine the TAOSC statements during a period of time

indicated that the Nurturant Parent lexeme 同情 *tong2 qing2* "sympathy" was not used in a typical Nurturant Parent context.

when the cross-strait relationship was relatively warmer to see whether different patterns of lexical use related to the STRICT FATHER/NURTURANT PARENT models would be found.

In sum, the results of the lexical frequency patterns found in our study not only reinforce the viability and replicability of this methodology in its extension to other political contexts but also provide empirical linguistic evidence of how political aims may influence lexical patterns depending on the audience to whom the speech is directed.

Acknowledgments We appreciate comments from the anonymous reviewers as well as participants of the CKIP 30th Anniversary Workshop on Chinese Lexicon, including Professor Chu-Ren Huang. We also appreciate Professor Janice Fon, Professor Siaw-Fong Chung, Yu-Xian Chen, Yong-Quan Chen, and Long-Hao Li for their comments on the statistics, as well as Jia-Fei Hong, Katarzyna Horszowska, Sheng-hsiu Chiu, Ren-Feng Duann, Shirley Liang, and Ying-Yu Lin for their comments on the study. This research was partially funded by General Research Fund Project no. 1210014 from the Hong Kong University Grants Council to the first author. Any and all errors are our own.

References

Ahrens, Kathleen. 2011. Examining conceptual metaphor models through lexical frequency patterns: A case study of US presidential speeches. In *Windows to the mind: Metaphor, metonymy and conceptual blending* (Vol. 48), ed. Sandra Handl and Hans-Jörg Schmid, 167–184. Berlin: De Gruyter Mouton.

Ahrens, Kathleen, and Sophia Yat Mei Lee. 2009. Gender versus politics: When conceptual models collide in the US Senate. In *Politics, gender, and conceptual metaphors*, ed. Kathleen Ahrens, 62–82. London: Palgrave Macmillan.

Charteris-Black, Jonathan. 2011. *Politicians and rhetoric: The persuasive power of metaphor.* London: Palgrave Macmillan.

Cienki, Alan J. 2004. Bush's and Gore's language and gestures in the 2000 US presidential debates: A test case for two models of metaphors. *Journal of Language and Politics* 3(3):409–440.

Echterhoff, Gerald, René Kopietz, and E. Tory Higgins. 2013. Adjusting shared reality: Communicators' memory changes as their connection with their audience changes. *Social Cognition* 31(2):162–186.

Flowerdew, John, and Solomon Leong. 2007. Metaphors in the discursive construction of patriotism: The case of Hong Kong's constitutional reform debate. *Discourse & Society* 18(3): 273–294.

Huang, Su-Fang (黃素芳). 2011. *Research for the response of Taiwan and Penghu about China's psychological warfare strategy (中共對臺心理戰策略與臺澎防衛作戰因應之研究). Master's thesis, National Chengchi University, Taipei.*

Jing-Schmidt, Zhou, and Xinjia Peng. 2017. Winds and tigers: Metaphor choice in China's anti-corruption discourse. *Lingua Sinica* 3(1):2.

Kan, Shirley A. 2014. *China/Taiwan: Evolution of the "one China" policy—Key statements from Washington, Beijing, and Taipei.* Washington D.C.: Library of Congress. Congressional Research Service.

Kilgarriff, Adam, Pavel Rychly, Pavel Smrz, and David Tugwell. 2004. *The Sketch Engine.* Paper presented at the *EURALEX 2004*, Lorient, France. Available at https://euralex.org/publications/the-sketch-engine/. Accessed 11 March 2019.

Lakoff, George. 2002. *Moral politics: How liberals and conservatives think* (2nd ed.). Chicago and London: University of Chicago Press.

Le, Elisabeth. 2004. Active participation within written argumentation: Metadiscourse and editorialist's authority. *Journal of Pragmatics* 36(4):687–714.

Lim, Elvin T. 2002. Five trends in presidential rhetoric: An analysis of rhetoric from George Washington to Bill Clinton. *Presidential Studies Quarterly* 32(2):328–348. doi:https://doi.org/10.1111/j.0360-4918.2002.00223.x.

Lin, Bao-Hua (林保華). 2007. Hu Jintao becomes hard-lined to Taiwan again (胡錦濤對台灣又強硬起來了). *The Epoch Times*. Available at http://hk.epochtimes.com/news/2007-01-11/胡錦濤對台灣又強硬起來了-18843. Accessed 2 May 2008.

McAdams, Dan P., Michelle Albaugh, Emily Farber, Jennifer Daniels, Regina L. Logan, and Brad Olson. 2008. Family metaphors and moral intuitions: How conservatives and liberals narrate their lives. *Journal of Personality and Social Psychology* 95(4):978–990.

Menegatti, Michela, and Monica Rubini. 2013. Convincing similar and dissimilar others: The power of language abstraction in political communication. *Personality and Social Psychology Bulletin* 39(5):596–607. doi:https://doi.org/10.1177/0146167213479404.

Musolff, Andreas. 2006. Metaphor scenarios in public discourse. *Metaphor and Symbol* 21(1): 23–38.

Musolff, Andreas. 2016. *Political metaphor analysis: Discourse and scenarios*. London and New York: Bloomsbury Publishing.

Scott, Alastair J., and George A. F. Seber. 1983. Difference of proportions from the same survey. *The American Statistician* 37(4a):319–320.

Tu, Sheng-Tsung (杜聖聰). 2008. *The code of the cross-strait truth—China's propaganda towards Taiwan: Policies, action and channels (兩岸真相密碼: 中共對台宣傳的政策、作為與途徑). Taipei: Showwe Information Co., Ltd.*

Zeng, Yu-Jhen (曾郁甄). 2012. *The analysis of China's Taiwan policy—The case of the important speech which published on the Taiwan Affairs Office's website (1996–2011) (中共對台政策之研究—以國台辦網站公佈之「黨和國家領導人重要講話」為例(1996年至2011年)). Master's thesis, Tamkang University, Taipei.*

Chapter 23
Linking Comprehension and Production: Frequency Distribution of Chinese Relative Clauses in the Sinica Treebank

Chien-Jer Charles Lin and Hai Hu

Abstract This chapter presents the distribution of Chinese relative clauses in the Sinica Treebank (Chen et al., Sinica corpus: Design methodology for balanced corpora, 1996; Huang et al., *Mandarin Chinese words and parts of speech: A corpus-based study*, Taylor & Francis, 2017). We extracted 3081 relative clauses from the treebank and classified the relative clauses into six types, including gapless relative clauses, possessive relative clauses, descriptive relative clauses, passive relative clauses, subject relative clauses, and object relative clauses. Each type of relative clause will be discussed regarding the length and syntactic complexity of prenominal clauses, the length and animacy/humanness of head nouns, the part-of-speech categories of embedded verbs, and the position of complex noun phrases in matrix clauses. The issues of the classifier phrase position in relation to relative clauses, the use of *suo* in object relative clauses, and cases where the head nouns are omitted will also be discussed. Based on the corpus distributions, we consider the implications for the comprehension of Chinese relative clauses.

Keywords Treebank · Chinese relative clauses · Sentence processing · Production-distribution-comprehension model · Corpus linguistics

C.-J. C. Lin (✉)
Department of East Asian Languages and Cultures, Indiana University Bloomington, Bloomington, IN, USA
e-mail: chiclin@indiana.edu

H. Hu
School of Foreign Languages, Shanghai Jiao Tong University, Shanghai, China
e-mail: hu.hai@sjtu.edu.cn

C.-R. Huang et al. (eds.), *Chinese Language Resources*, Text, Speech and Language Technology 49, https://doi.org/10.1007/978-3-031-38913-9_23

23.1 Introduction: The Corpus's Role in Sentence Processing

An important topic in linguistic research concerns the interface issue, namely, how a language system interacts with computation, expressive content, and articulation. Two dimensions of linguistic processing—language comprehension and language production—are particularly important. Language comprehension revolves around how the mind perceives and interprets linguistic signals, whereas language production entails how the mind generates linguistic codes for articulation. These dual facets of language processing serve as the foundation for the development of various theories concerning language.

While it might appear evident that there should be a connection between language comprehension and language production, the precise nature of this connection remains less clear. A conventional model like the Speech Chain (Denes and Pinson 1993) sees comprehension and production as inseparable facets of the same coin. Language production corresponds to the speaker (i.e., encoding) aspect of the chain while language comprehension corresponds to the listener (i.e., decoding) aspect of the chain. Such models typically assume a symmetrical relation between comprehension and production, with these two aspects linked through shared linguistic representations. Accordingly, if a linguistic expression is difficult to encode, it is also taken to be difficult to decode. The complexity of linguistic representations and language users' experience with language comprehension and language production can both account for the symmetrical processing effects in comprehension and production. Linguistic materials that are more complex are expected to be harder to interpret and produce (Ferreira 1991; Gibson and Warren 2004). Similarly, less frequently encountered/produced expressions are expected to be more demanding to understand (Reali and Christiansen 2007).

The Production-Distribution-Comprehension (PDC) model (MacDonald 2013) represents a significant endeavor to directly bridge the realms of sentence production and sentence comprehension. According to the PDC model, the distributional regularities in corpora provide valuable insights into the mechanisms at play during utterance planning. This involves organizing information based on processing ease, with a tendency to reuse recently employed structures. Distributional regularities can also be used to predict how utterances may unfold (Hale 2001, 2006; Levy 2008). Distributional regularities from corpora therefore serve as an important resource for making inferences about grammar. On the one hand, corpus data can be seen as a snapshot of collective language production, revealing what structures and expressions are favored in a given context. On the other hand, corpus data illuminates the probabilistic underpinnings of grammar based on which parsing decisions are made.

23.2 Processing Relative Clauses

Taking relative clauses (RCs) as an example, a common finding in English is that subject-extracted relative clauses (SRCs) like (1) below are easier to process than object-extracted relative clauses (ORCs) like (2) both for comprehension and for production (Gibson et al. 2005; King and Just 1991; Traxler et al. 2002; see Lin and Bever 2006 and O'Grady 2011 for a typological overview). Multiple factors contrasting SRCs and ORCs can account for the processing advantage of (1) over (2), including, for instance, the shorter distance between the head and the gap in SRCs compared with that in ORCs (Gibson 1998) and the canonical thematic order of Noun-Verb-Noun (NVN) or Agent-Verb-Patient found in SRCs but not in ORCs (Bever 1970; Lin 2014, 2015).

(23.1)	The harpist$_i$ who [GAP$_i$] knows the composer received good reviews.
(23.2)	The harpist$_i$ who the composer knows [GAP$_i$] received good reviews.

The processing advantage of SRCs is predicted based on the formal property of the linguistic material, namely, a shorter filler-gap distance and the canonicity of word orders found in SRCs. Intriguingly, this processing asymmetry is also consistent with the distributional dominance of SRCs in corpora. Roland et al. (2007), for instance, reported that ORCs are less frequent than SRCs in English written corpora. Considering production, distribution, and comprehension, therefore, RCs in English show a rather consistent pattern; that is, SRCs exhibit higher frequency and are generally easier to process compared to ORCs.

The underlying reasons for this correlation, however, remain a subject of debate, given the presence of multiple factors that can make similar predictions. One potential scenario considers production as the foundation for distributional dominance and, consequently, ease of comprehension. In this view, due to factors like locality and word order canonicity, planning the production of an SRC is inherently more straightforward than that of an ORC. Consequently, SRCs tend to appear more frequently in corpora. As language users encounter SRCs more often, they become more adept at both producing and comprehending them, creating a self-reinforcing cycle. Another plausible scenario involves inferring from frequency distribution that SRCs serve a more functional role in discourse than ORCs. Given their higher frequency of use, SRCs are not only easier to produce or reuse but are also more likely to be expected and comprehended by language users. Several other explanations could account for this correlation, but the linked observations in comprehension, production, and corpus distribution have yet to definitively establish the causal relationships among them.

This chapter will report the distributional frequencies of Chinese relative clauses in the Sinica Treebank 3.0 (http://turing.iis.sinica.edu.tw/treesearch/; Chen et al. 1996, 2003) and discuss these distributions in light of their significance in sentence processing. In recent years, researchers have increasingly focused on the processing of head-final relative clauses, where RCs appear before the head nouns they modify.

Chinese, in particular, has garnered attention in sentence processing research. While the basic word order of Chinese is Subject-Verb-Object (SVO) as it is in English, the noun phrase (NP) structure in Chinese is head-final. The embedded clause in a Chinese NP appears before the noun it modifies. Owing to this typological particularity, SRCs and ORCs in Chinese present distinct filler-gap relations than those in English. Specifically, Chinese RCs feature gaps that precede fillers in terms of linear order, and SRCs entail longer dependency distances compared to ORCs as shown in (3-4). Furthermore, ORCs, but not SRCs, adhere to the canonical NVN order in Chinese. These considerations related to locality and word order suggest a processing advantage for ORCs over SRCs, in contrast to the observations in English.

(23.3) [GAP$_i$]認識作曲家的豎琴家$_i$獲得好評。

[GAP$_i$]__renshi__zuoqujia__de__shuqinjia$_i$__huode__haoping

[GAP$_i$]__know__composer__DE__harpist$_i$__win__good.review

The harpist$_i$ who [GAP$_i$] knows the composer received good reviews.

(23.4) 作曲家認識 [GAP$_i$]的豎琴家$_i$獲得好評。

zuoqujia__renshi__[GAP$_i$]__de__shuqinjia$_i$__huode__haoping

composer__know__[GAP$_i$]__DE__harpist$_i$__win__good.review

The harpist$_i$ who the composer knows [GAP$_i$] received good reviews.

Head-final relative clauses like those in Chinese therefore offer an intriguing arena for the various comprehension and production factors that have otherwise been complicated in head-initial RCs. While locality and word order canonicity both predict easier comprehension of SRCs in English, they predict easier comprehension of ORCs in Chinese. Interestingly, the distribution of relative clauses in Chinese corpora does not consistently align with these processing predictions as observed in English. Frequency distributions have quite consistently indicated higher occurrence of SRCs than ORCs in the corpora (e.g., Wu et al. 2011), thus predicting an SRC advantage. In fact, research on Chinese RC processing has yielded mixed results. In terms of comprehension, some studies have reported that SRCs are easier (Chen et al. 2012; Jäger et al. 2015; Lin and Bever 2006), while others have reported that ORCs are easier (Gibson and Wu 2013; Hsiao and Gibson 2003; Lin 2014; Lin and Garnsey 2011; Packard et al. 2011; Qiao et al. 2012; Sung et al. 2016). In terms of RC production, SRCs have been found to take a shorter time to initiate than ORCs (Lin 2013).

The dominance of SRCs in corpora is in line with the SRC advantage in sentence planning (Lin 2013) and in some comprehension studies (Chen et al. 2012; Jäger et al. 2015; Lin and Bever 2006) but in conflict with the ORC advantage in other comprehension studies (Gibson and Wu 2013; Hsiao and Gibson 2003; Lin 2014; Lin and Garnsey 2011; Packard et al. 2011; Qiao et al. 2012; Sung et al. 2016). In light of this, our study aims to delve deeper into the distributions of Chinese RCs while considering their relevance to critical issues in RC processing. Subsequent sections will dissect the corpus data extracted from the Sinica Treebank and explore

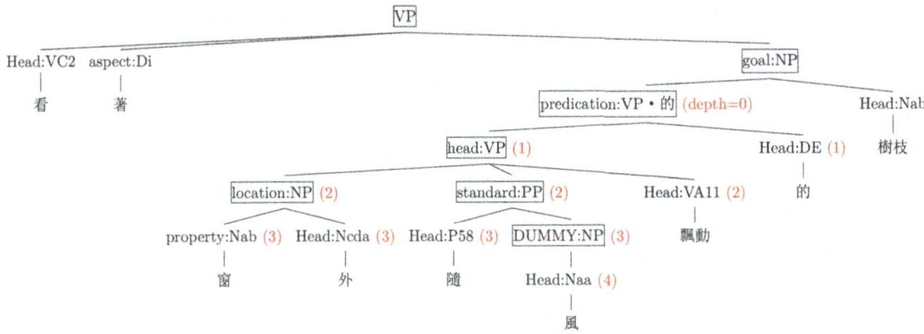

Fig. 23.1 Example of a Sinica tree structure of a relative clause, with depths in parentheses and phrasal nodes in boxes

the intricate connections between sentence comprehension, sentence production, and linguistic representation.

23.3 Distributional Regularities of Chinese Relative Clauses in the Sinica Treebank

Chinese relative clauses were extracted from the Sinica Treebank 3.0, which is based on the Sinica Corpus (http://asbc.iis.sinica.edu.tw/; Chen et al. 1996), a balanced corpus of contemporary Chinese texts produced between 1981 and 2007 (Huang et al. 2017). The Sinica Treebank 3.0 is composed of 361,834 words automatically parsed into 61,087 syntactic trees, which were manually checked and corrected before public release. Our corpus searches targeted NPs that contained prenominal modifier phrases headed by 的 *de* where the prenominal modifier contained a clause, a verb phrase (VP), or a verb. A sample tree diagram is provided in Fig. 23.1.

Our search yielded 3081 tokens, which were manually coded based on various syntactic and semantic properties of the head nouns, the prenominal clauses, and the location of complex NPs in the matrix clauses. The coding process was carried out and reviewed by native speakers of Standard Chinese (i.e., Mandarin), including both authors and several linguists. The coding guidelines were established by the first author. Cases where *de* served as a genitive marker (e.g., 人性的黑暗面 *renxing de heianmian* "the dark side of human nature") or appeared as part of an idiom (e.g., 所謂的 *suowei de* "so-called") as well as cases that contained incomplete RC fragments were excluded from further analysis ($N = 106$, 3% of all tokens). As a result, 2975 RCs were retained for subsequent analyses.

In addition to manually coding the syntactic and semantic properties of the RCs, we extracted the parts-of-speech (POS) tags of the embedded verbs based on verb classification in the Sinica Corpus and measured the syntactic complexity of the embedded clauses based on several metrics.[1] These metrics included (a) the length of the prenominal RCs in terms of the number of characters and number of words, (b) the syntactic depth of the prenominal clauses in terms of the number of syntactic layers, and (c) syntactic complexity in terms of the number of phrasal nodes in the prenominal clauses. We will use Fig. 23.1 above to illustrate these measures.

The number of syllables or characters is the most straightforward measure. In Fig. 23.1, the prenominal clause contains seven characters/syllables, including the relativizer *de*. In Standard Chinese, the number of syllables/characters is almost equivalent to the number of morphemes. Phonological lengths thus quite closely reflect the amount of lexical content. The number of words (six in Fig. 23.1) is based on word segmentation in the Sinica Corpus. The number of layers (or depth) of a prenominal clause indicates how deep the clause is, which is measured by the number of edges on the path from the head (VP·的 in Fig. 23.1) to its deepest word (Head:Naa 風). Note that we counted from the head node of the RC (VP·的), not the head node of the whole tree fragment (VP), so in Fig. 23.1, the number of edges on the path is four. Tokens where more than one RC was found were excluded from this analysis. An additional measure of syntactic complexity is the number of phrasal nodes, whereby all non-terminal (non-leaf) nodes are counted. In the tree in Fig. 23.1, the embedded clause has four phrasal nodes—head:VP, location:NP, standard:PP, and DUMMY:NP. These phrasal nodes are roughly equivalent to the constituents in the sentence, which we believe are a good indicator of RC complexity.

The RCs were classified into six distinct types, with a primary focus on how the head nouns are reconstructed in the embedded clauses. Head nouns can be modified by clauses that are devoid of missing arguments. These RCs are gapless and are integrated with the head nouns as clausal complements (see Sect. 23.3.1). In most cases, the embedded clause contains a missing argument, with which the head noun is identified. A complete clause can be reconstructed by interpreting the missing argument as being coreferential with the head noun. In these instances, a filler-gap dependency exists between the head and the missing argument. We considered five subtypes where the head holds a dependency with an NP in the subordinate clause. In possessive RCs, the head is coreferential with the possessor argument of an embedded NP. In descriptive RCs, the head serves as the NP that the descriptive RC predicates on. The remaining three subtypes of RCs contain more obvious missing arguments in the embedded clause. In passive RCs, the head noun is coreferential with the missing subject NP of the embedded passive clause. In SRCs, the head noun is coreferential with the subject NP in the embedded clause. Finally, in ORCs, the head noun is coreferential with the object NP in the embedded clause. Table 23.1 provides definitions for the six types of RCs, each of which will be introduced in more detail. Furthermore, their respective distributions in the corpus will be discussed in subsequent sections:

---

[1] The python script is available at https://github.com/huhailinguist/processSinicaTree. Accessed on 13 September 2023

Table 23.1 Definitions of the relative clause types

RC type	Definition	Example
1. Gapless RC	Subordinate clauses that do not contain a missing argument of the embedded verb	七十萬人居住的以色列境內各阿拉伯城鎮 "the Arabic cities inside Israel where 700,000 people live"
2. Possessive RC	Subordinate clauses where a noun phrase serves as the possessee of the head noun. Usually, these possessee NPs form a part/whole or kinship relation with the head noun and subcategorizes for the head nouns as their inalienable possessor argument	一位身材魁梧、手持鐵椎的大力士 "a strong guy whose figure is stout and whose hand holds a hammer"
3. Descriptive RC	Subordinate modifiers that are headed by stative intransitive verbs, which can usually be modified by an intensifier like 很 *hen* "very"	年輕的一代 "the young generation"
4. Passive RC	Subordinate clauses that contain a passive structure headed by *bei* and a missing subject argument	被列為觀光區的原住民部落 "the aboriginal sites that have been designated as tourist districts"
4. SRC	Subordinate clauses where the subject argument of the embedded verb is empty and coreferential with the head noun	唱歌的小河 "the river that sings"
6. ORC	Subordinate clauses where the object argument of the embedded verb is empty and coreferential with the head noun	人類共同追求的目標 "the goal that all mankind pursues"

Figure 23.2 presents the percentile distributions of the different types of RCs. The majority (87%) of the RCs fell within two types of gapped RCs—SRCs (53%) and ORCs (34%), with SRCs outnumbering ORCs. The embedded clauses clearly showed the tendency of having missing subject or object arguments that were coreferential with the head nouns.

To get an initial glimpse of the complexity of the prenominal clauses, Table 23.2 shows the clausal lengths in terms of syllables/characters and words, the syntactic depths, and the syntactic complexity of the six types of RCs. The overall pattern was consistent across all four metrics ($ps < 0.05$, paired comparisons with Tukey correction). Descriptive RCs were the shortest and least complex, while passive RCs were the longest and most complex. SRCs were longer and more complex than ORCs.

Given that the syntactic category of the embedded verb plays an important role in selecting arguments, we further extracted the POS of the main verbs in the embedded clauses based on verb classification in the Sinica Corpus (Huang et al. 2017). The distribution of verb classes in the different RC types is presented in Table 23.3. The following sections will further discuss the POS properties of the different RC types using the information in Table 23.3.

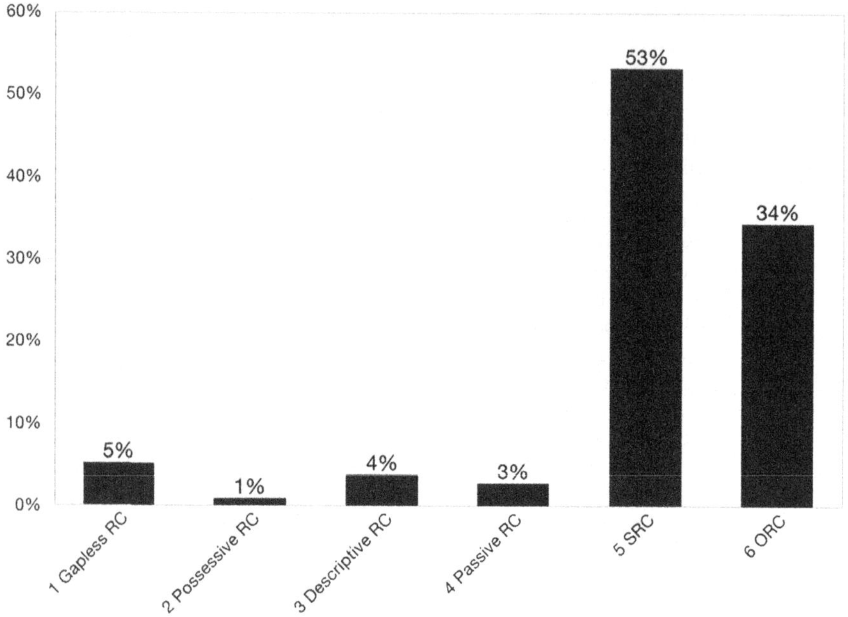

Fig. 23.2 Percentile distribution of relative clauses

Table 23.2 Length and complexity of relative clauses

	Gapless RC	Possessive RC	Descriptive RC	Passive RC	SRC	ORC
RC length: Number of characters	7.03	6.84	4.65	8.01	7.66	6.99
RC length: Number of words	4.37	4.48	3.09	5.30	4.70	4.40
Depth: Number of layers	3.10	3.09	2.23	3.85	3.24	3.04
Number of phrasal nodes	2.53	2.57	1.47	3.61	2.53	2.32

23.3.1 Gapless Relative Clauses and Possessive Relative Clauses

Both gapless RCs, exemplified in (5) to (7) below, and possessive RCs, as illustrated in (8), present themselves as complete clauses without obvious missing arguments or gaps. This section will distinguish these two types of RCs and compare their distributions in the corpus. Gapless RCs encompass three distinct types of compositional relations between the head noun and the embedded clauses. When the head noun functions as a relational noun (e.g., "time" and "space"), it takes an event argument and the prenominal clause fulfills the event argument requirement of the relational noun and serves as a clausal complement of the head noun. RCs like (5) are

Table 23.3 POS distributions of the embedded verbs of relative clauses (the most common categories are boldfaced)

POS	Gapless RC (%)	Possessive RC (%)	Descriptive RC (%)	Passive RC (%)	SRC (%)	ORC (%)
VA: Active intransitive verb	10	4	4	0	15	3
VB: Active pseudo-transitive verb	0	0	0	4	1	1
VC: Active transitive verb	**40**	26	9	**35**	**34**	**49**
VD: Ditransitive verb	4	0	0	0	1	4
VE: Active verb with a sentential object	6	0	0	6	4	11
VF: Active verb with a verbal object	2	0	0	5	1	1
VG: Classificatory verb	2	13	5	16	8	2
VH: Stative intransitive verb	17	**52**	**57**	11	7	7
VI: Stative pseudo-transitive verb	2	0	7	0	1	1
VJ: Stative transitive verb	10	4	9	15	17	9
VK: Stative verb with a sentential object	4	0	5	5	5	8
VL: Stative verb with a verbal object	2	0	5	1	6	2

commonly referred to as gapless relative clauses (Tsai 1997; Zhang 2008) or adjunct relative clauses (Lin 2018) in the literature. Gapless relative clauses also encompass *sloppy* relative clauses like (6), where the head noun is coerced into a relational noun, and it becomes integrated with a clausal complement to arrive at a sense of aboutness—akin to the function of "of" in English (Cheng and Sybesma 2005). Additionally, appositive relative clauses, exemplified by (7), fall under the category of gapless RCs. Together, gapless relative clauses accounted for approximately 5% of the relative clauses found in the Sinica Treebank.

(23.5) 七十萬人居住的以色列境內各阿拉伯城鎮
qishiwan__ren__juzhu__de__yiselie__jingnei__ge__alabo__chengzhen
700,000__people__live__DE__Israel__inside__each__Arabic__city
the Arabic cities inside Israel where 700,000 people live
(23.6) 昨日盤面拉高出貨的味道濃厚
zuori__panmian__lagao__chuhuo__de__weidao__nonghou
yesterday__stock.index__rise__sell__DE__taste__strong
The feel of stocks rising and being sold was strong yesterday.
(23.7) 民不與官鬥的道理

(continued)

min__bu__yu__guan__dou__de__daoli
civilian__not__with__ government.officials__fight__DE__principle
the principle that civilians should not fight against government officials

In contrast, in some gapless prenominal clauses, the head noun is non-relational and does not take the entire embedded clause as its complement or argument. Instead, the head noun forms a possessive association with a nominal argument located within the embedded clause. These RCs are classified as possessive RCs, as shown in (23.8) below. In these instances, the head noun is interpreted as the possessor argument of an embedded inalienable noun (e.g., *shencai* "figure" and *shou* "hand") (following Lin 2011). Possessive RCs constituted only 1% of the relative clauses extracted from the Sinica Treebank.

(23.8) 一位身材$_i$魁梧、手$_i$持鐵椎的大力士$_i$
yi__wei__shencai$_i$__kuiwu__shou$_i$__chi__tiechui__de__dalishi$_i$
one__CL__figure$_i$__stout__hand$_i$__hold__hammer__DE__strong.guy$_i$
a strong guy whose figure is stout and whose hand holds a hammer

Distinctive reading patterns have been observed in gapless relative clauses like those in (23.5) to (23.7) and possessive relative clauses like (23.8) (Lin 2018) owing to the head nouns holding different dependency relations with the embedded clauses. Since the entire gapless RC is integrated with the adjunctive relational head noun, the complexity and frequency of the prenominal clause influence the processing difficulty of the complex NP. Conversely, the comprehension of possessive RCs is sensitive to the structural position of the dependent noun (possessee) in the prenominal clause. Dependent nouns located at subject positions as seen in (23.8) are generally easier to comprehend than those at lower syntactic positions such as objects. Gapless and possessive relative clauses are otherwise comparable in terms of pronominal clause lengths and syntactic complexity, and the lengths of the head nouns. All instances of possessive RCs found in our study involved an inalienable noun located in the subject position like in (23.8).

Furthermore, the animacies of the head nouns were distinctive between the two types of RCs. The majority (97%) of the head nouns in the gapless RCs were non-human relational nouns, while 53% of the head nouns in the possessive RCs were human possessors. Comparing the main verbs in gapless RCs and those in possessive RCs, it was observed that over half (52%) of the main verbs in the possessive RCs were stative intransitive verbs (VH), suggesting that possessive RCs mainly serve the function of describing the individual-level properties of the human head nouns.

23.3.2 Subject and Object Relative Clauses: Matrix Position, Animacy, and Complexity

The most common relative clauses are those where the head noun is interpreted as a key argument of the main verb in the embedded clause. These relative clauses typically contain a missing argument that is coreferential with the head noun. The highest grammatical functions in the Keenan-Comrie Accessibility Hierarchy (Keenan and Comrie 1977) shown in (23.9) below, namely, the subject and the object, are also the positions most frequently relativized in Chinese. These two types of relative clauses (not including descriptive SRCs and passive SRCs) account for over 87% of the relative clauses in the Sinica Treebank.

(23.9) Keenan-Comrie Accessibility Hierarchy (1977: 66):
subject > direct object > indirect object > oblique NP > genitive NP > object of comparison

Our study classified RCs that involved subject extraction into three subtypes: subject relative clauses that contain a missing subject argument (53%) like in (23.10) below, RCs that contain a passive structure (3%) like in (11), and prenominal modifiers that involve descriptive predicates (4%) like in (23.12). A typical RC that involved the extraction of a noun from an object position (34%) is exemplified by (23.13) below.

(23.10) [GAP$_i$]唱歌的小河$_i$
[GAP$_i$]__changge__de__xiaohe $_i$
[GAP$_i$]__sing__DE__river $_i$
the river that sings
(23.11) [GAP$_i$]被列為觀光區的原住民部落$_i$
[GAP$_i$]__bei__liewei__guanguangqu__de__yuanzhumin__buluo$_i$
[GAP$_i$]__BEI__designate.as__tourist.district__DE__aboriginal__site$_i$
the aboriginal sites that have been designated as tourist districts
(23.12) [GAP$_i$]年輕的一代$_i$
[GAP$_i$]__nianqing__de__yi__dai$_i$
[GAP$_i$]__young__DE__one__generation$_i$
the young generation
(23.13) 人類共同追求[GAP$_i$]的目標$_i$
renlei__gongtong__zhuiqiu__[GAP$_i$]__de__mubiao$_i$
mankind__together__pursue__[GAP$_i$]__DE__goal$_i$
the goal that all mankind pursues together

Passive relative clauses, with a word order like that in (23.14) below and an additional functional head such as 被 *bei*, 受 *shou*, 為 *wei*, 由 *you*, 遭 *zao*, etc., are distinctive from SRCs and ORCs. Notably, in the so-called "short passives", the agent NP may be absent, and the head noun typically assumes the role of the theme

Table 23.4 Distribution of relative clauses as a function of extraction types and position in matrix clauses

	S-SRC (%)	S-ORC (%)	O-SRC (%)	O-ORC (%)	Total
Wu et al. (2011)	39.5	26.5	21.3	12.7	347
Our study	31.8	19.2	26.2	22.8	1542

S-SRC SRC in matrix subject position, *S-ORC* ORC in matrix subject position, *O-SRC* SRC in matrix object position, *O-ORC* ORC in matrix object position

or patient NP of the embedded verb. Due to these distinctions, we have categorized passive RCs separately and will discuss their distributional properties in Sect. 23.3.3.

(23.14) [GAP$_i$]__*bei/zao/shou*__(Agent.NP)__Verb__DE__Patient.NP$_i$

Given that stative verbs in Chinese are typically predicative of subject NPs, as in (15) below, they can be regarded as RCs that involve subject extractions. However, they also diverge quite significantly from the typical gapped relatives like SRCs and ORCs, which entail the relativization of a key argument of the embedded verb. Based on the information provided in Table 23.2, descriptive relative clauses were notably shorter in length (averaging 4.65 characters) and displayed a higher degree of simplicity (averaging 1.47 phrasal nodes) compared to RCs that involved extractions from subject or object positions. They can thus be taken as simple predicates that are integrated with the head nouns without having to involve a structure-based filler-gap dependency, much like gapless relative clauses and adjectives in English. Notably, the embedded verbs in these descriptive RCs were mainly stative intransitive verbs (57% being VH verbs).

(23.15) 這些孩子還很年輕
zhe__xie__haizi__hai__hen__nianqing
this__CL__kids__still__very__young
These kids are still young.

We will now turn to the distributional properties of RCs that involve the extraction of subject and object arguments. As introduced, SRCs and ORCs are among the most commonly studied sentence structures. Of the relative clauses extracted from the Sinica Treebank, SRCs (53%) appeared more frequently than ORCs (34%), which is consistent with findings in other languages and in other studies on the Chinese language. Table 23.2 also shows that SRCs were longer and more complex than ORCs. Sentence comprehension studies on Chinese RCs have yielded a mix of SRC advantages and ORC advantages, as reviewed in Sect. 23.2. The corpus distributions suggest that Chinese language users may, on the whole, be more experienced with SRCs than ORCs.

One important discourse function of RCs is to reference information already present in the background and present the focused NP for predication. The RC's position in the matrix clause therefore plays a pivotal role for understanding the discourse functions. Typically, the subject position of a sentence imparts grounding

Table 23.5 Distribution of relative clauses as a function of extraction types, position in matrix clauses, and existence of *shi* in matrix predicates

	S-SRC (%)	S-ORC (%)	O-SRC (%)	O-ORC (%)	Total
N-*shi*-N	12.2	29.3	33.0	25.5	482
SV(O)	40.8	14.6	23.1	21.5	1060

S-SRC SRC in matrix subject position, *S-ORC* ORC in matrix subject position, *O-SRC* SRC in matrix object position, *O-ORC* ORC in matrix object position

information shared by interlocutors whereas the object position provides new and focused information. Sentence processing research has revealed that, overall, Chinese RCs are more frequently expected in the subject position (Lin 2012). Table 23.4 summarizes the findings of Wu et al. (2011), who extracted 1218 relative clauses from the first 1000 files in the Chinese Treebank 5.0 (Xue et al. 2005), and compares them with the distributions in our study based on the Sinica Treebank.

The general distributions were similar in both studies, with RCs appearing more often in the subject positions of matrix clauses than in the object positions. Furthermore, there were more SRCs than ORCs in both positions. However, our study differs from Wu et al. (2011) in that the SRCs in our study were more inclined to modify matrix subject NPs, while the ORCs tended to modify matrix object NPs. This contrast was even more pronounced when we differentiated between matrix clauses that contained the presentative copula *shi* and those that did not, as shown in Table 23.5.

Sentences containing non-*shi* predicates presented a stronger tendency for an SRC to modify a subject NP (41% vs. 23%) and for an ORC to modify an object NP (22% vs. 15%). This interplay between the presence of the presentative copula *shi* and the distribution of RCs in matrix clauses underscores the importance of differentiating sentences containing *shi* and those that do not when studying RC positions. It also implies that the grammatical function of the head noun in the RC interacts with its function in the matrix clause. When considering sentences without *shi* it becomes apparent that head nouns tend to fulfill the same grammatical functions in both the subordinate and matrix clauses. This observation can be explained by two plausible accounts. First, in terms of production, it may be more efficient to maintain consistent grammatical functions in both the embedded clause and the matrix clause. Secondly, this distribution also aligns with the general semantic tendency that NPs in the subject position tend to be human and those in the object position tend to be non-human entities, as proposed by Traxler et al. (2002). The humanness/animacy factor can lead to the tendency for the heads of SRCs to be human nouns, which are also preferably located in the subject position of the matrix clause. On the other hand, the heads of ORCs are more likely to be inanimate and preferably located in the object position of the matrix clause.

To delve deeper into these two accounts, we further conducted an analysis of the animacy distribution of the head nouns in relation to the types of grammatical extractions (SRC vs. ORC) and their matrix positions (Subject vs. Object). In terms of animacy and humanness, the head nouns were classified into five categories,

Table 23.6 Examples and distribution of head noun animacy/humanness

Animacy/humanness	Example	%
Inanimate	所費的功夫 "the effort it takes"	58.0
Human	她教過的學生 "the students that she taught"	37.0
Animal	觀賞到的動物 "the animals that people see"	3.1
Plant	這種種子所長成的草 "the kind of grass that this kind of seed turns into"	1.1
Metaphorical animate	唱歌的小河 "the stream that sings"	0.5
Unclassifiable or mixed		0.3

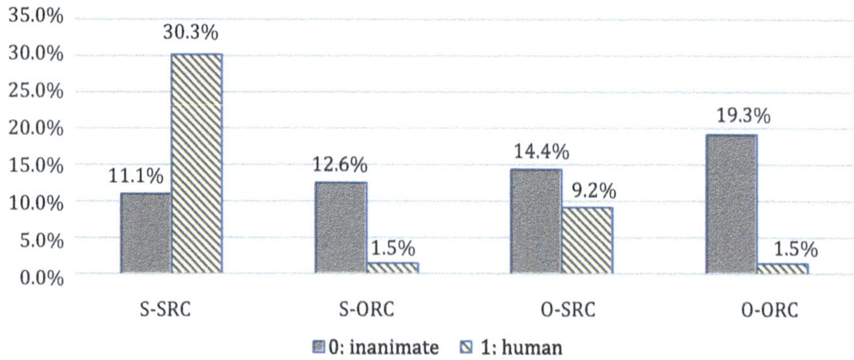

Fig. 23.3 Percentile distribution of head noun animacy/humanness, RC matrix positions, and RC types

as shown in Table 23.6. We focused on the distribution of inanimate NPs (58%) and human NPs (37%) because these two categories accounted for the majority (95%) of the data.

Figure 23.3 presents the percentile distribution of SRCs and ORCs ($N = 997$, where the head noun is either inanimate or human) as a function of head noun animacy/humanness and matrix positions, excluding the matrix sentences that contained *shi*.

The distribution percentages shown in Fig. 23.3 affirm the overall animacy/humanness asymmetry in terms of grammatical positions, which has been observed across languages (Fox and Thompson 1990). Specifically, subject positions are more likely to be occupied by human nouns and object positions are more likely to be occupied by inanimate nouns. This asymmetry was also evident in RC extraction types, as both SRCs and ORCs showed distinctive animacy preferences.

As shown in Fig. 23.3, in the matrix subject position, while SRCs mainly modified human NPs, only very few ORCs modified human NPs. In the matrix object position, the proportion of inanimate NPs increased for both SRCs and ORCs and the proportion of human NPs decreased, especially in SRCs. The animacy

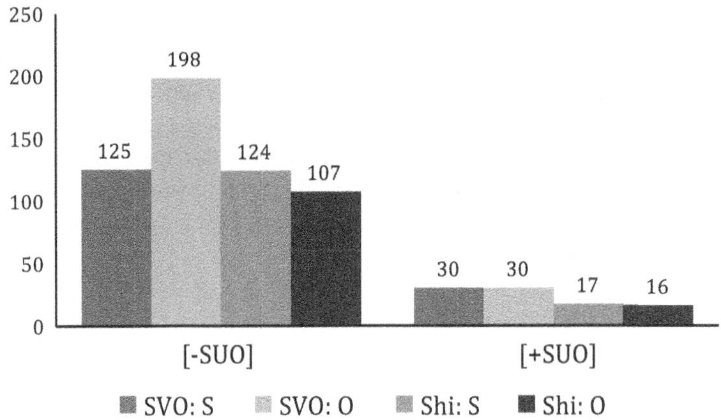

Fig. 23.4 Distribution of RC matrix positions as a function of the existence of *suo* in ORCs (numbers indicate instances)

preference within the matrix clauses and that within the embedded clauses presented an intriguing interaction, resulting in a competition between the two levels of grammatical functions based on their animacy preferences. In the matrix subject position, the animacy preference of the embedded RC type determined the tendency, while in the matrix object position, that of the matrix clause determined the tendency. In both matrix positions, ORCs modified inanimate head NPs more frequently than SRCs, while SRCs featured a higher proportion of human head nouns than ORCs only in the matrix subject position.

Regarding the POS of the embedded verbs (see Table 23.3), in both SRCs and ORCs, transitive action verbs (VC) were the most common. The different verb classes were fairly evenly distributed in SRCs but more skewed toward transitive verbs that required an object argument in ORCs. Compared with ORCs, SRCs had more intransitive action verbs like *pao* "to run" (VA: 15%) that required only one subject argument, classification verbs like *xing* "to be named as" (VG: 8%), and stative verbs that required only one object argument like *daibiao* "to stand for" (VJ: 17%).

Finally, ORCs in Standard Chinese are known to sometimes appear with the particle *suo* located before the main verb, as in (16) below, which is associated with greater formality and literary style. Among the RCs in our study, 164 RCs (5.5%) featured the particle *suo*. ORCs with *suo* were longer than those without *suo* in the embedded clauses (9.7 vs. 6.8 characters, $t = 5.92$, $p < 0.001$), which is consistent with the notion that constituent length serves as an indicator of formality in Standard Chinese, with longer constituents generally conveying a higher degree of formality.

(23.16)	專家所具備的投資能力比一般人高。
	zhuanjia__suo__jubei__de__touzi__nenngli__bi__yiban__ren__gao
	expert__SUO__have__DE__invest__ability__compare__regular__person__high
	The ability to invest that experts have is higher than that of regular people.

Upon comparing ORCs with *suo* and ORCs without *suo* in terms of whether they modify a matrix subject NP or a matrix object NP in Fig. 23.4, a noteworthy observation emerged. While ORCs without *suo* tended to appear in the matrix object position in sentences that did not involve *shi*, ORCs with *suo* are equally distributed in subject and object positions. This finding suggests that the enhanced formality associated with *suo* in an ORC overrides the animacy propensity that was discussed above and leads to a more balanced appearance of an ORC in the subject and object positions of matrix clauses.

23.3.3 Passive Relative Clauses

Due to the increased syntactic complexity associated with an additional functional head (e.g., *bei*), passive RCs are longer and more complex than SRCs and ORCs (see Table 23.1). Passive RCs, as exemplified in (11), stand between SRCs and ORCs as a third category that involves the relativization of a key argument associated with the embedded verb. In terms of thematic content, passive RCs are similar to ORCs as it is the patient NP of the embedded clause that is relativized. In terms of the grammatical position of the relativized gap, a passive RC is more similar to an SRC, where the gap is located in the subject position.

We looked at the position of passive RCs in matrix clauses and found that, like ORCs, the majority (69%) of passive RCs were located at the matrix object position. Further exploring the animacy distribution of the head nouns in SRCs, ORCs, and passive RCs, as shown in Table 23.7 below, based on the coding scheme in Table 23.6, we found that passive RCs were more similar to ORCs, with the head noun more likely to be an inanimate NP, though the tendency of having an inanimate head noun was not as strong as that of ORCs. These observations suggest that relativized patient NPs tend to be inanimate nouns. Moreover, ORCs and passive RCs were similar in terms of their thematic content and animacy preferences.

On the other hand, there appeared to be more human head nouns in passive RCs (31%) than in ORCs (7%), suggesting that a human patient noun is more likely to be relativized if it appears in the subject position of a passive clause than if it appears in the object position of an SVO clause. This finding suggested that passivization promoted the saliency of a patient NP for relativization.

Table 23.7 Animacy distribution of SRCs, ORCs, and passive RCs

Animacy of head	SRC (%)	ORC (%)	Passive RC (%)
0: Inanimate	40	89	58
1: Human	55	7	31
2: Animal	4	2	8
3: Plant	1	2	3
4: Metaphorical animate	1	0	0
5: Unclassifiable or mixed	0	1	1

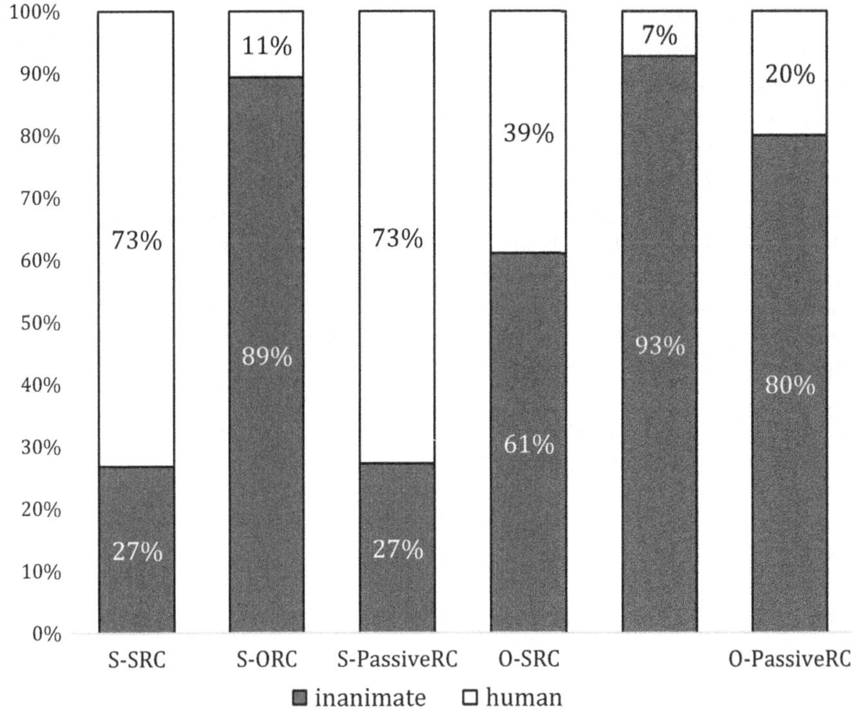

Fig. 23.5 Percentile distribution of animacy/humanness, RC matrix positions, and RC types

Turning now to the interplay between the animacy of the head noun and the position of the complex NP in the matrix clause in Fig. 23.5, the head nouns of passive RCs were predominantly human NPs in matrix subject positions (i.e., S-PassiveRC) but inanimate NPs in matrix object positions (i.e., O-PassiveRC). This distribution again confirms that passive RCs fall between SRCs and ORCs. The animacy of its head noun mirrors that of an SRC in the matrix subject position but aligns more closely with that of an ORC in the matrix object position.

The POS distribution of the embedded verbs in passive RCs was similar to those of ORCs. Unlike SRCs, passive RCs did not contain any intransitive action verbs (VA) and had more instances of classification verbs like *chengwei* "to call" (VG) serving as the main verb. In terms of thematic ordering, passive RCs presented the canonical order of Agent-Verb-Patient, similar to that of an ORC. Lin (2015) compared the reading patterns of passive RCs, RCs that involved the disposal marker *ba*, as shown in (23.17) below, and normal SRCs. The study's findings indicated that passive RCs exhibited the shortest reading times. This outcome underscores the importance of thematic ordering in processing relative clauses.

(23.17) [GAP$_i$]__*ba*__Patient.NP__Verb__DE__Agent.NP$_i$

23.4 Classifier Position in Relative Clauses

One important function of RCs in discourse is to serve the restrictive function; that is, RCs help bring attention to particular referents already present in the background knowledge. One well-known proposal about how restrictiveness is expressed in Standard Chinese focuses on the position of the determiner-classifier phrase in relation to the relative clause (Chao 1968). When a relative clause precedes a determiner-classifier phrase, as in (18a) below, it is considered restrictive because the pre-determiner-classifier position is an edge-position that marks focus. When a relative clause appears after a determiner-classifier phrase, as in (18b), it lacks the focus marking and can be interpreted either as restrictive or non-restrictive (Lin 2012).

(23.18a)	他在台北拇指山下許的那個願
	ta__zai__taibei__muzhishan__xuxia__de__na__ge__yuan
	he__at__Taipei__Mt.Muzhi__make__DE__that__CL__wish
	the wish that he made on Mt. Muzhi in Taipei
(23.18b)	這場可能贏的球
	zhe__chang__keneng__ying__de__qiu
	this__CL__likely__win__DE__ball.game
	the ball game that (I am) likely to win

Over the years, this proposal has sparked controversy. One way to test Chao's (1968) proposal is to examine whether the position of determiner-classifier (CL) phrases interacts with the matrix positions of complex NPs since restrictive relative clauses are more likely to appear in subject positions to ground referents (Gibson et al. 2005). Following this logic, we expected to find more occurrences of RCs that appeared before classifier phrases than RCs that appeared after classifier phrases in subject positions.

Focusing on the matrix positions of RCs that co-occurred with classifier phrases ($N = 174$) and distinguishing sentences that contained *shi* from those that did not, we found that RCs were generally more likely to appear after CL phrases, except when they appeared in the subject position of a sentence containing *shi* (see Fig. 23.6).

The finding that RCs were, overall, more likely to appear after classifiers suggests that the post-classifier position (i.e., CL-RC) is an unmarked position for RCs. The greater occurrences of RCs in the pre-classifier position when complex NPs appeared in the matrix subject position of a sentence with *shi* suggest that (i) the subjects in sentences with *shi* are preferred for grounding referents and (ii) RCs appearing in pre-classifier positions are indeed more likely to be used in a restrictive sense. These findings are consistent with Chao's (1968) proposal and further specify that grounding most likely happens in the subject position of a sentence containing *shi*.

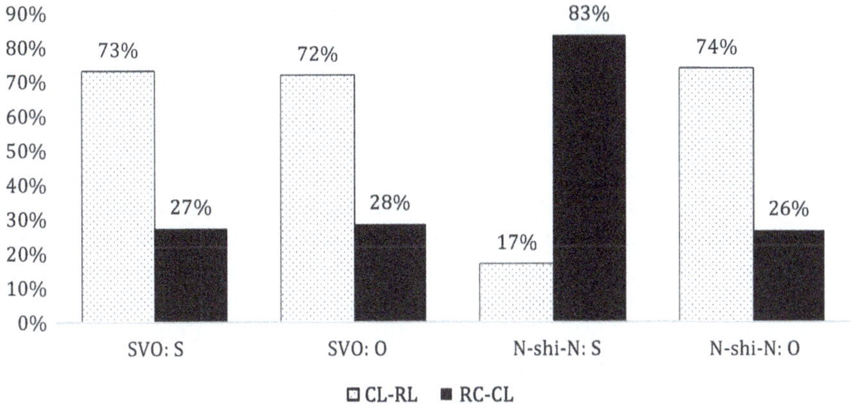

Fig. 23.6 Position of RCs in relation to CL phrases as a function of matrix positions

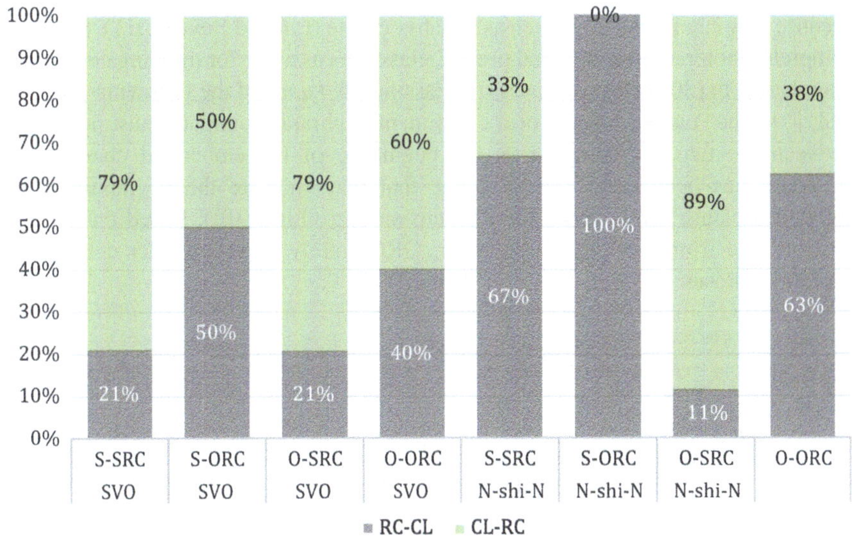

Fig. 23.7 Position of RCs and CL phrases as a function of matrix positions and RC types

Figure 23.7 further breaks down the distributions in Fig. 23.6 as a function of RC types (SRCs vs. ORCs) and shows an overall trend where ORCs appeared in the marked pre-classifier position more often than SRCs did.

To understand this finding, we schematically sketched the linear sequencing of classifier phrases in relation to RCs in (19) below:

(23.19a) CL-SRC:	CL [_ V N1 de] N2
(23.19b) CL-ORC:	CL [N1 V _ de] N2
(23.19c) SRC-CL:	[_ V N1 de] CL N2
(23.19d) ORC-CL:	[N1 V _ de] CL N2

Our observation in Fig. 23.7 was that, relative to (19b) and (19a), respectively, (19d) appeared more often than (19c), which suggests the possibility that language users may have attempted to avoid the potential classifier-noun clash in the CL-ORC condition in (19b) by moving the ORC to a pre-classifier position—assuming that a decision was made between (19a) and (19c) as well as between (19b) and (19d). Wu (2011) similarly found less than 5% of classifier phrases before ORCs in the corpus and interpreted this as a production strategy to avoid ambiguity between the classifier and the first noun in the relative clause. Interestingly, passive RCs where no semantic clash exists after the classifier displayed the same pattern as SRCs in preferring the unmarked position (88% vs. 12%) in classifier phrases, further supporting the notion of ambiguity avoidance in ORCs.

Being prenominal, Chinese RCs often present a challenge for comprehension because they can initially be taken as a matrix clause (Lin and Bever 2011). Sentence comprehension research has used pre-RC classifiers as a cue for marking constituent boundaries. In (20) below, because the classifier 塊 *kuai* and the following pronominal 他 *ta* "he" cannot form a local constituent, a phrasal boundary must be created between the two, signaling *ta* as the beginning of the embedded clause. This boundary has been employed as a cue that may indicate the beginning of an embedded clause for sentence comprehension (e.g., Lin 2018). Based on the production data from the corpus, however, ORCs rarely appeared after determiner-classifier phrases.

(23.20)	一塊他喜歡[GAP$_i$]的石頭$_i$
	yi__kuai__ta__xihuan__[GAP$_i$]__de__shitou$_i$
	one__CL__he__like__[GAP$_i$]__de__rock$_i$
	a rock that he likes

23.5 Headless Relative Clauses

The head nouns of RCs can be left empty, as in (21) below, when they can be easily reconstructed from context or are of generic nature. Among the collected tokens, 303 RCs (10%) were headless. The majority (95%) of headless RCs were either SRCs or ORCs. Interestingly, in contrast to the overall distribution of RC types where we found more SRCs than ORCs (see Fig. 23.1), headless RCs were more often found in ORCs (58%) than in SRCs (37%) (see Table 23.8). This pattern suggests that head nouns that are coreferential with the object of the embedded

Table 23.8 Distribution of headless RCs as a function of RC types

Gapless RC	Possessive RC	Descriptive RC	Passive RC	SRC	ORC
0.99%	2.31%	0.66%	0.99%	37.29%	57.76%

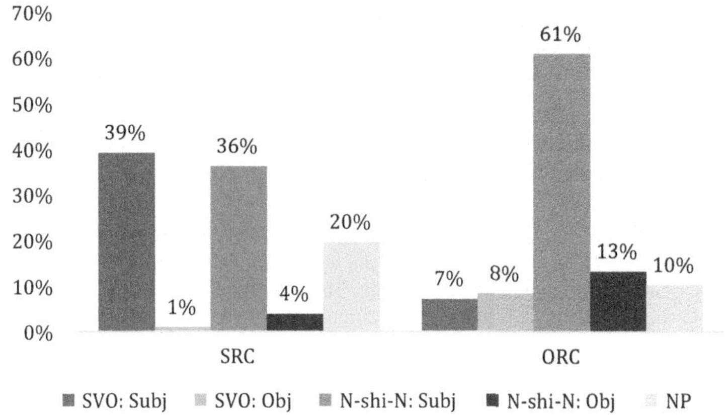

Fig. 23.8 Position of headless RCs as a function of matrix positions

clause are more likely to be omitted given their lower saliency in discourse. These omitted head nouns were more likely to be inanimate (65%) than human (30%).

(23.21)	所以真正賺錢的都是這些廠商
	suoyi__zhenzheng__zhuanqian__de__dou__shi__zhe__xie__changshanng
	therefore__really__make.profit__DE__DOU__SHI__this__CL__merchant
	Therefore, those who really make a profit are the merchants.

Focusing on SRCs and ORCs, headless SRCs (20%) were more likely to appear as an independent topicalized NP than headless ORCs (10%). In matrix clauses, headless SRCs appeared more often in the subject position, which is consistent with the overall preference for SRCs to appear in the matrix subject position (see Fig. 23.8). Interestingly, headless ORCs did not show the same preference for the matrix object position. For sentences with *shi*, in particular, headless ORCs were more likely to appear in the subject position. The tendency for a headless RC to appear in the subject position of a sentence with *shi* suggests that headless RCs are mainly used for grounding referents that already exist in the background.

23.6 Concluding Remarks

This chapter presented topics on the comprehension of Chinese relative clauses in relation to the distributional properties of Chinese relative clauses in the Sinica Treebank. The data were analyzed regarding structural dimensions such as the length and complexity of relative clauses, their positions in matrix clauses, semantic dimensions regarding the animacy of head nouns, and the position of classifier phrases in relation to relative clauses. These corpus data, which serve as a snapshot of collective sentence production, have contributed to our understanding of the relation between production and comprehension. Moreover, they have raised intriguing questions about sentence processing for further exploration.

Acknowledgments We thank Li-Hsin Ning and Yu-Jung Lin for contributing to the coding of the Sinica Treebank data. The first author, Charles Lin, was sponsored by Chiang Ching-kuo Foundation's Scholar Grant while writing the manuscript. The second author, Hai Hu, was supported by China Scholarship Council for his graduate education at Indiana University Bloomington.

References

Bever, Thomas G. 1970. The cognitive basis for linguistic structures. *Cognition and the Development of Language* 279(362):1–61.

Chao, Yuen Ren. 1968. *A grammar of spoken Chinese*. University of California Press.

Chen, Keh-Jiann, Chu-Ren Huang, Li-Ping Chang, and Hui-Li Hsu. 1996. Sinica corpus: Design methodology for balanced corpora. In *Proceedings of the 11th Pacific Asia Conference on Language, Information and Computation*, ed. Byung-Soo Park and Jong-Bok Kim, 167–176. Seoul, Korea.

Chen, Keh-Jiann, Chu-Ren Huang, Feng-Yi Chen, Chi-Ching Luo, Ming-Chung Chang, Chao-Jan Chen, and Zhao-Ming Gao. 2003. Sinica treebank: Design criteria, representational issues and implementation. In *Building and using parsed corpora*, ed. Anne Abeille, 231–248. Dordrecht: Kluwer.

Chen, Zhong, Lena Jäger, and Shravan Vasishth. 2012. How structure-sensitive is the parser? Evidence from Mandarin Chinese. In *Empirical approaches to linguistic theory: Studies of meaning and structure*, 43–62. Berlin: Mouton de Gruyter.

Cheng, Lisa Lai-Shen, and Rint Sybesma. 2005. A Chinese relative. In *Organizing grammar: Linguistic studies in honor of Henk van Riemsdijk*, ed. Hans Broekhuis, Norbert Corver, Rint Huybregts, Ursula Kleinhenz, and Jan Koster, 69–76. Berlin: Mouton de Gruyter.

Denes, Peter B., and Elliot Pinson. 1993. *The Speech Chain*. Macmillan.

Ferreira, Fernanda. 1991. Effects of length and syntactic complexity on initiation times for prepared utterances. *Journal of Memory and Language* 30(2):210–233.

Fox, Barbara A., and Sandra A. Thompson. 1990. A discourse explanation of the grammar of relative clauses in English conversation. *Language* 66:297–316.

Gibson, Edward. 1998. Linguistic complexity: Locality of syntactic dependencies. *Cognition* 68(1): 1–76.

Gibson, Edward, and H.-H. Iris Wu. 2013. Processing Chinese relative clauses in context. *Language and Cognitive Processes* 28(1–2):125–155.

Gibson, Edward, and Tessa Warren. 2004. Reading time evidence for intermediate linguistic structure in long-distance dependencies. *Syntax* 7(1):55–78.

Gibson, Edward, Timothy Desmet, Daniel Grodner, Duane Watson, and Kara Ko. 2005. Reading relative clauses in English. *Cognitive Linguistics* 16(2):313–353.
Hale, John. 2001. A probabilistic Earley parser as a psycholinguistic model. In *Proceedings of the Second Meeting of the North American Chapter of the Association for Computational Linguistics on Language Technologies*, 1–8. Pittsburgh, Pennsylvania.
Hale, John. 2006. Uncertainty about the rest of the sentence. *Cognitive Science* 30(4):643–672.
Hsiao, Franny, and Edward Gibson. 2003. Processing relative clauses in Chinese. *Cognition* 90(1): 3–27.
Huang, Chu-Ren, Shu-Kai Hsieh, and Keh-Jiann Chen. 2017. *Mandarin Chinese words and parts of speech: A corpus-based study*. Taylor & Francis.
Jäger, Lena, Zhong Chen, Qiang Li, Chien-Jer Charles Lin, and Shravan Vasishth. 2015. The subject relative advantage in Chinese: Evidence for expectation-based processing. *Journal of Memory and Language* 79:97–120.
Keenan, Edward L., and Bernard Comrie. 1977. Noun phrase accessibility and universal grammar. *Linguistic Inquiry* 8(1):63–99.
King, Jonathan, and Marcel Adam Just. 1991. Individual differences in syntactic processing: The role of working memory. *Journal of Memory and Language* 30(5):580–602.
Levy, Roger. 2008. Expectation-based syntactic comprehension. *Cognition* 106(3):1126–1177.
Lin, Chien-Jer Charles. 2011. Processing (in)alienable possessions at the syntax-semantics interface. In *Interfaces in Linguistics: New research perspectives*, ed. Raffaella Folli and Christiane Ulbrich, 351–367. New York: Oxford University Press.
Lin, Chien-Jer Charles. 2012. Restrictiveness and information status of Chinese relative clauses: Evidence from discourse comprehension. Paper presented at the *Pragmatics Festival*. Bloomington, Indiana.
Lin, Chien-Jer Charles. 2013. Effects of syntactic complexity and animacy on the initiation times for head-final relative clauses. Poster presented at the *26th Annual CUNY Conference on Human Sentence Processing*. Columbia, South Carolina.
Lin, Chien-Jer Charles. 2014. Effect of thematic order on the comprehension of Chinese relative clauses. *Lingua* 140:180–206.
Lin, Chien-Jer Charles. 2015. Thematic orders and the comprehension of subject-extracted relative clauses in Mandarin Chinese. *Frontiers in Psychology* 6:1255. (*Special research topic on encoding and navigating linguistic representations in memory*, ed. Claudia Felser, Colin Phillips, and Matthew Wagers).
Lin, Chien-Jer Charles. 2018. Subject prominence and processing filler-gap dependencies in prenominal relative clauses: The comprehension of possessive relative clauses and adjunct relative clauses in Mandarin Chinese. *Language* 94:758–797.
Lin, Chien-Jer Charles, and Thomas G. Bever. 2006. Subject preference in the processing of relative clauses in Chinese. In *Proceedings of the 25th West Coast Conference on Formal Linguistics*, 254–260. Somerville, Massachusetts.
Lin, Chien-Jer Charles, and Thomas G. Bever. 2011. Garden path in the processing of head-final relative clauses. In *Processing and producing head-final structures*, ed. Yuki Hirose, Hiroko Yamashita, Jerome Packard, 277–297.
Lin, Yow-Yu, and Susan Garnsey. 2011. Verb bias in Mandarin relative clause processing. *Concentric: Studies in Linguistics* 37(1):73–91.
MacDonald, Maryellen C. 2013. How language production shapes language form and comprehension. *Frontiers in Psychology* 4:226.
O'Grady, William. 2011. Relative clauses: Processing and acquisition. In *The acquisition of relative clauses: Processing, typology and function*, ed. Evan Kidd, 13–38. Amsterdam and Philadelphia: John Benjamins Publishing Company.
Packard, Jerome L., Zheng Ye, and Xiaolin Zhou. 2011. Filler-gap processing in Mandarin relative clauses: Evidence from event-related potentials. In *Processing and producing head-final structures*, ed. Yuki Hirose, Hiroko Yamashita, Jerome Packard, 219–240.

Qiao, Xiaomei, Liyao Shen, and Kenneth I. Forster. 2012. Relative clause processing in Mandarin: Evidence from the Maze Task. *Language and Cognitive Processes* 27:611–630.

Reali, Florencia, and Morten H. Christiansen. 2007. Processing of relative clauses is made easier by frequency of occurrence. *Journal of Memory and Language* 57(1):1–23.

Roland, Douglas, Frederic Dick, and Jeffrey L. Elman. 2007. Frequency of basic English grammatical structures: A corpus analysis. *Journal of Memory and Language* 57(3):348–379.

Sung, Yao-Ting, Jih-Ho Cha, Jung-Yueh Tu, Ming-Da Wu, and Wei-Chun Lin. 2016. Investigating the processing of relative clauses in Mandarin Chinese: Evidence from eye-movement data. *Journal of Psycholinguistic Research* 45:1089–1113.

Traxler, Matthew J., Robin K. Morris, and Rachel E. Seely. 2002. Processing subject and object relative clauses: Evidence from eye movements. *Journal of Memory and Language* 47(1): 69–90.

Tsai, Wei-Tien Dylan. 1997. On the absence of island effects. *Tsing Hua Journal of Chinese Studies* 27:125–149.

Wu, Fuyun. 2011. Frequency issues of classifier configurations for processing Mandarin object-extracted relative clauses: A corpus study. *Corpus Linguistics and Linguistic Theory* 7: 203–227.

Wu, Fuyun, Elsi Kaiser, and Elaine Andersen. 2011. Subject preference, head animacy and lexical cues: A corpus study of relative clauses in Chinese. In *Processing and producing head-final structures*, ed. Yuki Hirose, Hiroko Yamashita, Jerome Packard, 173–94.

Xue, Naiwen, Fei Xia, Fu-Dong Chiou, and Marta Palmer. 2005. The Penn Chinese treebank: Phrase structure annotation of a large corpus. *Natural Language Engineering* 11(2):207–238.

Zhang, Niina. 2008. Gapless relative clauses as clausal licensers of relational nouns. *Language and Linguistics* 9:1005–1028.

Chapter 24
Perception Correlated Information Allocation and Pattern Convergence for Discourse Prosody

Helen Kai-Yun Chen and Chiu-Yu Tseng

Abstract This chapter will present a study that explored speech expressiveness and information arrangement in relation to discourse prosody in continuous Mandarin speeches. Based on corpus data from four diverse speech genres, our study examined perceived prosodic highlights in correlation with speech expressiveness and the convergence of prominence patterns for discourse prosody. Using the corpus linguistic approach and quantitative analyses, we first summarized the number of perceived emphasis token patterns and their distribution across speech genres. Then, we conducted two experiments: (i) speech expressiveness by information weighting calculation that is based on prosodic highlights allocation and (ii) discourse prosody through the convergence of patterned prosodic highlights in limited degrees of contrastive strength. The results from the first experiment pinpointed major differences across speech genres in terms of expressiveness, demonstrating that the most spontaneous type of speech carried the largest amount of information. The second experiment found that a limited number of intonation patterns converged for higher-level discourse prosody. Ultimately, our research uncovered the sources contributing to speech expressiveness and diversity across speech genres, while at the same time showed successful convergence of divergent surface variations from speech signals to deduce systematic and predictable patterns of discourse-level global prosody.

Keywords Speech expressiveness · Discourse prosody · Perceived prosodic highlight patterns and convergence · Information allocation and deployment

H. K.-Y. Chen (✉)
National Central University, Taoyuan City, Taiwan
e-mail: helenkychen@ncu.edu.tw

C.-Y. Tseng
Institute of Linguistics, Academia Sinica, Taipei, Taiwan
e-mail: cytling@sinica.edu.tw

C.-R. Huang et al. (eds.), *Chinese Language Resources*, Text, Speech and Language Technology 49, https://doi.org/10.1007/978-3-031-38913-9_24

24.1 Introduction

One of the major challenges to natural language processing and speech understanding nowadays is how language-processing systems capture and represent aspects of continuous speech, especially those occurring in a context that is mostly unplanned and highly spontaneous. The main challenge of processing spontaneous speech is its expressive nature, which leads to highly variant surface realizations from speech signals. Many times, speech signals, especially their prosodic realizations, are considered and processed by sound segments that may have been further dissected to their bare meta forms or from units predefined and constrained by syntax-based constituents. Not much attention, however, has been paid to the processing of speech prosody with the largest discourse-based units or levels of multiple-phrase paragraphs, which may depart considerably from the bare forms at times. Given that the larger the unit being processed, the more speech context needs to be covered, hence more expressiveness is delivered. As a result, it is easily assumed that the surface realizations of discourse prosody are highly variant or divergent, which in turn poses a potential problem for language processing and generalization.

Discourse prosody, though diverse in its surface realizations, can nevertheless be accounted for by systematic yet simple underlying representations in association with information allocation and planning. In our study, we were mainly concerned with patterns and features derived from speaking (the "parole" in de Saussure 1966) and speaking more than one phrase/sentence at a time, which is, after all, the essence of continuous speech. The objective of our study thus focused on information attributed speech expressiveness in interaction with discourse prosody in Mandarin spontaneous speeches from diverse genres. Specifically, our study was built on the assumption that a direct correlation exists between the allocation and weighting of information and perceived prosodic highlights[1] in limited levels of contrastiveness in speech. It has been suggested that both speech expressiveness and discourse prosody are closely associated with information allocation and distribution at different discourse-prosodic levels in a hierarchical relationship[2] across speech genres, especially higher-level context prosody. Based on this assumption, our exploration in terms of speech expressiveness centered on perceived prosodic highlights correlated information load at higher-level discourse-prosodic units. Furthermore, we

[1] The term "prosodic highlights" in our study refers to the prosody-related prominence through perception, which is based on the speech context. Prosodic highlights are defined in terms of features in perceivable higher/lower pitch and/or relatively stronger/weaker loudness, as well as degrees of contrast (see Sect. 24.2.2. for the definitions of annotating levels of perceived emphases). In this chapter, we use perceived prosodic highlights, perceived prominence, and emphasis interchangeably.

[2] The hierarchical relationship of discourse-prosodic units is presented in the spirit of the hierarchical prosodic phrase grouping (HPG) framework (Tseng 鄭秋豫 2010; Tseng et al. 2005a, 2005b; Tseng and Su 2008) that our study adopted when annotating the discourse-prosodic units/boundaries in the continuous speeches. Please refer to Sect. 24.2.2 for a brief introduction of the framework.

demonstrated the convergence, or merging of perceived emphasis patterns from lower-level discourse-prosodic units for discourse prosody.

By ways in which perceived prosodic highlights are configured and patterned, therefore, our study offers an alternative account of the sources that contribute to realistic speech expressiveness and relevant prosodic variations that are derived from the underlying emphasis patterns of discourse prosody. We hold that realistic speech expressiveness and relevant prosodic variations are, in principle, information-oriented and correlated. Our results were drawn from the context of diverse speech genres, revealing how prominence-attributed information loading varies at higher-level discourse-prosodic units across speech genres, while simultaneously foregrounding the successful convergence of perceived prominence patterns that reflect the coarsely-graded nature of discourse prosody.

The speech data incorporated in our study were culled from corpora of continuous Mandarin speeches, including two types of read speeches and two spontaneous ones. All selected data underwent the same preprocessing procedures and labor-intensive annotations for the annotations of discourse-prosodic levels and perceived prosodic highlights. Combining both the corpus linguistic approach and quantitative analyses, we first summarized the number of perception-based emphasis token patterns and their distribution by discourse-prosodic units at the phrasal level.[3] Then, two experiments were conducted to explore speech expressiveness and discourse prosody. The first experiment involved the calculation of information load by higher-level discourse-prosodic units. As for discourse prosody, the second experiment attempted the convergence of emphasis token patterns from lower-level discourse-prosodic units. Not limited by sentence-level- or intonation-unit-based prosody, we aimed to derive systematic and predictable patterns of *context prosody* from divergent prosodic variations on the surface.

24.1.1 Speech Expressiveness

Expressiveness as the center of speech prosody studies has long been associated with the paralinguistic aspects of speech. As suggested in some earlier studies on expressive speech (e.g., Campbell 2002; Tatham and Morton 2004), spontaneous speech itself carries richer paralingual information that provides listeners with means for expressiveness. It was not until Fujisaki (2004: 1) that clearer definitions for linguistic and paralinguistic information have been proposed: the former is defined by "discrete symbols and linguistic rules from written texts," while the latter refers to information "that is not inferable from the text but rather added deliberately by speakers onto the linguistic information." As has been suggested, expressive speech encompasses aspects of a language system that should cover at least both linguistic

[3] More precisely, phrasal-level discourse-prosodic units refer to prosodic phrase units (PPh) in the HPG framework. Please refer to Sect. 24.2.2 for further details.

and paralinguistic information (Erickson 2005). Erickson (2005) provided a thorough review of previous studies on expressive speech up until early 2000. However, the majority of studies cited concentrated on emotion-related expressions and their features in association with identifiable suprasegmental acoustic characteristics and variations.

Adhering to Erickson (2005), we held similarly that expressive speech is associated with both linguistic and paralinguistic information. Alternatively, we believe that in addition to emotion, other expressions also exist in the same identifiable suprasegmental acoustic variations. Specifically, we considered perceived prosodic highlights as another source that expresses additional yet structured paralinguistic information. The first experiment, therefore, focused on weighted information loading by perceived prominence across speeches from multiple genres. We arbitrarily assigned weighting scores by perceived prominence levels and calculated the information loading scores according to the levels of the discourse-prosodic units. From the standpoint of analyzing speaking/parole, we approached the weighting assignment in terms of its density distributed across the context of continuous speech. As such, the scoring assignment did not correspond to the mapping between discrete preprocessed units and absolute acoustic values but instead reflected diffused information allocation in the relative prominence deployment. The ultimate goal was to contribute to the understanding of context prosody in continuous speech.

With the assumption regarding a direct association between prosodic highlights and information allocation, it has been hypothesized that the larger the planning size of discourse-prosodic units, the heavier its information load will be. This follows from the rationale that a larger planning unit allows for more ups and downs (such as prosodic highlights and reductions) in perceived prominence pattern deployment and hence more expressiveness. As will be demonstrated, the results from the first experiment showed that the most spontaneous speech genre carried the most amount of information content but only when examined by the highest-level discourse-prosodic planning unit. Thus, the findings from our first experiment advance the exploration of expressive speech via evidences based on the unique association between information content and prosodic expression in continuous speech.

24.1.2 *Discourse Prosody*

The examination of discourse prosody is based on the assumption that the allocation of perceived prosodic highlights in continuous speech can be converged or merged into limited patterns of prosodic variations.[4] The viability of such convergence is further built on a coarsely-graded distinction of prosodic contrastiveness at higher discourse levels in speech. In other words, we adopted a viewpoint similar to melody

[4] We adopted the term "variation" not with its traditional sense in linguistics but rather in the sense from music studies; thus, it is more similar to the concept of melodic variations.

perception in music studies regarding the identifiability of motivic similarities among different parts of the overall melody (Patel 2008). As explained by Patel (2008), listeners recognize these similarities without identity, as similarity itself is a graded feature influenced by many factors within music perception.

Drawing on a parallel mechanism from music perception for speech, Patel (2008: 197) further suggested that a language has "only a limited number of linguistically distinctive intonation contours." Supporting evidence has been drawn from the claim by Halliday (1970) regarding the possibility of grouping large sets of pitch contours based on a small number of distinct pitch contours. Other relevant perceptual research (e.g., 't Hart et al. 1990) has shown that a limited number of basic intonation patterns for discourse prosody can be identified by specific types of rises and falls within pitch contours. Nevertheless, these previous studies have focused mostly on Indo-European languages such as English and Dutch; hence, much of the discussions have been framed by sentence-level prosody and, especially, the concept of "supradeclination" (Wichmann 2014). Turning to Mandarin speech, it is debatable whether supradeclination serves as a major feature that defines higher-level prosodic units. As demonstrated by Tseng and Su (2014) in Mandarin continuous speech, prosodic contrastiveness in higher-level intonation variations is not as distinct as it is in English as the overall intonation contour tends to be much flatter; instead, a sharper F0 contrast is required for lower-level prosodic word units that are mostly tone-bearing. These findings on language-specific prosody realizations at discourse levels thus call for an alternative exploration of the coarsely-graded nature of discourse prosody, especially for our Mandarin data.

Driven by the suggestion regarding a limited number of intonation contours for discourse prosody, we attempted the convergence of perceived prosodic highlight allocations. Particularly in the second experiment, we examined discourse prosody in Mandarin speeches through the method of convergence of patterns that were based on the relative up- and down-stepping of perceived prosodic highlight allocations by lower-level discourse units. The main questions included: can perceived prosodic highlight allocations from lower-level prosodic units be converged into a limited number of prosodic variations to reflect discourse prosody; and what are some of the factors that influence successful convergence, as well as factors for the divergence found among prosodic variations that cannot be merged further? As will be shown, while major results have demonstrated successful convergence and hence narrowed down prosodic patterns, divergence was found to be related to the planning size of the discourse-prosodic units. In other words, it will be shown that the larger the planning size, the more divergence will be found in the prosodic highlight patterns that cannot be merged. The results will thus shed light on systematic and patterned discourse prosody with the coarsely-graded nature of the Mandarin speech.

This chapter is organized as follows. Section 24.2 will describe the speech data, data preprocessing, and the annotation schemes, while Sect. 24.3 will introduce the methodologies incorporated in the two experiments. In Sect. 24.4, the preliminary results from cross-genre comparisons and from the merging of emphasis token patterns will be presented. Sections 24.5 and 24.6 will provide details of the experiment results, focusing on speech expressiveness and prominence pattern

Table 24.1 Summary of total time and number of syllables from the four speech genres

Read speech	Total time (min.)	Total number of Syl	Spontaneous speech	Total time (min.)	Total number of Syl
CNA	50	22,988	**SpnL**	145	33,306
WB	28	14,083	**SpnC**	54	10,756

convergence, respectively. Finally, Sect. 24.7 will present a general discussion and summary.

24.2 Speech Data and Preprocessing

In this section, we will first present the speech data incorporated for the current analyses and experiments. The Mandarin data that will be introduced in Sect. 24.2.1 covered a wide variety of speech genres, including data from both read and spontaneous speeches. All selected data underwent the same procedures of preprocessing and annotation prior to further analyses. Layers of annotations, including discourse-prosodic boundaries and perception-based prosodic highlights, were manually tagged across all data. The procedures for the preprocessing and annotation schemes will be described in Sect. 24.2.2.

24.2.1 Speech Data

Two sets of read and spontaneous speech data, respectively, were incorporated in our study. The read speech data were culled from Sinica COSPRO[5] (Tseng et al. 2003; Tseng et al. 2005a; Tseng and Su 2008), including (i) speeches produced via prose reading tasks (CNA) by one male and one female native Mandarin speaker and (ii) speeches derived from simulating weather forecast tasks (WB) by one male and one female. As for the spontaneous speeches, one was a university classroom lecture in the form of a spontaneous monologue (SpnL) delivered by a male professor, while the second one was a piece of naturally occurring spontaneous conversation (SpnC) taken from a corpus of Mandarin interactions (cf. Chen et al. 2012). The data from one female speaker from one segment of a dyadic interaction was selected. Table 24.1 summarizes the total duration time of each speech genre and the equivalent number of syllables.

The main difference between the two sets of read and spontaneous speeches is that both CNA and WB were continuous speeches produced via reading tasks, and

[5] As introduced in Tseng et al. (2003) and Tseng et al. (2005a), Sinica COSPRO is an intonation balanced speech corpus originally designed to examine the role of intonation and prosodic grouping in Mandarin continuous speech.

the reading materials were presented to the subjects in the format of written text. As for the spontaneous lecture SpnL, the instructor delivered the whole lecture in a form close to spontaneous speech, yet the content from each lesson in general followed preplanned topics from the course syllabus and was well structured by topics. Finally, for the spontaneous conversation SpnC, the interaction between speakers was of high spontaneity since they were given minimal instructions as to any specific topic to cover during the course of the recordings (Chen et al. 2012). The SpnC data, therefore, represented the least constrained speech genre compared with the read CNA and WB speeches, and the lecture SpnL with more spontaneity fell somewhere in between. It was thus expected that SpnC would be the most expressive among all speeches and that each speech genre would display unique prosodic realizations by various degrees of spontaneity and hence expressiveness.

24.2.2 Data Preprocessing and Annotations

The speech data first underwent the procedures of both automatic and manual preprocessing, followed by the manual annotation of perception-based prosodic information. For the preprocessing procedures, speech signals from all selected data were first force-aligned into segments using the Hidden Markov Model Toolkit (HTK). The next step involved labor-intensive manual spot-checking by trained transcribers. Annotations by experienced annotators were then performed independently in separate layers for discourse-prosodic units and perceived prosodic highlights. Next, details of the annotation procedures will be discussed.

Annotation of Discourse-Prosodic Units

The key to our annotation of discourse-prosodic units was the rationale that prosody-based breaks and boundaries are not limited by lower word or phrase levels. Instead, we simultaneously considered the boundaries at higher levels of paragraph- and discourse-associated units. Following the framework of hierarchical prosodic phrase grouping (HPG, Tseng 鄭秋豫 2010; Tseng et al. 2005a, 2005b; Tseng et al. 2008), five levels of discourse-prosodic units in a hierarchical relationship were annotated across all speech data.[6] These levels were marked B1 through B5, corresponding,

[6]As explained by Tseng (2013), in utilizing the HPG framework for the annotation of discourse-prosodic units, the main strength is that such a framework is not text-bounded, nor is it syntactically predetermined. While the framework purposely distances itself away from the possible connotations associated with other levels of linguistic information (Tseng 2013), it pays further attention to units of higher discourse-prosodic levels. Since the main focus of our study was to capture the features of speech expressiveness and discourse prosody, it was essential that we incorporated such a framework, which takes into consideration prosodic features from units whose size reaches beyond that of the sentential level.

respectively, to syllable (SYL), prosodic word (PW), prosodic phrase (PPh), breath group (BG), and multiple-phrase speech paragraph (PG). In the HPG framework (e.g., Tseng 鄭秋豫 2010; Tseng et al. 2005a, 2005b), BG, by definition, corresponds to a psycholinguistic unit constrained by changes in breath while speaking continuously; as for PG, it is at the highest level, corresponding mostly to discourse paragraphs and sometimes also associated with major topic changes. By default, the boundary breaks, prosodic units, and their relationship in the HPG framework can be stated as

$$\mathrm{SYL/B1} < \mathrm{PW/B2} < \mathrm{PPh/B3} < \mathrm{BG/B4} < \mathrm{PG/B5}.$$

The discourse units of the perceived prosodic boundaries and breaks were manually tagged by experienced annotators in one individual layer. Methods of tagging followed conventions similar to the ToBI system (Silverman et al. 1992) in that speech strings were divided into discourse-prosodic units of various sizes via marking boundary breaks in a hierarchical relationship instead of identifying only a single prosodic unit bounded by syntactic units at a time. During the annotation process and afterward, we also constantly checked for both intra- and inter-annotator consistency to make sure that both reached at least 80% of consistency and that the finalized boundary segmentations would reach at least 95% of agreement among all annotators.

Annotations of Emphases by Degrees of Perceived Prominence

The same speech data were further tagged manually by trained annotators into perception-based emphasis/non-emphasis tokens (ETs). For the perceived strength of prominence, the data were tagged, based on four relative degrees, from reduction (E0) to the most emphasized degree (E3) (cf. Tseng 2013; Tseng et al. 2011) as follows:

- E0—reduced pitch, lowered volume, and/or contracted segments
- E1—normal pitch, normal volume, and clearly produced segments
- E2—raised pitch, louder volume, irrespective of the speaker's tone of voice
- E3—higher raised pitch, louder volume, with noticeable change in tone of voice

With this annotation scheme, we note specifically that only a limited number of contrastive degrees of prominence were consistently perceived by listeners while processing continuous speech signals. When annotating perceived prominence, the annotators simply tagged the speech data into a string consisting of ETs (E2 and E3)/non-ETs (E0 and E1) in an independent layer.

Since Mandarin does not actually carry pitch accents on individual words, our annotation scheme was distinguished from the model of prosody-related prominence annotation proposed by Kohler (1997) and as recently discussed by Baumann et al. (2016). In other words, our tagging of perceived emphasis did not follow any predefined prosody-based units, nor was it syntactically constrained; rather, the

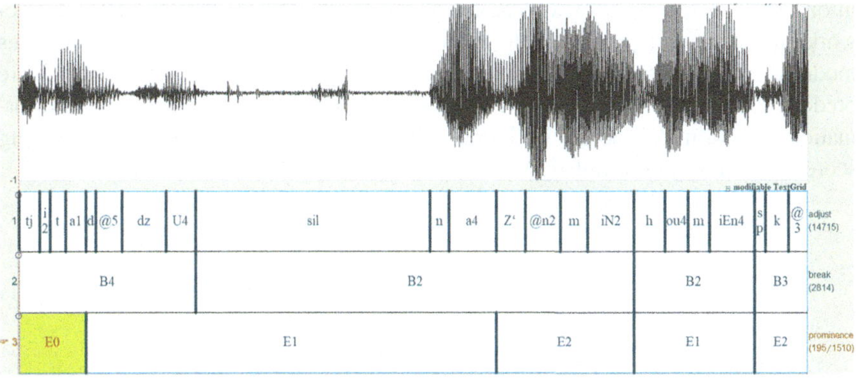

Fig. 24.1 An illustration of our annotation schemes for discourse-prosodic units (second layer beneath the spectrogram) and prominence (thrid layer beneath the spectrogram) using Praat (© Boersma and Weenink 2015)

tagging maintained perceived degrees that were largely intra- and inter-annotator consistent (over 80%). As explained by Tseng (2013), information regarding perceived emphasis was tagged independently to allow for further examination of any possible interaction between perceived prosodic highlights with respect to higher-level paragraph/discourse structures. One additional note is that, among the four speech genres, only SpnL and SpnC were annotated with the reduction (E0) tag, as it was assumed that the speakers in the reading tasks rarely reduced any part of their speech production. Finally, Fig. 24.1 provides an example to illustrate our annotations for discourse-prosodic units and levels of prominence:

24.3 Methodology

In our study, we incorporated mainly quantitative analyses and basic pattern merging to examine patterns of perceived prosodic highlights in association with information allocation and distribution. Then, two experiments were conducted: first, to calculate the weighting scores in reflecting information load and allocation and, second, to converge perceived prominence for discourse prosody. In the following, details of the experimental methodologies will be presented.

24.3.1 Weighting Scores of Information Allocation by Levels of Perceived Prominence

The calculation of the information attributed weighting scores was based on patterns composed of emphasis/non-emphasis tokens (ETs) annotated in the data. The information weighting scores were calculated by the PPh unit in the HPG framework. In particular, possible information weighting of perceived emphases was modeled, whereby scores corresponding to degrees of emphases were predetermined. Following a similar rationale for modeling prominence-based information weighting proposed in Tseng (2013), we arbitrarily assigned weighting scores according to Formula (24.1):

$$\text{Score}\,(t_n) = \begin{matrix} 0, \text{if label} = \text{E0} \\ 0, \text{if label} = \text{E1} \\ 1, \text{if label} = \text{E2} \\ 2, \text{if label} = \text{E3} \end{matrix} \tag{24.1}$$

in which t stands for each emphasis token. One additional note is that, as explained in Sect. 24.2.2, for the annotation of perceived prominence degrees, both spontaneous speeches were tagged with one additional level of reduction (E0). To calculate the weighting scores of information allocation on the same basis of prominence levels, initially, we merged the E0 tag with E1 in SpnL and SpnC and assigned a score of 0 to both. This also followed the assumption that the distinction between E0 and E1 by prominence level would be perceived as a minimum difference.

After the scoring assignments, we then calculated the average weighting scores at the BG level in the HPG framework by further removal of the length effect,[7] following Steps One through Three:

Step One. To remove the length effect from the PPh and BG units, each PPh weighing (ω) was normalized by the number of ETs within the unit, as shown in (24.2):

$$\text{Nor.\_PPh\_}\omega_n = \sum_{m=1}^{M} \text{Emphasis\_Score}_m / M \tag{24.2}$$

in which M is the total number of ETs in each PPh.

Step Two. Each BG weighing (ω) was normalized by the number of PPhs within it, following (24.3):

$$\text{Nor.\_BG\_}\omega_o = \sum_{n=1}^{N} \text{Nor.\_PPh\_}\omega_n / N \tag{24.3}$$

in which N is the total number of PPhs in each BG.

Step Three. The average weighting score at the BG level was derived following (24.4):

[7] As will be shown in Sect. 24.4.1, the chunking sizes at different discourse-prosodic levels differed drastically across speech genres. This is the main reason that we had to remove the length effect.

$$\text{Ave.\_BG\_}\omega = \sum_{o=1}^{O} \text{Nor.\_PPh\_}\omega_o / O \quad (24.4)$$

in which O is the total number of BG units.

Finally, we carried out the calculation of average weighting scores of information allocation at the top PG level that had also been normalized by PPh in accordance with the same steps above.

24.3.2 Converging Perceived Prosodic Highlights for Discourse Prosody

To converge the prosodic highlight allocations from lower-level discourse-prosodic units, we started with perceived prosodic highlights allocated by PPh. Following the rationale of Tseng and Su (2014), we paid special attention to the patterns of prosodic highlights via adopting the relative high/low (H/L) concept in phonology (i.e., similar to the ToBI system in Silverman et al. 1992). In other words, the patterns derived using our methodology did not simply stand for the independent occurrence of a certain pattern in direct correspondence to the prominence allocations; rather, each pattern reflected an up- or down-stepping tendency of relative prosodic prominence in the PPh unit (Tseng and Su 2014). In the spirit of the same rationale, we attempted to converge prosodic highlight allocations at the PPh level, aiming at deriving a limited number of prosodic pattern variations[8] in BG as a higher-level discourse-base unit. We adhered to the following steps for the convergence process:

Step One. First, we transcribed ETs in sequences by PPh into a number of strings consisting of 0 and 1: the first PPh within each BG was always assigned a 1, which served as the initial anchor point. In cases where the following PPh of the same BG corresponded to the same ET pattern as its preceding PPh, the number 0 was assigned; otherwise, 1 was assigned. As a result, we captured the up- and down-stepping relativeness in adjacent ET patterns in BG via a string of 0/1, as demonstrated by the "0/1 assignment" layer shown in Fig. 24.2a.

Step Two. As the F0 contour in each BG was now represented by a string of 0/1, the next step involved arbitrarily breaking up the string into subgroups to facilitate further convergence of the allocation of perceived prosodic highlights. We simply broke up the string whenever a change from 0 to 1 occurred.

Step Three. Considering that the 0/1 string could only provide an observation about the F0 realizations in between adjacent PPhs, we transformed the number string into alphabetic order following the rules:

[8] Again, we used the term "variation" in the sense of melodic variation in music studies.

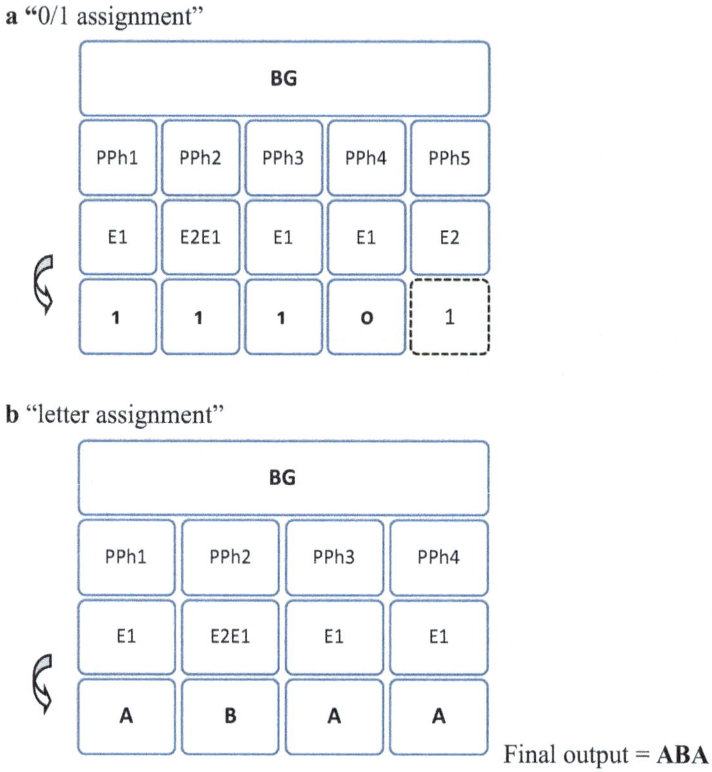

Fig. 24.2 (**a**) Illustration of convergence procedures: Steps One and Two; (**b**) illustration of convergence procedures: Steps Three and Four

- The first PPh without any relative value was always set as "A".
- If the following PPh corresponded to an ET pattern that was different from any of the ET patterns that had already occurred, a new letter was assigned; otherwise, the PPh corresponding to a repeating ET pattern was labeled with the same letter.[9]

Step Four. The alphabetic sequence was further narrowed down via collapsing two or more occurrences of the same letter into one so that the final output was derived.

[9]Figure 24.2b demonstrates the "letter assignment" in Step Three. We took the first four PPhs in Figure 24.2a to illustrate the procedure of the letter assignment. As explained, whenever the following PPh corresponded to a different ET pattern, a new letter was assigned. As a result, the

Table 24.2 Chunking size by mean syllables

Genres	PW (SD)	PPh (SD)	BG (SD)	PG (SD)
CNA	2.2 (0.7)	7.5 (4.1)	24 (13)	78 (49)
WB	2.3 (0.5)	9.6 (5.2)	38 (24)	95 (66)
SpnL	2.4 (0.9)	7.3 (5.7)	121 (99)	629 (516)
SpnC	2.2 (0.9)	7.8 (7.0)	36 (29)	1160 (595)

SD standard deviation

Table 24.3 Chunking size by DPUs at the immediately lower level

Genres	PW/PPh (SD)	PPh/BG (SD)	BG/PG (SD)
CNA	3.27 (1.8)	3.29 (1.9)	3.17 (1.8)
WB	4.20 (2.2)	4.00 (3.1)	2.47 (1.6)
SpnL	3.11 (2.3)	16.60 (13.7)	5.17 (3.8)
SpnC	3.60 (2.8)	3.34 (3.2)	44.44 (13.8)

SD standard deviation

24.4 Cross-Genre Comparison of Discourse-Prosodic Unit Size and Preliminary Convergence of Emphasis Token Patterns

24.4.1 Chunking Size

First, we calculated the chunking size of the discourse-prosodic units (DPUs) at each HPG level. The purpose of the estimation, on the one hand, was to provide information regarding the planning size of DPUs; on the other hand, the summary served as a reference point for following analyses. The chunking size was calculated by the average number of syllables within each unit (see Table 24.2). The results were further validated by calculating the size of each discourse-prosodic level by the unit immediately lower than the current one (see Table 24.3).

Discussion

As shown in Tables 24.2 and 24.3, we found that the chunking sizes of units below the PPh level (inclusive of PW) were rather consistent across the different speech genres. Moving up to the higher levels of BG and PG, however, the sizes of the planning units varied significantly. Most of all, at the BG and PG levels of SpnL and SpnC, the chunking size differed drastically, and this was mainly reflected in the largest planning size at the BG level in SpnL and the largest planning size at the PG level in SpnC, respectively. Based on this observation, clearly the distinction

final alphabetic sequence was not limited to merely A/B combinations as illustrated in Figure 24.2b, as more complex patterns did exist.

Table 24.4 (a) Summary of total number of ET patterns (without E0); (b) summary of total number of ET patterns (with E0)

(a)				(b)		
DPU/ET pattern	CNA	WB	SpnL	DPU/ET pattern	SpnL	SpnC
# of PPh	3065	1467	4535	**# of PPh**	4535	1379
# of ET patterns (w/o E0)	46	32	72	**# of ET patterns (with E0)**	219	161

between the read and spontaneous speeches was mainly in the planning size, especially in terms of higher level DPUs. In the end, cross-genre comparison pinpointed specifically the largest DPU for speech planning across all data, namely, the multiple-phrase discourse-based unit PG in spontaneous conversation.

24.4.2 Summary of Emphasis Token Patterns in the Prosodic Phrase PPh

This section will summarize the total number of emphasis token patterns in PPh across speech genres. The results are listed in Table 24.4a and b, without and with E0 annotation, respectively[10].

Discussion

Table 24.4a demonstrates that the ET patterns derived from the lecture speech SpnL outnumbered that of CNA and WB. Most of all, the number of patterns identified by PPh for SpnL was twice as many as those identified in the read speeches. This finding is actually in line with results previously reported in Tseng and Su (2012) and thus has already shown the richer varieties in emphasis patterns used in SpnL. When taking into consideration the annotation of reduction in Table 24.4b, the results showed a significant increase in the varieties of ET patterns in both spontaneous speeches. Interestingly, for SpnL alone, the ET patterns with reduction were almost three times that of the total patterns without E0 annotation. While it is within expectations that adding one more level to the prominence annotation would lead to an increase in the varieties of emphasis token combinations and hence total number of ET patterns, the results nevertheless show the enriched nature of expressiveness in spontaneous speeches based solely on ET pattern counts.

[10]Since the spontaneous speeches SpnL and SpnC were annotated with the reduction E0, we calculated the total number of ET patterns separately for the read and lecture speeches together (see Table 24.4a, without reduction) and spontaneous speeches (see Table 24.4b, with reduction).

24.4.3 Distribution of Emphasis Token Patterns

To follow up on the results above, we attempted the preliminary convergence or clustering of ET patterns to find out the distribution of major emphasis patterns across speech genres. Previously, Tseng and Su (2012) provided similar analyses regarding genre-related prosodic expressiveness by examining the distribution of emphasis token patterns.[11] In their study (Tseng and Su 2012), it was reported that six unique patterns could be derived out of 70% of PPhs across the speech data from CNA, WB, and SpnL (i.e., the same speeches used in our study). It was further demonstrated that these shared ET patterns across speech data actually took on quite distinct and diverse distributions from genre to genre (Tseng and Su 2012).[12] To take this work a step further, we paid particular attention to the spontaneous speeches, namely, the lecture SpnL and conversation SpnC data, and simultaneously took into consideration the annotation of reduction. Figure 24.3 thus presents the frequency count of the most commonly occurring ET patterns and their distributions in PPh.

Discussion

In Fig. 24.3, first, aside from the pattern "other," about 60 to 70% of both spontaneous speech data could be accounted for over six major emphasis token (ET) patterns. Among them, four patterns were shared, namely, "E1," "E2 E1," "E1 E0 E1," and "E2." The other two patterns were unique to each genre, respectively. From those shared patterns, the one composed solely of "E1" took on a significant proportion from both genres (SpnL: 42% vs. SpnC: 31%). Actually, in Tseng and Su (2012), it was indicated that "E1" would be the pattern that singled out spontaneous speech SpnL from the two read speeches.[13] The same observation still held when we added one more spontaneous conversation speech genre.

Outside of the "E1" pattern, we further noticed that none of the other five ET patterns took up more than 10% of the overall distribution. Yet another observation that stood out was the increasing usage of reduction. This was especially salient with SpnC, in which at least three out of six major ET patterns actually involved E0, including "E0 E1" (7%), "E0" (5%), and "E1 E0 E1" (4%). In other words, leaving "other" and "E1" patterns aside, for SpnC, at least 16% of the ET patterns were composed by E0. Compared with SpnL, only one major pattern, namely, "E1 E0 E1"

[11] In Tseng and Su (2012), the speech data incorporated in their analyses included the two read speech genres CNA and WB, as well as the spontaneous lecture SpnL. However, the degree of prominence levels did not cover reduction E0 in their study.

[12] In their findings, Tseng and Su (2012) suggested that the six major ET patterns are (1) "E1"; (2) "E2 E1"; (3) "E1 E2 E1"; (4) "E1 E2"; (5) "E2"; and (6) "E2 E1 E2". The cross-speech genre analyses showed that CNA and WB were further distinguished by the "E2 E1" and "E1 E2" patterns, respectively, whereas the lecture data was dominated by the "E1" pattern (Tseng and Su 2012).

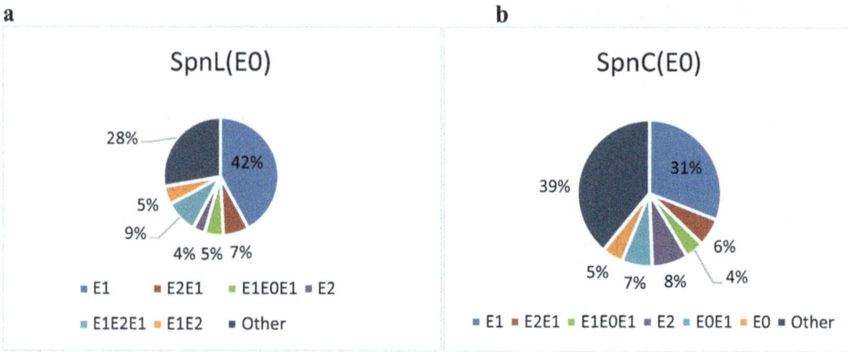

Fig. 24.3 (**a**) Commonly occurring ET patterns for SpnL; (**b**) commonly occurring ET patterns for SpnC

(5%), contained E0. Thus, the finding further established the prevailing use of reduction in SpnC as the token that distinguished the two spontaneous speeches.

Based on our analyses, not only did we sustain the observation that "E1" was the pattern that foregrounded the spontaneous speeches, it was also demonstrated that reduction was the perceived prominence level discriminating the two spontaneous speeches. While both spontaneous speeches incorporated E0, the proportion of patterns with reduction further distinguished the two genres. Moreover, to take the finding from Tseng and Su (2012) further, our analysis showed the unique role of reduction in spontaneous speeches, which could otherwise correspond to surface realizations such as fillers, filled pauses, and/or other semantically reduced elements. It has been suggested that elements with reduced prominence can fill in spaces between focal information allocations in ongoing speech planning and create sharper prosodic contrast for more varied expressiveness as a result of their reduced nature.

24.4.4 Interim Summary

In the preliminary cross-speech genre comparison, we started by examining the unit planning size at each HPG level. Then, we summarized the number of emphasis token patterns and the distribution of major ET patterns. In terms of planning size, a drastic difference in chunking sizes was demonstrated, especially at higher discourse levels in the spontaneous speeches. As for the number of ET patterns and their distribution, it was shown that expressiveness was reflected mainly in more varieties of ET patterns in both spontaneous speeches, as well as more major patterns with

[13] In Tseng and Su (2012), it was shown that the pattern "E1" only took up about 10% of the total ET patterns in CNA and WB, compared to about 39% of the "E1" pattern found in the total ET patterns in the SpnL data.

reduction, which further distinguished SpnL and SpnC. In the following, we will turn to the two experiments regarding speech expressiveness and discourse prosody.

24.5 Emphasis Weighting Scores of Expressiveness

The first experiment explored speech expressiveness by calculating emphasis weighting scores. As explicated in the Introduction section, this experiment was built on the hypothesis that the larger the discourse-prosodic unit size for speech planning, the heavier its information content load will be. A relevant rationale follows in that the unit of larger planning size corresponds to more room for ups and downs in the configuration of prosodic highlights for output production; hence, more expressiveness will be delivered through more complex information structures as a result of such deployment. To test this hypothesis, we carried out the calculation of the weighting scores of information allocation following the methodology described in Sect. 24.3.1.

24.5.1 Results

The average weighting scores of the discourse-prosody levels BG and PG[14] across all speech genres are summarized in Table 24.5. Furthermore, as explained in Sect. 24.3.1, when calculating the scores of information allocation, we initially combined reduction E0 with E1 tags in the perceived prominence annotations. However, considering that both SpnL and SpnC were annotated with reduction, we tried to adjust the weighting score assignment by reassigning a -1 value to all the E0 tags, while the scores assigned to E1 through E3 remained the same. Tables 24.5 and 24.6 present respectively the results of the mean scores for all four speeches and readjustment for SpnL and SpnC.

In Table 24.5, it is noteworthy that a clear distinction can be drawn between the two read speeches and spontaneous speeches. Specifically, both read speeches were noticeably distinguished from the spontaneous speeches according to the higher mean weighting scores and thus heavier information loading. Of the two read and spontaneous speeches, respectively, CNA (prose reading) and SpnL (classroom lecture) demonstrated higher mean scores and hence the most amount of information content at normalized BG and PG levels.

After readjusting the weighting score assignments, in Table 24.6, we found that the mean scores of SpnL were still larger than that of SpnC at both normalized BG and PG levels. Interestingly, when assigning E0 a negative score, the mean scores at

[14]The calculation of the weighting scores of information allocation was based on normalized BG/PG units.

Table 24.5 Summary of mean weighting scores of BG/PG across speech genres

Genres	BG-Mean[a] (SD)	PG-Mean[a] (SD)
CNA	0.49 (0.12)	0.49 (0.08)
WB	0.45 (0.11)	0.45 (0.07)
SpnL	0.22 (0.08)	0.22 (0.05)
SpnC	0.19 (0.21)	0.22 (0.04)

SD standard deviation
[a]In arbitrarily assigned weighting scores: E3 = 2; E2 = 1; E1=E0=0

Table 24.6 Summary of mean weighting scores of BG/PG for SpnL and SpnC after readjusting

Genres	BG-Mean[a] (SD)	PG-Mean[a] (SD)
SpnL	0.14 (0.10)	0.13 (0.06)
SpnC	0.01 (0.28)	0.03 (0.08)

SD standard deviation
[a]Inarbitrarily assigned weighting scores: E3 = 2; E2 = 1; E1 = 0; E0 = −1

Table 24.7 Summary of actual amount of information content at BG/PG levels across speech genres

Genres	BG	PG
CNA	1.62	5.15
WB	1.79	4.43
SpnL	3.73	18.61
SpnC	0.63	32.56

normalized BG/PG levels for SpnC dropped significantly; compared with Table 24.5, there was a drop from 0.19 to 0.01 at the BG level and 0.22 to 0.03 at the PG level. After reassignment, the mean scores at the BG/PG levels for SpnC approached 0. In other words, when taking reduction into consideration, information loading at both levels in SpnC dropped to the minimum.

Given that the results in Tables 24.5 and 24.6 are based on mean weighting scores at normalized BG/PG levels, we wondered what the actual amount of information load at these levels would be. Thus, we carried out one additional calculation to find out the actual amount of information load at these levels by simply multiplying the results of the mean scores from Table 24.5 by the chunking size reported in Table 24.3. The findings are provided in Table 24.7.

At the BG level, the actual amount of information through comparison can be stated as SpnL > SpnC for the spontaneous speeches and WB > CNA for the read speeches. Surprisingly, moving up to the multiple-phrase discourse-oriented PG level, we found that the rank was reversed as SpnC carried the most amount of information content. When cross-referring to the chunking size of the discourse-prosodic units summarized in Table 24.3, recalling that it was SpnL at the BG level and SpnC at the PG level, respectively, that corresponded to the largest chunking size. The results therefore confirmed our hypothesis that the larger planning size of the discourse-prosodic unit entailed heavier information content loading. The correlation between perceived prominence and information weighting thus led to the further establishment of information loading as a direct association with the discourse unit size in planning during speech production.

24.5.2 *Discussion*

After calculating the emphasis weighting scores, the results from our experiment demonstrated that at normalized BG/PG levels, a clear distinction could be drawn between the read and spontaneous speeches. Considering that the original annotation scheme of perceived prominence did include reduction in the spontaneous speeches, we otherwise singled out E0 and arbitrarily assigned a negative score to it. In the end, the recalculation reflected the average scores at the BG/PG levels as approaching 0 in SpnC, which was the speech genre with the most spontaneity. This was most likely due to the incorporation of far more reduced tokens in SpnC. The observation also echoes the findings of the richer variations in emphasis patterns identified and patterns with reduction in SpnC as discussed in Sect. 24.4.3. In terms of surface realizations, again, this corresponded to the more frequent uses of reduced fragments, such as fillers, in the conversation data.

The proposed hypothesis of perceived prominence correlated with information weighting was confirmed through the calculation of the actual amount of information load of the discourse-based units at the BG/PG levels. Interestingly, our findings illustrated that for SpnC, only at the highest discourse-prosodic level did we find a correspondence of the largest amount of information load. Most of all, it was only by comparing multiple speech genres that we were able to arrive at this conclusion. On the other hand, the results indicated that at the BG level, SpnL and WB, respectively, carried the most amount of information. Therefore, the comparison based on different levels in the hierarchical prosody-based framework enabled the identification of discrepancy in planning size as the major factor contributing to the amount of information load in summation. Overall, the same evidence further illustrates the contribution and significance of large-scale discourse-level context prosody.

24.6 Emphasis Pattern Convergence for Discourse Prosody

The second experiment examined discourse prosody in Mandarin speeches through the method of convergence, which merged prosodic highlight patterns from lower-level discourse-prosodic units. This experiment attempted convergence, with the ultimate goal of identifying representations of discourse-level prosody, following the assumption that only coarsely-graded prosodic contrastiveness is required for prosodic realization at higher discourse levels. In addition to exploring the convergence of perceived prosodic highlight allocations, we also looked at factors that influenced the successful narrowing down of emphasis patterns, as well as factors for the divergence found among patterns that could not be merged further.

24.6.1 Converging Perceived Emphasis Token Patterns at the BG Level

Following the methodology in Sect. 24.3.2, we started by testing the feasibility of converging the ET patterns at lower-level PPh for the relative prosodic variations at the BG level. Table 24.8 summarizes the number of patterns/variations before/after the convergence. The distribution of converged emphasis variations is also presented in Fig. 24.4.

Results

Table 24.8 demonstrates that the number of variations after the convergence were narrowed down considerably, except for the spontaneous lecture SpnL. As for the other three speech genres, we were able to narrow down around 70% to 85% of the perceived emphasis patterns, and the number of variations identified was around 50. Turning to Fig. 24.4, we found that these 50 or so emphasis patterns in CNA/WB/SpnC were distributed among a limited number of variations. Aside from the category "other," at least 80% of the emphasis patterns were merged into four major variations in common, namely, "A," "AB," "ABC," and "ABA." Therefore, convergence worked effectively in merging emphasis patterns into identifiable prosodic variations at the BG level for discourse prosody.

Table 24.8 Summary of the number of perceived emphasis patterns before and after convergence

Pattern/variation	CNA	WB	SpnL	SpnC
#Before converging	373	201	454	181
# After converging	56	52	205	52

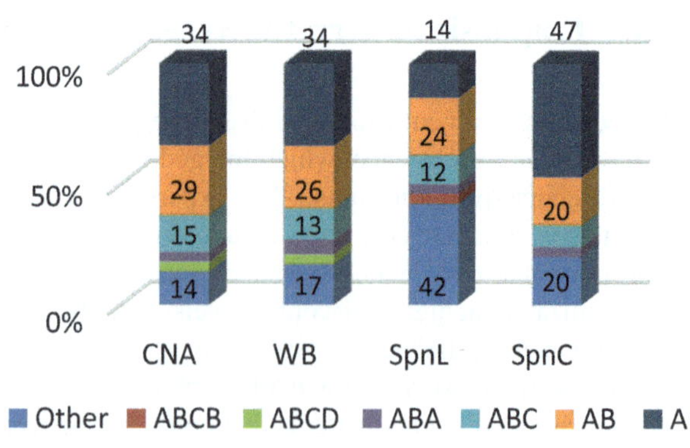

Fig. 24.4 Distribution of prosodic variations after convergence at the BG level

Discussion

The results above exhibit the successful convergence of perceived ET patterns for discourse prosody following the proposed methodology. As for the spontaneous classroom lecture SpnL, surprisingly, it was an exception and we were able to narrow down about only half of the emphasis patterns. Turning to distribution, although those four major variations identified in the other three genres still held for SpnL, at least 40% of the patterns were from the category "other," meaning that they could not be merged further. To uncover the reason for the incongruity of SpnL, we considered two possible contributing factors: (i) annotation of reduction in perceived prominence levels and (ii) differences in chunking sizes of discourse-prosodic units. We examined them in the following tests.

24.6.2 Considering Reduction for Convergence

We first tested whether reduction (E0) might be responsible for the divergence found in the results for SpnL. As was demonstrated in Sect. 24.4.2, the addition of the E0 tag to both spontaneous speeches indeed led to an increase in varieties of ET patterns. Thus, we followed up by testing whether the merging of tags E0 and E1 in the spontaneous speeches contributed to a better result after convergence. In other words, we tried to find out whether the emphasis patterns could be further merged after decreasing the contrastive levels in the perceived prominence annotations from a four-way distinction down to three.

Results

We first combined E0 and E1 tags into one level, followed by the execution of the same convergence procedures. The results are presented in Fig. 24.5:

In Fig. 24.5, we found that the four major variations as a result of convergence remained unchanged. Moreover, the percentages in the category "other" for SpnL and SpnC were indeed narrowed down. A cross-comparison with Fig. 24.4, however, indicated that by combining E1 and E0, it did not seem to contribute to an effective convergence (i.e., the proportion in the category "other" could only be narrowed down by less than 10%: for SpnL, it dropped from 42% to 33% and for SpnC from 20% to 13%). In the end, decreasing the perceived prominence levels did not seem to be a major factor in changing the overall results.

Discussion

Our first attempt at improving the results of the convergence procedures focused on narrowing down the prominence levels to a three-way distinction. As a result, the major prosodic variations remained the same and the proportion in the category "other" did not change much. Most of all, this still did not offer a satisfying explanation of why SpnL would be the style with the most divergent "other" category across all genres. It was thus concluded that decreasing prominence levels did not have a significant impact on the convergence of emphasis patterns.

24.6.3 Converging Perceived Emphasis Token Patterns at the PG Level

The second test examined whether the results above might be related to the planning size at different discourse-prosodic levels. Following the same convergence procedures, we attempted the feasibility of merging the relative prosodic highlight patterns at the top discourse-based PG level. The results are presented in Fig. 24.6.

Results

Figure 24.6 exhibits that after convergence, the major variations were further narrowed down to only three, namely "A," "AB," and "ABC." However, none of those took up more than 25% of the overall distribution within each genre. Another noticeable finding was that the proportion in the "other" category increased significantly, which could be understood as the patterns derived as a result of convergence were simply too diverse to be collapsed into one unique variation.

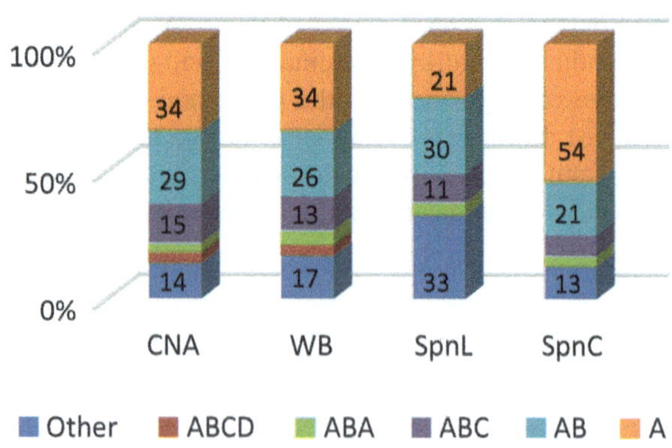

Fig. 24.5 Distribution of prosodic variations after convergence based on combining E1 and E0 (The percentages were excluded in this figure if they were under 10%)

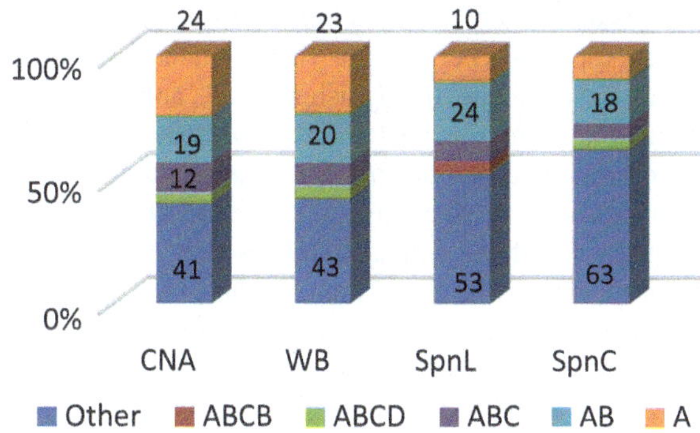

Fig. 24.6 Distribution of prosodic variations after convergence at the PG level (The percentages were excluded in this figure if they were under 10%)

Discussion

In the second test, we attempted convergence at the PG level, and the results illustrated that convergence yielded three shared variations, although none accounted for more than a quarter of the overall distribution. From the growing number of patterns in the category "other," it was clearly shown that at the PG level the SpnC data displayed the largest proportion of emphasis patterns after converging (e.g., 63% of the emphasis patterns were simply different from one another and could not be further merged into a unique variation). Interestingly, turning to the chunking size of the discourse-prosodic units summarized in Tables 24.2 and 24.3, SpnC indeed corresponded to the largest planning unit at the top PG level. These findings, therefore, demonstrate most notably that the larger the chunking size, the more diverse variations we should arrive at after convergence. One of the key factors influencing the successful convergence of prosodic highlights, therefore, was the chunking size (i.e., how speakers plan for the unit at each discourse-prosodic level). When the size of higher-level discourse units grew, it involved more complex production planning and allowed for more room to manipulate and allocate the ups and downs of intonation contours, which resulted in divergence. This provided solid explanations for why we found the highest percentage of the category "other" at the BG level in SpnL, while at the PG level it was found in SpnC.

24.7 General Discussion and Summary

Our study centered on perceived prominence patterns for speech expressiveness in relation to discourse prosody in continuous Mandarin speeches. Our analyses and experiments were framed by the comparison across continuous speeches of diverse genres, which underwent the same annotation procedures for discourse-prosodic units from the hierarchical HPG framework and perceived prominences in limited contrastive degrees. Using quantitative analysis, we preliminarily merged emphasis patterns at the PPh level and the results pinpointed major differences across speech genres, especially between the two spontaneous speeches. While identifying reduction as the main cue distinguishing SpnL and SpnC, we further explored the role of reduction. From the viewpoint of perception, the more frequently incorporated reductions were responsible for creating larger contrasts in the physical signals from surface realizations. As a consequence, frequent reductions further foregrounded those emphasis tokens that carried actual prominence, resulting in enriched expressiveness. Thus, by the initial clustering of emphasis patterns, we identified how the contrastiveness in prominence perceived from speech signals contributes to expressiveness.

Turning to the two experiments, one of the shared observations involved the role of planning size among discourse-prosodic units at different levels. In the first experiment, we substantiated the hypothesis regarding the positive correlation between perceived prominence and information weighting, showing that the most spontaneous type of speech genre carried the largest amount of information loading but only when examined at the highest discourse level and in the largest planning unit. A noteworthy uptake of the validation was that the data with the most spontaneity should not be treated simply as unplanned and random speech production. On the contrary, spontaneity is reflected in well-preplanned, goal-oriented interaction, in which speakers accommodate large quantities of information to reach projected goals and thus communicate efficiently.

Moreover, in the second experiment, we attempted the convergence of prominence patterns. In addition to successfully narrowing down prosodic highlight variations, it was further identified that planning size was directly associated with the divergence found in the category "other" (i.e., patterns could not be merged further). Again, what we found in common regarding planning size was that the larger discourse-prosodic unit size from higher levels implied more complex production planning and room needed for configuring the ups and downs of pitch contours. Most of all, these findings would not have surfaced had we only examined fragments lifted out of only one type of speech data, nor would we have made these observations had we left out the discourse-level context or simply examined each discourse-prosodic unit in isolation. In short, we provided a systematic account of the composition of global prosody and the reason behind phrasal intonational variations that seem to be highly varied on the surface in continuous speech prosody. These accounts offer solid explications of why, in realistic speech, meta forms require modifications.

Finally, parallel to motivic similarity found in music perception (Patel 2008), our second experiment showed that perceived prosodic highlight allocations could be converged in reflecting the nature of overall discourse prosody. Above all, the discussion of discourse prosody focused on the granularity of intonational variations grounded in prosodic contrastiveness, which was realized at only a limited number of levels. Although speech signals in their surface realizations were deemed highly variant, we were able to locate and pinpoint from their surface realizations limited and invariant patterns for higher-level discourse- and context-based prosody. Based on these findings, for future research we plan to explore further how information load and coarsely defined context prosody via convergence interact more precisely with the allocation of information by content and status. Particular interests have been drawn to contrastiveness as a result of perceived "ups" and "downs" in speech signals, in which the "ups" from the prosodic highlights have been shown to associate with information projection, and we are currently working on the "downs" such as prosodic reduction. We believe that these ups and downs co-construct contrastiveness and belong to part of the blueprint of context prosody. As for implementation, we aim to incorporate the exploration of expressiveness in spontaneous speech as well as the features of discourse prosody in speech understanding, recognition, modeling, and synthesis for speech technology.

References

't Hart, Johan, René Collier, and Antonie Cohen. 1990. *A perceptual study of intonation: An experimental-phonetic approach to speech melody*. Cambridge: Cambridge University Press.

Baumann, Stefan, Oliver Niebuhr, and Bastian Schroeter. 2016. Acoustic cues to perceived prominence levels: Evidence from German spontaneous speech. In *Proceedings of Speech Prosody 2016*, 711-715. Boston, Massachusetts.

Boersma, Paul, and David Weenink. 2015. *Praat: Doing phonetics by computer*. www.praat.org. (20 Nov, 2015.)

Campbell, Nick. 2002. Labeling natural conversational speech data. Paper presented at the *2002 Autumn Meeting of Acoustic Society of Japan (ASJ)*, 273-274. Akita, Japan

Chen, Helen K. Y., Laurent Prévot, Roxane Bertrand, Béatrice Priego-Valverde, and Philippe Blache. 2012. Toward a Mandarin-French corpus of interactional data. Paper presented at the *16th Workshop on the Semantics and Pragmatics of Dialogues*. Paris, France.

Erickson, Donna. 2005. Expressive speech: Production, perception and application to speech synthesis. *Acoustical Science and Technology* 26:317-325.

Fujisaki, Hiroya. 2004. Prosody, information, and modeling—With emphasis on tonal features of speech. In *Proceedings of Speech Prosody 2004*, ed. Bernard Bel and Isabelle Marlien, 1-10. Nara, Japan.

Halliday, Michael A. K. 1970. *A course in spoken English: Intonation*. London: Oxford University Press.

Kohler, Klaus J. 1997. Modelling prosody in spontaneous speech. In *Computing prosody*, ed. Sagisaka, Yoshinori, Nick Campbell, and Norio Higuchi, 187-210. New York: Springer.

Patel, Aniruddh D. 2008. *Music, language, and the brain*. New York: Oxford University Press.

de Saussure, Ferdinand. 1966. *Course in general linguistics*. (Wade Baskin, Trans.). New York: McGraw-Hill Book Company.

Silverman, Kim E., Mary Beckman, John Pitrelli, Mari Ostendorf, Colin Wightman, Patti Price, Janet B. Pierrehumbert, and Julia Hirschberg. 1992. ToBI: A standard for labeling English prosody. In *Proceedings of the 2nd International Conference on Spoken Language Processing* (ICSLP) 2: 867-870. Alberta, Canada.

Tatham, Mark, and Katherine Morton. 2004. *Expressive in speech: analysis and synthesis*. New York: Oxford University Press.

Tseng, Chiu-yu 鄭秋豫. 2010. An F0 analysis of discourse construction and global information in realized narrative prosody 語篇的基頻構組與語流韻律體現. *Language and Linguistics 語言暨語言學 11:183-218.*

Tseng, Chiu-yu. 2013. Output prosody—How information highlights are piggybacked by discourse structure. *Zhongguo Yuyin Xuebao 中國語音學報 4:109-124.*

Tseng, Chiu-yu, and Chao-yu Su. 2008. Discourse prosody and context—Global F0 and tempo modulations. In *Proceedings of Interspeech 2008*, 1200-1203. Brisbane, Australia.

Tseng, Chiu-yu, and Chao-yu Su. 2012. Information allocation and prosodic expressiveness in continuous speech: A Mandarin cross-genre analysis. In *Proceedings of the 8th International Symposium on Chinese Spoken Language (ISCSLP 2012)*, 243-246. Hong Kong.

Tseng, Chiu-yu, and Chao-yu Su. 2014. Where and how to make an emphasis? —L2 distinct prosody and why. In *Proceedings of the 9th International Symposium on Chinese Spoken Language (ISCSLP 2014)*, 633-637. Singapore.

Tseng, Chiu-yu, Yun-ching Cheng, Wei-shan Lee, and Feng-lan Huang. 2003. Collecting Mandarin speech databases for prosody investigation. In *Proceedings of the Oriental COCOSDA 2003*, 225-232. Singapore.

Tseng, Chiu-yu, Yun-Ching Cheng, and Chun-Hsiang Chang. 2005a. Sinica COSPRO and toolkit—Corpora and platform of Mandarin Chinese fluent speech. In *Proceedings of the Oriental COCOSDA 2005*, 23-28. Jakarta, Indonesia.

Tseng, Chiu-yu, Shao-huang Pin, Yeh-lin Lee, Hsin-min Wang, and Yong-cheng Chen. 2005b. Fluent speech prosody: Framework and modeling. *Speech Communication* 46:284-309.

Tseng, Chiu-yu, Lin-shan Lee, and Chao-yu Su. 2008. Spontaneous Mandarin speech prosody—the NTU DSP lecture corpus. In *Proceedings of the Oriental COCOSDA*, 171-174. Kyoto, Japan.

Tseng, Chiu-yu, Chao-yu Su, and Chi-Feng Huang. 2011. Prosodic highlights in Mandarin continuous speech—Cross-genre attributes and implications. In *Proceedings of Interspeech 2011*, 1381-1384. Florence, Italy.

Wichmann, Anne. 2014. *Intonation in text and discourse: Beginnings, middles and ends*. London: Routledge.

Part IV
Language Processing: Models and Applications

Chapter 25
Speech Recognition and Text-to-Speech Synthesis

Lifa Sun, Shiyin Kang, Xunying Liu, and Helen Meng

Abstract Automatic speech recognition (ASR) and text-to-speech (TTS) synthesis are two very important modules in human-computer communication. With the development of deep learning, the performance of ASR and TTS has improved significantly. In this chapter, widely used deep models will be introduced, including restricted Boltzmann machines (RBMs), deep belief networks (DBNs) and deep neural networks (DNNs), recurrent neural networks (RNNs), and long short-term memory recurrent neural networks (LSTM-RNNs), as well as their applications in ASR and TTS. The experimental results suggest that the accuracy of ASR and the speech quality of TTS can be improved.

Keywords Automatic speech recognition · Text-to-speech synthesis · Deep learning · Hidden Markov models

25.1 Introduction

Human-computer communication via speech has long been the desideratum of natural user interfaces. Speech input into computers is supported by automatic speech recognition (ASR), and speech output from computers is generated by text-to-speech (TTS) synthesis. ASR technologies must achieve high performance accuracies, while TTS technologies must achieve high degrees of intelligibility and naturalness. Both are challenging problems, as will be elaborated later. The Chinese language presents a unique context and related challenges for the research and development of speech technologies, such as its tonal syllable structure, lack of word delimiters, and ambiguities in the mapping between the written system (i.e., characters) and the spoken system (i.e., syllables). State-of-the-art deep learning

L. Sun (✉) · S. Kang · X. Liu · H. Meng
Department of Systems Engineering and Engineering Management, The Chinese University of Hong Kong, Hong Kong, China
e-mail: lfsun@dailylive.cn; shiyin.kang@kunlun-inc.com; xyliu@se.cuhk.edu.hk; hmmeng@se.cuhk.edu.hk

C.-R. Huang et al. (eds.), *Chinese Language Resources*, Text, Speech and Language Technology 49, https://doi.org/10.1007/978-3-031-38913-9_25

approaches have presented elegant and computationally efficient models for ASR and TTS, with significant performance improvements.

The following sections are organized as follows. Section 25.2 will review major deep models and architectures, while Sect. 25.3 will present an introduction to the Gaussian mixture model and hidden Markov model (GMM-HMM), as well as ASR systems. Section 25.4 will provide an overview of TTS systems, and Sect. 25.5 will present a brief discussion of the approaches and models used in the experiments. Finally, Sect. 25.6 will close the chapter with a summary and conclusion.

25.2 Basic Models for Deep Learning

Deep learning is a branch of machine learning based on learning representations of data whose architectures are composed of multiple levels of non-linear operations, such as neural networks with many hidden layers. Deep learning has a significant advantage of modeling highly complex unstructured sequences. In this section, we will introduce several basic deep architectures, including unconditional models, such as restricted Boltzmann machines (RBMs) (Smolensky 1986) and deep belief networks (DBNs) (Hinton et al. 2006), and conditional models, such as deep neural networks (DNNs) (Hinton and Salakhutdinov 2006), recurrent neural networks (RNNs) (Rumelhart et al. 1985; Schuster and Paliwal 1997), and long short-term memory recurrent neural networks (LSTM-RNNs) (Hochreiter and Schmidhuber 1997).

25.2.1 *Restricted Boltzmann Machines*

An RBM is a particular type of Markov random field (i.e., an undirected graphical model) that has one layer of stochastic visible units and one layer of stochastic hidden units. This two-layered architecture can model the dependency among a set of random variables. In an RBM, visible stochastic units $\boldsymbol{v} = [v_1, \ldots, v_V]^{\mathrm{T}}$ are connected to hidden stochastic units $\boldsymbol{h} = [h_1, \ldots, h_H]^{\mathrm{T}}$, as shown in Fig. 25.1,

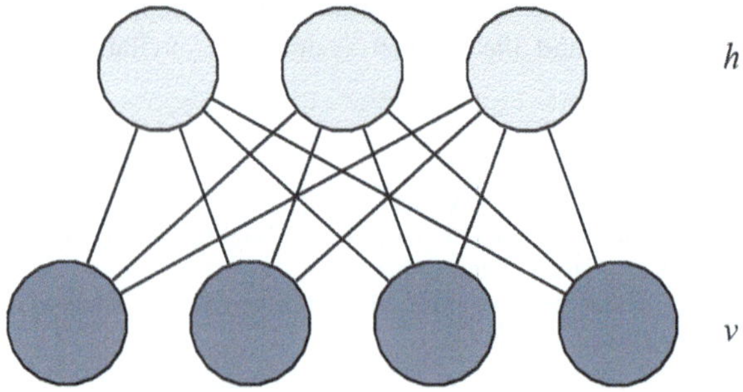

Fig. 25.1 Graphical model representation of an RBM

where h and v are the number of units at the hidden and visible layers, respectively. According to the type of visible stochastic units $\boldsymbol{v}$, RBM can be divided into Bernoulli RBM (B-RBM), Gaussian RBM (G-RBM), Gaussian-Bernoulli RBM (GB-RBM), and Categorical-Bernoulli RBM (CB-RBM).

25.2.2 Bernoulli RBM

For a B-RBM, $\boldsymbol{v} \in \{0, 1\}^V$ and $\boldsymbol{h} \in \{0, 1\}^H$ are both binary stochastic variables. The energy function $\{\boldsymbol{v}, \boldsymbol{h}\}$ is defined in Eq. (25.1),

$$E(\boldsymbol{v}, \boldsymbol{h}; \Theta) = -\boldsymbol{h}^T \boldsymbol{W} \boldsymbol{v} - \boldsymbol{a}^T \boldsymbol{h} - \boldsymbol{b}^T \boldsymbol{v} \tag{25.1}$$

where $\Theta = (\boldsymbol{W}, \boldsymbol{a}, \boldsymbol{b})$ is the set of model parameters, $\boldsymbol{W}$ represents the symmetric interaction between $\boldsymbol{v}$ and $\boldsymbol{h}$, $\boldsymbol{a}$ is the hidden unit bias, and $\boldsymbol{b}$ is the visible unit bias. The conditional probability density function can be calculated as shown in Eqs. (25.2) and (25.3) (a detailed derivation process can be found in Li 2015),

$$p(h_j = 1 | \boldsymbol{v}; \Theta) = \frac{e^{a_j + \sum_i w_{ij} v_i}}{1 + e^{a_j + \sum_i w_{ij} v_i}} = \sigma\left(a_j + \sum_i^V w_{ij} v_i\right) \tag{25.2}$$

$$p(v_j = 1 | \boldsymbol{h}; \Theta) = \frac{e^{b_i + \sum_j w_{ij} h_j}}{1 + e^{b_i + \sum_j w_{ij} h_j}} = \sigma\left(b_i + \sum_j^H w_{ij} h_j\right) \tag{25.3}$$

where $\sigma(x) = (1 + e^{-x})^{-1}$.

The update rule for RBM parameters (e.g., w_{ij}) can be derived by taking the gradient of the $log\ p(\boldsymbol{v}|\Theta)$, defined in Eq. (25.4),

$$\Delta w_{ij} = \frac{\partial \log p(\boldsymbol{v}|\Theta)}{\partial w_{ij}} = E_{\text{data}}(v_i h_j) - E_{\text{model}}(v_i h_j) \tag{25.4}$$

where $E_{\text{data}}(v_i h_j)$ denotes the expectation observed in the training data and $E_{\text{model}}(v_i h_j)$ is the expectation under the distribution defined by the model. Because $E_{\text{model}}(v_i h_j)$ is intractable to compute directly, an efficient approximation method (i.e., contrastive divergence, CD) has been proposed, where $E_{\text{model}}(v_i h_j)$ is replaced by running the Gibbs sampler (Hinton 2002), as shown in Fig. 25.2:

$$hj^{(0)} \sim p\left(h_j | \mathbf{v}^{(0)}\right) h_j^{(1)} \sim p\left(h_j | \mathbf{v}^{(1)}\right) h_j^{(\infty)}.$$

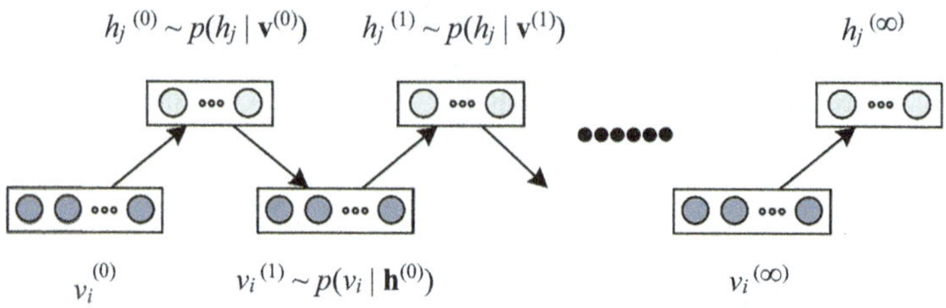

Fig. 25.2 Graphical representation of Gibbs sampling

25.2.3 Other RBMs

For a G-RBM, the type of visible units is under Gaussian distribution (real-valued data, e.g., mel-frequency cepstral coefficients, MFCCs, in ASR). The visible units in a GB-RBM are a mixture of real-valued data (under Gaussian distribution) and binary data (under Bernoulli distribution). For a CB-RBM, the visible units are a mixture of categorical data (e.g., some linguistic context features in TTS) and binary data. Different RBMs have different forms of energy functions (Kang et al. 2013; Ling et al. 2015). Here, we will use a G-RBM as an example of the other types of RBMs. For a G-RBM, which means $v \in \mathcal{R}^V$ are real-valued and $h \in \{0,1\}^H$ are binary, the energy function is defined Eq. (25.5),

$$E(\boldsymbol{v},\boldsymbol{h};\Theta) = -\boldsymbol{h}^T\,\boldsymbol{W}\,\mathrm{diag}(\boldsymbol{\sigma})^{-1}\boldsymbol{v} + \frac{\mathbf{1}}{\mathbf{2}}(\boldsymbol{v}-\boldsymbol{\mu})^T\,\mathrm{diag}\left(\boldsymbol{\sigma}^2\right)^{-1}(\boldsymbol{v}-\boldsymbol{\mu}) - \boldsymbol{a}^T\boldsymbol{h} \tag{25.5}$$

where μ is the mean of $\boldsymbol{v}$ and diag($\boldsymbol{\sigma}$) is the diagonal covariance matrix of $\boldsymbol{v}$. For simplicity, diag($\boldsymbol{\sigma}$) is commonly fixed to an identity matrix. Then, the energy is modified, as shown in Eq. (25.6),

$$E(\boldsymbol{v},\boldsymbol{h};\Theta) = -\boldsymbol{h}^T\,\boldsymbol{W}^{-1}\boldsymbol{v} + \frac{\mathbf{1}}{\mathbf{2}}(\boldsymbol{v}-\boldsymbol{\mu})^T\,\mathrm{diag}\left(\boldsymbol{\sigma}^2\right)^{-1}(\boldsymbol{v}-\boldsymbol{\mu}) - \boldsymbol{a}^T\boldsymbol{h} \tag{25.6}$$

While training a G-RBM using the CD algorithm, the two conditional probability density functions (PDFs) for Gibbs sampling are derived as Eqs. (25.7) and (25.8),

$$p\left(h_j = 1|\boldsymbol{v};\Theta\right) = \sigma\left(a_j + \sum_i^V w_{ij}v_i\right) \tag{25.7}$$

$$p\left(v_j|\boldsymbol{h};\Theta\right) = \mathcal{N}\left(\mu_i + \sum_j^H w_{ij}h_j, 1\right) \tag{25.8}$$

where σ is a sigmoid function and $\mathcal{N}$ is a Gaussian function.

25.2.4 Deep Belief Networks

A DBN is a probabilistic generative model that is composed of many layers of hidden units (Hinton et al. 2006). DBNs can be viewed as a composition of stacked RBMs, as shown in Fig. 25.3. The top two layers have an undirected, symmetric connection between them, while the lower layers receive top-down, directed connections to generate the visible units. In this model, abstract features can be learned from complex unstructured data. A DBN with $L + 1$ layers models the joint distribution over the visible and hidden units, as shown in Eq. (25.9):

$$P\left(v, \mathbf{h}^{(0)}, \ldots, \mathbf{h}^{(L)} \mid \Theta\right) = \mathrm{P}\left(v \mid \mathbf{h}^{(0)}, \Theta\right) \prod_{l=1}^{L-1} P\left(\mathbf{h}^{(l-1)} \mid \mathbf{h}^{(l)}, \Theta\right) \cdot P\left(\mathbf{h}^{(L-1)} \mid \mathbf{h}^{(L)}, \Theta\right) \tag{25.9}$$

where $P(\boldsymbol{h}^{(l-1)} \mid \boldsymbol{h}^{(l)}, \Theta)$ is a visible-given-hidden conditional distribution in the layer l RBM of the DBN, $P(\boldsymbol{h}^{(L-1)}, \boldsymbol{h}^{(L)} \mid \Theta)$ is the joint distribution in the top-level RBM, and $L + 1$ is the number of hidden layers, including the top one.

The generative model is defined by the conditional distribution $P(\boldsymbol{h}^{(l-1)} \mid \boldsymbol{h}^{(l)}, \Theta)$ and the top-level joint distribution (an RBM) $P(\boldsymbol{h}^{(L-1)}, \boldsymbol{h}^{(L)} \mid \Theta)$. Because of the complex model structure with many hidden layers, it is difficult to estimate the model parameters directly by the maximum likelihood (ML) criterion. A greedy

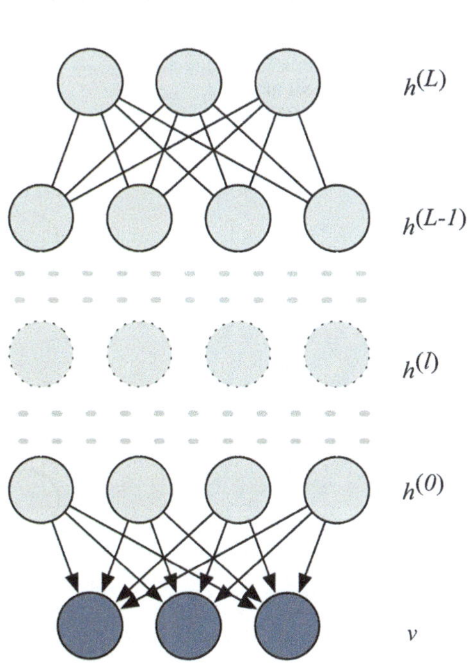

Fig. 25.3 Graphical model representation of a DBN

layer-wise learning algorithm has been proposed and widely applied to train DBNs (Hinton et al. 2006). First, we used the training algorithm (CD) to train the parameters ($\boldsymbol{W}^{(1)}$, $\boldsymbol{a}^{(1)}$, $\boldsymbol{b}^{(1)}$) of the first layer. Then, we fixed the first layer parameter ($\boldsymbol{a}_{(1)}$, $\boldsymbol{b}_{(1)}$) and derived samples from $p(\boldsymbol{h}^{(1)} \mid \boldsymbol{v}; \Theta)$ to train the parameters ($\boldsymbol{W}^{(2)}$, $\boldsymbol{a}^{(2)}$, $\boldsymbol{b}^{(2)}$) of the second layer. This training procedure continued until it reached the top layer.

Some of the major advantages of generative models (e.g., DBNs) are summarized as follows: (i) generative models can learn abstract features without any labels, which can obtain many more parameters than a discriminative model; and (ii) it is possible to interpret the non-linear representations in the deep hidden layers (Hinton et al. 2006; Salakhutdinov 2009).

25.2.5 Deep Neural Networks

A DNN is a feed-forward, artificial neural network (ANN) that has multiple hidden layers of units between its input and output layers (Hinton et al. 2012). DNN models the conditional probability density function of output given to the input (visible layer), while DBN models their joint probability density function. A model representation of a DNN is shown in Fig. 25.4:

Generally, the training process of a DNN can be divided into two stages (i.e., pre-training stage and fine-tuning stage). Pre-training a DNN is achieved by maximizing the average log-likelihood of each RBM, excluding the top one. This popular training technique is called contrastive divergence, as mentioned in the RBM and

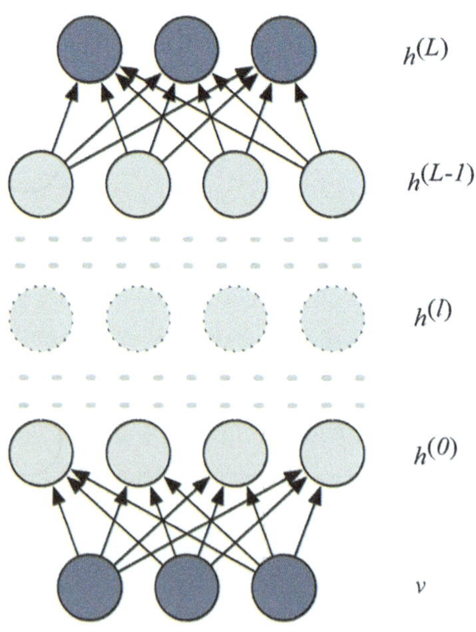

Fig. 25.4 Graphical model representation of a DNN

DBN sections. In the fine-tuning stage, the target (i.e., expected value) of the output layer is required. For example, the expected recognized words are the target of the output in ASR and the real output is the real value. Then, a cost function (e.g., cross-entropy error) is used to measure the distance between the expected value and the real value. The DNN model can be optimized in a supervised way by minimizing the cost function using the back-propagation algorithm (Rumelhart et al. 1986), which is divided into two phases: propagation and weight update.
Phase 1: Propagation

- Obtain the output from the initialized neural network using forward propagation.
- Compute the distance between the expected and real output values to generate the deltas using backward propagation.

Phase 2: Weight Update

- Calculate the gradient of the weight using the deltas.
- Update the current weight using a ratio of the gradient.

Phases 1 and 2 are repeated until convergence or a specific number of iterations is reached. The size of this ratio, called the learning rate, can influence learning speed and quality.

25.2.6 Recurrent Neural Networks

An RNN is a particular type of artificial neural network in which a directed cycle is used to connect between hidden units in the same layer. The idea behind RNNs is to make use of context dependency information in the sequence. In the other neural networks (e.g., DBNs and DNNs), it is assumed that all the inputs are independent of each other. For a standard RNN, given the input sequence $\boldsymbol{v} = (v_1,\ldots, v_T)$, the hidden vector $\boldsymbol{h} = (h_1,\ldots, h_T)$ and the output vector $\boldsymbol{y} = (y_1,\ldots, y_T)$ can be computed by $t = 1$ to T according to Eqs. (25.10) and (25.11),

$$h_t = H(W_{vhvt} + W_{hhht-1} + b_h) \tag{25.10}$$

$$y_t = W_{hy}h_t + b_y \tag{25.11}$$

where H is the activation function of the hidden layer, W is the weight matrix (e.g., W_{vh} is the input-hidden-weight matrix), and b is the bias vectors (e.g., b_h is the hidden bias vectors).

To make full use of the context of speech sequences in both preceding and succeeding directions, bidirectional RNNs (BRNNs) were proposed by Schuster and Paliwal (1997).

As shown in Fig. 25.5, BRNNs compute the forward sequence $\overleftarrow{h}$ and the backward sequence $\overrightarrow{h}$ by iterating the forward layer from $t = T$ to 1 and the

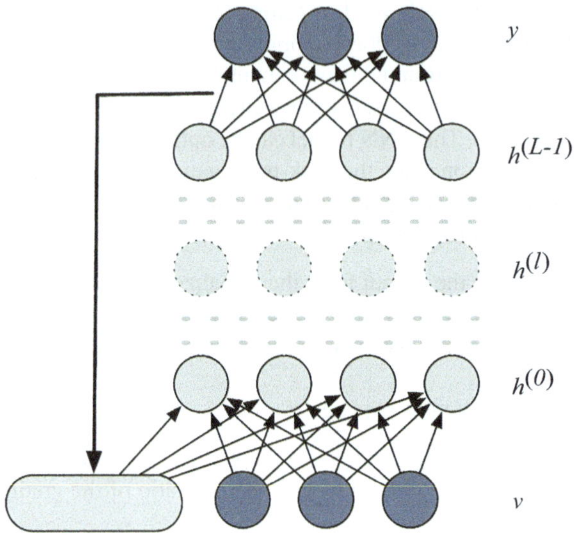

Fig. 25.5 Graphical model representation of an RNN

backward layer from $t = 1$ to T. The iterating functions are shown in Eqs. (25.12), (25.13), and (25.14):

$$\overrightarrow{h}_t = \mathcal{H}\left(W_{v\overrightarrow{h}} v_t + W_{\overrightarrow{h}\overrightarrow{h}} \overrightarrow{h}_{t-1} + b_{\overrightarrow{h}}\right) \tag{25.12}$$

$$\overleftarrow{h}_t = \mathcal{H}\left(W_{v\overleftarrow{h}} v_t + W_{\overleftarrow{h}\overleftarrow{h}} \overleftarrow{h}_{t+1} + b_{\overleftarrow{h}}\right) \tag{25.13}$$

$$y_t = W_{\overrightarrow{h}y} \overrightarrow{h}_t + W_{\overleftarrow{h}y} \overleftarrow{h}_t + b_y \tag{25.14}$$

25.3 Conventional GMM-HMM

The HMM is a statistical Markov model in which the observed data samples of a discrete-time series are characterized by a Markov process with hidden states. The HMM is widely used for modeling speech signals (e.g., automatic speech recognition, speech synthesis, speech enhancement, and spoken language understanding).

Figure 25.6 presents an example of a three-state, left-to-right HMM. In it, state-transition probabilities are represented by a_{ij}. For example, there are two options at *state-1*, the probability of moving to *state-1* is a_{11} and that of moving to *state-2* is a_{12}. Initial-state prob- abilities are denoted by π_i. State-output probabilities are represented by b_i. To simplify HMM modeling, b_i is assumed to be Gaussian distributions. All the parameters of HMM, including a_{ij}, b_i, and π_i, are represented by λ. The training process of HMM is shown in Eq. (25.15),

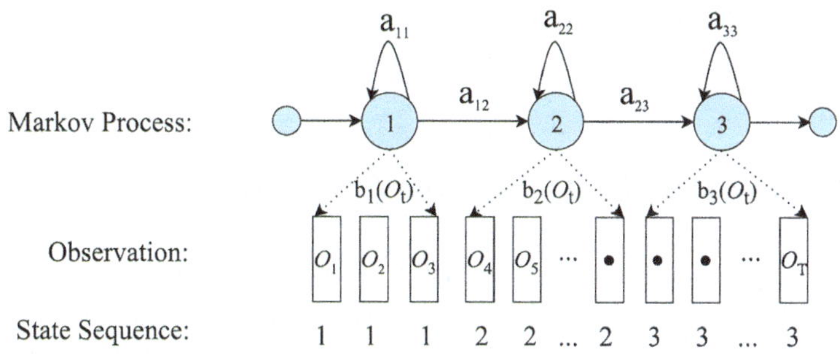

Fig. 25.6 Three-state, left-to-right HMM (Ling et al. 2015)

$$\lambda_{\max} = \frac{\operatorname{argmax} p(\boldsymbol{O} \mid \lambda, W)}{\lambda} \tag{25.15}$$

where $\boldsymbol{O} = \left[\boldsymbol{O}_1^T, \boldsymbol{O}_2^{\mathrm{T}}, \ldots, \boldsymbol{O}_T^{\mathrm{T}}\right]^{\mathrm{T}}$ and W are speech parameters (i.e., linguistic features). For speech recognition, speech parameters ω are computed by the observation sequence $\boldsymbol{O}$, as shown in Eq. (25.16); for speech synthesis, the observation sequence $\boldsymbol{O}$ is calculated by speech parameters ω, as shown in Eq. (25.17):

$$\boldsymbol{\omega}_{\max} = \frac{\operatorname{argmax} p(\boldsymbol{\omega} \mid \lambda_{\max}, \boldsymbol{O})}{\boldsymbol{\omega}} \tag{25.16}$$

$$\boldsymbol{O}_{\max} = \frac{\operatorname{argmax} p(\boldsymbol{O} \mid \lambda_{\max}, \boldsymbol{\omega})}{\boldsymbol{\omega}} \tag{25.17}$$

25.3.1 Automatic Speech Recognition Systems

This section will present an example of a state-of-the-art Mandarin Chinese ASR system featuring a range of deep learning approaches previously presented in Sect. 25.2. This Mandarin Chinese conversational telephone ASR system was developed by Cambridge University (CU) for the 2014 Defense Advanced Research Projects Agency (DARPA)-sponsored Broad Operational Language Translation (BOLT) evaluation. A range of advanced modeling techniques was employed to both improve the Chinese speech recognition performance and provide a suitable integration with the translation system that produced the final English outputs. These included an improved system combination technique using a frame-level acoustic model combination approach. The sequence level discriminatively trained the DNN hybrid, and tandem DNN-HMM systems were combined on-the-fly to produce consistent decoding output during the search. A multilevel paraphrastic RNNLM (language modeling) toolkit was also used to provide both alternative paraphrase expressions and character sequences while preserving consistent character-to-word segmentation.

25.3.2 Task Description and Data Resources

Acoustic models were trained with 301 h of Mandarin Chinese conversational telephone speech data released by the Linguistic Data Consortium (LDC) for the DARPA BOLT program, "bolt14train." These included 32 h of Call Home Mandarin data (CHM), 56 h of Call Friend Mandarin data (CFM), and an additional 213 h of Mandarin conversational telephone speech collected by the Hong Kong University of Science and Technology (HKUST). The training data set consisted of a total of 1479 conversations. Among these, 253 CHM and CFM conversations contained multiple speakers per conversation side. A 4.5-h BOLT development set of Mandarin Chinese conversational telephone speech data, "dev14," consisting of 57 speakers and a total of 19 conversations, was used for performance evaluation. Manual audio segmentation was also used to allow translation outputs to be accurately scored. A 72-h training subset of the 301-h full set used in the National Institute of Standards and Technology (NIST) Rich Transcription 2004 Evaluation (RT04) Mandarin system, "rt04train," and an associated 2-h development set, "dev04," containing 24 conversations were also used in the initial system development.

A word recognition list with 63,000 words was used for decoding. The list consisted of a total of approximately 52,000 multiple-character Chinese words, 5000 single-character Chinese words, and an additional 5000 frequent English words. A 44,000-word subset of the 52,000 multiple-character Chinese words was obtained using an LDC-released Mandarin Chinese lexicon. A left-to-right maximum word-length-based character-to-word segmentation method (Sinha et al. 2006) based on the 52,000 multiple-character words was applied to the text data. The resulting character-to-word segmented acoustic transcripts contained an average of 1.426 characters per word. A base phone set containing 46 toneless (124 tonal) phones was also used (Sinha et al. 2006).

The baseline 4-gram back-off LM was trained using a total of one billion words of text data from the following two types of text sources: 2.6 million words of data from the acoustic transcripts; and one billion words of additional web data collected by various research sites, including CU, IBM Research, SRI, and the University of Washington, under the DARPA Effective, Affordable, Reusable Speech-to-Text (EARS) and Global Autonomous Language Exploitation (GALE) programs (Olive et al. 2011). Numeric terms were first converted into spoken forms before the left-to-right maximum word-length-based character-to-word segmentation scheme described above was applied. A 120-million-word subset of the one-billion-word full set used in the earlier RT04 CU Mandarin system (Gales et al. 2005) was also used in the initial system development.

25.3.3 Acoustic Modeling

Acoustic Front-End Processing

An important part of speaker-level diversity in conversational speech is attributed to the variation of the vocal tract length (Lee and Rose 1996). The first-order effect of a difference in vocal tract length can be approximated via a scaling of the formant positions. A female speaker, for example, can exhibit formants roughly 10% to 20% higher than those of a male speaker. To handle this problem, vocal tract length normalization (VTLN) (Lee and Rose 1996) was performed in a supervised mode for the training data and an unsupervised manner for the test data. An ML frequency scaling factor of the speech spectrum was estimated at the speaker level before being applied to the spectrum to produce normalized perceptual linear prediction (PLP) features (Woodland et al. 1997). Cepstral mean and variance normalization was also used to further remove speaker-level variability. The advantage of VTLN lies in its low complexity and effectiveness. It can also be efficiently implemented and applied to a range of back-end acoustic models considered here, such as conventional GMM-HMMs and DNN hybrid and tandem systems.

In tonal languages like Mandarin Chinese, prosodic pitch variation occurs at the sentence level in the form of long and smooth contours, where short and sharp lexical tones are super- imposed. It is therefore important to incorporate pitch features into the acoustic front-end. Pitch features were extracted and smoothed using the Kaldi toolkit (Povey et al. 2011). The pitch parameters, along with the first- and second-order differentials, were mean and variance normalized at the speaker level before being augmented to the heteroscedastic linear discriminant analysis (HLDA) (Kumar and Andreou 1997; Liu et al. 2003) and projected in the speaker-level normalized PLP. This resulted in a feature vector with 42 dimensions.

Baseline GMM-HMM Systems

Baseline tonal triphone context-dependent GMM-HMM systems were constructed using the front-end processing described in the previous section. Phonetic decision tree state clustering (Young et al. 1994) was used. To model complex phonological variation patterns such as tone sandhi and glottalization, word position information was also used during decision tree tying (Liu et al. 2011). After incorporating word-level position information, the number of tonal phones was increased from 124 to 293. As expected, the use of tonal- and word-position-dependent questions dramatically increased the number of context-dependent phone units to consider during both training and decoding. As not all of them were allowed according to the lexicon, only the valid subset under lexical constraint was retained after applying the context filtering approach proposed in Liu et al. (2011). The system contained a total of 12,000 tied HMM states, with 28 Gaussians per state on average. Minimum probability error (MPE)-based HMM parameter estimation and speaker adaptive training (SAT) (Povey and Woodland 2002) were performed. Constrained maximum likelihood linear regression (CMLLR)-based SAT (Gales 1998) was also used, as was unsupervised maximum likelihood linear regression (MLLR)-based SAT (Leggetter and Woodland 1995).

Hybrid DNN-HMM Systems

Hybrid DNN-HMM acoustic models with five hidden layers were first trained using the cross-entropy (CE) criterion on a GPU before MPE-based sequence-level discriminative training was performed. A layer-by-layer discriminative pre-training was used. The first four hidden layers had 2000 nodes, while the fifth hidden layer had 1000 nodes, and 12,000 output-layer context-dependent state targets were used. Fifty-six dimensional input features including normalized PLP features with their differentials up to the third order and pitch parameters were used. The input vector thus had 504 dimensions, which was produced by concatenating the current frame with four frames from both left and right contexts. A tenth of the training set was randomly selected as the held-out set for cross-validation. An example of a hybrid DNN-HMM acoustic model is shown in Fig. 25.7:

Tandem Systems

An alternative approach to incorporating DNNs into HMM-based acoustic models is to use a DNN as a feature extractor trained to produce phoneme posterior probabilities. The resulting probabilistic features (Hermansky et al. 2000) and bottleneck features (Grézl et al. 2007; Yu and Seltzer 2011) were used to train standard GMM-HMMs in a tandem fashion. As these features capture additional discriminative information complementary to the standard front-ends, they were often

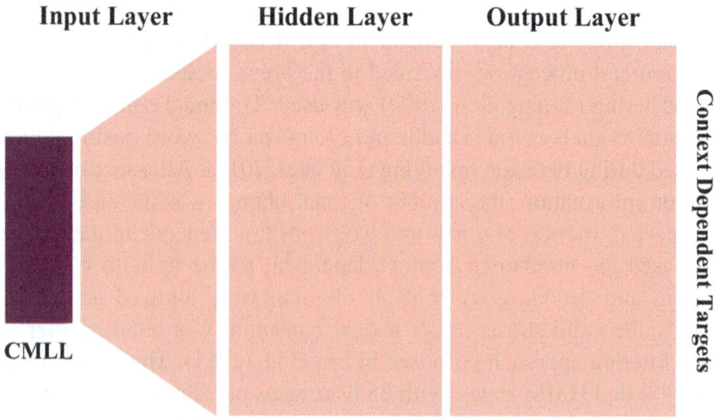

Fig. 25.7 Example of a hybrid DNN-HMM acoustic model

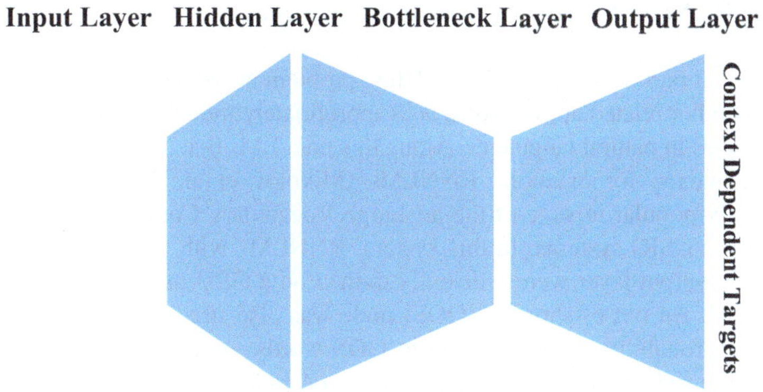

Fig. 25.8 Example of a tandem DNN-HMM acoustic model

combined via feature concatenation. As a GMM-HMM is a back-end classifier, the tandem approach required minimum changes to the downstream techniques, such as speaker adaptation and decoding, while the useful information represented by the bottleneck features was also retained. The GMM-HMMs also provided additional useful system diversity for combination with hybrid DNN-HMM systems (Swietojanski et al. 2013). DNNs with an additional bottleneck layer were trained using the same procedure described above, and 26 dimensional bottleneck features were extracted. The resulting features were then normalized at the speaker level before being decorrelated via an semi-tied covariance matrices (Gales 1999), transformed and augmented to the standard acoustic front-ends, and used in training for the back-end GMM-HMMs. An example of this tandem DNN-HMM acoustic model is shown in Fig. 25.8:

25.3.4 Language Modeling

Baseline Interpolated 4-Gram LM

The baseline 4-gram word-level LM was trained using the one-billion-word text data and the list of 63,000 words described in Sect. 25.3.2. Modified Kneser-Ney (KN)-smoothed 4-gram LMs were estimated for the acoustic transcription data and web data sources separately before a linear interpolation was used to combine them. The interpolation weights were perplexity optimized with "dev14," "dev04," and additional CHM and CFM data from the earlier NIST evaluation sets "eval03" and "eval97." The interpolated 4-gram LM had a total of 48 million 2-grams, 133 million 3-grams, and 143 million 4-grams, with a perplexity of 151 for "dev14."

Efficient RNNLM Training and Lattice Rescoring

An important part of the language modeling problem in speech recognition systems, and many other related applications, is to appropriately model long-distance context dependencies in natural languages. Along this line, LMs that can model longer-span history contexts, for example, RNNLMs (Mikolov et al. 2010), have become increasingly popular in state-of-the-art Large Vocabulary Continuous Speech Recognition (LVCSR) systems. In this system, RNNLMs with a non-class-based full vocabulary output layer were efficiently trained on a GPU in a bunch mode (Chen et al. 2014). An out-of-shortlist (OOS) node was also used at the output layer to model the probability mass assigned to OOS words. A total of 512 hidden layer nodes were used. A 27,000-word input layer vocabulary and a 20,000-word output layer shortlist were also used. An example of this RNN-based language model is shown in Fig. 25.9.

As RNNLMs use a complex vector space representation of full history contexts, it is non-trivial to apply them in the early stage of ASR systems or to directly rescore the word lattices produced by them. Instead, N-best list rescoring is normally used (Mikolov et al. 2010; Si et al. 2013). This practical constraint limits the possible improvements that can be obtained from RNNLMs for downstream applications that favor a more compact lattice representation, for example, confusion network (CN) decoding techniques (Evermann and Woodland 2000; Mangu et al. 2000). To address this issue, two efficient RNNLM lattice rescoring algorithms were proposed by Liu et al. (2014a). The first uses an *n*-gram style approximation of history contexts. In this system, our RNNLM rescoring approach was used.

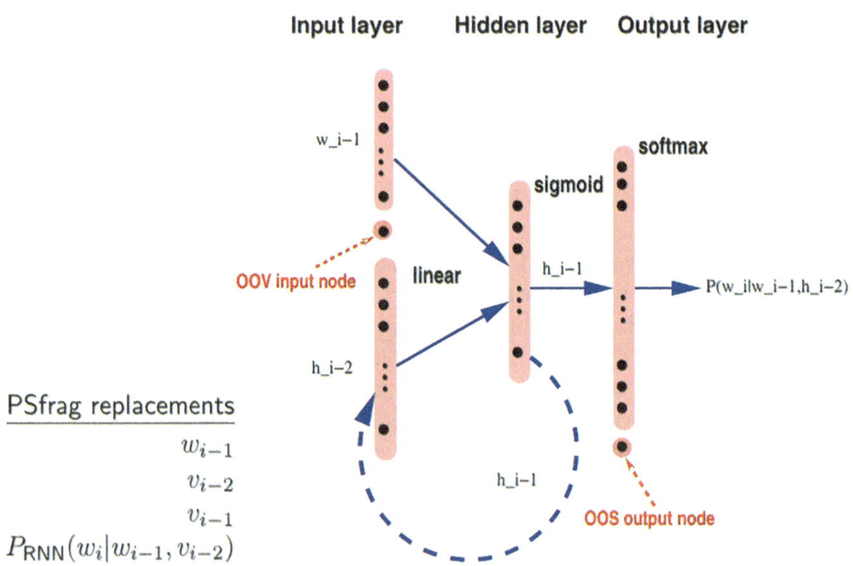

Fig. 25.9 An example of an RNN language mode

Multilevel Paraphrastic RNNLMs

Linguistic factors that influence the realization of surface word sequences, for example, expressive richness, are only implicitly learned by RNNLMs. Observed sentences and their associated alternative paraphrases representing the same meaning are not explicitly related during training. An example of paraphrases of one Chinese sentence is shown in Fig. 25.10. To further improve the RNNLM's coverage and generalization, the 2.6 million words of acoustic transcripts data were augmented with 15 million words of its paraphrase variants. These paraphrases were automatically produced using the statistical paraphrase induction and generation method described in (Liu et al. 2014b). The combined data set above was then used to train a paraphrastic RNNLM (Liu et al. 2015). To incorporate richer linguistic constraints, LMs that model different units, for example, syllables, words, or phrases, can be log-linearly combined in the form of a multilevel LM (Liu et al. 2013a; Liu et al. 2013b; Liu et al. 2013c) to improve discrimination. In our work, a multi-level paraphrastic RNNLM modeling both word and character sequences was constructed, which aimed to implicitly model alternative character-to-word segmentations, while retaining consistent character-to-word segmentation. This is a useful feature for downstream applications such as machine translation.

25.3.5 System Combination

State-of-the-art ASR systems often use system combination techniques (Schwartz et al. 2004; Woodland et al. 2004). Two major categories of techniques are often used: hypothesis-level combination and cross-system adaptation. The former

Original Sentence:			
霍华德	对此	表示	感谢
Paraphrases:			
霍华德	对此	表达	高度 赞赏
霍华德	对 这 一 事件	表示	十分 感谢
霍华德	为此	致辞 说	感谢
霍华德	对此	致 以	感谢
霍华德	为此	声明	致谢
霍华德		表示	将 始终 铭记
霍华德		说	感谢
霍华德		表示	衷心 感谢
霍华德		说	感恩戴德
...	...	...	...

Fig. 25.10 Example set of paraphrases of a Chinese sentence

exploits the consensus among component systems using voting as well as confidence measures, such as Recognizer Output Voting Error Reduction (ROVER) (Fiscus 1997) and confusion network combination (CNC) (Evermann and Woodland 2000). Hypothesis-level combination in general is unable to retain consistent decoding output from component systems. Alternatively, the second category based on cross-adaptation (Prasad et al. 2005; Schwartz et al. 2004; Woodland et al. 2004; Woodland et al. 1995) can be used. The acoustic and/or language models (Liu et al. 2013a) of one system are adapted to the recognition outputs of another. Consistent decoding output can then be produced by decoding using the cross-adapted system.

To be effective in combination, cross-adaptation further requires that the component system to be adapted has a comparable or lower error rate than the supervision system. To address this issue, an improved system combination based on frame-level acoustic model combination was used. The state output probabilities of the hybrid DNN-HMM system and a comparable tandem system were log-linearly combined with a weighting of 1:0.4 on-the-fly for joint decoding (Soltau et al. 2014; Swietojanski et al. 2013).

25.3.6 System Architecture and Performance

The CU evaluation system used a multi-pass recognition framework. In the first pass, the hybrid speaker independent (SI) system described in Sect. 25.3.3.3 and the baseline 4-gram LM presented in Sect. 25.3.4.1 were used to produce initial recognition outputs. Together with recognition outputs separately produced by collaborating teams at IBM research and Johns Hopkins University, these outputs were then used to adapt both the hybrid SAT and tandem SAT systems. The joint decoding method described in Sect. 25.3.5 was then used to combine these two systems on-the-fly at test time. After lattice rescoring using a paraphrastic multilevel RNNLM, CN decoding produced the final system outputs. The overall system architecture is shown in Fig. 25.11, with a character error rate (CER) score of 27.4% for the "dev14" set, as shown in the last line in the table included in Fig. 25.11. Compared with the baseline GMM-HMM system performance shown in the top line in the same table, a total error rate reduction of 20.9% absolute (43% relative) was obtained by applying DNN- and RNN-based deep learning techniques to the system.

25.4 Text-to-Speech Synthesis Systems

In this section, a state-of-the-art Chinese TTS system will be presented that makes use of the advantages of the DBN model (mentioned in Sect. 25.2.4) in modeling high-dimensional data with cross-dimensional correlations. To evaluate the performance of the proposed DBN-based approach, it was compared with the HMM-based approach, which is a dominant "shallow" method.

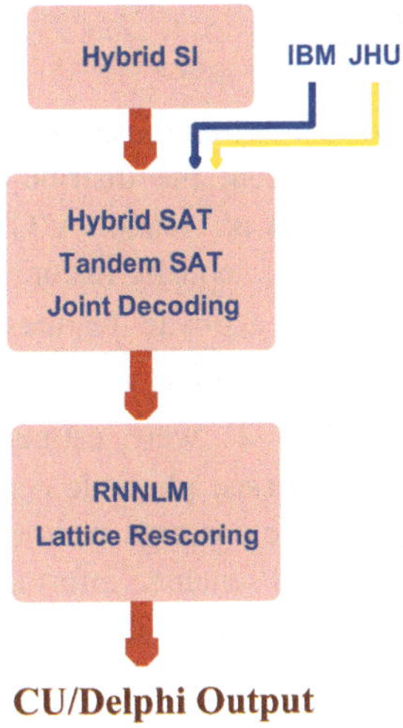

Pass	CU System	CER%
-	GMM-HMM SAT baseline	43.8
Pass1	Hybrid DNN-HMM SI	31.8
Pass2	Hybrid SAT⊗Tandem	28.7
Pass3	SAT +RNNLM rescoring	27.4

Fig. 25.11 Overall system architecture and CER for "dev14"

Table 25.1 Summary of TH-CoSS Corpus (Female)

	Utterances	Prosodic phrases	Prosodic words	Syllables
No.	5406	16,769	44,658	98,749

```
/为临帖/他还|远游|西安|碑林/龙门|石窟/泰山|摩崖|石刻/./
wei4 lin2 tie4 ta1 hai2 yuan3 you2 xi1 an1 bei1 lin2
long2 men2 shi2 ku1 tai4 shan1 mo2 ya2 shi2 ke4
```

Fig. 25.12 Example of the annotation file

25.4.1 Data Resources

The TsingHua-Corpus of Speech Synthesis (TH-CoSS) Chinese Corpus (Cai et al. 2007) was used for the experiments. This corpus has about 20,000 Chinese sentences read by one female and one male. Table 25.1 shows a summary of the TH-CoSS Corpus (Female Part). The annotation files contain segmental and prosodic tags, as shown in Fig. 25.12. The first line is the corresponding text of waveforms and the boundaries of the prosodic phrases (denoted as "/") and prosodic words (denoted as "|"). The second line is the corresponding pinyin annotations.

25.4.2 Baseline HMM-Based Approach

In the speech synthesis system (see Fig. 25.13), decision-tree-clustered context-dependent phoneme HMMs were widely used to represent the distributions of acoustic features given linguistic features (Yoshimura et al. 1999). A Gaussian distribution (e.g., GMM) was used to represent the PDF of acoustic features as the leaf node of the decision trees. At the training stage, acoustic features $\mathbf{y} = \left[\mathbf{y}_1^{\mathrm{T}}, \mathbf{y}_2^{\mathrm{T}}, \ldots, \mathbf{y}_T^{\mathrm{T}}\right]^{\mathrm{T}.}$ were extracted from the speech waveforms and context features $\mathbf{x} = \left[\mathbf{x}_1^{\mathrm{T}}, \mathbf{x}_2^{\mathrm{T}}, \ldots, \mathbf{x}_T^{\mathrm{T}}\right]^T$ context-dependent HMMs λ^* were estimated by $\lambda^* = \arg\max_\lambda p(y \mid x, \lambda)$. In HMM-based speech synthesis, phonetic context is very complicated when considering prosodic and linguistic contexts such as stress, tone, accentual phrases, parts-of-speech, breath group, and sentence information. It is important to obtain training data covering all the possible context-dependent units. To deal with this issue, a decision-tree-based clustering technique (Yu et al. 2011) was widely used after the initial training. That is, the PDFs of context-dependent HMMs with similar context descriptions shared the same distribution. In the synthesis stage, front-end text analysis was conducted to obtain the context features $x^{\sim}$. The corresponding HMM parameters were derived from the training stage, according to the decision trees. Finally, a vocoder was used to synthesize the speech waveform from the generated parameters.

Although the speech synthesis approaches using GMMs and HMMs were successfully applied to generate highly intelligible speech, the generated speech sounds were muffled and some detailed characteristics were often lost. The possible reasons

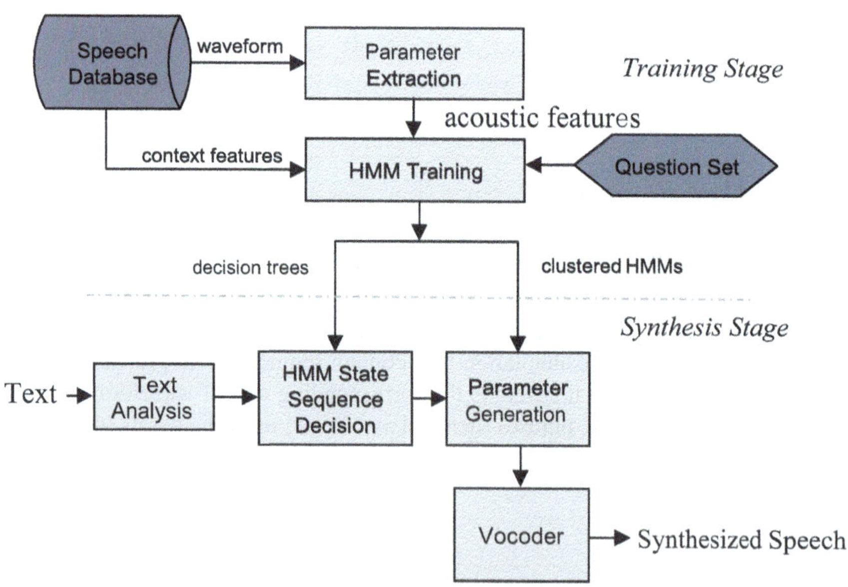

Fig. 25.13 Block diagram of a typical HMM-based speech synthesis system

for these results are as follows: (i) the GMMs could not model the PDF distributions precisely because of the limitation of the "shallow" architecture (Chen et al. 2013; Ling et al. 2013a, 2013b; Nakashika et al. 2013); and (ii) in the HMMs, the decision trees were inefficient in expressing complex context dependencies such as exclusive or (XOR), parity, and multiplex problems. The fragmentation of the training data to each node of the decision tree resulted in an overfitting problem (Kang and Meng 2014; Kang et al. 2013; Zen et al. 2013).

25.4.3 DBN-Based Approach

The architectures of deep learning are composed of many hidden layers of non-linear operations, which can be used for supervised or unsupervised feature representation and transformation. Compared with the conventional "shallow" models, deep models are more effective in the aspects of learning representations and mapping non-linear relationships. Taking DBN as an example, of which other deep models can easily be applied in a similar manner, Kang et al. (2013) proposed a synthesis method using multi-distribution DBN, which was the first attempt to apply a DBN to speech synthesis. The text-to-acoustic mapping was achieved by modeling the joint distribution between the input contextual factors and the output acoustic parameters with the DBN.

To build a multi-distribution DBN, as shown in Fig. 25.14, three types of RBMs were involved: (i) a GB-RBM, for spectrum, log F0, and voiced-unvoiced (V/UV) representation with Gaussian or Bernoulli distributions; (ii) a CB-RBM, to capture the correspondence between syllable identities and the binary data derived from the linguistic context; and (iii) B-RBMs, which were used to encode binary data:

For this approach, the input was linguistic context features that were the tonal syllable labels $\boldsymbol{l}^c$ in Mandarin Chinese. The syllable labels were encoded with a 1-of-k code following the categorical distribution. The output acoustic features were 50 uniformly spaced frames of 24-order mel-generalized cepstrum coefficients (MGCs) plus log-energy, 200 uniformly spaced frames of V/UV decisions, and the corresponding log F0 values within the syllable boundaries. The MGCs, log F0s, and V/UV units were concatenated to form a 1650-dimensional supervector for each syllable, which was used as the visible layer $\boldsymbol{v}$ for the GB-RBM. The posteriors of the hidden layer $P\ (h^{(L)} \mid \boldsymbol{v}_g, \boldsymbol{v}_b)$ were used as the visible data to train the immediate upper-layer B-RBM. Likewise, as many layers of B-RBMs as needed were stacked in a similar manner. That is, the depth of the model could easily be controlled. Finally, the joint distribution of the top hidden layer's posteriors and the corresponding syllable label were modeled by a CB-RBM.

At synthesis time, for an arbitrary text, text analysis was first used to obtain the context feature $\boldsymbol{l}^c$. Then, alternative Gibbs sampling using $P\ (h_i^{(L)} = 1 \mid \boldsymbol{x}, \boldsymbol{h}^{(L-1)})$ and $P\ (h_j^{(L-1)} = 1 \mid \boldsymbol{h}^{(L)})$ was conducted with the clamped $\boldsymbol{l}^c$ to update $\boldsymbol{h}^{(L-1)}$. This procedure continued until convergence or a maximum number of iterations was reached. Then, the acoustic feature supervectors were predicted as the mean vector

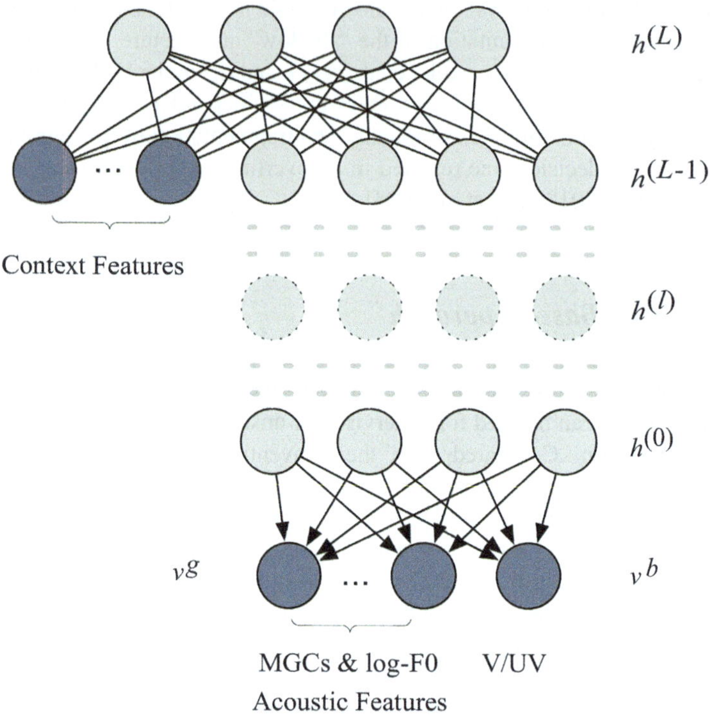

Fig. 25.14 Model structure of input-to-feature mapping using a DBN for speech synthesis (Kang et al. 2013)

of $p(\boldsymbol{v} \mid \boldsymbol{h}^{(1)})$, which was determined by recursively generating hidden variables from $\boldsymbol{h}^{(L-1)}$ to $\boldsymbol{h}^{(1)}$. The duration of each syllable was the average estimated from the training data. Finally, the generated acoustic features were interpolated according to the estimated durations and were fed into the Mel log spectrum approximation (MLSA) filter (Fukada et al. 1992) for the speech waveforms.

25.4.4 *Experiments*

Experimental Setup

The TH-CoSS Chinese Corpus (Female Part) (Cai et al. 2007) was used for the experiments. The training set contained 1000 utterances (about 80.9 min), including 23,727 syllable samples, which were divided into 1364 classes of tonal syllables. A test set with 100 utterances was used for the evaluation. Three systems were implemented for comparison:

- **HMM:** HMM-based approach in which MGCs and log F0s were all predicted by an HMM, which was the baseline.
- **DBN** (MGCs): DBN-based approach in which MGCs were predicted by a DBN and log F0s were predicted by an HMM.
- **DBN** (MGCs + log F0): DBN-based approach in which MGCs and log F0s were all predicted by a DBN.

The DBN-based approach contained four hidden layers and the number of units in each hidden layer was 2000. The DBN model was trained using stochastic gradient descent, with a mini-batch size of 200 training samples. The training procedure was carried out on one Tesla M2090 GPU system and it took about 1.1 h to complete.

For the HMM-based baseline approach, each syllable HMM was left-to-right, with 10 states. Initially, 416 monosyllable HMMs were estimated as the seeds to train the context-dependent HMMs. The question set for the decision-tree-based clustering contained 2596 effective questions. Other configurations, including syllable duration prediction and vocoder, were the same as those in the DBN-based approach.

Subjective Evaluation

A Mean Opinion Score (MOS) test was conducted to evaluate the quality of the synthesized speech. In this test, 10 experienced listeners were asked to rate 10 samples synthesized by these three systems using a 5-point scale (5 = excellent, 4 = good, 3 = fair, 2 = poor, 1 = bad). Table 25.2 shows the results of the MOS test. Comparing the DBN (MGCs) with the HMM, the DBN achieved better performance in modeling and predicting spectral features (MGCs). The score degradation comparing the DBN (MGCs) and the DBN (MGCs + log F0) shows that low-dimensional log F0 features could not model very well when combined with high-dimensional spectral features. Generally speaking, F0s contained more suprasegmental information, while more segmental information was included in MGCs. Thus, F0s were more difficult to model using the DBNs.

25.5 Discussion

As shown in the experiments section, the DBN-based approach achieved better performance in modeling high-dimensional features than the baseline HMM-based approach. The two main advantages of deep models over HMM-based models can

Table 25.2 Subjective evaluation results for DBN-based speech synthesis (Kang et al. 2013)

System	MOS
HMM	2.86
DBN (MGCs)	3.09
DBN (MGCs + log F0)	2.88

be summarized as: (i) they model all the training data using an integrated framework, thus avoiding data partitioning of decision trees as in the HMM-based approach; and (ii) they can model the correlations between spectral coefficients within a single frame in the frequency domain. However, in the HMM-based approach, it was assumed that spectral coefficients within a single frame were independent.

25.6 Summary and Conclusion

In this chapter, state-of-the-art ASR and TTS systems using deep learning models were presented. Deep models have a great advantage in modeling non-linear relationships of high-dimensional features and context dependency of speech signals. To evaluate the performance of the deep models (e.g., DBNs, DNNs, and RNNs), some experiments were conducted. The results of the ASR system showed that deep models (DNN + RNN) reduced CERs from 43.8% to 27.4%, which was a significant improvement compared with the conventional GMM-HMM baseline approach. The experiments with the TTS systems suggest that deep architecture (i.e., DBN) can improve the quality of synthesized speech by modeling high-dimensional spectral features, as shown in the increase of the MOS, from 2.86 to 3.09.

References

Cai, Lianhong, Dandan Cui, and Rui Cai. 2007. TH-CoSS, a Mandarin speech corpus for TTS. *Journal of Chinese Information Processing* 21(2):94. Available at http://jcip.cipsc.org.cn/EN/abstract/abstract724.shtml. Accessed 31/10/2018.

Chen, Linghui, Zhenhua Ling, Yan Song, and Lirong Dai. 2013. Joint spectral distribution modeling using restricted Boltzmann machines for voice conversion. In *Proceedings of the 14th Annual Conference of the International Speech Communication Association (INTERSPEECH 2013)*, 3052–3056. Lyon, France.

Chen, Xie, Yongqiang Wang, Xunying Liu, Mark J. F. Gales, and Philip C. Woodland. 2014. Efficient GPU-based training of recurrent neural network language models using spliced sentence bunch. In *Proceedings of the 15th Annual Conference of the International Speech Communication Association (INTERSPEECH 2014)*, 641–645. Singapore.

Evermann, Gunnar, and Philip C. Woodland. 2000. Posterior probability decoding, confidence estimation and system combination. In *Proceedings of the Speech Transcription Workshop*, vol. 27. Baltimore, Maryland.

Fiscus, Jonathan G. 1997. A post-processing system to yield reduced word error rates: Recognizer output voting error reduction (ROVER). In *Proceedings of the 1997 IEEE Workshop on Automatic Speech Recognition and Understanding*, 347–354. Santa Barbara, California.

Fukada, Toshiaki, Keiichi Tokuda, Takao Kobayashi, and Satoshi Imai. 1992. An adaptive algorithm for mel-cepstral analysis of speech. In *Proceedings of the IEEE International Conference on Acoustics, Speech and Signal Processing (ICASSP 1992)*, 1:137–140. San Francisco, California.

Gales, Mark J. F. 1998. Maximum likelihood linear transformations for HMM-based speech recognition. *Computer Speech & Language* 12(2):75–98.

Gales, Mark J. F. 1999. Semi-tied covariance matrices for hidden Markov models. *IEEE Transactions on Speech and Audio Processing* 7(3):272–281.

Gales, Mark J. F., Bin Jia, Xunying Liu, Khe Chai Sim, Philip C. Woodland, and Kai Yu. 2005. Development of the CU-HTK 2004 RT04 Mandarin conversational telephone speech transcription system. In *Proceedings of the IEEE International Conference on Acoustics, Speech and Signal Processing (ICASSP 2005)*, 841–844. Philadelphia, Pennsylvania.

Grezl, Frantisek, Martin Karafiat, Stanislav Kontar, and Jan Cernocky. 2007. Probabilistic and bottle-neck features for LVCSR of meetings. In *Proceedings of the IEEE International Conference on Acoustics, Speech and Signal Processing (ICASSP 2007)*, 4: IV-757. Honolulu, Hawai'i.

Hermansky, Hynek, Daniel W. Ellis, and Shantanu Sharma. 2000. Tandem connectionist feature extraction for conventional HMM systems. In *Proceedings of the IEEE International Conference on Acoustics, Speech, and Signal Processing (ICASSP 2000)*, 3:1635–1638. Istanbul, Turkey.

Hinton, Geoffrey E. 2002. Training products of experts by minimizing contrastive divergence. *Neural Computation* 14(8):1711–800.

Hinton, Geoffrey E., and Ruslan R. Salakhutdinov. 2006. Reducing the dimensionality of data with neural networks. *Science* 313(5786):504–507.

Hinton, Geoffrey E., Simon Osindero, and Yee-Whye Teh. 2006. A fast learning algorithm for deep belief nets. *Neural Computation* 18(7):1527–1554.

Hinton, Geoffrey, Li Deng, Dong Yu, George E. Dahl, Abdel-rahman Mohamed, Navdeep Jaitly, Andrew Senior, Vincent Vanhoucke, Patrick Nguyen, Tara N. Sainath, and Brian Kingsbury. 2012. Deep neural networks for acoustic modeling in speech recognition. *IEEE Signal Process Magazine* 29(6):82–97.

Hochreiter, Sepp, and Jurgen Schmidhuber. 1997. Long short-term memory. *Neural Computation* 9(8):1735–1780.

Kang, Shiyin, and Helen Meng. 2014. Statistical parametric speech synthesis using weighted multi-distribution deep belief network. In *Proceedings of the 15th Annual Conference of the International Speech Communication Association (INTERSPEECH 2014)*, 1959–1963. Singapore.

Kang, Shiyin, Xiaojun Qian, and Helen Meng. 2013. Multi-distribution deep belief network for speech synthesis. In *Proceedings of the IEEE International Conference on Acoustics, Speech and Signal Processing (ICASSP 2013)*, 8012–8016. Vancouver, Canada.

Kumar, Nagendra, and Andreas G. Andreou. 1997. Investigation of silicon auditory models and generalization of linear discriminant analysis for improved speech recognition. Ph.D. dissertation. Johns Hopkins University, Baltimore, Maryland.

Lee, Li, and Richard C. Rose. 1996. Speaker normalization using efficient frequency warping procedures. In *Proceedings of the IEEE International Conference on Acoustics, Speech, and Signal Processing (ICASSP 1996)*, 1:353–356. Atlanta, Georgia.

Leggetter, Christopher J., and Philip C. Woodland. 1995. Maximum likelihood linear regression for speaker adaptation of continuous density hidden Markov models. *Computer Speech & Language* 9(2): 71–185.

Li, Kun. 2015. The use of multi-distribution deep neural networks for segmental and suprasegmental mispronunciation detection and diagnosis in L2 English speech. Ph.D. dissertation. The Chinese University of Hong Kong.

Ling, Zhenhua, Li Deng, and Dong Yu. 2013a. Modeling spectral envelopes using restricted Boltzmann machines and deep belief networks for statistical parametric speech synthesis. *IEEE Transactions on Audio, Speech and Language Processing* 21(10):2129–2139.

Ling, Zhenhua, Li Deng, and Dong Yu. 2013b. Modeling spectral envelopes using restricted Boltzmann machines for statistical parametric speech synthesis. In *Proceedings of the IEEE International Conference on Acoustics, Speech and Signal Processing (ICASSP 2013)*, 7825–7829. Vancouver, Canada.

Ling, Zhenhua, Shiyin Kang, Heiga Zen, Andrew Senior, Mike Schuster, Xiaojun Qian, Helen M. Meng, and Li Deng. 2015. Deep learning for acoustic modeling in parametric speech generation: A systematic review of existing techniques and future trends. *IEEE Signal Processing Magazine* 32(3):35–52.

Liu, Xunying, Mark J. F. Gales, and Philip C. Woodland. 2003. Automatic complexity control for HLDA systems. In *Proceedings of the IEEE International Conference on Acoustics, Speech, and Signal Processing (ICASSP 2003)*, 1: I-132. Hong Kong, China.

Liu, Xunying, Mark J. F. Gales, Jim L. Hieronymus, and Philip C. Woodland. 2011. Investigation of acoustic units for LVCSR systems. In *Proceedings of the IEEE International Conference on Acoustics, Speech and Signal Processing (ICASSP 2011)*, 4872–4875. Prague, Czech Republic.

Liu, Xunying, Mark J. F. Gales, and Philip C. Woodland. 2013a. Use of contexts in language model interpolation and adaptation. *Computer Speech & Language* 27(1):301–321.

Liu, Xunying, Mark J. F. Gales, and Philip C. Woodland. 2013b. Language model cross adaptation for LVCSR system combination. *Computer Speech & Language* 27(4):928–942.

Liu, Xunying, James L. Hieronymus, Mark J. F. Gales, and Philip C. Woodland. 2013c. Syllable language models for Mandarin speech recognition: Exploiting character language models. *The Journal of the Acoustical Society of America* 133(1):519–528.

Liu, Xindong, Yannan Wang, Xia Chen, Mark J. F. Gales, and Philip C. Woodland. 2014a. Efficient lattice rescoring using recurrent neural network language models. In *Proceedings of the IEEE International Conference on Acoustics, Speech and Signal Processing (ICASSP 2014)*, 4908–4912. Florence, Italy.

Liu, Xindong, Yannan Wang, Xia Chen, Mark J. F. Gales, and Philip C. Woodland. 2014b. Paraphrastic language models. *Computer Speech & Language* 28(6):1298–1316.

Liu, Xunying, Xie Chen, Mark J. F. Gales, and Philip C. Woodland. 2015. Paraphrastic recurrent neural network language models. In *Proceedings of the IEEE International Conference on Acoustics, Speech and Signal Processing (ICASSP 2015)*, 5406–5410. Brisbane, Australia.

Mangu, Lidia, Eric Brill, and Andreas Stolcke. 2000. Finding consensus in speech recognition: Word error minimization and other applications of confusion networks. *Computer Speech & Language* 14(4):373–400.

Mikolov, Tomas, Martin Karafiat, Lukas Burget, Jan Cernocky, and Sanjeev Khudanpur. 2010. Recurrent neural network based language model. In *Proceedings of the 11th Annual Conference of the International Speech Communication Association (INTERSPEECH 2010)*, 2:3. Makuhari, Chiba, Japan.

Nakashika, Toru, Ryoichi Takashima, Tetsuya Takiguchi, and Yasuo Ariki. 2013. Voice conversion in high-order eigen space using deep belief nets. In *Interspeech* 369–372.

Olive, Joseph, Caitlin Christianson, and John McCary. 2011. *Handbook of natural language processing and machine translation: DARPA global autonomous language exploitation.* Springer Science & Business Media.

Povey, Daniel, and Philip C. Woodland. 2002. Minimum phone error and I-smoothing for improved discriminative training. In *Proceedings of the IEEE International Conference on Acoustics, Speech, and Signal Processing (ICASSP 2002)*, 1:I-105. Orlando, Florida.

Povey, Daniel, Arnab Ghoshal, Gilles Boulianne, Lukas Burget, Ondrej Glembek, Nagendra Goel, Mirko Hannemann, Petr Motlicek, Yanmin Qian, Petr Schwarz, Jan Silovsky, Georg Stemmer, and Karel Vesely. 2011. The Kaldi speech recognition toolkit. Paper presented at the *IEEE 2011 Workshop on Automatic Speech Recognition and Understanding*. EPFL-CONF-192584. IEEE Signal Processing Society. Big Island, Hawai'i.

Prasad, Rohit, Spyros Matsoukas, Chia-Lin Kao, Jeff Z. Ma, Dongxin Xu, Thomas Colthurst, Owen Kimball, Richard M. Schwartz, Jean-Luc Gauvain, Lori Lamel, Holger Schwenk, G. Adda, and Fabrice Lefèvre. 2005. The 2004 BBN/LIMSI 20xRT English conversational telephone speech recognition system. In *Proceedings of INTERSPEECH 2005—Eurospeech, 9th European Conference on Speech Communication and Technology*, 1645–1648. Lisbon, Portugal.

Rumelhart, David, Geoffrey Hinton, and Ronald Williams. 1985. Learning internal representations by error propagation. In *Parallel distributed processing: Explorations in the microstructure of cognition* (Vol. 1: Foundations), (ed.) David E. Rumelhart and James L. McClelland. Cambridge, MA: Bradford Books/MIT Press.

Rumelhart, D., Geoffrey Hinton, and Ronald Williams. 1986. Learning representations by back-propagating errors. *Nature* 323(6088):533–536.

Salakhutdinov, Ruslan. 2009. Learning deep generative models. Ph.D. dissertation. University of Toronto, Canada.

Schuster, Mike, and Kuldip K. Paliwal. 1997. Bidirectional recurrent neural networks. *IEEE Transactions on Signal Processing* 45(11):2673–2681.

Schwartz, Richard, Thomas Colthurst, Nicolae Duta, Herbert Gish, Rukmini Iyer, Chia-Lin Kao, Daben Liu, Owen Kimball, Jeff Ma, John Makhoul, Spyros Matsoukas, Long Nguyen, Mohamed Noamany, Rohit Prasad, Bing Xiang, DanXia Xu, Jean-Luc Gauvain, Lori Lamel, Holger Schwenk, G. Adda, and L. Chen. 2004. Speech recognition in multiple languages and domains: The 2003 BBN/LIMSI EARS system. In *Proceedings of the IEEE International Conference on Acoustics, Speech and Signal Processing, (ICASSP 2004)*, 3:iii-753. Montréal, Québec, Canada.

Si, Yujing, Qingqing Zhang, Ta Li, Jielin Pan, and Yonghong Yan. 2013. Prefix tree based n-best list rescoring for recurrent neural network language model used in speech recognition system. In *Proceedings of the 14th Annual Conference of the International Speech Communication Association (INTERSPEECH 2013)*, 3419–3423. Lyon, France.

Sinha, Rohit, Mark J. F. Gales, D. Y. Kim, X. Andrew Liu, Khe Chai Sim, and Philip C. Woodland. 2006. The CU-HTK Mandarin broadcast news transcription system. In *Proceedings of the IEEE International Conference on Acoustics, Speech and Signal Processing (ICASSP 2006)*, 1:I-I. Toulouse, France.

Smolensky, Paul. 1986. Information processing in dynamical systems: Foundations of harmony theory. In *Parallel distributed processing: Explorations in the microstructure of cognition* (Vol. 1: Foundations), (ed.) David E. Rumelhart and James L. McClelland. 1:194–281. Cambridge, MA: Bradford Books/MIT Press.

Soltau, Hagen, George Saon, and Tara N. Sainath. 2014. Joint training of convolutional and non-convolutional neural networks. In *Proceedings of the IEEE International Conference on Acoustics, Speech and Signal Processing (ICASSP 2014)*, 5572–5576. Florence, Italy.

Swietojanski, Pawel, Arnab Ghoshal, and Steve Renals. 2013. Revisiting hybrid and GMM- HMM system combination techniques. In *Proceedings of the IEEE International Conference on Acoustics, Speech and Signal Processing (ICASSP 2013)*, 6744–6748. Vancouver, Canada.

Woodland, Philip C., Christopher J. Leggetter, Julian J. Odell, Valtcho Valtchev, and Steve J. Young. 1995. The 1994 HTK large vocabulary speech recognition system. In *Proceedings of the IEEE International Conference on Acoustics, Speech, and Signal Processing (ICASSP 1995)*, 1:73–76. Detroit, Michigan.

Woodland, Philip C., Mark J. F. Gales, David Pye, and Steve J. Young. 1997. The development of the 1996 HTK broadcast news transcription system. Paper presented at the *DARPA Speech Recognition Workshop*, 73–78. Chantilly, Virginia.

Woodland, Philip C., Ricky Ho Yin Chan, Gunnar Evermann, Mark J. F. Gales, D. Kim, Xunying Liu, David Mrva, Khe Chai Sim, Lan Wang, Kai Yu, John Makhoul, and Richard Schwartz. 2004. SuperEARS: Multi-site broadcast news system. Paper presented at the *Rich Transcription (RT-04F) Workshop*. Palisades, New York.

Yoshimura, Takayoshi, Keiichi Tokuda, Takashi Masuko, Takao Kobayashi, and Tadashi Kitamura. 1999. Simultaneous modeling of spectrum, pitch and duration in HMM-based speech synthesis. In *Proceedings of the Sixth European Conference on Speech Communication and Technology (Eurospeech 1999)*, 2347–2350. Budapest, Hungary.

Young, Steve J., Julian J. Odell, and Philip C. Woodland. 1994. Tree-based state tying for high accuracy acoustic modeling. In *Proceedings of the Workshop on Human Language and Technology*, 307–312. Plainsboro, New Jersey.

Yu, Dong, and Michael L. Seltzer. 2011. Improved bottleneck features using pretrained deep neural networks. In *Proceedings of the 12th Annual Conference of the International Speech Communication Association (INTERSPEECH 2011)*, 237:240. Florence, Italy.

Yu, Kai, Heiga Zen, Francois Mairesse, and Steve Young. 2011. Context adaptive training with factorized decision trees for HMM-based statistical parametric speech synthesis. *Speech Communication* 53(6):914–923.

Zen, Heiga, Andrew Senior, and Mike Schuster. 2013. Statistical parametric speech synthesis using deep neural networks. In *Proceedings of the IEEE International Conference on Acoustics, Speech and Signal Processing (ICASSP 2013)*, 7962–7966. Vancouver, Canada.

Chapter 26
A Semi-supervised Approach for Chinese Noun Phrase Chunking

Zhao-Ming Gao, Yen-Hsi Lin, and Ruben G. Tsui

Abstract This chapter addresses Chinese noun phrase chunking with special reference to nominalizations based on a semi-supervised approach. It uses YamCha, a support vector machine (SVM) toolkit, to train the model. In addition to the IOB scheme and the two words before and after the target word, we experimented with new features and exploited unlabeled data from web pages to enhance the performance of the model. The result of our experiments showed that our proposed method of semi-supervised learning is effective in tackling a variety of complex Chinese noun phrases that have been largely unexplored in previous research. An important bi-product of our approach is the identification of Chinese nominalized verbs, which are indistinguishable from verbs in terms of their morphology and part-of-speech tags. The findings of this research may shed light on more recent approaches to similar problems.

Keywords Chinese noun phrase chunking · Semi-supervised learning · Chinese nominalized verbs

26.1 Introduction

Phrasal chunking has always been a critical step in natural language processing (NLP) and related fields, such as web mining and text categorization. Despite its importance, chunking is a problem that has largely eluded a satisfactory solution in the Chinese language. In question answering systems, the majority of keywords and

Z.-M. Gao (✉)
Department of Foreign Languages and Literatures, National Taiwan University, Taipei, Taiwan
e-mail: zmgao@ntu.edu.tw

Y.-H. Lin
Delta Electronics, Inc., Taipei, Taiwan
e-mail: r95944002@ntu.edu.tw

R. G. Tsui
Graduate Program in Translation and Interpretation, College of Liberal Arts, National Taiwan University, Taipei, Taiwan

C.-R. Huang et al. (eds.), *Chinese Language Resources*, Text, Speech and Language Technology 49, https://doi.org/10.1007/978-3-031-38913-9_26

key phrases used in searches are mostly nouns or noun phrases. Even if an input consists of a simple and natural question, what these systems focus on in the analysis step are in fact, noun phrases. In terms of Internet search engines, keywords and key phrases supplied by users or those automatically suggested by search engines based on statistical analysis are indeed mostly noun phrases.

When producing indexes for databases as large as those behind major search engines and as small as those created with ordinary texts, noun phrases are used more often than other types of phrases. In addition, semantic role labeling, named entity recognition, and coreference resolution all involve the identification of noun phrases. Undoubtedly, the availability of a good noun phrase (NP) identification program will significantly contribute to NLP research and related applications.

In our study, we first employed the support vector machine (SVM) algorithm as a starting model. In addition to the IOB tagging approach used in many studies, we also experimented with different tagging methods. Our study posited that the IOE representation scheme as well as a simplified tagset would produce a better classifier for Chinese noun phrase identification in both closed and open tests. We also used sentences from Word Sketch Engine (WSE), a large corpus with part-of-speech (POS) and grammatical dependency information, as well as extracted unlabeled data from web pages to complement the limited data in the Sinica Treebank. The purpose of using more data from WSE and web pages was to improve the chunker implemented with supervised learning methods by employing the self-learning concept in semi-supervised learning.

We collected an additional set of different types of noun phrases for the open tests to compare the effects of supervised and semi-supervised approaches in NP chunking. The results of our experiments showed that the parameters that we adopted for the Chinese data produced more favorable results than those produced by conventional parameters. In the open tests, the F-measure of the supervised approach was only 70%, but the semi-supervised learning approach increased the F-measure to 78.79%, which significantly enhanced the performance of noun phrase identification.

26.2 Literature Review

Most research on noun phrase identification has centered on chunking. A "chunk" typically refers to a phrase that does not contain other types of chunks. In other words, a chunk is a non-overlapping and non-recursive combination of words (cf. Tjong and Buchholz 2000). An NP chunk is different from a noun phrase in that the former does not contain nested noun phrases (including possessive NPs), prepositional phrases, or subordinate clauses. Consider the Chinese sentence 噴灑農藥危害到生物多樣性 *pēnsǎ nóngyào wéihài dào shēngwù duōyàngxìng* "spraying agricultural pesticides harms biodiversity," which can be analyzed as a tree structure based on the Sinica Treebank format shown in Fig. 26.1 below. In this sentence, 農

Fig. 26.1 Syntactic tree structure of 噴灑農藥危害到生物多樣性

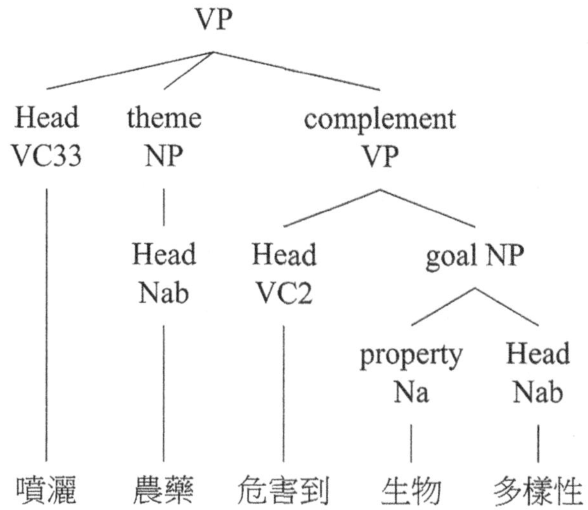

藥 *nóngyào* "agricultural pesticide" and 生物多樣性 *shēngwù duōyàngxìng* "biodiversity" are both NP chunks.

Considering the sentence 再想到蝴蝶會生滿屋的毛蟲 *zài xiǎngdào húdié huì shēng mǎn wū de máochóng* "then thinking of the fact that butterflies will produce a house full of caterpillars," as shown in Fig. 26.2 below, the syntactic tree structure of 滿屋的毛蟲 *mǎn wū de máochóng* "a house full of caterpillars" is not an NP chunk, as the phrase contains two base noun phrases 滿屋 *mǎn wū* "a house full of" and 毛蟲 *máochóng* "caterpillars."

The task of NP chunking is more challenging in Chinese than in English for several reasons. Unlike English, Chinese does not have delimiters between words. Chinese parts-of-speech are also much more difficult to decide contextually than those in English (cf. CKIP 詞庫小組 1993; Huang and Shi 2016; Huang et al. 2017) because of the absence of morphological cues in Chinese, which can distinguish verbs from nouns. In addition, errors in word segmentation and part-of-speech tagging inevitably reduce the accuracy rate of NP chunking in Chinese. Compared with the chunking specifications, data sets, and solutions for English in the CoNLL-2000 Shared Task (http://www.cnts.ua.ac.be/conll2000/chunking/), the corresponding information for Chinese is less consistent. As it is necessary to label the structural information of each chunk in a sentence, researchers in Chinese text processing tend to employ treebanks such as the Sinica Treebank and the Penn Chinese Treebank. It should be noted that the Sinica Treebank and the Penn Chinese Treebank differ significantly. They not only have different tagsets but also different structures due to the different grammatical frameworks they adopted. This means that neither the extraction of the same syntactic structure from the two treebanks nor the direct comparison of the two treebanks is straightforward. A detailed discussion of the design criteria and annotation guidelines of the Sinica Treebank can be found in Huang and Chen (2017).

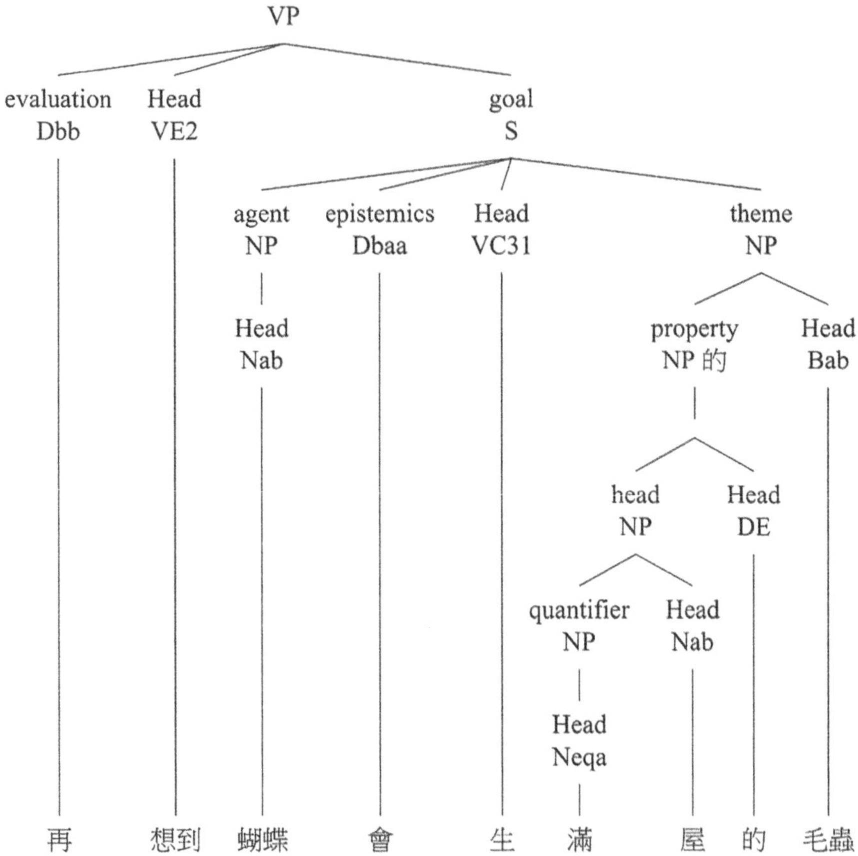

Fig. 26.2 Syntactic tree structure of 再想到蝴蝶會生滿屋的毛蟲

Abney (1996) utilized finite state machines to implement a regular parser by testing both English and German and was able to successfully and quickly extract phrases in major syntactic categories, such as verb, noun, and prepositional phrases, with an approach that emphasized the importance of grammar. Kinyon (2001) proposed a rule-based chunker that worked across a number of languages, and the methods could even be used in the absence of a large training corpus, as long as rules for identifying structural boundaries were available. These experiments showed that rule-based chunkers, which have been mostly overlooked in recent years, are not at all inferior to statistical chunkers; in fact, their performance can be superior in terms of both their recall and F-measure.

Before the advent of large-scale text corpora, structural rules for NP chunking were often used to identify appropriate patterns by means of finite-state machines. These patterns were retrieved statistically from the corpora, either annotated with POS tags or in conjunction with linguistic rules and corpus statistics. Following the release of the Penn Chinese Treebank to the general public, solutions for phrasal

Word:	w_{i-2}	w_{i-1}	w_i	w_{i+1}	w_{i+2}
POS:	t_{i-2}	t_{i-1}	t_i	t_{i+1}	t_{i+2}
Chunk:	c_{i-2}	c_{i-1}	$\boxed{c_i}$		

Fig. 26.3 Features proposed in Kudo and Matsumoto (2000)

Table 26.1 Sample vectors for the sentence 這是詞組範例標記 corresponding to Kudo and Matsumoto's (2000) algorithm

Target word category	w_i	w_{i-2}	w_{i-1}	w_{i+1}	w_{i+2}	t_i	t_{i-1}	t_{i+1}
B	1: 這	1:0	1:0	1: 是	1: 詞組	1: NES	1: 0	1: SHI
O	1: 是	1:0	1: 這	1: 詞組	1: 範例	1: SHI	1: NES	1: NA
B	1: 詞組	1: 這	1: 這	1: 範例	1: 標記	1: NA	1: SHI	1: NA

chunking have been increasingly based on machine learning techniques, including transformation-based learning, maximum entropy, memory-based learning (MBL), hidden Markov models (HMMs), and the SVM algorithm. Kudo and Matsumoto (2000, 2001), for example, applied weighted voting to eight SVM-based systems trained with distinct chunk representations. These algorithms have long been used in other topics related to natural language processing.

Kudo and Matsumoto (2000) used SVM effectively in phrase identification tasks. The features included the surrounding words of a word, the POS, and the predicted phrase category. To identify the phrase category of the *i*th word (also called C_i), it employed the features shown in Fig. 26.3 below:where $w_i p_{q \in Q}$ is the word occurring at the i th position, t_i represents the POS tag for w_i, and c_i is the chunk label of the i th word. In addition, the authors converted (c_{i+1}, c_{i+2}) in the feature set into (c_{i-1}, c_{i-2}) to achieve the effects of backward parsing. During testing, each chunk label (c_{i-1}, c_{i-2}) for forward parsing; (c_{i+1}, c_{i+2}) for backward parsing), regarded as a feature, was not predetermined but was instead the result of the model currently being used, and the corresponding labels w_i and t_i were static features. Table 26.1 below shows the corresponding sample vectors for the sentence 這/是/詞組/範例/標記 *zhè/shì/cízǔ/fànlì/biāojì*; in particular, B and O indicate whether each word in the question is at the beginning (B) or outside (O) of the NP:

In recent years, Deep Neural Network (DNN) models have largely replaced traditional machine learning approaches in NLP and other subfields of AI. These models include various types of neural networks such as Recurrent Neural Networks (RNNs), Convolutional Neural Networks (CNNs), Long Short-Term Memory (LSTM), Transformers, and Bidirectional Encoder Representations from Transformers (BERT).

RNNs are a type of DNN that can be used for NP chunking. RNNs can model sequential data by keeping an internal state that enables them to memorize prior inputs. Word embeddings are used as input to the RNN. In the case of NP chunking (cf. Collobert & Weston, 2008), the output of RNNs consists of a series of labels indicating whether each word is part of a noun phrase.

CNNs are another type of neural network that can be used for NP chunking. CNNs can identify patterns in data by using filters. In such an approach, a CNN is applied to a sequence of word embeddings as input to identify sequences of words that are likely to form noun phrases.

LSTM is a type of RNN that can address the problem of vanishing gradients that can occur when learning on long sequences. LSTMs consist of cells connected by gates, including an input gate, an output gate, and a forget gate. The gates control the flow of information, allowing the LSTM to learn long-term dependencies in a sequence.

Chiu and Nichols (2015) propose a combination of LSTMs and CNNs for Named Entity Recognition (NER) to capture character-level information. A bidirectional LSTM (BiLSTM) is employed in the model to label the sequence after a CNN extracts local features from the input text. Zhai et al. (2017) introduce a novel method for sequence chunking by treating each chunk as a separate unit for labeling. Instead of using the standard IOB (Inside, Outside, Beginning) labels, this study adopts an encoder-decoder-pointer framework and a BiLSTM for segmentation. Experimental results show that the proposed neural sequence chunking models can achieve state-of-the-art performance on chunking.

Vaswani et al. (2017) present the Transformer model, a neural network architecture that employs a self-attention mechanism to compute input sequence representations. The Transformer model was developed to address the shortcomings of previous sequence modeling approaches, such as RNNs and CNNs, which are difficult to capture long-term dependencies in sequential data. The authors demonstrate that the Transformer model outperforms previous models based on recurrent or convolutional architectures on a variety of NLP tasks.

The BERT model is an example of a Transformer-based approach. Devlin et al. (2019) introduce the BERT model, which was pre-trained on large amounts of unlabeled text data using a masked language modeling task and a next sentence prediction task. The authors demonstrate that fine-tuning BERT for a variety of downstream NLP tasks can lead to state-of-the-art performance on numerous benchmark data sets, outperforming previous models trained on task-specific labeled data. Since then, BERT has become one of the most widely used language models for a variety of NLP tasks.

Compared with the research on English NP chunking, studies on Chinese NP chunking are relatively scarce. Zhao and Huang (1999) described the structural rules for several types of phrases but abandoned the rule-based approach and adopted the memory-based learning approach. The experiments reported in the study indicated that if no information about the words themselves was provided and only their POS information was used, the results were less satisfactory.

The study conducted by Wang and Chi (2003) is an early investigation into Chinese NP chunking using neural networks. They use a three-layer neural network with input, output, and hidden layers and train it with the backpropagation algorithm. The input data includes information on character segmentation and its neighboring characters in a Chinese sentence, while the output comprises the segmentation outcomes of every character in the sentence. The model can determine whether a Chinese character is at the left boundary, right boundary, or in the middle of a chunk.

Chang et al. 張席維等 (2005) adopted the algorithm proposed by Kudo and Matsumoto (2000, 2001) to train a model for Chinese NP chunking using the Sinica Treebank as the training data. Although the studies by Kudo and Matsumoto (2000, 2001) achieved about 94% accuracy for the English data, Chang et al. 張席維等 (2005) managed only 87.43% accuracy, suggesting that NP chunking is indeed more challenging in Chinese than in English. Zhou et al. (2012) formulated phrase chunking as a joint segmentation and labeling task and proposed a dynamic programming algorithm with pruning for decoding, allowing the direct employment of features that described the internal characteristics of a chunk and captured the correlations between adjacent chunks. Using the unannotated Chinese text of a parallel Chinese-English corpus, Zhu et al. (2014) presented an unsupervised shallow parsing model trained by exploiting graph-based label propagation for bilingual knowledge transfer, achieving high F1 scores compared with conventional approaches. Zhu et al. (2015) developed a syntactic and semantic parsing toolkit called NiuParser for Chinese, including a chunker that implemented a linear-chain conditional random field (CRF) algorithm based on Lafferty et al. (2001) for sequence labeling.

Wu et al. (2019) present a BiLSTM-CRF with self-attention mechanism (Att-BiLSTM-CRF) model for Chinese Clinic Named Entity Recognition (CNER) to overcome the problems arising from long-term dependencies, lexical ambiguities, and the lack of word boundaries in Chinese. Self-attention is used to capture long-term dependencies by directly linking each character. A character-level representation approach, along with part-of-speech information, is proposed to identify more semantic information about Chinese characters.

The research by Wang et al. (2021) on relation extraction for Chinese noun phrases differs from most recent studies on similar topics because it utilizes an unsupervised approach that does not rely on deep learning. Instead, the study uses a three-layer data-driven architecture that includes a modifier-sensitive phrase segmenter, a candidate relation generator, and a missing relation predicate detector. The system first segments Chinese noun phrases into modifiers and headwords, which are then used to create potential relation triples through a graph clique mining approach.

As shown in the review above, most recent studies focus on name entity recognition (NER). There has been little research on the identification of NP chunking, which is a more general issue than NER in NLP. NER is arguably simpler than NP chunking, because NER is shorter and less complex in structure. This is especially the case for Chinese, as Chinese has very complex nominalizations, where a verb can be nominalized without any morphological change. This makes the part-of-speech (POS) tags of both verbs and nominalized verbs identical in many cases, increasing the difficulty of Chinese NP chunking. Since the nominalization problem in Chinese NP chunking has not been properly addressed in previous research, it is unclear if deep learning approaches can outperform traditional machine learning methods. In the following, we will describe a semi-supervised approach to Chinese NP chunking using SVM. We hope our study may shed light on more recent approaches to similar problems.

26.3 Support Vector Machine and YamCha

SVM is a machine learning algorithm widely used for classification problems. Compared with other traditional classifiers, such as decision tree learning and maximum entropy, SVM offers the following advantages:

1. Good performance, even in high-dimensional feature spaces.
2. Kernel functions are capable of projecting data onto an even higher-dimensional space, without increasing computational complexity.

The main goal of SVM is to produce an optimal hyperplane to separate the training sample vectors into two categories (positive and negative) to maximize the margin. In Fig. 26.4 below, each solid line represents a hyperplane that separates the data into two categories. The distance between the two parallel dotted lines represents the margin, which is the quantity that SVM aims to maximize. The sample points located on the dotted lines are called the support vectors, and only those support vectors that are localized will affect the results of the entire model.

Although SVM is capable of achieving a high level of accuracy in classification, its computational complexity is also higher than those of other machine learning algorithms. Under circumstances where a large amount of training data is required, the SVM training process is not efficient enough. In addition, it is also possible that the results will not be available until after an excessive amount of training time has elapsed.

YamCha (Yet Another Multipurpose CHunk Annotator) is a toolkit designed by Taku Kudo (2001), based on Kudo and Matsumoto (2000), to solve NLP-related

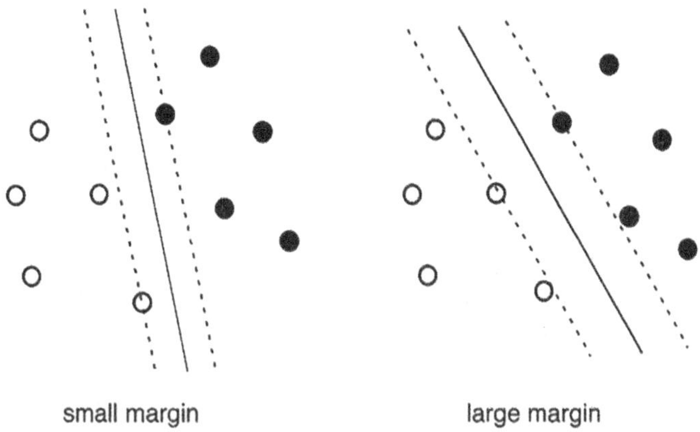

Fig. 26.4 Two possible hyperplanes for separating data

He	PRP	B-NP
reckons	VBZ	B-VP
The	DT	B-NP
current	JJ	I-NP
account	NN	I-NP
deficit	NN	I-NP
will	MD	B-VP
narrow	VB	I-VP

Fig. 26.5 YamCha's input file format is the same as that of the CoNLL-2000 Shared Task (see Table 26.2), where the symbols B, I, and O represent whether each word is at the NP's beginning, inside, or outside, respectively

problems such as phrase chunking, part-of-speech tagging, and text classification applications. YamCha utilizes SVM as the classification method. Unlike the simple SVM classifier, the input files required by YamCha have a more intuitive format. Users simply need to prepare the data to be processed in the format illustrated in Fig. 26.5 below, arrange the relevant features of each word in a straightforward order, and then use the file as YamCha's input. If none of the parameters are altered, the tool will take the default values specified and train the data by treating the words at the $(n-2, n-1, n, n+1, n+2)$ positions and their features as the feature sets of the target words.

How YamCha differs from traditional toolkits is that the tool takes care of the problem of data format for the user. Another point worth noting is that, although SVM performs very well on classification tasks, the amount of computation and running time are also greater than those required by other algorithms. YamCha has made improvements on this front and has achieved at least a threefold increase in speed in terms of training and classification time.

26.4 Semi-supervised Learning

As suggested by its literal meaning, semi-supervised learning (SSL) methods lie somewhere between supervised and unsupervised learning methods: a large amount of unlabeled data is combined with some labeled data for training purposes to address the issue of data sparseness. Given a certain amount of labeled data, is it possible to take advantage of the vast amounts of readily available unlabeled data to build a classifier with higher accuracy? This problem is commonly classified as one that can be handled using semi-supervised learning techniques. Manually annotating data is a time-consuming and costly endeavor in practice. On the other hand, data that has not been checked manually is plentiful and readily available. For this reason, being able to utilize unlabeled data is important in machine learning. For example, a large number of web pages gathered from the Internet via computer programs can be stored, but manual processing is required to correctly classify them. In speech recognition research, it is relatively simple to collect voice recordings, but annotating these audio files word by word requires large amounts of time and manual labor. Under these circumstances, if unlabeled data can contribute to more efficient models, semi-supervised learning is a very useful approach.

Table 26.2 Different schemes for annotating the phrases in the sentence 這是詞組範例標記說明

	IOB1	IOB2	IOE1	IOE2
這 *zhè* "this"	I	B	I	E
是 *shì* "be"	O	O	O	O
詞組 *cízǔ* "phrase"	I	B	I	I
範例 *fànlì* "example"	I	I	I	I
標記 *biāojì* "label"	I	I	E	E
說明 *shuōmíng* "description"	B	B	I	E

In semi-supervised learning, matching data types with models based on different algorithms is a very important step, as mismatching may lead to counterproductive and undesirable results. The expectation-maximization (EM) algorithm with a generative mixture model, the transductive support vector machine (TSVM) algorithm, graph-based algorithms, self-training, and co-training are all commonly used methods in semi-supervised learning, and each offers its own set of advantages. If the labels can clearly separate the data into distinct categories, it is better to employ EM with a generative mixture model. However, if the feature set is sufficient in breaking down the data into two groups, co-training is more suitable as this algorithm makes certain assumptions about the separate features, and for different feature sets, different learning tools are used. Any points with the same features will be grouped into the same category, and when the current model cannot be improved further, graph-based methods such as min-cuts, Boltzmann machine, and tree-based Bayes are more appropriate. More discussions on semi-supervised learning in NLP can be found in Abney (2007), Zhu and Goldberg (2009), and Søgaard (2013).

The earliest attempts at applying the concept of utilizing unlabeled data for classification were perhaps self-learning algorithms. As a first step, only a small amount of labeled data is used for training. Next, suitable points are identified from the unlabeled data with the current decision function and added to the collection of (labeled) training data for the next round of training to arrive at a new decision function. This is repeated until it is no longer possible to find data that can be labeled from the remaining unlabeled data, or until a certain threshold has been reached.

Yarowsky (1995) is a well-known and often cited work on the topic of "self-learning." Employing only 2% of annotated data, this approach to word sense disambiguation even outperformed approaches that require labeled data. Ando and Zhang (2005) is another good example of using additional unlabeled data to improve the performance of the classifier using structural learning. The basic idea of such an approach is to create auxiliary problems that are related to the target problem and have the same predictive structure. The proposed method first trained different predictors from different auxiliary problems and then combined all the problems using singular value decomposition (SVD). The algorithm automatically generated labeled data for the auxiliary problems from unlabeled data. In experiments on name entity chunking and syntactic chunking, Ando and Zhang (2005) reported a better performance than that in previous studies.

26.5 Experiments

26.5.1 Data Sets Used in the Experiments

In our study, we utilized the Sinica Treebank (Version 3.0) for the data required for the supervised and semi-supervised learning experiments. The sources of textual data in this corpus include articles from the Academia Sinica Balanced Corpus of Modern Chinese (Sinica Corpus), elementary school textbooks, *Taiwan Panorama* magazine, and the balanced speech files provided by the Institute of Linguistics, Academia Sinica. Computer analysis was performed on these files and corrections were made manually in the construction of the treebank, resulting in six files with a total of 65,434 Chinese syntactic structure trees and 392,237 words (six words per structure tree on average). We extracted 70% of the data from each file in the database to use as our training data. The remaining 30% was used as test data in closed tests. Apart from the structural information, we also obtained Chinese semantic roles (cf. the treebank below). The POS tagset used in the Sinica Treebank is discussed in CKIP 詞庫小組 (1993) and Huang et al. (2017). The original tagset is very fine-grained, and for each syntactic category, it has at most three subcategories; for example, the tag for personal pronouns is `Nhaa`. The sentences in the files are represented in the following format:

```
#S(agent:NP(Head:Nca:觀光局)|evaluation:Dbb:還|quantity:Daa:另|
Head:VE12:安排|aspect:Di:了|theme:NP(property:NP(quantifier:DM:幾
處|Head:Ncb:市郊)|property:Nv4:遊覽|Head:Nac:活動))#。
(PERIODCATEGORY)
```

There were approximately 45,000 sentences in the training data. We extracted 65,009 NP chunks, with each containing only 1.59 words on average. This suggests that the NP chunks annotated in the Sinica Treebank consist mainly of single words. With respect to the sentence above, represented by the treebank diagram, the words/phrases 觀光局 *guānguāng jú* "Tourism Bureau," 幾處市郊 *jǐ chù shìjiāo* "several suburban locations," and 活動 *huódòng* "activity" are separate chunks according to the structure specified in the treebank. Note that 遊覽活動 *yóulǎn huódòng* "sightseeing activities" and 幾處市郊遊覽活動 *jǐ chù shìjiāo yóulǎn huódòng* "sightseeing activities in several suburban locations" are not annotated as NPs because the Sinica Treebank uses Information-based Case Grammar (ICG), which is different from traditional grammatical formalisms (cf. Huang and Chen 2017). Moreover, noun phrases consisting of an adjective or noun followed by the marker 的 *DE* followed by a noun are not identified as NPs in the Sinica Treebank. While this is in line with the definition of NP chunking in most research, it does not conform to the traditional notion of a noun phrase. Since noun phrase identification was an intermediate step to parsing in our approach, we aimed to identify as many complete NPs as possible to facilitate parsing. For this reason, when labeling the answers for the NP chunks, we made changes to several structures and created answers that were more consistent with the traditional definition of NPs, including the following:

1. Noun + 的 DE + Noun
`#1:1.[0] S(agent:NP(Head:Nhaa:他)|Head:VC31:拿|aspect:Di:了|theme:NP(possessor:N‧的(head:Nhaa:我|Head:DE:的)|Head:Naeb:錢))#。(PERIODCATEGORY)`
2. Adjective + 的 DE + Noun
`#1:1.[0] S(theme:NP(Head:Nep:這)|Head:V_11:是|range:NP(property:VP‧的(head:VP(degree:Dfa:很|Head:VH11:有名)|Head:DE:的)|Head:Ncb:餐廳))#。(PERIODCATEGORY)`
3. Classifier + 的 DE + Noun
`#VP(Head:VC2:承擔|goal:NP(possessor:NP‧的(head:NP(quantifier:Neu:千萬| Head:Nab:窮人)|Head:DE:的)|Head:Nad:苦難))#`

From their syntactic tree structures, the three sentences above contain only the following NP chunks: 他 *tā* "he," 這 *zhè* "this," 錢 *qián* "money," 餐廳 *cāntīng* "restaurant," and 苦難 *kǔ'nàn* "suffering." We combined these with their modifiers in the manner described above for the three types of NP chunks and arrived at 我的錢 *wǒ de qián* "my money," 很有名的餐廳 *hěn yǒumíng de cāntīng* "a very famous restaurant," 千萬窮人的苦難 *qiānwàn qióngrén de kǔ'nàn* "suffering of thousands of poor people," etc.

Potential Issues

1. Unlike English and many other languages, Chinese is a language that has no inflectional morphemes. In English, for example, verbs in the passive voice are inflected, and when they are converted to nouns, suffixes such as "-ing" and "-tion" are added. In Chinese passives, on the other hand, there are no morphological cues within verbs. The Chinese passive is typically marked by the insertion of 被 *bèi* in front of the verb. In addition, unlike English, nominalization in Chinese is not revealed by morphological information. Consider the English sentence below:
   The experiment involved the *combining* of the two chemicals.
   It is apparent that *combining* here is used as a nominal, but in the following Chinese sentences, it is unclear which parts of speech 進口 *jìnkǒu* "import/imported" and 喜愛 *xǐ'ài* "affinity, preference, affection" belong to:

政府編定汽車管理制度使進口汽車得以合法化。
zhèngfǔ__biāndìng__qìchē__guǎnlǐ__zhìdù__shǐ__jìnkǒu__qìchē__déyǐ__héfǎhuà
government__develop__automobile__management__system__cause__import__automobile__become__lawful
The government has set up a car management system to legitimize imported cars.
他深得學生的喜愛。
tā__shēn__dé__xuéshēng__de__xǐ'ài
he__deeply__receive__student__DE__affection
He has won the affection of the students.

This is also the nominalization phenomenon mentioned in Chang et al. 張席維等 (2005), Ding et al. (2005), and Ma and Huang 馬偉雲, 黃居仁 (2006). Phrases that exhibit this particular characteristic in the Sinica Treebank number fewer than 3000. As a result, Chang et al. 張席維等 (2005) also emphasized that, based on their experimental results, when using supervised learning techniques to identify Chinese NPs, the key to improving accuracy is to decide correctly whether the verbs have been nominalized.

2. The average length of the annotated chunks extracted from the Sinica Treebank was less than two words. Cheng et al. (2005) mentioned that there are actually quite a few NPs consisting of several words in the Chinese language. Examples include 行政院/國家/科學/委員會 *Xíngzhèngyuàn/guójiā/kēxué/wěiyuánhuì* "National Science Council, Executive Yuan" and 電腦/人體/模型 *diànnǎo/réntǐ/móxíng* "human computer model." These chunks are quite commonly encountered in daily life. Therefore, using the Sinica Treebank as a gold standard or training corpus will not solve the problem of long chunks.
3. Even more challenging scenarios may involve a mixture of the two situations above, examples of which include 汽車/強制/責任/險 *qìchē/qiángzhì/zérèn/xiǎn* "compulsory automobile liability insurance," 營建/工程/研究所 *yíngjiàn/gōngchéng/yánjiūsuǒ* "construction engineering research institute," and 台灣/大學/進修/推廣/部 *Táiwān/Dàxué/jìnxiū/tuīguǎng/bù* "School of Professional Education and Continuing Studies, National Taiwan University." Note that examples like these are quite common in Chinese texts but few researches have addressed the complexity of Chinese NPs. Most of these examples are also excluded in NP chunking.

Representations of Noun Phrases

Ramshaw and Marcus (1995) proposed the following chunk tagset {I, O, B} to represent the position of a word within a phrase:

- I: Word is inside a particular phrase.
- O: Word is outside of all phrases.
- B: Word is at the leftmost (beginning) position of the phrase.

This scheme was referred to as IOB1 by Tjong (2000), who additionally proposed IOB2/IOE1/IOE2:

- IOB2: "B" refers to the start (beginning) of any phrase.
- IOE1: "E" refers to the end that immediately follows another phrase.
- IOE2: "E" refers to the end of any phrase.

Table 26.2 below shows several examples of these schemes. Furthermore, a "start/end" scheme also exists, but the experiments using this approach in Kudo and Matsumoto (2000) did not produce satisfactory results.

With respect to the experimental results, we adopted the same evaluation approach used in the CoNLL-2000 Shared Task, which provides a tool to compute tag accuracy, precision (*P*), recall (*R*) and the *F*-measure, which is defined as *F*-measure = 2PR/(*P* + *R*). The *F*-measure was our principal standard of evaluation.

26.5.2 Available Resources

In subsequent experiments, we used a number of well-known and popular tools and resources:

1. Sinica Chinese word segmentation system (http://ckipsvr.iis.sinica.edu.tw): The output contains segmented words with their corresponding POS tags; unknown words can also be handled.
2. Word Sketch Engine (WSE) (`http://www.sketchengine.co.uk`). This is a large corpus analysis system (cf. Huang et al. 2005; Kilgarriff et al. 2004) containing a number of languages, including Chinese, English, French, and German. In addition, the corpus data has been annotated with POS tags and grammatical dependency information, and the sentences in this corpus are automatically annotated with POS tags and grammatical information. Apart from segmented words, their POS tags can also be looked up, as shown in the following two examples:

稅捐處 工商 稅科 、 財產稅科 、 稽徵 科 及 稅務 管理 科 等 依照 權責 , 將 分別 全面 查緝 逃漏稅 。
shuìjuān__chù__gōng__shāng__shuì__kē, cáichăn__shuì__kē,
jīzhēngkē__jí__shuìwù__guănlǐ__kē__děng__yīzhào__quán__zé,
jiāng__fēnbié__quánmiàn__chájī__táolòushuì.
taxation__department__industry__commerce__property__tax__section,
tax collection__and__section__tax__management__section__etc.__follow__authority__
responsibility__, will__separately__fully__investigate-and-prosecute__tax evasion*The Industrial and Commercial Tax Section, Property Tax Section, Tax Collection Section and Taxation Management Section of the Revenue Service Department will fully investigate and prosecute all tax evasion cases according to each division's authority and responsibilities.*
在/P21賦稅/Naeb 方面/Nac, /COMMACATEGORY 查緝/VC2 逃漏稅/Na 及/Caa 進行/VC2 會計師/Nab 評鑑

With respect to POS tagging, WSE differs from Sinica's Chinese word segmenter in that when assigning a POS tag to a word, the Sinica system takes into account the context of the sentence, whereas WSE does not. Therefore, for non-function words (i.e., words that potentially belong to several different categories), WSE performs less favorably in terms of accuracy and is therefore less valuable compared with its Sinica counterpart.

3. Google search engine. As WSE was not a large enough corpus, we used the Google search engine to extract example sentences to complement the data in WSE.

26.5.3 Supervised Learning Experiment

There are in fact three versions of the CKIP POS tagset. The original tagset used in the Sinica Corpus and Sinica Treebank is the most elaborate one (cf. the tags in the second column in Table 26.3). The three versions of POS tagsets differ in the number of subcategories as well as the level of sophistication. Tags in the first column in Table 26.3 belong to the simplified tagset, which is less fine-grained than the original POS tagset yet more fine-grained than the reduced tagset. Table 26.3 below shows a comparison between CKIP tagsets and the simplified labels, as well as the interpretations from CKIP 詞庫小組 (1993) and Huang et al. (2017):

Chang et al. 張席維等 (2005) experimented with Chinese NP chunking using the simplified and the reduced tagsets, showing that the information in the subcategories of verbs is useful for distinguishing verbs from nominalization. The finding was also supported by the experiments by Ma and Huang 馬偉雲, 黃居仁 (2006), which pointed out that the verb subcategories of the CKIP tagset are conducive to the identification of nominalization in Chinese. However, do finer details in verb subcategories result in better performance? Will the most fine-grained tagset perform the best? Table 26.4 below shows that the values of the F-measure for the original and the simplified tagsets did not differ significantly.

As for the open test, it included some of the following sentences:

我們買了一張很貴的票。
wǒmen__mǎi__le__yī__zhāng__hěn__guì__de__piào
we__buy__ASP__one__CL__HEN__expensive__DE__ticket
We bought a very expensive ticket.
我聘了一個很優秀的職員。
wǒ__pìn__le__yī__gè__hěn__yōuxiù__de__zhíyuán.
I__hire__ASP__one__CL__HEN__excellent__DE__employee
I hired an excellent employee.
阿忠的那一間房子。
Ā-zhōng__de__nà__yī__jiàn__fángzi.
A-Zhong__DE__that__one__CL__house.
A-Zhong's house.

Chang et al. 張席維等 (2005) already pointed out that models trained using supervised learning methods do not perform satisfactorily in the identification of nominalization. Therefore, in the open test, we only selected sentences with NPs in basic forms, such as Classifier + Noun, Adjective + Noun, and Classifier + Adjective + Noun, along with sentences that contained long composite NPs and possessives. Table 26.5 below illustrates the results of this experiment:

In Table 26.4, (1) the use of the original CKIP POS tags did not produce a performance superior to that of the simplified tags, and (2) although in the closed test both representations were comparable in terms of accuracy, from the results of the open test shown in Table 26.5, the IOE scheme produced more accurate results than

Table 26.3 CKIP tagsets (Academia Sinica)

Simplified symbols	Symbols in treebank	Interpretation	Simplified symbols	Symbols in treebank	Interpretation
A	A	Non-predicative adjective 非謂形容詞	P	P*	Preposition 介詞
CAA	CAA	Coordinating conjunction, e.g., 和 *he* "and", 跟 *gen* "and" 對等連接詞	SHI	V_11	*shì* (to be) 是
CAB	CAB	Conjunction, e.g., 等等 *dengdeng* "etc." 連接詞	T	Ta, Tb, Tc, td	Final particle 語助詞
CBA	CBAB	Conjunction, e.g., 的話 *dehua* "if" 連接詞	VA	VA11, 12, 13, VA3, VA4	Active intransitive verb 動作不及物動詞
CBB	Cbaa, Cbba, Cbbb, Cbca, Cbcb	Correlative conjunction 關聯連接詞	VAC	VA2	Active causative verb 動作使動動詞
D	Dab, Dbaa, Dbab, Dbb, Dbc, dc, Dd, dg, dh, Dj	Adverb 副詞	VB	VB11, 12, VB2	Active transitive verb 動作類及物動詞
DA	DAA	Quantitative adverb 數量副詞	VC	VC2, VC31, 32, 33	Active transitive verb 動作及物動詞
DE		Particle DE and its functional equivalents 的, 之, 得, 地	VCL	VC1	Active verb with a locative object 動作接地方賓語動詞
DFA	DFA	Pre-verbal adverb of degree 動詞前程度副詞	VD	VD1, VD2	Ditransitive verb 雙賓動詞
DFB	DFB	Post-verbal adverb of degree 動詞後程度副詞	VE	VE11, VE12, VE2	Active verb with a sentential object 動作句賓動詞
DI	DI	Aspectual adverb 時態副詞	VF	VF1, VF2	Active verb with a verbal object 動作謂賓動詞
DK	DK	Sentential adverb 句副詞	VG	VG1, VG2	Classificatory verb 分類動詞
FW		Foreign word 外來語	VH	VH11, 12, 13, 14, 15, 17, VH21	Stative intransitive verb 狀態不及物動詞
I	I	Interjection 感嘆詞	VHC		

(continued)

Table 26.3 (continued)

Simplified symbols	Symbols in treebank	Interpretation	Simplified symbols	Symbols in treebank	Interpretation
				VH16, VH22	Stative causative verb 狀態使動動詞
NA	Naa, nab, Nac, Nad, Naea, Naeb	Common noun 普通名詞	VI	VI1,2,3	Stative pseudo-transitive verb 狀態類及物動詞
NB	Nba, Nbc	Proper noun 專有名詞	VJ	VJ1, 2, 3	Stative transitive verb 狀態及物動詞
NC	Nca, Ncb, Ncc, Nce	Place noun 地方名詞	VK	VK1, 2	Stative verb with a sentential object 狀態句賓動詞
NCD	Ncda, Ncdb	Localizer 位置詞	VL	VL1, 2, 3, 4	Stative verb with a verbal object 狀態謂賓動詞
ND	Ndaa, Ndab, Ndc, Ndd	Time noun 時間名詞	V_2	V_2	*yǒu* (to have) 有
NEU	NEU	Numeral determinative 數詞定詞	NH	Nhaa, Nhab, Nhac, Nhb, Nhc	Pronoun 代名詞
NEP	NEP	Demonstrative determinative 指代定詞			
NF	Nfa, Nfb, Nfc, Nfd, Nfe, Nfg, Nfh, Nfi	Classifier, measure 量詞			
NG	NG	Postposition 後置詞			

those of the IOB scheme. As a result, we combined these two types of parameters in our subsequent experiments (including those conducted with semi-supervised learning methods). Another advantage of using the simplified tags is that when we employed the Sinica Chinese word segmenter to preprocess the data for the open test, the tags produced were consistent with those from the trained model. We also discovered the following from the open test:

1. The initial model was not sufficiently sensitive to long phrases. The test data contained the following two NPs: (a) 一名騎機車的年輕人 *yī míng qí jīchē de niánqīng rén* "a young person riding a motorcycle" and (b) 一名高級官員 *yī míng gāojí guānyuán* "a senior official." In these two cases, 一名 *yī míng* (*míng* is a classifier for "person" to describe his/her occupation, etc.) is part of an NP, but

Table 26.4 Comparison of results of features from IOB, IOE, CKIP, and simplified in the closed test

Feature combination	Tag accuracy (%)	Precision (%)	Recall (%)	*F*-measure (%)
(*n* – 2 . . . *n* + 2), (*n* – 2 . . . *n* + 2), (*n* – 2 . . . *n* – 1), IOB, simplified	91.21	84.85	86.98	85.90
(*n* – 2 . . . *n* + 2), (*n* – 2 . . . *n* + 2), (*n* – 2 . . . *n* – 1), IOB, CKIP	90.89	84.44	86.60	85.50
(*n* – 2 . . . *n* + 2), (*n* – 2 . . . *n* + 2), (*n* – 2 . . . *n* – 1), IOE, simplified	92.06	84.65	86.28	85.46
(*n* – 2 . . . *n* + 2), (*n* – 2 . . . *n* + 2), (*n* – 2 . . . *n* – 1), IOE, CKIP	91.93	84.34	86.09	85.20

Table 26.5 Preliminary comparison of open test results between IOB and IOE

Feature combination	Accuracy (%)	Precision (%)	Recall (%)	*F*-measure (%)
(*n* – 2 . . . *n* + 2), (*n* – 2 . . . *n* + 2), (*n* – 2 . . . *n* – 1), IOE, simplified	92.95	86.67	89.66	88.14
(*n* – 2 . . . *n* + 2), (*n* – 2 . . . *n* + 2), *T*(*n* – 2 . . . *n* – 1), IOB, simplified	88.93	68.75	75.86	72.13

in the first instance, it is labeled 一 O/ 名 O, whereas in the second instance, it is labeled 一 I / 名 I. For this reason, the part-of-speech of the word following a classifier being considered by the tagging process is very important. As our initial model incorporated into the feature set a window of only two words on either side of each target word, in the phrase 有一間很漂亮的教師休息室 *yǒuyī jiàn hěn piàoliang de jiàoshī xiūxí shì* "there is a very nice-looking teacher lounge" in the open test, it was possible to tag 一間 *yī jiàn* (*jiàn* is a classifier for "room") incorrectly since a noun was nowhere to be found by looking at the following two words.

2. Even if there were sentences with very similar patterns (e.g., 很漂亮的衣服 *hěn piàoliang de yīfú* "nice-looking clothes" and 很貴的票 *hěn guì de piào* "expensive ticket"), the model outputted different results. For example, we found that 很漂亮 *hěn piàoliang* "nice-looking, pretty" appeared in the training set as part of a noun phrase yet 貴 *guì* "expensive" was treated only as a verb.

Therefore, we considered the following:

1. Altering the size of the window around the target word and consider NPs of different lengths and their semantic features as the feature set; and.
2. Words in particular positions and their semantic features did not necessarily have to exist at the same time.

Table 26.6 Representative feature symbols adopted in the experiment and their significance

Feature rep-resentative	Feature description	Feature rep-resentative	Feature description
W_n	*n*th word	IOB	The IOB scheme to label an NLP
L_n	POS of the *n*th word	IOE	The IOB scheme to label an NLP
T_n	Tag of the *n*th word	*Hn*	Semantic feature of the *n*th word
			According to HowNet
Simplified	Simplified label	CKIP	CKIP label
F	Forward parsing	B	Backward parsing

Table 26.7 Comparison of features used in the models

Model 1	F, $W_{i-2}, \ldots W_{i+2}, P_{i-2} \ldots P_{i+2}, T_{i-2} \ldots T_{i-1}$
Model 2	F, $W_{i-2}, \ldots W_{i+2}, P_{i-2} \ldots P_{i+2}, H_{i-2} \ldots H_{i+2}, T_{i-2} \ldots T_{i-1}$
Model 3	F, $W_{i-4}, \ldots W_{i+2}, P_{i-4} \ldots P_{i+2}, T_{i-2} \ldots T_{i-1}$
Model 4	F, $W_{i-1}, \ldots W_{i+1}, P_{i-1} \ldots P_{i+1}, T_{i-2} \ldots T_{i-1}$
Model 5	F, $Wi, P_{i-2} \ldots P_{i+2}, T_{i-2} \ldots T_{i-1}$
Model 6	B, $W_{i-2}, \ldots W_{i+2}, P_{i-2} \ldots P_{i+2}, T_{i-2} \ldots T_{i-1}$
Model 7	F, $P_{i-2} \ldots P_{i+2}, T_{i-2} \ldots T_{i-1}$

In addition, we also took into consideration the semantic information from HowNet. Table 26.6 below shows the symbols used in the feature set and their meanings:

Table 26.7 below lists the feature combinations for different models; as these combinations produced similar results in the closed test, not all combinations are shown:

Table 26.8 below shows a sample of sentences used in the open test as well as the output results of various models. From these results, each model exhibited obvious shortcomings, and none of them were able to completely determine the NPs correctly. For example, the phrase 監察人員 *jiānchá rényuán* "inspector, supervisor" was not identified by any of the models.

In the sentences in the open test, many words (or the POS sequence) were repeated. Adding different collocates or modifiers, or using a different word order, tested the accuracy and stability of the models for different types of expressions.

Apart from the issue of the limited training corpus and its shortcomings, which was mentioned previously, word sense ambiguity, nominalization, unknown words, and other difficulties encountered in practice were not observed in the corpus. In other words, the data was somewhat unrealistic. As the corpus consists mostly of long articles broken down into sentences, certain usages or expressions are repeated many times simply because they occur in the same articles. The actual quantity of training data was in fact less than what was nominally reported. Although the Sinica Treebank reportedly contains over 60,000 sentences, many of the so-called

Table 26.8 An excerpt of the results of the open test

Sample sentences in open test	我們買了一張很貴的票	一間很漂亮的教師休息室	一輛很貴的車	昨天的報紙登出一則有趣的廣告	監察人員發現重大弊端
Tokenized (segmented)	我們 (Nh)/買 (VC)/了 (Di)/一 (Neu)/張 (Nf)/很 (Dfa)/貴 (VH)/的 (DE)/票 (Na)	一 (Neu) 間 (Nf)很 (Dfa) 漂亮 (VH) 的 (DE) 教師 (Na) 休息室 (Nc)	一 (Neu) 輛 (Nf) 很 (Dfa) 貴 (VH) 的 (DE) 車 (Na)	昨天 (Nd)/的 (DE)/報紙 (Na)登出 (VC)/一 (Neu)/則 (Nf)/有趣 (VH)/的 (DE)/廣告 (Na)	監察 (VC)/人員 (Na)/發現 (VE)/重大 (VH)/弊端 (Na)
Model 1	1. 我們	1. 一間	1. 一輛	1. 報紙	1. 人員
	2. 一張很貴的票	2. 教師休息室	2. 車	2. 一則有趣的廣告	2. 重大弊端
Model 2	1. 我們	1. 一間	1. 一輛	1. 報紙	1. 人員
	2. 一張 3 票	2. 教師休息室	2. 車	2. 一則有趣的廣告	2. 重大弊端
Model 3	1. 我們	1. 一間	1. 一輛	1. 報紙	1. 人員
	2. 一張很貴的票	2. 教師休息室	2. 車	2. 一則有趣的廣告	2. 重大弊端
Model 4	1. 我們	1 很漂亮的教師休息室	1. 一輛	1. 報紙	1. 人員
	2. 一張 3 票		2. 車	2. 一則有趣的廣告	2. 重大弊端
Model 5	1. 我們	1. 一間	1. 一輛	1. 報紙	1. 人員
	2. 一張很貴的票	2. 教師休息室	2. 車	2. 一則有趣的廣告	2. 重大弊端
Model 6	1. 我們	1. 一間	1. 一輛	1. 昨天的報紙	1. 人員
	2. 一張很貴的票	2. 教師休息室	2. 很貴的車	2. 一則有趣的廣告	2. 重大弊端
Model 7	1. 我們	1. 一間	1. 一輛	1. 昨天的報紙	1. 人員
	2. 一張很貴的票	2. 教師休息室	2. 車	2. 一則有趣的廣告	2. 重大弊端

sentences actually contain only single words or consist of nouns entirely, or they are shorter than normal written expressions. In such cases, the so-called sentences were noise for the classifier as no discernible structures could be obtained from them.

For example, the string 爸爸說:山路不難走 *Bàba shuō: Shānlù bù nán zǒu* "Father says, the mountain paths are not difficult to traverse" in the corpus is broken down into two sentences, 爸爸/說 and 山路/不/難/走. In practice, however, longer sentences are preferred. In addition, in the Sinica Treebank, the word and phrase labels were manually checked and corrected, so the corpus offers a high degree of accuracy and credibility. In actual tests, however, words tokenized with the Sinica Chinese word segmenter were not accurate, or their POS tags were wrong. For example, in the corpus, there are words in the NV category, such as 電腦 (NA) *diànnǎo* "computer" / 打字 (NV4) *dǎzì* "typing" / 及 (CAA) *jí* "and" / 排版 (NV4) *páibǎn* "typesetting". However, the Sinica Chinese word segmenter was unable to recognize instances of nominalization (NV), and therefore the resulting tokens were as follows: 電腦 (Na) 打字 (VA) 及 (Caa) 排版 (VA). In the training set, the sentence 兩 (NEU) *liǎng* "two" / 者 (NA) *zhě* "thing, person" / 同等重要 *tóngděng zhòngyào* "equally important" was tokenized by the Sinica Chinese word segmenter as 兩者 (NH) *liǎngzhě* "both" / 同等重要, which indicates that there were considerable differences between the data in the open test and those in the closed test.

Nevertheless, the data used in this experiment indicated that when using supervised learning to perform Chinese noun phrase identification, if the training data is the only information available, the IOE NP scheme, simplified POS tags, target words, and words in the two-word before-and-after window around each target word, as well as the POS tags of these words, are the best feature combinations. Therefore, we combined several features as the basic feature set for the next experiments.

26.5.4 Semi-supervised Learning Experiment

From the last experiment, we found that simply using information from the Sinica Treebank and looking up meanings in a lexical semantic database such as HowNet were not very useful in determining nominalized expressions, so we aimed to utilize external resources to help us obtain new information. This inspiration came from the self-training idea mentioned earlier.

From the sentences in the training corpus, we were able to observe several rules regarding the combinations of verbs followed by nouns. Table 26.9 below shows sample sentences and our conjectures, followed by rules deduced from the corpus and from Table 26.9 as shown in Table 26.10:

First, we randomly selected two types of phrases from the corpus—verbs (as modifiers) followed by nouns (e.g., 採購人員 *cǎigòu rényuán* "procurement staff" and 運動精神 *yùndòng jīngshén* "sportsmanship") and verbs followed by objects (e.g., 祭拜祖先 *jìbài zǔxiān* "worshipping ancestors" and 來自家人 *láizì jiārén* "[coming] from the family")—with 100 bigrams from each category. Then, using WSE, we searched for 50 sentences that contained these bigrams. As an example, the following sentences contain the bigram 採購人員 *cǎigòu rényuán* "procurement staff":

... 團體 [之] 採購人員。
... 需要仰賴的不只有 [總務] 採購人員 [自身]。
... 又蘊含 [了] 採購人員 [對] 他人和社會...
... 大多數 [的] 採購人員 [會] 蕭規曹隨...

After we gathered a predetermined number of sentences, we then collected statistics regarding the parts-of-speech of the words that immediately preceded and followed the bigrams of interest. Even if a large variety of parts-of-speech were

Table 26.9 Some sentences in the corpus and their characteristics

Sample sentences	Conjecture
導遊 發 給 每人 一 本 導覽 手冊。	An NP often follows classifiers.
dǎoyóu fā gěi měirén yī **běn** dǎolǎn shǒucè	
Tour guide__distribute__give__everyone__one__CL__guide__manual	
The tour guide hands out a guidebook to each person.	
這個 報導 給予 我們 無限 的 想像 空間。	的 DE is often followed by an NP.
zhège bàodǎo jǐyǔ wǒmen wúxiàn **de** xiǎngxiàng kōngjiān	
this__report__give__we__unlimited__DE__imagine__space	
This report gives us unlimited room for imagination.	
大家 看 了 宣導 短片 之後 有 什麼 感想 呢?	A temporal word is often followed by an NP.
dàjiā kàn **le** xuāndǎo duǎnpiàn zhīhòu yǒu shénme gǎnxiǎng ne	
everyone__watch__ASP__advocacy__video__afterwards__YOU__what__impression__NE	
What is everyone's impression after watching the educational video?	
我們 今天 只 能 採買 一千 元 以下 的 東西。	An adverb has a good chance of being followed by a verb.
wǒmen jīntiān zhǐ **néng** cǎimǎi yīqiān yuán yǐxià de dōngxī	
we__today__only__can__purchase__1,000__yuan__under__DE__things	
Today we can only purchase items under a thousand dollars.	
大家 申請 補助 的 報告 都 還 沒 寫。	If a personal pronoun is followed by a verb, then it is not likely that this verb will modify a noun.
dàjiā shēnqǐng bǔzhù de bàogào dōu hái méi xiě	
everyone__apply__subsidy__DE__report__all__yet__not__write	
No one has written the report required for the subsidy application yet.	

Table 26.10 Rules deduced from the corpus and from Table 26.9

Categories of words that can follow verbs	NEQA, NEP, NEU and other classifiers
	NG: temporal postposition
	NC: locative
	NH: pronoun

Table 26.11 Comparison of the parts-of-speech of words before verbs of various functions

Type	Word classes that can follow verbs
Verb	D
Verb as modifier	DE, DI, NEQA, NEP

CNA19931119.0012	的設計能力，決定專款補助八名優秀	設計人員	每人最高
CNA19931119.0012	設計人才培訓計畫」，甄選具潛力的	設計人員	赴歐洲做一
CNA19941104.0028	</p><p>該報告對「狂風號」戰機研究	設計人員	的未來出路
CNA19941117.0477	實行的是單位資格認證制度，但對	設計人員	的個人技術
CNA19941216.0337	升高。此外，五年內也培植農機開發	設計人員	約七十人。
CNA19950118.0234	是在輸出船長、工程師、計算機軟體	設計人員	、飛機維修
CNA19950316.0355	有鑑於此，高雄捷運的設計費用是按照實際設	設計人員	的薪資加上
CNA19950720.0266	航鑑交易。</p><p>分析家說，海軍的	設計人員	已草繪出航
CNA19951025.0336	設計資格管理是只管單位的資格，對	設計人員	的個人技術

Fig. 26.6 Sample sentences extracted from Word Sketch Engine

found in these words, we were able to generalize a few possible common features between these two types of phrases. The findings are summarized in Table 26.11 below:

Next, we proceeded to conduct a preliminary small-scale test, where we selected combinations consisting of a verb followed immediately by a noun (V1N1) from the closed test data. Then, as before, we extracted sentences from WSE based on these combinations to obtain words that immediately preceded and followed the target phrases. Lastly, we found the distribution of the parts-of-speech of these neighboring words and determined which category each instance of (V1N1) fell under based on the features previously inferred from the data. In the following, we looked up sentences from WSE that contained the string 設計人員 *shèjì rényuán* "designer, design staff" (see Fig. 26.6):

After tallying the word counts, we found that the number of occurrences of "DE," "DI," and classifiers that occurred before the target phrases was higher than that of adverbs "D." For this reason, we categorized 設計人員 *shèjì rényuán* "designer, design staff" as a Class A phrase consisting of a modifier and a noun. For sentences that contained the phrase 採購汽車 *cǎigòu qìchē* "procure cars," the number of occurrences immediately preceding adverbs "D" was higher than that of "DE," "DI," and classifiers in the same position. Therefore, we categorized 採購汽車 *cǎigòu qìchē* "procure cars" as a Class B phrase consisting of a verb and an object. There was also a third category, exemplified by the phrase 服務社會 *fúwù shèhuì* "serve the society." This bigram did not occur verbatim in any sentence within the WSE corpus (but in a slightly different form in only four or five sentences). In this situation, we categorized it as a Class C case (insufficient data). In the data for the closed test, after cases of insufficient data were removed, the remaining 443 Verb + Noun combinations allowed us to collect adequate data for analysis. When utilizing the approach in the first experiment, only 169 VC + N combinations were correctly identified, whereas 274 such combinations were not. With the method used in this experiment, 218 cases that were previously misidentified were be modified and were correct; 145 combinations that were correctly identified previously remained unchanged, although around an eighth of the cases were misidentified. Overall, the results improved. The step above confirmed our initial conjectures and, furthermore, we were able to extract even more common features from the large amount of data that we collected.

WSE, as mentioned, is an annotated corpus. However, it suffers from limited vocabulary, as well as the issue of timeliness: certain words are relatively new and are used by relatively few people, or they might have been too colloquial and were considered unsuitable for incorporation into the corpus. To address the data sparseness issue, we collected and utilized a large amount of web-derived content as unlabeled data to classify phrases that did not obtain good results from WSE.

With respect to word combinations that did not occur in WSE, such as 服務社會 *fúwù shèhuì*, or those with very low frequencies and thus would not contribute to sufficiently objective analysis, such as 紅燒牛肉 *hóngshāo niúròu* "braised beef," we used the Google search engine to locate pages that contained these phrases and obtained short sentences, similar to those available in WSE, that contained our target phrases. Like WSE, we collected the top 50 snippets returned by the Google search, which contained the summaries of the web pages. The disadvantages, of course, were that, unlike those from WSE, these summaries were just raw data that had neither been tokenized (with segmented words) nor labeled with POS tags. The newly obtained Chinese raw data should have been, in principle, tokenized into separate words as a first step. It should be noted that except for some pre-verbal adverbs, the patterns that we identified were mostly function words that co-occurred with target phrases, such as 的 *DE* and pronouns, which tended to be closed sets and rarely included new members.

After collecting and processing all the required web data, we then found the counts and frequencies of word classes that preceded the target phrases, as we did with WSE. Regarding the combinations of function words, which were previously mentioned, they consisted mostly of one or two words. Therefore, after word segmentation and POS tagging, the part-of-speech of the word preceding each target phrase and the parts-of-speech of the two words preceding the target phrase were checked to see whether the results were consistent with the patterns in our hypothesis.

Continuing with the data used in the previous experiment, the number of word combinations with very low frequencies in WSE was 670,569, which were modified and corrected after data was collected from the web based on those to be analyzed.

Table 26.12 Results of the supervised and semi-supervised learning experiments

Feature combination	Tag accuracy (%)	Precision (%)	Recall (%)	*F*-measure (%)
Closed test				
Supervised	92.06	84.65	86.28	85.46
Semi-supervised	92.19	84.85	86.64	85.73
Open test				
Supervised	89.03	67.31	72.92	70
Semi-supervised	91.61	76.47	81.25	78.79

As these two steps, which involved using external data sources, were only capable of classifying the functions of certain words with a verb as their part-of-speech, the results of this experiment were regarded as a feature to be used as part of the training data for the SVM-based NP labeling process, and the SVM software employed remained the principal tool for analysis.

At this point, the results showed that the input data format was compliant with YamCha's requirements. The features used for semi-supervised learning included the tags I, O, and E from the supervised learning experiment, two words before and after the target word, and the tags A, B, and C, which represented nominalization, verb, and any part-of-speech except a verb, respectively. Note that the tags A, B, and C were derived from unlabeled data, as shown below:

W_n	POS_n	V_n	C_n
設計	VC	A	I
人員	NA	C	E
做好	VC	B	O
拍賣	VC	A	I
網站	NA	C	E

We also performed closed and open tests based on this approach. As the focus was to improve the identification of nominalized verbs, apart from the test data used in the last experiment, the open test portion also incorporated sentences containing VPs with nominalized verbs, which accounted for 50% of the entire test data set. Table 26.12 below shows the results of this experiment. In the closed test, the F-measure produced by the semi-supervised learning experiment was 85.46%, which was only 0.2 percentage points higher than that of the supervised learning experiment. However, in the open test, the corresponding F-measure from the semi-supervised learning method outperformed the supervised learning approach significantly by 8.79% points.

From the data analysis above, similar methods yielded more accurate results from the WSE data compared with the general Internet sources. Apart from the fact that data from WSE was processed by a word segmentation program and POS tagging, there were several other reasons as well. First, while the sentences from WSE were carefully selected and were more consistent in format, the web data was from diverse and dissimilar sources. Second, a single web search may have yielded duplicate

請提出具具體可行保障婦女權益之政見-呂健吉的愛情憤哲學、時評論壇、部落...
實言之，婦女權益之保障必須要落實在整個意識形態的改變，首先就要破除男尊女卑的觀念，從教育上做起，讓男女平等的觀念從小培養起來；其次則是就工作權的保障，要就法令...
blog.udn.com/luching/16S0S07 - 44k - 頁庫存檔-類似網頁

轉載-保障婦女權益之政見應具體可行文/人間福報社論 @ 妙音害院::PIXNET...
保障婦女權益之政見應具體可行 2008/3/7 | 作者: | 點閱次數: 31 | I 推薦朋友 I 新聞評分 I 環保列印明日是三月八日婦女節，行政院長於日前行政院會上宜示將在婦女
blog.pixnet.net/famscl/post/15133738 - 24k - 頁庫存檔-類似網頁

妙音書院: 轉載-保障婦女權益之政見應具體可行文/人間福報社論-yam 天空部落
2008 年 3 月 7 日... 保障婦女權益之政見應具體可行 2008/3/7 I 作者：| 點閱次陖: 31| 推薦朋友 | 新聞評分 | 環保列印明日是三月八日婦女節，行政院長於日前行政院會上…
blog.yam.com/fams：cl2/article/141564S5 - 51k -頁庫存檔-類似網頁

台灣婦女資訊網～婦女運動【附錄】
積極輔導婦女就業，保障婦女工作權，使免於因性別、婚姻、懷孕、生產而受任何歧視。... 一、支持保障婦女工作權益，促進婦女福利制度化、立法化的各項行舫。...
taiwan.yam.org.tw/womenweb/outmov_7.htm - 16k - 頁庫存檔-類似網頁

Fig. 26.7 One of the issues of using the web as a data source

entries. For example, an expression or sentence that was particularly popular at the moment or was quoted extensively by many may have ended up verbatim in many web articles. Figure 26.7 below shows that the search for the phrase 保障婦女 *bǎozhàng fùnǚ* "guaranteeing (the rights of) women," for example, returned a few pages that actually contained the same web article. It was therefore possible that the patterns found around our target phrases were unexpected or unusable. These represented situations where the data contained too many errors and too little usable data, respectively, and the end result was that sufficient data that fit our requirements could not be located within the scope of our search.

26.6 Conclusions and Future Research

We employed different features in our models, which were augmented based on existing ones. The supervised learning methods used in a small-scale open test produced an F-measure of 70%, but after we added the features drawn from unlabeled data from the web, the F-measure improved by 8.79% points to 78.79%.

Although the performance of the models was subject to the training data and the tests may have produced unstable results and occasionally unexpected situations, the semi-supervised learning approach that we proposed took advantage of readily available data from the Internet and indeed made improvements in NP chunking overall. The contributions of our studies are as follows:

1. Phrasal chunking has always been an important step in many natural language processing tasks but studies specific to the Chinese language that involves nominalizations have been lacking. Compared with other languages, the structures of Chinese NPs are much more complex. Our study, therefore, focused mainly on NP identification with special reference to nominalizations and provided evidence that features widely adopted previously for chunking in other languages were not suitable in the case of Chinese. We also identified more suitable features.
2. We proposed a simple semi-supervised learning method that addressed the issues of data sparseness and reliance on labeled data in supervised learning. In addition, compared with previous NP chunkers, our noun phrase identification system could deal with a variety of complex noun phrases previously unexplored, which will provide practical utility to some NLP tasks that require the application of a higher proportion of NPs such as parsing, semantic role labeling, and text categorization.

In the future, we hope to discover even better features and explore different machine learning methods to deal with very long phrases consisting of two or more nominalized verbs. Meanwhile, we will continue to experiment with deep learning algorithms that have the potential for better performance, given their ability to capture long-term dependency without the need for feature engineering. It is, however, noteworthy that recent breakthroughs in deep learning related to this study have so far been limited to name entity recognition (NER), which is only a smaller and simpler subset of NP chunking. The complex cases of Chinese NP chunking involving nominalizations still have not been addressed in recent deep learning approaches. As large unlabeled data is readily available, we also hope to be able to design unsupervised learning algorithms to overcome the problem of limited labeled data. While this study employs traditional machine learning methods, it remains to be seen how well deep learning approaches can tackle the problems noted in this study.

References

Abney, Steven. 1996. Partial parsing via finite-state cascades. *Journal of Natural Language Engineering* 2(4):337–344.

Abney, Steven. 2007. *Semisupervised learning for computational linguistics.* Chapman & Hall/ CRC.

Ando, Rie Kubota, and Tong Zhang. 2005. A high-performance semi-supervised learning method for text chunking. In *Proceedings of the 43rd Annual Meeting on Association for Computational Linguistics*, 1–9. Ann Arbor, Michigan.

Chang, Hsi-Wei, Zhao-Ming Gao, Chao-Lin Liu 張席維, 高照明, 劉昭麟. 2005. A preliminary study on Chinese base NP detection using SVM 利用向量支撐機辨識中文基底名詞組的初步研究. In *Proceedings of the 17th Conference on Computational Linguistics and Speech Processing* 第十七屆自然語言與語音處理研討會, 317–332. Tainan, Taiwan.

Cheng, Yuchang, Masayuki Asahara, and Yuji Matsumoto. 2005. Machine learning-based dependency analyzer for Chinese. *Journal of Chinese Language and Computing* 15(1): 13–24.

Chiu, Jason P. C., and Nichols, Eric. 2015. Named entity recognition with bidirectional LSTM-CNNs. Transactions of the Association for Computational Linguistics, 4, 357–370.

CKIP 詞庫小組 1993. *Analyses of parts-of-speech in Chinese* (3rd ed.) 中文詞類分析(三版) Technical Report no. 93–05. Academia Sinica. Taipei, Taiwan.

Collobert, Ronan, and Weston, Jason. 2008. A unified architecture for natural language processing: Deep neural networks with multitask learning. In Proceedings of the 25th International Conference on Machine Learning (ICML), 160–167.

Devlin, Jacob, Chang, Ming-Wei, Lee, Kenton, and Toutanova, Kristina. 2019. BERT: Pre-training of deep bidirectional transformers for language understanding. In Proceedings of the 2019 Conference of the North American Chapter of the Association for Computational Linguistics: Human Language Technologies (NAACL-HLT), 4171–4186.

Ding, Bing-Gong, Chang-Ning Huang, and De-Gen Huang. 2005. Chinese main verb identification: From specification to realization. *Computational Linguistics and Chinese Language Processing* 10(1):53–94.

Huang, Chu-Ren, and Keh-Jiann Chen. 2017. Sinica treebank. In *Handbook of linguistic annotation*, ed. Nancy Ide and James Pustejovsky, 641–657. New York: Springer.

Huang, Chu-Ren, and Dingxu Shi. 2016. *A reference grammar of Chinese*. Cambridge, UK: Cambridge University Press.

Huang, Chu-Ren, Adam Kilgarriff, Yiching Wu, Chih-Ming Chiu, Simon Smith, Pavel Rychly, Ming-Hong Bai, and Keh-Jiann Chen. 2005. Chinese sketch engine and the extraction of grammatical collocations. In *Proceedings of the Fourth SIGHAN Workshop on Chinese Language Processing*, in association with IJCNLP. Jeju Island, Korea.

Huang, Chu-Ren, Shu-Kai Hsieh, and Keh-Jiann Chen. 2017. *Mandarin Chinese words and parts of speech: A corpus-based study*. London: Routledge.

Kilgarriff, Adam, Pavel Rychly, Pavel Smrz, and David Tugwell. 2004. Sketch engine. In *Proceedings of Euralex*, 105–116. Lorient, France. Reprinted in *Lexicology: Critical concepts in linguistics*, ed. Patrick Hanks. London: Routledge.

Kinyon, Alexandra. 2001. A language-independent shallow-parser compiler. In *Proceedings of the 39th ACL Conference*, 322–329. Toulouse, France.

Kudo, Taku. 2001. YamCha: Yet Another Multipurpose CHunk Annotator. Available at http://chasen.org/~taku/software/YamCha/. Accessed 22 August 2018.

Kudo, Taku, and Yuji Matsumoto. 2000. Use of support vector learning for chunk identification. In *Proceedings of CoNLL-2000*, 142–144. Lisbon, Portugal.

Kudo, Taku, and Yuji Matsumoto. 2001. Chunking with support vector machine. In *Proceedings of NAACL 2001*, 192–199. Pittsburgh, Pennsylvania.

Lafferty, John D., Andrew McCallum, and Fernando C. N. Pereira. 2001. Conditional random fields: Probabilistic models for segmenting and labeling sequence data. In *Proceedings of the 18th International Conference on Machine Learning 2001 (ICML 2001)*. Williamstown, Massachusetts.

Ma, Wei-Yun, and Chu-Ren Huang, 馬偉雲, 黃居仁. 2006. The design of a statistic model for identifying Chinese nominalizations 中文動詞名物化判斷的統計式模型設計. In *Proceedings of the 17th Conference on Computational Linguistics and Speech Processing* 第十八屆自然語言與語音處理研討會. Hsinchu, Taiwan.

Ramshaw, Lance, and Mitchell Marcus. 1995. Text chunking using transformation-based learning. In *Proceedings of the Third Workshop on Very Large Corpora*, 82–94. Cambridge, Massachusetts.

Søgaard, Anders. 2013. *Semi-supervised learning and domain adaptation in natural language processing*. Morgan & Claypool.

Tjong, Kim Sang Erik. 2000. Noun phrase recognition by system combination. In *Proceedings of the 1st North American Chapter of the Association for Computational Linguistics Conference*, 50–55. Seattle, Washington.

Tjong, Kim Sang Eric, and Sabine Buchholz. 2000. Introduction to the CoNLL-2000 shared task: Chunking. In *Proceedings of CoNLL-2000 and LLL-2000*, 127–132. Lisbon, Portugal.

Vaswani, Ashish, et al. 2017. Attention is all you need. Advances in Neural Information Processing Systems 30, 5998–6008. Long Beach, CA.

Wang, Rongbo and Chi, Zheru. 2003. Automatic segmentation of Chinese chunks using a neural network. IEEE Inernational Conference Neural Networks & Signal Processing, 14–17. Nanjing. China.

Wang, Chengyu, He, Xiaofeng, and Zhou Aoying 2021. Open relation extraction for Chinese noun phrases. IEEE Transactions on Knowledge and Data Engineering, 33(6): 2693–2708.

Wu, et al. 2019. An Attention-based BiLSTM-CRF model for Chinese clinic named entity recognition. IEEE Access, Special Section on Data-enabled Intelligence for Digital Health, 7, 113942–113949.

Yarowsky, David. 1995. Unsupervised word sense disambiguation rivaling supervised methods. In *Proceedings of the 33rd Annual Meeting of the Association for Computational Linguistics*, 189–196. Cambridge, Massachusetts.

Zhai, Feifei et al. 2017. Neural models for sequence chunking. Proceedings of the Thirty-First AAAI Conference on Artificial Intelligence (AAAI-17), 3365–3371. San Francisco, California.

Zhao, Jun, and Chang-ning Huang. 1999. The model of Chinese base NP analysis. *Chinese Journal of Computers* 22(2):141–146.

Zhou, Junsheng, Weiguang Qu, and Fen Zhang. 2012. Exploiting chunk-level features to improve phrase chunking. In *Proceedings of the 2012 Joint Conference on Empirical Methods in Natural Language Processing and Computational Natural Language Learning*, 557–567. Jeju Island, Korea.

Zhu, Xiaojin, and Andrew Goldberg. 2009. *Introduction to semi-supervised learning*. Morgan & Claypool.

Zhu, Ling, Derek F. Wong, and Lidia S. Chao. 2014. Unsupervised chunking based on graph propagation from bilingual corpus. *The Scientific World Journal*, 2014:1–10.

Zhu, Jingbo, Muhua Zhu, Qiang Wang, and Tong Xiao. 2015. NiuParser: A Chinese syntactic and semantic parsing toolkit. In *Proceedings of ACL-IJCNLP 2015 System Demonstrations*, 145–150. Beijing, China.

Chapter 27
A Study on the Semantic Interpretation of Chinese Noun Compounds

Meng Wang and Lulu Wang

Abstract Noun compound interpretation is determined by implicit semantic relations encoded by constituent nouns. In this chapter, we will present preliminary research on the interpretation of Chinese noun compounds (NCs) using two different strategies. For the abstract relation strategy, we proposed a novel taxonomy of Chinese noun compounds and a method for interpreting Chinese NCs based on word similarity. For the verbal paraphrasing strategy, we proposed the simple dynamic approach of using paraphrasing verbs, which not only provided possible interpretations of noun compounds but also captured the subtle semantic differences of similar NCs. Both strategies can be applied in other fields, such as question answering, information retrieval, and lexicography.

Keywords Chinese noun compounds · Interpretation · Semantics

27.1 Introduction

A noun compound (NC) is a sequence of two or more nouns that functions as a single noun (Downing 1977). The use of NCs is very frequent in English-written text, including press and technical materials, newswires, and fictional prose. In other languages, such as Chinese, NCs are also abundant in texts since the compounding of nouns is the most common way of naming new things. The syntax and semantics of noun compounds has remained an active research field in linguistics, which includes the broader research of multiword expressions (MWEs). As a well-established subtask of language understanding, the interpretation of noun compounds involves uncovering the underlying semantic relations encoded by

M. Wang (✉)
School of Humanities, Jiangnan University, Wuxi, China

L. Wang
Department of Linguistics, Communication University of China, Beijing, China
e-mail: lulu.wang@cuc.edu.cn

C.-R. Huang et al. (eds.), *Chinese Language Resources*, Text, Speech and Language Technology 49, https://doi.org/10.1007/978-3-031-38913-9_27

constituent nouns. For example, 爱情故事 *aiqing gushi* "love story" can be illustrated as 讲述爱情的故事 *jiangshu aiqing de gushi* "a story that tells about love" and 别墅女人 *bieshu nvren* "villa woman" means 住在别墅的女人 *zhuzai bieshu de nvren* "a woman living in a villa." Understanding the semantic relations between noun compounds is helpful for many tasks, such as machine translation, information retrieval, and question answering, among others.

In this chapter, we will focus on the semantic interpretation of Chinese noun compounds. The remainder is organized as follows: Section 27.2 will describe related work, while Sect. 27.3 will present a novel taxonomy of Chinese noun compounds based on the transparency of the compounds. In Sect. 27.4, a method for predicting the semantic relations of novel NCs based on word similarity will be introduced. Section 27.5 will illustrate how to interpret noun compounds using verbal paraphrasing, while Sect. 27.6 will offer the conclusion and future work.

27.2 Previous Studies

In theoretical linguistics, there are contradictory views regarding the semantic interpretation of NCs. Most linguists describe the semantics of noun compounds via a set of abstract relations, as represented in the work of Levi (1978), who presented nine recoverable deletable predicates (RDPs)—be, cause, have, make, use, about, for, from, and in—that are universal and primitive in generating noun compounds, and Warren (1978), who proposed a four-level hierarchical taxonomy derived from the Brown Corpus. Following this tradition, some scholars in the computational field have focused on the taxonomies of noun compounds. Ó Séaghdha (2007) proposed six semantic relations—BE, HAVE, IN, ACTOR, INST(-RUMENT), and ABOUT—and each relation was subdivided into subcategories. For example, HAVE is subdivided into the possession, condition-experiencer, property-object, part-whole, and group-member subcategories. Tratz and Hovy (2010) presented a large, fine-grained taxonomy of 43 noun compound relations, which were notably tested by Amazon's Mechanical Turk service. However, there is still no consensus as to which set of relations binds nouns in a noun compound.

Overall, the semantic relations proposed by different scholars have ranged from general to more specific, with the general ones aiming for broad-coverage analysis of unrestricted text and the specific ones aiming for specialized applications in some domains. In this line of research, the semantic interpretation of NCs is viewed as a multiclass classification problem, where the predefined semantic relations are the categories to be assigned. However, the approach of abstract relations is problematic in several ways. As Nakov and Hearst (2013) pointed out, it is unclear which relation inventory is best, as relations capture only part of the semantics and multiple relations are possible. For example, Wei (2012) assumed that 中国电影 *zhongguo dianying* "Chinese movies" is classified into the categories of LOCATION and CONTENT.

Considering these drawbacks, other researchers have used verbal paraphrasing to interpret noun compounds (Girju et al. 2005; Nakov and Hearst 2006; Nakov 2008;

Table 27.1 Levi's (1978) transparency scale for noun compounds

	Types	Examples
a	Transparent	*Orange peel*
b	Partly opaque	*Grammar school*
c	Exocentric	*Ladybird*
d	Partly idiomatic	*Flea market*
e	Completely idiomatic	*Honeymoon*

Ó Séaghdha 2008). Finn (1980) interpreted "salt water" with "dissolved in." Butnariu and Veale (2008) summarized eight relational possibilities, for example, "headache pill" might be paraphrased as "headache-inducing pill," "headache prevention pill," "pill for treating headaches," "pill that causes headaches," "pill that is prescribed for headaches," and "pill that prevents headaches." With these verbs, the paraphrases are more specific than that of the abstract relations. Following this view, the SemEval 2010 task 9 "Noun Compound Interpretation Using Paraphrasing Verbs and Prepositions" and SemEval 2013 task 4 "Free Paraphrases of Noun Compounds" both intended to promote a paraphrase-based approach to this problem.

Accordingly, there are two ways to interpret noun compounds in Chinese. Theoretically, there have been some achievements in the analysis of semantic relations, while very little work on the automatic semantic interpretation of Chinese NCs has been done. Zhao et al. (2007) focused on a subset of Chinese NCs in which the head word is a verb nominalization, such as 血液循环 *xueye xunhuan* "blood circulation," and four coarse-grained semantic roles were proposed for the classification of noun modifiers in compound nominalization. Our study took a static approach in which the interpretation was viewed as a classification problem. As for the second line of research, Wang (2010) and Wang et al. (2014) adopted a bottom-up strategy to capture the verbs of noun compounds and provided four types of paraphrase patterns. As Wei (2012) pointed out, these four types are not specific enough to give proper interpretations. Instead, Wei (2012) classified the noun compounds into eight major types and 346 subcategories, which proved to be fine-grained.

27.3 Taxonomy of Chinese Noun Compounds

Whether using abstract relations or verbal paraphrasing, there are still some noun compounds that are not interpretable. We hypothesized that this is due to the lack of consideration of the decomposable possibilities and the semantic transparency of noun compounds. Taking the noun compound 夫妻肺片 *fuqi feipian* "pork lungs in chili sauce" as an example, it is not decomposable; that is, the meaning of the compound is not simply the combination of the literal meanings of the parts. Levi (1978) proposed a transparency scale for noun compounds, as shown in Table 27.1.

In Table 27.1, Levi (1978) summarized five types of noun compounds based on semantic transparency, each type showing a different interpretation pattern of the

Table 27.2 Basic types of noun compounds

	Transparency scale	Examples
a	Transparent	机组人员
		jizu renyuan
		"crew member"
b	Partly opaque	钻石戒指
		zuanshi jiezhi
		"diamond ring"
c	Partly idiomatic	试管婴儿
		shiguan yinger
		"test tube baby"
d	Completely idiomatic	夫妻肺片
		fuqi feipian
		"the spouse pork lung"

noun compounds. For example, "orange peel" is simply the combination of "orange" and "peel." However, "grammar school" cannot be combined literally because there is a hidden verb in this compound, as in "grammar teaching school." In contrast, the other types cannot be combined literally or be interpreted by hidden verbs. For instance, "ladybird" is not a kind of bird but a kind of bug, "Coccinellidae,"[1] and "honeymoon" has nothing to do with "honey" or "moon" but instead refers to the vacation that brides and grooms take to celebrate their marriage. The type "partly idiomatic" is special because it is partly idiomatic that verbs are not easy to recover. For example, it is not acceptable to say "flea selling market" for the market selling small commodities.

In light of Levi's (1978) transparence scale and Nunberg et al.'s (1994) claims on idioms, we collected 428 noun-noun compounds (N1-N2) and classified them into the following four categories shown in Table 27.2.

As Table 27.2 shows, the first three types are decomposable at the syntagmatic level, but the last one is non-decomposable. Initially, we decided that non-decomposable idioms should be analyzed as a whole unit both syntactically and semantically, and since the other types were decomposable, they could be divided into N1 and N2. However, the semantic relations of these types are different in terms of semantic transparency. Therefore, we proposed a novel taxonomy of Chinese noun compounds based on semantic transparency. Table 27.3 summarizes 11 subcategories of noun compounds based on their semantic relations.

To interpret the noun compounds in Table 27.3, we created different interpretation patterns with different conditions. Category 1 corresponds to the noun compounds of type a in Table 27.2, which can be interpreted as the literal meanings of the parts, for example, 机组人员 *jizu renyuan* "crew members" in the paraphrased 属于机组的人员 *shuyu jizu de renyuan* "the members that belong to the crew."

[1] Here, "lady" refers to the "Virgin Mary"; see more at http://www.hkhk.edu.ee/nature/ladybird_legends.html

Table 27.3 Semantic relations of NCs

	Semantic relations	Interpretation patterns	Examples
1	Possessive	N2 belongs to N1	机组人员 *jizu renyuan* "crew member"
2	Property	N2's property is N1	股份制企业 *gufenzhi qiye* "joint stock company"
3	Locative	N2 is located in N1	印尼火山 *yinni huoshan* "Indonesia volcano"
4	Time	N2 is made in N1	清代家具 *qingdai jiaju* "Qing Dynasty furniture"
5	Content	N2 is about N1	爱情故事 *aiqing gushi* "love story"
6	Material	N2 is made of N1	钻石戒指 *zuanshi jiezhi* "iamond ring"
7	Patient	V-N1-N2	围棋高手 *weiqi gaoshou* "Chess master"
8	Actor	N1-V-N2	教委文件 *jiaowei wenjian* "the board of education document"
9	Cause	N1 causes N2	考试焦虑 *kaoshi jiaolv* "exam anxiety"
10	Partly idiomatic	Metaphoric or metonymic meaning of N1	试管婴儿 *shiguan yinger* "test tube baby"
11	Idiomatic	Idiomatic meaning of N1-N2	夫妻肺片 *fuqi feipian* "pork lungs in chili sauce"

In categories 2 to 5, these four types correspond to both type a and type b, since the meaning of the compounds can be interpreted by the fixed pattern of the components and can also be predicted by hidden verbs. For instance, the paraphrased verb of the compound 雅典奥运会 *yadian aoyunhui* "Athens Olympics" could be 举办 *juban* "to hold," and thus the paraphrased sentence would be 在雅典举办的奥运会 *zai yadian juban de aoyunhui* "The Olympic Games that were held in Athens." As for 爱情故事 *aiqing gushi* "love story," it could be paraphrased as 关于爱情的

故事 *guanyu aiqing de gushi* "the story about love" and 讲述爱情的故事 *jiangshu aiqing de gushi* "the story telling about love."

Moreover, categories 6 to 9 correspond to type b, in which the hidden verb must be revealed. In this group, the qualia roles of the head noun are different for each type. For example, the qualia role in category 6 is AGE because "material" usually relates to the MAKE relation, and the relation of "patient" in category 7 relates more with TELIC roles,[2] which are interpreted as the function of N1. For example, 围棋高手 *weiqi gaoshou* "chess master" could be paraphrased as 下围棋的高手 *xia weiqi de gaoshou* "the masters of playing chess." Here, 下 *xia* "to play" is the TELIC role of 围棋 *weiqi* "chess."

The last two categories correspond to type c and the non-decomposable idioms separately. Noun compounds in category 10 should be interpreted as having a metaphoric meaning, and thus they cannot be interpreted by hidden verbs. Taking 试管婴儿 *shiguan yinger* "test tube babies" as an example, the compound cannot be illustrated using expressions like 在试管里 孕育的婴儿 *zai shiguan li yunyu de yinger* "the babies that are fertilized in test tubes." The word 试管 *shiguan* "test tubes" has the metonymic meaning of 试管孕育技术 *shiguan yunyu jishu* "in glass fertilization." Therefore, the metaphoric meaning of the compound needs to infer 用试管技术孕育的婴儿 *yong shiguan jishu yunyu de yinger* "the babies that are fertilized by the technique of using test tubes." For these types of idioms, they are not decomposable at all and should be treated as a whole unit. For example, 夫妻肺片 *fuqi feipian* "pork lungs in chili sauce" refers only to the name of the dish.

27.4 Interpretation Based on Word Similarity

Kim and Baldwin (2005) introduced a method for interpreting novel English noun compounds with semantic relations using WordNet: Similarity. Based on the taxonomy above, we proposed a method using word similarity to predict the semantic relations of novel Chinese NCs. Given an NC in the testing data, we calculated the similarities between the correspondence nouns in the training data to acquire the semantic relation, which was our first strategy.

27.4.1 Word Similarity Measures

HowNet-based similarity. HowNet is a commonsense knowledge base of interconceptual relations and inter-attribute relations of concepts as connoted in lexicons of Chinese and their English equivalents (Dong and Dong 2005). As a knowledge base, the knowledge structured by HowNet is represented by a graph

[2]Pustejovsky (1995) proposed four qualia roles of nouns: formal, constitutive, agentive, and telic.

```
NO.=095550
W_C=学校
G_C=N
W_E=school
G_E=N
DEF=InstitutePlace|场所,@teach|教,@study|学,education|教育
```

Fig. 27.1 Definition of the Chinese word 学校 "school" in HowNet

```
Aa01A01= 人 士 人物 人士 人氏 人选
Aa01A02= 人类 生人 全人类
Aa01A03= 人手 人员 人口 人丁 口 食指
Aa01A04= 劳力 劳动力 工作者
Aa01A05= 匹夫 个人
Aa01A06= 家伙 东西 货色 厮 崽子 兔崽子 狗崽子 小子 杂种 畜生 混蛋 王八蛋 竖子 鼠辈 小崽子
Aa01A07= 者 手 匠 客 主 子 家 夫 翁 汉 员 分子 鬼 货 棍 徒
```

Fig. 27.2 Examples in *Cilin*

rather than a tree, and it is devoted to demonstrating the general and specific properties of concepts. For every word sense c_i (i.e., concept), its definition is composed of a set of sememes and corresponding relations. For instance, the Chinese word 学校 "school" is defined as follows in Fig. 27.1.

HowNet allows users to measure the semantic similarity and relatedness between a pair of two concepts based on the overlapping of sememes. In our study, we adopted a similarity measure provided by Liu and Li (2002) to achieve the similarity of two nouns.

***Cilin*-based similarity.** *Cilin* is a Chinese thesaurus that defines and describes "concepts" and reveals their relations using Synset. The semantic category of words (i.e., concepts) is encoded by a five-layer tree, as shown in Fig. 27.2.

The similarity of two words in *Cilin* is measured by the distance in the tree. Formally, it is defined using Formula (27.1):

$$\text{sim}_{\text{cilin}}(w_1, w_2) = 1 - \frac{\text{pathlen}(w_1, w_2)}{\text{pathlen}(w_1, \text{Root}) + \text{pathlen}(w_2, \text{Root})} \tag{27.1}$$

where pathlen(w_1, w_2) is the minimum path length of (w_1, w_2) to their common parent node, and Root represents the root of the tree.

27.4.2 Method

The similarity between NCs (t_1, t_2) and (n_1, n_2) was calculated by the similarities of the component nouns. Formally, the similarity of each NC pair was defined using Formula (27.2):

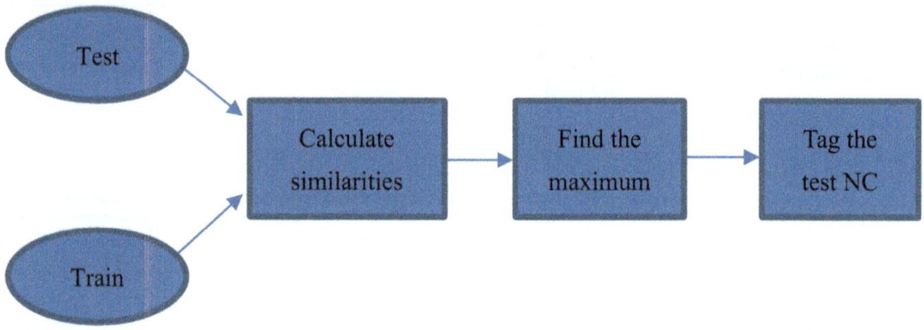

Fig. 27.3 The procedure of our method

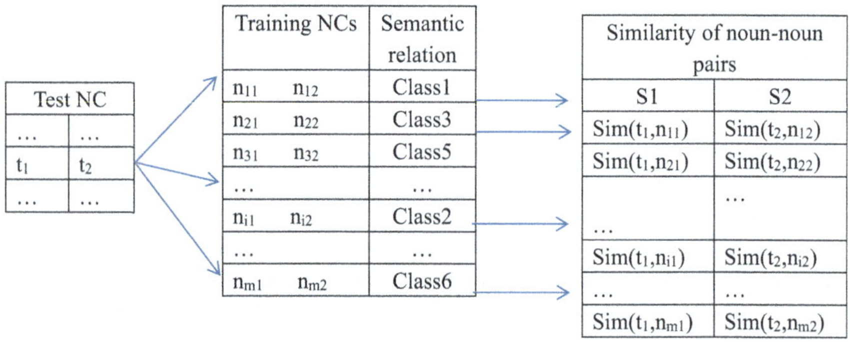

Fig. 27.4 Detailed similarities between the test NC and training NCs

$$\text{Sim}((t_1, t_2)\ (n_1, n_2)) = \frac{(\alpha \text{S1} + \text{S1}) \times ((1 - \alpha)\text{S2} + \text{S2})}{2} \tag{27.2}$$

where S1 is the modifier similarity (i.e., Sim(t_1, n_1)) and S2 is the head similarity (i.e., Sim(t_2, n_2)), while $\alpha \in [0, 1]$ is the weighting factor that balances the contributions of the modifier and head.

For each test NC, we calculated the similarities of all NCs in the training data. Then, we chose the NC in the training data that had the highest similarity and labeled it the test NC according to the sematic relation associated with that training data. Formally, the semantic relation of the test NC (t_1, t_2) was determined using Formula (27.3):

$$\begin{aligned} \text{Relation}\ (t_1, t_2) &= \text{Relation}\ (n_{i1}, n_{i2}), \text{ where } i \\ &= \underbrace{\text{argmax}}_{i}\ \text{Sim}\ ((t_1, t_2), (n_{i1}, n_{i2})) \end{aligned} \tag{27.3}$$

Figure 27.3 shows the complete procedure of our method, while Fig. 27.4 illustrates in detail how we calculated the similarities between a test NC (t_1, t_2) and the NCs in the training data.

As can be seen, the test NC is associated with a total number of "m" similarities, where "m" is the number of NCs in the training data. Then, the semantic relation of the test NC was determined by the training instance with the highest similarity.

27.4.3 *Experiments and Evaluation*

We retrieved two-word Chinese NCs from the *People's Daily* of 1998 and 2000, which were segmented and POS tagged (Yu et al. 2002). After excluding proper nouns and coordinate constructions, we obtained 1483 NCs for our experiment. The semantic relations of all the NCs were judged by two annotators who had majored in linguistics. Overall, we used 978 NCs for the training data and 505 NCs for the testing data.

We experimented with the two similarity methods introduced above, assuming that the contribution of the head and modifier noun was equal ($\alpha = 0.5$). Table 27.4 shows the experimental results. Note that the HowNet and *Cilin* similarities were based on dictionary-based methods. Thus, if the test word did not appear in HowNet or *Cilin*, our method could not tag the test NC (i.e., unlabeled data) because of the lack of similarities. The performances of HowNet and *Cilin* similarity were very close, and they each classified 35% of the NCs correctly.

Table 27.5 lists some test NCs and the most similar NCs found in the training data. As can be seen, our method provided reasonable interpretations, which is very useful in understanding novel NCs. For instance, if a reader did not know the meaning of the novel NC 网络医生 *wangluo yisheng* "network doctor," our method provided NCs such as 出租车司机 *chuzuche siji* "taxi driver," which were easy to understand. Our method could also help a reader to predict the semantic relation of two nouns. Taking 布料玩具 *buliao wanju* "cloth toy" and 黄金首饰 *huangjin shoushi* "gold treasury" as an example, they both shared the same semantic relation of "material," and thus their similarity was very high, so with our method, a reader could learn the semantic relation of the former and the unfamiliar relation of the latter, as well as the more frequently used relation.

27.5 Interpretation Using Verbal Paraphrasing

In linguistic theories, it has been proven that verbs play an important role in the process of noun compound derivation. In this section, we will present a simple and unsupervised approach for characterizing the semantic relations held in two-word

Table 27.4 Accuracy based on HowNet and *Cilin* similarity

Similarity measure	Unlabeled	# Correct (accuracy)
HowNet	25	174 (34.46%)
Cilin	16	178 (35.25%)

Table 27.5 The most similar NCs based on the two similarity measures

Test NCs	The most similar NCs in the training data	
	HowNet similarity	*Cilin* similarity
残疾儿童	白内障患者	白内障患者
canji ertong	*baineizhang huanzhe*	*baineizhang huanzhe*
"disabled children"	"cataract patient"	"cataract patient"
玻璃茶几	水晶花瓶	钻石戒指
boli chaji	*shuijing huaping*	*zuanshi jiezhi*
"glass table"	"crystal vase"	"diamond ring"
网络医生	因特网用户	出租车司机
wangluo yisheng	*yintewang yonghu*	*chuzuche siji*
"network doctor"	"Internet user"	"taxi driver"
蔬菜收入	水果价格	水果价格
shucai shouru	*shuiguo jiage*	*shuiguo jiage*
"vegetable income"	"fruit price"	"fruit price"
大学校长	中学教师	政府领导
daxue xiaozhang	*zhongxue jiaoshi*	*zhengfu lingdao*
"university president"	"middle school teacher"	"government leader"
布料玩具	黄金首饰	冰秋千
buliao wanju	*huangjin shoushi*	*bing qiuqian*
"cloth toy"	"gold treasury"	"ice swing"

Chinese NCs. What is especially novel about this approach is that NCs are interpreted in terms of verbal phrases, rather than by a set of concrete verbs. This is a richer and more flexible paraphrasing model in the sense that one semantic relation can be expressed by different verbal phrases.

27.5.1 Acquisition of Paraphrasing Verbs

In English, popular approaches to the acquisition of paraphrasing verbs have searched for snippets that have both nouns as endpoints as well as collected verbs from intervening materials. For example, Nakov and Hearst (2006) used the phrase "noun2 THAT * noun1" for Google queries and extracted verbs between THAT and noun1 from the returned pages. However, there are neither inflections nor clear form markers in Chinese, such as the complementizers that indicate relative clauses, which is why it is difficult to acquire Chinese verbs using explicit clues.

Semantic relations between words should be expressed through certain syntactic forms and structures. The semantic relations held between nouns, and verbs are directly expressed by "Verb-Object" and "Subject-Verb" structures, in which the noun acts as the subject or object of the verb. For example, the Verb-Object structure 切割钻石 *qiege zuanshi* "cut the diamond" shows that 钻石 *zuanshi* "diamond" is a solid substance that can be cut. Thus, we aimed to acquire concept-related verbs for the nouns using the two grammatical relations above. It was determined that a large-scale corpus with phrase-structure annotation was necessary for this task. However, such resources in Chinese are limited, resulting in a lack of coverage of the acquired verbs. Therefore, we adopted a backward strategy that extracted the verbs from specific grammatical relations (i.e., Subject-Verb and Verb-Object) in terms of collocation using Chinese Word Sketch (CWS).

Chinese Word Sketch. CWS[3] is a combination of the Chinese Gigaword Corpus and the corpus management tool in Sketch Engine (Kilgarriff et al. 2004; Huang et al. 2005). The Chinese Gigaword Corpus (second edition) is a comprehensive archive of newswire text data in Chinese containing about 1.4 billion Chinese characters. All the texts have been segmented and POS tagged automatically. We included all the data in our study. The main functionality of Sketch Engine includes KWIC displays, co-occurrence statistics, grammatical relations, and word sketches, which provide grammatical descriptions of a word in terms of corpus collocations. For nouns, the grammatical description includes nine relations: "A_Modifier/N_Modifier/Modifies," "Subject_of," "Object_of," "And/Or," and "Possession/Possessor." All the collocations were formalized as triples of Rel; Word1; Word2, where Rel is a relation, Word1 is a keyword of a query, and Word2 is the collocation involved with respect to the relation in question.

We used a two-step procedure to acquire the verbs that were related to the compound "n1 n2." First, we collected the collocations with "Subject_of" and "Object_of" relations using n1 and n2 as the keywords of the queries, respectively. We chose only the top 200 words with the highest salience for each relation. Thus, we obtained two sets of collocating verbs denoted as VerbSet1 and VerbSet2 for n1 and n2. Then, we found the intersection of VerbSet1 and VerbSet2, which provided the final paraphrasing verbs. Table 27.6 shows an example of the procedure.

We used this method for 电影公司 *dianying gongsi* "film company" and 啤酒公司 *pijiu gongsi* "beer company," which have the same head. The paraphrasing verbs are shown in Table 27.7, which shows that the two similar compounds have very few common verbs. Fine-grained semantic distinctions were captured with our approach.

27.5.2 Generating Verbal Paraphrases

Yuan (1995) proposed four typical Chinese syntactic patterns for the recovery of the implied predicates, as shown in Table 27.8. In our approach, we used those patterns to generate verbal paraphrases for a compound based on the acquired paraphrasing verbs. We obtained the verbal paraphrases to the maximum using those patterns; however, many of them did not make sense. Next, we filtered out the inappropriate paraphrases via search engines.

[3] http://wordsketch.ling.sinica.edu.tw/

Table 27.6 Verbs acquired for the noun compound 钻石戒指 *zuanshi jiezhi* "diamond ring"

VerbSet1	镶有 *xiangyou* "embed with"
钻石	盛产 *shengchan* "be rich in"
zuanshi	镶 *xiang* "embed"
"diamond"	镶满 *xiangman* "be studded with"
	走私 *zousi* "smuggle"
	镶嵌 *xiangqian* "inlay"
	打磨 *damo* "polish"
VerbSet2	戴上 *daishang* "wear"
戒指	戴 *dai* "wear"
jiezhi	定情 *dingqing* "promise"
"ring"	戴有 *daiyou* "wear"
	试戴 *shidai* "try on"
	抢走 *qiangzou* "snatch"
	交换 *jiaohuan* "exchange"
	镶 *xiang* "encrust"
	镶嵌 *xiangqian* "encrust"
Intersection	拥有 *yongyou* "own"
钻石戒指	获得 *huode* "get"
zuanshi jiezhi	购买 *goumai* "buy"
"diamond ring"	镶嵌 *xiangqian* "encrust"
	戴 *dai* "wear"
	抢走 *qiangzou* "snatch"
	镶 *xiang* "encrust"
	包括 *baokuo* "contain"

Table 27.7 Examples of paraphrasing verbs for 电影公司 *dianying gongsi* "film company" and 啤酒公司 *pijiu gongsi* "beer company"

Noun compounds	Paraphrasing verbs				
电影公司	发行	制作	投资	进出口	服务
dianying gongsi	*faxing*	*zhizuo*	*touzi*	*jinchukou*	*fuwu*
"film company"	"distribute"	"produce"	"invest"	"import and export"	"serve"
啤酒公司	销售	制造	经销	代理	经营
pijiu gongsi	*xiaoshou*	*zhizao*	*jingxiao*	*daili*	*jingying*
"beer company"	"sell"	"make"	"distribute"	"import and distribute"	"manage"

Table 27.8 Patterns used to generate verbal paraphrases

No.	Pattern
P1	n1 + v + 的 *de* + n2
P2	n1 + v + n2
P3	n2 + v + n1
P4	v + n1 + 的 *de* + n2

Table 27.9 Top five verbal paraphrases ranked by Baidu and Google

Rank	钻石 戒指 *zuanshi jiezhi* "diamond ring"	
	Baidu	Google
1	带钻石的戒指 743	*买钻石的戒指 452,000*
	dai zuanshi de jiezhi	*mai zuanshi de jiezhi*
	"ring with diamond"	*"buy diamond ring"*
2	钻石镶嵌戒指 627	钻石镶嵌的戒指 362,000
	zuanshi xiangqian jiezhi	zuanshi xiangqian de jiezhi
	"diamond inlaid ring"	"ring embedded with diamond"
3	*买钻石的戒指 249*	镶嵌钻石的戒指 325,000
	mai zuanshi de jiezhi	xiangqian zuanshi de jiezhi
	"buy diamond ring"	"ring with inlaid diamond"
4	镶钻石的戒指 197	镶钻石的戒指 203,000
	xiang zuanshi de jiezhi	xiang zuanshi de jiezhi
	"ring embedded with diamond"	"ring embedded with diamond"
5	钻石镶戒指 173	*没有钻石的戒指 132,000*
	zuanshi xiang jiezhi	*meiyou zuanshi de jiezhi*
	"diamond inlaid ring"	*"ring without diamond"*

27.5.3 Filtering Verbal Paraphrases

The goal of this process aimed to remove the noise (i.e., inappropriate paraphrases) and retain the most reasonable verbal paraphrases by assigning a higher rank to them. For this purpose, we validated these paraphrases by finding evidence in a large corpus. The greater the evidence, the more appropriate a given paraphrase should be.

The notion of "Web as a corpus" has been widely accepted by researchers. Keller and Lapata (2003) applied web counts to a wide variety of NLP tasks involving syntax and semantics and demonstrated that realistic NLP tasks can benefit from web counts. In our approach, we viewed all the candidate paraphrases as queries, and all queries were submitted to the search engines and performed as exact matches. Thus, we obtained the web counts of the paraphrases. For each noun compound, the paraphrases were ranked by descending order of web counts. The paraphrases with a higher ranking were considered more reasonable than those with a lower ranking.

Baidu (www.baidu.com) and Google (www.google.com) were the most popular search engines for our Chinese search. We conducted experiments based on the web counts obtained from the two search engines, respectively. The number of hits from Baidu and Google was not identical, which resulted in some differences in the ranking. Table 27.9 shows the top five paraphrases for 钻石戒指 *zuanshi jiezhi* "diamond ring" based on Baidu and Google, respectively (incorrect phrases are in italics).

Table 27.10 Accuracy based on Google and Baidu

Google	Top *n*	1	3	5	10
	Accuracy (%)	68.79	90.28	93.35	96.41
Baidu	Top *n*	1	3	5	10
	Accuracy (%)	71.09	89.25	92.83	96.67

27.5.4 Experiments and Evaluation

We randomly selected 391 Chinese noun compounds from the newswire corpus *People's Daily* to test our approach. For each compound, the top 10 candidate paraphrases were collected. All the paraphrases were judged by three human subjects.[4] They were asked to make binary judgments (yes or no) for each paraphrase, that is, whether the paraphrases expressed a meaning similar to that of the compound. If more than two subjects labeled the paraphrase yes, it was viewed as correct. We defined the accuracy of the compounds using Formula (27.4):

$$\text{Accuracy} = \frac{\text{the number of compounds with correct interpretation}}{\text{the total number of compounds}} \times 100\% \tag{27.4}$$

Table 27.10 shows the different accuracy rates, where "*n*" equals 1, 3, 5, and 10. As shown, the performances based on Google and Baidu were very similar. Thus, our method provided correct interpretations for almost 70% of the compounds when only the topmost paraphrase was given, and accuracy increased with the number of candidate paraphrases.

27.6 Conclusion

In this chapter, we presented our preliminary research on the interpretation of Chinese noun compounds using two different strategies. For the abstract relation strategy, we proposed a novel taxonomy of Chinese noun compounds based on the transparency of the compounds. Then, we proposed a method for interpreting Chinese NCs based on word similarity. Our experimental results showed that word similarity provided useful information in solving interpretation problems. In the future, we plan to use corpus-based similarity methods such as word2vec to solve the out-of-vocabulary (OOV) problem. Moreover, the voting strategy can be used to determine the semantic relations of the test NCs since we chose only those NCs with the highest similarity.

[4]One of the subjects was a Ph.D. student in linguistics, and the other two had master's degrees in computational linguistics.

For the verbal paraphrasing strategy, we proposed the simple dynamic approach of using paraphrasing verbs, which could be useful in many NLP tasks. This approach not only provided possible interpretations of noun compounds but also captured interesting fine-grained semantic differences of similar noun compounds. In the future, we plan to acquire more verbs using web data, such as the Google 5-gram web index. We also plan to expand the paraphrasing patterns. Finally, we are also very interested in applying the methods proposed here to information retrieval.

Acknowledgments This work was supported by the National Natural Science Foundation of China (No. 61300152, No. 61300156). We would like to thank the anonymous reviewers for their comments.

References

Butnariu, Cristina, and Tony Veale. 2008. A concept-centered approach to noun-compound interpretation. In *Proceedings of the 22nd International Conference on Computational Linguistics*, 81–88. Manchester, United Kingdom.

Dong, Zhendong, and Qiang Dong. 2005. HowNet. Available at http://www.keenage.com. Accessed:10 Oct. 2015

Downing, Pamela. 1977. On the creation and use of English compound nouns. *Language* 53(4): 810–842.

Finn, T. 1980. The semantic interpretation of compound nominals. Ph.D. dissertation. University of Illinois, Urbana.

Girju, Roxana, Dan Moldovan, Marta Tatu, and Daniel Antohe. 2005. On the semantics of noun compounds. *Journal of Computer Speech and Language—Special Issue on Multiword Expressions* 4(19):479–496.

Huang, Chu-ren, Adam Kilgarriff, Yiching Wu, Chih-Ming Chui, Simon Smith, Pavel Rychly, Ming-Hong Bai, and Keh-Jiann Chen. 2005. Chinese sketch engine and the extraction of grammatical collocations. In *Proceedings of the Fourth SIGHAN Workshop on Chinese Language Processing*. Jeju Island, Korea.

Keller, Frank, and Mirella Lapata. 2003. Using the web to obtain frequencies for unseen bigrams. *Computational Linguistics* 29(3):459–484.

Kilgarriff, Adam, Pavel Rychly, Pavel Smrz, and David Tugwell. 2004. The sketch engine. In *Proceedings of Euralex*, 105–116. Lorient, France.

Kim, Su Nam, and Timothy Baldwin. 2005. Automatic interpretation of noun compounds using WordNet similarity. In *Proceedings of the Second International Joint Conference on Natural Language Processing*, 945–956. Jeju Island, Korea.

Levi, Judith N. 1978. *The syntax and semantics of complex nominals*. New York: Academic Press.

Liu, Qun, and Sujian Li. 2002. Word similarity computing based on HowNet. *International Journal of Computational Linguistics & Chinese Language Processing* 7(2):59–76.

Nakov, Preslav. 2008. Noun compound interpretation using paraphrasing verbs: Feasibility study. In *LNAI* (Vol. 5253). In *Proceedings of the 13th International Conference on Artificial Intelligence: Methodology, Systems and Applications (AIMSA 2008)*, 103–117 Varna, Bulgaria.

Nakov, Preslav, and Marti A. Hearst. 2006. Using verbs to characterize noun-noun relations. In *LNCS* (Vol 4183). In *Proceedings of the 12th International Conference on Artificial Intelligence: Methodology, Systems and Applications (AIMSA 2006)*, 233–244. Varna, Bulgaria.

Nakov, Preslav, and Marti A. Hearst. 2013. Semantic interpretation of noun compounds using verbal and other paraphrases. *ACM Transactions on Audio, Speech, and Language Processing* 10(3):Article 13.

Nunberg, Geoffrey, Ivan A. Sag, and Thomas Wasow. 1994. Idioms. *Language* 70(3):491–538.

Ó Séaghdha, Diarmuid. 2007. Designing and evaluating a semantic annotation scheme for compound nouns. In *Proceedings of the 4th Corpus Linguistics Conference*. University of Birmingham, United Kingdom.

Pustejovsky, James. 1995. *The generative lexicon*. Cambridge, MA: The MIT Press.

Ó Séaghdha, Diarmuid. 2008. Learning compound noun semantics. Ph.D. dissertation. University of Cambridge.

Tratz, Stephen, and Hovy, Eduard. 2010. A taxonomy, dataset, and classifier for automatic noun compound interpretation. In *Proceedings of the 48th Annual Meeting of the Association for Computational Linguistics*, 678–687. Uppsala, Sweden.

Wang, Meng 王萌. 2010. Linguistic knowledge acquisition of noun for the construction of probabilistic lexical knowledge-based 面向概率型词汇知识库建设的名词语言知识获取. Ph.D. dissertation. Peking University, China.

Wang, Meng, Chu-ren Huang, Shiwen Yu, and Shiyong Kang. 2014. Chinese noun compound interpretation using verbal paraphrases. *ICIC Express Letters, Part B: Applications* 5(5): 1377–1382.

Warren, Beatrice. 1978. Semantic patterns of noun-noun compounds. Ph.D. thesis. Acta Universitatis Gothoburgensis, Sweden.

Wei, Xue. 魏雪. 2012. Research on Chinese noun compound interpretation for semantic-query. 面向语义搜索的汉语名名组合的自动释义研究. Master's thesis. Peking University, China.

Yu, Shiwen, Huiming Duan, Xuefeng Zhu, and Bin Sun 俞士汶, 段慧明, 朱学锋, 孙斌. 2002. The basic processing of contemporary Chinese corpus at Peking University SPECIFICATION 北京大学现代汉语语料库基本加工规范. *Journal of Chinese Information Processing 中文信息学报 16(5):49–64.*

Yuan, Yulin 袁毓林. 1995. Implying predicate and its syntactic implementation 谓词隐含及其句法后果—"的"字结构的称代规则和"的"的语法、语义功能 *Studies of the Chinese Language 中国语文 4:241–255.*

Zhao, Jinglei, Hui Liu, and Ruzhan Lu. 2007. Semantic labeling of compound nominalization in Chinese. In *Proceedings of the Workshop on a Broader Perspective on Multiword Expressions*, 73–80. Prague, Czech Republic.

Chapter 28
Reducing Approximation and Estimation Errors with Heterogeneous Annotations

Weiwei Sun

Abstract This chapter will present the methods for building natural language processing (NLP) systems using heterogeneous linguistic annotations. Considering that heterogeneous annotations are usually systematically different but highly compatible, we proposed to use them to reduce two main types of errors in statistical NLP, namely, approximation and estimation errors. To support our proposal, we studied Chinese word segmentation and part-of-speech tagging, and then empirically analyzed the diversity between two representative corpora—Chinese Treebank and PKU's *People's Daily*—using the manually mapped data collected. The analysis was further exploited to improve the subword-based lexical processing system by (1) integrating systems that were respectively trained by heterogeneous annotations to reduce approximation errors, and (2) retraining models using high-quality automatically converted data to reduce estimation errors.

Keywords Word segmentation · Part-of-speech tagging · Heterogeneous annotations · Approximation error · Estimation error

28.1 Introduction

The majority of data-driven natural language processing (NLP) systems rely on large-scale, manually annotated corpora that are important for training statistical models but are very expensive to build. Nowadays, multiple heterogeneous annotated corpora have been built and publicly available for many NLP tasks. For example, the Penn Treebank (Marcus et al. 1993) is popular for training context-free grammar (CFG)-based parsers; the Redwoods Treebank is well known for systems grounded in head-driven phrase structure grammar (HPSG) (Pollard and Sag 1994); the Propositional Bank (PropBank) (Palmer et al. 2005) is favored in building general semantic role labeling systems; and FrameNet (Baker et al. 1998) is

W. Sun (✉)
Department of Computer Science, University of Cambridge, Cambridge, UK
e-mail: ws390@cam.ac.uk

C.-R. Huang et al. (eds.), *Chinese Language Resources*, Text, Speech and Language Technology 49, https://doi.org/10.1007/978-3-031-38913-9_28

preferred for predicate-specific labeling. The annotation schemes in past projects mostly differed since the underlying linguistic theories varied, resulting in different ways of explaining the same language phenomena. Though statistical NLP systems are usually not bound to specific annotation standards, almost all of them use homogeneous annotation in the training corpus. The coexistence of heterogeneous annotation data therefore presents a new challenge to the consumers of such resources.

There are two essential characteristics of heterogeneous annotations that can be utilized to reduce two main types of errors in statistical NLP, namely, approximation errors due to the intrinsic suboptimality of a model and estimation errors due to having only finite training data. First, heterogeneous annotations are (similar but) different as a result of different annotation schemata. Therefore, systems respectively trained by heterogeneous data can produce different but relevant linguistic analysis. This suggests that complementary features from heterogeneous analysis can be derived for disambiguation, and therefore approximation errors can be reduced. Second, heterogeneous annotations are (different but) similar because their linguistic analysis is highly correlated. This implies that appropriate conversions between heterogeneous corpora are reasonably accurate, and therefore estimation errors can be reduced by reason of the increase of reliable training data.

This chapter will explore heterogeneous annotations to reduce both approximation and estimation errors in Chinese word segmentation and part-of-speech (POS) tagging, which are fundamental steps in more advanced Chinese language processing tasks. We empirically analyzed the diversity between two popular representative heterogeneous corpora—the Chinese Treebank (CTB) (Xue et al. 2005) and PKU's *People's Daily* (PPD). To that end, we manually labeled 200 sentences from the CTB with PPD-style annotations.[1] Our analysis confirmed the aforementioned two properties of heterogeneous annotations. We proposed a structure-based stacking model to fully utilize heterogeneous word structures to reduce approximation errors. In particular, joint word segmentation and POS tagging were addressed as a two-step process. First, character-based taggers were respectively trained using heterogeneous annotations to produce multiple analyses. The outputs of these taggers were then merged into subword sequences, which were further resegmented and tagged by a subword tagger. The subword tagger was designed to refine the tagging results with the help of heterogeneous annotations. To reduce estimation errors, we employed a learning-based approach to convert complementary heterogeneous data to increase labeled training data for the target task. Both the character-based tagger and the subword tagger were refined by retraining using the automatically converted data.

We conducted experiments on the CTB and PPD data and compared our system with other state-of-the-art linear-model-based systems. Our structure-based stacking model achieved an f-score of 94.36, which was superior to the feature-based stacking

[1]The first 200 sentences in the development data for the experiments were selected. This data set is available at http://www.aclweb.org/anthology/attachments/P/P12/P12-1025 (datasets.zip).

model introduced in Jiang et al. (2009). The converted data also enhanced the baseline model. A simple character-based model improved from 93.41 to 94.11. Since the two treatments were concerned with reducing different types of errors and thus were not fully overlapping, the combination of the treatments led to further improvement. Our final system achieved an f-score of 94.68, which yielded a relative error reduction of 11% over the best published result (94.02). Our study has been partially published in Sun (2011) and Sun and Wan (2012).

The remaining parts of the chapter are organized as follows. Section 28.2 will review related supervised segmentation and tagging methods, and then introduce our novel subword tagging model. Section 28.3 will present a diversity analysis of two popular lexical annotation resources, while Sects. 28.4 and 28.5 will describe the details of our new methods. Section 28.6 will present the experimental results and analysis, and Sect. 28.7 will conclude the chapter.

28.2 Joint Chinese Word Segmentation and POS Tagging

28.2.1 The Problem

Word segmentation and POS tagging are fundamental steps in more advanced Chinese language processing tasks, such as syntactic parsing and semantic role labeling. Joint approaches that resolve the two tasks simultaneously have received much attention in recent research. Previous work has shown that joint solutions led to accuracy improvements over pipelined systems by avoiding segmentation error propagation and exploiting POS information to help segmentation. A challenge for joint approaches is the large combined search space, which makes efficient decoding and structured learning of parameters difficult to achieve. Moreover, the representation ability of models is limited because using rich contextual word features makes the search intractable. To overcome such efficiency and effectiveness limitations, approximate inference and reranking techniques have been explored in previous work (Jiang et al. 2008b; Zhang and Clark 2010).

Given a sequence of characters $\mathbf{c} = (c_1, \ldots, c_{\#\mathbf{c}})$, the task of word segmentation and POS tagging is to predict a sequence of word and POS tag pairs with the formula $\mathbf{y} = (\langle w_i, p_i, w_{\#\mathbf{y}}, p_{\#\mathbf{y}} \rangle)$, where w_i is a word, p_i is its POS tag, and the # symbol denotes the number of elements in each variable. To avoid error propagation and to make use of POS information for word segmentation, the two tasks should be resolved jointly. Previous research has shown that integrated methods outperformed pipelined systems (Jiang et al. 2008a; Zhang and Clark 2008). A major challenge for such joint systems is the large search space for the decoder, which may lead to decoding inefficiency.

28.2.2 Character-Based and Word-Based Methods

Similar to word segmentation, both word-based (semi-Markov tagging) and character-based (Markov tagging) methods are popular for joint word segmentation and POS tagging. Word segmentation can be viewed as a bracketing problem, while joint segmentation and tagging can be viewed as a labeled bracketing problem.

In the word-based approach, the basic predicting units are the words themselves. This kind of word-based solver sequentially decides whether the local sequence of characters makes up a word as well as its possible POS tag. In particular, a word-based solver reads the input sentence from left to right and predicts whether the current chunk of continuous characters is a word token and which class it belongs to. Word-based solvers may use previously predicted words and their POS information as clues to find a new word. After one word has been found and classified, word-based solvers move on and search for the next possible word. This word-by-word method for segmentation was first proposed in Zhang and Clark (2007), and was then further used in POS tagging in Zhang and Clark (2008).

In the character-based approach, the basic processing units are characters that compose words, and joint word segmentation and tagging are formulated by the classification of characters into POS tags with boundary information. For example, the label B-NN indicates that a character is located at the beginning of a noun. Using this method, POS information interacts with segmentation. This character-by-character method for segmentation was first proposed in Xue (2003), and was then further used in POS tagging in Ng and Low (2004). One main disadvantage of this model is the difficulty in incorporating whole-word information. Note that the hybrid approach described in Nakagawa and Uchimoto (2007) and Kruengkrai et al. (2009) is also a character-based approach since the word information used was word-type information.

28.2.3 Subword Tagging Model

Motivation

In this chapter, we will present a novel stacked subword model for joint word segmentation and POS tagging, concerning both efficiency and effectiveness. Our work was motivated by several characteristics of this problem. First, the majority of words in a segmentation problem are easy to identify. For example, a simple maximum matching segmenter can achieve an f-score of about 90. Our study showed that it is possible to improve efficiency and accuracy using different strategies for different words. However, previous approaches have treated all possible words equally. The basic strategy in our work was to identify "simple" and "difficult" words first and to integrate them at the subword level. To identify simple words, we borrowed ideas from system ensembles.

Second, segmenters designed with different views have complementary strengths. Our study argued that the agreements and disagreements of different solvers can be used to construct an intermediate subword structure for joint word segmentation and POS tagging. Since the subwords were large enough in practice, the decoding for the POS tagging of subwords was efficient. In particular, our study showed that heterogeneous corpora can be utilized to train diverse segmenters.

Finally, the Chinese language is characterized by a lack of morphology that often provides important clues for POS tagging, and POS tags contain much syntactic information that needs contextual information within a large window for disambiguation. For example, Huang et al. (2007) showed the effectiveness of utilizing syntactic information to rerank POS tagging results and that the capability to represent rich contextual features is crucial for a Chinese POS tagger. In our work, we used a representation-efficiency tradeoff through stacked learning, which is a way of approximating rich non-local features.

Framework

Given multiple word segmentations of one sentence, we formally defined a subword structure that maximized the agreement of non-word-break positions. Based on the subword structure, joint word segmentation and POS tagging were addressed as a two-step process: (1) coarse-grained word segmentation and tagging; and (2) fine-grained subword tagging. The workflow is shown in Fig. 28.1. In the first phase, multiple segmenters were applied to produce multiple segmentation predictions. Take the particular system in Fig. 28.1, for example. One word-based segmenter (Seg_W) and one character-based segmenter (Seg_C) were trained to produce word boundaries. Additionally, a local character-based joint word segmentation and POS tagging solver ($SegTag_L$) was used to provide word boundaries as well as find inaccurate POS information. Here, the word "local" means that the labels of nearby characters were not used as features. In other words, the local character classifier assumed that the tags of the characters were independent of each other. Note that this framework can be integrated with various word segmenters. Section 28.4 will show how segmenters trained by heterogeneous corpora can be applied in this phase.

In the second phase, our system first combined the three segmentation and tagging results to retrieve subwords that maximized the agreement between word boundaries. Finally, a fine-grained subword tagger (SubTag) was applied to bracket subwords into words and to obtain their POS tags.

In our model, word segmentation and POS tagging interacted with each other in two processes. First, although Seg_L was locally trained, it resolved the two subtasks simultaneously. Therefore, in the subword generating stage, word segmentation and POS tagging helped each other. Second, in the subword tagging stage, the bracketing and the classification of subwords were jointly resolved as one sequence-labeling problem.

Our experiments using the CTB and PPD showed that statistical segmenters on their own produced high-quality word boundaries. As a result, the oracle

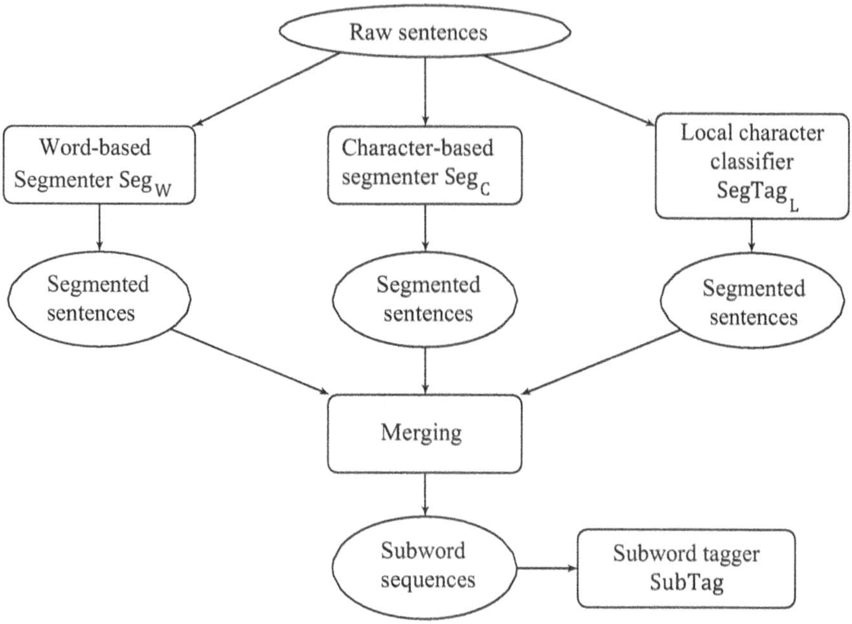

Fig. 28.1 Workflow of the stacked subword model

performance of recovering words from a subword sequence was very high. The quality of the final tagger relied on the quality of the subword tagger. The findings showed that constructing a high-performance subword tagger well resolved the whole task. The statistics also empirically showed that subwords were significantly larger than characters and only slightly smaller than words. As a result, the search space of the subword tagging decreased significantly, and exact Viterbi decoding without approximate pruning was efficiently processed. This property made nearly all the popular sequence labeling algorithms applicable.

Generating Subword Sequences

The majority of words were easy to identify in the segmentation process. We favored the idea of treating different words using different strategies. In our work, we tried to identify simple and difficult words first and then integrate them at the subword level. Inspired by previous work, we constructed this subword structure using multiple solvers designed from different views. If a piece of continuous characters was consistently segmented by multiple segmenters, it would not be separated in the subword tagging step. The intuition was that strings that are consistently segmented by different segmenters tend to be correct predictions. The key point for the intermediate subword structures was to maximize the agreement between the three

	以	总	成绩	3	5	5	.	3	5	分	居
Answer:	[P]	[JJ]	[NN]	[			CD		]	[M]	[VV]
Segw:	[]	[]	[ ]	[		]	[		]	[	]
Segc:	[]	[]	[ ]	[						]	[]
SegTagL:	[P]	[JJ]	[NN]	[	CD		]	[NT]	[CD]	[NT]	[VV]
Subwords:	[P]	[JJ]	[NN]	[	B-CD	]	[I-CD]	[NT]	[CD]	[NT]	[VV]

Fig. 28.2 Example phrase 以总成绩 355.35 分居领先地位 (in front, with a total score of 355.35 points)

coarse-grained systems. In other words, the goal was to make merged subwords as large as possible without overlapping with any predicted word produced by the three coarse-grained solvers. In particular, if the position between two continuous characters was predicted as a word boundary by any segmenter, this position was taken as a separation position in the subword sequence. This strategy ensured that it was still possible to resegment the strings of boundaries in disagreement with the coarse-grained segmenters at the fine-grained tagging stage.

The formal definition is as follows. Given a sequence of characters $\mathbf{c} = (c_1, \ldots, c_{\#\mathbf{c}})$, let $c[i{:}\ j]$ denote a string that is made up of characters between c_i and c_j (including c_i and c_j); then, a partition of the sentence can be written as $c[0, e_1]$, $c[e_1 + 1{:}\ e_2], \ldots, c[e_m{:}\ \#\mathbf{c}]$. Let $s_k = \{c[i{:}\ j]\}$ denote the set of all segments of a partition. Given multiple partitions of a character sequence $\mathcal{L} = \{s_k\}$, there is one and only one merged partition $s_{\mathcal{L}} = \{c[i{:}\ j]\}$:

s.t.
1. $\forall c[i : j] \in s_{\mathcal{L}}, \forall s_k \in \mathcal{L}, \exists c[s : e] \in s_k, s \le i \le j \le e.$
2. $\forall\ \mathcal{I}$ 'satisfies the above condition, $\lvert \mathcal{I}' \rvert > \lvert \mathcal{I} \rvert$.

The first condition ensures that all segments in the merged partition can only be embedded in but not overlapped with any segment of any partition from $\mathcal{L}$. The second condition promises that segments of the merged partition will achieve the maximum length.

Figure 28.2 illustrates the procedure of our method. The lines Seg_W, Seg_C, and SegTag_L are the predictions of the three coarse-grained solvers. The open square brackets and the closed square brackets, respectively, indicate the beginning and the end of a word. For the three words at the beginning and the two words at the end, the three predictors agreed with each other, so these five words were kept as subwords. For the character sequence "355 35," the predictions were very different. Because there were no word-break predictions among the first three characters "355," they together were taken as one subword. For the other five characters, either the left position or the right position was segmented as a word break by at least one predictor, so the merging processor separated them and took each one as a single subword. The last line shows the merged subword sequence with their inaccurate POS tags. The coarse-grained POS tags with positional information were derived from the labels provided by SegTag_L.

28.2.4 Stacked Learning for Parameter Estimation

Stacked generalization is a meta-learning algorithm that was first proposed in Wolpert (1992) and Breiman (1996). The idea is to include two "levels" of predictors. The first level includes one or more predictors $g_1, \ldots g_K$: $\mathbb{R}^d \rightarrow \mathbb{R}$; each receives input $\mathbf{x} \in \mathbb{R}^d$ and outputs the prediction $g_k(\mathbf{x})$. The second level consists of a single function h: $\mathbb{R}^{d+k} \rightarrow \mathbb{R}$ that takes as its input $\langle \mathbf{x}, g_1(\mathbf{x}), \ldots, g_K(\mathbf{x}) \rangle$ and outputs the final prediction $\hat{y} = h(\mathbf{x}, g_1(\mathbf{x}), \ldots, g_K(\mathbf{x}))$.

Training is performed as follows. The training data $S = \{(\mathbf{x}_t, \mathbf{y}_t): t \in [1, T]\}$ is split into $L1$ equal-sized disjoint subsets $S_1, \ldots, S_L$. Then, functions $\mathbf{g}_1, \ldots, \mathbf{g}_L$ (where $\mathbf{g}_l = \langle g_1^l, \ldots, g_K^l \rangle$) are separately trained by $S - S_l$ and are used to construct the augmented data set $\hat{S} = \{(\langle \mathbf{x}_t, \hat{\mathbf{y}}_t^1, \ldots, \hat{\mathbf{y}}_t^K \rangle, \mathbf{y}_t): \hat{\mathbf{y}}_t^k = g_K^l(\mathbf{x}_t) \text{ and } \mathbf{x}_t \in S_l\}$. Finally, each g_k is trained by the original data set, and the second level predictor h is trained by $\hat{S}$. The intent of the cross-validation scheme is that $\mathbf{y}_t^k$ is similar to the prediction produced by the predictor, which is learned by a sample that does not include $\mathbf{x}_t$.

Stacked learning has been applied as a system ensemble method in several NLP tasks, such as named entity recognition (Wu et al. 2003) and dependency parsing (McDonald and Nivre 2011). This framework has also been explored as a solution for learning non-local features in Torres Martins et al. (2008). In machine learning research, stacked learning has been applied to structured prediction (Cohen and Carvalho 2005). In our work, stacked learning was used to acquire extended training data for subword tagging.

The three coarse-grained solvers Seg_W, Seg_C, and SegTag_L were directly trained by the original training data. When these three predictors were used to produce the training data, the performance was perfect. However, this did not hold when these models were applied to the test data. When we directly applied Seg_W, Seg_C, and SegTag_L to extend the training data to generate subword samples, the extended training data for the subword tagger were very different from the data in the run time, resulting in poor performance.

One way to correct the training/test mismatch is to use the stacking method, where a K-fold *cross-validation* of the original data is performed to construct the training data for subword tagging. Algorithm 28.1 illustrates the learning procedure. First, the training data $S = \{(\mathbf{c}_t, \mathbf{y}_t)\}$ was split into L equal-sized disjointed subsets $S_1, \ldots, S_L$. For each subset S_l, the complementary set S-S_l was used to train the three coarse-grained solvers $\text{Seg}_\text{W}{}^l$, $\text{Seg}_\text{C}{}^l$ and $\text{SegTag}_\text{L}{}^l$, which processed S_l and provided inaccurate predictions. Then, the inaccurate predictions were merged into subword

Algorithm 28.1 The stacked learning procedure for the subword tagger.

Input: Data $S = \{(\mathbf{c}_t, \mathbf{y}_t), t = 1, 2, \ldots, \text{n}\}$
Split S into L partitions $\{S_1, \ldots, S_\text{L}\}$
for $l = 1, \ldots, L$ **do**
Train $\text{Seg}_\text{W}{}^l$, $\text{Seg}_\text{C}{}^l$ and $\text{SegTag}_\text{L}{}^l$ using S - S_l.
Predict S_l using $\text{Seg}_\text{W}{}^l$, $\text{Seg}_\text{C}{}^l$ and $\text{SegTag}_\text{L}{}^l$.
Merge the predictions to get subwords training sample S_l'.
Train the subword tagger SubTag using S'.

sequences and S_l was extended to $S_l^{'}$. Finally, the subword tagger was trained by the whole extended data set $S^{'}$.

28.2.5 *Evaluation*

Set-up

Previous studies on joint Chinese word segmentation and POS tagging have used the CTB in experiments. We followed this set-up to evaluate the effectiveness of the subword tagging framework. We used CTB 5.0 as our main corpus and defined the training, development, and test sets according to Jiang et al. (2008a, 2008b), Kruengkrai et al. (2009), and Zhang and Clark (2010). Table 28.1 shows the statistics of our experimental settings:

Three metrics were used for evaluation: precision (P), recall (R), and balanced f-score (F), defined by $2PR/(P + R)$. Precision represented the relative amount of correct words in the system output, and recall represented the relative amount of correct words compared to the gold-standard annotations. For segmentation, a token was considered to be correct if its boundaries matched the boundaries of a word in the gold-standard annotations. For the whole task, both the boundaries and the POS tag had to be correctly identified.

Performance of the Three Coarse-Grained Solvers

Table 28.2 shows the performance of the development data set of the three coarse-grained solvers. In our study, we used 20 iterations to train Seg_{W} and Seg_{C} for all experiments. Even though they were only locally trained, the character classifier SegTag_{L} still significantly outperformed the two state-of-the-art segmenters Seg_{W}

Table 28.1 Training, development, and test data using CTB 5.0

Data set	CTB files	# Of sent	# Of words
Training	1–270	18,089	493,939
	400–931		
	1001–1151		
Devel.	301–325	350	6821
Test	271–300	348	8008

Table 28.2 Performance of the development data set of the three coarse-grained solvers

Devel. data	Task	*P* (%)	*R* (%)	*F*
Seg_{W}	Seg	94.55	94.84	94.69
Seg_{C}	Seg	95.10	94.38	94.73
SegTag_{L}	Seg	95.67	95.98	95.83
	Seg&tag	87.54	91.29	89.38

and Seg_C. This good performance indicates that POS information is very important for word segmentation.

Usefulness of Rich Contextual Features

Table 28.3 shows the effect that features within different window sizes had on the subword tagging task. In this table, C represents subword content features, while T represents IOB-style (inside, outside, beginning) POS tag features. The number indicates the length of the window. For example, C:±1 means that the tagger used one preceding subword and one succeeding subword as features. In Table 28.3, the impact of the features derived from the neighboring subwords can be clearly seen, as in the significant increase between the C:±2 and C:±1 models. This confirmed our hypothesis that a longer history and future features are crucial to the Chinese POS tagging problem. The main advantage of our model was that it made rich contextual features applicable. In all previous solutions, only features within a short history could be used due to the efficiency limitation. Performance was further slightly improved when the window size was increased to 3. Using the labeled bracketing f-score, the evaluation showed that the C:±3T:±1 model performed the same as the C:±3T:±2 model. However, the subword classification accuracy of the C:±3T: ±1 model was higher, so in the following experiments and the final results reported on the test data set, we chose this setting.

Table 28.3 also suggests that the IOB-style POS information of the subwords did not contribute to the increased performance for two main reasons: (1) the POS information provided by the local classifier was inaccurate; and (2) the structured learning of the subword tagger used "real" predicted subword labels during its decoding time, since this learning algorithm was influenced during the training time. It is still an open question whether more accurate POS information on rich contexts can help in this task. If the answer is "yes," how can these features be efficiently incorporated?

Table 28.3 Performance of the stacked subword model ($K = 5$) with features in different window sizes

Devel. data	P (%)	R (%)	F
C:±0T:±0	92.52	92.83	92.67
C:±1T:±0	92.63	93.27	92.95
C:±1T:±1	92.62	93.05	92.83
C:±2T:±0	93.17	93.86	93.51
C:±2T:±1	93.27	93.64	93.45
C:±2T:±2	93.08	93.61	93.34
C:±3T:±0	93.12	93.86	93.49
C:±3T:±1	93.34	93.96	93.65
C:±3T:±2	93.34	93.96	93.65

Usefulness of Stacked Learning

Table 28.4 shows the comparison of the performance of the C:±3T:±1 model trained with no stacking, as well as different folds of cross-validation. Although it was still possible to improve the word segmentation and POS tagging performance compared with the local character classifier, the whole task benefitted only a little from the subword tagging procedure when the stacking technique was not applied. The stacking technique significantly improved system performance, both for word segmentation and POS tagging. This experiment confirmed the theoretical motivation of using stacked learning, which simulated the test-time setting when a subword tagger was applied to a new instance. Moreover, there was not much difference between the 5-fold and the 10-fold cross-validation.

Results of the Test Set

Table 28.5 summarizes the performance of our final system on the test data and other systems reported in the majority of previous work. The final results of our system were achieved using 10-fold cross-validation of the C:±3T:±1 model. The left-most column indicates the references for previous systems that achieved state-of-the-art results. The comparison of the accuracy between our stacked subword system and the state-of-the-art systems in the literature indicates that our method was competitive with the best systems. Our system obtained the highest f-score performance on both word segmentation and the whole task, resulting in error reductions of 14.1% and 5.5%, respectively.

Table 28.4 Performance of the development data when no stacking and different folds of cross-validation were separately applied

Devel. data	Task	*P* (%)	*R* (%)	*F*
No stacking	Seg	95.75	96.48	96.12
	Seg&Tag	91.42	92.13	91.77
$K = 5$	Seg	96.42	97.04	96.73
	Seg&Tag	93.34	93.96	93.65
$K = 10$	Seg	96.67	97.11	96.89
	Seg&Tag	93.50	94.06	93.78

Table 28.5 F-scores of the test data

Test	Seg	Seg&Tag
Jiang et al. (2008a)	97.85	93.41
Jiang et al. (2008b)	97.74	93.37
Kruengkrai et al. (2009)	97.87	93.67
Zhang and Clark (2010)	97.78	93.67
Our system	**98.17**	**94.02**

28.3 Heterogeneous Annotations

28.3.1 Annotation Ensemble

In general, the corpus annotation not only presented a variety of explanatory linguistic information but also helped promote different learning algorithms that usually depended on large-scale corpora, especially today's popular deep learning methods. The process of annotation has attracted more and more attention now that these algorithms have been developed. For example, Ide and Pustejovsky (2017) provided a comprehensive survey of the development of state-of-the-art linguistic annotations of language resources.

For Chinese word segmentation and POS tagging, supervised learning has become a dominant paradigm. Much of the progress is due to the development of both corpora and machine learning techniques. Although several institutions to date have released their segmented and POS tagged data, acquiring sufficient quantities of high-quality training examples is still a major bottleneck. The annotation schemes of existing lexical resources are different, since the underlying linguistic theories vary. Despite the existence of multiple resources, such data cannot simply be put together for training systems because almost all of the statistical NLP systems assume homogeneous annotation. Therefore, it is not only interesting but also important to study how to fully utilize heterogeneous resources to improve Chinese lexical processing. There is currently a feature-engineering solution for segmentation and POS tagging, as presented in Jiang et al. (2009). Different from their work, we incorporated heterogeneous taggers into our subword tagging model, which more explicitly explored the relation between heterogeneous annotations.

28.3.2 Analysis of CTB and PPD Standards

Our study focused on two popular representative corpora for Chinese lexical processing: the CTB and PPD. To analyze the diversity between these annotation standards, we retrieved 200 sentences from the CTB and manually labeled them according to the PPD standard. Specifically, we employed a PPD-style segmentation and tagging system to automatically label these 200 sentences. A linguistic expert who deeply understands the PPD standard then manually checked the automatic analysis and corrected its errors.

These 200 sentences were segmented into 3886 and 3882 words, respectively, according to the CTB and PPD standards. The average length of the word tokens was almost the same. However, the word boundaries and the definitions of words were different, resulting in 3561 word tokens that were consistently segmented by both standards. In other words, 91.7% of the CTB word tokens shared the same word boundaries with 91.6% of the PPD word tokens. Among these 3561 words, 552 punctuation marks were consistently segmented. When the punctuation marks were filtered out to avoid overestimation of consistency, 90.4% of the CTB words had the same boundaries as 90.3% of the PPD words. The boundaries of the words that were differently segmented were compatible. Among all annotations, only one cross-bracketing occurred. These statistics indicate that the two heterogeneous segmented corpora were systematically different, which confirmed the aforementioned two properties of heterogeneous annotations.

Table 28.6 shows the mapping between CTB-style tags and PPD-style tags. For a definition and illustration of these tags, please refer to the annotation guidelines.[2] The statistics after the colons represent how many times the POS tag pair appeared among the 3561 words that were consistently segmented. In Table 28.6, it can be seen that (1) there is no one-to-one mapping between the heterogeneous word classification and (2) the mapping between heterogeneous tags is not very clear. This simple analysis indicates that the two POS-tagged corpora also hold the two properties of heterogeneous annotations. The differences between the POS annotation standards are systematic. The annotations in the CTB are treebank-driven, and thus are considered more functional (dynamic) information of basic lexical categories. The annotations in PPD are lexicon-driven, and thus focus on more static properties of words. Due to limited space, we only illustrated the annotation of verbs and nouns to better understand the differences.

- The CTB tag VV indicates common verbs that are mainly labeled as verbs (V) according to the PPD standard. However, these words can also be tagged as nominal categories (A, VN, N)[3]A. The main reason is that there are a large number of Chinese adjectives and nouns that can be realized as predicates without linking verbs.
- The tag NN indicates common nouns in the CTB. Some of them are labeled as verbal categories (VN, V).[4] The main reason is that a majority of Chinese verbs can be realized as subjects and objects without form changes.

28.3.3 Two Essential Characteristics

There are two main types of errors in statistical NLP: (1) approximation errors due to the intrinsic suboptimality of a model; and (2) estimation errors due to having only finite training data. Take Chinese word segmentation, for example. Our previous analysis (Sun 2010) showed that one main intrinsic disadvantage of the character-based model is the difficulty in incorporating whole-word information, while one main disadvantage of the word-based model is the weak ability to express word formation. In both models, the significant decrease in the prediction accuracy of

---

[2]Available at http://www.cis.upenn.edu/~chinese/posguide.3rd.ch.pdf and http://www.icl.pku.edu.cn/icl_groups/corpus/spec.htm.

[3]A: adjective, N: noun; VN: normalization of a verb.

[4]V: verb.

Table 28.6 Mapping between the CTB and PPD POS tags

AS ⇒ u:44;	CD ⇒ m:134;
DEC ⇒ u:83;	DEV ⇒ u:7;
DEG ⇒ u:123;	ETC ⇒ u:9;
LB ⇒ p:1;	NT ⇒ t:98;
OD ⇒ m:41;	PU = w:552;
SP ⇒ u:1;	VC ⇒ v:32;
VE ⇒ v:13;	BA p:2; d:1;
CS ⇒ c:3; d:1;	DT ⇒ r:15; b:1;
MSP ⇒ c:2; u:1;	PN ⇒ r:53; n:2;
CC ⇒ c:73; p:5; v:2;	M ⇒ q:101; n:11; v:1;
LC ⇒ f:51; Ng:3; v:1; u:1;	P ⇒ p:133; v:4; c:2; Vg:1;
VA ⇒ a:57; i:4; z:2; ad:1; b:1;	NR ⇒ ns:170; nr:65; j:23; nt:21; nz:7; n:2; s:1;
VV ⇒ v:382; i:5; a:3; Vg:2;	JJ ⇒ a:43; b:13; n:3; vn:3;
vn:2; n:2; p:2; w:1;	d:2; j:2; f:2; t:2; z:1;
AD ⇒ d:149; c:11; ad:6; z:4;	NN ⇒ n:738; vn:135; v:26;
a:3; v:2; n:1; r:1; m:1; f:1; t:1;	j:19; Ng:5; an:5; a:3; r:3; s:3; Ag:2; nt:2; f:2; q:2; i:1; t:1; nz:1; b:1;

out-of-vocabulary (OOV) words indicates the impact of estimation errors. These two essential characteristics of the systematic diversity of heterogeneous annotations can be utilized to reduce both approximation and estimation errors. On the one hand, heterogeneous annotations are (similar but) different considering different annotation schemata. As a result, systems respectively trained by heterogeneous annotation data can produce different analyses. Auxiliary features from heterogeneous analyses can be derived for disambiguation, and therefore approximation errors can be reduced. On the other hand, heterogeneous annotations are (different but) similar in the sense that the corresponding linguistic analysis is highly correlated. An auxiliary corpus can be converted with a high precision rate for model retraining, and therefore estimation errors can be reduced. Note that different annotated corpora are usually based on different texts.

28.4 Structure-Based Stacking

28.4.1 Reducing Approximation Errors via Stacking

Each annotation data set alone can yield a predictor that can be taken as a mechanism to produce structured texts. With different training data, multiple heterogeneous systems can be constructed. These systems produce similar linguistic analyses that hold the same high-level linguistic principles but differ in detail. A very simple way to take advantage of heterogeneous structures is to design a predictor that can predict a more accurate target structure based on the input, the less accurate target structure, and complementary structures. This idea is very close to stacked learning (Wolpert 1992), which has been well developed for ensemble learning and successfully applied to some NLP tasks, such as dependency parsing (Torres Martins et al. 2008).

Formally speaking, our idea was to include two "levels" of processing. The first level included one or more base predictors $f_1, \ldots, f_K$ that were independently built with different training data. The second level of processing consisted of an inference function h that took as its input $\langle \mathbf{x}, f_1(\mathbf{x}), \ldots, f_K(\mathbf{x}) \rangle$[5] and output the final prediction $h(\mathbf{x}, f_1(\mathbf{x}), \ldots, f_K(\mathbf{x}))$. The only difference between the model ensemble and the annotation ensemble was that the output spaces of the model ensemble were the same, while the output spaces of the annotation ensemble were different. This framework is general and flexible in the sense that it assumes almost nothing about the individual systems and takes them as black boxes.

[5] $\mathbf{x}$ is a given Chinese sentence.

28.4.2 Character-Based Tagger

With IOB2 representation (Ramshaw and Marcus 1995), the problem of joint segmentation and tagging can be regarded as a character classification task. Previous work has shown that the character-based approach is an effective method for Chinese lexical processing. Both of our feature- and structure-based stacking models employed character-based taggers to generate multiple segmentation and tagging results. Our base tagger used a discriminative sequential classifier to predict the POS tag with positional information for each character. Each character was assigned one of two possible boundary tags: B for a character that begins a word and I for a character that occurs in the middle of a word. We denoted a candidate character token c_i with a fixed window $c_{i\ 2}c_{i\ 1}c_i\ c_{i+1}c_{i+2}$. The following features were used for classification:

- Character unigrams: $c_k\ (i - l \leq k \leq i + l)$
- Character bigrams: $c_k\ c_{k+1}\ (i - l \leq k < i + l)$

28.4.3 Feature-Based Stacking

Jiang et al. (2009) introduced a feature-based stacking solution for annotation ensemble. In their solution, an auxiliary tagger CTag_{ppd} was trained by a complementary corpus (i.e., PPD) to assist with the target CTB-style tagging. To refine the character-based tagger CTag_{ctb}, PPD-style character labels were directly incorporated as new features. The stacking model relied on the ability of the discriminative learning method to explore informative features, which played a central role in boosting tagging performance. To compare their feature-based stacking model with our structure-based model, we implemented a similar system $\text{CTag}_{\text{ppd} \rightarrow \text{ctb}}$. Apart from character uni/bigram features, PPD-style character labels were used to derive the following features to enhance our CTB-style tagger,

- Character unigrams: $C_k^{ppd}\left(i - l^{ppd} \leq k < i + l^{ppd.}\right)$
- Character bigrams: $C_k^{ppd} C_{k+1}^{ppd}\left(i - l^{ppd} \leq k < i + l^{ppd}\right)$

where l and $l^{\,ppd}$ are the window sizes of the features that can be tuned by the development data.

28.4.4 Structure-Based Stacking

We proposed extending our structured-based stacking model for the task, in which heterogeneous word structures were used not only to generate features but also to derive a subword structure. Previous work was motivated by the diversity of

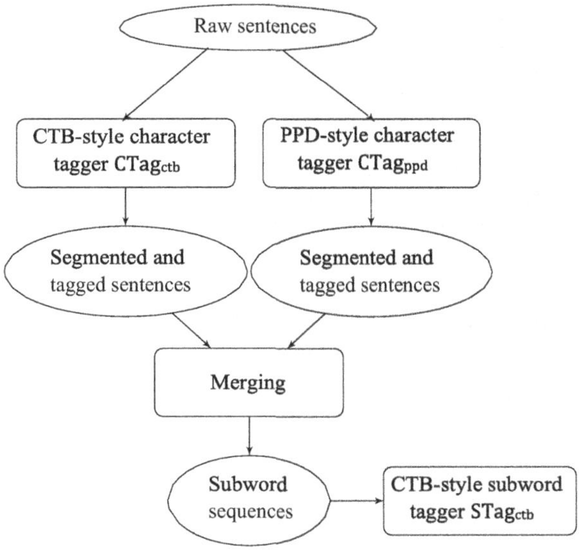

Fig. 28.3 Workflow of the heterogeneous annotation-based subword tagging model

heterogeneous models, while our work was motivated by the diversity of heterogeneous annotations. The workflow of our new system is shown in Fig. 28.3. In the first phase, one character-based CTB-style tagger ($CTag_{ctb}$) and one character-based PPD-style tagger ($CTag_{ppd}$) were respectively trained to produce heterogeneous word boundaries. In the second phase, this system first combined the two segmentation and tagging results to retrieve subwords that maximized the agreement between word boundaries. Finally, a fine-grained subword tagger ($STag_{ctb}$) was applied to bracket subwords into words and to label their POS tags. We also applied a PPD-style subword tagger. To compare with previous work, we specifically concentrated on the PPD-to-CTB adaptation.

Following Sect. 28.2, the intermediate subword structures were defined to maximize the agreement between $CTag_{ctb}$ and $CTag_{ppd}$. In other words, the goal was to make the merged subwords as large as possible without overlapping with any predicted words produced by the two taggers. If the position between two continuous characters was predicted as a word boundary by any segmenter, this position was taken as a separation position of the subword sequence. This strategy ensured that it was still possible to correctly resegment the strings of which the boundaries disagreed with by the heterogeneous segmenters at the subword tagging stage.

To train the subword tagger $STag_{ctb}$, features were formed making use of both CTB-style and PPD-style POS tags provided by the character-based taggers. In the following description, C refers to the content of a subword; T_{ctb} and T_{ppd} refer to the positional POS tags generated from $CTag_{ctb}$ and $CTag_{ppd}$; and l_C, l_T^{ctb} and l_T^{ppd} are the window sizes. For convenience, we denoted a subword with its context $\ldots s_{i-1}, s_i, s_{i+1} \ldots$, where s_i is the current token. The following features were applied:

- Unigram features: $C(s_k)$ $(i - l_C \leq k \leq +l_C)$, $T_{ctb}(s_k)$ $(i - l_T^{ctb} \leq k \leq i + l_T^{ctb})$, $T_{ppd}(s_k)$ $(i - l_T^{ppd} \leq k \leq i + l_T^{ppd})$.
- Bigram features: $C(s_k)C(s_{k+1})$ $(i - l_C \leq k < i + l_C)$, $T_{ctb}(s_k)T_{ctb}(s_{k+1})$ $(i - l_T^{ctb} \leq k < i + l_T^{ctb})$, $T_{ppd}(s_k)T_{ppd}(s_{k+1})$ $(i - l_T^{ppd} \leq k < i + l_T^{ppd})$.
- $C(s_{i-1})C(s_{i+1})$ (if $l_C \geq 1$), $T_{ctb}(s_{i-1})T_{ctb}(s_{i+1})$ (if $l_T^{ctb} \geq 1$), $T_{ppd}(s_{i-1})$ $T_{ppd}(s_{i+1})$ (if $l_T^{ppd} \geq 1$).
- Word formation features: Character *n*-gram prefixes and suffixes for *n* up to 3.

Cross-validation

$CTag_{ctb}$ and $CTag_{ppd}$ were directly trained by the original training data (i.e., the CTB and PPD data). The cross-validation technique was necessary to generate the training data for subword tagging since it dealt with the training/test mismatch problem. To construct the training data for the new heterogeneous subword tagger, a 10-fold cross-validation of the original CTB data was also performed.

28.5 Data-Driven Annotation Conversion

It is possible to acquire high-quality labeled data for a specific annotation standard by exploring existing heterogeneous corpora since the annotations are normally highly compatible. Moreover, the exploitation of additional (pseudo) labeled data aims to reduce estimation errors and enhances an NLP system in a different way from stacking. We therefore expected that the improvements would not overlap much and their combination would lead to further improvement.

Stacking models can be viewed as annotation converters, as they take as inputs complementary structures and produce output target structures. In other words, stacking models actually learn statistical models to transform lexical representations. We acquired informative extra samples by processing the PPD data with our stacking models. Though the converted annotations were imperfect, they were still helpful in reducing estimation errors.

28.5.1 Character-Based Conversion

The feature-based stacking model $CTag_{ppd \rightarrow ctb}$ mapped the input character sequence **c** and its PPD-style character label sequence to the corresponding CTB-style character label sequence. This model by itself can be taken as a corpus conversion model to transform a PPD-style analysis to a CTB-style analysis. By processing the auxiliary corpus D_{ppd} with $CTag_{ppd \rightarrow ctb}$, we acquired a new labeled data set $D'_{ctb} = D_{ppd \rightarrow ctb}^{CTag_{ppd \rightarrow ctb}}$.We retrained the $\mathrm{CTag_{ctb}}$ model with both original and converted data $D_{ctb} \cup D'_{ctb}$.

28.5.2 Subword-Based Conversion

Similarly, the structure-based stacking model can also be taken as a corpus conversion model. By processing the auxiliary corpus D_{ppd} with $\mathrm{STag_{ctb}}$, we acquired a new labeled data set $D''_{ctb} = D_{ppd \rightarrow ctb}^{STag_{ctb}}$. We retrained the $STag_{ctb}$ model with $D_{ctb} \cup D''_{ctb}$. When we used the gold-standard PPD-style labels of D''_{ctb} to extract subwords, the new model overfit the gold-standard PPD-style labels, which were unavailable at test time. To avoid this training/test mismatch problem, we also employed a 10-fold cross-validation procedure to add noise.

It is not new to convert a corpus from one formalism to another. A well-known work is the transformation of the Penn Treebank into resources for various deep linguistic processing, including lexicalized tree adjoining grammar (LTAG) (Xia 1999), combinatory categorial grammar (CCG) (Hockenmaier and Steedman 2007), head-driven phrase structure grammar (HPSG) (Miyao et al. 2005), and lexical functional grammar (LFG) (Cahill et al. 2002). Such work for corpus conversion mainly leverages rich sets of handcrafted rules to convert corpora. The construction of linguistic rules is usually time-consuming and the rules are not full coverage. Compared with rule-based conversion, our statistical converters were much easier to build and empirically performed well.

28.6 Experiments

28.6.1 Set-up

To demonstrate the impact of heterogeneous data on reducing both approximation and estimation errors for Chinese lexical processing, we conducted experiments using the CTB and PPD. The CTB set-up was exactly the same as the experiments in Sect. 28.2.5. Jiang et al. (2009) presented a preliminary study of the annotation adaptation topic and conducted experiments with extra PPD data.[6] In other words, the CTB-style annotation was the target analysis, while the PPD-style annotation was the complementary/auxiliary analysis. Our experiments for annotation ensemble followed Jiang et al.'s (2009) setting to lead to a fair comparison between our system and theirs. A CRF learning toolkit, wapiti (Lavergne et al. 2010),[7] was used to

[6] http://icl.pku.edu.cn/icl_res/

[7] http://wapiti.limsi.fr/

Table 28.7 Performance of the development data of different stacking models

Devel. data	*P* (%)	*R* (%)	*F*
$CTag_{ctb}$	93.28	92.58	92.93
$CTag_{ppd \rightarrow ctb}$	93.89	93.46	93.67
$STag_{ctb}$	94.07	93.99	94.03

resolve sequence labeling problems. Among several parameter estimation methods provided by wapiti, our auxiliary experiments indicated that the "rprop-" method worked best. Three metrics were used for evaluation: precision (P), recall (R), and balanced f-score (*F*), defined by $2PR/(P + R)$. Precision represented the relative amount of correct words in the system output, and recall represented the relative amount of correct words compared with the gold-standard annotations. A token was considered to be correct if its boundaries matched the boundaries of a word in the gold-standard annotations and their POS tags were identical.

28.6.2 Results of Stacking

Table 28.7 summarizes the segmentation and tagging performance of the baseline and different stacking models. The baseline of the character-based joint solver ($CTag_{ctb}$) was competitive and achieved an f-score of 92.93. Using the character labels from a heterogeneous solver ($CTag_{ppd}$), which was trained by the PPD data set, the performance of this character-based system ($CTag_{ppd \rightarrow ctb}$) was improved to 93.67. This result confirmed the importance of a heterogeneous structure. Our structure-based stacking solution was effective and outperformed feature-based stacking. By better exploiting the heterogeneous word boundary structures, our subword tagging model achieved an f-score of 94.03 (l^{ctb} and l^{ppd} were tuned by the $T \quad T$ development data and both set to 1).

The contribution of the auxiliary tagger was twofold. On the one hand, the heterogeneous solver provided structural information, which was the basis on which to construct the subword sequence. On the other hand, this tagger provided additional POS information, which was helpful for disambiguation. To evaluate these two contributions, we performed another experiment using just the heterogeneous word boundary structures without the POS information. The f-score of this type of subword tagging was 93.73. This result indicates that both the word boundary and POS information were helpful.

28.6.3 Learning Curves

We performed additional experiments to evaluate the effect of heterogeneous features as the amount of PPD data was varied. Table 28.8 summarizes the f-score changes. The feature-based model worked well only when a considerable amount of

Table 28.8 F-scores relative to the sizes of the training data (sizes, shown in columns #CTB and #PPD, represent the number of sentences in each training corpus)

PPD → CTB			
#CTB	#PPD	CTag	Stag
18,104	7381	92.21	93.26
18,104	14,545	93.22	93.82
18,104	21,745	93.58	93.96
18,104	28,767	93.55	93.87
18,104	35,996	93.67	94.03
9052	9052	92.10	92.40

Table 28.9 F-scores with gold-standard PPD-style tagging of the manually converted data

Data	Auto PPD	Gold PPD
$CTag_{ppd \rightarrow ctb}$	93.69	95.19
$STag_{ctb}$	94.14	94.70

heterogeneous data was available. When a small set was added, the performance was even lower than the baseline (92.93). The structure-based stacking model was more robust and obtained consistent gains regardless of the size of the complementary data.

28.6.4 Results of Annotation Conversion

The stacking models can be viewed as data-driven annotation converting models. However they were not trained by "real" labeled samples. Although the target representation (CTB-style analysis in our case) was the gold standard, the input representation (PPD-style analysis in our case) was labeled by the automatic tagger $CTag_{ppd}$. To make clear whether these stacking models trained with noisy inputs could tolerate perfect inputs, we evaluated the two stacking models based on our manually converted data. The accuracies presented in Table 28.9 indicate that although the conversion models were learned by applying noisy data, they refined target tagging with gold-standard auxiliary tagging. Another interesting finding was that the gold-standard PPD-style analysis did not help the subword tagging model as much as the character-tagging model.

28.6.5 Results of Retraining

Table 28.10 shows the accuracies of the retrained models. Note that a subword tagger was built on character taggers, so when we retrained a subword system, we considered whether to retrain the base character taggers. The error rates decreased as automatically converted data was added to the training pool, especially for the

Table 28.10 Performance of the development data of the retrained models

CTag_{ctb}	STag_{ctb}	*P* (%)	*R* (%)	*F*
$D_{ctb} \cup D'_{ctb}$	–	94.46	94.06	94.26
$D_{ctb} \cup D'_{ctb}$	D_{ctb}	94.61	94.43	94.52
D_{ctb}	$D_{ctb} \cup D''_{ctb}$	94.05	94.08	94.06
$D_{ctb} \cup D'_{ctb}$	$D_{ctb} \cup D''_{ctb}$	94.71	94.53	94.62

Table 28.11 Performance of the test data of the different systems

Test data	*P* (%)	*R* (%)	*F*
Character model	93.31	93.51	93.41
+Retraining	93.93	94.29	94.11
Subword model	94.10	94.62	94.36
+Retraining	**94.42**	**94.93**	**94.68**

character-based tagger CTag_{ctb}. When the CTB-style tagging was improved, the final tagging was improved in the end. The retraining did not help the subword tagging much, as improvement was very modest.

28.6.6 Results of the Test Set

Table 28.11 summarizes the tagging performance of the different systems. The baseline of the character-based tagger was competitive and achieved an f-score of 93.41. By better using the heterogeneous word boundary structures, our subword tagging model achieved an f-score of 94.36. Both the character and subword tagging models were enhanced by the automatically converted corpus. With the pseudo labeled data, the performance increased to 94.11 and 94.68.

28.7 Conclusion

Our theoretical and empirical analyses of two popular representative corpora highlighted the two essential characteristics of heterogeneous annotations that were explored to reduce approximation and estimation errors for Chinese word segmentation and POS tagging. We employed stacking models to incorporate features derived from heterogeneous analysis and applied them to convert heterogeneous labeled data for retraining. The appropriate application of heterogeneous annotations led to a significant improvement compared with various strong baselines. Although our discussion focused on a specific task, the key idea of leveraging heterogeneous annotations to reduce approximation errors with stacking models and estimation errors with automatically converted corpora is very general and applicable to other NLP tasks.

Acknowledgements This work was mainly finished when the author was attending Saarland University and the Research Center for Artificial Intelligence (DFKI). At that time, the author was funded by the DFKI and the German Academic Exchange Service (DAAD).

References

Baker, Collin F., Charles J. Fillmore, and John B. Lowe. 1998. The Berkeley FrameNet project. In *Proceedings of the 36th Annual Meeting of the Association for Computational Linguistics and 17th International Conference on Computational Linguistics, Volume 1*, Association for Computational Linguistics, 86–90. Montréal, Québec, Canada.

Breiman, Leo. 1996. Stacked regressions. *Machine Learning* 24:49–64.

Cahill, Aoife, Mairead McCarthy, Josef Van Genabith, and Andy Way. 2002. Automatic annotation of the Penn Treebank with lfg f-structure information. In *Proceedings of the LREC Workshop on Linguistic Knowledge Acquisition and Representation: Bootstrapping Annotated Language Data*, 8–15. Las Palmas, Canary Islands.

Cohen, William W., and Vitor R. Carvalho. 2005. Stacked sequential learning. In *Proceedings of the 19th International Joint Conference on Artificial Intelligence*, 671–676. San Francisco, California.

Hockenmaier, Julia, and Mark Steedman. 2007. CCGbank: A corpus of CCG derivations and dependency structures extracted from the Penn Treebank. *Computational Linguistics* 33(3): 355–396.

Huang, Zhongqiang, Mary Harper, and Wen Wang. 2007. Mandarin part-of-speech tagging and discriminative reranking. In *Proceedings of the 2007 Joint Conference on Empirical Methods in Natural Language Processing and Computational Natural Language Learning (EMNLP-CoNLL)*, Association for Computational Linguistics, 1093–1102. Prague, Czech Republic.

Ide, Nancy, and James Pustejovsky. 2017. *Handbook of linguistic annotation*. Dordrecht: Springer.

Jiang, Wenbin, Liang Huang, Qun Liu, and Yajuan Lü. 2008a. A cascaded linear model for joint Chinese word segmentation and part-of-speech tagging. In *Proceedings of ACL-08: HLT*, Association for Computational Linguistics, 897–904. Columbus, Ohio.

Jiang, Wenbin, Haitao Mi, and Qun Liu. 2008b. Word lattice reranking for Chinese word segmentation and part-of-speech tagging. In *Proceedings of the 22nd International Conference on Computational Linguistics*, Coling 2008 Organizing Committee, 385–392. Manchester, United Kingdom.

Jiang, Wenbin, Liang Huang, and Qun Liu. 2009. Automatic adaptation of annotation standards: Chinese word segmentation and POS tagging—A case study. In *Proceedings of the Joint Conference of the 47th Annual Meeting of the ACL and the 4th International Joint Conference on Natural Language Processing of the AFNLP*, Association for Computational Linguistics, 522–530. Suntec, Singapore.

Kruengkrai, Canasai, Kiyotaka Uchimoto, Jun'ichi Kazama, Yiou Wang, Kentaro Torisawa, and Hitoshi Isahara. 2009. An error-driven word-character hybrid model for joint Chinese word segmentation and POS tagging. In *Proceedings of the Joint Conference of the 47th Annual Meeting of the ACL and the 4th International Joint Conference on Natural Language Processing of the AFNLP*, Association for Computational Linguistics, 513–521. Suntec, Singapore.

Lavergne, Thomas, Olivier Cappé, and François Yvon. 2010. Practical very large scale CRFs. In *Proceedings of the 48th Annual Meeting of the Association for Computational Linguistics*, 504–513. Uppsala, Sweden.

Marcus, Mitchell P., Mary Ann Marcinkiewicz, and Beatrice Santorini. 1993. Building a large annotated corpus of English: The Penn Treebank. *Computational Linguistics* 19(2):313–330.

Torres Martins, André Filipe, Dipanjan Das, Noah A. Smith, and Eric P. Xing. 2008. Stacking dependency parsers. In *Proceedings of the 2008 Conference on Empirical Methods in Natural Language Processing*, Association for Computational Linguistics, 157–166. Honolulu, Hawai'i.

McDonald, Ryan T., and Joakim Nivre. 2011. Analyzing and integrating dependency parsers. *Computational Linguistics* 37(1):197–230.

Miyao, Yusuke, Takashi Ninomiya, and Jun'ichi Tsujii. 2005. Corpus-oriented grammar development for acquiring a head-driven phrase structure grammar from the Penn Treebank. In *Proceedings of the Second International Joint Conference on Natural Language Processing (IJCNLP 2005)*, 684–693. Jeju Island, Korea.

Nakagawa, Tetsuji, and Kiyotaka Uchimoto. 2007. A hybrid approach to word segmentation and POS tagging. In *Proceedings of the 45th Annual Meeting of the Association for Computational Linguistics, Companion Volume Proceedings of the Demo and Poster Sessions*, Association for Computational Linguistics, 217–220. Prague, Czech Republic.

Ng, Hwee Tou, and Jin Kiat Low. 2004. Chinese part-of-speech tagging: One-at-a-time or all-at-once? Word-based or character-based? In *Proceedings of EMNLP 2004*, Association for Computational Linguistics, ed. Dekang Lin and Dekai Wu, 277–284. Barcelona, Spain.

Palmer, Martha, Daniel Gildea, and Paul Kingsbury. 2005. The proposition bank: An annotated corpus of semantic roles. *Computational Linguistics* 31:71–106.

Pollard, Carl, and Ivan A. Sag. 1994. *Head-driven phrase structure grammar*. Chicago: The University of Chicago Press.

Ramshaw, Lance, and Mitch Marcus. 1995. Text chunking using transformation-based learning. In *Proceedings of the Third Workshop on Very Large Corpora*, Association for Computational Linguistics, ed. David Yarowsky and Kenneth Church, 82–94. Somerset, New Jersey.

Sun, Weiwei. 2010. Word-based and character-based word segmentation models: Comparison and combination. In *Proceedings of the 23rd International Conference on Computational Linguistics (Coling 2010)*, Coling 2010 Organizing Committee, 1211–1219. Beijing, China.

Sun, Weiwei. 2011. A stacked sub-word model for joint Chinese word segmentation and part-of-speech tagging. In *Proceedings of the 49th Annual Meeting of the Association for Computational Linguistics: Human Language Technologies*, Association for Computational Linguistics, 1385–1394. Portland, Oregon.

Sun, Weiwei, and Xiaojun Wan. 2012. Reducing approximation and estimation errors for Chinese lexical processing with heterogeneous annotations. In *Proceedings of the 50th Annual Meeting of the Association for Computational Linguistics*, Association for Computational Linguistics. Jeju Island, Korea.

Wolpert, David H. 1992. Original contribution: Stacked generalization. *Neural Networks* 5:241–259.

Wu, Dekai, Grace Ngai, and Marine Carpuat. 2003. A stacked, voted, stacked model for named entity recognition. In *Proceedings of the Seventh Conference on Natural Language Learning at HLT-NAACL 2003*, ed. Walter Daelemans and Miles Osborne, 200–203. Edmonton, Alberta, Canada.

Xia, Fei. 1999. Extracting tree adjoining grammars from bracketed corpora. In *Proceedings of the Sixth Natural Language Processing Pacific Rim Symposium*, 398–403. Beijing, China.

Xue, Nianwen. 2003. Chinese word segmentation as character tagging. In *International Journal of Computational Linguistics and Chinese Language Processing*.

Xue, Naiwen, Fei Xia, Fu-dong Chiou, and Martha Palmer. 2005. The Penn Chinese Treebank: Phrase structure annotation of a large corpus. *Natural Language Engineering* 11:207–238.

Zhang, Yue, and Stephen Clark. 2007. Chinese segmentation with a word-based perceptron algorithm. In *Proceedings of the 45th Annual Meeting of the Association of Computational Linguistics*, Association for Computational Linguistics, 840–847. Prague, Czech Republic.

Zhang, Yue, and Stephen Clark. 2008. Joint word segmentation and POS tagging using a single perceptron. In *Proceedings of ACL-08: HLT*, Association for Computational Linguistics, 888–896. Columbus, Ohio.

Zhang, Yue, and Stephen Clark. 2010. A fast decoder for joint word segmentation and POS-tagging using a single discriminative model. In *Proceedings of the 2010 Conference on Empirical Methods in Natural Language Processing*, Association for Computational Linguistics, 843–852. Cambridge, Massachusetts.

Chapter 29
A Quadratic Assignment Decipherment and Graduated Assignment Solution for Ontology Matching

Kexiang Wang, Baobao Chang, and Zhifang Sui

Abstract Ontology matching aims at seizing semantically similar correspondences between different ontologies. Once ontology matching problems are successfully solved, the heterogeneity problem of large-scale ontologies from multiple sources can be handled. Different from the previous works, we proposed a system of generalized quadratic assignment decipherment for ontology matching and assigned a compatibility matrix in a customizable way to include both local and global ontology information. Moreover, we refined the original graduated assignment algorithm with personalized disturbance and matrix padding in the ontology matching setting. Experiments using the Ontology Alignment Evaluation Initiative (OAEI) datasets have proved our method's competitive performance compared with state-of-the-art systems, even though additional resources were not incorporated into our system. In addition, the formulation of quadratic assignment decipherment provided ontology matching with ready-made algorithms rooted in the optimization theory for a graduated assignment solution.

Keywords Quadratic assignment problem · Graduated assignment · Ontology matching

29.1 Introduction and Related Work

Ontologies, to some extent, are resources of general and special knowledge that pave the way for many artificial intelligence tasks, such as information retrieval and natural language processing. In recent years, ontologies have been increasingly utilized in other fields to make the whole system more intelligent. However, due to the non-uniform standards that ontologies are based on, heterogeneity problems

---

K. Wang · B. Chang · Z. Sui (✉)
Key Laboratory of Computational Linguistics, Peking University, Ministry of Education, Beijing, China

School of Electronic Engineering and Computer Science, Peking University, Beijing, China
e-mail: ayanami@vip.163.com; chbb@pku.edu.cn; szf@pku.edu.cn

C.-R. Huang et al. (eds.), *Chinese Language Resources*, Text, Speech and Language Technology 49, https://doi.org/10.1007/978-3-031-38913-9_29

between ontologies are frequently encountered, which hinders the knowledge-sharing process of ontologies. Hence, bridging the gap between different ontologies in an accurate and automatic way rises as a key problem. Ontology matching (or ontology mapping) is one of the most promising solutions to linking ontologies.

Generally speaking, ontology matching is the process of finding semantic correspondences between different ontologies. Correspondence aligns the entities in one ontology with another, which plays a role as an intermediate language. There can be many types of entities in an ontology, such as class entities, property entities, and individual entities. The two entities of a correspondence are expected to be of the same type. In this chapter, we will mainly focus on the matching case that enforces the two-way one-to-one matching constraint between two ontologies. In other words, when two ontologies are matched, the entity in one ontology has at most one matching pair in the other ontology. This ontology matching case is similar to graph matching, which is a common practice in ontology matching.

Many methods have been proposed to solve ontology matching problems. Among them, graph-based matching methods are the most promising solutions. Ontologies using these methods are treated as graphs (Euzenat and Shvaiko 2007; Hu et al. 2005), in which the node represents the entity and the edge represents the relationship between entities. Graph-based matching methods are more competitive than other methods according to the experimental results reported by the Ontology Alignment Evaluation Initiative (OAEI[1]) and other researchers. Examples include the similarity propagation method (Li et al. 2009; Ngo and Bellahsene 2012) and the affinity-preserving random walk method (Xiang et al. 2015). Similarity propagation, which originated from schema matching in the database literature, has been utilized to solve problems in ontology matching. This method gives a ranking score for every possible correspondence between two ontologies, which represents the confidence of a correspondence. The ranking score is computed based on the iterative propagation from a node to its neighboring node. Affinity-preserving random walk also gives a ranking score to a possible correspondence but in a reweighted random walk view. This method performs quite well and shows strong robustness in the deformation of ontologies. Other notable methods include Anchor-PROMPT (Noy and Musen 2001) and GMO (Hu et al. 2005).

In this chapter, we will propose a novel method for ontology matching. The key aspect of our method is the decipherment of ontology matching as a quadratic assignment problem (QAP) (Lawler 1963) and a graduated assignment (GA) algorithm (Gold and Rangarajan 1996a, 1996b) as a solution to QAPs. The formulation of a QAP is an attempt to handle ontology matching in a unified and global framework that adopts both the local features such as entity similarity and the global features such as the compatibility value of two correspondences. According to our method, all these features can be embedded in a customizable compatibility

[1]The OAEI is a coordinated international initiative that organizes annual campaigns to evaluate ontology matching systems. All of the ontologies in the OAEI are described in the OWL-DL and serialized in the RDF/XML format.

matrix. A matching matrix between the two ontologies was adopted to represent the matching results, and our goal was to solve a QAP to obtain a correct matching matrix. The QAP was NP-hard (non-deterministic polynomial-time hard) and GA was the approximation algorithm used to solve the QAP. In this chapter, the original GA algorithm will be refined with a personalized disturbance step to enforce the matching constraint and a matrix padding operation to deal with the case in which the matching matrix is not a square matrix. Our contributions are summarized as follows: (1) an elegant QAP decipherment for ontology matching, (2) a novel and sophisticated way to set up a compatibility matrix, and (3) a modification of the GA algorithm for ontology matching. As for the evaluation of our method, standard benchmark datasets from the OAEI were used. The experimental results justified the effectiveness of our method when compared with state-of-the-art systems.

The chapter is organized as follows. Section 29.2 will present the formal definition of the ontology matching problem. Then, Section 29.3 will explain QAP-based ontology matching, while Sect. 29.4 will focus on the construction of the compatibility matrix. Section 29.5 will introduce the GA algorithm and the two refined strategies used to make it applicable for ontology matching. The experimental results will be presented in Sect. 29.6, and Sect. 29.7 will conclude the chapter.

29.2 Definition of the Ontology Matching Problem

Ontology matching aims at finding the semantic correspondences between ontologies. Correspondence is a pair that specifies the matching relationship between two entities from different ontologies. There are three kinds of typical entities in ontologies: class, property, and individual. Matching can only occur in the same type of entities, for example, there can be a correspondence between a class entity in one ontology and a class entity in another ontology. Correspondence is defined as a four-tuple (shown in Eq. [29.1]), where e^1 and e^2 represent the two entities that are matched between ontologies O^1 and O^2, respectively, r is the relation type between e^1 and e^2, and $k \in [0, 1]$ is the confidence score of this correspondence (Mao et al. 2010).

$$m = < e^1 e^2, r, k > \tag{29.1}$$

For simplicity, we only conducted ontology matching for class entities and property entities. In other words, we neglected the matching scenario for individual entities. We found only one relation type that was the equivalence relation. The aim of the matching process was to find equivalent entities between the two ontologies, so e^1 and e^2 in the correspondence in Eq. (29.1) are equivalent to each other. As required by the OAEI, the matching is considered with a two-way one-to-one matching constraint between the two ontologies.

29.3 QAP Decipherment for Ontology Matching

As a bridge between two ontologies, the correspondence is supposed to be a reflex of the overall information of ontologies. It is insufficient to conduct the matching process based only on the local information of the entities. Global information that captures the pairwise relationship between entities is also crucial for the matching performance. Unlike most previous works, we designated a compatibility matrix that embedded both local and global ontology information and viewed ontology matching with the two-way one-to-one matching constraint as a QAP. Once formulated as a QAP, the mature and effective algorithms designed for the QAP using the optimization theory were utilized to solve ontology matching, and the result was an effective and efficient algorithm for ontology matching. In our work, we adopted the GA algorithm as a QAP solver and showed its state-of-the-art performance for ontology matching. The standard QAP is stated as follows in Eq. (29.2):

$$\begin{aligned} &\min_{M} E_{\text{qap}}(M) = -\frac{1}{2}\sum_{aibj} C_{ai;\,bj} M_{ai} M_{bj} \\ &\text{subject to } \sum_{a} M_{ai} = 1, \sum_{i} M_{ai} = 1, \ \text{ and } M_{ai} \in \{0, 1\}. \end{aligned} \tag{29.2}$$

The optimization problem shown in Eq. (29.2) aims at finding the constrained matching matrix M with a minimal objective function (Rangarajan et al. 1997). M is a binary matrix that stands for the matching result between the two ontologies. If M_{ij} is 1, the entity e_i matches with the entity e_j. Otherwise, e_i does not match with e_j. C is the quadratic assignment benefit matrix, which is called a compatibility matrix for ontology matching in this chapter. C is an $n_1 n_2 \times n_1 n_2$ matrix when there are n_1 entities in O_1 and n_2 entities in O_2. The element $C_{ai;bj}$ can be interpreted as the compatibility value between the correspondence $<e_a, e_i>$ and the correspondence $<e_b, e_j>$. The matrix M should satisfy the two-way one-to-one matching constraint and integrality constraint as shown in Eq. (29.2). E_{qap} is the quadratic objective function of M. Taking into account the presence of missing and extra nodes, M is required to satisfy the inequality constraints: $\sum_{a} M_{ai} \leq 1$ and $\sum_{i} M_{ai} \leq 1$. When all the elements in a row or a column of M are zero, the corresponding entity has no matching entity. Without loss of universality, we mainly focused on the cases with equality constraints because we could introduce slack variables (Bertsekas and Tsitsiklis 1989) into M to transform the inequality constraint to an equality one.

On the whole, ontology matching with QAP decipherment is an optimization problem that belongs to integer quadratic programming (IQP). Unlike integer linear programming (ILP), IQP is competent in characterizing the complicated interrelationships between variables, such as the co-occurrence case of two variables. When the variable in IQP is the matching matrix that assigns entities in one ontology to those in another, the IQP problem becomes a QAP. Conducting ontology matching from a QAP perspective has the following advantages:

(i) The essentials of ontology matching can be elegantly characterized in a QAP. For example, the quadratic objective function E_{qap} is an overall measure of the consistency of all correspondences. A good matching matrix M is expected to guarantee that all correspondences are consistent with each other. The objective function in the QAP sums compatibility among all correspondences specified by M and guides the ontology matching process in a meaningful direction. Meanwhile, the two-way one-to-one matching constraint is also included in a QAP. Thus, the QAP is a suitable mathematical form for ontology matching.

(ii) The QAP explicitly provides the enforcement of matching constraint. According to the work of Cho et al. (2010), how to use matching constraint is key to the performance of a matching system. However, most systems in the current OAEI campaigns used the matching constraint only as a post-processing discretization step, which reduced the effect of the matching constraint. These systems generally gave every possible correspondence a confidence score without taking the matching constraint into consideration. This could lead to a continuous solution and a poor matching performance. Comparatively, the QAP-based matching method was more effective at finding a discrete solution that was likely to be a good approximate to the global extremum of the quadratic objective function.

(iii) Compared with the emerging topic of ontology matching, QAP is a well-studied one from both theoretical and practical points of view, offering an in-depth understanding of the QAP. Many widely used QAP solvers such as GA are reliable and effective in solving ontology matching within our framework. A few other methods that have been put forward for ontology matching in recent years could be flawed because their convergence property is not guaranteed. Comparatively, a QAP solver like GA is a better choice.

(iv) Local and global features can be encoded in the compatibility matrix C as illustrated in the following section. C can be set by experience or learned from training examples. The QAP offers the possibility of setting C in a suitable way and designates itself as a highly customizable method for ontology matching.

For convenience, we transformed the standard QAP in (2) to a maximization problem by removing the minus sign from the objective function. In this maximization formulation, the more the two correspondences $<e_a, e_i>$ and $<e_b, e_j>$ are consistent with each other, the larger $C_{ai;bj}$ is. This formulation is a more natural one for ontology matching. As mentioned above, class matching and property matching were both implemented in our method, and these two kinds of matching were conducted simultaneously, although most methods match classes and properties separately. The key is that the M matrix consists of two non-zero submatrices: the one for class matching in the upper-left corner and the other for property matching in the bottom-right corner. The remaining two submatrices in the upper-right and bottom-left corners are a zero matrix. In the QAP-based ontology matching, the consistency between class correspondence and property correspondence can both be taken into account. Class matching and property matching can influence each other,

Algorithm 29.1 Computing C

Input: The number of entities in O_1 and O_2, n_1 and n_2; the list that contains all possible correspondences, M; the array that contains the corresponding entity similarity, ES;
Output: The compatibility matrix, C

for *the ai-th correspondence* m_{ai} *in* M **do**
    $(e_a, e_i) \leftarrow$ the entities of m_{ai} in O^1 and O^2;
    if $EntityType(e_a) \neq EntityType(e_i)$ **then**
        continue;
    for *the bj-th correspondence* m_{bj} *in* M **do**
        $(e_b, e_j) \leftarrow$ the entities of m_{bj} in O^1 and O^2;
    if $EntityType(e_b) \neq EntityType(e_j)$ **then**
        continue;
    if $(<e_a, e_i>,<e_b, e_j>) \in RelationType$ **then**
        $C_{ai;bj} \leftarrow (\exp(ES_{ai}) + \exp(ES_{bj}))/2$;
    else
        $C_{ai;bj} \leftarrow 1.0/(n_1 \times n_2)$;
return C;

which leads to a better matching performance. For example, two class entities with semantically similar property entities are likely to form a correct correspondence.

29.4 Customization of the Compatibility Matrix

The compatibility matrix C with the objective function shown in Eq. (29.2) recorded the compatibility of every two possible correspondences, and our matching method made use of C to find the correct correspondence. A good compatibility matrix here means that the compatibility value is a good measure of the consistency of two correspondences. Only a good measure of consistency between correspondences can ensure a good matching performance. The compatibility matrix C was set according to Algorithm 29.1. First, we initialized C as a zero matrix, gave all possible correspondences in M an index, and filled the entity similarity (ES) array with similarity values between entities from O^1 and O^2. Entity similarity is represented by the cosine value of two term frequency-inverse document frequency (tf-idf) vectors constructed from the entity's descriptions: *local name*, *label*, *comment*, *subterms*, *superterms* (both for classes and properties), *properties*, *instances* (for classes), *domain*, and *range* (for properties). For *label* and *comment* texts, preprocessing according to Cheatham and Hitzler (2013) is needed, which includes tokenization, lemmatization, stop word removal, and translations.

In Algorithm 29.1, the function *EntityType* returns the type of entity (class or property). A detailed description of the function of *RelationType* is as follows. *RelationType* is the pairwise consistent relationship between two correspondences, $<e_a, e_i>$ and $<e_b, e_j>$. This pairwise relationship $(<e_a, e_i>,<e_b, e_j>)$ is judged according to the topological structure of the ontologies. *RelationType* checks whether these two correspondences are consistent. When the two correspondences

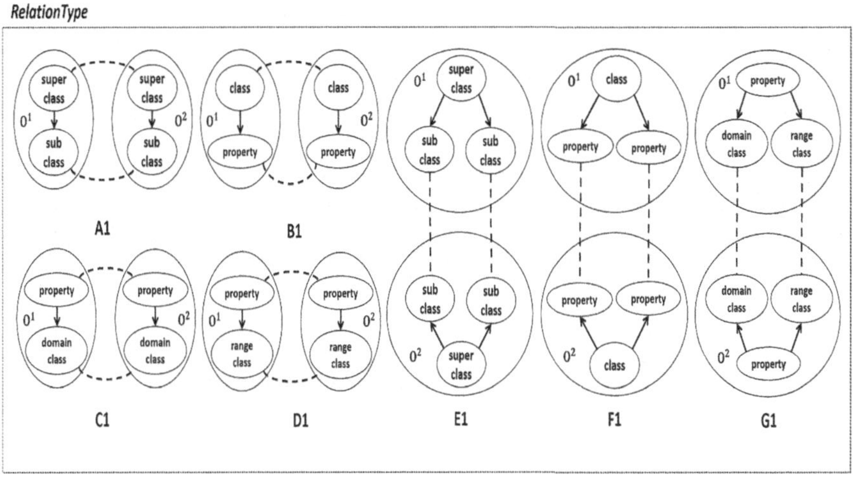

Fig. 29.1 Graph for RelationType

are consistent, the binary relation between e_a and e_i is equivalent to that between e_b and e_j. There are seven binary relation types, as shown in Fig. 29.1 above: superclass and subclass; class and its own property; property and its own domain class; property and its own range class; two classes that have the same superclass; two properties that belong to the same class; and domain class and range class that belong to the same property. Relation types from $A1$ to $D1$ are cases with only the relevant four entities (e_a, e_b, e_i, and e_j), while those from $E1$ to $G1$ are assisted by other entities. We focused on the original relation types defined by Web Ontology Language (OWL) semantics (from $A1$ to $D1$) and the types that can be induced with the help of another upper entity in common. More complicated relation types were ignored for their rareness and *RelationType* covered most of the possible binary relation types of two entities in a correspondence. All of the seven binary relation types represented in *RelationType* can lead to a consistent pairwise relationship between the two correspondences. For this reason, the exponential function exp() was adopted in Algorithm 29.1 to extend the effect of consistent correspondences. If a pairwise relationship of two correspondences is not *RelationType* (i.e., the two correspondences are not consistent), the compatibility value will be $1.0/(n_1 \times n_2)$, and when the corresponding entities are of the same type but are not consistent, the compatibility value will be 0. The compatibility matrix C was constructed in this way to make consistent correspondences prominent so that the matching algorithm could easily locate them.

When assigning the compatibility matrix as described in Algorithm 29.1, C will be an $n_1n_2 \times n_1n_2$ matrix containing much information from the original ontologies O^1 and O^2. Furthermore, diagonal elements represent the pairwise relationship between one correspondence and itself, which is controlled by the corresponding entity similarity. Most graph matching algorithms will set zero diagonal elements. However, the diagonal element has a clear definition and can be larger than zero for the case of ontology matching. It can also be interpreted as the local feature of two ontologies. Non-diagonal elements represent the pairwise relationship between one correspondence and another different correspondence, which represents the inter-compatibility of correspondences and the global feature of ontology. C encodes both the local and global features of O^1 and O^2. With many zero elements, as seen in Algorithm 29.1, C is a sparse matrix. The sparsity of a compatibility matrix can improve the efficiency of the QAP solver. In constructing the compatibility matrix in this way, C is a good reflection and "skeleton" of original ontologies, which differs from simplest ways of constructing it in the previous works.

29.5 The Refined Graduated Assignment Solution for Ontology Matching

When the decipherment in a QAP and the customization of the compatibility matrix are finished, a QAP solver must be chosen to solve the QAP-based ontology matching. The graduated assignment was our choice for its deep theoretical basis and excellent effectiveness in practical use. GA transforms the original quadratic assignment problem to a series of linear assignment problems (LAP) with an increasing value of the control parameter β. GA is a deterministic annealing algorithm and a continuation method. If the minus sign is removed, the objective function becomes the form shown in Eq. (29.3) (Gold and Rangarajan 1996a), which has an $x\log(x)$ smoothing function and Lagrange multipliers μ and ν to enforce the matching constraint. The GA algorithm can be deduced from this complete objective. Although the QAP is NP-hard, it is guaranteed to find the optimal solution for an LAP in polynomial time (Bertsekas and Tsitsiklis 1989). The two-way one-to-one matching constraint is enforced by the softassign process. The matching matrix M is a doubly stochastic matrix with continuous elements. As β increases and becomes infinite, M will become a permutation matrix that satisfies the matching constraint and makes S_{qap} relatively large. It has been proven that the softassign quadratic assignment algorithm has the property of convergence to a fixed point with the exact and approximate doubly stochastic constraint satisfaction (Rangarajan et al. 1997). The pseudo-code of the GA algorithm can be found in Gold and Rangarajan (1996a).

$$\begin{aligned} S_{\text{qap}} &= \frac{1}{2}\sum_{aibj} C_{ai;bj} M_{ai} M_{bj} + \frac{1}{\beta}\sum_{ai} M_{ai}(\log M_{ai} - 1) \\ &+ \sum_{a} \mu_a \left(\sum_{i} M_{ai} - 1 \right) + \sum_{i} \upsilon_i \left(\sum_{a} M_{ai} - 1 \right). \end{aligned} \tag{29.3}$$

However, the GA algorithm has some problems when used for the ontology matching scenario. First, in the initial iterations, β is small and M will be close to M^0

of the first iteration (or $|M - M^0| < \sigma$) and the effect of the matching constraint will be suppressed. Small β is an obstacle for the discretization solution. A permutation matrix M is what we expected, not a doubly stochastic matrix ensured by Sinkhorn's (1964) theorem. Equation (29.4) is deduced from Eq. (29.3) in the odd row normalization with respect to μ (Rangarajan et al. 1996). In Eq. (29.4), exp() is originated from the barrier function $x\log(x)$ and β controls how far the softassign result is from the initial M^0. Only when β becomes larger can the matching constraint take effect. From our viewpoint, the initial iterations of GA are crucial to the matching performance (Gold and Rangarajan 1996a), but the small control parameter β can cause problems. When O^2 is much dissimilar from O^1, GA is likely to plunge to a local maximum, and it will not take full advantage of the matching constraint. Second, GA cannot handle the general case in which two ontologies have different numbers of entities because Sinkhorn's theorem is the theoretical foundation of softassign and it is correct only if the matching matrix is a square matrix.

$$\frac{M_{ai}^{(2k)}}{M_{ai}^{(2k+1)}} = \exp\left(-\beta\left[\mu_a^{(k)} - \mu_a^{(k+1)}\right]\right) \tag{29.4}$$

For the first problem, a strategy called personalized disturbance was adopted to accelerate the effect of the matching constraint, especially in the initial stage when β is small. Equation (29.5) shows this main point. M is the matching matrix after softassign is applied to the iteration at each value of β. Disturbance is a function that returns the matrix, satisfying the two-way one-to-one matching constraint. We chose a simple greedy algorithm (Leordeanu and Hebert 2005) as the linear assignment solver to enforce the matching constraint in Disturbance in Eq. (29.5). The disturbed matrix became a permutation matrix (i.e., it is a permutation matrix when the two ontologies have equal numbers of entities). This method is an approximately good solution based on the iterations that GA has worked through. α is a parameter that trades off between the original M and the disturbed one, which can be a constant or variable that is relevant to β. The averaged matching matrix M' solves the dilemma in which small β cannot enforce the matching constraint and GA is likely to plunge to a local maximum.

$$M' = (1 - \alpha)M + \alpha\,\text{Disturbance}(M) \tag{29.5}$$

For the second problem, we proposed an easy-to-implement strategy called matrix padding. As depicted in Fig. 29.2, the class and property submatrices were padded with 1 to extend into a square matrix, and the whole matching matrix M became a larger square matrix. The padding operation was performed only after all the elements in M were enlarged to a positive number (i.e., exponential form of M). The padding number 1 was the minimum of $\exp(x)$ when $x \geq 0$. Matrix padding can make M a square matrix, and in this way, GA is applicable to the general case in which O^1 and O^2 have different numbers of entities.

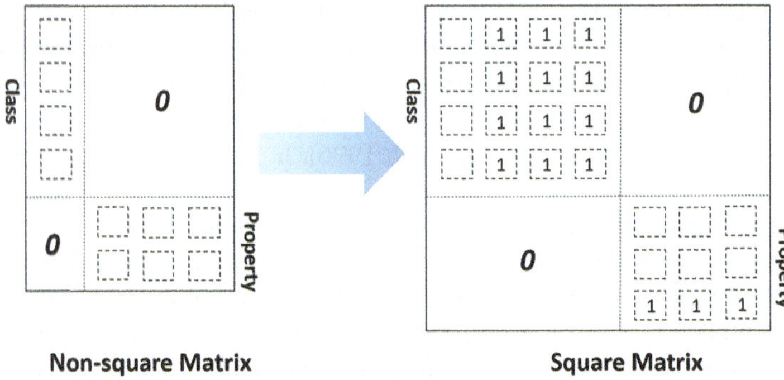

Fig. 29.2 Graph for the matrix padding process for M. The dotted boxes with 1 inside are the padding elements, and those with no number inside are the original elements of the exponential form of M. ***0*** represents the zero matrix

29.6 Experiments Using OAEI Datasets

Ontology matching experiments are mainly based on the OAEI's datasets. Every year the OAEI organizes an ontology matching contest and makes public the results of the participants. We implemented our method into two datasets and compared our results with those of the OAEI participants. The datasets were (1) the Benchmark-Biblio 2012 dataset, which consists of one reference ontology and 94 target ontologies, and (2) the Benchmark-Biblio 2013 dataset, which consists of five subdatasets with one reference ontology and 94 target ontologies in each subdataset. Our goal was to match the target ontology with the reference ontology, and we only focused on the correspondence between class and property entities. We chose the standard benchmark dataset to tune the parameters of our method, for example, α and β in GA. The standard benchmark dataset was provided by the OAEI to assist participants in adjusting their systems. The OAEI compares all kinds of matching methods based on the harmonic mean values of recall, precision, and F1-measure.

We implemented a QAP-based method for ontology matching. We set parameter α at 0.85 and made the personalized disturbance step take effect from the second iteration at each value of the control parameter β. Other parameters of the GA algorithm included $\beta_0 = 1.0$, $\beta_f = 3.0$, $\beta_r = 1.05$, $I_0 = 40$, and $I_1 = 100$. For the clean-up heuristic in the last part of GA, we adopted the Stable Marriage algorithm, which is a widely used LAP solver. Correct correspondences were what we expected to obtain after running the refined GA algorithm.

Table 29.1 summarizes the matching performance of our method and other leading participants in the OAEI contest according to the F1-measure, as well as the results of edna, which is a simple edit distance method on labels, as a baseline for comparison. Table 29.1 shows that our method resulted in a competitive performance. On average, all of the systems, including ours, had a far better performance than the baseline and they behaved relatively stable across all the datasets, except that MapSSS had an extremely low F1-measure on the 2013 benchmark. Our method

Table 29.1 Experiments using the OAEI datasets and comparison with the participants of the OAEI contest. The last one, edna, a simple matcher, served as the baseline

Matching systems	2012 Biblio	2013 Biblio
YAM++	0.83	0.89
Our method	0.87	0.88
CroMatcher	[a]	0.88
MapSSS	0.87	0.14
edna	0.41	0.41

[a] Unreported result

and MapSSS performed the best on the 2012 benchmark, while YAM++ performed the best on the 2013 benchmark. YAM++ is a pipeline system that combines candidate filtering, terminological matcher, instance matcher, structural matcher, and the post-processing of correspondences. CroMatcher is a weighted aggregation of basic matchers such as terminological matcher and structural matcher. In a word, these leading systems are either a composition of weak matchers or a pipeline that requires many steps. However, our method unified ontology matching into a compact framework that performed the best on one benchmark dataset. To the best of our knowledge, the method we proposed resulted in the best performance if only one matcher could be used.

29.7 Conclusion

In this chapter, we advanced ontology matching using a novel quadratic assignment problem perspective. Enhanced by the customizable design of the compatibility matrix and the adoption of graduated assignment, ontology matching lent itself well to an effective and elegant solution. To enforce the two-way one-to-one matching constraint early in the matching process, we proposed a step called personalized disturbance, and using a matrix padding strategy, we made graduated assignment applicable to the matching case in which ontologies had a different number of entities. Experiments using the datasets of the OAEI campaigns demonstrated our method's competitive performance with the leading participants in the OEAI contest. In the future, the compatibility matrix element will be learned from training examples.

Acknowledgments This research was supported by the National Key Basic Research Program of China (No. 2014- CB340504) and the National Natural Science Foundation of China (No. 61375074, 61273318).

References

Bertsekas, Dimitri P., and John N. Tsitsiklis. 1989. *Parallel and distributed computation: Numerical methods* (Vol. 23). Englewood Cliffs, NJ: Prentice Hall.

Cheatham, Michelle, and Pascal Hitzler. 2013. String similarity metrics for ontology alignment. In *International Semantic Web Conference*. Berlin and Heidelberg: Springer. Available at https://link.springer.com/chapter/10.1007/978-3-642-41338-4_19. Accessed 26 April 2017.

Cho, Minsu, Jungmin Lee, and Kyoung Mu Lee. 2010. Reweighted random walks for graph matching. In *European Conference on Computer Vision*. Berlin and Heidelberg: Springer. Available at https://link.springer.com/chapter/10.1007/978-3-642-15555-0_36. Accessed 26 April 2017.

Euzenat, Jrme, and Pavel Shvaiko. 2007. *Ontology matching* (Vol. 18). Heidelberg: Springer.

Gold, Steven, and Anand Rangarajan. 1996a. A graduated assignment algorithm for graph matching. *IEEE Transactions on Pattern Analysis and Machine Intelligence*, 18(4):377–388.

Gold, Steven, and Anand Rangarajan. 1996b. Graph matching by graduated assignment. In *Proceedings of the CVPR'96, 1996 IEEE Computer Society Conference on Computer Vision and Pattern Recognition*.

Hu, Wei, Ningsheng Jian, Yuzhong Qu, and Yanbing Wang. 2005. GMO: A graph matching for ontologies. In *Proceedings of K-CAP Workshop on Integrating Ontologies*.

Lawler, Eugene L. 1963. The quadratic assignment problem. *Management Science* 9(4):586–599.

Leordeanu, Marius, and Martial Hebert. 2005. A spectral technique for correspondence problems using pairwise constraints. In the *Tenth IEEE International Conference on Computer Vision (ICCV)* (Vol. 2). Available at https://ieeexplore.ieee.org/abstract/document/1544893/. Accessed 26 April 2017.

Li, Juanzi, Jie Tang, Yi Li, and Qiong Luo. 2009. RiMOM: A dynamic multistrategy ontology alignment framework. *IEEE Transactions on Knowledge and Data Engineering* 21(8): 1218–1232.

Mao, Ming, Yefei Peng, and Michael Spring. 2010. An adaptive ontology mapping approach with neural network based constraint satisfaction. *Web Semantics: Science, Services and Agents on the World Wide Web* 8(1):14–25.

Ngo, DuyHoa, and Zohra Bellahsene. 2012. Yam++—A combination of graph matching and machine learning approach to ontology alignment task. *Journal of Web Semantics* 16.

Noy, Natalya F., and Mark A. Musen. 2001. Anchor-PROMPT: Using non-local context for semantic matching. In *Proceedings of the Workshop on Ontologies and Information Sharing at the International Joint Conference on Artificial Intelligence (IJCAI)*.

Rangarajan, Anand, Steven Gold, and Eric Mjolsness. 1996. A novel optimizing network architecture with applications. *Neural Computation* 8(5):1041–1060.

Rangarajan, Anand, Alan Yuille, Steven Gold, and Eric Mjolsness. 1997. A convergence proof for the softassign quadratic assignment algorithm. *Advances in Neural Information Processing Systems* 620–626.

Sinkhorn, Richard. 1964. A relationship between arbitrary positive matrices and doubly stochastic matrices. *Annals of Mathematical Statistics* 35(2):876–879.

Xiang, Chuncheng, Baobao Chang, and Zhifang Sui. 2015. An ontology matching approach based on affinity-preserving random walks. In *Proceedings of the International Joint Conference on Artificial Intelligence (IJCAI)*.

Chapter 30
Automated Answer Type Recognition for Primary School Students' Question Sentences

Ru-Yng Chang, Kai-Chun Chang, Nien-Chi Liu, Bo-Lin Lin, Yu-Hsuan Chen, and Liang-Chih Yu

Abstract Answer type recognition (ATR) can improve the precision rate of answer extraction, giving it an important role in question answering systems. Experiments on ATR in the study presented in this chapter were conducted based on a pupil question answering corpus from students at an elementary school in Taipei County, Taiwan. The questions corresponded to six answer types—"PERSON," "EVENT," "TIME," "PLACE," "OBJECT," and "OTHER." To identify the best-performing ATR module, we used several different combinations of six basic approaches, including Distinguished Question Words (DQW), Contextual Rules (CR), Maximum Entropy Classifiers (ME), Support Vector Machine (SVM), Binary Classifiers (BC), and Binary Classifiers with Filtered Training Data (BCF). Among the probability modules and hybrid approaches, CR + ME had the highest precision rate, followed closely by CR + SVM and CR + ME + SVM. A comparison of the single ME and SVM models showed that CR raised the precision rate, while CR + ME + BC had the highest recall rate. Finally, DQW + ME was found to have the highest average F1 score and thus provided the most stable performance.

R.-Y. Chang (✉)
HowiseAI International Co. LTD., New Taipei City, Taiwan

Computational Intelligence Technology Center, Industrial Technology Research Institute, Hsinchu, Taiwan

K.-C. Chang · L.-C. Yu
Department of Information Management, Yuan Ze University, Taoyuan, Taiwan

N.-C. Liu · B.-L. Lin
Computational Intelligence Technology Center, Industrial Technology Research Institute, Hsinchu, Taiwan

Department of Information Management, Yuan Ze University, Taoyuan, Taiwan

Y.-H. Chen
Computational Intelligence Technology Center, Industrial Technology Research Institute, Hsinchu, Taiwan

C.-R. Huang et al. (eds.), *Chinese Language Resources*, Text, Speech and Language Technology 49, https://doi.org/10.1007/978-3-031-38913-9_30

Keywords Question answering system · Answer type recognition · Pupil · Social studies textbooks

30.1 Introduction

Our study was part of Taiwan's "Humanistic Perceptions and Wisdom Life Integration Services Development Project—Interactive Knowledge Question Answering System (1/4)." This vision for creating smart campuses and homes entails building a pupil question answering system for primary school students, teachers, and parents (see Fig. 30.1). Primary school students can use Voice over IP (VOIP) through a phone or use texts through a computer or mobile device to ask the system questions about textbook contents and receive an immediate response, thus providing a more engaging and interactive way of acquiring knowledge. Elementary school textbooks cover a wide range of knowledge. The first goal of this pupil question answering system is to help primary school students to better learn material from their social studies course books. Teachers and parents can track student-system interaction to assess learning status and attitudes. The system focuses on providing factual responses to questions; for example, when a student asks 至聖先師是哪一位? *Zhìshèng xiānshī shì nǎ-yī-wèi* "Who is the greatest sage and teacher?", the system responds 孔子 *Kungtzu* "Confucius." Figure 30.2 illustrates the question answering process:

Jurafsky and Martin (2009) suggested that query processing, passage retrieval, and answer processing are three common and basic technological phases in the framework of factoid question answering systems. Query processing attempts to understand input query and is often composed of two modules: query formulation

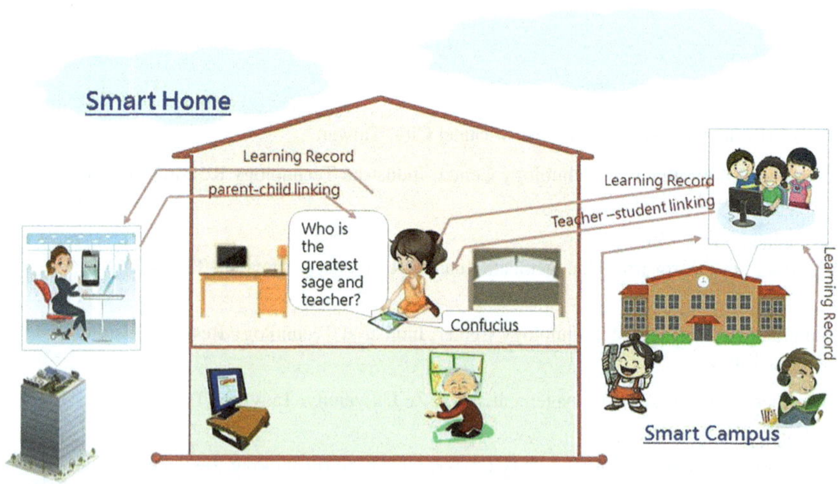

Fig. 30.1 Pupil question answering system

Fig. 30.2 Student interface

and answer type recognition (ATR). ATR is also called query classification, and it classifies queries by expected answer type. For example, a query like 台灣最高的山叫什麼? *Táiwān zuì gāo de shān jiào shénme* "What is the highest mountain in Taiwan?" would return an answer extracted from the "PLACE" answer type. ATR can improve response precision rates and reduce the search time for answer extraction in a question answering system. Therefore, our study focused on ATR.

30.2 Related Works

Table 30.1 summarizes related works, where ME stands for Maximum Entropy Classifiers and SVM stands for Support Vector Machine, classifiers that are frequently used for answer type recognition tasks. An automatic pattern-mining approach was used to identify question patterns (Hui et al. 2011). In recent years, answer type recognition has been conducted in several languages, including English and Mandarin Chinese. A question word is not necessary in a Mandarin Chinese question, and this is a significant difference between English and Mandarin Chinese questions, for example, a student query of 台灣最大的水庫? *Táiwān zuì dà de shuǐkù* "What is Taiwan's largest reservoir?". Thus, answer type recognition in Mandarin Chinese questions is difficult to achieve. ME and SVM have delivered

Table 30.1 Summary of related works

Method	Features	Language	Authors/Year
SVM	Adopts sequence kernels (SK), syntactic tree kernels (STK) (2002), and partial tree kernels (PTK) (2006) to generate sequences of words (WS), part-of-speech (POS) tags (PS), and different kinds of trees	English	Alessandro et al. (2011)
DS-SRM (distance sensitive sequential rule miner) to find ExCSR (extended class sequential rule)		English	Hui et al. (2011)
ME	Question wh-words, head words, WordNet hypernyms, unigram words, and word shape	English	Huang et al. (2009)
ME or SVM	Question wh-words, N-grams, word shape, and head words and their hypernyms	Mandarin Chinese	Huang et al. (2008)
INFOMAP (taxonomy rule) + SVM	Character-based bigrams, word-based bigrams, POS, HowNet main definitions and HowNet definitions	Mandarin Chinese	Day et al. (2005)
Naïve Bayes, kernel Naïve Bayes, rule induction or decision tree classifiers	Wh-words, wh-word positions, wh-types, question length, end marker, word shape, POS tags, head words, related words, and named entity results	Bengali	Banerjee and Bandyopadhyay (2013)
Decision tree, Naïve Bayes, SVM or voting	Bag-of-words, keywords	Vietnamese	Tran et al. (2013)

stable performances in previous related ATR tasks, and the automatic pattern-mining approach has improved question pattern identification. Therefore, combinations of ME, SVM, and the pattern-mining approach were proposed and experimented in our study.

30.3 Methodology

30.3.1 Corpus Collection

Experiments on ATR were conducted based on a pupil question answering corpus collected from fifth- and sixth-grade students at Tinghsi Elementary School in

Taipei. The corpus collection included answer types, terms, and sentences, examples of which are shown in Table 30.2.

APPROACH I. Sentences with a "PERSON," "EVENT," "TIME," "PLACE," or "OBJECT" term were extracted from the social studies textbooks. Students were asked to rewrite the sentences to generate a question that answered the keyword or phrase in the original sentence. An example of an extracted sentence is 賽德克族人莫那魯道鼓動族人抵抗日軍不合乎人道的管制，史稱「霧社事件」。 *Sàidékè-zú-rén Mònàlǔdào gǔdòng zúrén dǐkàng rìjūn bù héhū réndào de guǎnzhì, shǐchēng "Wù-shè-shìjiàn"* "Mona Rudo, chief of the Seediq tribe, led his people to revolt against inhuman treatment by the Japanese army in the so-called 'Musha incident'." Students then rewrote this sentence as a question that could be answered by the term 霧社事件 *Wù-shè-shìjiàn* "Musha incident."

APPROACH II. Terms associated with "PERSON," "EVENT," "TIME," "PLACE," and "OBJECT" were extracted from the social studies textbooks, and students were asked to generate questions that could be answered using those terms. For example, students were given the term 霧社事件 *Wù-shè-shìjiàn* "Musha incident" and were asked to write a question for which 霧社事件 *Wù-shè-shìjiàn* "Musha incident" is the answer.

APPROACH III. Students could generate any questions about the terms associated with "PERSON," "EVENT," "TIME," "PLACE," and "OBJECT" that were extracted from the social studies textbooks. For example, students could write other questions about the term 霧社事件 *Wù-shè-shìjiàn* "Musha incident," such as 霧社事件是什麼時代發生的? *Wù-shè-shìjiàn shì shénme shídài fāsheng de?* "When happened in the Musha incident?" and 誰帶領賽德克族參與霧社事件? *Shéi dàilǐng Sàidékè-zú cānyù Wù-shè-shìjiàn?* "Who led the Seediq tribe in the Musha incident?", which are both possible and reasonable student questions about the Musha incident.

Figure 30.3 illustrates the corpus collection results for APPROACHES I, II, and III.

APPROACH IV. Students were asked to think of questions that followed or approximated the pattern "What is the [superlative adjective] [noun] in Taiwan?", such as 台灣最高的山叫什麼? *Tái wān zuì gāo de shān jiào shén me*? "What is Taiwan's highest mountain?"

APPROACH V. Students were provided with statements and were asked to write corresponding questions.

Because of the uniqueness of the Chinese language, some Chinese knowledge base information was also employed in our study.

30.3.2 Six Basic Approaches

To identify the best ATR module performance, experiments were conducted using different combinations of the following six basic approaches.

Table 30.2 Examples of sentences and terms used for corpus collection

Answer type	Term	Sentence	Source (Kang Hsuan Publisher Version)[a]
PERSON	孫中山	清代末年孫中山提倡革命, 創建中華民國	Appendix of fifth grade, first semester; unit 5-1 of fourth grade, first semester; appendix of fourth grade, 1st semester
	Sūn Zhōngshān	*Qīngdài mònián Sūn Zhōngshān tíchàng gémìng, chuàngjiàn Zhōnghuámínguó*	
	Sun Yat-sen	"Sun Yat-sen promoted the revolution and established the Republic of China in the late Qing Dynasty"	
EVENT	霧社事件	賽德克族人莫那魯道鼓動族人抵抗日軍不合乎人道的管制, 史稱「霧社事件」	Unit 4-1 of fifth grade, second semester
	Wù-shè-shìjiàn	*Sàidékè-zú-rén Mònàlǚdào gǚdòng zúrén dǐkàng rìjūn bù héhū réndào de guǎnzhì, shǐchēng "Wù-shè-shìjiàn"*	
	Musha Incident	"Mona Rudo, the chief of the Seediq tribe, led his people to revolt against inhuman treatment by the Japanese army in the so-called 'Musha incident'"	
TIME	端午節	端午節是為了紀念愛國詩人屈原	Unit 5-1 of fourth grade, first semester
	Duānwǚjié	*Duānwǚjié shì wéiliǎo jìniàn àiguó shīrén Qūyuán*	
	Dragon Boat Festival	"The Dragon Boat Festival commemorates the patriotic poet Qu Yuan"	
PLACE	玉山	玉山主峰海拔 3952 公尺, 是台灣第一高山	Unit 1-1 of fifth grade, first semester
	Yùshān	*Yùshān zhǚfēng hǎibá 3952 gōngchǐ, shì táiwān dìyī gāoshān*	
	Yushan	"Mt. Yu has a peak elevation of 3952 meters, making it Taiwan's tallest mountain"	
OBJECT	望遠鏡	伽利略利用自己發明的望遠鏡, 觀察並證明了哥白尼地球繞著太陽運行的說法	Unit 1-1 of sixth grade, second semester
	Wàngyuǎnjìng	*Jiālìlüè lìyòng zìjǐ fāmíng de wàngyuǎnjìng, guānchá bìng zhèngmíng le Gēbáiní dìqiú rào zhe tàiyang yùnxíng de shuōfǎ*	
	Telescope	"Galileo invented the telescope, and his Observations proved Copernicus's belief that the Earth orbits the sun"	

[a]In Taiwan, elementary school textbooks are published in different editions by multiple publishing houses; thus, students in different schools may use different books for the same subject

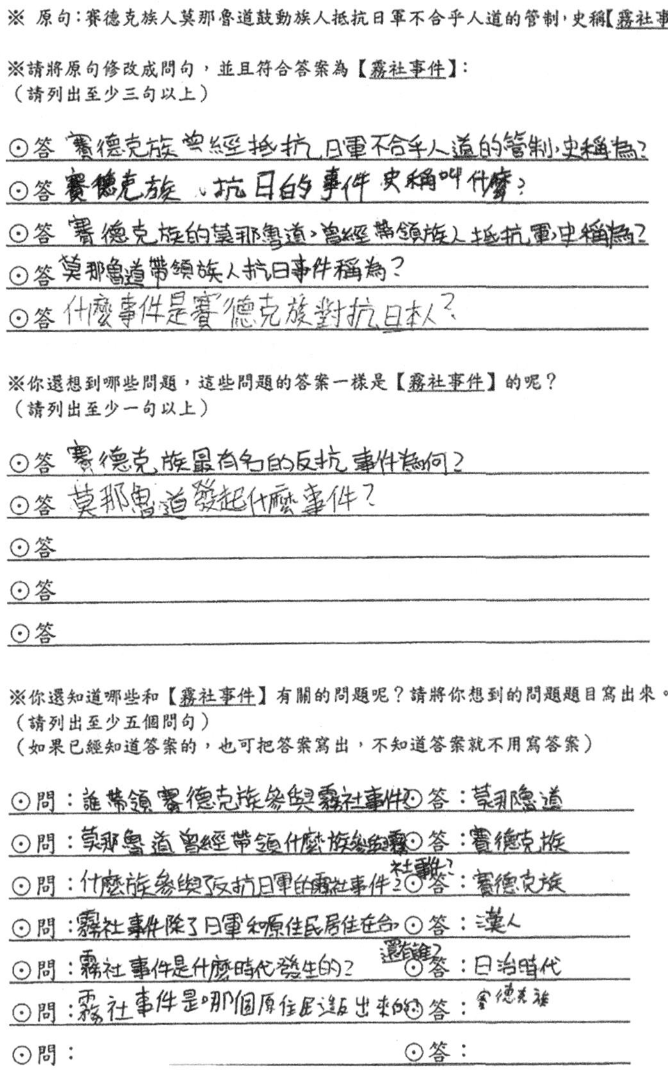
※ 原句：賽德克族人莫那魯道鼓動族人抵抗日軍不合乎人道的管制，史稱【霧社事件】。

※請將原句修改成問句，並且符合答案為【霧社事件】：
（請列出至少三句以上）

⊙答 賽德克族曾經抵抗日軍不合乎人道的管制，史稱為？
⊙答 賽德克族、抗日的事件史稱叫什麼？
⊙答 賽德克族的莫那魯道，曾經帶領族人抵抗日軍，史稱為？
⊙答 莫那魯道帶領族人抗日事件稱為？
⊙答 什麼事件是賽德克族對抗日本人？

※你還想到哪些問題，這些問題的答案一樣是【霧社事件】的呢？
（請列出至少一句以上）

⊙答 賽德克族最有名的反抗事件為何？
⊙答 莫那魯道發起什麼事件？
⊙答
⊙答
⊙答

※你還知道哪些和【霧社事件】有關的問題呢？請將你想到的問題題目寫出來。
（請列出至少五個問句）
（如果已經知道答案的，也可把答案寫出，不知道答案就不用寫答案）

⊙問：誰帶領賽德克族參與霧社事件？⊙答：莫那魯道
⊙問：莫那魯道曾經帶領什麼族參與霧社事件？⊙答：賽德克族
⊙問：什麼族參與了反抗日軍的霧社事件？⊙答：賽德克族
⊙問：霧社事件除了日軍和原住民居住在台，還有誰？⊙答：漢人
⊙問：霧社事件是什麼時代發生的？⊙答：日治時代
⊙問：霧社事件是哪個原住民族發出來的？⊙答：賽德克族
⊙問：⊙答：

Fig. 30.3 Corpus collection results for APPROACHES I, II, and III

Distinguished Question Words (DQW). In Mandarin Chinese, some question words are highly indicative of different answer type questions. For instance, if a sentence contains 誰 *Shéi* "who," then the answer type should be "PERSON." Such question words are called Distinguishing Question Words (DQW), and they were collected for the ATR tasks (see Table 30.3).

Contextual Rules (CR). In Mandarin Chinese, question words can constitute question sentences, but they do not have enough information to determine the associated answer type. For example, contextual information is needed when a

Table 30.3 Examples of distinguished question words for the ATR tasks

Question words		Answer type
誰 (Who)...	→	PERSON
何 (What)/啥事 (What happened)...	→	EVENT
何時 (When)...	→	TIME
哪裡/裏/兒/邊 (Where)...	→	PLACE
何物 (What is <Noun>)...	→	OBJECT
是不是 (Is it?)、為什麼會 (Why?)...	→	OTHER

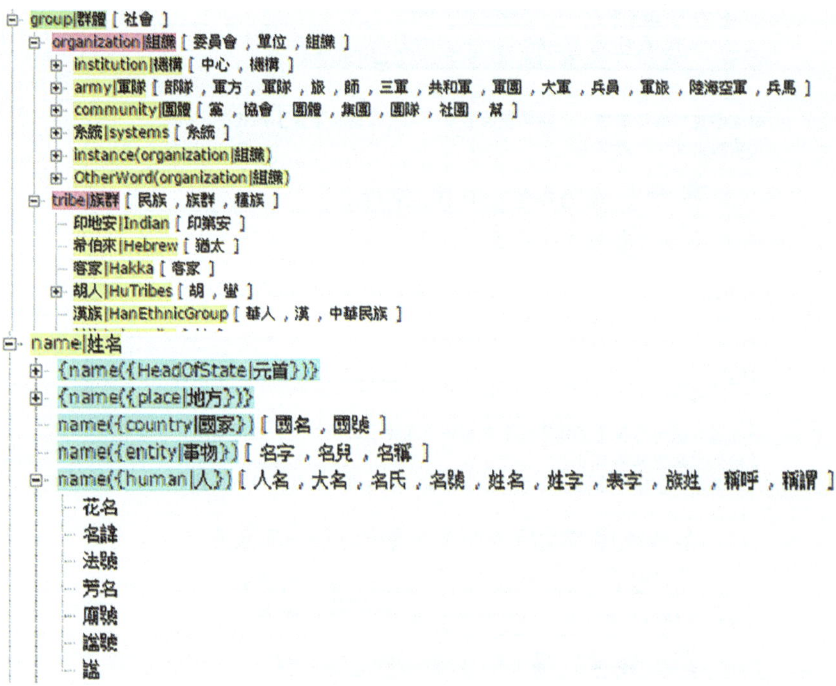

Fig. 30.4 E-HowNet

sentence contains the question word 什麼 *shénme* "what" for ATR because it implies doubt, meaning that it does not explicitly note what information is desired. In Mandarin Chinese, placing 什麼 *shénme* "what" before 族群 *Zúqún* "tribe," 民族 *Mínzú* "nationality," or 種族 *Zhǒngzú* "race" implies the answer type "PERSON." Word contextualization provides more information for ATR. Converting contextual words into concepts can reduce the number of required rules. Because the concept of the words 族群 *Zúqún* "tribe," 民族 *Mínzú* "nationality," and 種族 *Zhǒngzú* "race" is the same as 族群 *Zúqún* "tribe" in E-HowNet (see Fig. 30.4) (Chen et al. 2005; CKIP Group 2009; http://ehownet.iis.sinica.edu.tw), the concept 族群 *Zúqún* "tribe" can represent the words 族群 *Zúqún* "tribe," 民族 *Mínzú* "nationality," and 種族 *Zhǒngzú* "race" in the rules. Parts of speech (POS) generated by the Chinese Knowledge and Information Processing (CKIP) POS tagger (Tsai and Chen 2003)

Table 30.4 Examples in the Contextual Rules reference table

A list	B list	Relative position of B and A lists	Answer type
什麼 (What)	Organization|組織、個人,人,族、@tribe|族群	Behind	PERSON
什麼 (What)	@name({human|人})	Front/behind	PERSON

also provide important cues for ATR. For example, for 台北 *Táiběi* "Taipei," the CKIP POS tagger generates a POS "Nc," which represents a place or location (CKIP Group 1993). Multilevel contextual information is important for ATR. Therefore, the CR approach considers multilevel contextual information within a sentence, such as words, parts of speech, relative position, and word concepts. E-HowNet organizes and provides information on concepts, hierarchical relations between concepts, and related words, as can be seen in Fig. 30.4. For the CR approach, E-HowNet was used to acquire information about concepts and related words, and the CKIP POS tagger was used to generate information about word boundaries and their corresponding POS.

A reference table was created for the generation of Contextual Rules that included the following categories: "A list," "B list," "relative position of B and A lists," and "answer type." Each value in the "A list" and "B list" categories is separated by a comma and can be a word, part of speech, or word concept. Concepts are represented by a string containing "|" in the "A list" and "B list" categories. For example, "Organization|組織" represents words related to the concept "Organization|組織" and its children concepts, while "@tribe|族群" denotes words related to the concept "@tribe|族群" in CR. The values in the "relative position of B and A lists" category can be front, behind, and front/behind. When a value in the "relative position of B and A lists" category is front/behind, it means that the values in the "B list" category can be either in front of or behind the values in the "A list" category. When a value in the "relative position of B and A lists" category is front, it means that the values in the "B list" category must be in front of the values in the "A list" category. The contents of Table 30.4 were used to generate the corresponding Contextual Rules shown in the Fig. 30.5.

Maximum Entropy Classifiers (ME). ME classifiers are based on the Principle of Maximum Entropy, and from all the models that fit the training data, it selects the one that has the largest entropy. ME classifiers can be used to solve a large variety of text classification problems. To address the wide variety of question sentences, ME was adopted for the ATR experiments.

Support Vector Machine (SVM). ME and SVM achieved good performance in previous related studies and were therefore used as two of the six basic approaches in our study.

Binary Classifiers (BC). Binary classifiers outperform multiclass classifiers. Each answer type recognition model was built using one binary classifier. The "PERSON" type model was built based on SVM, while the other type models

IF sentence contains "什麼 *shénme* 'what'"
IF sentence contains [words of the concept "Organization|組織" and its children concepts] **AND** the position of [words of the concept "Organization|組織" and its children concepts] > the position of "什麼 *shénme* 'what'" **THEN**
answer type=PERSON
ELSE IF sentence contains ["個人" or "人" or "族"] **AND** the position of ["個人" or "人" or "族"] > the position of "什麼 *shénme* 'what'" **THEN**
answer type=PERSON
ELSE IF sentence contains [the words of concept "tribe|族群"] and the position of [the words of concept "tribe|族群"] > the position of "什麼 *shénme* 'what'" **THEN**
answer type=PERSON
ELSE IF sentence contains [the words of concept "name({human|人})"] **THEN**
answer type=PERSON

Fig. 30.5 Contextual Rules

were built based on ME. During testing, the recognized answer type was "OTHER" when the output of each BC was "OTHER."

Binary Classifiers with Filtered Training Data (BCF). BCF classifiers can assemble several binary classifiers, but these binary classifiers do not include all question types. The difference between BC and BCF is that the top-two confused types are excluded from the training data in each binary classifier of BCF for one answer type. For example, questions with "TIME" and "OTHER" answer types are often confused with questions with the "PERSON" answer type. Therefore, the training data did not include questions with "TIME" and "OTHER" answer types in the "PERSON" classifier of BCF. Questions with "EVENT," "PLACE," and "OBJECT" answer types are transformed into the "OTHER" answer type after the "PERSON" BCF classifier has been built. The "PERSON" classifier of BCF is then trained using the answer types "PERSON" and "OTHER," which are transformed from "EVENT," "PLACE," and "OBJECT" answer types. This approach was adopted during the BCF training phase. The "PERSON" classifier of BCF was an SVM-based classifier and the other classifiers of BCF were ME-based classifiers. SVM achieved good performance for "PERSON" in the following ATR experiments. The purpose of BCF is to reduce training data confusion. Table 30.5 provides a detailed description of the training methods.

30.3.3 Features of ME Classifiers and SVM

Dictionary POS and semantic class information are traditional and powerful feature types for ATR classifiers. Table 30.6 summarizes the feature types adopted for the ATR experiments using ME classifiers and SVM. Some domain lexicons were used for feature generation, including the Academia Sinica Chinese Historical Place

Table 30.5 Detailed training methods of all BCF

BCF	Model	Training data
PERSON	SVM	PERSON
		OTHER: Original answer types EVENT, PLACE, and OBJECT
EVENT	ME	EVENT
		OTHER: Original answer types PERSON, TIME, and PLACE
TIME	ME	TIME
		OTHER: Original answer types PERSON, EVENT, and PLACE
PLACE	ME	TIME
		OTHER: Original answer types PERSON, EVENT, and TIME
OBJECT	ME	OBJECT
		OTHER: Original answer types PERSON, TIME, and PLACE

Table 30.6 ATR feature types

Which question words are included in the sentence?	
Does the sentence contain vocabulary from the special domain lexicon?	
	Does the sentence contain a word from the Academia Sinica Chinese Historical Place Lexicon?
	Does the sentence contain a word from the Taiwan Place Data Set?
	Does the sentence contain a word from the Historical Figures of Modern Taiwan in Taiwan Pedia?
	Does the sentence contain a noun class from Taiwan Pedia?
Does the sentence contain question words or special POS?	
	Does the sentence contain the POS "Nf" (quantifier) and question words?
	Does the sentence contain the POS "Ncd" (locative marker) and question words?
Which semantic classes of textbook words belonging to PERSON, EVENT, TIME, PLACE, and OBJECT types are included in the sentence?	
	For example, the sentence contains a textbook word "孫中山 *sun chung-shan* 'Sun Yat-sen'" and the semantic class of the word "孫中山 *sun chung-shan* 'Sun Yat-sen'" is "PERSON." Therefore, the value of the feature is "PERSON"
Special position noun concept in E-HowNet	
	To which E-HowNet concept does the last noun in the sentence belong?
	To which E-HowNet concept does the first noun following the question word in the sentence belong?
	To which E-HowNet concept does the noun before the question word in the sentence belong?

Lexicon,[1] the Taiwan Place Data Set,[2] and Taiwan Pedia.[3] The CKIP POS tagger was also used to generate parts of speech. In the CKIP POS tagger, the POS "Nf" represents a quantifier, with examples including 顆 *Kē* "a grain," 位 *Wèi* "a person," and 年 *Nián* "a year" as illustrative words for the POS "Nf." The POS "Ncd" denotes a locative marker, with examples including 前 *Qián* "front" and 後 *Hòu* "behind"

[1]Available at http://archive.ihp.sinica.edu.tw/hplname/. Accessed 10 May 2014.

[2]Available at http://data.gov.tw/node/7711. Accessed 10 May 2014.

[3]Available at http://taiwanpedia.culture.tw/. Accessed 10 May 2014.

Table 30.7 Features explored by AprioriAll

Nc → Nep → [event|事件]	Na[animal|獸] → Nc
Nc → Nep → [function|活動]	Na[animal|獸] → Nep
Nc → Nep → [習俗]	Na[tool|用具] → Nep
Nb → Nep → [event|事件] → 是	Na[thing|萬物] → Nep
Nc → Nep → [戰爭|war] → 是	Na[edible|食物] → Nc
Nc → Nep → [event|事件]	Na[animal|獸] → Nc

(CKIP Group 1993). Words with the POS "Nf" or "Ncd" can provide a cue for ATR and were thus used as features in our study. Texts from the social studies textbooks were also collected and manually classified into "PERSON," "EVENT," "TIME," "PLACE," "OBJECT," and "OTHER" answer types. For example, the textbook word 孫中山 *Sūn Zhōngshān* "Sun Yat-sen" is the name of a famous Chinese statesman. This word and its semantic class "PERSON" were used for ATR feature generation. The word concept in E-HowNet also was used for the feature generation of ATR classifiers.

To avoid missing new ATR features, AprioriAll, a sequential pattern-mining algorithm, was used for feature generation. Table 30.7 shows some of the features explored by AprioriAll, where a string containing "|" represents an E-HowNet concept, POS "Nc" represents a location noun, POS "Nep" represents a pronoun, POS "Na" represents a common noun, and POS "Nb" represents a proper noun.

30.3.4 Proposed Methodologies

To find the best-performing ATR module, experiments were conducted with different combinations of the six basic approaches, and the following methodologies were proposed:

METHODOLOGY I: Individual Basic Approaches. Each basic approach described in Sect. 30.3.2 was applied in isolation to each ATR module.

METHODOLOGY II: DQW + ME, DQW + SVM, DQW + BC, and DQW + BCF. ME, SVM

BC, and BCF were individually combined with DQW. Figures 30.6 and 30.7, respectively, illustrate DQW + SVM and DQW + BC and their corresponding algorithm pseudocodes.

METHODOLOGY III: CR + ME, CR + SVM, CR + BC, CR + BCF. ME, SVM, BC, and BCF were individually combined with CR. Figures 30.8 and 30.9, respectively, illustrate CR + ME and CR + BC and their corresponding algorithm pseudo codes.

METHODOLOGY IV: ME + SVM. ME and SVM were used individually to predict questions. When the predictive results from ME and SVM were different, the result with the higher confidence score was selected as the output. Figure 30.10 shows the ME+SVM methodology and corresponding algorithm.

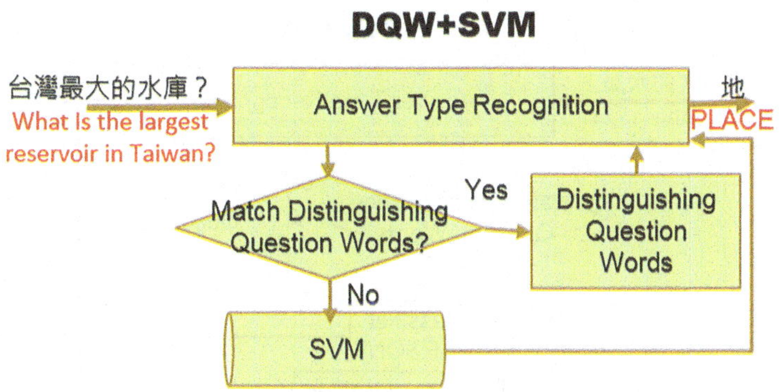


```
INPUT: question
IF the sentence contains Distinguished Question Word of DQW THEN APPLY
   DQW
   Result = result from DQW
ELSE
   APPLY SVM
   Result = result from SVM
END IF
OUTPUT Result
```

Fig. 30.6 DQW + SVM and corresponding algorithm

METHODOLOGY V: CR + ME + SVM. The difference between ME+SVM and CR + ME + SVM is that the first step of CR + ME + SVM is applying CR. Figure 30.11 illustrates CR + ME + SVM and its corresponding algorithm pseudo code.

METHODOLOGY VI: CR + ME + BC. ME was combined with CR + BC because the average performance of ME for ATR was better than that of SVM. Figure 30.12 illustrates CR + ME + BC and its corresponding algorithm pseudocode.

30.4 Experiments

30.4.1 Experimental Setting

A total of 5413 question sentences were collected from the corpus, with data distribution summarized in Table 30.8. For ATR assessment, 80% of the corpus was used for training data and the remaining 20% was used for testing. The proposed methodologies were implemented based on fivefold cross-validation, and assessment was based on the recall, precision, and F1 measure for ATR outside testing.

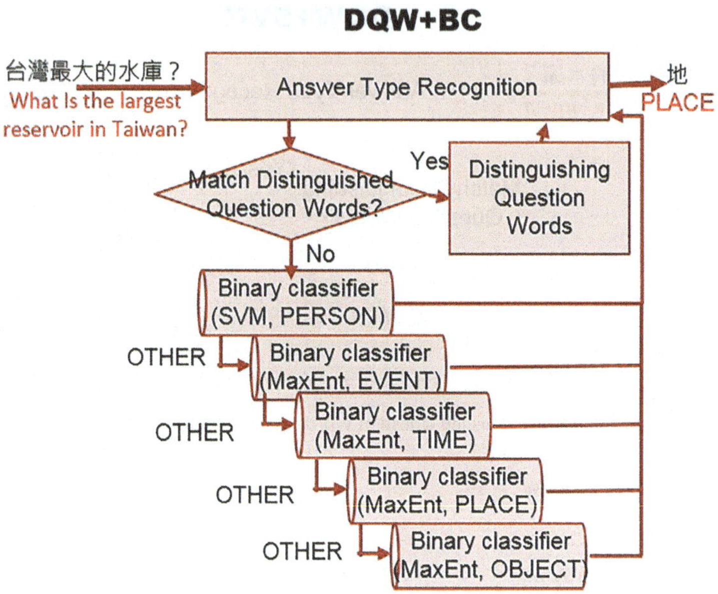


```
INPUT: question
IF the sentence contains Distinguished Question Word of DQW THEN APPLY
   DQW
   Result= result from DQW
ELSE
   APPLY Binary Classifier on PERSON
   Result= result from Binary Classifier on PERSON
   IF Result = "OTHER" THEN
      APPLY Binary Classifier on EVENT
      Result= result from Binary Classifier on EVENT
   ELSE IF Result = "OTHER" THEN
      APPLY Binary Classifier on TIME
      Result= result from Binary Classifier on TIME
   ELSE IF Result = "OTHER" THEN
      APPLY Binary Cla ssifier on PLACE
      Result= result from Binary Classifier on PLACE
   ELSE IF Result = "OTHER" THEN
      APPLY Binary Classifier on OBJECT
      Result= result from Binary Classifier on OBJECT
   END IF
END IF
OUTPUT Result
```

Fig. 30.7 DQW + BC and corresponding algorithm

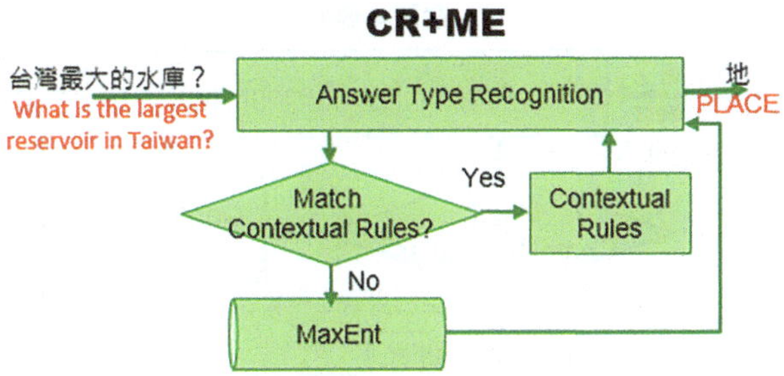

INPUT: question
IF the sentence matches Contextual Rules of CR **THEN**
    APPLY CR
    Result= result from CR
ELSE
    APPLY ME
    Result= result from ME
END IF
OUTPUT Result

Fig. 30.8 CR + ME and corresponding algorithm

30.4.2 Experimental Results

The first experiment compared the performance of the six basic approaches. Figures 30.13, 30.14, 30.15, 30.16, 30.17, and 30.18, respectively, show the performance of DQW, CR, ME, SVM, BC, and BCF. In the DQW and CR results, the precision and recall results of the "PERSON" answer type were reasonably good, indicating that questions with the "PERSON" answer type had distinguishing features from questions with other answer types. The DQW and CR approaches both achieved the best precision rate (100) but obtained very low recall rates for the "EVENT" and "OBJECT" types. Few question words could be used to identify "EVENT" and "OBJECT" questions, but their corresponding answer types were easily differentiated. Contextual information may have improved the recall rate for the "EVENT" type, but not for the "OBJECT" type. "OTHER" answer type questions had high levels of ambiguity, resulting in a high recall rate but a low precision rate in the DQW and CR results. Aside from the "PERSON" type, ME outperformed SVM for other types, and SVM showed only a slightly better result for the "PERSON" type. The average performance of BC did not exceed that of SVM or ME. Moreover, the average performance of BCF did not exceed that of BC. For the "EVENT" type, BC produced a better precision rate than SVM and a slightly better rate than ME. For the "TIME" and "PLACE" types, BC slightly outperformed SVM, but with a lower recall rate. Compared to BC, precision and recall were reduced significantly in BCF, especially for the "OBJECT" type, possibly because of insufficient training data. Of the six methods, ME was found to be the most stable for ATR.

The second experiment evaluated the impact of the other four basic approaches (ME, SVM, BC, and BCF, respectively) combined with DQW and CR, with the

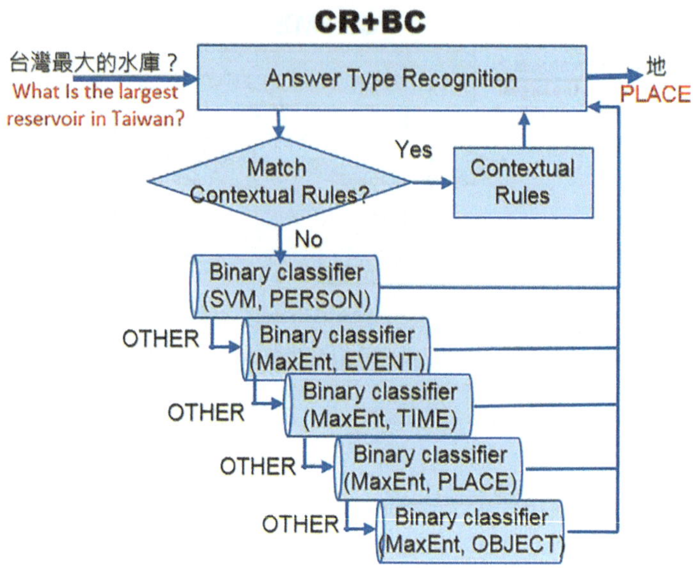


```
INPUT: question
IF the sentence matches Contextual Rules of CR THEN
  APPLY CR
  Result= result from CR
ELSE
  APPLY Binary Classifier on PERSON
  Result= result from Binary Classifier on PERSON
  IF Result= "OTHER" THEN
    APPLY Binary Classifier on EVENT
    Result= result from Binary Classifier on EVENT
  ELSE IF Result= "OTHER" THEN
    APPLY Binary Classifier on TIME
    Result= result from Binary Classifier on TIME
  ELSE IF Result= "OTHER" THEN
    APPLY Binary Classifier on PLACE
    Result= result from Binary Classifier on PLACE
  ELSE IF Result= "OTHER" THEN
    APPLY Binary Classifier on OBJECT
    Result= result from Binary Classifier on OBJECT
  END IF
END IF
OUTPUT Result
```

Fig. 30.9 CR + BC and corresponding algorithm

results shown in Figs. 30.19, 30.20, 30.21, 30.22, 30.23, 30.24, 30.25, and 30.26. For both BC and BCF, coupling with DQW increased the overall F1 scores, and coupling with CR was more effective than coupling with DQW for promoting the overall F1 scores. This means that CR was more effective in enhancing the precision

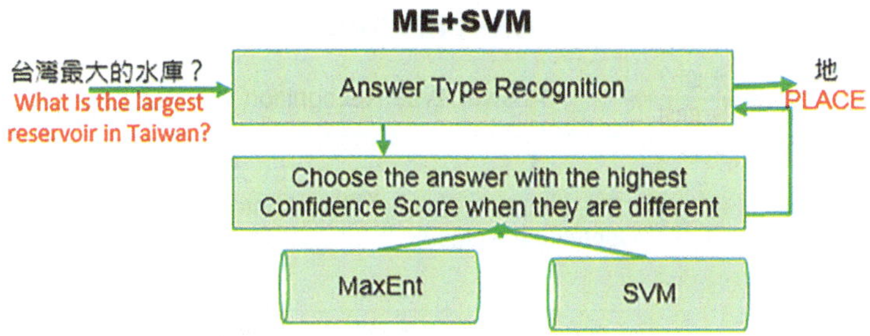


```
INPUT: question
APPLY ME
Result1= result from ME
ME_Score= confidence score of result from ME
APPLY SVM
Result2= result from SVM
SVM_Score= confidence score of result from SVM
IF Result1 != Result2 THEN
   IF ME_Score > SVM_Score THEN
   Result= Result1
   ELSE
   Result= Result2
   END IF
END IF
OUTPUT Result
```

Fig. 30.10 ME + SVM and corresponding algorithm

and recall rates than DQW when coupled with BC or BCF. Compared with the results for BC, CR improved the precision rate in the CR + BC results, indicating that CR provided robust information for accurate ATR.

Figures 30.27, 30.28, and 30.29, respectively, show the performance of ME +SVM, CR + ME + SVM, and CR + ME + BC. ME + SVM achieved a better precision rate than ME for all answer types but had a lower recall rate than ME for "PLACE," "OBJECT," and "OTHER," resulting in a low average F1 score for ME. Because the proposed confidence-score-based model selection did not work well, the confidence scores of SVM and ME did not equal their predictive capability. Therefore, another model selection approach is needed when the results of SVM and ME differ. From the results of ME+SVM and CR + ME + SVM, CR improved the precision rates of all answer types but reduced the recall rates of "EVENT," "PLACE," and "OBJECT," leading to a fall in F1 scores. Moreover, the Contextual Rules of "EVENT" did not improve. Compared to CR + ME, CR + ME + BC showed a substantial increase in the recall rate, except for the "PERSON" type. The experimental results showed that CR and ME can handle most questions types.

The experimental results showed that the system encountered problems when dealing with question sentences with complex structures. One possible reason is that a question may have more than one answer type. For example, the question 哪個節日有喝什麼的習俗, 據說可以驅邪解毒? *Nǎgè jiérì yǒu hē shénme de xísú, jùshuō*

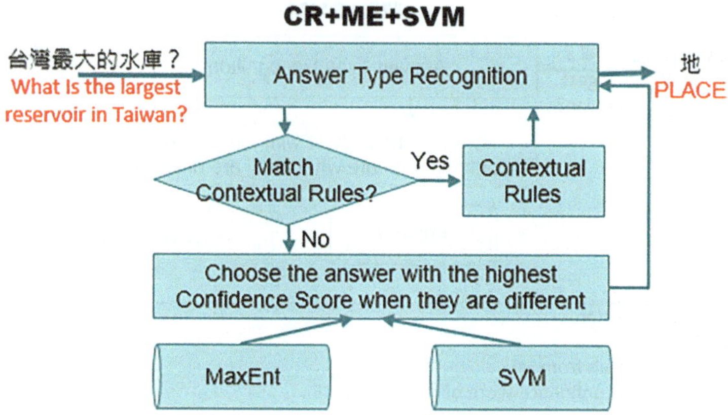


```
INPUT: question
IF the sentence matches Contextual Rules of CR THEN
  APPLY CR
  Result= result from CR
ELSE
  APPLY ME
  Result1= result from ME
  ME_Score= confidence score of result from ME
  APPLY SVM
  Result2= result from SVM
  SVM_Score= confidence score of result from SVM
  IF Result1 != Result2 THEN
    IF ME_Score > SVM_Score THEN
    Result= Result1
    ELSE
    Result= Result2
    END IF
  END IF
END IF
OUTPUT Result
```

Fig. 30.11 CR + ME + SVM and corresponding algorithm

kěyǐ qūxié jiědú? "Which festival is associated with drinking beverages for exorcism and detoxification?" has two answer types—"TIME" and "OBJECT." Sometimes students ask questions using informal statements, including error words, Zhuyin text,[4] unsuitable lexical choices, missing words, and redundant words, as shown in Table 30.9.

[1] Zhuyin text is a special network culture in Taiwan and refers to words in a sentence that are replaced with Mandarin phonetic symbols. A word may be replaced in whole or part by corresponding [4] Mandarin phonetic symbols. For example, the Mandarin phonetic symbol for the word 你 *Nǐ* 'You' is "ㄋㄧˇ" and that for 嗎 *Ma* '?' is "ㄇㄚ˙". Therefore, 你看得懂這句話嗎? *Nǐ kàn dé dǒng zhè jù huà ma* 'Can you read this sentence?' may be written as "ㄋ看得懂這句話ㄇ?"

```
INPUT: question
IF the sentence matches Contextual Rules of CR THEN
   APPLY CR
   Result= result from CR
ELSE
   APPLY ME
   Result= result from ME
   IF Result = "OTHER" THEN
   APPLY Binary Classifier on PERSON
   Result= result from Binary Classifier on PERSON
   ELS IF Result= "OTHER" THEN
      APPLY Binary Classifier on EVENT
      Result= result from Binary Classifier on EVENT
   ELSE IF Result= "OTHER" THEN
      APPLY Binary Classifier on TIME
      Result= result from Binary Classifier on TIME
   ELSE IF Result= "OTHER" THEN
      APPLY Binary Classifier on PLACE
      Result= result from Binary Classifier on PLACE
   ELSE IF Result= "OTHER" THEN
      APPLY Binary Classifier on OBJECT
      Result= result from Binary Classifier on OBJECT
   END IF
END IF
OUTPUT Result
```

Fig. 30.12 CR + ME + BC and corresponding algorithm

30.5 Conclusion

Distinguishing Question Words (DQW), Contextual Rules (CR), Maximum Entropy Classifiers (ME), Support Vector Machine (SVM), Binary Classifiers (BC), and Binary Classifiers with Filtered Training Data (BCF) were combined and assessed for answer type recognition to facilitate query processing in a pupil question answering system. Combinations including DQW + ME, DQW + SVM, DQW + BC, DQW + BCF, CR + ME, CR + SVM, CR + BC, CR + BCF, ME + SVM, CR + ME + BC, and CR + ME + SVM were presented and evaluated. The features used in ME and SVM included question words, special domain dictionaries, special POS, and the semantic class of special position nouns. The AprioriAll algorithm was used to explore the sequential patterns of question sentences, which were then used as features in ME and SVM. The experimental results showed that the proposed DQW + ME approach achieved the best F1 score in the ATR tasks.

Table 30.8 Data distribution of the pupil question answering corpus

Percentage	Type	Example of question sentence	Answer
21.30%	PERSON	創建中華民國的是誰?	孫中山
		Chuàngjiàn Zhōnghuámínguó de shì shéi?	*Sūn Zhōngshān*
		"Who established the Republic of China?"	Sun Yat-sen
2.46%	EVENT	台東元宵節會做什麼活動?	炸寒單
		Táidōng Yuánxiāojié huì zuò shén me huódòng?	*Zhà hán dān*
		"What activity takes place in Taitung during the Lantern Festival?"	Firecrackers at Master
9.31%	TIME	哪一個節日要喝菊花酒?	重陽節
		Nă-yī-ge jiérì yào hē júhuā-jiŭ?	*Chóngyángjié*
		"Which festival features drinking chrysanthemum wine?"	Chung Yeung Festival
19.12%	PLACE	台灣東部有哪個海?	太平洋
		Táiwān dōngbù yǒu nă-gè hǎi?	*Tàipíngyáng*
		"What ocean lies to the east of Taiwan?"	Pacific Ocean
8.72%	OBJECT	那本書是儒家思想最重要的典籍?	論語
		Nà-běn shū shì rújiāsīxiăng zuì zhòngyào de diănjí?	*Lúnyŭ*
		"What is the most important book on Confucianism?"	Analects of Confucius
39.09%	OTHER	卑南族的傳統語言是什麼?	卑南語
		Bēinánzú de chuántŏng yŭyán shì shénme	*Bēinányŭ*
		"What is the traditional language of the Puyuma?"	Pinuyumayan
100% (5413)			

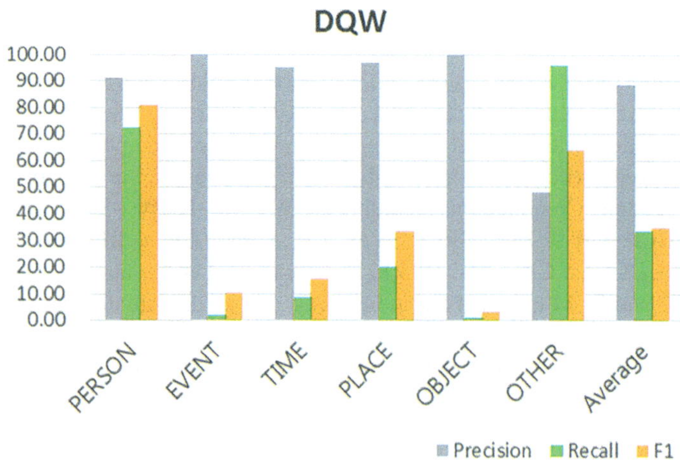

Fig. 30.13 DQW performance

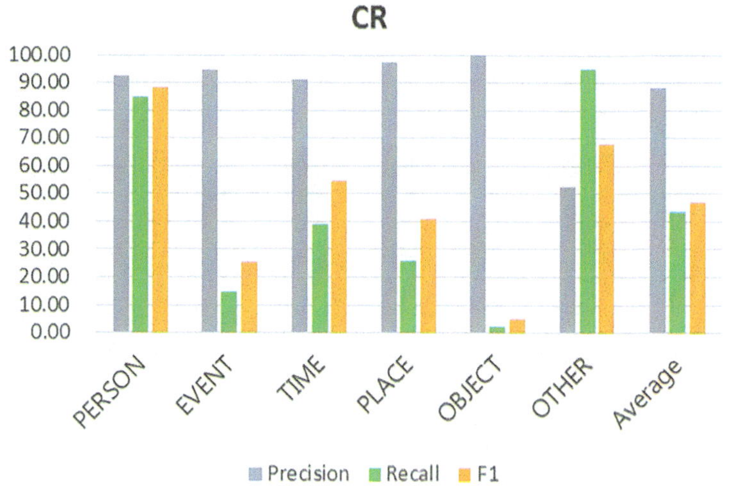

Fig. 30.14 CR performance

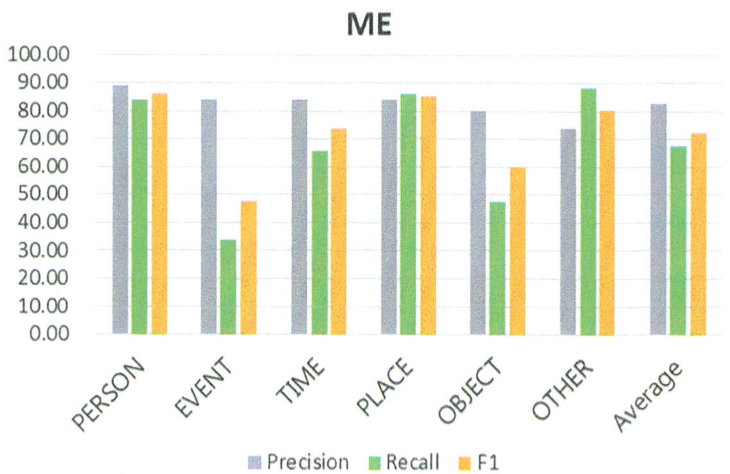

Fig. 30.15 ME performance

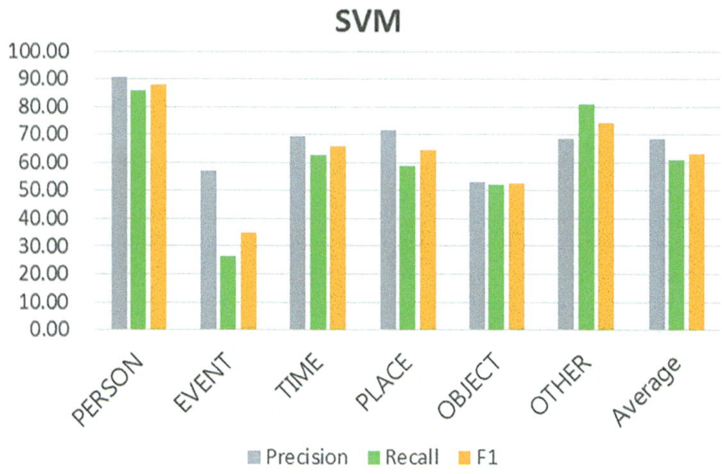

Fig. 30.16 SVM performance

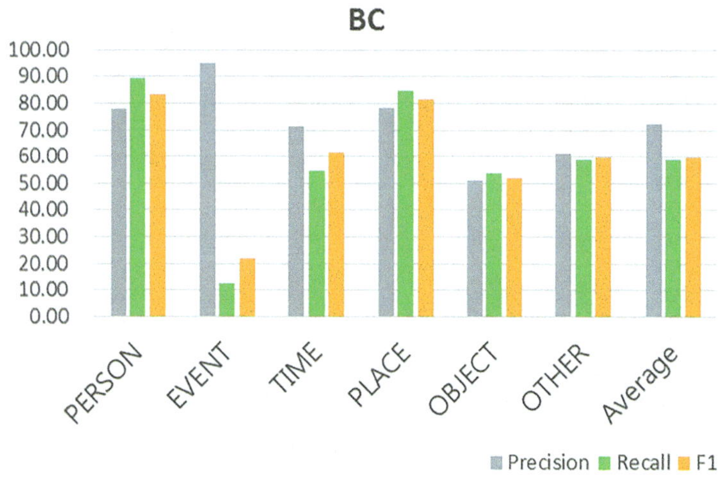

Fig. 30.17 BC performance

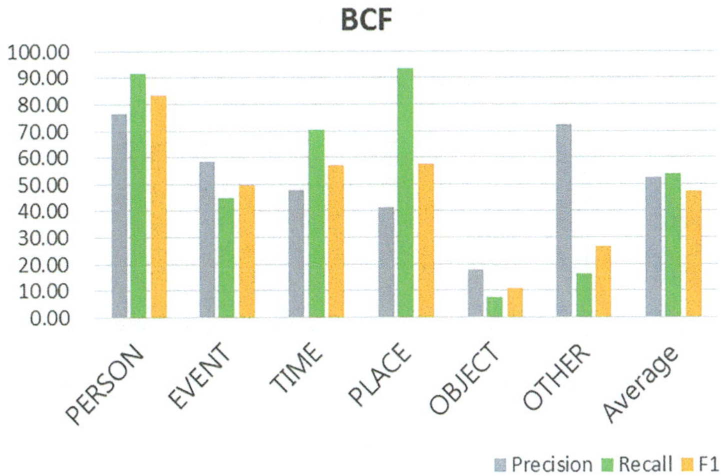

Fig. 30.18 BCF performance

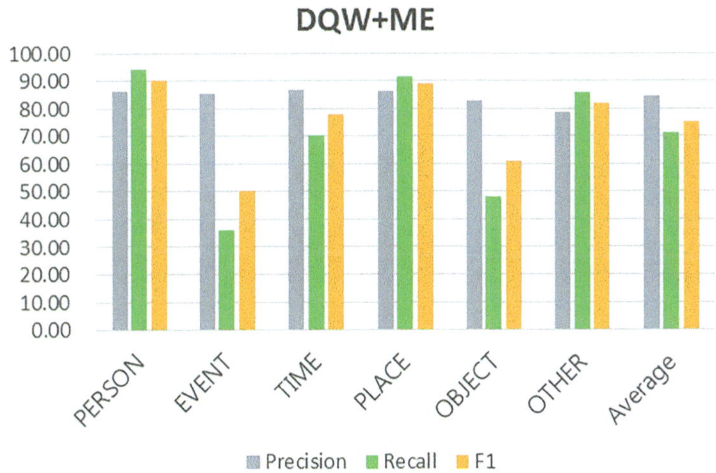

Fig. 30.19 DQW + ME performance

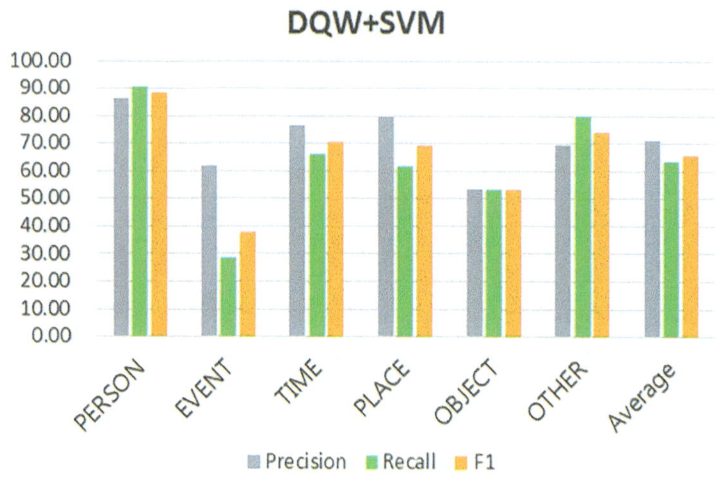

Fig. 30.20 DQW + SVM performance

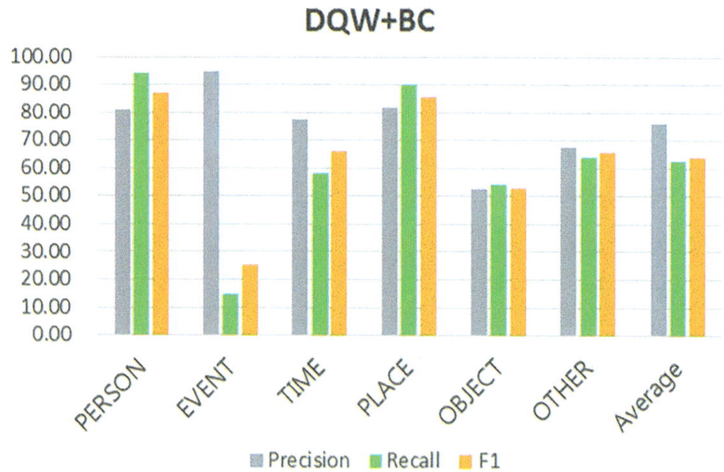

Fig. 30.21 DQW + BC performance

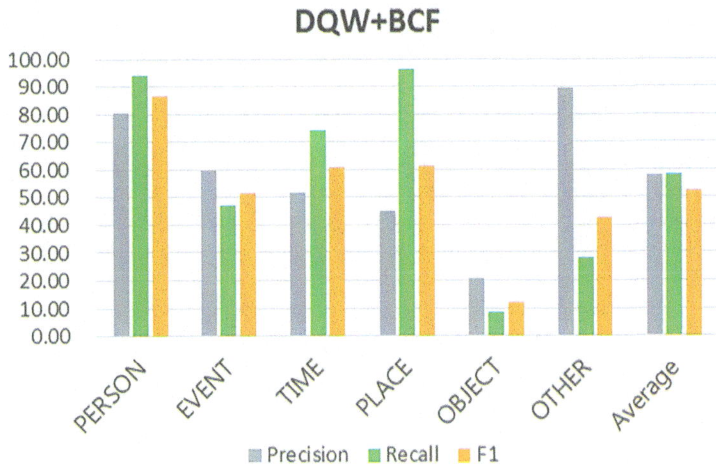

Fig. 30.22 DQW + BCF performance

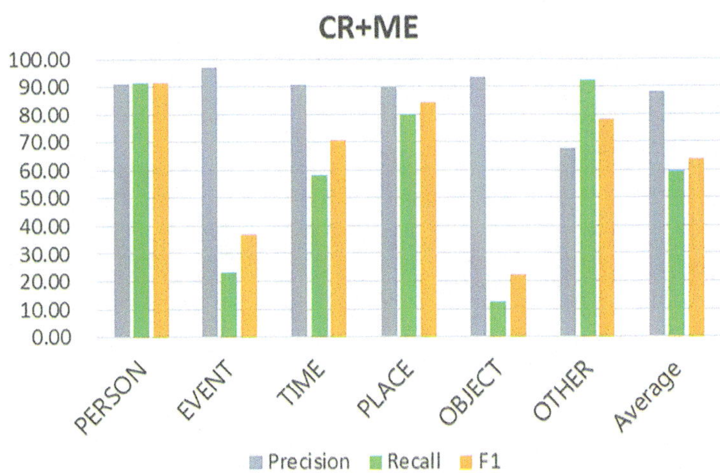

Fig. 30.23 CR + ME performance

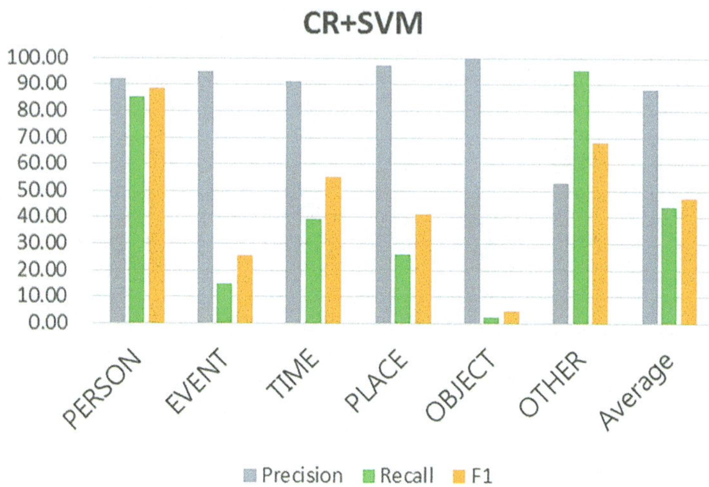

Fig. 30.24 CR + SVM performance

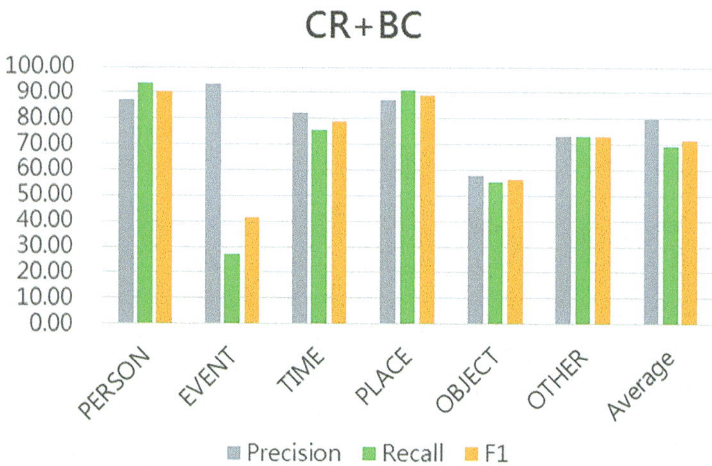

Fig. 30.25 CR + BC performance

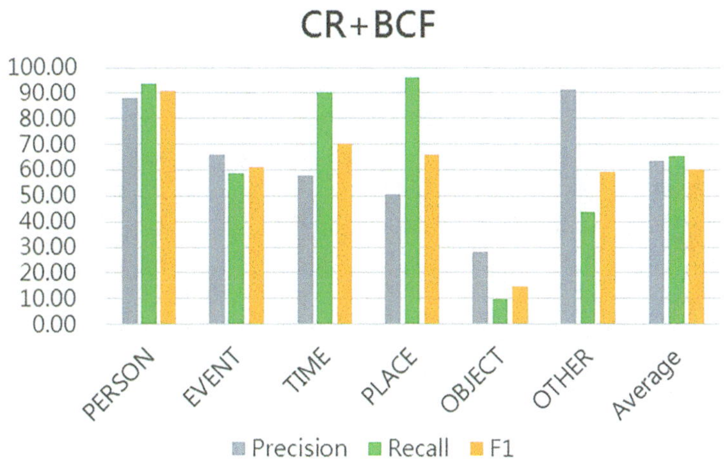

Fig. 30.26 CR + BCF performance

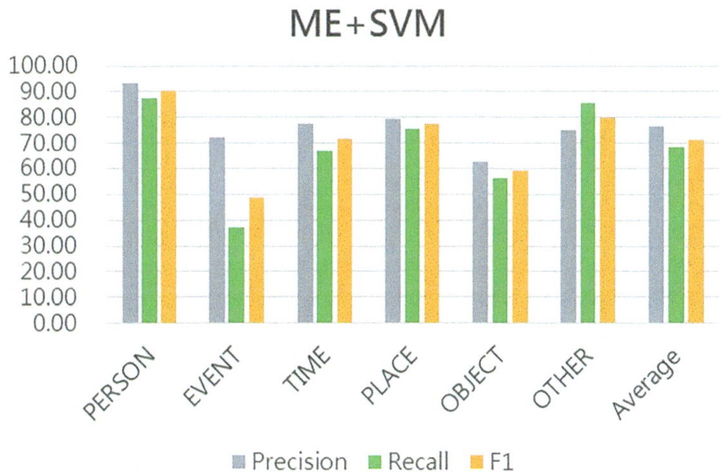

Fig. 30.27 ME + SVM performance

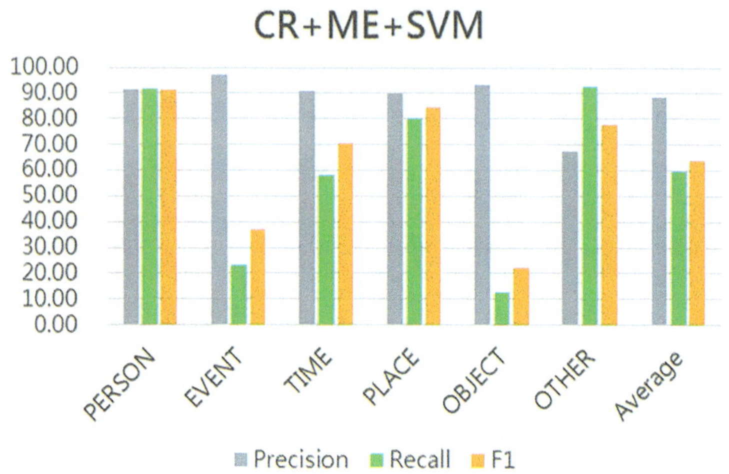

Fig. 30.28 CR + ME + SVM performance

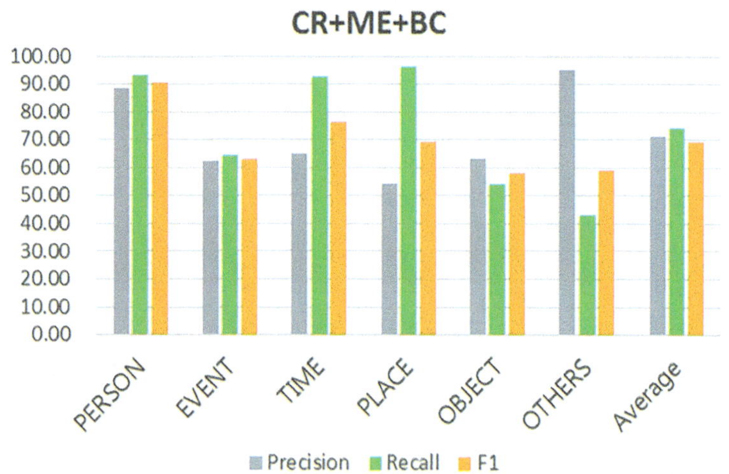

Fig. 30.29 CR + ME + BC performance

Table 30.9 Examples of problematic questions

Error words	*舍*時武昌起義?
	* Shě * shí wǔchāngqǐyì?
	She →(When) is Wuchang uprising?
Zhuyin sentences	鄭成功的* ㄐㄩˋ*點在哪裡?
	Zhèng Chénggong de * jù *diǎn zài nǎ-lǐ?
	Where is Zheng Chenggong's *chu tien (→stronghold)?
Unsuitable lexical choices	張飛*什麼*死的?
	Zhāng Fēi * shénme * sǐ de
	*What (→Why)*did Chang Fei die?
Missing words	誰被稱為*聖先師*?
	Shéi bèi chēngwéi * shèngxiānshī *
	Who is called the *great (→greatest)* sage and teacher?
Redundant words	*什麼的*哪裡是新北市政府所在地, 也是林家花園所在地?
	* Shénme de * Nǎlǐ shì xīnběi shì zhèngfǔ suǒ-zài-dì, yě shì línjiā huāyuán suǒ-zài-dì?
	what and→(~~What and~~) where is New Taipei City government and Lin family mansion and garden?

References

Alessandro, Moschitti, Jennifer Chu-Carroll, Siddharth Patwardhan, James Fan, and Giuseppe Riccardi. 2011. Using syntactic and semantic structural kernels for classifying definition questions in "Jeopardy!" In *Proceedings of the 2011 Conference on Empirical Methods in Natural Language Processing*, ed. Association for Computational Linguistics, 712–724. Edinburgh, Scotland.

Banerjee, Somnath, and Sivaji Bandyopadhyay. 2013. An empirical study of combining multiple models in Bengali question classification. Paper presented at the *International Joint Conference on Natural Language Processing*, 892–896. Nagoya, Japan. Available at https://aclweb.org/anthology/I13-1113. Accessed 9 April 2019.

Chen, Keh-Jiann, Shu-Ling Huang, Yueh-Yin Shihand, and Yi-Jun Chen. 2005. Extended-HowNet—A representational framework for concepts. Paper presented at *OntoLex 2005—Ontologies and Lexical Resources IJCNLP-05 Workshop*. Jeju Island, South Korea. Available at https://www.researchgate.net/publication/239753241_Extended-HowNet-_A_Representational_Framework_for_Concepts. Accessed 9 April 2019.

Chinese Knowledge Information Processing (CKIP) Group of the Academia Sinica Institute of Information Science. 1993. Technical report no. 93-05: Part-of-speech analysis of Mandarin Chinese. Available at http://ckip.iis.sinica.edu.tw/CKIP/tr/9305_2013%20revision.pdf. Accessed 30 November 2018.

Chinese Knowledge Information Processing (CKIP) Group of the Academia Sinica Institute of Information Science. 2009. Technical report no. 09-01: Lexical semantic representation and semantic composition: An Introduction to E-HowNet. Available at http://ckip.iis.sinica.edu.tw/CKIP/tr/200901_2016b.pdf. Accessed 30 November 2018.

Day, Min-Yuh, Cheng-Wei Lee, Shih-Hung Wu, Chorng-Shyong Ong, and Wen-Lian Hsu. 2005. An integrated knowledge-based and machine learning approach for Chinese question classification. In *Proceedings of the 2005 IEEE International Conference on Natural Language Processing and Knowledge Engineering*. Wuhan, China.

Huang, Zhiheng, Marcus Thint, and Zengchang Qin. 2008. Question classification using head words and their hypernyms. In *Proceedings of the 2008 Conference on Empirical Methods in Natural Language Processing*, ed. the Association for Computational Linguistics, 927–936. Honolulu, Hawai'i.

Huang, Zhiheng, Marcus Thint, and Asli Celikyilmaz. 2009. Investigation of question classifier in question answering. In *Proceedings of the 2009 Conference on Empirical Methods in Natural Language Processing*, ed. the Association for Computational Linguistics and the Asian Federation of Natural Language Processing, 543–550. Singapore.

Hui, Zijing, Juan Liu, and Lumei Ouyang. 2011. Question classification based on an extended class sequential rule model. In *Proceedings of the 5th International Joint Conference on Natural Language Processing*, ed. Asian Federation of Natural Language Processing, 938–946. Chiang Mai, Thailand.

Jurafsky, Daniel, and James H. Martin. 2009. *Speech and language processing: An introduction to natural language processing, computational linguistics, and speech recognition*. Pearson Education.

Tran, Dang Hai, Cuong Xuan Chu, Son Bao Pham, and Minh Le Nguyen. 2013. Learning based approaches for Vietnamese question classification using keywords extraction from the web. Paper presented at the *International Joint Conference on Natural Language Processing*, 14–18. Nagoya, Japan. Available at https://www.aclweb.org/anthology/I13-1088. Accessed 9 April 2019.

Tsai, Yu-Fang, and Keh-Jiann Chen. 2003. Reliable and cost-effective POS-tagging. In *Proceedings of ROCLING XV*, ed. the Association for Computational Linguistics and Chinese Language Processing, 161–174. Taiwan, ROC.

Chapter 31
Information Diffusion Prediction Based on Social Representation Learning with Group Influence

Zhitao Wang, Chengyao Chen, and Wenjie Li

Abstract In this chapter, we will introduce a social representation learning model with group influence to address the issue of information diffusion prediction in social media. The model aimed at projecting social media users into a latent representation in a continuous space, where their closeness in the information propagation process could be measured directly. The proposed model translated the specific diffusion process as a dynamic group formation based on a certain message under group influence and explained the diffusion closeness among users based on the order and time that they adopted the message (i.e., joined the group). Additionally, the model applied graph information by introducing pre-trained network embeddings and utilizing the adaptive margin function to enhance generalization ability. The diffusion prediction method was then developed based on the learned representations. We evaluated the proposed method using a real-world social media diffusion dataset. Our experimental results demonstrated higher performance compared with previous methods.

Keywords Information diffusion · Representation learning

31.1 Introduction

With a drastic boost in users, online social media has brought about fundamental changes in information diffusion, which has enabled online information to propagate and evolve dynamically. However, the mechanisms behind these changing

Z. Wang (✉)
Wechat Pay, Tencent Inc., Shenzhen, China
e-mail: zhitaowang@tencent.com

C. Chen
JP Morgan Asset Management, Hong Kong, China
e-mail: stacy.chen@jpmchase.com

W. Li
Department of Computing, The Hong Kong Polytechnic University, Hong Kong, China
e-mail: cswjli@comp.polyu.edu.hk

C.-R. Huang et al. (eds.), *Chinese Language Resources*, Text, Speech and Language Technology 49, https://doi.org/10.1007/978-3-031-38913-9_31

information diffusion patterns are still not well understood. Recently, researchers have paid particular attention to the problem of temporal diffusion modeling for social media, which is a very important problem underlying information diffusion. Diffusion modeling aims at studying the mechanisms underpinning information propagation through users' interactions (e.g., retweets on Twitter) and predicting users' temporal adoption (order) in future diffusion processes.

The majority of previous work on social media has referred to classical diffusion models, especially the independent cascade (IC) model, for information diffusion modeling. For example, Saito et al. (2008) proposed an expectation-maximization algorithm to estimate the discrete IC model, while Guille and Hacid (2012) proposed to integrate more features into basic IC models for diffusion prediction. These IC-based methods focused on explaining how an "infected" node (i.e., sender) activates its neighbor, which required sufficient observations of historical diffusion paths along network links. Unfortunately, in most cases, no exact explicit paths were observed in social media, only temporal propagation orders. Hence, the prediction ability of these models was inevitably limited.

Recently, the work of Bourigault et al. (2014) provided a new view of this problem by applying the representation learning model. Based on the work of Lafferty and Lebanon (2005), Bourigault et al. (2014) proposed to model information diffusion as a heat diffusion process, in which the first user is regarded as a heat source and other users adopt the information through the heat diffusion effect. Although this work achieved better performance than the IC-based models, the assumption that users are influenced only by the source user still violates the mechanisms of the diffusion process in social media.

Additionally, all the methods above focused on node-to-node diffusion (e.g., the sender and its neighbor or the source and other users), which led to them ignoring the influence of a group during diffusion. In fact, group influence is a common phenomenon. For example, on microblogging websites, users can add their own opinions and comments when reposting. When a user receives a reposted message, he/she may be interested in both the original message and some pieces of added comments from the previously infected users. In this case, the user is influenced by a group.

In our study, we captured group influence during the diffusion process and integrated it into a diffusion model. We regarded temporal diffusion as a group formation process (i.e., the adoption of the original message by a user represented his/her participation in the group) and proposed a representation learning model with group influence to explain these processes. Specifically, we applied the time-decay function to measure the different influences of early adopter group members based on their adoption time and explored how likely a user would adopt the information under these influences. The model learned the users' representation in a latent space, where some metrics (e.g., Euclidean distance and cosine similarity) directly reflected the users' closeness in diffusion. This type of representation has a stronger ability to encode latent features of diffusion relationships than the sparse representation in traditional IC-based models. For example, in the continuous latent space, the closeness of any pair of indirectly linked nodes can be measured by distance metrics, while sparse representation requires a more complex procedure to discover the nodes' closeness.

Graph information is an important factor of diffusion but was barely used by previous representation learning model. Therefore, we integrated the static graph structural information into the model to enhance its generalization ability. The pre-trained network embeddings and an adaptive margin function based on a network structure were introduced as learning supervision. We compared the proposed approach with alternative methods using real-world social media data, and the experimental results demonstrated that our model had a promising information diffusion prediction performance.

31.2 Method

First, a specific diffusion process was denoted as a cascade $c = \{(u_1^c, t_1^c), \ldots, (u_i^c, t_i^c), \ldots\}$ with a sequential structure, where the element (u_i^c, t_i^c) indicated that the i th adopter (or infected user) in cascade c was u_i^c and its adoption time was t_i^c. The elements were ranked by their adoption time; thus, it satisfies $t_i^c < t_j^c$ if $i < j$. Additionally, the early adopters group before timestamp t_i^c in cascade c was defined as $E(t_{i-1}^c) = \{(u_1^c, t_1^c), \ldots, (u_{i-1}^c, t_{i-1}^c)\}$, representing the set of infected users who participated in cascade c earlier than u_i^c. The problem of temporal propagation prediction was formulated as, given the social network G with N users and an observed diffusion processes set C_l, the goal is to learn a predictive model and validate it with a future cascades set C_t. Note that G represents a directed graph, where the graph links are created for the following relationships in the microblog network. As for test set C_t, it should include the diffusion processes that happen after the cascades in C_l so that the prediction ability for the future can be evaluated.

31.2.1 Representation Learning Model

Representation learning aims at projecting each social network user into a latent representation vector $\mathbf{z}$ with n dimensions ($\mathbf{z} \in \mathbb{R}^n$) such that the relationships of representations (i.e., embeddings) for a given metric can explain the closeness of the diffusion relationships among users. Therefore, extracting diffusion relationships from diffusion data is of great significance in representation learning. Inspired by Bourigault et al. (2014), we regarded the actual temporal order of infected users in a specific cascade as a reflection of the diffusion relationships. Additionally, due to the characteristics of the social media diffusion data, it is more reasonable to consider the diffusion process from a receiver-centric view, that is, how a user is influenced by the group of previous infected users in a specific cascade. Therefore, we assumed the correlation between the diffusion relationships among users and the temporal orders of cascades as follows: (1) given two users u_i^c and u_j^c in the same cascade c, if $t_i^c < t_j^c$, then u_i^c has a closer diffusion relationship with its early adopters set $E(u_i^c)$ than u_j^c at the fixed timestamp t_i^c; and (2) given a user u_i^c in cascade c and another user $u_j \notin c$, u_i^c has a closer diffusion relationship with its early adopters set $E(u_i^c)$ than u_j at the fixed timestamp t_i^c.

Apart from the temporal order, the time interval between two users in a specific cascade can also reflect their different diffusion influence. To measure this influence, we introduced two time-decay models, the Exponential model and the Rayleigh model (Gomez-Rodriguez et al. 2011), which made full use of the infection timestamps in the diffusion data. The Exponential model is one of the most classic monotonic models. It assumes that when the time interval between an infected node and the sample node rises, the diffusion influence between them drops continuously. The Exponential time-decay function is defined in (1):

$$\Delta_E(t_i, t_j) = e^{-\frac{(t_i - t_j)}{\tau}} \tag{31.1}$$

where $t_i > t_j$, $\tau > 0$. Respectively, t_i and t_j represent the contamination time of the sample user u_i and one of his/her early adopters u_j in a specific cascade. If the time interval is large, then the diffusion influence between them decreases and vice versa. Since the unit of contamination time is millisecond in the observed data, a parameter τ was defined to control the time scale. However, temporal infection in social media does not seem to follow this monotonic rule all the time. To address this problem, the non-monotonic Rayleigh model, which is well-adapted to modeling diffusion fads, was used. In this model, propagation influence climbs to a peak and then decreases rapidly by time, which is defined in Eq. (31.2):

$$\Delta_R(t_i, t_j) = \frac{t_i - t_j}{\tau} e^{-\frac{(t_i - t_j)^2}{2\tau^2}} \tag{31.2}$$

where $t_i > t_j$, $\tau > 0$. Respectively, t_i and t_j represent the contamination time of the sample user u_i and one of his/her early adopters u_j in a specific cascade, and τ was defined to control the time scale. Unlike the exponential model, if the time interval is too small, this function will give a small value correspondingly, which can avoid some random situations where two users without a strong relationship participate in the diffusion almost simultaneously.

Given the time-decay functions above, we encoded the group of early adopters $E(u_i^c)$ of user u_i^c as follows in Eq. (31.3):

$$\mathbf{z}_{E(u_i^c)} = \sum_{k=1}^{i-1} \frac{\Delta(t_i^c, t_k^c)}{\sum_{p=1}^{i-1} \Delta(t_i^c, t_p^c)} \mathbf{z}_k \tag{31.3}$$

where $\Delta\left(t_i^c, t_k^c\right)$ can be either Δ_E or Δ_R, and the time-decay weights were normalized by all the early adopters.

Combined with the time-decay diffusion influence, the diffusion relationships extracted from the infected temporal orders above were translated to the constraint condition for representation learning in a latent space with the L2-Norm metric. For user u_i^c who was infected in cascade c and another user u_j, if they satisfied one of the following conditions:

- user u_j was also infected in the same cascade c and $t_i^c < t_j^c$
- user u_j was not infected in cascade c, that is, $u_j \notin c$

then we derived the following constraint condition:

$$\left\| \mathbf{z}_{E\left(u_i^c\right)} - \mathbf{z}_i \right\|^2 < \left\| \mathbf{z}_{E\left(u_i^c\right)} - \mathbf{z}_j \right\|^2$$

The left part of the two inequations above represents the closeness of the diffusion relationship between u_i^c and its early adopters $E\left(u_i^c\right)$ with different diffusion influence, while the right part denotes the closeness between u_j^c and $E\left(u_i^c\right)$ in the latent space. The smaller the value, the closer they are. The fraction in the left (right) part represents a normalized diffusion influence received by u_i^c (u_j) from $u_k^c \in E\left(u_i^c\right)$. Utilizing these diffusion influences as weights of the representations of different early adopters, all early adopters $E\left(u_i^c\right)$ were composed as one representation with group influence.

To learn the representations above, the classical margin-based loss function was applied such that the constraint conditions were regarded as the diffusion order criterion, as shown in Eq. (31.4):

$$\mathcal{L} = \sum_{c \in C_l} \sum_{\substack{u_i^c \in c \\ u_j \in \mathcal{N}\left(u_i^c\right)}} \left(\gamma\left(u_i^c, u_j\right) + \left\| \mathbf{z}_{E\left(u_i^c\right)} - \mathbf{z}_i \right\|^2 - \left\| \mathbf{z}_{E\left(u_i^c\right)} - \mathbf{z}_j \right\|^2 \right)_+ \quad (31.4)$$

where we regarded user u_i^c as a positive sample who followed the actual temporal order of a specific cascade, while regarded u_j as a negative sample who should not have appeared in c at timestamp u_i^c according to the observed order. Therefore, $\mathcal{N}\left(u_i^c\right)$ represents the negative sample set of the positive sample u_i^c, where the elements should be the users later infected or never infected in c. The two $\|\cdot\|^2$ parts indicate the diffusion closeness of the fixed early adopters set $E\left(u_i^c\right)$ with a positive sample u_i^c and a negative sample u_j, respectively. The function $\gamma\left(u_i^c, u_j\right)$ provides an adaptive margin value according to the network relationships of u_i^c, $E\left(u_i^c\right)$, and u_j, which will be introduced subsequently. The plus function $(x)_+$ denotes the positive part of x. The loss function favors lower values of the metric $\|\cdot\|^2$ for positive samples than for negative ones such that the constraint conditions are satisfied. The objective is thus to learn representations $\mathbf{z}$ for all users in the given network G to minimize the loss function $\mathcal{L}$.

The classical stochastic gradient descent method was applied to figure out this optimization problem. All users were projected into the latent space with an initial representation. For each iteration, a pair of positive and negative users as well as the early adopters of the positive users were sampled. The steepest gradients of the parameters (i.e., the representations of all the sampled users) were calculated using Eq. (31.4). The parameters were then updated by taking a gradient step with a constant learning rate with these gradients.

31.2.2 Social Graph Guidance

Graph information is very crucial for diffusion modeling, but it cannot be directly introduced into the latent continuous space. In our study, we introduced graph information by introducing network embeddings in initialization and utilizing an adaptive margin function.

Most representation learning models randomly initialize the embeddings, which may lead to weak robustness, especially for diffusion modeling. For instance, given randomly initialized representations $\mathbf{z}_i$ and $\mathbf{z}_j$ for users u_i and u_j, and u_i has a link with u_j, if there was no diffusion interactions between them in the training data, then the closeness measured for $\mathbf{z}_i$ and $\mathbf{z}_j$ may be weak. However, the link indicates that their closeness is limited to a certain range rather than too far away. Based on this observation, we proposed to use pre-trained network embeddings as the initialization of representation since they reflect perfectly the static relationships among users in a latent space. In this way, diffusion was regarded as dynamic processes in which users change their closeness with others according to their interactions.

Different choices of margins are suitable for embedding learning into different data, which has been proven in previous work (Bordes et al. 2013). However, fixed margins without considering graph information for all data in diffusion modeling cannot distinguish closeness differences. For example, if u_j and u_k are both negative samples of u_i^c in c but have a large difference in graph distance compared with the early adopters set $E(u_i^c)$, then it is difficult for a model with a fixed margin to recognize this difference only from observations of diffusion. Thus, an adaptive margin function based on graph information was adopted in the model to improve distinguishing ability. Shortest path is a natural metric for margin selection as it clearly shows the different costs of two paths with the same source node but different target node, which corresponds to the difference of closeness in the diffusion process. The adaptive margin function was defined in Eq. (31.5):

$$\gamma\left(u_i^c, u_j\right) = \gamma + \max\left(\sum_{k=1}^{i-1} \frac{\Delta\left(t_i^c, t_k^c\right)}{\sum_{p=1}^{i-1} \Delta\left(t_i^c, t_p^c\right)} \left(p_{jk} - p_{ik}\right), 0\right) \tag{31.5}$$

where γ is a basic margin parameter assigned with 1 in our study. p_{jk} (p_{jk}) denotes the shortest path length from u_i^c (u_j) to one of the early adopters u_k^c. We considered all directed edges as having the same length with 1, so the length of a shortest path equals the number of edges on this path. Corresponding to the loss function $\mathcal{L}$, this function is concerned with the difference between the length from a positive user u_i^c to its early adopters set $E\left(u_i^c\right)$ and the length from a negative user u_j to its early adopters set $E\left(u_i^c\right)$. To measure the length of the shortest paths from a node to a set of nodes, time-decay influence was used to obtain the weighted average value. max $(x, 0)$ retains the positive part of x, which means that the margin is changed only if the positive user is truly closer to the early adopters set than the negative user in the graph.

31.2.3 Diffusion Prediction

Based on learned representation and the learning model, we proposed a corresponding diffusion prediction method. Given a source user u_1^c in a test diffusion cascade c, we predicted diffusion using the following steps:

- Initialize the infected users set as $U_{in}^c = \left\{u_1^c\right\}$ and the uninfected users set as $U_{un}^c = U - \left\{u_1^c\right\}$;
- For a given prediction timestamp t_i, select the most possible user $u_i \in U_{un}^c$ for the current U_{in}^c based on:

$$u_i = \underset{u_{potential}}{argmin} \left\| \sum_{k=1}^{i-1} \frac{\Delta\left(t_i^c, t_k^c\right)}{\sum_{p=1}^{i-1} \Delta\left(t_i^c, t_p^c\right)} \mathbf{z}_k - \mathbf{z}_{potential} \right\|^2$$

- Update $U_{in}^c = U_{in}^c \cup \left\{u_i\right\}$, $U_{un}^c = U_{un}^c - \left\{u_i\right\}$. Repeat steps 2 and 3, until $U_{un}^c = \varnothing$.

Consistent with the learning process, time-decay influence was also considered in the predicting process, which predicted infected users iteratively according to the given timestamp. These timestamps were observed for the infected users of each cascade in the test data, while for other uninfected users in that cascade, we set a fixed discrete time interval. The prediction process stopped after all users in the given network G were infected.

31.3 Experiments

We evaluated our method using a real-world social media dataset (Zhang et al. 2013) extracted from Sina Weibo, a Twitter-like microblogging site, where users are connected by directed following relationships. Information was propagated through the users' reposting behavior based on their followees. Therefore, the reposting log essentially represents an information diffusion process with only temporal orders. The whole dataset contains about 170,000 users and the complete reposting logs of 300,000 original posts among these users. To reduce the effect of sparsity, some preprocesses were conducted on the original dataset: we extracted a subset of the original network by filtering users who appeared less than 30 times in all the reposting logs or had no links with others; and then we selected the corresponding reposting logs related only to these users for the experiment. We chose a time point to partition datasets and used the cascades with the original posts before this time point for training; the remaining cascades were used for testing. The detailed statistics of the experimental dataset are shown in Table 31.1. This sub-network was relatively dense. Benefiting from this dense structure, the diffusion processes were relatively long, with the average cascade length reaching more than 20 in both the training and testing data.

Given a source user of an original post, we aimed to predict users who will most likely to repost this piece of information iteratively. In the diffusion prediction algorithm, we posited that users would repost each message only once; therefore, the final prediction cascades are regarded as ranked lists of all users in this sub-network. We evaluated the performance by three retrieval metrics: Mean Average Precision (MAP), Precision at 5 (P@5), and Precision at 10 (P@10).

To achieve the best performance of our method using this data, we first explored the optimized settings for the experiments, including the choice of initialization and the dimension of representation. As shown in Fig. 31.1, we attempted three ways of initializing the representation: Random, DeepWalk (Perozzi et al. 2014), and Line (Tang et al. 2015), where Line-Order1, Line-Order2, and Line-Both are different settings in Line. Consistent with our expectations, utilizing pre-trained network embeddings as initializations attained higher performances than random initialization. According to this result, we selected Line-Order1 for initialization and set the dimension size of representation at 64 for the following experiments.

We compared the prediction performance with the following methods: Basic Rank, the IC model, and the Content Diffusion Kernel (CDK). Basic Rank represents the method of selecting the next user who had the most diffusion interactions with the current infected users set in the training data iteratively to predict each cascade. The IC model is the most classic one. The CDK refers to the diffusion

Table 31.1 Statistics of the Weibo diffusion data

#Users	# Directed links	# Train cascades	Avg. train cascade length	# Test cascades	Avg. test cascade length
8190	148,752	34,692	20.55	8673	24.47

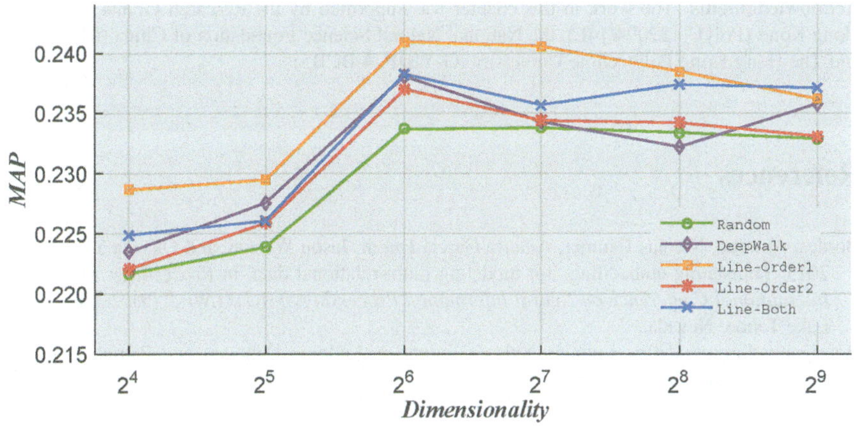

Fig. 31.1 Initialization and dimension settings

Table 31.2 Prediction results of the different methods

Model	Dimensionality	P@5	P@10	MAP
Basic rank	Not available	0.127	0.065	0.155
IC	Not available	0.174	0.092	0.195
CDK	256	0.192	0.109	0.215
Our method	64	**0.226**	**0.125**	**0.241**

representation learning model proposed by Bourigault et al. (2014), whose work is the most relevant to ours.

Table 31.2 shows the performance of our method and other baselines in the temporal prediction task. As mentioned above, the IC model is not very fit for such data, but its performance was a little better than that of Basic Rank. Diffusion representation learning methods showed a better prediction ability. In this experiment, we tuned the parameters of the CDK and found that it required a dimension of 256 to achieve the best performance. However, our method still outperformed that of the CDK, with a relatively smaller latent space.

31.4 Conclusion

In this chapter, we addressed the information temporal diffusion prediction problem on social media data. We proposed a representation learning model and a corresponding prediction method to translate the diffusion relationships among users in a continuous space by combining the time-decay group influence and the graph information appropriately. The experimental results witnessed better performance of our method than the other representative methods. For future work, we expect to establish a synthetic learning model that can jointly learn diffusion relationships and graph embeddings.

Acknowledgments The work in this chapter was supported by the Research Grants Council of Hong Kong (PolyU 152094/14E), the National Natural Science Foundation of China (61272291), and The Hong Kong Polytechnic University (G-YBJP, 4-BCB5).

References

Bordes, Antoine, Nicolas Usunier, Alberto Garcia-Duran, Jason Weston, and Oksana Yakhnenko. 2013. Translating embeddings for modeling multi-relational data. In *Proceedings of the 26th International Conference on Neural Information Processing Systems (NIPS'13)*, 2:2787–2795. Lake Tahoe, Nevada.

Bourigault, Simon, Cedric Lagnier, Sylvain Lamprier, Ludovic Denoyer, and Patrick Gallinari. 2014. Learning social network embeddings for predicting information diffusion. In *Proceedings of the 7th ACM International Conference on Web Search and Data Mining (WSDM 2014)*, 393–402. New York City, New York.

Gomez-Rodriguez, Manuel, David Balduzzi, Bernhard Schölkopf, and Getoor T. Scheffer. 2011. Uncovering the temporal dynamics of diffusion networks. In *Proceedings of the 28th International Conference on Machine Learning (ICML 2011)*, 561–568. Bellevue, Washington.

Guille, Adrien, and Hakim Hacid. 2012. A predictive model for the temporal dynamics of information diffusion in online social networks. In *Proceedings of the 21st International Conference on World Wide Web*, 1145–1152. Lyon, France.

Lafferty, John, and Guy Lebanon. 2005. Diffusion kernels on statistical manifolds. *Journal of Machine Learning Research* 6(6):129–163.

Perozzi, Bryan, Rami Al-Rfou, and Steven Skiena. 2014. DeepWalk: Online learning of social representations. In *Proceedings of the 20th ACM SIGKDD International Conference on Knowledge Discovery and Data Mining*, 701–710. New York City, New York.

Saito, Kazumi, Ryohei Nakano, and Masahiro Kimura. 2008. Prediction of information diffusion probabilities for independent cascade model. In *Proceedings of the 12th International Conference on Knowledge-Based and Intelligent Information and Engineering Systems (KES 2008)*, 67–75. Zagreb, Croatia.

Tang, Jian, Meng Qu, Mingzhe Wang, Ming Zhang, Jun Yan, and Qiaozhu Mei. 2015. Line: Large-scale information network embedding. In *Proceedings of the 24th International Conference on World Wide Web*, 1067–1077. Florence, Italy.

Zhang, Jing, Biao Liu, Jie Tang, Ting Chen, and Juanzi Li. 2013. Social influence locality for modeling retweeting behaviors. In *Proceedings of the Twenty-Third International Joint Conference on Artificial Intelligence*, 2761–2767. Beijing, China.

Part V
Chinese Language Resources

Chapter 32
Chinese Language Resources: A Comprehensive Compendium

Anran Li, Weidong Zhan, Jia-Fei Hong, Zhao-Ming Gao, and Chu-Ren Huang

Abstract This chapter will present a collective effort to compile a comprehensive repository of accessible Chinese language resources that can be used online, licensed for use, or accessed in published form. The compendium will be presented in three parts according to each language resource's type of accessibility, which is a direct consequence of the type of relevant information provided for each resource. Within each accessibility type, the resources were then further divided according to the following resource types: integrated resources, corpora, lexical resources, and wordnet/ontology. We believe that this four-way classification system will facilitate intuitive searches. However, this design will make it difficult to search for a resource within the same class due to having to rely on the alphabetic order of the titles of the resources. Lastly, it is important for our readers to bear in mind that such a repository is bound to be incomplete given the scale and distributional nature of the resources and the productivity of new resource construction. We plan to post this compendium online to allow easier access and provide updates in the future.

Keywords Repository of resources · Corpora · Mandarin · Languages in China

A. Li (✉) · C.-R. Huang
Department of Chinese and Bilingual Studies, The Hong Kong Polytechnic University, Hong Kong, China
e-mail: 17903045r@connect.polyu.hk; churen.huang@polyu.edu.hk

W. Zhan
Department of Chinese Language and Literature, Peking University, Beijing, China
e-mail: zwd@pku.edu.cn

J.-F. Hong
Department of Chinese as a Second Language, National Taiwan Normal University, Taipei, Taiwan
e-mail: jiafeihong@ntnu.edu.tw

Z.-M. Gao
Department of Foreign Languages and Literatures, National Taiwan University, Taipei, Taiwan
e-mail: zmgao@ntu.edu.tw

C.-R. Huang et al. (eds.), *Chinese Language Resources*, Text, Speech and Language Technology 49, https://doi.org/10.1007/978-3-031-38913-9_32

32.1 Online Resources

32.1.1 Integrated Resources

Resource title	Developer and maintainer/author/host	Web sites	Notes
Adventures in Wen-Land 文國尋寶記—中小學語文知識網路	Institute of Linguistics, Academia Sinica, 中央研究院語言學研究所/ Chu-Ren Huang, Feng-Ju Lo et al. 黃居仁, 羅鳳珠 等	http://wen.ling.sinica.edu.tw/ http://cls.lib.ntu.edu.tw/wen	This is an integrated resource, including corpora of elementary school textbooks, lexica, classical Chinese literature, and references such as dictionaries, as well as language learning games and tools. This resource is intended to be used by advanced learners as well as teachers (for the preparation of teaching materials). As this is an integrated resource, some external links do not function now but the two mirror sites have preserved some unique functions
Audio Media Center of the National Language Resource Monitoring and Research Center 国家语言资源监测与研究中心有声媒体分中心	Communication University of China 中国传媒大学	http://ling.cuc.edu.cn	This platform has eight language resources and/or language tools: homophone auto-generation software, parallel corpus retrieval software (CUC_ParaConc), multilingual corpus processing software (HyConc), resources for neology research, charts for diachronic changes in media language, a national public opinion database of language and characters, a media language corpus, media language corpus segmentation, and an annotation system

(continued)

Resource title	Developer and maintainer/author/host	Web sites	Notes
Buddhist Electronic Texts Integration of the Chinese Buddhist Electronic Texts Association (CBETA) 中華電子佛典協會電子佛典集成	Chinese Buddhist Electronic Texts Association 中華電子佛典協會	http://www.cbeta.org/ http://cbetaonline.dila.edu.tw/	The CBETA aims to digitalize and share all Chinese Buddhist texts. The CBETA database can be accessed online, freely downloaded after registration, or obtained on a CD. The online search tools meet state-of-the-art corpus linguistic requirements and are essential resources for religion, culture, and language studies, especially in terms of the impact of Buddhism on Chinese. This is also one of the largest historical corpora of translated texts in the world
Chinese Classics on the Web 網路展書讀	Yuan Ze University, 元智大學/Feng-ju Lo 羅鳳珠	http://cls.lib.ntu.edu.tw/	This is the aggregated website of Feng-ju Lo's life-long dedication to digital humanities for classical Chinese literature. The content ranges from the Four great books to Tang and Song poetry, Ming Dynasty plays, the great Chinese novels, and Southern-Min vernacular literature. Each web site explores different technologies and showcases different ways to integrate texts for reading, teaching, and research
Chinese-English Index System of the National Academy for Educational Research (Trial Version) 國家教育研究院華英雙語索引典系統(試用版)	National Academy for Educational Research 國家教育研究院	http://coct.naer.edu.tw/bc/	This corpus contains a collection of articles from the fields of literature, science, finance and economics, the arts, ideology, culture, global, and entertainment over the past

(continued)

Resource title	Developer and maintainer/author/host	Web sites	Notes
			20 years. These articles have both Chinese and English versions. The Chinese parts of the articles are shown in traditional Chinese and the means of expression is Taiwan Chinese
Digital Resources Center for Global Chinese Teaching and Learning 全球華語文數位教與學資源中心	Institute of Linguistics, Academia Sinica 中央研究院語言學研究所/ Chin-Chuan Cheng, Chu-Ren Huang et al. 鄭錦全, 黃居仁 等	http://elearning.ling.sinica.edu.tw	This resource center is linked to multiple corpora. The central piece is a platform that provides *Word-Focused Extensive Reading* (一詞泛讀) to guide learners automatically through corpus-generated data in small chunks. It is also linked to the Key Word in Context (KWIC) interfaces of multiple Academia Sinica corpora and generates only three sentences at a time based on several user-designated criteria (such as easiness, synonyms, etc.)
Minority Languages Center of the National Language Resource Monitoring and Research Center 国家语言资源监测与研究中心少数民族语言分中心	Minzu University of China 中央民族大学	http://nmlr.muc.edu.cn/ziyuanzhongxin/	This platform contains several minority language corpora, including Mongol, Tibetan, the Uygur language, the Kazak language, etc.
Overseas Chinese Center of the National Language Resource Monitoring and Research Center 国家语言资源监测与研究中心海外华语研究分中心	Jinan University 暨南大学	https://huayu.jnu.edu.cn/source.aspx	This platform contains many corpora, word lists, language tools, and many other language resources, which are mainly focused on the teaching of Chinese as a foreign language, especially in Southeast Asia's condition

(continued)

Resource title	Developer and maintainer/author/host	Web sites	Notes
Print Media Center of the National Language Resource Monitoring and Research Center 国家语言资源监测与研究中心平面媒体分中心	Beijing Language and Culture University 北京语言大学	http://cnlr.blcu.edu.cn/	This platform has five parts: the National Language Resources Dynamic Circulation Corpus (DCC, 10 billion characters from 18 newspapers over the past 10 years); the Traditional Culture Diachronic Corpus (CCC, corpus of ancient books and records); the Semantic Cloud Platform (SCP, enables people to see the collocation conditions of the DCC and has a word-embedding function); the Language Calculation Lab (LC-LAB); and the Green Book of Chinese Language Usage Condition
Scripta Sinica 漢籍全文資料庫計畫	Academia Sinica 中央研究院	hanchi.ihp.sinica.edu.tw	Scripta Sinica is the largest Chinese full-text database and it encompasses an enormous breadth of historical materials, such as almost all the important Chinese classics, especially those related to Chinese history. It started in 1984 as the first major Chinese digital archives project and now contains 1173 titles and more than 665 million characters
SouWenJieZi—A Linguistic KnowledgeNet 搜文解字 - 語文知識網路	Institute of Linguistics, Academia Sinica, 中央研究院語言學研究所/ Chu-Ren Huang, Feng-ju Lo et al. 黃居仁, 羅鳳珠 等	http://words.sinica.edu.tw	This platform contains an electronic dictionary, a literature knowledge center, an ancient writing and Chinese characters evolution knowledge base, and several language games. This is

(continued)

Resource title	Developer and maintainer/author/host	Web sites	Notes
			part of the Language Archives Project
Taiwan Digital Archives Program: Language Archives (Phase I, II) 語言典藏計畫(第一期、第二期)	Institute of Linguistics, Academia Sinica 中央研究院語言學研究所/ Chu-Ren Huang et al. 黃居仁 等	http://languagearchives.sinica.edu.tw/cht/index.php.html	This is the first integrated language archiving project in greater China. The coverage includes Pre-Qin excavated texts, Classical Chinese, Modern Mandarin, Taiwan Southern-Min and Hakka from historical perspectives, and endangered Formosan languages
Taiwan Southern Min and Hakka Archives 台灣閩客語語言典藏	Institute of Linguistics, Academia Sinica 中央研究院語言學研究所/ Chin-Chuan Cheng, Min-hua Chiang et al. 鄭錦全, 江敏華 等	http://museum02.digitalarchives.tw/ndap/2003/banlamgu	This site contains language resources for both Taiwan Southern Min and Taiwan Hakka. The content includes fieldwork data as well as historical data in searchable corpus format
The Global Database of Events, Language, and Tone Project 事件、语言与音调全球数据库项目	Kalev Leetaru (from Yahoo!) Kalev Leetaru (雅虎) and Georgetown University 乔治城大学	https://www.gdeltproject.org/data.html	This corpus is part of the Google GDELT Project. The 2015 data alone has recorded nearly three quarters of a trillion emotional snapshots and more than 1.5 billion location references, while its total archives span more than 215 years. The corpus enables users to retrieve and analyze tasks

32.1.2 Corpora

Resource title	Developer and maintainer/author/host	Web sites	Notes
A Collection of Chinese Corpora and	The University of Leeds 利兹大学		This corpus contains three subcorpuses: the

(continued)

Resource title	Developer and maintainer/author/host	Web sites	Notes
Frequency Lists Sharoff 汉语综合语料库		http://corpus.leeds.ac.uk/query-zh.html	Chinese Internet Corpus (280 million words); the Lancaster Corpus of Mandarin Chinese; and the Chinese Business Corpus (30 million words)
Academia Sinica Tagged Corpus of Ancient Chinese 中央研究院上古漢語標記語料庫	Institute of Linguistics, Institute of Information Science, Academia Sinica 中央研究院資訊科學研究所, 語言學研究所/Pei-Chuan Wei, Paul Thompson, Chenghui Liu, Chu-Ren Huang, Keh-Jiann Chen 魏培泉, Paul Thompson, 劉承慧, 黃居仁, 陳克健	http://lingcorpus.iis.sinica.edu.tw/ancient/	This is part of the historical Chinese tagged corpus from Academia Sinica, the first segmented and PoS-tagged corpus of Classical Chinese corpora in the world. The Ancient Chinese Corpus covers Pre-Qin and Western Han texts, which represent some of the oldest (near) vernacular texts of Chinese
Academia Sinica Tagged Corpus of Early Mandarin Chinese 中央研究院近代漢語標記語料庫	Institute of Linguistics, Institute of Information Science, Academia Sinica 中央研究院資訊科學研究所, 語言學研究所/Pei-Chuan Wei, Paul Thompson, Chenghui Liu, Chu-Ren Huang, Keh-Jiann Chen 魏培泉, Paul Thompson, 劉承慧, 黃居仁, 陳克健	http://lingcorpus.iis.sinica.edu.tw/early/	This is part of the historical Chinese tagged corpus from Academia Sinica, the first segmented and PoS-tagged corpus of Classical Chinese corpora in the world. The Middle Chinese Corpus covers the Wei and Jin Dynasties to the Northern and Southern Dynasties and focuses on vernacular texts, including many translated Buddhist texts. This represents the period in which the Chinese language underwent critical changes
Academia Sinica Tagged Corpus of Middle Chinese 中央研究院中古漢語標記語料庫	Institute of Linguistics, Institute of Information Science, Academia Sinica 中央研究院資訊科學研究所, 語言學研究所/Pei-chuan Wei, Paul Thompson,	http://lingcorpus.iis.sinica.edu.tw/middle/	This is part of the historical Chinese tagged corpus from Academia Sinica, the first segmented and PoS-tagged corpus of Classical Chinese

(continued)

Resource title	Developer and maintainer/author/host	Web sites	Notes
	Chenghui Liu, Chu-Ren Huang, Keh-Jiann Chen 魏培泉, Paul Thompson, 劉承慧, 黃居仁, 陳克健		corpora in the world. The Early Mandarin Chinese Corpus covers Yuan to Qing vernacular texts, mostly novels and plays. This represents the period in which Mandarin Chinese was established as the common spoken language for the educated
Asian Scientific Paper Excerpt Corpus-JC 亚洲科技文献摘要语料库	Japan Science and Technology Agency 日本科学技术振兴处 National Institute of Information and Communications Technology, Japan 日本国立情报通信研究所	http://lotus.kuee.kyoto-u.ac.jp/ASPEC/	This platform consists of a Japanese-English paper abstract corpus (ASPEC-JE, three million parallel sentences) and a Japanese-Chinese paper excerpt corpus (ASPEC-JC, 680,000 parallel sentences)
Balanced Corpus of Ancient Chinese (State Language Commission) 国家语言文字工作委员会古籍语料库	State Language Commission 国家语言文字工作委员会	http://www.aihanyu.org/cncorpus/ACindex.aspx	This Ancient Chinese corpus contains nearly 100 million characters, including most of the ancient texts in *Si Ku Quan Shu* (四库全书), which includes different kinds of ancient books and records from the Zhou Dynasty to the Qing Dynasty
Balanced Corpus of Modern Chinese (State Language Commission) 国家语言文字工作委员会现代汉语平衡语料库	State Language Commission 国家语言文字工作委员会	http://www.aihanyu.org/cncorpus/CnCindex.aspx	This Modern Chinese corpus contains 9487 writings. The corpus has 19,455,328 characters (including Chinese characters, alphabets, numbers, punctuation marks, etc.), 12,842,116 tokens (including monosyllabic words, disyllabic words, polysyllabic words, letter words, foreign words, numeric strings, punctuation

(continued)

Resource title	Developer and maintainer/author/host	Web sites	Notes
			marks, etc.), and 162,875 types. Among all the 162,875 word forms, 151,300 are Chinese words
BCC Online Corpus 北京语言大学汉语语料库	Beijing Language and Culture University 北京语言大学	http://bcc.blcu.edu.cn/	This Chinese corpus contains about 15 billion characters. It includes writings from many different fields (two billion from newspapers, three billion from literature, three billion from Weibo, three billion from the science and technology fields, two billion from Ancient Chinese, and two billion from other sources)
Bilingual Laws Information System (BLIS) 香港律政司雙語法例資料系統	Department of Justice, The Government of Hong Kong SAR 香港律政司	https://www.elegislation.gov.hk/search	This corpus provides current and past versions of consolidated legislation dating back to June 30, 1997, and PDF copies marked "verified copy" have official legal status
CCL Chinese-English Aligned Parallel Corpus 北京大学中国语言学研究中心汉英对齐平行语料库	Center for Chinese Linguistics, Peking University 北京大学中国语言学研究中心/Weidong Zhan, Rui Guo et al. 詹卫东, 郭锐 等	http://ccl.pku.edu.cn:8080/ccl_corpus/index_bi.jsp	This parallel corpus has 233,589 sentence pairs in 2374 aligned documents. In the corpus, there are 259,425 Chinese sentences and 287,924 English sentences, which cover both written language and spoken language. It also contains practical writings, literature works, and news from different domains, such as politics, science, sports, social culture, industry and commerce, the arts, and movies

(continued)

Resource title	Developer and maintainer/author/host	Web sites	Notes
CCL Online Corpus 北京大学中国语言学研究中心语料库	Center for Chinese Linguistics, Peking University 北京大学中国语言学研究中心/Weidong Zhan, Rui Guo et al. 詹卫东, 郭锐 等	http://ccl.pku.edu.cn:8080/ccl_corpus	The scale of this corpus is 700 million characters. The articles cover different kinds of registers and date from the eleventh century B.C. to the contemporary era. The content is raw materials
Chinese Academic Journal Corpus (Chinese Texts) 中文學術語料庫	National Taiwan Normal University 國立臺灣師範大學	http://140.122.83.220:5566/cqpweb/chineseall/	This corpus contains 1000 articles from the core journals of the humanities and social science fields in Taiwan. Its scale is about nine million characters
Chinese Discourse Annotated Corpus of the Harbin Institute of Technology 哈尔滨工业大学中文篇章关系语料库	Harbin Institute of Technology 哈尔滨工业大学	http://ir.hit.edu.cn/hit-cdtb/	This corpus contains 525 annotated texts. The raw texts are from four kinds of texts in OntoNotes 4.0: "broad news," "magazines," "news wires," and "web." For each of the texts, the corpus can annotate three kinds of discourse relations: clause discourse relations; complex sentence discourse relations; and sentence group discourse relations
Chinese Interlanguage Corpus 華語仲介語語料庫	National Academy for Educational Research 國家教育研究院	http://coct.naer.edu.tw/cqpweb/learners/	The language materials in this corpus mainly came from non-native Chinese speakers' essays (from universities in Taiwan) and a testing corpus that is accredited by the Steering Committee for the Test of Proficiency—Huayu (Taiwan)

(continued)

Resource title	Developer and maintainer/author/host	Web sites	Notes
Chinese-English Parallel Corpus 中英雙語平行語料庫	National Taiwan Normal University 國立臺灣師範大學	http://140.122.83.198:7002/	This corpus contains materials from English film subtitles and Hong Kong news. Based on alignment technology, it enables users to retrieve both Chinese and English materials
COCT Spoken Language Corpus COCT 口語語料庫	National Academy for Educational Research 國家教育研究院	http://coct.naer.edu.tw/cqpweb/bl/	This corpus contains a collection of different kinds of programs, including law, politics, military science, finance and economics, current events, science, culture, education, lifestyles, and the arts, from the past 10 years. The language that is used in the programs is limited to Mandarin Chinese in Taiwan
COCT Written Language Corpus COCT 書面語語料庫	National Academy for Educational Research 國家教育研究院	http://coct.naer.edu.tw/cqpweb/yl2016/	This corpus contains articles from many different fields, including philosophy, religion, science, applied science, social sciences, history, geography, language and literature, the arts, finance, and entertainment, from the past 10 years. All these articles came from books with an ISBN code. The corpus also contains news from *United Daily News* and *China Times* from 1999 to 2016. The language that is used in the programs is limited to Mandarin Chinese in Taiwan
Corpus of Political Speeches 政治演講語料庫	Hong Kong Baptist University 香港浸會大學/Kathleen Ahrens	http://digital.lib.hkbu.edu.hk/corpus/index.php	This is a comparable corpus of political speeches from four different jurisdictions: the Corpus of

(continued)

Resource title	Developer and maintainer/author/host	Web sites	Notes
			U.S. Presidential Speeches (1789–2015); the Corpus of Policy Addresses by Hong Kong Governors (1984–1996) and Hong Kong Chief Executives (1997–2014); the Corpus of Speeches Given on New Year's Day and Double Tenth Day by Taiwan Presidents (1978–2014); and the Corpus of Reports on the Work of the Government by Premiers of the People's Republic of China (1984–2013)
Early Cantonese Colloquial Texts: A Database 早期粵語口語文獻資料庫	Hong Kong University of Science and Technology 香港科技大學	http://ccl.ust.hk/ccl/useful_resources/useful_resources.html	This corpus contains a collection of seven kinds of Cantonese teaching dictionaries and textbooks compiled by early Western scholars: *Vocabulary of the Canton Dialect*; *Chinese Chrestomathy in the Canton Dialect*; *Cantonese Made Easy* (four editions); and *A Chinese and English Phrase Book in the Canton Dialect*
Early Cantonese Tagged Database 早期粵語標注語料庫	Hong Kong University of Science and Technology 香港科技大學	http://ccl.ust.hk/ccl/useful_resources/useful_resources.html	This corpus contains is a collection of 10 literatures, including *The Gospel According to St. Mark* (in English and Cantonese), *Easy Phrases in the Canton Dialect of the Chinese Language*, *A Chinese and English Phrase Book in the Canton Dialect*,

(continued)

Resource title	Developer and maintainer/author/host	Web sites	Notes
			Progressive and Idiomatic Sentences in Cantonese Colloquial, and so on. Its scale is about 160,000 characters
English-Chinese Parallel Concordancer 漢英平行語料庫	The Hong Kong Institute of Education 香港教育學院	http://ec-concord.ied.edu.hk/paraconc	The scale of this corpus is 576,724 Chinese characters (413,823 words). It enables users to search for concordances and see the translation of texts
HSK Learner Corpus of Composition Texts 北京语言大学 HSK 汉语水平考试动态作文语料库	Beijing Language and Culture University 北京语言大学	http://bcc.blcu.edu.cn/hsk	This is an interlanguage corpus collection of 11,569 Chinese essays (about 4.3 million characters) that were written by non-native speakers. All the essays were collected from the essay test of the Chinese Proficiency Test (HSK) from 1992 to 2005
Intelligent Collocation Search Engine 智慧搭配詞搜尋引擎	National Taiwan Normal University 國立臺灣師範大學	http://140.122.83.243:8000/ICE/Index.htm	This corpus contains a collection of articles from the fields of business, journalism, justice, academic research, finance and economics, and travel. It has the function of collocation word retrieval
Korean-Chinese Parallel Corpus 韩汉平行语料库	Korea Advanced Institute of Science and Technology 韩国科学技术学院	http://semanticweb.kaist.ac.kr/home/index.php/KAIST_Corpus	This platform has many corpora, including a Chinese-English-Korean multilingual corpus that contains 60,000 sentences, a DongaKorean-English-Japanese-Chinese multilingual newspaper corpus that

(continued)

Resource title	Developer and maintainer/author/host	Web sites	Notes
			contains 1791 files, and so on
Learn Chinese Online via Podcast and MP3 洛杉矶汉语学习中心语音学习资料库	Los Angeles Chinese Learning Center, USA 洛杉矶汉语学习中心	http://chinese-school.netfirms.com/learn-Chinese-online.html	This recorded corpus enables users to learn Chinese online. It contains recordings of pinyin, vocabularies, phrases, and so on
Linguistic Variation in Chinese Speech Communities (LIVAC) 香港城市大學泛華語共時同題語料庫	City University of Hong Kong 香港城市大學	http://www.livac.org/search.php	This is a synchronous Chinese corpus, with a scale of 2.5 billion characters. Six hundred million characters have been processed and analyzed. The texts are from different Chinese communities. It also possesses an ever-expanding Pan-Chinese dictionary of more than two million entries
NICT Japanese-Chinese Parallel Corpus 日本国立情报通信研究所日汉平行语料库	National Institute of Information and Communications Technology, Japan 日本国立情报通信研究所	http://universal.elra.info/product_info.php?cPath=42_43&products_id=2044	This corpus contains 38,383 sentence pairs collected from Japanese newspapers and manually translated into Chinese. Its scale is 947,066 Japanese words and 877,859 Chinese words, all encoded in Unicode. The corpus is aligned at word and phrase levels. The texts are segmented and annotated with part-of-speech tags, morphological structures, and syntactic structures
NTU Multilingual Corpus 南洋理工大学多语语料库	Nanyang Technological University 南洋理工大学	http://compling.hss.ntu.edu.sg/ntumc/	This corpus contains 375,000 words (15,000 sentences) in six languages (English, Chinese, Japanese, Korean, Indonesian, and Vietnamese). It enables

(continued)

Resource title	Developer and maintainer/author/host	Web sites	Notes
			users to retrieve words by concepts, word, lemmas, parts-of-speech, etc.
Sinica Corpus 中央研究院現代漢語平衡語料庫	Chinese Language and Knowledge Processing Group, Institute of Information Science, and Institute of Linguistics, Academia Sinica 中央研究院資訊科學研究所, 語言學研究所 中文詞知識庫小組/Keh-Jiann Chen, Chu-Ren Huang 陳克健, 黃居仁	http://asbc.iis.sinica.edu.tw/ http://lingcorpus.iis.sinica.edu.tw/modern/ (five million word version)	The Academia Sinica Balanced Corpus of Modern Chinese (Sinica Corpus) is the first PoS-tagged balanced corpus of Mandarin Chinese, as well as the first Chinese corpus on the web (since 1997). The current version (4.0) contains more than 10 million words (with more than 14 million characters). The corpus search interface allows KWIC searches (both with or without PoS) and has many collocation calculation tools, such as Mutual Information (MI) calculation
Spoken Language Corpus of Chinese Learners (Spoken Language Test) 華語學習者口語語料庫(口語考試)	National Taiwan Normal University 國立臺灣師範大學	http://140.122.83.243/mp3c/	The spoken language materials in this corpus are from the recorded documents of the spoken language test in the Test of Chinese as a Foreign Language (TOCFL, the test for Teaching Chinese as a Second Language [TCSL] learners) from 2008 to April 2011. Its scale is 770,000 characters. The corpus enables users to retrieve the usage conditions and phonological representations of learners
Taiwan Corpus of Child Mandarin	National Taiwan University, Education	http://tccm.corpus.eduhk.hk/	This corpus contains the CHILDES-style

(continued)

Resource title	Developer and maintainer/author/host	Web sites	Notes
(TCCM) 台灣兒童語言語料庫	University of Hong Kong 國立臺灣大學 香港教育大學/Hintat Cheung 張顯達		language acquisition corpus Children Learning Mandarin in Taiwan
Taiwan Presidential Corpus 遷台後歷屆總統元旦及國慶文告資料庫	Institute of Linguistics, Academia Sinica 中央研究院語言學研究所/Chu-Ren Huang, Kathleen Ahrens, Weilun Lu 黃居仁, Kathleen Ahrens, 呂維倫	http://140.109.19.114/president/	This corpus consists of all major announcements on New Year's Day, national days, etc. by the first four presidents of Taiwan
The Hong Kong Bilingual Child Language Corpus 香港雙語兒童語言資料庫	Chinese University of Hong Kong 香港中文大學	http://www.cuhk.edu.hk/lin/home/bilingual.htm	This corpus contains longitudinal speech data from six bilingual children exposed to Cantonese and English from birth. These children grew up in a one-parent-one-language environment where each parent was a native speaker of the respective language
The UCLA Written Chinese Corpus 加州大学洛杉矶分校汉语书面语语料库	University of California Los Angeles 加州大学洛杉矶分校 University Centre for Computer Corpus Research on Language of Lancaster University 兰开斯特大学计算机语料库及语言研究中心/Hongyin Tao, Richard Xiao 陶红印, 肖忠华	http://www.lancaster.ac.uk/fass/projects/corpus/UCLA/default.htm	This corpus is the Chinese counterpart of the Freiburg-LOB Corpus of British English (FLOB) and the Brown corpora of British and American English. The samples in the corpus were collected from written Modern Chinese available from the Internet from 2000 to 2012. Its scale is 1,119,930 words
Web-based Chinese Corpus 臺灣網路語料庫	National Taiwan Normal University 國立臺灣師範大學	http://140.122.83.220:5566/cqpweb/chacademicjournal/	Based on the concept of "Web as Corpus," this corpus directly uses web resources as materials. Its scale is 400 million characters
Wikidata Corpus 维基百科语料库	Wikimedia Foundation 维基媒体基金会	https://github.com/Samurais/wikidata-corpus	This corpus trains data from Chinese Wikidata using the

(continued)

Resource title	Developer and maintainer/author/host	Web sites	Notes
			word2vec method for word-embedding tasks
Written Language Corpus of Chinese Learners (Writing Practice and Writing Test) 華語學習者書面語語料庫(寫作練習與 寫作考試)	National Taiwan Normal University 國立臺灣師範大學	http://kitty.2y.idv.tw/~hjchen/cwrite-mtc/main.cgi http://kitty.2y.idv.tw/~hjchen/cwrite/main.cgi	These two corpuses contain Chinese essays written by non-native Chinese learners. The first one is a collection of the practice writing essays of non-native Chinese learners in National Taiwan Normal University from 2010 to 2012. Its scale is two million characters. The second one is comprised of materials from the writing test of the TOCFL (the test for TCSL learners) from 2006 to 2012. The scale of the corpus is 1.5 million characters. Both corpuses enable users to perform online retrieval

32.1.3 Lexical Resources

Resource title	Developer and maintainer/author/host	Web sites	Notes
Data Bank of Common First and Last Characters of Chinese Words 常用詞首、詞尾字資料庫	Chinese Language and Knowledge Processing Group, Institute of Information Science, Academia Sinica 中央研究院資訊科學研究所 中文詞知識庫小組/Keh-Jiann Chen, Chu-Ren Huang 陳克健, 黃居仁	http://140.109.19.103/affix/	This knowledge base is a collection of 4025 commonly used first and last characters of nouns and verbs from the Sinica Corpus. All the characters are provided with senses, categories in *Tong Yi Ci Ci Lin* (for nouns), word formation rules (for verbs), and examples

(continued)

Resource title	Developer and maintainer/author/host	Web sites	Notes
Lexicon of Pre-Qin Oracle, Bronze Inscription and Bamboo Scripts 先秦甲骨金文簡牘詞彙庫	Institute of History and Philology, Academia Sinica 中央研究院歷史語言研究所/Chao-Jung Chen, Bo-Sheng Jhong, Guo-Hua Yuan, Ming-chorng Hwang 陳昭容, 鍾柏生, 袁國華, 黃銘崇	http://inscription.asdc.sinica.edu.tw/	This is an online lexicon of words from original excavated Pre-Qin scripts written on oracle bones, bronze inscription, and bamboo. Actual graphic forms, variants, and PoS are presented. This is one of the Language Archives projects
Online Dictionary of Taiwan Sign Language 台灣手語線上辭典	The Taiwan Sign Language Research Group, Institute of Linguistics, National Chung Cheng University 國立中正大學語言學研究所 臺灣手語研究小組/James H.-Y. Tai and S. C. Jane Tsay	http://tsl.ccu.edu.tw/web/chinese/	This digital dictionary contains video files of Taiwan Sign Language words
Word Index of the Balanced Corpus of Modern Chinese (State Language Commission) 国家语言文字工作委员会现代汉语平衡语料库字词索引	State Language Commission 国家语言文字工作委员会	http://www.aihanyu.org/cncorpus/WDindex.aspx	This is a word list extracted from the Balanced Corpus of Modern Chinese (State Language Commission). Each of the items has information on part-of-speech and word frequency

32.1.4 *Wordnet/Ontology*

Resource title	Developer and maintainer/author/host	Web sites	Notes
Chinese Open WordNet 汉语开放词网	Nanyang Technological University 南洋理工大学	http://compling.hss.ntu.edu.sg/cow/	This wordnet is based on the concepts of the Princeton WordNet and the Global WordNet Grid. It contains 42,315 synsets, 79,812 senses, and 61,536 unique words

(continued)

Resource title	Developer and maintainer/author/host	Web sites	Notes
Chinese WordNet 中文詞彙網路	Institute of Linguistics, Academia Sinica 中央研究院語言學研究所 National Taiwan University 臺灣大學/Chu-Ren Huang, Shu-Kai Hsieh 黃居仁, 謝舒凱	http://cwn.ling.sinica.edu.tw/ http://lope.linguistics.ntu.edu.tw/cwn/ Version 2.0. http://lope.linguistics.ntu.edu.tw/cwn2/	This wordnet, based on the idea of English WordNet, aims to offer integrated materials to distinguish Chinese word senses. Based on the construct of lexical semantics and ontology, it is an effective reference for linguistics researches. It has 5600 word forms and 13,160 senses
CoreNet 核心词网	Korea Advanced Institute of Science and Technology 韩国科学技术学院	http://semanticweb.kaist.ac.kr/home/index.php/CoreNet_Corpus	This is a net of words based on their semantics. It contains a Word-to-Concept System that includes 23,938 Korean words with 58,985 senses and 34,409 Chinese words with 39,352 senses. It also contains a Predicate Case Frame that includes 973 Korean words with 1909 senses and 368 Chinese words
E-HowNet Ontology 廣義知網知識本體架構	Chinese Language and Knowledge Processing Group, Institute of Information Science, Academia Sinica 中央研究院資訊科學所中文詞知識庫小組/Keh-Jiann Chen 陳克健	http://ehownet.iis.sinica.edu.tw/index.php	This knowledge base connects more than 90,000 entries in the Chinese Knowledge Information Processing (CKIP) Chinese Lexical Knowledge Base to HowNet nodes. It aims to build a vocabulary knowledge base that can express the relationships between

(continued)

Resource title	Developer and maintainer/author/host	Web sites	Notes
			concepts and the relationships among the properties of the concepts
Emotion Ontology of Chinese Words 情感词汇本体库	Dalian University of Technology 大连理工大学	http://ir.dlut.edu.cn/EmotionOntologyDownload	This ontology describes Chinese words and phrases from many different aspects, including part-of-speech, emotion category, emotion intensity, polarity, etc. The ontology is based on Ekman's emotion classification system (six basic emotions: anger, disgust, fear, happiness, sadness, and surprise). It classifies emotions into seven main classes and 21 subclasses
Hantology 漢字知識本體	Institute of Linguistics, Academia Sinica 中央研究院語言學研究所/Ya-Min Chou, Chu-Ren Huang 周亞民, 黃居仁	http://hantology.ling.sinica.edu.tw/index.htm	This ontology enables users to search for Chinese characters by semantic symbol or input a Chinese character to get the main semantic symbol, and it is composed of semantic symbols and their original senses
The Academia Sinica Bilingual Ontological WordNet (Sinica BOW) 中央研究院中英雙語知識本體詞網	Institute of Linguistics, Institute of Information Science, Academia Sinica 中央研究院語言學研究所, 資訊科學研究所/Chu-Ren Huang 黃居仁	http://bow.ling.sinica.edu.tw	This platform integrates three main resources, which are WordNet, Suggested Upper Merged Ontology (SUMO), and the English-Chinese Translation Equivalents Database (ECTED). Sinica

(continued)

Resource title	Developer and maintainer/author/host	Web sites	Notes
			BOW functions both as an English-Chinese bilingual wordnet and bilingual lexical access to SUMO

32.1.5 Treebanks

Resource title	Developer and maintainer/author/host	Web sites	Notes
Sinica Treebank Version 3.0 中文句結構樹資料庫	Chinese Language and Knowledge Processing Group, Institute of Information Science, Academia Sinica 中央研究院資訊科學所中文詞知識庫小組/Keh-Jiann Chen, Chu-Ren Huang et al. 陳克健, 黃居仁 等	http://turing.iis.sinica.edu.tw/treesearch/	This database includes six documents, 61,087 Chinese tree graphs, and 361,834 words. All the language materials were extracted from the Sinica Corpus. The tree graphs were automatically generated and manually amended. These graphs show the syntactic and semantic information of sentences

32.1.6 Chinese Information Processing Tools

Resource title	Developer and maintainer/author/host	Web sites	Notes
Chinese Segmentation System 中文斷詞系統	Chinese Language and Knowledge Processing Group, Institute of Information Science, Academia Sinica 中央研究院資訊科學所中文詞知識庫小組/Keh-Jiann Chen 陳克健	http://ckipsvr.iis.sinica.edu.tw/	This language tool can extract unknown words from inputted texts and segment the texts (including unknown words). It not only shows the segmentation results and the unknown word list but also shows the operational procedures of the program

(continued)

Resource title	Developer and maintainer/author/host	Web sites	Notes
Chinese Synonyms for Natural Language Processing and Understanding 中文近义词工具包	Hai Liang Wang, Hu Ying Xi	https://github.com/huyingxi/Synonyms	This toolkit can extract Chinese synonyms automatically and calculate the similarity between two Chinese words or sentences
CKIP Chinese Parser 中文剖析系統	Chinese Language and Knowledge Processing Group, Institute of Information Science, Academia Sinica 中央研究院資訊科學所中文詞知識庫小組/Keh-Jiann Chen 陳克健	http://parser.iis.sinica.edu.tw/	This is an online parser that can segment and parse inputted sentences automatically. It can also automatically label the semantic roles of the sentence components
FudanNLP 复旦大学自然语言处理工具包	Fudan University 复旦大学	https://github.com/FudanNLP/fnlp	This toolkit has the functions of Chinese word segmentation, part-of-speech tagging, named entity recognition, keyword extraction, dependency grammar analysis, text categorization, and so on
HanLP: Han Language Processing 汉语言处理系统	Shanghai Linrun Information Technology Ltd. 上海林原信息科技有限公司	http://hanlp.linrunsoft.com/	This is an open-source language tool that can perform multiple tasks, including Chinese word segmentation, part-of-speech tagging, named entity recognition, keyword extraction, auto-abstraction, dependency grammar analysis, text categorization, and so on
ictclas4j Segmenter ictclas4j 中文分词系统	Ying Jiang 姜赢	https://code.google.com/archive/p/ictclas4j/	This segmenter is an open-source project based on FreeICTCLAS (Institute of Computing Technology, Chinese Lexical Analysis System)
Language Cloud of the Harbin Institute of Technology 哈尔滨工业大学语言云	Harbin Institute of Technology 哈尔滨工业大学	http://www.ltp-cloud.com/	This is a language processing platform based on the "Language Technology Platform" (LTP) of the

(continued)

Resource title	Developer and maintainer/author/host	Web sites	Notes
			Harbin Institute of Technology. It offers plenty of NLP technologies such as Chinese word segmentation, part-of-speech tagging, named entity recognition, dependency parsing, and semantic role labeling. It comes in the Python version and the Docker version at https://github.com/HIT-SCIR/pyltp and https://github.com/HIT-SCIR/ltp, respectively
Lingpipe	Alias-i	http://alias-i.com/lingpipe/demos/tutorial/chineseTokens/read-me.html	This is a toolkit for processing text using computational linguistics methods. It can be used to perform tasks such as finding the names of people, organizations, or locations in the news; carrying out classification tasks for Twitter search results automatically; and giving spelling suggestions for queries
NAER Segmentor 國家教育研究院中文分詞系統	National Academy for Educational Research 國家教育研究院	https://github.com/naernlp/Segmentor	This segmentor uses the part-of-speech marking system of Sinica. It can segment traditional Chinese text very quickly, but users cannot use their own dictionaries
Natural Language Toolkit (NLTK) 自然语言处理工具包	Department of Computer and Information Science, University of Pennsylvania 宾夕法尼亚大学计算机与信息科学系/Steven Bird, Edward Loper	http://www.nltk.org/install.html	This is a suite of libraries and programs for symbolic and statistical natural language processing that is written in Python. It has the functions of classification, tokenization, stemming, tagging, parsing,

(continued)

Resource title	Developer and maintainer/author/host	Web sites	Notes
			and semantic reasoning. It contains Chinese data (treebank, segmenter, parser, etc.) from the CKIP group of Academia Sinica
NiuParser 1.3.0 中文句法语义分析系统	Northeastern University, China 东北大学	http://www.niuparser.com	This platform has the functions of Chinese word segmentation, part-of-speech tagging, named entity recognition, machine translation, public opinion analysis, dependency grammar analysis, semantic role labeling, automatic writing, knowledge graphs, and a question-answering system.
NiuTrans 东北大学统计机器翻译系统	Natural Language Processing Laboratory of Northeastern University, China 东北大学自然语言处理实验室	http://www.niutrans.com/niutrans/NiuTrans.ch.html	This is an open-source statistical machine translation system that is written in C++
NLPIR-ICTCLAS Chinese Lexical Analysis System NLPIR-ICTCLAS 汉语分词系统	Hua-Ping Zhang 张华平	http://ictclas.nlpir.org	This segmenter has the functions of Chinese and English word segmentation, part-of-speech tagging, named entity recognition, new word recognition, keyword extraction, and Weibo analysis. It permits users to use their own dictionaries
Polyglot	Rami Al-Rfou	https://pypi.python.org/pypi/polyglot	This is a natural language pipeline that supports massive multilingual applications, including tokenization, language detection, named entity recognition, part-of-speech tagging, sentiment analysis, word embedding, morphological analysis, and transliteration

(continued)

Resource title	Developer and maintainer/author/host	Web sites	Notes
SnowNLP: Simplified Chinese Text Processing 简体中文文本处理工具包		https://github.com/isnowfy/snownlp	This is a class lib for Python. It offers the functions of Chinese word segmentation, part-of-speech tagging, emotion analysis, text categorization, keyword and abstract extraction, and so on
The Stanford Parser 斯坦福句法分析器	Stanford University 斯坦福大学	https://nlp.stanford.edu/software/lex-parser.html	This probabilistic parser gains knowledge from training sets and produces the most likely analysis of new sentences. This is a multilingual parser that can parse different languages, including Chinese, English, German, French, and so on
The Stanford Word Segmenter 斯坦福分词系统	Stanford University 斯坦福大学	https://nlp.stanford.edu/software/segmenter.shtml	This segmenter can perform Chinese word segmentation tasks automatically

32.2 Licensable Resources

32.2.1 Integrated Resources

Resource title	Developer and maintainer/author/host	Web sites	Notes	How to use
Chinese LDC 中文语言资源联盟	Chinese Information Processing Society of China 中国中文信息学会	http://www.chineseldc.org/resource_list.php	This platform creates and collects systematic speech data that can be used in lexicon, language corpus, and instrumental reference researches. It can distribute existing data to departments for education, scientific research, governmental purposes, and the development of industrial technology	Apply and pay

(continued)

Resource title	Developer and maintainer/author/host	Web sites	Notes	How to use
Chinese Lexicons 中文詞知識庫	Chinese Language and Knowledge Processing Group, Institute of Information Science, Academia Sinica 中央研究院資訊科學所中文詞知識庫小組/Keh-Jiann Chen 陳克健	http://ckip.iis.sinica.edu.tw:8080/license/	This platform has several language resources, including Chinese Parser, Sinica Treebank, a Chinese segmentation system, E-HowNet, Chinese word sketches, a public opinion analysis system, a Chinese word-embedding corpus, a Chinese segmentation corpus, and a Chinese news corpus	Apply
Linguistic Data Consortium (LDC) 语言资源联盟	University of Pennsylvania 宾夕法尼亚大学	https://www.ldc.upenn.edu/language-resources	This platform contains a great deal of different language resources that can meet different requirements of users	Apply and pay
Natural Language Toolkit (NLTK) Corpora 自然语言处理工具包数据平台	Natural Language Toolkit (NLTK) 自然语言处理工具包	http://www.nltk.org/nltk_data/	This platform contains dozens of corpora and trained models that can help users to use the Natural Language Toolkit more efficiently	Apply

32.2.2 Corpora

Resource title	Developer and maintainer/author/host	Web sites	Notes	How to use
Chinese Gigaword Corpus Edition 5.0 中文亿词语料库第五版	Linguistic Data Consortium, University of Pennsylvania 宾夕法尼亚大学语言数据联盟/Robert Parker et al.	https://catalog.ldc.upenn.edu/LDC2011T13	The Chinese Gigaword Corpus is the largest Chinese Corpus in the world collected by the LDC. Each new edition is larger than the previous one. Edition 5.0 contains over eight billion (8000 million) characters from *Agence France Presse*, the Central News	Apply and pay

(continued)

Resource title	Developer and maintainer/author/ host	Web sites	Notes	How to use
			Agency (Taiwan), China News Service, *Guangming Daily*, *People's Daily*, *People's Liberation Army Daily*, the Xinhua News Agency, and *Zaobao Newspaper* (Singapore). The only version of the Chinese Gigaword Corpus is Version 2.0	
Chinese Speech Corpus 中文語音語料庫	National Taiwan Normal University 國立臺灣師範大學	http://140.122.83.243/ac/query.php	This corpus contains materials from several Chinese teleplays, which users can retrieve online	Register
CORPUS Program 中文新聞語料庫	Chinese Language and Knowledge Processing Group, Institute of Information Science, Academia Sinica 中央研究院資訊科學所中文詞知識庫小組/Keh-Jiann Chen, Chu-Ren Huang et al. 陳克健, 黃居仁 等	http://www.aclclp.org.tw/use_cp_c.php	This corpus has 14 million characters. The material was collected from *United Daily News*, *China Times*, *Liberty Times*, and *CommonWealth Magazine*	Apply and pay
Standard Segmentation Corpus 中文分詞語料庫	Chinese Language and Knowledge Processing Group, Institute of Information Science, Academia Sinica 中央研究院資訊科學所中文詞知識庫小組/Chu-Ren Huang, Keh-Jiann Chen 黃居仁, 陳克健	http://www.aclclp.org.tw/use_ssc_c.php	This corpus has two million words, which are segmented only; the words do not have part-of-speech tags.	Apply and pay
Tagged Chinese Gigaword Corpus Version 2.0 中文億詞標注語料庫第二版	Linguistic Data Consortium, University of Pennsylvania 賓夕法尼亞大學語言資料聯盟/Chu-Ren Huang et al. 黃居仁 等	https://catalog.ldc.upenn.edu/LDC2009T14	The Tagged Chinese Gigaword Corpus Version 2.0, processed and PoS tagged by the Academia Sinica team, is the largest tagged	Apply and pay

(continued)

Resource title	Developer and maintainer/author/host	Web sites	Notes	How to use
			Chinese Corpus in the world. Collected by the LDC, version 2.0 is from the Central News Agency (Taiwan), the Xinhua News Agency, and *Zaobao Newspaper* (Singapore). This version contains more than 1100 million characters and more than 831 million words	
The Babel English-Chinese Parallel Corpus Babel 英汉平行语料库	Lancaster University 兰开斯特大学/ Richard Xiao 肖忠华	http://www.lancaster.ac.uk/fass/projects/corpus/babel/babel.htm	This corpus contains 327 English articles and their translation in Mandarin Chinese. These articles are from the *World of English* and *Time*. The scale of this corpus is 544,095 words (253,633 English words and 287,462 Chinese tokens). The corpus is annotated with part-of-speech tags. Sentence alignment was performed automatically and corrected by hand	Apply
The Lancaster Corpus of Mandarin Chinese 兰开斯特大学中文语料库	Lancaster University 兰开斯特大学/ Tony McEnery, Richard Xiao	http://www.lancaster.ac.uk/fass/projects/corpus/LCMC	This corpus is the Chinese version of the FLOB. Its contents are segmented and annotated with part-of-speech tags	Apply
The Lancaster Los Angeles Spoken Chinese Corpus 兰开斯特洛杉矶汉语口语语料库	Lancaster University 兰开斯特大学/ Richard Xiao 肖忠华	http://www.lancaster.ac.uk/fass/projects/corpus/LLSCC/	This is a corpus of spoken Mandarin Chinese. Its scale is 1,002,151 words from dialogues and monologues, with 73,976 sentences and 49,670 paragraphs. The materials are from	Apply

(continued)

Resource title	Developer and maintainer/author/ host	Web sites	Notes	How to use
			conversations, telephone calls, play and movie transcripts, TV talk show transcripts, debate transcripts, oral narratives, and edited oral narratives	
The PDC2000 Corpus of Chinese News Text 2000 年《人民日报》全年语料库	Lancaster University 兰开斯特大学/ Richard Xiao 肖忠华	http://www.lancaster.ac.uk/fass/projects/corpus/pdc2000/	This corpus contains a whole years' worth of data from the *People's Daily* (2000). Its scale is about 15 million words in 366 files. Each file consists of a corpus header and the corpus text proper. The content of the corpus is annotated with part-of-speech tags	Apply

32.2.3 Lexical Resources

Resource title	Developer and maintainer/author/ host	Web sites	Notes	How to use
Chinese Electronic Dictionary 中文詞庫(八萬目詞)	Chinese Language and Knowledge Processing Group, Institute of Information Science, Academia Sinica 中央研究院資訊科學所中文詞知識庫小組/Keh-Jiann Chen, Chu-Ren Huang 陳克健, 黃居仁	http://www.aclclp.org.tw/use_ced_c.php	This electronic dictionary has 80,000 entries, which include common words, commonly used proper nouns, idioms, idiomatic phrases, derivates, heterographies, terms, and Ancient Chinese words. Each entry includes phonetic notation, frequency, part-of-speech, and semantic class.	Apply and pay

(continued)

Resource title	Developer and maintainer/author/host	Web sites	Notes	How to use
Reference Lexicon for Segmentation Standard Dictionary 中文分詞詞庫	Chinese Language and Knowledge Processing Group, Academia Sinica 中央研究院中文詞知識庫小組/Chu-Ren Huang 黃居仁	http://www.aclclp.org.tw/use_rlssd_c.php	This word list was extracted from the Standard Segmentation Corpus. It has 42,138 entries, with their frequencies.	Apply and pay
Sinica Chinese Core Vocabulary 中央研究院中文核心詞彙表	Chinese Language and Knowledge Processing Group, Academia Sinica 中央研究院中文詞知識庫小組/Chu-Ren Huang et al. 黃居仁等	http://www.aclclp.org.tw/use_sccv_c.php	This word list includes 1121 high-frequency Chinese words. These words are the intersection of the first 2000 high-frequency words in the Sinica Corpus and the Modern Chinese Dialogue Speech Corpus. Each word includes part-of-speech, frequency (in both corpuses), frequency rank (in both corpuses), English translation, and Chinese and English example sentences.	Apply and pay
The Grammatical Knowledge-base of Contemporary Chinese 北京大学现代汉语语法信息词典	Peking University 北京大学/Shi-Wen Yu et al. 俞士汶 等	http://opendata.pku.edu.cn/dataset.xhtml?persistentId=doi:10.18170/DVN/EDQWIL	This dictionary is based on Prof. Zhu De-xi's theories and contains 73,000 items. For each item, it offers homographs, pinyin, senses, multi-category conditions, and much more syntactic information. It aims to analyze and generate Chinese sentences automatically.	Apply
Word List with Accumulated Word Frequency in the Sinica Corpus 中央研究院平衡語料庫詞集及詞頻統計	Chinese Language and Knowledge Processing Group, Institute of Information Science, Academia Sinica 中央	http://www.aclclp.org.tw/use_wlawf_c.php	This word list was extracted from the Sinica Corpus. It shows the part-of-speech, word frequency, and	Apply and pay

(continued)

Resource title	Developer and maintainer/author/host	Web sites	Notes	How to use
	研究院資訊科學所中文詞知識庫小組/Keh-Jiann Chen, Chu-Ren Huang 陳克健, 黃居仁		cumulative frequency of each item.	

32.2.4 Wordnet/Ontology

Resource title	Developer and maintainer/author/host	Web sites	Notes	How to use
HowNet 知网	Language Knowledge Department, Computer and Language Information Research Centre, Chinese Academy of Sciences 中国科学院计算机语言信息中心语言知识研究室/Zhendong Dong 董振东	http://www.keenage.com/html/e_index.html	This is an online common-sense knowledge base of interconceptual relations and interattribute relations of concepts as connoted in Chinese lexicons and their English equivalents	Apply and pay
The Academia Sinica Bilingual Ontological Database 中英雙語知識本體資料庫	Institute of Linguistics, Academia Sinica, 中央研究院/Chu-Ren Huang 黃居仁	http://www.aclclp.org.tw/use_bd_c.php	This database contains a bilingual ontology of about 110,000 Chinese words. The ontology is based on the Institute of Electrical and Electronics Engineers (IEEE)-approved SUMO. It offers not only the bilingual ontology of concepts but also the infrastructure of knowledge management, which can transfer knowledge from different sources into interoperable information	Apply and pay

32.2.5 Treebanks

Resource title	Developer and maintainer/author/host	Web sites	Notes	How to use
Chinese Syntactic Treebank of Tsinghua University 清华大学汉语句法树库	Tsinghua University 清华大学	http://cslt.riit.tsinghua.edu.cn/~qzhou/papers/TCTScheme.pdf	This treebank contains parsed texts from literature, academic fields, news, and practical writings. Its scale is about one million words	Apply and pay
CoNLL X Shared Task Chinese Treebank CoNLL X 中文句結構樹資料庫	Chinese Language and Knowledge Processing Group, Institute of Information Science, Academia Sinica 中央研究院資訊科學研究所中文組實驗室中文詞知識庫小組	http://www.aclclp.org.tw/use_conll_c.php	The materials in this treebank are from the Chinese CoNLL X corpus competition (2006). The tree graphs from the Sinica Treebank are presented in dependency-tree form. The test corpus is free to download, but the training corpus requires payment to use	Apply and pay

32.2.6 Sketch Engine

Resource title	Developer and maintainer/author/host	Web sites	Notes	How to use
Chinese Word Sketch Engine 中文詞彙特性速描系統	Institute of Linguistics, Academia Sinica 中央研究院/Chu-Ren Huang, Adam Kilgarriff et al.	http://wordsketch.ling.sinica.edu.tw/	This system is connected to the LDC Chinese Gigaword Corpus (1.4 billion characters). It can provide users with word sketch information, grammatical relations, synonym analysis, and other lexical and syntactic knowledge of inputted words.	Register
Word Sketch Engine 词汇特征素描系统	Lexical Computing Limited, UK 英国词汇计算有限公司	https://www.sketchengine.co.uk/	Word Sketch Engine contains 500 corpora, each of which contains up to 30 billion words, in more than 90 languages. These corpora show users the grammatical and collocational behavior of words.	Free for 30 days, then pay

32.2.7 Evaluation Resources

Resource title	Developer and maintainer/author/host	Web sites	Notes	How to use
Chinese Information Retrieval Benchmark Version 3.0 中文資訊檢索標杆測試集第三版	Department of Library and Information Science, National Taiwan University 國立臺灣大學圖書資訊學系/Chen Kuang-Hua 陳光華	http://www.aclclp.org.tw/use_cir_c.php	The material in this corpus was collected according to information retrieval evaluation theories. The corpus aims to be a reliable testing resource for Chinese information retrieval. It includes three parts: documents set, topics (questions) set, and answers set	Apply and pay
DoLWS-MAN: Database of Word-level Statistics (Mandarin)	The Hong Kong Polytechnic University 香港理工大學/Karl David Neergaard, Hongzhi Xu, Chu-Ren Huang, 許洪志, 黃居仁	Available soon from the LDC, University of Pennsylvania	This database provides the lexical characteristics of a descriptive and statistical nature for Mandarin Chinese words and non-words. It was designed for researchers who are particularly concerned with the language processing of isolated words. The database is basically a set of phonological neighborhood data in Mandarin Chinese collected through experiments and fitted with statistical models, and it is searchable by Speech Assessment Methods Phonetic Alphabet (SAMPA), characters, or pinyin	To be determined

(continued)

Resource title	Developer and maintainer/author/ host	Web sites	Notes	How to use
EVALution and EVALution-MAN	The Hong Kong Polytechnic University 香港理工大學/Enrico Santus, Hongchao Liu, Chu-Ren Huang et al. 劉洪超, 黃居仁 等	Available soon from the LDC, University of Pennsylvania	This repository contains different versions of EVALution, a dataset containing Semantic Relations and Metadata for Training and Evaluating Distributional Semantic Models. EVALution contains English data while EVALution-MAN contains Mandarin Chinese data	To be determined
SemTransCNC 1.0: Semantic Transparency Dataset of Chinese Nominal Compound	The Hong Kong Polytechnic University 香港理工大學/Shichang Wang, Chu-Ren Huang et al. 王世昌, 黃居仁 等	To be available soon from LDC, University of Pennsylvania	This dataset was built using a series of Mechanical Turk-based experiments. It consists of the overall and the constituent semantic transparency (OST and CST, respectively) data of 1176 dimorphemic Chinese nominal compounds that consist of free morphemes and have mid-range frequencies	To be determined
SIGHAN Bakeoff 2012 SIGHAN 繁體中文剖析資料集 2012 版	Academia Sinica 中央研究院	http://www.aclclp.org.tw/use_bakeoff_c.php	This database has three parts: training set, dry-run set, and testing set. The first two sets are extended from the Sinica Treebank, while the testing set has 1000 new Chinese sentences (annotated), which can be used as testing materials for parsing and Semantic Role Labeling tasks	Apply and pay

32.3 Published Resources/Technical Reports[1]

32.3.1 Segmentation and Part-of-Speech Analysis

1. Chinese Language and Knowledge Processing Group 中央研究院資訊科學所中文詞知識庫小組. 1993. Technical report: Chinese part of speech analysis 詞庫小組技術報告 - 中文詞類分析. In *CKIP technical report* 中文詞知識庫小組技術報告. Taipei: Academia Sinica. http://ckip.iis.sinica.edu.tw/CKIP/tr/9305_2013%20revision.pdf
2. Computational Linguistics Laboratory of the Institute of Applied Linguistics 教育部语言文字应用研究所计算语言学研究室. 2001. Standardized set of Chinese POS markers for computational uses 信息处理用现代汉语词类标记集规范. *Applied Linguistics* 语言文字应用. 03:16–20.
3. Huang, Chu-Ren, Keh-Jiann Chen, and Chinese Language and Knowledge Processing Group 黃居仁, 陳克健, 中央研究院資訊科學所中文詞知識庫小組. 1996. Technical report: SouWenJieZi—Chinese word boundary research and word segmentation specification for information processing 詞庫小組技術報告 -「搜」文解字-中文詞界研究與資訊用分詞標準. In *CKIP technical report* 中文詞知識庫小組技術報告. Taipei: Academia Sinica. https://www.researchgate.net/publication/301699745_souwenjiezi-_zhongwencijieyanjiuyuzixunyongfencibiaozhun
4. Huang, Chu-Ren, Shu-Kai Hsieh, and Keh-Jiann Chen. 2017. *Mandarin Chinese words and parts of speech: A corpus-based study*. Routledge.
5. Huang, Chu-Ren, and Nianwen Xue. 2012. Words without boundaries: Computational approaches to Chinese word segmentation. *Language and Linguistics Compass* 6(8):494–505.
6. Institute of Computational Linguistics of Peking University (ed.) 北京大学计算语言学研究所 编制. 1999. *Contemporary Chinese corpus processing specification—Word segmentation and part-of-speech tagging* 现代汉语语料库加工规范——词语切分与词性标注. Beijing: Institute of Computational Linguistics of Peking University (technical report, unpublished). http://www.docin.com/p-1074544403.html
7. Jin, Guang-Jing, Hang Xiao, and Li Fu 靳光瑾, 肖航, 富丽. 2005. Standardized set of Chinese POS markers for computational uses (revised ed.) 信息处理用现代汉语词类标记规范(修订). In *Proceedings of the 4th National Applied Linguistics Workshop* 第四届全国语言文字应用学术研讨会论文集, 9. Beijing: Institute of Applied Linguistics, Ministry of Education.
8. Liu, Yuan, Qiang Tan, and Xu-Kun Shen 刘源, 谭强, 沈旭昆. 1994. *Contemporary Chinese language word segmentation specification and automatic word*

[1] For papers and reports that were written in English, the titles and publication information are listed in English only. For papers and reports that were written in Chinese, the titles and publication information are listed in both English and Chinese.

segmentation methods for information processing 信息处理用现代汉语分词规范及自动分词方法. Beijing: Tsinghua University Press.
9. Yu, Shi-Wen, Hui-Ming Duan, Xue-Feng Zhu, Bin Sun, and Bao-Bao Chang 俞士汶, 段慧明, 朱学锋, 孙斌, 常宝宝. 2003. Corpus processing specification of Peking University: Segmentation, part-of-speech tagging and phonetic notation 北大语料库加工规范: 切分· 词性标注· 注音. *Journal of Chinese Language and Computing* 汉语语言与计算学报 13(2):121–158.

32.3.2 Word List/Dictionary

1. Huang, Chu-Ren, Keh-Jiann Chen, Zhao-Ming Gao, Feng-Yi Chen, and Jheng-Jhong Shen. 1998. Technical report: Accumulated frequency of Sinica Corpus. In *CKIP technical report*. Tai Pei: Academia Sinica.
2. Huang, Chu-Ren, Keh-Jiann Chen, Zhao-Ming Gao, Feng-Yi Chen, and Jheng-Jhong Shen 黃居仁, 陳克健, 高照明, 陳鳳儀, 沈正中. 1998. Technical report: Word frequency dictionary 詞庫小組技術報告 - 詞頻詞典. In *CKIP technical report* 中文詞知識庫小組技術報告. Tai Pei: Academia Sinica. http://ckip.iis.sinica.edu.tw/CKIP/tr/9801_2013.pdf
3. Ji, Chun-Sing 紀春興. 1995. Technical report: Mandarin Chinese character frequency list based on national phonetic alphabets 詞庫小組技術報告 - 注音檢索現代漢語字頻表. In *CKIP technical report* 中文詞知識庫小組技術報告. Tai Pei: Academia Sinica. http://ckip.iis.sinica.edu.tw/CKIP/tr/9501_2013.pdf
4. McEnery, Tony, Richard Xiao, and Paul Rayson. 2015. *A frequency dictionary of Mandarin Chinese: Core vocabulary for learners*. Routledge.
5. Shen, Jheng-Jhong, Zhao-Ming Gao, and Chu-Ren Huang 沈正中, 高照明, 黃居仁. 1998. Technical report: An English-Chinese glossary of NLP and CL related terms 詞庫小組技術報告 - 自然語言處理及計算語言學相關術語中英對譯表. In *CKIP technical report* 中文詞知識庫小組技術報告. Tai Pei: Academia Sinica.
6. Wei, Pei-Chuan, Cheng-Huei Liou, Chu-Ren Huang, and Syueh-Ru Wu 魏培泉, 劉承慧, 黃居仁, 吳雪如. 2000. Technical report: Verb-complement word list of novels of Ming and Qing Dynasties 詞庫小組技術報告 - 明清小說動補詞語表. In *CKIP technical report* 中文詞知識庫小組技術報告. Tai Pei: Academia Sinica.
7. Wei, Pei-Chuan, Cheng-Huei Liou, Pu-Sen Tan, and Chu-Ren Huang 魏培泉, 劉承慧, 譚樸森, 黃居仁. 1994. Technical report: Character frequency list of Ancient Chinese 詞庫小組技術報告 - 古漢語字頻表. In *CKIP technical report* 中文詞知識庫小組技術報告. Tai Pei: Academia Sinica.
8. Wei, Pei-Chuan, Cheng-Huei Liou, Pu-Sen Tan, and Chu-Ren Huang 魏培泉, 劉承慧, 譚樸森, 黃居仁. 1997. Technical report: Word frequency list of Ancient Chinese 詞庫小組技術報告 - 古漢語詞頻表(甲). In *CKIP technical report* 中文詞知識庫小組技術報告. Tai Pei: Academia Sinica.

9. Wei, Pei-Chuan, Cheng-Huei Liou, Pu-Sen Tan, and Chu-Ren Huang 魏培泉, 劉承慧, 譚樸森, 黃居仁. 1997. Technical report: Word frequency list of "The Analects of Confucius" 詞庫小組技術報告 - 論語詞頻表. In *CKIP technical report* 中文詞知識庫小組技術報告. Tai Pei: Academia Sinica.
10. Yu, Shi-Wen, Xue-Feng Zhu, Elisabeth Kaske, and Zhi-Wei Feng 俞士汶, 朱学锋, Elisabeth Kaske, 冯志伟. 1996. *English-Chinese lexicon of computational linguistics* 英汉对照计算语言学词语汇编. Beijing: Peking University Press.
11. Yu, Shi-Wen, Xue-Feng Zhu, Hui Wang, Hua-Rui Zhang, Yun-Yun Zhang, De-Xi Zhu, Jian-Ming Lu, and Rui Guo 俞士汶, 朱学锋, 王惠, 张化瑞, 张芸芸, 朱德熙, 陆俭明, 郭锐. 2003. *The grammatical knowledge-base of contemporary Chinese—A complete specification* (version 2) 现代汉语语法信息词典详解 (第二版). Beijing: Tsinghua University Press.
12. Yu, Shi-Wen, Xue-Feng Zhu, Hui Wang, and Yun-Yun Zhang 俞士汶, 朱学锋, 王惠, 张芸芸. 1998. *The grammatical knowledge-base of contemporary Chinese—A complete specification* 现代汉语语法信息词典详解. Beijing: Tsinghua University Press.

32.3.3 Corpus Construction

1. Chen, Keh-Jiann, and Chu-Ren Huang. 2017. Modern Chinese balanced corpus of Academia Sinica. In *Encyclopedia of Chinese language and linguistics*, ed. Rint Sybesma. Leiden: Brill Publishers. https://doi.org/10.1163/2210-7363_ecll_COM_000191
2. Chinese Language and Knowledge Processing Group 中央研究院資訊科學所中文詞知識庫小組. 1998. Technical report: The content and instruction of Sinica Corpus 詞庫小組技術報告 - 中央研究院平衡語料庫的內容與說明. In *CKIP technical report* 中文詞知識庫小組技術報告. Tai Pei: Academia Sinica. http://ckip.iis.sinica.edu.tw/CKIP/tr/9804_2013.pdf
3. Huang, Chu-Ren 黃居仁. 2016. Corpus and language resources construction in Taiwan 臺灣語料庫與語言資源建設. In *The language situation in China (2016)* 中國語言生活狀況報告 *(2016)*, ed. Department of Language Information Management of Ministry of Education 教育部語言文字資訊管理司 編撰, 259–267. Beijing: Commercial Press.
4. Huang, Chu-Ren, Keh-Jiann Chen, and Zhao-Ming Gao 黃居仁, 陳克健, 高照明. 2016. Language processing research and language resources construction motivated by linguistic characteristics of Chinese 兼顧漢語語言特色的語言資訊化建設研究. *The Journal of Chinese Sociolinguistics* 中國社會語言學 02: 13–25.
5. Tseng, Shu-Jyuan, and Yi-Fen Liou 曾淑娟, 劉怡芬. 2002. Technical report: Instruction of spoken Mandarin Chinese corpus annotation system 詞庫小組技術報告 - 現代漢語口語對話語料庫標注系統說明. In *CKIP technical report* 中文詞知識庫小組技術報告. Tai Pei: Academia Sinica. http://ckip.iis.sinica.edu.tw/CKIP/tr/0201_2013.pdf

6. Yu, Shi-Wen, Hui-Ming Duan, Xue-Feng Zhu, and Bin Sun 俞士汶, 段慧明, 朱学锋, 孙斌. 2002. The basic processing of Contemporary Chinese corpus at Peking University SPECIFICATION 北京大学现代汉语语料库基本加工规范. *Journal of Chinese Information Processing* 中文信息学报. 16(5):49–64.

32.3.4 Semantic Representation

1. Chinese Language and Knowledge Processing Group. 2009. Technical report: Lexical semantic representation and semantic composition—An introduction to E-HowNet. In *CKIP technical report*. Tai Pei: Academia Sinica. http://ckip.iis.sinica.edu.tw/CKIP/tr/200901_2016b.pdf
2. Huang, Chu-Ren 黃居仁. 2007, 2006, 2005, 2004. Technical report: Meaning in sense in Mandarin Chinese version 4.0/3.0/2.0/1.0 詞庫小組技術報告 - 中文的詞義小辭典 4.0/3.0/2.0/1.0 版. In *CKIP technical report* 中央研究院文獻語料庫與詞庫小組技術報告. Tai Pei: Academia Sinica.
3. Huang, Chu-Ren (ed.) 黃居仁 主編. 2007, 2006, 2005, 2004. Technical report: Differentiation and description principles of Chinese lexical meaning version 4.0/3.0/2.0/1.0 詞庫小組技術報告 - 中文的詞彙意義的區辨與描述原則 4.0/3.0/2.0/1.0版. In *CKIP technical report* 中央研究院文獻語料庫與詞庫小組技術報告. Tai Pei: Academia Sinica.
4. Huang, Chu-Ren, Shu-Kai Hsieh, Jia-Fei Hong, Yun-Zhu Chen, I-Li Su, Yong-Xiang Chen, and Sheng-Wei Huang 黃居仁, 謝舒凱, 洪嘉馡, 陳韻竹, 蘇依莉, 陳永祥, 黃勝偉. 2010. Chinese Wordnet: Design, implementation, and application of an infrastructure for cross-lingual knowledge processing 中文詞彙網路:跨語言知識處理基礎架構的設計理念與實踐. *Journal of Chinese Information Processing* 中文資訊學報 24(2):14–23.
5. Huang, Shu-Ling, Su-Chu Lin, and Keh-Jiann Chen. 2014. Technical report: Sense representations for extended modalities in E-HowNet. In *CKIP technical report*. Tai Pei: Academia Sinica. http://ckip.iis.sinica.edu.tw/CKIP/tr/201401-tech_report_modality.pdf
6. Huang, Shu-Ling, Su-Chu Lin, and Keh-Jiann Chen. 2014. Technical report: The interactions among syntax, semantics, and morphology— How lexical structures affect verbal semantics and syntax. In *CKIP technical report*. Tai Pei: Academia Sinica. http://ckip.iis.sinica.edu.tw/CKIP/tr/201402-tech_report_morphology.pdf
7. Huang, Shu-Ling, Su-Chu Lin, Wei-Yun Ma, and Keh-Jiann Chen. 2015. Technical report: Semantic roles and semantic role labeling. In *CKIP technical report*. Tai Pei: Academia Sinica. http://ckip.iis.sinica.edu.tw/CKIP/tr/20151215-final-tech_report_semantic%20roles%20and%20semantic%20role%20labeling.pdf
8. Mei, Jia-Ju, Yi-Ming Zhu, Yun-Qi Gao, and Hong-Xiang Yin 梅家驹, 竺一鸣, 高蕴琦, 殷鸿翔. 1983. *TongYiCi CiLin* 同义词词林. Shanghai: The Commercial Press.

9. Xue, Nian-Wen, and Martha Palmer. 2009. Adding semantic roles to the Chinese Treebank. *Natural Language Engineering* 15(1):143–172.
10. Yuan, Yu-Lin 袁毓林. 2014. The description system and usage cases of qualia structure of the Chinese nouns 汉语名词物性结构的描写体系和运用案例. *Contemporary Linguistics* 当代语言学. 16(01):31–48, 125.

32.3.5 Treebank Construction

1. Chen, Keh-Jiann, Chi-Ching Luo, Ming-Chung Chang, Feng-Yi Chen, Chao-Jan Chen, Chu-Ren Huang, and Zhao-Ming Gao. 2003. Sinica treebank: Design criteria, representational issues and implementation. In *Treebanks: Building and using parsed corpora*, ed. Anne Abeillé, 231–248. Dordrecht and Boston: Kluwer Academic Publishers.
2. Chen, Keh-Jiann, Chi-Ching Luo, Zhao-Ming Gao, Ming-Chung Chang, Feng-Yi Chen, Chao-Jan Chen, and Chu-Ren Huang. 1999. The CKIP Chinese treebank: Guidelines for annotation. In *Proceedings of ATALA Workshop–Treebanks*, 85–96. Paris, France.
3. Chinese Language and Knowledge Processing Group 中央研究院資訊科學所中文組實驗室中文詞知識庫小組. 2013. Technical report: Semantic roles in Sinica Treebank 詞庫小組技術報告 - 句結構樹中的語義角色. In *CKIP Technical Report* 中文詞知識庫小組技術報告. Taipei: Academia Sinica. http://ckip.iis.sinica.edu.tw/CKIP/tr/201301_20140813.pdf
4. Huang, Chu-Ren, Feng-Yi Chen, Keh-Jiann Chen, Zhao-Ming Gao, and Kuang-Yu Chen. 2000. Sinica treebank: Design criteria, annotation guidelines, and on-line interface. In *Proceedings of the Second SIGHAN Workshop on Chinese Language Processing*, 29–37. Sapporo, Japan.
5. Huang, Chu-Ren, and Keh-Jiann Chen. 2017. Sinica treebank. In *Handbook of linguistic annotation*, ed. Nancy Ide and James Pustejovsky, 641–657. Dordrecht: Springer.
6. Xue, Nian-Wen, and Fei Xia. 2000. The bracketing guidelines for the Penn Chinese treebank (3.0). *IRCS Technical Reports Series* 39.
7. Xue, Nian-Wen, Fei Xia, Fu-Dong Chiou, and Martha Palmer. 2005. The Penn Chinese treebank: Phrase structure annotation of a large corpus. *Natural Language Engineering* 11(2):207–238.
8. Zhan, Weidong 詹卫东. 2009. Contemporary Chinese treebank processing specification (version 1.0) 现代汉语树库加工规范 (version 1.0). Department of Chinese Language and Literature of Peking University (technical report, unpublished). http://www.docin.com/p-475935862.html
9. Zhan, Weidong 詹卫东. 2009. Frequently asked questions of Contemporary Chinese treebank annotation 现代汉语树库标注常见问题举例. Department of Chinese Language and Literature of Peking University (technical report, unpublished). http://www.docin.com/p-469628749.html

10. Zhou, Qiang 周强. n.d. Technical report of Tsinghua Chinese treebank 清华大学汉语树库构建技术报告. Department of Computer Science and Technology of Tsinghua University (technical report, unpublished). http://www.docin.com/p-598594922.html

The manufacturer's authorised representative in the EU is Springer Nature Customer Service Centre GmbH, Europaplatz 3, 69115 Heidelberg, Germany. If you have any concerns regarding our products, please contact ProductSafety@springernature.com

Printed and bound by CPI Group (UK) Ltd, Croydon, CR0 4YY

30/09/2026

02225314-0020